MW01039033

Robert Parris Moses

Robert Parris Moses

A Life in Civil Rights and Leadership at the Grassroots

Laura Visser-Maessen

The University of North Carolina Press CHAPEL HILL

This book was published with the assistance of the Fred W. Morrison Fund of the University of North Carolina Press.

© 2016 The University of North Carolina Press
All rights reserved
Set in Espinosa Nova by Westchester Publishing Services

The paper in this book meets the guidelines for permanence and durability of the Committee on Production Guidelines for Book Longevity of the Council on Library Resources. The University of North Carolina Press has been a member of the Green Press Initiative since 2003.

Cover illustration: *Remembering Slain Comrades*. Bob Moses addressing demonstrators during Boardwalk demonstration, Atlantic City, N.J., August 10, 1964. Photo © Matt Herron/Take Stock.

Library of Congress Cataloging-in-Publication Data
Visser-Maessen, Laura, author.
    Robert Parris Moses : a life in civil rights and leadership at the grassroots / Laura Visser-Maessen.
        pages cm
    Includes bibliographical references and index.
        ISBN 978-1-4696-2798-4 (cloth : alk. paper) — ISBN 978-1-4696-6650-1 (pbk. : alk. paper) — ISBN 978-1-4696-2799-1 (ebook)
    1. Moses, Robert Parris. 2. African American civil rights workers—Mississippi—Biography. 3. Civil rights workers—Mississippi—Biography. 4. African Americans—Mississippi—Biography. 5. African Americans—Civil rights—Mississippi. 6. Civil rights movements—Mississippi—History—20th century. 7. Mississippi—Race relations. I. Title.
    E185.97.M89V57 2016
    323.092—dc23
    [B]

2015031955

To my parents,
Thei and Marietta,
My husband, Martijn,
and our beautiful children,
Emma and Jesse

This Band of Brothers was led by Bob Moses
Who was fought by all of the official forces
He was silent in manner
But his strength and determination were like a
      waving banner
In his work he was persistent
And met his opposition with nonviolent resistance.

—DORIE LADNER, December 22, 1964

Contents

Illustrations

Preface

Writing a life history is always a difficult enterprise. Not only does someone's life and meaning have to be reduced to a few hundred pages, but they also have to be placed within a larger frame of history, even if focusing on an individual actor within a broad movement underscores how history often developed without the grand designs historians read into it post facto; Moses's entrance into Mississippi testifies to this. I have therefore built my story predominantly around archived material produced during the movement's heyday, that is, the late 1950s to mid-1960s, such as correspondence, project files, reports, and minutes from Student Nonviolent Coordinating Committee (SNCC) workers, federal and local officials, and workers from other organizations, like the National Association for the Advancement of Colored People and the Southern Christian Leadership Conference. To provide a sense of how outsiders witnessed movement activism, I have included contemporary press reports, although fully aware that what is depicted and how is influenced by their authors' subjectivity and civil rights groups' interference.[1]

As a method of testing my own views, filling gaps in my knowledge, and bringing more flavor to the events and people described, I have relied heavily on oral history, memoirs, and other ego documents by movement veterans and conducted in-person and email interviews myself. But wary of the fact that oral history is liable to factual errors, memory lapses, and shifts in interpretations due to the benefit of hindsight, I have generally accorded greater weight to interviews recorded at the time. Veterans' present-day circumstances, like prominent positions in mainstream American life, might influence what they remember or choose to reveal. Likewise, it is logical to assume that where Moses is today determines his interpretations of how he got there.[2]

Yet oral history proved a valuable addition because Moses has kept his personal records private. Much knowledge pertaining to his background and evaluations of movement events are captured primarily in the rare interviews he granted to historians such as Clayborne Carson, Taylor Branch, William Chafe, and Charles Payne in the 1980s and 1990s. But he has mostly resisted invitations to participate in the telling of his story. Reflecting the difficulties attached to history writing as well as his singular fascination with truth telling and (moral) purity in language, he has explained this reluctance through his realization that "historians and the other activists, educators, and academicians have to tell a story, the story has to have 'characters,' and in some sense there has to be 'steady states' which run into 'trouble' and get 'resolved.'" He attributed this resentment for the crafting of stories to the 1960s, when romanticized northern and biased southern newspaper accounts of the movement provided him with "my first insights into the difficult question of 'getting the story straight' as I tried to 'understand' the various stories reporters crafted about movement 'events' in which I played a part and/or was even a central 'character.'" As such, "all historical 'evidence,'" he believed, "comes with 'background' information so there are virtually no 'observation sentences' whose truth or falsity are evident without appeal to some 'background' information and/or some theory." Even in the heyday of his life, he still had "great difficulty reading" about himself, a fact that cannot be understood without "background" either, even if that background is his own subjective interpretation.[3]

But Moses was fully aware of the fact that his words, always carefully chosen, influence interpretations of history, too. From its inception, SNCC was overly conscious of how the movement was depicted; part of its, and especially Moses's, emphasis on grassroots leadership was rooted in this. In the 1960s, he even deliberately reached out to sympathetic media outlets to make sure their reports reflected the message he wanted to convey and, consciously or subconsciously, adjusted his speech and behavior in public accordingly. SNCC still has an active veteran community that plays a dominant role in shaping history and conceptualizing the movement through conferences, memoirs/books, and talks at schools and other venues. Interpretations of pivotal incidents in SNCC's history, like the events in Albany or Atlantic City, have been repeated over and over, even by workers who were not present as they became part of a collective "SNCC identity." Moreover, SNCC workers have come to use historical works to legitimize their own interpretations and memories by reacting to and, more often, against what historians have written. Consequently, their stories exist in part due to, and are both formed and limited by, what others have said about the movement.[4]

Since this might precipitate changes in interpretation over time, their words should be analyzed with caution. This extends to Moses, especially because no trail exists of his thoughts between his departure from the movement in 1965 and his return from Africa almost fifteen years later. This, for instance, allowed for a fairly consistent trajectory of his organizing views in his *Radical Equations* (2001). The book, partly coauthored by SNCC worker Charles Cobb, is a call to action to support Moses's Algebra Project that he developed in the 1980s. The story told on the movement is merely a stepping stone to the tale of his Algebra Project that is discussed in the second part of the book. This enabled him to solely discuss the movement experiences relevant for understanding his most recent work and gloss over his daily, behind-the-scenes activities that spurred the movement. The story even stops short after 1964, avoiding any discussion of his departure from SNCC. As such, the form and content of the book skillfully mirror his self-effacing organizing message, whereas the archival evidence of the time itself indicates that his activities extended beyond just using one's skills and power to facilitate local groups.

Yet to understand Moses and evaluate his work accurately, his own interpretations of what he did, and how he chose to (re)present himself then and now are just as important as what he actually did. In this, my interviews and correspondence with Moses, conducted between 2010 and 2014, proved indispensable. Involving him, however, was not an easy feat. After two years of requests—perhaps a sign of him trying to "read" me—he finally agreed to an interview at SNCC's fiftieth anniversary reunion in Raleigh, North Carolina, in 2010. The opportunity provided a chance to get a personal insight into his personality and organizing skills. The experience supported historic accounts of him as being calm, patient, gentle, and always on the lookout for what the person in front of him has to offer by building personal relations, like inquiring about my life and the social struggles in my home country.

Noteworthy was how he tried to activate my own thinking process—in a similar way as he did with Mississippi locals in the 1960s—by regularly asking me, like a teacher, "Why do you phrase [a question or comment] like that?" Forcing me to be as precise as I could be, he asked me about my sources and even to send him any documents I had about his 1960s activities, as if he was as interested in reconstructing his own life as I was. This reflected his preoccupation with truth telling, but also his educational training, including the academic's inherent tendency to question everything. Since then, Moses has kindly answered several follow-up questions and commented on some parts of my work because, he said, my effort to base his "story" into the available archival evidence made it "readable" for him, although his responses were sparse and far between.[5]

While I was grateful and honored to have Moses's cooperation, this is not a sanctioned biography. I have applied the same caution to his own words as to the rest of my sources by inserting them only when other (archival) evidence, particularly sources recorded at the time, supported them. He has also refrained from helping me reconstruct what he termed "the depiction of the characters or the structuring of 'steady states,' 'troubles,' and 'resolutions.'" Considering the interpretation of his story "*my freedom*" as a historian, he rather helped me "get the story straight" by eliminating tales that did not happen, working out the timeline of events, and providing other useful factual background to shape my interpretations. This means that much of his story remains hidden, in particular his own interpretations of movement events and emotions at the time. One caveat concerns the activities of, and Moses's views on, black women in SNCC and the movement, especially those of his ex-wife Dona Richards and second wife, Janet Jemmott, since little archival evidence was available to back up my depictions; that story is for others to tell, perhaps these women themselves if and when they feel the need to. Yet Moses's painstaking efforts to keep his personal views and experiences private for over fifty years should only deserve our respect. The decision what to disclose deservedly had to be his alone, and I can only hope that what I have disclosed does justice to his life's work.[6]

Capturing Moses and his leadership as realistically as possible—that is, what he factually did or did not do and to what effect—was my main goal in writing this book, although I realize that my story inevitably is guilty of crafting a certain image, too. Sharing Moses's ambivalence toward theory to account for human behavior, I have abstained from linking his story and character to social movement and (charismatic) leadership models or psychoanalysis; this is a job better left to sociologists and psychologists. As a historian, I have only felt fit to place my findings in movement historiography and give some suggestions as to how to interpret his leadership within this body of work. My thoughts on this are found in the bibliographic essay at the end of the book, although I acknowledge that presenting other scholars' views in such a restricted format unavoidably leads to generalization.

Ultimately, to assess Moses's legacy and leadership, it is best just to follow French philosopher Albert Camus's credo of defining a man merely by what he did and thereby consider the fact *that* he acted more valuable than anything he might or might not have accomplished. As William Heath, author of the historical novel *The Children Bob Moses Led*, has said, "The real Moses is impressive enough, he doesn't need to be mythologized." Indeed, let his actions speak for themselves.[7]

ALBERT CAMUS, whose existentialist philosophies run through this manuscript, has also once said that "your successes and happiness are forgiven you only if you generously consent to share them." I therefore would like to take this opportunity to acknowledge my gratitude to everyone who has had a stake in the realization of this book.

Foremost my appreciation should go to Brandon Proia of the UNCP for taking on this project and for the wonderful job he and his coeditors have done in shaping this book into its current form. Particular thanks should also be directed toward Prof. Adam Fairclough of the History Department at Leiden University (the Netherlands). Without his invaluable insights, faith, and support, this manuscript would not have come into being as it is. I am also grateful to Dr. Damian Pargas for his unbridled encouragement and assistance. Outside the Leiden community, I owe particular gratitude to the staff of the American Studies Department of the Radboud University Nijmegen (the Netherlands), especially Prof. Hans Bak, Dr. Mathilde Roza, and Drs. Nicole Verberkt. Special mention should also go to the Roosevelt Study Center in Middelburg, the Netherlands, with its exceptional and friendly staff, most notably Prof. Cornelis van Minnen and Dr. Hans Krabbendam, for all their support, financial and otherwise.

I would also like to show my appreciation for several American scholars who in one way or another have contributed to this end result: Robert Allen and Charles Henry of the African American Studies Department at the University of California, Berkeley, for spurring my interest in African American history, writing letters of recommendation, and interest in my personal life; John Dittmer, Charles Payne, and David Garrow for sharing their interviews with Bob Moses; Todd Moye for his useful comments on my work at the 2009 Southern Historical Association conference in Louisville, Kentucky; and William Chafe for his elaborate advice and help in getting this book published. Furthermore, I want to thank William and Roser Heath. Not only have they given me relentless support and useful insights on my work, but they have also opened their home, hearts, and personal archives to me. I hope we'll stay in touch for many years to come.

I also would like to extend my appreciation to Henry Grossberg, former executive director of the Stuyvesant High School Alumni Association; the wonderful and always helpful Katherine Collett, archivist of the Hamilton College Library, and Donald Davis, archivist of the American Friends Service Committee in Philadelphia for helping me uncover new details about Bob Moses's life before he joined SNCC, as well as the New York–based Gilder Lehrman Institute of American History for its financial donations to support my research.

Exceptional thanks should be given to everyone in the SNCC community who embraced me and my project. I feel lucky and honored to have had the chance of getting to know each of you. Listening to you all sing Freedom Songs during SNCC's 50th Anniversary Reunion Conference is something I'll never forget. With fondness I remember the heartfelt concern many of you showed when it became apparent that I was stranded in North Carolina due to the volcano eruption in Iceland, which disrupted international flights for days. Within less than a day, I had several offers to stay in your homes or those of your family members as well as John Doar's private phone number.

I am especially grateful to those of you who have so warmly given me your time to discuss your memories, donated useful material, and helped me understand both the grandness and pain of your efforts to achieve equality and justice for all (in alphabetical order): Julian Bond, Heather Tobis Booth, Luvaughn Brown, Bell Chevigny, John Cumbler, David Dennis, John Doar, Matt Herron, Janice Goodman, Jim Kates, Ed King, Mary King, Dorie Ladner, Paul Lauter, John Lewis, Sheila Michaels, Mike Miller, Robert Parris Moses, Joan Mulholland, Alvin Poussaint, Wally Roberts, Phil Alden Robinson, and Lisa Anderson Todd. I can only hope this manuscript does justice to your lives, work, and sacrifices.

But even in the best academic environments, a scholar can only survive the long hours of solitude behind the computer screen through the presence of a loving network of family and friends. Special recognition should go to Jorrit van den Berk, Albertine Bloemendal, Lenny van Bussel, Maayke van Halbeek, Patrick Haarsma, Mandy Gooßen, Christian Borrman, and Cindy Storms for their encouragement and friendship over the years. I am also very fortunate to have family members whom I consider close friends. I would particularly like to acknowledge my sisters Andrea Rösken-Maessen and Christa Verkoulen-Maessen, as well as my incredible parents, Thei and Marietta Maessen. Whenever I need a word of advice, a laugh, or any other type of backing, you are there. I love you dearly. This also includes my brothers- and sisters-in-law, Ron Verkoulen, Wil Rösken, Rienk Visser, Gerrie Visser, and Yvette Linders, and my parents-in-law, Wilma and Klaas Visser.

But I am especially indebted to my husband, Martijn Visser, for his relentless love, support, and patience. I cannot express how much I love sharing my life with you and our beautiful children, Emma and Jesse. Everything I am today is because of you.

Introduction

> In the movement there are great examples of organizers and
> their efforts, and this is not emphasized. It doesn't make good
> copy, but it made the movement. It was the tissues and the
> bones, the inner structure of the movement. So these ideas
> about organizing versus leading, and the complex roles that
> people played both as organizers and leaders, need to be
> examined.
>
> —ROBERT PARRIS MOSES, 1986

Throughout his life, Robert Parris Moses faced the same dilemma, again
and again: that of organizing versus leading.[1]

Moses emerged as one of the most prominent individuals between
1961 and 1965 within the group-centered leadership of the Student Nonviolent Coordinating Committee (SNCC). SNCC evolved out of the
1960 sit-in movement and worked in eleven southern states, enjoying particular success in direct action and voter registration. The latter resulted
largely from Moses's activism in Mississippi, where he exemplified an
approach for social change that he called the community organizing tradition. This complemented the media-centered community-mobilizing
tradition associated with Martin Luther King Jr., which focused on mass-
based, short-term mobilization for high-profile confrontations like
marches. According to Moses's approach, the role of civil rights organizers was to develop local initiatives and local leadership, rather than
making decisions on behalf of local people.[2]

To facilitate the organization of local communities, Moses and
SNCC not only built on the foundations laid by older local activists,
mostly from the National Association for the Advancement of Colored
People (NAACP), but also implemented new techniques. This culminated in SNCC's most ambitious project, Freedom Summer, and the
formation of the Mississippi Freedom Democratic Party (MFDP) in
1964. These projects brought widespread attention to conditions in
the state and formed key incentives for the passage of the 1965 Voting
Rights Act.

With his shy, self-effacing character and soft voice, Moses exemplified his organizational philosophy. He emphasized the inherent worth of each person, careful listening, and an identification with the working class. Promoting "moral leadership by example," he presented himself as a facilitator of indigenous black leadership rather than a figure of authority. He thereby challenged conventional concepts of leadership and rejected the distinction between leaders and followers.

Yet Moses constantly struggled with the realization that the special qualities he brought to the practice of organizing provided him with the conventional power he sought to avoid. His advice, organizing style, and example in Mississippi helped spur SNCC's transition from a campus-based student movement centered on integrating urban public facilities to a group of full-time organizers working with the rural poor on voter registration and political organizing in the Deep South. He was accorded a cult status among the generation of activists within the New Left and the Mississippi rural poor. SNCC workers and local blacks alike revered him. Several considered him to be "Jesus Christ in the flesh"; others underscored that "if there would have been no Bob Moses there would have been nothing."[3]

The singular attributes Moses brought to his organizing work—his intelligence, determination, audacity, resources, sense of direction, and self-effacing style—evolved into what became known as the Bob Moses Mystique. Even Moses's internal struggles with leadership, culminating in his decision to change his name and flee to Africa to avoid the draft in the mid-1960s, played an essential part in the myth making. Some admirers described him as a "tragic hero," an idealist who, like the movement itself, became so discouraged by future possibilities for social change that he turned inward. In the words of one awed white liberal in 1964, "The more he withdraws to the last row at meetings, the more he broods and introspects, the more he lives with the people who are his sustenance, the less he says to anyone, the more his legend grows."[4]

But in reality, Moses was neither a saint nor the unassuming facilitator he prefers to see himself as but rather a remarkable and perceptive man who cared deeply about leadership, thought profoundly about ways to develop and project it, and utilized his unique abilities to spur this along while trying to safeguard his ideals. Although he sought to avoid manipulation and autocratic means of decision making, through indirection and subtle use of logic and his personal strength, he nonetheless managed to accomplish goals he believed were necessary.

BOB MOSES IS WIDELY acknowledged as one of the civil rights movement's most compelling and beloved characters. Nevertheless—or perhaps *because* he yields such admiration—he remains relatively understudied and not fully understood. To assert the true value of the leadership and organizing approach he personified, it is necessary to uncover what he actually did and how the inherent contradictions in his leadership played out in practice.

The contradictions between Moses's visions of leadership and reality are plentiful, and although he managed to overcome many, he certainly did not overcome all. For starters, his path into the civil rights movement was an unusual one, which played a major role in the mystique that formed around him. While the roots of his organizing approach are found in the black community of Harlem in which he grew up in the 1930s and 1940s and in the rapport he had with black civil rights activists Amzie Moore and Ella Baker, the cosmopolitan influences he garnered from his time spent at elite white educational institutions in the 1950s were crucial to shaping his activism. His fascination with existentialism, particularly Albert Camus's emphasis on walking a fine line between being neither a victim nor an executioner, sharpened his commitment to nonviolence and sensitivity to the question of avoiding leadership roles that carried the potential of manipulation. As his SNCC colleague Stokely Carmichael noted, Moses believed "strongly that we are what we do. . . . If you exploit others, you are an exploiter. If you oppress, you are an oppressor. . . . It is only in the act of rebellion—not in talking or posturing—that you become a rebel. And there is a human moral imperative to rebel against all injustice. Simple enough, right? Well, try to live by those precepts. Bob really seemed to try." Yet the fact that he even posed his and African Americans' struggles into such frames set him apart from most in the movement and undermined his claim that credentials like his were no prerequisites for leadership.[5]

Moses addressed the situation in Mississippi by forming small groups of full-time workers who utilized a unique organizational culture based in personal relationships and democratic procedures. For everyone's survival, it was imperative that all were in agreement and that one could move flexibly based on one's own and locals' insights. Considering the limited gains of the established civil rights organizations and the fail-ures of SNCC's direct action proponents, grassroots leadership was the only logical approach for attaining civil rights in the Mississippi context. Projecting individual leaders or organizations threatened the unity and scale of the local movement, while its survival in the state's distinctive racist environment hinged on consensus and the involvement of as many participants as possible. The absence of visible leaders was also a safety measure. It was thus also out of pragmatism, rather than sheer idealism, that Moses saw the dependency of social change on a common program for and by all blacks in the community's social strata. Because locals risked their lives, they could only be moved to participate for a long period of time if they fully internalized the movement. This could merely be ac-complished if full-time workers operated on locals' and not their own agendas. As Moses said, an organizer "could not create consensus, an or-ganizer had to find it."[6]

Yet the fact that Moses was there risking his life *with* them while he did not *have* to was enough to exalt him over others. By following the advice of experienced grassroots organizers like Amzie Moore, going into one of the most hardcore racist places in the nation and renouncing all comfort for years on end, Moses, as well as the SNCC workers who followed him into the state, attained great moral power. Such acts—especially of courage and self-sacrifice—contributed powerfully to a "movement" culture. Martin Luther King Jr. and his Southern Christian Leadership Conference (SCLC) popularized the existentialist idea that leaders had to suffer along-side locals during protests rather than remaining safely within their head-quarters. This distinguished the movement that emerged in the South after 1955 from the tradition of activism associated with the nation's oldest civil rights organization, the NAACP. By going into *Mississippi*, notorious for its extreme racial violence and the almost absolute exclusion of blacks in the political process, Moses took this idea to new levels and effectively changed the meaning of what commitment to the struggle meant.[7]

Moses's seemingly exceptional example not only complicated his mes-sage that social change depended on black Mississippians alone, but also underscored how much his perspective differed from that of his colleagues in SNCC. Most were southern black college students who emphasized de-segregation campaigns in urban areas. By moving from the North to the South, Moses advocated the idea that even while racism was a national phenomenon, the base of the black freedom struggle must be situated in the South. But rather than just seeking an end to segregation, he considered his work in the South, especially his activity with the Democratic Party, to be a prerequisite for a better quality of life in the urban black North. Such insights relied on his direct knowledge of Harlem life combined with his ambivalent experiences in white middle-class institutions, thus motivating his interest in voting rights and economic issues. Moreover, Moses's northern encounters with the Old Left had influenced his stance on allowing activists with alleged Communist pasts to work freely in the movement, something most of his southern coworkers found difficult to accept.

Although Moses tried to unite local blacks around the goals of voter registration and ending racial violence, his ideas of leadership and voting rights as being universal met staunch opposition from more conservative and middle-class blacks. He succeeded in allying the different groups within the black community—and their representative local and national organizations—into the Council of Federated Organizations (COFO), an umbrella group created by and for "the people." Yet in the process of developing local leadership, Moses acknowledged, "One of the hardest things to know was when to back away. There's always a feeling that you know what is right." He also reckoned with the moral issue of personal responsibility. If local blacks lost their jobs, homes, or even their lives due to their encouragement, did this equate Moses and his colleagues with Camus's dreaded imagery of an executioner?[8]

What made Moses's leadership conundrum worse was his realization that SNCC needed to forge an allegiance between North and South, but in a way that strengthened rather than undermined grassroots leadership. The movement had evolved out of southern black society, but it had to create new networks and resources based on the recognition that northern involvement was vital for the survival of the movement. Those participants who were not chased out or assassinated depended for their survival on outside assistance. To forge social change on a long-term basis, SNCC had to include other resources: the largely forgotten population of the southern black poor *and* the growing segment of northern white liberals, particularly students, who sought avenues to get involved in the movement. In enterprises like the 1963 Freedom Vote and the 1964 Freedom Summer, he then had to merge the vastly different needs of local blacks, professional activists, and white liberals without sacrificing the ideal of grassroots leadership.

Moses's idea of facilitation as augmenting—not directing—locals' initiatives increasingly rubbed against the reality that the strategy went beyond the mere notion of using one's skills and power to assist local groups. Although he responded to Mississippi blacks' needs, his behind-the-scenes work to translate them to northerners with resources was a significant factor in SNCC's success in developing grassroots leadership. A large part of his job eventually became mediating between southern blacks and their northern allies. In this, his particular talents, consensus-seeking character, contacts, and experiences in the North played a key role.

With its dependency on hundreds of educated, mostly white northerners and on national goodwill and publicity, Freedom Summer and the MFDP's challenge to the seating of the regular Mississippi state Democrats at the 1964 Democratic National Convention especially exacerbated Moses's leadership dilemmas. He strongly believed in their necessity but struggled to convince his colleagues to orchestrate these programs without disregarding their opposition and concern for what the presence of hundreds of whites would do to black leadership.

Moses found himself in a complex situation where locals and full-time civil rights workers had to rely on each other to get the job done, but to get anything with a long-term effect done, the emphasis needed to be on grassroots leadership. To combat the oppression that had strangled Mississippi's earlier activists and to expand movement participation beyond the traditional leadership of the black middle class, locals needed SNCC to accelerate the degree, intensity, and effectiveness of their own protests. SNCC's corps of full-time organizers who worked on subsistence pay, combined with its flexible structure and tapping of the groups of working-class blacks that established organizations ignored, proved more effective in this than the tiny field staff of the long-active NAACP.

SNCC could thus *generate* a local movement by drawing "ordinary" citizens *into* the movement; it had the time and numbers to show them, systematically, how to organize through workshops and meetings. Many, like Fannie Lou Hamer, were *ready* to participate but proved much more responsive to organizers who became part of the community and stayed with them in the aftermath of protests. Other national organizations then followed SNCC's example. What was new in the 1960s then was the scale and character of support that national organizations afforded local ones, with SNCC setting the tone. The resources it brought locals and the humble manner in which SNCC made them available proved crucial in attracting local blacks' sustained involvement.

SNCC's self-abdicating, consensus-based approach effectively complemented the methods of prior activists, but Moses could not escape the fact that the presence of SNCC workers in itself was another catalyst, especially if their class or educational backgrounds or personalities, like his own, represented something else. Most locals were eager to "grow" and feel connected to a world outside their own. Moses and SNCC then catered to this with systematic provisions of workshops and leadership trainings inside and outside the state. Although native workers often started and sustained projects without his presence and locals and workers merged in mutually reinforcing roles, even he acknowledged that for locals, and especially native students who joined SNCC, the organization served as "a Petri dish from which their own sense of themselves evolved."[9]

In this, Moses's example proved directive. Unlike SNCC's direct-action proponents, he felt that his destiny was intertwined with that of black Mississippians. Seeing his prime allegiance to Amzie Moore instead of to an organization (SNCC), he was able to genuinely see locals as family and move along flexibly on their initiatives even if he did not always consider these wise. Building these relationships then became SNCC's primary job and engaging in it a political act in itself that bolstered locals' confidence. Moses's personal fascination with exposure, ownership in learning, and "credentials" accelerated this development. While SNCC often used older tactics—like meetings, voter registration drives, citizenship schools, the running of black candidates for office, and direct aid—his emphasis on turning these efforts into organizing tools *in themselves* represented a new dimension in the freedom struggle that effectively expanded movement participation and increased the depth of participants' commitment.

Moses's example gave him leverage not only with black Mississippians but also within SNCC. Like him, SNCC operated through participatory democracy and dealt with internal conflict through a quest for consensus. Because SNCC workers felt they were held together by a shared sense of "spirit" rather than a defined ideology, they tried to treat everyone's opinion as equally worthy of consideration. Although SNCC's loose organization at times hindered its effectiveness, it allowed for flexibility and diversity. In fact, SNCC did not see itself as an organization made to last but rather as a "movement" in which Martin Luther King Jr.'s dream of the beloved community—a society in which genuine interpersonal living based in justice as well as love was possible—was already acted out.[10]

Because Moses projected a sense of humility as a leader that enhanced his moral influence, he exemplified SNCC's organizational philosophy like no other. Yet despite their self-negating organizational leadership model, SNCC workers paradoxically felt a great need for leadership and structure. Moses's talents and background then played an important role in the universal projection of leadership onto him. His intrinsically shy character and soft speech fitted his message of self-effacing leadership. Moreover, his "outsider" status and the fact that he had academic titles mattered to northern white liberals and southern blacks alike, even if he did not flaunt his credentials. So did his boldness, which owed a large part to his family's struggles to become part of the middle class and his experiences in white institutions. The latter had unleashed a sense of entitlement and aspirations in him that many of his southern colleagues to a larger degree had been forced to contain. But Moses mostly derived his influence from his keen sense of direction and what one worker termed "the sheer degree of thought [he] put into creating" the Mississippi movement. While he combined his organic and cosmopolitan experiences into a singular philosophy that movement participants could not always follow—like his 1965 merger with the anti–Vietnam War movement—it was his breadth of vision and his ability to explain it in a way that crossed racial, geographical, and class boundaries that impressed other workers.[11]

Although Moses has been depicted as an "unmitigated idealist," in reality he was an effective hands-on organizer. He executed a significant number of behind-the-scenes responsibilities that were crucial for SNCC's and COFO's daily operations. Workers needed someone whose pragmatic capabilities they could trust because often their physical and mental survival depended on it; only rarely are people willing to risk life and limb for someone's charisma alone. Still, his example in risking life and limb *with them* helped others in reaching the courage to risk theirs.

In addition, Moses's unassuming personality and pragmatic reminders to focus on what *was* under workers' control often helped smooth over conflicts with workers from other civil rights organizations, with locals, and within SNCC. In this, workers indicated that they particularly appreciated his ability to see the broader picture in motivating them to continue their work and reaching out to their colleagues. Field workers as well as SNCC headquarters actually demanded of him that he played this intermediary role; he even occasionally acted as a disciplinarian. He did so at times because headquarters ordered it and at other times of his own accord because he recognized that certain degrees of discipline were needed for effective organizing. Yet Moses differed from most of his colleagues in approaching discipline as another organizing tool that could help individuals grow rather than as a means for expediency, which enhanced his charisma and attractiveness as a leader.[12]

These inherent contradictions in Moses's leadership philosophy became increasingly untenable from 1965 onward. His power within SNCC and the movement at large following the effective display of his hands-on organizing, mediating, and networking skills during Freedom Summer essentially made him a national movement leader, threatening to eclipse his preferred roles as facilitator and organizer. Moreover, after having been in the national spotlight, neither the grassroots leadership in Mississippi nor SNCC wanted to return to the slow organizing approach that he had made so successful and that he felt needed to be continued. The Mississippi movement became more moderate in its direction while SNCC increasingly sought a black nationalist course. Moses was left caught in the middle. Emotionally and physically exhausted, he withdrew from the organization. Yet he retained his faith in his leadership approach. By combining his lessons learned from the Mississippi movement with his subsequent experiences as a school teacher in Tanzania, he was then able to reapply it successfully in a new activist career in math literacy that has spanned his life from the 1980s onward.

By uncovering how Moses tried to operate without resorting to a hierarchical style but simultaneously could wield power effectively, it is possible to show that exceptional individuals within the civil rights movement could play decisive roles without this taking away the rightful ownership of the Mississippi movement from the locals who spearheaded it. It also sheds light on the multifaceted relationship between the origins of ideas and subsequent activism of movement participants, as well as on the role SNCC's exceptional organizational culture played in allowing individuals, like Moses, to thrive and in making facilitation as an organizing approach work. Emphasizing Moses's own views, preconceptions, skills, and background influences that played a part in the decisions he made gives a more realistic appraisal of his leadership and restores him to his own unique self. His life story helps us understand how those "complex roles that people played as organizers and leaders" contributed to the social change the 1960s civil rights movement generated.

CHAPTER ONE

The Making of a Mind

Two months after Robert Moses was born in Harlem on January 23, 1935, a race riot erupted that left three dead, some sixty injured, and seventy-five arrested. Although it started over a rumor that a white policeman had killed a black youth, the *New York Times* held the Depression's "many economic ills" accountable. The black *Amsterdam News* went further, blaming "the discrimination, exploitation and oppression of 204,000 American citizens in the most liberal city in America," New York.[1]

Since World War I, Harlem had functioned as the so-called mecca of the New Negro, an exciting place for cosmopolitan-minded and race-conscious blacks that attracted thousands of migrants and immigrants. As of 1930, only 21.2 percent of Manhattan's blacks had been born there. The rest were foreign born or born elsewhere in the United States, with nearly 50 percent of the latter coming from the South. Between 1916 and 1930, 1.6 million southern blacks moved north in what became known as the Great Migration. Another 5 million followed between 1940 and 1970, seeking to find their fortune in northern industrial jobs as their farms suffered from credit loss and natural disasters, such as flooding and the boll weevil, and to escape increased racial animosity. After Booker T. Washington's death and much of his constituency's move northward, the focus of black leadership also shifted to the North. Harlem emerged as the political capital of black America. Its heavy concentration of black activism included NAACP headquarters, Marcus Garvey's Universal Negro Improvement Association, and A. Philip Randolph's Brotherhood of Sleeping Car Porters. The center of a new black cultural "renaissance," Harlem's institutions such as jazz clubs and social and literary organizations flourished as well, drawing even a large white clientele.[2]

This expansion was dramatic. As in most northern cities, housing segregation had firmly been encoded in New York. Blacks accordingly could not rent outside Harlem's edges. Within its perimeters, landlords kept blacks' rents artificially high, while white storeowners did the same with food prices. Consequently, adequate minimum incomes needed to be higher than in the rest of the city, leading to overcrowding and higher crime rates. In the 1920s, Harlem became a slum in every sense of the word, but its internal divisions, based on class and nativity, prevented united protest. By the time the riot broke out in 1935, conditions had worsened. Due to the Great Depression, 60 percent of Harlem's population was unemployed, and those with jobs faced severe wage cuts.[3]

After the riot, the city government realized it needed to invest in the neighborhood. One means was building four-story public housing projects, the Harlem River Houses, which opened in 1937. In total, 574 black families out of 11,500 applicants could rent a small apartment at $7 a room per month. The project had a nursery school, health clinic, and laundry facilities. The tenants chosen, mostly unskilled or semi-skilled workers, needed an average family income of $1,340. Among them were Bob Moses, his parents Gregory H. and Louise Parris Moses, and his older brother Gregory. In 1941, the family was extended with another son, Roger.[4]

MOSES'S FAMILY HISTORY was also rooted in the Great Migration and the proud black self-help tradition that thrived in places like Harlem. His grandfather, William Henry Moses, was a prominent southern Baptist preacher whose career reflected a strong affiliation with black-led initiatives for social change. He was educated at Virginia Seminary in Lynchburg and was a one-term president of Guadalupe College for Baptist ministers in Texas, both strong black independent institutions founded to counter black moderates' cooperation with white Baptists. He also became the vice-president of the predominantly black National Baptist Convention, then the nation's third largest religious organization. Unsurprisingly, William Moses was a supporter of Marcus Garvey, although Pan-Africanism was not regularly discussed in his home. In 1925, he gained national stature for his progressive views regarding the controversial Scopes trial,[5] which he attended.[6]

Grandfather Moses wrote homiletic reviews and held pastorates in the South, in Washington, D.C., and Philadelphia, to advance his family into the middle class. The ancestry of his wife, Julia Trent, went back to a white plantation owner's son, Peter Trent, from Cumberland, Virginia. The Moses couple eventually settled with their six children in New York, where Grandfather Moses's church did well. This allowed his children to attend good schools.[7]

Shortly after the move, however, William Moses fell ill. Moses's father, the fourth in line, helped his mother maintain the household. After bell hopping at fancy hotels in Saratoga, Gregory Moses accepted a steady blue-collar job at Harlem's 369th Armory. Maintaining he got "shortchanged,"[8] he always looked enviously at his older brothers. One, William (Uncle Bill), a Pennsylvania State College graduate, worked in New York as an architectural draftsman, designed buildings in Virginia, and then taught courses at the state's black Hampton Institute. Uncle Bill was Moses's only immediate family member living in the South.[9] Another brother, DeMaurice, a former lawyer who had attended Columbia University, was a lieutenant colonel. He had led a black battalion in the Pacific during World War II. Afterward, he became commander of the 369th Armory, where Gregory worked as a maintenance man. He and his wife, Aunt Doris, sent their children through expensive schools and into Harvard and Yale. Gregory's strong and independent-minded sisters, Ethel, Lucia, and Julia, were—against their father's wishes—in show business. Their careers spanned the renowned Cotton Club Girls lineup, touring the globe with Broadway shows, and acting in Black cinema.[10,11]

Gregory Moses had only completed high school. Until his marriage in 1932, he lived with his father. His wife, Moses's mother, Louise Parris, grew up in Jamaica, Long Island, the daughter of a domestic worker in Queens. Louise graduated from high school as well, a feat she was very proud of. She, "the prettiest thing on 111th Avenue in Jamaica," was making plans to go to college when Gregory, the family story went, "snapped her up." Gregory did not want Louise to work when the children were young, although she had cherished her previous job at Chock Full of Nuts, a coffee chain Jackie Robinson helped to market in New York's black neighborhoods. "She was proud of how she managed her counter and her regular customers," Moses recalled. Consequently, life was difficult for the Moses family, even though having a steady job during the Great Depression made one part of the black middle class, and the move to the public housing projects was considered an improvement in the black community. Gregory even dipped into his pension to make sure his family could celebrate Christmas and Easter every year.[12]

When the nation recovered through the wartime economic boom, blacks hardly profited. Whites worked in the thriving defense industries, but many of its jobs were closed to blacks. When Harlem subsequently experienced another race riot in 1943, the then eight-year-old Moses "knew what was going on but didn't have a clue about what it meant." Peering out their fourth-floor living room window with his mother and older brother, he just watched a "sea of young black boys" and was not able to "see the end of them as they flowed with an unrelenting roar on the street" below.[13]

Moses's sense of the war itself was just as basic, which was reflected in the games he played outside the housing projects with his brothers and neighborhood friends. They marched to the commands of one of them, or they each pretended to be a country, threw a ball in the air, and whoever it hit could then declare war on another "country" and that person had to fetch the ball. Rather than on freedom and democracy, his understanding of the war's significance mostly centered on the issue of scarce goods. He regularly stood in long lines to get rationed products like margarine and sugar and listened to his aunts complain about the lack of nylon stockings. Because his father could not afford to attend the pricy local grocery stores, twice a month Moses, his mother, and older brother had to walk several miles to the nearest A&P in Brooklyn—trips they had to continue for the remainder of his childhood.[14]

Throughout the forties, the Moses family experienced hardship. Like most in Harlem, it had to find ways of supplementing the family income to survive. Moses, his mother, and brothers therefore sold milk from a black-owned cooperative in the housing projects before school. If they were lucky and sold two boxes, they could buy two quarts of milk for themselves. As teenagers, Moses and his brother delivered laundry in the housing projects as well to supplement the family's income. These early encounters with self-help impressed young Moses deeply. Harlem was filled with such examples, especially by the black church and other black self-help organizations. The co-op experience gained in significance as Moses grew older. "It later made a very deep impression as I learned more about the whole process of setting up businesses and the problems of black people in getting started in the economy in this country."[15]

Harlem's black culture thus introduced Moses to a type of activism that stressed self-empowerment, although he did not adopt the language of its most well-known institution, the black church. Church did not play a traditional role in his early life, but he neither rejected his Baptist family background. Many migrants from the South did not feel at ease in northern black churches due to the sobriety of their services, which contradicted the emotional southern rural way of holding mass, and the hostility that some congregants displayed toward newcomers. Consequently, migrants often left, shopped around for other churches, or started new ones. Practicing religion, like everything in the North, became a more fluid experience.[16]

Consequently, while Grandfather Moses and Grandma Johnson, Moses's grandmother on his mother's side, lived for the church, neither of Moses's parents attended church. While religious themselves, they chose not to push institutionalized religion on their sons' lives, although Moses attended Sunday school occasionally. Nonetheless, Moses was influenced by his Uncle Bill's stories about the small Universalist church he attended in Hampton. Having always been interested in what he would "loosely call spiritual notions," Moses adopted a loose approach to religion that allowed him to evade dogmatic denominational entanglements while remaining open to nonconventional forms of Christianity later in life.[17]

Rather than on biblical doctrine, Moses based the hallmarks of his later activist philosophy—agency, ownership in learning, grassroots leadership, the inherent worth of each man, self-determination, careful listening, and an identification with the working class—on those around him. Notions of community and racial solidarity were central in the lives of those Moses associated with during his childhood. Even the Harlem River Houses themselves were designed to foster the sense of community and black self-help that he found admirable and sought to emulate throughout his life. For example, vigilant adults living in the Projects once returned the abandoned tricycles of Moses and his brother Gregory to their apartment, albeit to the wrong one. Another neighbor organized a baseball team, the only organized black team in town that entered tournaments. Moses was a member, and his father, who attended every game, served as the players' mentor. The team had their own outfits and traveled to the tournaments on city buses with funds raised by themselves. From fourth grade onward, Moses played baseball with the team every summer, and during the winter he participated in organized basketball at the YMCA.[18]

Particularly the members of Moses's immediate family served as social consciousness-raising examples who proudly and unmistakably espoused these ideals, leaving an indelible impression on Moses as he grew up. He admired his Uncle Bill, who headed the NAACP in Hampton, Virginia, and in the 1930s had played in an integrated theater production but refused to accept lower wages than his white coworkers. During the war, he had organized a petition for integration of the armed forces, which he sent to President Roosevelt, and the police once escorted Moses's Aunt Ethel out when she protested against the Nazis at a German Bund meeting in Madison Square Garden. But the importance of human dignity and agency also became apparent to him through smaller instances. It, for example, deeply affected Moses to witness the great pains his Aunts Lucia and Julia took to have their mother Julia Trent's family established as "legitimate," since she was the descendent of a slave and one of the white slave master's sons. During an emotional scene in Moses's home, Julia referred repeatedly to a court document that listed Julia Trent's mother as wife—not property—of the slave master's son to emphasize her personhood and dignity.[19,20]

Politics were never distant. Moses mentioned that in his grandmother's "kitchen there was always this running conversation about the state of the country. Even when my aunts talked about big names like Lena Horne or Duke Ellington whom they had worked with, [it] was really political dialogue about other Black talent they knew who were unable to emerge." When Jackie Robinson began to play for the Brooklyn Dodgers in 1947, Moses's father, a huge fan of the Giants' white right fielder Melvin Ott, instantly switched allegiance to Robinson and the Dodgers. The twelve-year-old Moses immediately grasped that "something momentous had taken place." He came to understand that the debates in his family carried an important message. "[T]heir discussions were like one long discussion on the larger issue of race. Inevitably they would turn to me. 'You're going to be whatever you want to be.' "[21]

Above all, Moses learned from observing his father. While Gregory Moses's Armory post was considered a worthy job, he derived little satisfaction from it; his main activities included operating switchboards and shoveling snow. Like him, 50 percent of Harlem blacks worked in the service sector, but those were generally jobs without further career prospects. Gregory's frustrations grew when his brother became the Armory's commander. This, Moses disclosed, "ate at him," but he "never expressed [such personal issues] in terms of frustration at society as a whole." Instead, he became an alcoholic. Although alcoholism was a common problem in the black community, most considered it a personal shortcoming. According to Moses's neighborhood friend Alvin Poussaint, he never spoke about his father's drinking but never hid the fact. The drinking affected everyone in the family. "It was hard, it was hard on my mother," Moses admitted, "What it means is that we can't count on him."[22]

Yet being funny and "in some sense gregarious," Moses saw in his father a "working class public speaker" who demonstrated that anyone who lacked an education could nonetheless be politically perceptive. At parent teacher meetings, Gregory would be the first to stand on his feet, and he would deliberately include his sons in his social encounters with the people in his personal network, such as family members, associates of Uncle Bill, and colleagues. Young Moses loved these meetings, which he said taught him how to listen. Such exchanges were "not just gossip talk. [They're] talking about issues of the day . . . related to the job and how it is that you can't really somehow make this job work." Gregory analyzed these discussions with Moses afterward. He would ask pointed questions, such as "What does this mean for the little guy? How does this translate out?"[23]

During these analyses, Gregory tried to teach his son how to "read" people by pointing out who they had just spoken with and what was "real" about them. His father, Moses said, was always "willing to look for and respond to the human qualities of that person [in front of him], so he was not predisposed to try to put that person down." This played a part in Moses's lifelong identification with the common man. After all, his father looked "at life from these different perspectives, so he was here at the bottom, but there were also people who are closely connected with him who had these connections at higher levels, so this [idea of] looking at the environment in Harlem and the structure . . . from the point of view of the man in the street . . . affected my whole interest in, [and] attraction to working [at the] grassroots." But Moses's later modus operandi in Mississippi also reflected his father's limitations. "What is lacking in my father is this exposure to a sustained struggle which has involved a large network of people. . . . He never got a chance to . . . turn his own personal struggles into this larger struggle." As an organizer in the 1960s, Moses therefore made "exposure," "education," and "connecting up with" key components.[24]

Moses of course did not develop this sophisticated analysis of his father, American society, race, and individual agency until later in life. As a child, he simply knew that his father had "sacrificed his talents for the sake of his family." Even Uncle Bill had faced the constraints of black professional success. He designed the award-winning Virginia Pavilion for the 1939 World Fair in an anonymous competition, but when the Virginia World Fair's Commission discovered the architect was black, it denied him his award and employed a white one. The white *Virginian Pilot* even apologized to its readers for having announced the winner on its front page and having addressed him as "Mister." Afterward, Bill spent days at Moses's house. While cooking food and drinking whiskey with Gregory, they repetitively tried to explain the meanings of the incident to five-year-old Moses. But the message he got away with was not entirely negative. After all, Bill had known that he probably would lose, but he entered the competition anyway because "he wanted to know that he could win." Yet Moses eventually concluded his family's misfortune stood not by itself. "There was a lot of that middle class frustration—a whole generation of people who were intelligent, rooted in family, and industrious, for who there was just no opportunity. You'd always hear, 'It's gonna be different when *you* grow up.' So you had a slow buildup of frustration," which became Moses's own as well.[25]

Moses's parents, like most in the black middle class, stressed the value of education as key to overcoming these frustrations, even as black schools nationwide were considered inferior to white ones at all levels. At PS-90, the black elementary school Moses attended in Harlem's center, black students were expected to attend vocational school afterward. Until the fourth grade, Moses had only white teachers, and no efforts were undertaken to encourage students to participate in advancement tests. This systematic attitude was disastrous for black students' confidence. It was not apathy that prevented them from taking such tests, Moses knew, but a haunting feeling that "it was something out of their range."[26]

According to Aunt Doris, school accordingly was "awful" for Moses, although he loved learning. He attributed this love to his mother, an avid reader. Every Friday, she took him to the library, and his best memories include reading with her in the living room on cold winter evenings. He also loved mathematics, which taught him logic and perseverance. Noting his skills, some teachers began giving him extra assignments. In the sixth grade, talent scouts picked him, along with other exceptional sixth graders from elementary schools in Harlem and the South Bronx, to attend rapid advancement classes at Edward W. Stitt junior high school, on the edges of Harlem. This special treatment even included a German teacher for algebra, which gave Moses a more optimistic appraisal of his school days from then on.[27]

One elementary teacher in particular, Mrs. Stuart, stimulated Moses's thinking. She translated Harlem's popular political manifestations of the day, emphasizing black nationalism and self-empowerment, to her class by making them recite James Henry Leigh Hunt's poem *Abou Ben Adhem* each day. The poem relates the story of Abou Ben Adhem, who is visited by an angel holding a list of all the men who love God. When he hears he is not on it, Adhem replies to record him as one who loves his fellow men instead. When the angel returns the next night with a list of names whom the Lord upon review has blessed, Adhem finds his leading the rest. The poem's vision attracted Moses deeply. It was "the biggest expression of black consciousness, on the part of Mrs. Stuart, who wanted her students to have a very deep value that was spiritual, but was related to the idea of working for and with your people ... it's not an expression of overt nationalism, but in the context of PS-90 and Harlem, it's a message." To this idea of noninstitutional spirituality, with its pragmatic and humanistic though nonatheist bend, Moses felt closest throughout his life.[28]

Despite his teachers' help, Moses continued to lag behind white children his age. This was not uncommon. According to one historian, black students in northern states "were one to two years behind whites. . . . Even those with comparable educational levels . . . were not on the same educational playing field because of the disadvantages of separate and unequal northern schools." This gave Moses a lifelong sense of insecurity about his academic capabilities.[29]

Nevertheless, in 1948, his hard work paid off. A high score on a city-wide examination allowed him to attend the exclusive Peter Stuyvesant High School, like his brother Gregory a year earlier. There he would learn to translate the elements of Harlem's black culture—humanism, self-help, solidarity, and spirituality—into a more concrete political vision. His transition to Stuyvesant, however, also introduced him to a new, cosmopolitan world full of whites.[30]

WHEN MOSES ATTENDED Stuyvesant, a public school for gifted children in lower Manhattan, between 1948 and 1952, it was still an all-boys school, renowned for its excellence in mathematics and science education combined with manual training. Its alumni include Thelonious Monk, civil rights activist Roy Innis, and four Nobel laureates. It was home to many students of left-leaning parents and openly endorsed liberal activism, a daring enterprise at a time when the repressive Cold War climate of the 1950s had already begun to manifest itself. Joseph McCarthy's witch hunt of organizations and individuals with existing or nonexisting ties to alleged or acknowledged Communist groups had become a rampant phenomenon in New York, especially in the public school system.[31]

In accordance with John Dewey's progressive ideals on which it had been founded, the school emphasized democracy and accepted a high number of immigrant children, Asians, Jews, and, uncommon in those days, African Americans. Moses's yearbook counts 23 blacks out of 758 graduating class students. Having inherited his family's independent-mindedness, this did not stop him from enthusiastically participating in all that Stuyvesant offered. Although his now fellow Stuyvesant student, and later renowned professor of psychiatry at Harvard Medical School, Alvin Poussaint noted that Moses had "always been self-effacing, quiet, and avoid[ing] the public spotlight," he was elected class president in his senior year. He also joined the basketball and track team, which earned him a Public School's Athletic League Award.[32]

Moses nevertheless spent most of his time with his Harlem playmates. From 1950, he and Poussaint shared a job at the New York University Medical Library, which allowed them to share their maturing views on society, including the frustrating racial and class realities at Stuyvesant. Moses's closest associates were his brother and Poussaint, since outside school hours, interracial social interaction was deemed unacceptable. Being the only black in an extra class for children with above-normal IQs, Moses was constantly picked on by its teacher, Mr. Eifert. But apart from a friend on the basketball team, no one interfered, Moses recalled, so they remained "kind of standoff enemies for the next two years, Mr. Eifert and myself." Poussaint was rejected for the Honor Society without reason despite being elected, and he felt chastised for his distinct East Harlem enunciation. Moreover, they were incensed when the school advisor directed all black students toward black schools when the college representatives came around. Poussaint nonetheless claimed that "juggling Harlem and Stuyvesant for me and Bob did not seem difficult." After school, they returned to Harlem, "where we did not feel like outsiders."[33]

These ambivalent encounters with white liberalism spurred Moses's openness to more left-leaning perspectives, although he did not yet foresee a future in political activism. He had neither been embedded in nor attracted to the nationalist politics he encountered in Harlem. This was not necessarily because of a lack of interest or approval but mere pragmatism; he was simply too taken up by his school work, traveling to and fro between Harlem and Manhattan, his job, and playing basketball at the Harlem YMCA three times a week. Nonetheless, Moses, Poussaint said, "was an idealist, even at Stuyvesant" and was "very politically aware [and] identified with groups that [fought] oppression and would talk about racial issues, socialism, and the shortcomings of capitalism."[34]

Moses's first introduction to leftist views came through Poussaint's father, a black printer who survived financially through left-leaning supporters and customers, many of them communists. In addition, Moses, his brother Gregory, Poussaint, and his sister Julie regularly went to hootenannies, or folk music parties, where Pete Seeger and other radical folk singers played. Moses even met Seeger, then still a member of the Communist Party, at a friend's apartment in Greenwich Village. Through this, he began to reflect on the state of the country, not the least because of the exaggerated presence of Federal Bureau of Investigation (FBI) agents at the hootenannies. Such experiences influenced his political orientation, but Seeger intrigued him for another reason. "Seeger was always talking about the South."[35]

Aunt Doris said her nephew was at that time a restless kid in a "general mix-up of trying to understand what life was all about," although he felt "that too much was made of social status" and "thought he was as good as" anyone. A decisive moment came when his brother Gregory and Poussaint attended summer camps organized by left-wing trade unionists. By 1956, there were twenty-seven of such camps in New York State. Moses only went once, but Gregory and Poussaint became camp counselors. The camps were considered radical, with mostly children of leftist parents and Jews active in organizations that fought segregation attending. The Communist Party's newspaper, the *Daily Worker*, was readily available, and Paul Robeson, then blacklisted for his communist-leaning beliefs, sang to the campers, one-tenth of whom were black. Folk dances and songs celebrating socialism and the Soviet and Chinese revolutions were taught. The camps were attractive, Poussaint stated, "because they promoted interracial interactions. . . . We considered these white people to be progressive and admired them. Their cause was not a popular one even in New York"—a claim supported by a *New York Times* report of a cross burning at one such camp in New Jersey in 1948. It were also whites from these camps rather than their supposed liberal classmates from Stuyvesant with whom Moses, his brother, and Poussaint attended the hootenannies.[36]

At the camp, Moses met Young Socialists and other radical-minded student groups, although it is unclear to what degree distinctions between the Old Left groups entered his formative process. He was mainly intrigued by discussions that included lynching and purging the southern, pro-segregationist Dixiecrats from the Democratic Party. But these Old Leftist–related encounters sensitized him to issues of "red baiting," as he knew these camp visitors and people like his brother and Poussaint to be just that, *people*—not Soviet Union–controlled puppets.[37]

MOSES GRADUATED FROM Stuyvesant in 1952. Wanting to continue his studies, his parents encouraged him to select a white liberal arts college. Moses agreed; he did not want to go to one of the historically black colleges that were mostly located in the South and considered inferior. But not knowing what type of career he wanted, he just prioritized a small school where he could get "a good education" and "play ball." They eventually settled on Hamilton College in Clinton, New York, to which he had won a scholarship.[38]

This exclusive school played another formative role in his transition into a full-time organizer. It strengthened his race consciousness, showed him models of groups working for social change, taught him to work within *and* criticize white liberal institutions, and helped solidify the intellectual basis of his future leadership style. What is also striking about this time is his clear enjoyment in engaging in social activities, especially in organized structures. He evidently sought extended family networks of like-minded people and, in these activities, found comfort even if he was the only black person there. This foreshadowed what he looked for in SNCC when he finally joined the movement in 1960.[39]

Academically, Moses and Hamilton were a perfect match. Its scholastic environment was demanding. Hamilton annually accepted 175 of 1,000 applications, and classes were mandatory, including on Saturdays. Moses ably handled the workload, including extracurricular activities such as the Honor Court, and became vice-president of his senior class, head of the student advisors to freshmen, and a member of the choir. He received a prestigious $900 Rhodes Scholarship and for three years earned an additional salary by working as a waiter in the nonfraternity dining hall. Until 1954, he also continued his job at the NYU Medical Library. He joined baseball and was captain of the basketball team from 1955 to 1956. That season, the basketball team won the most matches in its history, with the yearbook praising his "playmaking techniques and his stabilizing influence on the team." He graduated in the upper quarter of his class with departmental honors in his favorite subject, philosophy, in 1956.[40]

Moses had discovered philosophy in high school, when he read Chinese philosopher Lao-Tse. At Hamilton, he studied other Eastern philosophers and became attracted to thinkers like Ludwig Wittgenstein, a language purist like Moses himself. But his favorites became the French existentialists, whom he read in French. One of his professors, Francis Tafoya, introduced him to Albert Camus, whose philosophies influenced Moses deeply.[41]

The teaching of existentialism and Camus in particular at Hamilton was not accidental. Existentialism flourished between the twentieth-century wars but became especially fashionable in academic settings after the massive destruction of World War II. Its disciples stressed the merit of individual existence and morality, although they differed in how one could give meaning to one's life. French Algerian Camus opposed nihilism, maintaining that the value of life asserted itself through one's actions if not through anything else. He demonstrated this through his own activism, which included joining the French Resistance during the war. This weight on following one's conscience as a means to personal freedom and on leading by one's life example profoundly attracted Moses.[42]

Camus provided practical answers that corresponded with how Moses remembered his father's teachings. Like Gregory Moses, Camus emphasized awareness and education as a virtue because only then individuals could make apt decisions. Moreover, Gregory had shown that every man could reflect sensibly on one's own position. By maintaining that "freedom was already within" each individual, Camus similarly affirmed the validity of self-empowerment. By extension, this justified bottom-up leadership. If individual agency was an end in its own right instead of a tool to a larger objective, then decisions ought to be made democratically. Consequently, Camus "urged a politics of small communities, where free individuals could discover their full selves and one another." Moses's identification with these principles allowed him to relate easily to SNCC workers, who had chosen a similar organizational leadership model.[43]

In collective struggles for social change, Camus stressed rationality and moral purity. He argued in *The Rebel* (1951) that historically, initiators of rebellion in trying to affirm their individual dignity in the face of those that deny their existence inevitably degraded the dignity of others through violence. "[T]he rebel rebelled in the name of the identity of man with man but sacrifices this identity by consecrating the difference in blood." Or: the victims became executioners. To salvage individual integrity, one should avoid being either one. This became Moses's credo too, he stated in 1964. "[Camus] comes out with something which I think is relevant in this struggle [for racial equality]. It's not a question that you just subjugate yourself to the conditions that are and don't try to change them. The problem is to go on from there, into something which is active, and yet the dichotomy is whether you can cease to be a victim anymore and also not be what he calls an executioner," that is, moving "Negro people from the place where they are now the victims of this kind of hatred, to a place where they don't in turn perpetuate this hatred."[44]

Moses's activist career became an exercise in living up to these beliefs. He was considered a moral purist and an idealist by admirers and critics alike. Yet his posturing should not be mistaken for naivety or lack of a keen sense of control or pragmatics. As his 1956 yearbook revealed, Moses might be an "unmitigated idealist," but he was "deliberately ambivalent about it," leaving his classmates to conclude that "in spite of the way he muddles his academic and human ideas he has quite a firm grip on that shy personality of his. In other words, there is something puckish behind that monk's façade." It included an apt example. "Were you to break into his 'philosopher's closet' by surprise, you would assuredly catch him conversing . . . with The Absolute; but if you questioned him on the spot, he would systematically doubt you out of affirming that a conversation was taking place when you entered. His retort to both idealist and skeptic is the same tongue-in-cheek: 'You know that what you believe is true, don't you?' "[45]

CAMUS ALSO SOLIDIFIED Moses's attraction to pacifism. When he entered Hamilton, he had not fully defined his position toward nonviolence, although in high school, he had immersed himself in Albert Schweitzer, another popular thinker in 1950s white academic settings. Like Camus, Schweitzer argued for ethics as instrumental in enduring peace. During his work at the NYU library, Moses renewed his interest in eastern nonviolent thought as well. In particular, his favorite, high school interest Lao-Tse, called for "action through inaction" and humility in leadership, mirroring the restraint and self-efficacy Moses later displayed as an organizer. Camus's stress on moral purity in the face of violence added a sensation of empowerment and human dignity to this.[46]

These ideas were easily aligned with the nonviolent tactics of Martin Luther King Jr. and those in the later student movement. Many of them had based their commitment to nonviolence on Gandhian principles or on traditional Christian thought, such as Jesus' Sermon on the Mount that taught "if someone strikes you on the right cheek, turn to him the other also" (Matthew 5:38–42) and the Sermon on the Plain to "Love your enemies" (Luke 6:27). This assignment, however, implied that non-violence was not just a tactic but a way of life—an assumption not all movement activists shared. Yet regardless of their final objective, as biographer Eric Burner observed, nonviolence in civil rights protests "amounted to a defiance of authority and custom and at the same time a refusal to strike back against attack" that "required precisely the self-knowledge and composure affirmed by *The Rebel*."[47]

Moses's attraction to pacifism also owed something to the Quakers. The Quakers, or Society of Friends, adhere to an unconventional form of Christianity that advocates freedom of conscience. Central to its theology is the innate presence of God, the "Inner Light," in each individual. Their validation of the godly existence in each individual could only be accomplished through nonviolence and a radical dismissal of religious symbolism and church leaders as necessary interpreters of the divine to the mortal. In secular terms, this echoed Camus's and Gregory Moses's insistence on individual agency and bottom-up leadership. Moreover, the Quaker worship style was one of silence (only then the "Inner Light" could be heard), which suited Moses's introverted personality.[48]

Moses befriended several Quakers who taught at Hamilton. He got especially close to Professor Channing Richardson, a conscientious objector during World War II, and his wife, for whom he worked as a babysitter. Richardson influenced Moses's intellectual and activist leanings in a time he characterized as still searching for an identity. He introduced him to the writings of Gandhi, whom Moses wrote a paper on in his junior year. At this time, Gandhi was popular among other young black activists, like Martin Luther King Jr., James Lawson, and Bayard Rustin, too. Lawson and Rustin had even been to India to study nonviolence; King followed in 1959.[49]

In 1953, Richardson steered Moses toward the Quaker-affiliated American Friends Service Committee (AFSC), to which Bayard Rustin was closely connected. A socialist Quaker pacifist from Pennsylvania, Rustin had strong ties to the Old Left through his 1930s and 1940s connections with the Young Communist League and A. Philip Randolph's labor movement (although he, like Randolph, later became a staunch anti-Communist). In 1941, Randolph and Rustin worked on the March on Washington movement, which induced President Roosevelt to ban racism in the defensive industry. In 1953, the eccentric Rustin, who spoke with a self-made British accent, was mostly known for his association with A. J. Muste's peace organization the Fellowship of Reconciliation (FOR), although he is now mostly remembered as the primary organizer of the 1963 March on Washington. From 1944 to 1946, he was jailed for draft resistance.[50]

Like the Quakers, the AFSC promoted social involvement and supported alternative military service by dismissing the draft as incompatible with individual freedom. Yet notions of conscientious objection (CO) were not commonly discussed in Moses's family, with one of his uncles holding a high army position. His two brothers joined the military as well, although not in active combat. Moses therefore did not have the "pacifist position worked out" when he was introduced to the AFSC. At best, he "was doing some searching about what I felt, and I guess what I felt strongest was that I didn't want to go in the Army." His Harlem and Stuyvesant experiences also played a role in this. One of his friends was killed during the Korean War. Moreover, he noted, "I'm thinking now about . . . what's going on in the country, what I'm learning through these hootenannies . . . I'm thinking back about Uncle Bill." Richardson therefore advised him to contact the AFSC in New York City, which sent him to Bayard Rustin. They met in the latter's apartment, where Rustin advised him and a few others about CO and other positions regarding the draft. While Rustin forgot this meeting ever occurred, it left an indelible impression on Moses. Not only was he amazed to "meet a black man raised in the U.S. with a pronounced English accent," but he especially revered his act as one of individual agency. "In showing up I became somebody because I was the only Black kid coming in."[51]

Moses applied for CO status shortly after the 1953 meeting with Rustin, although his move also had a distinctly religious undertone. He had become involved with the Intervarsity Christian Fellowship, a religious study group he had learned about through his job waiting tables. The head waiter, Corky, was the group's driving force, with whom Moses attended conferences and prayer meetings. After his junior year, he attended a summer camp in Canada with the group. His counselor was a German related to the neo-orthodox movement around Swiss protestant theologian Karl Barth. This taught him a whole new set of life theories. He also avidly discussed religion with Alvin Poussaint and with his two Jewish roommates.[52]

However, when he studied more philosophy during his sophomore year, he began to doubt what he had been absorbing. "[It] threw me off the track." But unwilling to give up his religious quest just yet, he sought new avenues to explore Christianity. He tried street preaching in New York with a group run by a black West Indian woman, but his shy personality and soft voice were incompatible with the job. To his later movement friends, who had grown up with bombastic, passionate preachers in the black church tradition, this fact seemed almost unbelievable. Dave Dennis, for instance, recounted his shock when he heard about it. "Moses standing on a corner of Times Square, preaching! I wish I could have seen it!"[53]

Yet this episode in Moses's life did not amount to a solid conversion to institutional religion. It was another stage in his overall search for a philosophy of his own, stitched together from dozens of different experiences. When his father told him that "the ministry was a calling, not just an occupation," Moses swiftly dropped the thought of becoming a minister himself. His experience with the Intervarsity Christian Fellowship nonetheless reinforced his budding views on pacifism. With them he entered into correspondence with the draft board, but his CO claim was denied since he could not provide evidence of a church he had been brought up in. Eventually, he was granted a student deferment.[54]

MOSES'S IDEAS ON PACIFISM and social activism developed further when his Quaker professors pushed him to attend AFSC camps abroad. The Richardsons helped him get accepted into these programs. For Moses, they were "consciousness-awakening[,] particularly in being able to look at the country, so to speak, from the 'outside.'" The trips provided him not only with an exhilarating, politically oriented social life with people from Africa, Europe, Australia, and Asia at the impressionable age of 20, but also with constructive models for working toward social change, especially from the bottom-up. The goal of the camps, an AFSC brochure reads, was stimulating "a higher sense of individual responsibility for society, and to create bonds of friendship between campers and the local community."[55]

In the summer of 1955, Moses attended these voluntary work camps in Europe, after having completed an orientation session at the AFSC's base near Philadelphia from June 28 to July 3. The AFSC had sent newsletters with instructions beforehand, advising attendees to be ready to explain the United States to outsiders, including "the negative things." It suggested studying the 1954 *Brown v. Topeka* Supreme Court ruling, organizations like the NAACP, and the Old Left cooperative and labor movements. The newsletters also explained good camp behavior, like not waiting for others to do the work, shedding materialism, and remembering "that the camp probably existed before you ever arrived and that there are others with different experiences and philosophies."[56]

On July 4, Moses embarked on the *Columbia* in Quebec, Canada, to arrive in Paris in time to witness the Bastille Day celebrations. He then left for Mont-de-l'Enclus in Belgium, where he helped erect a dormitory at an underprivileged children's summer camp. The project was small and offered little variety, including in the diet; they ate potato soup every night. He and nine volunteers from the United States, United Kingdom, Belgium, France, Germany, and Sweden stayed for a month. During a talk on his trips for Hamilton's International Relations Club on October 24, 1955, he noted that the Europeans took a special interest in him as a black American. Locals regularly approached him with shouts of "Congo, Congo," the African nation Belgium had colonized. When he put the AFSC's advice to the test, however, he was "surprised that they had not heard of the Supreme Court decision. . . . The people were full of questions about the Negro problem in America."[57]

After Belgium, he went to Metz in France to construct houses for the homeless with African, Middle Eastern, Ceylon, and French volunteers. Because there were no machines, they had to mix cement and pour foundations by hand. It was hard labor, but Moses liked it regardless. He had worthwhile encounters with the other volunteers, especially because he spoke French. The camp was bigger than the one in Belgium and organized by more skilled and politically experienced individuals. He stayed with pacifists who, like Camus, had been part of the French Resistance. Coming into contact with people who had lived through World War II impressed him, but overall he emphasized discovering a newfound feeling of personal worth reminiscent of his father's egalitarian teachings. "Mainly I got into a sense of what it meant to be in a kind of network of people who were open to you as a person . . . I didn't have that either at Stuyvesant [or] Hamilton."[58]

Moses ended the summer in Bremen, Germany, after a week of hitch-hiking through Switzerland. For a fortnight, he worked on a farm in Bremerhafen, digging up potatoes for a nearby missionary hospital with workers from the United States, Canada, France, Germany, the Netherlands, Spain, Australia, and Scandinavian countries. Among them was a white girl from the American South. Moses was especially intrigued by the "interesting discussions in which people were really sort of astounded by her description [of southern race relations and] *acceptance* of 'well, this is the way we live' . . . in this part of the United States."[59]

In 1956, Moses went to another AFSC camp in Japan, where he attended Quaker workshops and helped build a stairway on a steep hill near a children's mental hospital, so the patients could ascend the hill more safely during the rainy season. He deliberately went to the camp early, so he could experience more of Japanese life. With two other Japanese campers, he stayed at a Buddhist monastery for a week to study its beliefs and spent the night at the home of one of its monks. Besides marveling at his daily practice of religion, Moses was amazed to discover that the monk's wife nursed three daughters, of whom the oldest was at least five, and that the Japanese had different concepts about food.[60]

Overall, the trips strengthened Moses's beliefs in pacifism, internal peace through meditation, and working for people society liked to ignore. They raised his racial awareness and broadened his knowledge of progressive activist groups. Moreover, the trips provided an opportunity for reflection at a time when Moses was still trying to define his role in the world. "It was good being away and also being kind of alone, because particularly I didn't speak any Japanese [and] no-one spoke any English." The restlessness about his identity that had troubled Moses as a child had not eased much when he left Hamilton—ironically largely because of it.[61]

FEW ADOLESCENTS ESCAPE grappling with their identity in growing up, but the issue of race complicated Moses's situation. Being one of only three blacks in the college's 750 student body, he was far more isolated than he had been at Stuyvesant. Like his high school, however, Hamilton advocated some sense of social responsibility. In 1954, the college awarded McCarthy critic Edward Murrow an honorary degree, and Chief Justice Earl Warren, who in the *Brown* suit had ruled the "separate-but-equal" clause unconstitutional, was the speaker at Moses's 1956 commencement. Warren, the *New York Times* reported, told the students that "whatever you accomplish will depend largely on what you make of your government." In this, Warren echoed the progressive tradition of Stuyvesant, emphasizing democracy. Hamilton's acceptance of blacks in itself was progressive too, although Moses stressed that it had its limits. "When I was at Hamilton the white attitude was: 'Well . . . society has the overall problem, [and our part is] to try and open a door for two or three Negroes, and let's see what happens.' The difference from the period before is simply that earlier they weren't interested in even opening a door." When he, for instance, remarked to a professor after the *Brown* suit that he had attended segregated schools in Harlem too, the latter denied "that as an instance of racism." In addition, Moses was disappointed to find out that a professor had confided to Moses's roommate that he was uneasy, if not downright afraid, to call on Moses because of the color of his skin.[62]

Getting involved in Hamilton's student life therefore meant confronting his own internal struggles over race. Moses deliberately rejected offers from fraternities to join them as their "token Negro," although he had not expected to even get invited; when he applied, the interviewer had asked surprised if he had understood that Hamilton was a fraternity school, implying that he could never join any of those. It took two years before Moses accepted an invitation to join the student Emerson Literary Society, although it displayed an unusually high level of social consciousness. Overall, he withdrew into his own world. According to one student, Moses "lived in some isolation" because "many of us had never really related to blacks in any significant way before." While he characterized integration as positive, he was "deeply bitter about some of the realities of the campus" and believed that white middle-class culture was in "vital need of some kind of renewal." To survive campus life, he developed "the capacity . . . to pass through unobtrusively" by placing himself "in the role of observer, listening and watching, learning how the dominant society feels." He even taught himself to "repress my feelings or at least expression of my feelings whenever I felt humiliated," a mindset that fitted his already natural tendency for self-effacement.[63]

Moses's feelings were not uncommon for blacks who attended (disproportionally) white northern schools. "White liberalism was just a façade," SNCC worker Robert Wright said about his time at Harvard University, "Whereas people spoke to us and ate with us and laughed and talked with us and played football[,] they never invited us to their parties." Martin Luther King Jr., who excelled at Boston University at the same time, felt equally self-conscious. According to biographer David Lewis, "racial stereotypes beset him on all sides," so King took to "seriousness, personal neatness, and punctuality" to avoid the image of the "happy-go-lucky darky." Others, like Malcolm X, responded by rejecting integration altogether.[64]

Moses's and King's response can perhaps be considered a northern version of what Richard Wright called his Jim Crow education, that is, learning how to behave in the white world to survive. When Moses speaks of "passing through unobtrusively," it can literally refer to his self-effacing nature, but metaphorically it invokes the notion of a "racial passing," a term used when members of one racial group deliberately identify with an other. Historian Thomas Sugrue underscored that for many northern blacks, "the only way to cross the black-white [class] boundary was to adopt 'white' attitudes, lifestyles, and culture." In this light, Moses's attraction to Camus is hardly surprising either: his work was set against the independence struggle of his native Algeria from his home, France, which divided his loyalty.[65]

Simultaneously, Moses also appreciated internal struggles like his own and those of Camus, because they provided him with an idea of the individual within the larger society. After all, Moses explained, within that "struggle you find a broader identification . . . with individuals that are going through the same kind of struggle, so [it] doesn't remain just a question of racial struggle. Then you get a picture of yourself as a person [and the] problem of identifying yourself in Negro culture—or of integrating into the white society—that disappears."[66]

BUT IN HIS academic self-appraisal, Moses remained deeply insecure. Even when a fellowship granted him access to the doctoral philosophy program at Harvard University in 1956, he doubted his competence. This was because of the always present "race question: can you compete with whites? And there was a myth that you could find a place in which it was possible to get an 'objective assessment' of how well you could compete, and that was Harvard." Yet he remained "torn between belief in the myth [and] the myth itself," which "left him wondering whether he really couldn't do the work." He nonetheless persevered because he did not know what else to do. He moved to Cambridge, Massachusetts, and earned his MA in philosophy in June 1957 and then commenced a PhD. He also worked two nights a week as a night grill attendant at the Harvard Business School, from November 1956 to May 1957, and part-time as a maintenance man for a Quaker meeting house between October 1957 and March 1958. He regularly attended meetings but never became an official member.[67]

Harvard opened a new avenue of looking at life. Existentialism was replaced by analytical philosophers like Wittgenstein, who emphasized purity in language. This attracted the taciturn Moses, who took Wittgenstein's aphorism "whereof one cannot speak, thereof one must be silent" to heart. He also worked closely with Professor John Blythe, who had written on Alfred North Whitehead, then considered the ideal analytic logician.[68]

One existentialist, Paul Tillich, however, was teaching at Harvard and was still widely influential. Martin Luther King Jr. wrote his dissertation on him in 1955. Moses had read Tillich's major works too, which had deeply affected him. He decided to attend his lectures. Yet, Moses found, the lectures were "all poetry," relying on too many metaphors and other stylistic ornaments. He and other graduate students agreed "that according to Wittgenstein, [Tillich] hadn't said anything at all. He was just playing with words."[69]

While the analytic approach left permanent traces in his thinking, such as his fixation with clarity in language, overall his fascination with Tillich's hidden messages and his strong identification with existentialism remained. "I tired of thinking and [of] the meaning of meaning. I returned to Camus's dictum 'I rebel, therefore we exist' and to Lao-Tse, who taught that the way to wisdom consists in living one life well—starting small, a step at a time, with what is near, with what is at hand." What was at hand for Moses, however, soon changed.[70]

IN FEBRUARY 1958, Gregory and Louise Moses returned from their first ever vacation. Shortly after, Louise passed away at age forty-three. Because she had forbidden her husband to tell them the truth, the Moses children did not know she had been suffering from cancer. So when the news reached him at Harvard that month, Moses, who had been very close with his mother, was devastated. He had been especially impressed with how she dealt with her life's agony, dominated by her husband's drinking, financial strains, and disease. "She showed me how to live [in] silence, quietly." When he worked at the NYU library, he had arranged a front desk job for her there to provide her with a life outside the home. Her example had a lasting impact on him, which helped him in his future activism. "My mother influenced my way of being quietly circumscribed, grounded independent of a need for accumulating things." His choice to briefly adopt her middle name in 1965 was indicative of her significance to him.[71]

A month after his mother's passing, Moses dropped out of Harvard. His brother Gregory was in the Army and his younger brother Roger studied at Hamilton, so he returned home to be with their father. Gregory Moses had not coped well with his wife's passing. After the funeral, he suffered a mental breakdown caused by despair. He told his family he was leaving for a while, and he packed and left. Before the day was over, Moses, packing to return to Harvard, received a phone call from the police, who had found Gregory hallucinating, convinced that he was actor Gary Cooper. Moses's father stayed in Bellevue Hospital's psychiatric ward until summer. Such episodes were not uncommon in the black community, especially among the upper-middle class. In the mid-1940s, black admissions to New York mental hospitals was double that of whites', and blacks reportedly had more hallucinations, a condition associated with frustrations over their substandard living situations. Moses stayed to take care of his father, even when the latter eventually returned to work.[72]

Meanwhile, Moses needed employment for them to survive. He signed a three-year contract, from 1958 to 1961, as a mathematics teacher at Horace Mann high school, one of the country's top private schools, located in the Bronx. This also safeguarded Moses's CO status, because after the Russians had launched *Sputnik*, the U.S. government had qualified math and science teachers for deferment.[73]

Moses liked teaching, but the racial realities at the predominantly white school frustrated him. He was again confronted "at every point . . . that you [were] treated as a Negro and you couldn't really be accepted as an individual yet—even at any level of the society you happened to penetrate." When one Horace Mann alumnus, white liberal Allard Lowenstein, spoke at the school in 1959 about the need to establish the right to vote in communist-dominated Europe, Moses quarreled with a fellow teacher about it. When Moses interjected that blacks in the United States were disenfranchised as well, his coworker bluntly replied, "That's different." Consequently, Moses "got the feeling that no matter what I did it would always be there, even though things were better [than] in my father's time."[74]

Moses's racial consciousness grew when he accepted another job as the private tutor of Frankie Lymon, an African American teenage singer who had scored a number 6 position on the *Billboard* singles charts in 1956. Moses accompanied him when he toured the North by bus. Lymon, doing drugs, would not study, so Moses soon left. Yet traveling to the black neighborhoods of a dozen northern cities, including Chicago and Boston, proved revelatory. Despite his background, Moses recalled "not really awakening to the idea that there was an urban black archipelago" until now. Seeing these communities upset him. As historian Nicholas Lemann described, in "all these places there was a heady sense of the coming into being of an established black presence," but "it was plain that something was wrong. The poor sections were getting worse, the middle class felt stuck, and there was not a governing idea about what the problem was and what the reaction to it should be." This echoed witnessing his father and others in his personal network struggle to get ahead, a condition that, Moses now recognized, "exemplified the economic and emotional situation of many blacks in the cities."[75]

BUT MOSES DID NOT yet have any idea what to do about it. Although several historians claim that he participated in the 1959 Youth March for Integrated Schools, he did not know about it. He had not even closely followed events in the South, being "cocooned in the isolation of Hamilton . . . [T]he Emmet Till murder, the Montgomery boycott, the emergence of Dr. King were external happenings." Nor was he involved in New York's grassroots civil rights activism. His work at Horace Mann shielded him from most Harlem realities, although he realized its difficulties were enormous. Despite local newspapers' coverage of grassroots protests, he had no idea if anyone was doing something about them. Even if "New York became a ground zero for northern civil rights protests," as historian Thomas Sugrue maintained, for Moses the idea of an advanced racial movement in his hometown did not register. To be sure, New York had seen grassroots agency through direct action and legal protests and had a large civil rights organizational presence, including the NAACP's headquarters. Yet the widespread *feeling* of a mass movement for change appeared absent. To many ordinary northern blacks in the late 1950s like Moses, this budding sensation was rather associated with the South—about which they heard through television, newspapers, churches, and personal networks, including southern relatives—not their own region.[76]

In early February 1960, Moses read one such *New York Times* article on Greensboro, North Carolina, where four black A&T College students had staged a sit-in at a Woolworth's whites-only lunch counter. The A&T students had expanded their protests daily, catching the local media's attention. By the end of the week, sit-ins had exploded across Greensboro and elsewhere in the state. The sit-ins soon reached all southern states, although generally only in urban areas with colleges nearby. The North witnessed sympathy protests, and southern sit-in leaders came to New York to encourage rallies there. By the end of 1960, over 70,000 people had participated in sit-ins, leading to over 3,000 arrests and the dismissal of dozens of students and faculty from southern educational institutions.

Nonetheless, apart from the Deep South, the students' efforts proved successful: lunch counters in national chain stores and several southern ones were integrated. A national audience, which witnessed neatly dressed blacks studying at lunch counters who refused to retaliate when heckled by whites, generally received the sit-in students sympathetically.[77]

News coverage of the sit-ins riveted Moses. In this sense, the sit-ins posed an interesting example of the local influencing the national and vice versa, with students across the nation copycatting what they saw on the news in their own neighborhoods. Even if not prompted into action themselves, they broadened awareness of civil rights activities elsewhere. In *Freedom on My Mind*, one Mississippi teenager related how she "ran to read the stories" about the sit-ins. Another Mississippi local, Victoria Gray, was attracted to them because they uncovered "a support system that wasn't there before" or, rather, one that had been invisible. In 1962, Moses similarly validated the effect of news coverage on him. "I saw a picture in the *New York Times* of Negro college students 'sitting in' at a lunch counter. . . . [They] had a certain look on their faces—sort of sullen, angry, determined. Before the Negro in the South had always looked on the defensive, cringing. This time they were taking the initiative. They were kids my age, and I knew this had something to do with my own life."[78]

Moses experienced what many blacks would whenever they were confronted with a civil rights demonstration far from home but yet so close. "The pictures attracted me because I could feel myself in the faces of the people that they had there on the front pages. I could feel how they felt." As such, he attested, the sit-ins "hit me powerfully, in the soul as well as the brain. I was mesmerized by the pictures I saw." Other northern SNCC workers were similarly captivated. Stokely Carmichael called the sit-ins "spectacular," remarking he could not forget "looking with amazement and joy at . . . the *New York Times*." To Moses, identification with the students ran especially deep because of his immersion in white society. "Until then, my Black life was conflicted, [having moved] back and forth between the sharply contrasting worlds of Hamilton College, Harvard University, Horace Mann, and Harlem." In a W. E. B. DuBois-like explanation of double-consciousness, he continued, "It made me realize that for a long time I had been troubled by the problem of being a Negro [and] being an American. This was the answer."[79]

That answer corresponded with Moses's budding outlook on the generation of social change. First, the sit-ins exemplified Camus's credo of moral leadership by example. Second, they were a means of nonviolent protest, and third, they conformed to the American middle-class values that reflected the white environment Moses had become familiar with. Fourth, the sit-ins' public image was one of a decentralized, leaderless movement, which corresponded with Camus's and Gregory Moses's lessons on individual agency, self-empowerment, and bottom-up leadership.[80]

Later studies of the sit-ins qualified this image of youthful independence. Many sit-ins were preceded by careful planning, the creation of communication networks, and training in nonviolence and were aided through established organizations with resources like funds and lawyers. The tactic itself went back to the 1930s labor movement and the 1940s activities of the civil rights organization CORE (Congress of Racial Equality). In the late 1950s, sit-ins occurred in Kansas and Tennessee. But the 1960s sit-ins involved lawbreaking on an unprecedented scale. Moreover, students, rather than traditional middle-class adults, protesting nonviolently en masse was a new phenomenon. The general reaction to the sit-ins was therefore similar to Moses's. As historian Howard Zinn wrote in 1965, "A Negro never before seen . . . was brought into the national view," as "the idea so long cherished . . . that only a handful of agitators opposed the system of segregation, was swept aside."[81]

MOSES IMMEDIATELY WANTED to go south to participate in the sit-ins himself. "I was struck by the determination on their faces. They weren't cowed [or] apathetic—they meant to finish what they had begun. Here was something that could be done. I simply had to get involved." During spring break, Moses visited his Uncle Bill in Virginia. Reflecting the changing ties of northern blacks with their southern heritage, he had never had any interest in going south before, but now could not resist. When Moses witnessed students picketing a Woolworth's store in Newport News, he instantly joined them. The experience unleashed unexpectedly profound emotions. "From the first time a Negro gets involved in white society, he [starts] repressing, repressing, repressing. My whole reaction through life to such humiliation was to avoid it, keep it down, hold it in, play it cool. . . . But when you do something personally to fight prejudice there is a feeling of great release."[82]

The visit to Newport News was revealing in another respect. Moses and his uncle attended a mass rally in support of the student protests. There Wyatt T. Walker of SCLC spoke extensively about Martin Luther

King Jr. and the need to support a national leader, implying King. He also spoke of a new SCLC office in Harlem. Intrigued, Moses walked up to Walker afterward to ask him for contact information. Also remembering Walker's leadership comments, he asked him, "Don't you think we need a lot of leaders?" Walker's emphasis, he felt, seemed out of place since students from all over "were spreading, getting activated, and moving, [so] why put an emphasis then, on one person?" Perplexed by the question, Walker merely responded by saying that the general need to support King did not outweigh the legitimacy of other activist groups. Finding this reply inarguable, Moses left it at that and walked off.[83]

Historians like Taylor Branch have cited Moses's question to Walker as indicative of Moses's general philosophy, but he had not yet thought these leadership matters through. Although his father's egalitarian teachings, Camus, the Quakers, and the decentralized sit-ins primed him toward this position, the Walker incident was merely the beginning. "I hadn't worked out any notions of leadership, except that I guess I had a feeling for what people later termed grassroots leadership, that is, that there should be leadership all over. [Walker's emphasis just] struck me as wrong—that is, the emphasis, which I later came to learn was part of a pattern [of] the ways in which organizations are shaped and formed. And a lot has to do with the media, and the need for projection."[84]

Moses left Virginia with the contact information of the Harlem SCLC office and news of a civil rights rally at his father's workplace, the Armory, in May. After attending a Harlem church meeting chaired by Bayard Rustin that recruited organizers for the rally, he volunteered and decorated his neighborhood with posters announcing the event. The rally featured celebrity activists like Harry Belafonte and Sidney Poitier, but Moses also witnessed Malcolm X conversing with actor and social activist Ossie Davis. In addition, he volunteered at the SCLC office every day after school. While the work was not very eventful—ranging from stuffing envelopes to handing out flyers—being in an office run by veteran organizers, such as Bayard Rustin and Jack O'Dell, was. Filled with volunteers, the office buzzed with conversations about the freedom struggle. For him, it constituted the moment of becoming networked into a broader movement for social change. Yet despite all the buzz around him, no mention was made of SNCC, which had been founded just weeks before.[85]

CHAPTER TWO

A Movement Education

For Bob Moses, the summer of 1960 was a summer of firsts: his first extensive stay in the South, his first in-depth contact with the movement, and his first trip to Mississippi. Seeking a form of activism that suited his personality, skills, and beliefs, he got involved in direct action immediately. However, he soon discovered that this was not what he was looking for.

Moses longed to go south, preferably to the Deep South, and "see the movement for myself." Although some historians insist that the civil rights movement was national in scope, Moses clearly regarded the South as the stage for the most discernible force in civil rights activism. He told Bayard Rustin he desired to work for Martin Luther King Jr. in Montgomery, Alabama. Moses's choice illustrates his point about the power of media projection: while he could have joined any of the grassroots protests in the North or the sit-in students across the South, he nonetheless picked King's organization. While his stay with SCLC was brief, it was long enough to get acquainted with the major organizations working for social change and to discern their distinctive characteristics.[1]

SCLC WAS FOUNDED IN 1957 with Rustin's and Ella Baker's help after the Montgomery Bus Boycott. Unlike the integrated, members-only, nationally oriented NAACP, SCLC's focus was regional, all-black, and open to all. The NAACP maintained a strong central body headquartered in New York with relatively autonomous branches across the country. They were nonetheless subjected to the NAACP's national policies. Branches were responsible for collecting dues, although the national office could withdraw any support if their results were considered insufficient or deviated from its central focus on litigation or "respectable" tactics like voter registration. This often had disastrous consequences, especially in the Deep South, where known NAACP members were blacklisted from employment. As one Mississippi member begged Gloster Current, the director of Branch and Field Services, in 1964, "Mr. Current, to discontinue the assistance, means that everything I have built here will go to waste. I'll have to leave town and the state to find work, because I have a family to support."[2]

The NAACP had been in existence since 1909 and, partly due to that longevity, focused intently on organizational routine and survival, making it simultaneously democratic and bureaucratic. SCLC, in contrast, rejected internal democracy because it inhibited swift action during civil rights campaigns. The organization was designed to take advantage of the media attention that King had acquired through his participation in the Montgomery Bus Boycott and intended to make him the "star" of the movement. Although its Board of Directors had forty-three members (mostly male ministers from the urban South), in reality, King's word was final. Between 1957 and the sit-ins, however, SCLC accomplished little. Its Crusade for Citizenship generated few new voters because it lacked extensive local organization by full-time activists. During the sit-ins, SCLC's role was secondary to the students.[3]

Lacking a membership base, SCLC's money had to come through King's efforts. Rather than developing programs, he spent much time fundraising through speeches and writings. Simultaneously, SCLC's ability to make snap, top-down decisions allowed it to move flexibly and effectively, and with its 1957 Prayer Pilgrimage and other headline-grabbing civil rights gatherings, it seemed the new face of the southern movement. Moses therefore logically assumed that King equaled action. Visibility had to be central in his decision to join SCLC, because, despite all the civil rights activism in 1960, he still knew little about the movement and nothing about SNCC.[4]

SNCC was founded at Shaw University in Raleigh, North Carolina, during the Southwide Youth Leadership Conference of April 15–17, 1960, after the sit-ins had uncovered a widespread social network in need of communication. Ella Baker initiated the conference, with $800 of SCLC money, to determine whether the separate sit-in student centers wanted to become one coordinating body. Over 200 delegates attended; over half came from southern educational institutions, with the rest hailing from northern colleges or organizations like CORE, FOR, SCLC, NAACP, and the NSA (National Student Association). National press generally focused on well-known conference attendees, like Martin Luther King Jr. and James Lawson, a black Vanderbilt University divinity student. The sit-in students received King less favorably than Lawson, whose speech criticized middle-class black leadership—particularly that of the NAACP—for prioritizing fundraising, organizational structures, and gradualist tactics like litigation. The sit-ins, Lawson stated, were a "judg-ment upon middle class conventional, half-way efforts to deal with radical social evil." Having violated an unwritten rule that civil rights organizations always refrained from publicly criticizing each other, the action boded ill for the future. The *New York Times* reported alarmingly about "a struggle between two factions in the fight for civil rights," but it bolstered the sensation among conference participants of a break with previous activism and a "new wave" represented by the students.[5]

Nevertheless, between April and July 1960, SNCC was hardly in the news. Part of this lack in coverage was deliberate. SNCC had shielded press attendance from policy sessions for fear the presence of reporters inhibited open discussions. Moreover, SNCC had only one paid mem-ber, Jane Stembridge, and no clear identity. Although it considered its function to be the coordination of local student groups, finding imme-diate consensus about its goals, structure, and relations with SCLC was impossible due to the diversity of its participants. Yet despite geograph-ical, philosophical, race, and class differences, overall SNCC's founders were young, highly esteemed democracy, rejected gradualism, and were open to nonviolent direct action, irrespective of end goal (tactic or way of life) and motivation (religious or secular).[6]

Status in SNCC was related to one's activism during the sit-ins. In this, none carried more prestige than the disproportionally large Nash-ville group, associated with James Lawson. Between 1958 and 1960, Law-son had directed workshops in nonviolence, which later SNCC stalwarts like Diane Nash, John Lewis, Bernard Lafayette, James Bevel, and Mar-ion Barry attended. They orchestrated sit-ins in Nashville in 1959 and more after Greensboro, all the while instructing new students into the tactic.[7]

Still, many in SNCC questioned the group's insistence on nonviolence or accepted its emphasis on redemption merely because it was popular or out of pragmatism. Nonetheless, until 1962, the Nashville group's re-ligious commitment to nonviolence dominated SNCC's discussions, and at its first policy meeting on May 13–14, 1960, SNCC adopted the group's views into its official Statement of Purpose, written by Lawson. The Statement's usefulness as a reflection of SNCC's earliest constituency, however, has long been contested. Several founding members insist that SNCC's religious orientation has been exaggerated. As Julian Bond ar-gued, "Many of the people were religious, but the *organization* was not." Reflecting this divergence, the May meeting ended only with the bare essentials for functioning: hiring Jane Stembridge as executive secretary, arranging office space in SCLC's Atlanta office through Ella Baker, and securing usage of NSA equipment through Connie Curry of the National Student Association's Southern Project.[8]

ON JULY 4, Moses arrived by bus in Atlanta too. Rustin had advised him to go to SCLC's new headquarters instead of inactive Montgomery, but when he arrived, it proved an enormous letdown. He had hoped "to see 'the movement' as I idealized it," with "energetic volunteers getting out mailings, bold campaigners preparing to hit the streets," and "strategies for political struggle being conceived behind closed doors." But unlike the efficient New York office, there was little activity, and, despite Rustin's letters to King and Baker, he was not expected. Even the building was disappointing, with three small rooms occupied by only three workers: Baker, Stembridge, and King, who was rarely present. Only Stembridge, stuffing envelopes for SNCC, was there when Moses arrived. Feeling useless, he joined her without even asking if he could help.[9]

Moses immediately got along with Stembridge, the daughter of a progressive-minded southern white Baptist minister. The two shared interests in religion, philosophy, and Moses's hometown. She had interrupted her theological studies at Union Seminary in New York to join the movement to convert other southern whites. "I hurt for my people because they are liars, blind, and hypocrites [and] I came to speak to them," she explained in one letter that August. While licking envelopes, the two talked animatedly about Niebuhr, Tillich, Kant, Jewish existentialist Martin Buber, and Camus's and Gandhi's theories on nonviolence. Often their discussions continued in B. B. Beamon's restaurant, until late into the night. Connie Curry frequently joined them. "When it got to be about two o'clock in the morning, and you just thought you could not listen or do one other thing, we would order a chocolate nut sundae." Their conversations also turned to leadership issues, as they grudgingly awaited SCLC's replacement of Ella Baker with Wyatt T. Walker over the summer.[10]

Moses was particularly sad to see Baker preparing to leave the organization. They had spoken only a few times, but Moses instantly "had a very strong, and a very positive reaction to Ella. I felt that she was someone you could trust." She had confided to him that despite her role in SCLC's foundation, she was unhappy with its focus on King. She had accepted his symbolic value but was more concerned with building up grassroots leadership. This, she felt, could break the historic cycle where blacks "put all [their] hopes in a leader, but then that leader often turns out to have feet of clay." She stressed that "strong people don't need strong leaders." With Walker's appointment, however, SCLC moved farther away from facilitating grassroots initiatives and closer to a dependence on big names and male leadership. Baker's message resonated with Moses due to his experience with Walker in Newport News that spring. As she imparted her life experiences in diverse civil rights organizations—being fifty-six she could have been King's mother—to him, Moses's respect for her grew.[11]

Baker's susceptibility to grassroots leadership was rooted in her rural North Carolina middle-class upbringing. She always rebelled against middle-class notions that set her up as being "apart from" the black masses but embraced the tenet of servicing others. After graduating from Shaw University in 1927, she worked for organizations like the YWCA and the Workers Education Project in Harlem. In 1940, she joined the NAACP and, as its Director of Branches, traveled the country extensively to recruit new members. During these trips, she met numerous southern civil rights leaders, strengthening her faith in bottom-up organizing—that is, finding someone who already worked as an activist and then supporting him with whatever resources he was lacking. In 1956, she, Bayard Rustin, and Stanley Levison founded In Friendship, which provided financial assistance to southern activists suffering from reprisals for their activity. She had resigned from the NAACP in 1946 because she questioned its commitment to developing local programs and because she resented its centralized structure and the sexism of its Assistant National Secretary Walter White.[12]

Baker encountered similar problems with SCLC. Its hierarchical structure mirrored that of the church, with one front man to inspire and be obeyed. King intended SCLC to bring the church's leadership model into politics, earning King the nickname "the Lawd" from SNCC workers. Such ego glorification troubled King at times, as he wrote in 1960. "I have no Messiah complex, and I know that we need many leaders to do the job." But he rarely stopped it and occasionally even expected it.[13]

Baker had therefore been planning to leave SCLC long before Walker's appointment. Within movement folklore, however, her decision to leave organizations was less explained by her lifelong discomfort with structure or gender constraints but rather by her overall belief that "organizational loyalties could transplant ideals"—a notion

SNCC adopted as a rationale for developing local leadership. This perceived independence greatly attracted the students. Many SNCC workers desired to stay independent, and Baker encouraged these views. At Raleigh, she told the students to avoid personal leadership struggles and basing leadership on status. Yet in her conference speech, Baker acknowledged that the students were already "[inclined] toward group-centered leadership" and "intolerant of anything that smacked of manipulation or domination." The Nashville group, for example, had internalized Old Left icon Myles Horton's lessons on internal democracy that he had developed at Highlander Folk School, a controversial interracial leadership training school for labor and civil rights activists in Tennessee in the 1930s. Accordingly, the Nashville group functioned democratically without dependence on one individual, even an influential figure like Lawson. It had a rotating chairmanship devoid of any power, a model that it wanted SNCC to copy.[14]

Although Bob Moses had arrived at similar views through different experiences, he was naturally drawn to the students and Baker. At B. B. Beamon's, he and Stembridge eagerly discussed the students' views. They agreed that Wyatt Walker's approach was "too hero-worshipping, media-centered, preacher-dominated, and authoritarian." They found Baker's approach much more appealing. Moses especially applauded her role in SNCC. "If a different person had been in her position, it would've been extremely difficult to envisage SNCC being set up the way it was, independent of King, because even when I was there in the office, there was still the pressure on the students [to affiliate because] if they had to rely on King for fundraising, then they should be a part of his organization."[15]

BUT MOSES'S FRUSTRATIONS over SCLC's inactivity grew as the weeks went by. Throughout July, he worked on getting a fundraising letter out, which stifled his enthusiasm. "I had thought SCLC would have various projects popping up over the South and I could fit into one of these, not so however, and I was back stuffing envelopes." This could have been tolerable, "if it were not that there was . . . nothing larger cooking."[16]

Through Stembridge, Moses learned that plenty *was* boiling because of the SNCC-affiliated Atlanta student movement (ASM) of the historically black Atlanta University Center (AUC). The ASM emerged after students Julian Bond and Lonnie King had read about the Greensboro sit-ins. Inspired, they founded the Committee on Appeal for Human

Rights (COAHR), and on March 15, two hundred students commenced a protracted series of sit-ins. It also picketed an A&P store, located nearby the YMCA where Moses stayed, for job discrimination.[17]

The picket particularly excited Moses. Believing SCLC did not need him, he picketed the store daily, often alone and all day long. Biographer Eric Burner explained this as a conscious decision to "[express] himself by example." However, rather than being a well-thought-out plan by Moses to convert bystanders Camus-style, his one-man action had a more basic explanation. Despite the ASM's numbers, often no one else showed up. "They loved to have long meetings, but they didn't like to walk that long picket line in the heat." As Bond confessed, "[Moses] picketed . . . all day in the hot sun. *I* didn't want to do that. But he did."[18]

Lacking the "credentials" for credibility in the student movement— one's accomplishments and harassments endured during the sit-ins— Moses needed to convince the COAHR and SNCC students of his commitment. This was not easy. Because he was so reserved and did not party with the rest of them, they even believed he might be a Communist spy. After all, Bond clarified, "to us, as in southerners, this was a foreign idea, Communists. Who were they? We were told these were bad people and they're going [to trick] us into doing things that we shouldn't do, and they're northerners. [So] here's [a guy] from New York [who] wants to help us. And we knew why we were doing these things because we lived in the part of the country where segregation was rampant. And he didn't. So why would he care? So there must be something wrong with him."[19]

This kind of thinking reflected a Cold War mind-set among the students. Most SNCC-related sit-in leaders, like Diane Nash, Charles Sherrod, and Charles Jones, saw their movement as part of the fight against Communism; Jones even testified to the House of Un-American Activities Committee (HUAC) in 1959. They accordingly had no qualms about accepting one American Federation of Labor and Congress of Industrial Organizations (AFL-CIO) union's demand to disinvite Bayard Rustin to SNCC's 1960 October conference in exchange for financial support.[20] Given the fact that Rustin had left the Communist Party twenty years earlier, this decision was remarkable for its timidity; only Jane Stembridge resigned from SNCC in protest.[21]

The students' suspicion of Moses also underscored their perceived differences between northerners and southerners. Regardless of organizational connections between the regions, politically inexperienced southern blacks like themselves did not automatically accept northerners as allies. But Moses's view of southerners was equally influenced by regional stereotypes. He had always interpreted southern blacks as lacking in initiative. He told the *Village Voice* in 1964 that before the sit-ins, he "knew nothing about the South except for, like, folk-myths from a few crazy Negroes. My image of the southern Negro was fearful, cringing." This was not uncommon for northern blacks. SNCC's Charles McDew, who grew up in Ohio, similarly admitted he had "tended to look down on the South and on the southern Negro" before he became a student sit-in leader in South Carolina.[22]

The differences between northern and southern students were nonetheless often real. At the Raleigh conference, Baker had let northerners (who were mostly white) and southerners (who were overwhelmingly black) meet separately and emphasized that the northerners' role was considered supportive. "It wasn't a question of color [but] of retaining the character of a Southern-based movement . . . [northerners] were much more articulate in terms of certain social philosophies than the southern students [but] they had demonstrated . . . their capacity for suffering and confrontation to a degree that the Northern students had not." Even the election of southern black activist Marion Barry as SNCC's first chairman was a reflection of the desire to keep the movement under southern control.[23]

TO KEEP HIMSELF BUSY, Moses attended a lecture by Prof. Lonnie Cross, a black Muslim and distinguished mathematician at Clark Atlanta University, on the "Ramifications of Gödel's Theorem." There he heard about a picket to support a sit-in at Rich's department store. Moses decided to join, although it was sponsored by the predominantly white organization SCEF (Southern Conference Educational Fund). SCEF was the offshoot of the leftist Southern Conference for Human Welfare (SCHW), organized in 1938 to promote civil rights and labor causes. It was considered controversial because it worked with anyone regardless of (past) political associations. A 1947 HUAC report had named SCHW "the most deviously camouflaged Communist-front operation of the day." Even after it disbanded, SCEF, its tax-exempt educational branch, never entirely escaped its stains. Moreover, SCEF was run by Carl and Anne Braden, a white couple from Kentucky suspected of Communist Party membership.[24]

When Atlanta police arrested the demonstrators, Moses's association with SCEF logically fueled the students' suspicions of him. After several frantic meetings, Ruby Doris Smith and Lonnie King called him in to ask how he had learned about the picket. Convinced that any "hyper-intellectual Yankee" was potentially dangerous, his theorem answer "hardly reduced their suspicion." They then asked Martin Luther King Jr. to question him since the newspapers had identified him as "Robert Moses of SCLC."[25]

King called in Moses to see him at Ebenezer Baptist Church, where he was co-pastor alongside his father. It was their first meeting, and the conversation was awkward and filled with silences. King summarized SCEF's history while Moses listened quietly. Moses contended that "King wasn't particularly worried about the presence of Communists in the Communism-is-evil-and-going-to-take-over sense. And in this, ironically, he was ahead of many of the students." But the problem was that SCLC was in the middle of a fundraising campaign, so King advised him to stay away from SCEF demonstrations to keep up outward appearances.[26]

King's advice reflected his feel for expediency. He was ambivalent toward Marxism and sympathetic toward Scandinavian-style democratic socialism himself, but whenever SCLC's public image was concerned, he could be ruthlessly pragmatic. He had recently "purged" Rustin from SCLC and later broke off relations with Jack O'Dell and Stanley Levison under pressure from the Kennedy administration. The NAACP and others had adopted anti-Communist resolutions, and officials like Roy Wilkins even cooperated with the FBI about alleged Communists among its rank and file. Although the strength of anti-communism was waning, King's and the students' suspicion of SCEF and Rustin showed that Cold War politics still presented a minefield for such organizations.[27]

As an SCLC volunteer, Moses felt he had to follow King's advice. Moreover, he "was hardly going to argue with him. . . . This was Martin Luther King." To him it was a matter of respect resulting from King's experience and his own lack thereof, rather than being star-stricken by King's charismatic media personality, which appeared to be absent from the scene altogether. The affair seemed to bother King, too. To Moses's amazement, King spoke very slowly, whereas he had thought that "there was never a time when Dr. King was without melody in his voice." When Moses became a SNCC leader, he too faced the reality that his public image did not correspond with who he was in private, as King had realized of himself long ago. Yet the difference between the two was that

King was able to live with and distinguish between the two identities, whereas the purist Moses could and would not.[28]

MOSES FOUND IT DIFFICULT to develop a rapport with King, despite their similarities. Although his background was more humble and action oriented, they were both intellectuals who had attended northern white schools (King attended Pennsylvania's Crozer Theological Seminary and Boston University) and traveled abroad (King to Europe, Ghana, and India). Above all, their academic training was similar. King's philosophy, like Moses's, was a patchwork of cosmopolitan and life experiences. But King seemed indifferent to comparing notes. Moses left the meeting believing that King "wasn't that interested in who I was. . . . Not that he was superficial, but the conversation was superficial." Had his name not been published, he believed he never would have met King. This contrasted starkly with his talks with Baker. Even as she was in the process of leaving, she struck up a conversation with Moses whenever she could. "She asked me about my upbringing, my thoughts on Harlem, my entrance into the movement . . . Baker was actually talking to me. I felt [it] seemed important enough [for her to make] time for it."[29]

Baker's and King's different styles thereby underlined SNCC's and SCLC's organizational cultures. Moses instinctively detected a causal connection between these organizations' structures and individuals' ability to thrive within. While SNCC and Baker taught that "you make a personal connection whenever you really want to do something with somebody else," in SCLC he found that many in its upper circles had lost this ability. Accordingly, lower-placed employees' individual talent was often overlooked. In hindsight, Moses characterized the King meeting as a missed chance that helped him "understand how the voice of organizers differs from that of leaders." King did not say "well here's someone who has come down to work, how can we really use [him]? The mark of [someone] who has an instinct for organizing [is that] you've always got to be on the lookout for people who present themselves as potential organizers. And I don't think . . . that he [had that] kind of instinct."[30]

Baker's interest in him came when Moses was still at the impressionable age of twenty-five, was uprooted from his family, and had trouble fitting in with the students. They had also discovered a personal connection: the milk co-op he worked for as a child had grown out of the 1930s Harlem-based Young Negroes' Cooperative League, of which

Baker had been national director. To Moses, "it was very helpful and meaningful to find somebody . . . who was involved in the civil rights movement, that I [was] attracted to, who had also touched on my early life in a way that was very meaningful." After all, "in a sense, I used to joke with her, she helped put the milk on our table." Baker liked him too. According to her biographer, she placed "great confidence" in Moses, because in him "she saw the makings of the kind of leader she herself had striven to become: modest, principled, and able to empower others through the force of example."[31]

IT NONETHELESS TOOK great effort for the Atlanta students to overcome their suspicions of Moses. Before his departure to Atlanta, Moses's Uncle Bill had asked his friend Carl Holman to look after him. Holman, an AUC professor who published the movement newspaper the *Atlanta Inquirer*, vouched for Moses's bona fides. Moses then moved in with his family, which reassured the students. Ella Baker in turn explained the students' political inexperience to Moses and educated the others on the Communist issue. A good friend of the Bradens, she encouraged the students to work with them, although in the past she had displayed a similar ambivalence as King to working with alleged Communists. Moses admired this "about-face" due to his own experiences with the Old Left at Stuyvesant. He nonetheless would long remember this experience of being wrongfully accused.[32]

The Atlanta students' eventual acceptance of him, however, owed most to Moses himself. "He worked hard," Bond explained, "And we quickly discovered with him, and many, many others, that we should take people on the basis of what they were doing, not on who we thought they were." Such suspicions were also impractical, SNCC worker Charles Sherrod argued. "We were all looking at each other, wondering, 'Which rock are they under?' We wasted months that way before we finally decided to forget it and go after segregation."[33]

Yet from the start, Moses's involvement in SNCC was dual in nature. Ideologically, he and SNCC matched perfectly, but in reality, his age, geographical background, style, and broader political vision set him apart. According to Bond, Moses already "had a much broader view of social problems and social concerns than we did. We had tunnel vision. . . . We were convinced that we could knock [segregation] over with little effort and everything would then be okay. Bob Moses, on the other hand, had already begun to project a systematic analysis; not just of the South, but of the country, the world." While the students were content to work in Atlanta, SNCC worker Cleveland Sellers asserted that Moses was already arguing that the student movement should trade the southern urban centers for the rural areas to eliminate the competition with other organizations and aid the rural blacks who were now left out. Moses nonetheless did not force his views on the students. As such, Bond contended, he "stood out because he helped us think about what we were doing, and how we could do it," in the same suggestive manner as Ella Baker and James Lawson employed.[34]

Meanwhile, SCLC's fundraising letter still needed to get out, but Moses consistently met a wall of bureaucratic regulations. He wanted to do it "New York style" by enlisting a number of students at the YMCA, but leaving the office was against SCLC policy. The meeting with King then provided an opportunity to settle the matter. He outlined his plan, and after King consented, he and Stembridge recruited several students and YMCA personnel. Three days later, the job was done.[35]

The mailing incident underlines how SCLC's organizational culture stifled Moses's talents. Stembridge documented in August that he had "not been appreciated as he should have been," which left Moses thoroughly disappointed. Without any new work lined up, he continued to help Stembridge with her activities, including spreading protest letters and contacting congressmen. On August 10, she gratefully wrote that the "SNCC office, with the help of Bob Moses . . . has really been producing." Meanwhile, the ASM was organizing citywide "kneel-ins" that challenged segregated churches to invite blacks into their services. Nonetheless, Moses, likely questioning the kneel-ins' long-term impact, was anxious to leave Atlanta.[36]

MOSES SAW HIS OPPORTUNITY after attending a small SNCC meeting in Atlanta on August 5. The group decided to hold a conference in October to further define SNCC's objectives, for which it aimed to involve as many movement representatives as possible. Yet attendees worried that the sit-ins had barely touched the Deep South, leaving SNCC with few contacts there. Stembridge therefore asked Moses to gather names there as SNCC's first field representative. Moses was immediately excited, and Ella Baker strongly encouraged him. She gave him a list of southern local activists she had met during her travels, because she believed that Moses—and through him, SNCC—would be open to movement participants with different outlooks than SCLC's ministers. Moses toured the

Deep South for three weeks by bus: first to Talladega and Birmingham in Alabama, then to Clarksdale, Cleveland, and Jackson in Mississippi, followed by Alexandria, New Orleans, and Shreveport in Louisiana. He returned through Mississippi's Gulfport and Biloxi, and Mobile, Alabama. Since SNCC lacked funds, he paid for the trip from his own personal savings.[37]

Moses's trip astonished the students of SNCC. The idea of *voluntarily* entering "the belly of the beast" was something remarkable. Stembridge wrote Moses she had "trouble sleeping for [being] worried about you" and that she greatly admired his courage. She teasingly wrote Moses that she "was getting a Messiah complex" about him and awaited his "return from the land of bondage," to which Moses cunningly replied that indeed "Jehovah's witness just came: The Kingdom of God is at hand." Although aware of Mississippi's reputation, Moses admitted that his northern background shielded him. "I didn't know enough to be afraid." Those who did know southern formal and informal racial customs from personal experience, like Julian Bond, were baffled. "[Moses] was willing to do things that we weren't always willing to do ourselves, but we knew needed to be done. When he agreed to go on this trip to *Mississippi* . . . *I'd* never been to Mississippi. And I didn't *want* to go to Mississippi!" Moreover, "he went on a *bus*. I hated to ride buses. I didn't ride buses in the city, let alone from country to country."[38]

Moses soon discovered why. When he boarded the bus to Alabama on August 13, he needed to decide where to sit as Baker, Stembridge, and Curry watched him board. Because he now represented the sit-in movement, he felt he had to violate the segregated seating arrangements on southern buses by sitting in the "white" section. But fearing that this might harm his ability to accomplish his trip, he only sat in front until the Georgia border. Shortly after, highway patrolmen indeed stopped the bus following reports about a black rider in the front. Troopers got on but soon left, unable to figure out who it had been. Later in Clarksdale, Mississippi, local activist Aaron Henry and a few students who escorted him to the bus were also eager to see where he would sit, since "I was representing the sit-in movement, SNCC, and this new wave." He sat in front until Cleveland without difficulties. When he left for Shreveport, Louisiana, an African already sat in front of a white man, so Moses took the next available seat to a white. Near Monroe, police stopped the bus and asked them to get off. Being even more unfamiliar with southern law, the police's actions confused the African. They were in turn confused by his African passport and Moses's American one, which he had from his trips overseas, since most blacks never owned one. They let them go after shifting all the passengers around based on the "correct" seating pattern.[39]

Moses's state of mind and approach to activism were already evident on this first bus trip through the Deep South. His audacity would help form the legendary aura that began to surround him, even if it sprang from his naivety and ignorance of the South. He also demonstrated the impulse to live up to an ideal image and to engage in direct action when necessary. Nevertheless, although nonviolent direct action performed an important liberating function, he was also aware that its effect was only temporary; for the goal of creating long-term communication networks across the South, it provided no value. He also concluded that his job was not served by attracting attention to himself. For most of the trip, he sat in the back. "I didn't mind shifting gears when I left Atlanta. I had no intention of flaunting anything, and had no need to. I was sure of myself in that way . . . I understood [where] SNCC folk were coming from and I didn't want to [argue] with them. And I knew this job . . . needed someone who was going to merge with the people. I was going to figure out how to do that[,] get the names and come back out."[40]

MOSES'S ITINERARY was flexible. Stembridge sent a letter every few days to a local activist requesting accommodation for him and help with planning the rest of his trip and meeting students. She would then forward the information to Moses, who responded with detailed reports of his activities. Their correspondence accordingly exemplifies a crucial development in the civil rights movement: how patient networking laid the basis for SNCC's work in the rural South. In one letter to a grassroots activist, Stembridge envisioned how the "future of the movement everywhere depends on consolidated efforts. If the entire state of Louisiana is covered with a strong web of contacts who will write one another, much can be done." She therefore had high hopes for Moses's trip, she wrote on August 14. "This could prove to be one of the most important ventures we have undertaken, not only for getting people to the conference, but for the future communication of the movement. I'm really excited."[41]

Some activists Moses met, like Mississippi's Aaron Henry and Alabama's Fred Shuttlesworth, entered the history books. Others never gained any kind of national renown, like Birmingham's Jesse Walker,

Shreveport's Philip Pennywell, or Mississippi activists Irving Dent (Hattiesburg), J. M. Rudd (Batesville), Rev. Brown (Gulfport), Isaac Grey (Vicksburg), and Rev. Redmond (Greenville). Nevertheless, these meetings intensified Moses's understanding of the wide range of movement activism, its longevity, and its dependence on professional and informal networks—fitting Baker's description of it. Moreover, he discovered that there *were* networks in places like Mississippi, despite their invisibility to professional groups like SNCC.

Moses's trip also revealed his developing organizing skills, creativity, and propensity for hard work. Carrying only a typewriter and SNCC material, he usually contacted a student or minister first, explained his purpose, and listened to student reports about their plans. He then asked them to consider setting up a coordinating committee representing all the state's local groups, with each group sending two delegates to SNCC's October Conference. A good example is his stop in Talladega, Alabama, between August 14 and 16. Reverends Collins and Watts directed him to Talladega College, where he located the Alabama Student Union (ASU). He asked Stembridge to send them SNCC material and suggested appointing a field representative. He wrote letters introducing SNCC to nearly a dozen ASU associates and initiated negotiations with Talladega College for an ASU conference to discuss student activism. Yet from the start, he advocated own responsibility for the students' efforts, including finding their own financial resources.[42]

His work also revealed the extent to which Moses's mind was already focusing on the southern rural counties. In Talladega, for instance, he got one agricultural extension worker "to help parley information to the rural areas," an activity he hoped the ASU could take over once it got going. He was also already aware of the importance of maintaining an "underground" network, since the worker refused to connect formerly with any organization. Instead, she agreed to pick up mail via a local reverend, after Moses had instructed Stembridge not to write her name on the envelope or use the SNCC stamp whenever she communicated with them.[43]

Moses went to Birmingham next. Although he did not stay long, the experience made an impression that underscored his naivety of the South. "As I moved through, I could see that the South was not the same everywhere, Birmingham, Alabama, belching smoke and fire from surrounding steel plants, matched no image of the South we held in Harlem." Moreover, he noticed, "white power was clearly the dominant power, but every day was not roiled with lynchings. Black folks had a life and I began learning how to enter it."[44]

Nonetheless, Birmingham was notorious for its—often literally—explosive racial situation. Moses met one man who singlehandedly tried to publish pamphlets about the many bombings directed at blacks in the city, which he sent to SNCC. When he located the city's most well-known activist, Fred Shuttlesworth, he even found him under siege. To Moses's amazement, Shuttlesworth, despite his connection to the pacifist SCLC, had guards carrying guns patrolling their meeting places. It was Moses's first indication that in Deep South activism, nonviolent tactics and self-defense easily went hand in hand—a lesson that was reinforced at his next stop, Mississippi.[45]

MISSISSIPPI MORE APTLY FITTED Moses's romantic images of the South, with its big plantations and sharecroppers working the cotton fields. Their dilapidated, wooden shacks revealed the state's deep poverty, the worst in the nation. Often lacking necessary furniture, like beds, 90 percent of black homes were without indoor heating or toilets. Over half had no running water.[46]

Conditions in the Delta, situated in the northwest, were particularly bad. In 1960, 75 percent of Delta families lived below the $3,000 poverty line due to its extensive sharecropper system, in which farmers lived and worked on a white (cotton) plantation owner's land in exchange for a part of its proceeds. Sharecroppers had little security. While tenants exercised some control over their property by paying rent, sharecroppers, who paid in labor, could face evictions at a moment's notice. In Mississippi's ten most renowned cotton counties, all located in the Delta, 94 percent of farmers remained either tenants or sharecroppers. Overall in postwar Mississippi, almost two-thirds of all black males worked in agriculture; 80 percent of them on white plantations. In 1959, such farm laborers made $600 a year in the Delta, while whites earned $1,500.[47]

Although Mississippi's population was 42 percent black in 1960, this number was almost double in the Delta. As such, poverty disproportionally affected African Americans. The Delta's black infant mortality rate was the highest in the state. One black mother bemoaned the fate of her children who went "to bed hungry and get up hungry and don't ever know nothing else in between." Illiteracy was rule rather than exception. Moreover, the wartime boom and careful manipulation of New Deal money (more than $450 million between 1933 and 1939) by white planters ensured technological advancements, like mechanization and tractors. But while the introduction of the mechanical cotton picker in 1943 increased the planters' wealth, it further reduced unskilled blacks' prospects; by the 1960s, only a fifth of their workforce was needed. With planters additionally shifting to other, less labor-intensive crops like soybeans and with blacks unable to find work in the new defense industries or other factories, migrating north became an attractive alternative. In the 1940s, 300,000 blacks left the state.[48]

Those who remained continued to be at the mercy of the Delta planters, who had acquired a political hegemony in the state. Corruption reigned in the Delta. Able to control the opposition from poor whites across the state by appealing to their racial prejudices, the planters, with help from other ruling elites and institutions like the courts, managed to root their race-based class system deeply into the state's structure. They kept the federal government and progressive forces, like the CIO and other labor unions, out of the state. Many white moderates, who were too ingrained in the system to join forces with blacks, rather opted for advocating a type of gradualism that might end racist excesses but preserve the class system. Unsurprisingly, Stembridge wrote Moses that she was "very skeptical about what you could find in [Mississippi]."[49]

Even so, the abysmal economic prospects for blacks in Mississippi and across the South, particularly in light of the movement to fully mechanize cotton production, fostered their susceptibility to the civil rights movement. The Great Migration provided the opening wedge, as the increased northern black vote forced national politicians to take heed of what was happening in the South for the first time since Reconstruction. Calls for federal lynching bills bolstered southern blacks, as did the decline in racial violence now that planters no longer had to rely so heavily on black labor. The move to mechanization and black migration further threatened to weaken the planters' position and transfer political power to the cities. This widened blacks' possibilities but also intensified the opposition they met.[50]

But the generation of blacks who grew up in the disruptive interbellum, fought in the wars, and were exposed to new mass media like the radio were more prone to accept the fight than their parents. As one Jackson newspaper noted, they had "a gleam in their eyes and a feeling that they have a foot in the door." In the 1940s and 1950s, many now dared to mobilize politically, but their moves were always shaped and limited by the economic context in which they had to operate. It still remained to be seen what these new economic realities meant for blacks and what they entailed for the southern rural movement's means for fostering social change, if it was manageable and fully understood at all. What was clear was that Mississippi blacks had different objectives than the Atlanta students, who were primarily interested in access to segregated public facilities that many Mississippi blacks could not even afford to patronize.[51]

Moses did not immediately see this logic. He would learn to analyze Mississippi's "peculiar situation" through forty-nine-year-old Amzie Moore of Cleveland. Already known in northern civil rights circles, Moore had a long history of activism in the state, individually and organizationally with the NAACP and the Regional Council of Negro Leadership (RCNL), which he helped found in 1951. Between 1942 and 1946, he was in the Army, serving two years in Asia. As with many black soldiers, World War II provided a psychological turnaround for him. The Army's segregationist practices, Moore recalled, "kept [me] wondering, why were we fighting?" Moreover, Japanese propaganda about America's racist practices "simply reminded us daily that there would be no freedom, even after the war." After his return, he got a federal job at the post office and with SCEF money learned to operate a gas station, which also housed his soon-to-be ex-wife's beauty parlor. This made him part of Mississippi's small black middle class and, being financially independent, he was less likely to suffer economically from white retaliations for his activism.[52]

Stembridge introduced Moses to Moore as "an extremely perceptive person," but Moore was skeptical of Moses's overly educated background. Yet he soon found that "Bob was altogether different. Bob believed me and was willing to work with me. When I found out he was honestly seeking to help ... I was willing to help him."[53]

Moses was likewise impressed by Moore. In one letter to Stembridge, he called him "the best I've met yet ... I would trust him explicitly and implicitly.... Plan to be here at least a week to absorb as much as I can from Mr. Amzie Moore!" Yet Moore doubted whether Moses was up for Mississippi. Facing a boycott from Delta whites for refusing to put "white" and "colored" signs up near the entrances and toilets of his gas station, Moore expected white mob violence daily. Moses often fell asleep with Moore sitting "in his rear bedroom window, rifle at the ready and floodlights washing across his backyard." By association, Moses was now a target, too.[54]

To assess Moses's reliability, Moore did a "reading" of him, like Gregory Moses had done with the people in his Harlem network. This was an old trick, Moses learned, "characteristic of people who are living on the margins and are not beat-up or debilitated. In places like the Mississippi Delta . . . your life depends on being able to read people." Moore did this by letting Moses speak to church congregations about the movement and seeing how the audience reacted. His experience with street preaching and the Intervarsity Christian Fellowship now came in handy. Moses applied a stock message. "There's something coming. Get ready. It's inevitably coming your way whether you like it or not. It sent me to tell you that." Apparently, it worked, because, Moses proudly stated, "I got a few 'amens' too."[55]

Moore took Moses around the Delta to meet other locals and introduced him to the region's past. In analyzing the key players in the region, Moses recognized his father's method of explaining Harlem to him as a child. Yet his father and Moore differed in two respects. First, he noted, "Amzie was engaged and tested in the roughest of political waters where there was a level of danger that did not exist in Harlem. My father lacked this exposure." Second, "Amzie's range of contacts was wider than Pop's; he was more at ease with political ideas. Like Pop, Amzie had no college education [but] Amzie had no sense of being incapacitated intellectually or unable to understand and explore any concept in the broad world of politics, culture, history, and race. Ideas simply didn't intimidate him and I found conversation with him invigorating and liberating." Moses later called him his "father in the movement." Moore illustrated to him Ella Baker's ideas about leadership, making real what had formerly been abstract. After all, Moses observed, "You couldn't experience what Ella was talking about [because] she wasn't in a community. She was operating in this network world."[56]

After discussing local blacks' immense economic and educational setbacks, Moore showed Moses a booklet from the Southern Regional Council (SRC). It revealed that only 5 percent of Mississippi blacks were registered to vote and only a quarter of that number could actually exercise that right; Moore too had registered in 1935 but had only been allowed to vote in general elections. In five of the thirteen counties with a 50 percent black populace, no blacks were registered at all.[57]

Moses was startled. "I had never [translated this to] what the number of Blacks and their percentage to whites meant in terms of say voting, and electing people." This was ironic. "I had been sitting up hearing about oppression behind the *iron* curtain and the meaning of the vote for freedom all through my college years . . . without knowing about the Delta and its congressional district with a Black majority. I had not made the connection to the denial of the right to vote behind the *cotton* curtain. Like the sit-ins, Amzie's words slammed into me powerfully." This painfully revealed not only Moses's ignorance of the South but also his, and other SNCC workers', naivety about their abilities to solve the nation's racial inequalities. He admitted, "[Amzie] wasn't distracted at all about integration of public facilities. It was a good thing, but it was not going straight to the heart of what was the trouble in Mississippi. Somehow, in following his guidance there, we stumbled on the key—the right to vote and the political action that ensued."[58]

MOSES AND MOORE TAPED a map of Mississippi to the wall and while Moore talked about Delta life, Moses typed a draft of a voter registration project for SNCC's conference. The plan entailed citizenship classes during winter and spring to be held in the Catholic mission of Mound Bayou. Father John LaBauve of the Divine Word Ministry would run the classes with help from three students who could live at Moore's house and more during the summer of 1961, including Moses himself.[59]

When Moses described the project to Stembridge, it had near-magical proportions. "The idea is to tackle the 2nd and 3rd Congressional districts, about 25 counties in all. . . . The main thrust is to take place next summer; we need to round up 100 strong men and women[,] at least 25 cars and several buses and money for gas and oil." Classes would "serve upwards of 200,000 people," Moses gushed. "Nobody [is] starry eyed, these are nasty jobs but we're going to find some nasty people to do them, so put me down 'cause I'm not only getting mean I'm getting downright nasty . . .'cause I don't intend to be in this business all my life." This illustrated how Moses was already thinking "big" along the lines of concentrating (political) power in one area. Stembridge's excitement overflowed too. "I cannot believe your letters . . . I got so excited that things almost happened to my kidneys. This VOTER REGISTRATION project is IT! Bob, this is what you were looking for!" She instantly wrote Moore that the "worth of the project is unquestioned. . . . This could be the most significant undertaking of those fighting for freedom" in Mississippi.[60]

Moses's and Stembridge's correspondence belied their ignorance of what working in Mississippi entailed in practice; the project Moses described in fact never even materialized. But the plan is nonetheless exemplary of how the conjunction of two generations of activists paved the way for what would follow in the state in subsequent years.

The project was modeled on past activity as Moore and LaBauve had already experimented with a citizenship school a few years earlier, albeit unsuccessfully. This provided the basis and network for the work to come. Simultaneously, the plan used the "new" emphasis on nonviolence and redemptive suffering. It mentioned that blacks "must regain their self-respect and self-reliance. This can be done by teaching people the philosophy of nonviolence" and "how to willingly accept suffering." This input likely comes from Moses, who identified with such principles, rather than Moore, who carried guns everywhere.[61]

The means to realize the plan also signaled the movement's dependence on the correlation between grassroots leadership and outside help. On the one hand, it relied heavily on local organizers to ensure housing and the voting school's location. Moses believed in this type of ownership, meaning that the project should be locals' own responsibility because only this guaranteed their continued involvement. This also meant the project was less visible to outsiders, which decreased the possibility of white retaliation. He wrote Stembridge that "whoever wants to give QUIET help [is] welcome! The thing to do seems to be to get the people to come in here, to contact [locals] quietly and by word of mouth as much as possible, to get quiet money wherever possible and forget about all the other machinations machined by machiners." With the latter, he meant any professionalized, bureaucratized means of organizing, as displayed by existing organizations. To double-check, Stembridge asked if this implied SCLC. Representing an early example of the two organizations' future turf battle, Moses indeed insisted that "the project will be SNCC's."[62]

On the other hand, by insisting that the project was "SNCC's with whoever" willing to help, Moses and Moore accepted that full-time help was needed and in larger numbers than in the past. Moses wrote Stembridge, "Amzie thinks, and I concur, the adults here will back the young folks but will never initiate a program strong enough to do what needs to be done." Moore even *pressed* the issue of outside involvement, Moses claimed. "[Amzie] thought it fine for young folks from Mississippi to go to the October conference ... but more important, he thought, young people—'SNCCers' from other parts of the South—needed to begin planning to come *into* Mississippi." Moreover, the project needed outside sponsors to make up for the resources local activists lacked. Stembridge promised that SNCC would print and mimeograph 200,000 copies of the Mississippi Constitution, 1,000 affidavits, and 1,000 sample ballots for the classes and to recruit 100 students as the project's workforce. Moses even proposed to organize a conference at Mississippi's Campbell College, because he believed it "vital to bring to the students here a sense of being a part of a large movement and assurance of strong outside support about expulsions and bails." Still, this project had to be theirs. "We hope that at the [October] SNCC meeting, [Mississippi] will be able to form its own organization and work right in on this voter registration project." In Moses's view, SNCC was merely bringing help to expand Moore's and LaBauve's old project. "[While SNCC agreed] to sponsor this and develop it ... the actual line which historically developed the project [was that] the motivation for it and the whole conceptualization behind it was coming out of local initiative." It *was* a quintessential grassroots initiative but one that needed massive fulltime help. Moses then left Cleveland—with $50 less for Moore's transportation to the October conference.[63]

MOSES CONTINUED TO JACKSON, where he met Alfred Cook of Tougaloo College and Walter Williams of Jackson State College. Moses linked them with SNCC through copies of its newsletter, the *Student Voice,* for distribution at their colleges, pressed their students to attend SNCC's conference, and asked Dean Jones of Campbell College to sponsor a meeting there. With Moore, he had also discussed setting up a conference in Jackson with Medgar Evers, Mississippi's most well-known NAACP activist. When he left the state, he had gathered "carloads" of people for SNCC's conference, from areas like Greenville, Laurel, Clarksdale, Jackson, Biloxi, and Cleveland, leaving Stembridge to conclude that Moses had done "miracles."[64]

Moses's hard work continued in Louisiana, where he contacted student movements in Shreveport and attended a statewide NAACP Youth Conference. He got some participants to recruit students for SNCC's conference and the president of the Alexandria NAACP Youth Council to attend a SNCC meeting in September. Other networking activities included sending SNCC's newsletter to NAACP youth chapters and facilitating contacts between Stembridge and other local chapter presidents. Baker had advised Moses to contact NAACP activist C. O. Simpkins in Shreveport, whom she knew propagated voter registration and grassroots organizing as well.[65] Unfortunately, he was out of town, as was another likeminded activist, Jim McCain. Hearing about McCain's organizing views, Moses contemplated a meeting between him and Amzie Moore. It is unclear whether this meeting occurred, but Moore did spend a month in Louisiana's civil rights hotbed Baton Rouge during September, so there are likely more connections between the early Mississippi and Louisiana grassroots movements.[66]

Moses returned to Atlanta in early September, after stopping in Mobile, Alabama, where he met SCLC co-founder Joseph Lowery. Stembridge concluded that Moses had done "more work and a better job than anybody." He had gathered at least 200 new names for SNCC to coordinate new projects with. Stembridge accordingly wrote him, "Bob—did you know that you have done probably the most significant work since February 1, 1960 when four freshmen . . . and you know the rest." Moses was satisfied, too: voter registration not only complied with his budding beliefs about the long-term production of social change, but it was also a tactic in which his self-effacing personality and ability to listen were assets rather than liabilities.[67]

AT THE SUMMER'S END, Moses went back to New York to finish the final year of his teaching contract. He moved in with Bob Cohen, a white folk singer he had met in June at a three-week folk dance camp in Maine. Moses had had this hobby since attending the high school summer camp. The Maine camp, however, was less liberal. Its organizers were conservative whites and many of its attendees anti-communist emigrants from Eastern Europe. Moses was the only black but never felt uncomfortable. The experience increased his faith in the egalitarian principles of mankind, Cohen said. "We felt in those days that the ingesting of other people's cultures strengthened rather than weakened one's own, causing one to [feel] more in communication with the rest of humanity." The two rented a flat on the West Side of Manhattan with a Jewish man from Michigan and a female folk dancer, and they often frequented dance parties. "Bob's face really lit up when he was folk dancing. He loved it," Cohen recalled, "sometimes we would be coming home late from a party or something, and if Bob had had a good time, he would start dancing down Amsterdam Avenue. He could be very free and gay then."[68]

But Moses's mind remained fixed on Mississippi. He studied the Mississippi Constitution, its voter registration regulations, state maps, and voting statistics. He also nurtured his interest in pacifism. One member of the New York branch of the Fellowship of Reconciliation wrote Stembridge on October 1 that he "had dinner with Bob Moses yesterday—a hell of a nice guy—and a new FOR member!" During winter, Moses heard James Lawson speak in New York but found Lawson's views to be more developed than his. Moses and Moore kept each other updated on the voting project, too. Moore told him that he had received a $100 check, which he wanted to invest in a new building for the school since LaBauve's Catholic building was no longer available; the bishop from Mound Bayou had transferred him as a penalty for his activism. Pushing the need for outside help, Moore pressed Moses on whether he could still count on SNCC to provide the material for the citizenship classes. Moses also sent Moore money to fix his car and again for Christmas.[69]

To friends, family, and colleagues, Moses said nothing about his plans. He focused on his students, reread Bertrand Russell and Camus in French, and generally remained isolated from organized civil rights activities; he met Stembridge only once when she visited New York. She had meanwhile resigned from SNCC (but returned as a Mississippi volunteer in 1963) over Rustin's de-invitation to SNCC's October conference, a position with which Moses sympathized. She was replaced by Edward King, whom Moses did not know. He did not even attend the October conference. Instead, he stayed close to home and saved money to return to Mississippi. Cohen stated that "the only hint I got of a deep feeling he had about [this] was that he would sit for hours and listen to a record of Odetta singing, 'I'm going back to the Red Clay County.'" In a March 1961 letter to Ed King, Moses wrote that he did follow "events from the far" and that he would gladly spend a few years working in a southern project. King promised him that SNCC was "quite interested in doing whatever we can to see that the [Mississippi voting] program goes over." In its April/May 1961 issue, SNCC's newspaper the *Student Voice* indeed announced the project, asking students to enlist for three months doing voter registration work in the Delta, with the work ranging from collecting and filing affidavits on rights violations with the Justice Department to helping potential voters with their literacy skills.[70]

While some white liberals depicted Moses's return to Mississippi in 1961 as a seemingly spontaneous existentialist act, it in fact was not. If he went, Moore had taught him, he was going well prepared.

CHAPTER THREE

You Killed My Husband

It was not until he set to work on his first civil rights campaign in Mc-Comb that Bob Moses truly discovered what organizing on the ground in Mississippi entailed. He would experience everything from local people's courage to white violence, from slow organizing to direct action, from nonviolence to armed self-defense. Yet Moses acclimated to these conditions fairly quickly. While he considered the project a mere experiment, it proved his hypothesis that social change started with locals, who had to become engaged through personal interaction.

Simultaneously, McComb immediately lay bare the painful realities of Moses's maturing leadership approach. In countering the narrative white southerners used to explain local blacks' activism—pinning the blame on "outside agitators"—he and other SNCC workers discovered a powerful new storyline that masked their own involvement and pushed locals forward as the true instigators of social change. But in the blood-stained fields of Mississippi, Moses found that Camus's apprehensions about not becoming an executioner were not merely academic.

Moses faced daunting questions about his organizing ideals. Were locals indeed the wise forbearers who led the young, idealistic SNCC workers into the right direction? Or were they, as one judge charged, in fact "like sheep being led to the slaughter," with Moses leading the flock? While McComb showed that in reality neither outside organizer nor local could do without the other, Moses found that coming to terms with his own sense of responsibility and newfound image as a leader was more difficult than it appeared.[1]

MOSES RETURNED FROM NEW YORK to rejoin Amzie Moore in mid-1961. He was energized, although the prospects for their voter registration program were bleak. Moore had attended SNCC's October conference, but reactions had been lukewarm; many in SNCC considered voter registration less important than direct action. After LaBauve's transfer, Moore had tried to revive interest in the voting project but now warned Moses that they still lacked funds, equipment, and meeting space. Moses suspected that Delta locals had communicated to him that now was not the right time. The past year's civil rights activism, executed largely by SNCC, had fueled racial tensions everywhere. Although Moses found no indication of it, Moore might also have experienced difficulty with the national NAACP, which apprehensively watched all SNCC activity. Yet Moore, Moses said, "was the only one" willing "to break with the NAACP on SNCC. That was Amzie's greatness, because he really believed that the students were gonna do this thing."[2]

Moore's openness to SNCC reflected Mississippi's precarious movement history. The NAACP had been active in the state since 1918, albeit largely in secret. Organized activism grew between the 1930s and 1950s, spurred by the economic and social transformations wrought by the Great Depression, New Deal, and World War II. Middle-class blacks like Amzie Moore, Aaron Henry, Medgar Evers, and T. R. M. Howard toiled to cultivate this new political terrain, although the dangerous realities of Mississippi forced most to play within the "separate-but-equal" realm. New organizations, like the RCNL and Progressive Voters Leagues, emerged. The NAACP could operate semi-openly, new branches developed, and dormant ones revived. Its membership rose from 377 in 1940 to 1,600 in 1953 and voter registration from 2,000 to 22,000.[3]

The 1954 *Brown* school desegregation suit, however, halted most activism from 1955 onward. The NAACP, which filed the suit, was outlawed in Alabama and prosecuted in other states, causing membership to plummet. Voter registration in Mississippi dropped below 12,000. In the Delta town of Indianola, middle-class whites organized the Citizens' Council, which grew to 25,000 members within three months. It used "legal" tactics, like economic pressure, to stifle activism. KKK and other hate groups' membership also accelerated. In the 1956 *Southern Manifesto*, state politicians joined other southern congressmen and senators in their vow to "resist forced integration by any lawful means." They tightened voter registration requirements and adopted the "breach of the peace" statute that criminalized anyone encouraging "disobedience" to Mississippi laws and customs. The legislature also created the Mississippi State Sovereignty Commission (MSSC) to spy on "subversives," meaning anyone challenging the racial hierarchy. It soon dwarfed similar commissions in other southern states in its targeting of civil rights organizations; it even donated $350,000 to the Citizens' Council biannually.[4]

The national NAACP offered its Mississippi branches little assistance during these years, feeling that its resources could gain more results elsewhere. White economic pressure effectively intimidated black entrepreneurs like T. V. Johnson, and acts or threats of violence ran activists like T. R. M. Howard, Gus Courts, and Clinton Battle out of the state. NAACP activists George Lee and Lamar Smith were brutally murdered. Shot in plain view on a courthouse lawn, Smith's assassination particularly stands out for its insolence. Added to this was the notorious lynching of Emmett Till in 1955. In McComb in Pike County—a city regarded as fairly progressive for Mississippi with 250 black registered voters—the NAACP was forced underground. Only a few places, like state capital Jackson or Biloxi in the tourist-dependent Gulf Coast, evinced public activism. Amzie Moore wrote a Chicago friend in 1955 that he feared he too "might have to run away up there." That he was still in Mississippi he owed to Howard and his Tri-State Bank and to out-of-state financial assistance from SCEF, In Friendship, and the NAACP. Moore therefore knew from personal experience how valuable the cooperation of local activists and outside assistants were to movement survival.[5]

Realizing that the success of the Mississippi movement required connecting activists across regional and organizational boundaries, Medgar Evers and Aaron Henry likewise joined the RNCL, despite the national NAACP's objections. After its decline, they joined SCLC, but NAACP headquarters pressured Evers to resign. Henry, whose NAACP state presidency was voluntary, retained his SCLC membership and kept pushing for outside intervention. In 1960, he told Moses that he was willing to work with anyone. Nonetheless, Henry and Evers—who feared competition with his NAACP Youth Chapters—always remained apprehensive about allying with SNCC because of its militancy.[6]

MOSES TRIED TO MAKE the most of his time with Moore by "just picking up what I could, watching Amzie, going where he told me to go." Some distraction came when he received notice that, with the end of his teaching contract, his draft deferment was revoked. He appealed the decision by arguing that his pacifism had only strengthened and that his SNCC work could function as an "alternative service." In response, he was summoned to a hearing in New York, even though he was notified in advance that his case would not be reopened.[7]

On his way back, Moses attended a small SNCC meeting in Philadelphia, where he was introduced to newly elected chairman Charles McDew and workers Tim Jenkins, Charles Sherrod, and Charles Jones. He related his plans, after which they gave him the telephone number of John Doar, a white official of the Justice Department's Civil Rights

Division they had had contact with. This surprised Moses, who discovered that SNCC was quite different from just a year before. "I was struck by the amount of politics that was going on within SNCC. People were going to these very high level meetings, and having organizational discussions about priorities [and] fundraising."[8]

While it briefly engaged in political activity by addressing the Democratic and Republican conventions, SNCC had established its name through nonviolent direct action, particularly the Rock Hill "jail-ins"[9] and the Freedom Rides. CORE had instigated the Rides in May 1961, a test of the 1960 Supreme Court decision that ruled segregation in interstate public transportation unconstitutional. White violence halted the original Riders in Alabama, forcing them to abandon the protest. But SNCC immediately organized a group of replacements. Hundreds of young and adult men and women of both races followed SNCC's example for months. Most were jailed; in Jackson, Mississippi, a SNCC contingent including James Bevel, Stokely Carmichael, and Bernard Lafayette was sentenced to Parchman state prison, where their shared suffering forged a unique bond among them.[10,11]

When the Interstate Commerce Commission (ICC) ruled to enforce the *Boynton* decision, SNCC's direct action proponents sought new goals. Unknown to Moses, they contemplated a Move on Mississippi (MOM) but gained little ground in Jackson due to competition with the local NAACP. Meanwhile, the Kennedy administration engaged other SNCC students in talks about sponsoring the "safer" tactic of voter registration. Charles Jones and Tim Jenkins tried to convince SNCC that it should follow this line. Backed by McDew and Sherrod, they sought Moses's endorsement in Philadelphia. This taught him that "there were always people in SNCC who, though they seemed pure and counter-ambitious, were extremely 'political.'" Sherrod even visited Cleveland to learn more about Moses's project. Most direct action advocates, however, felt that voter registration was a "copout." Eventually, SNCC decided to have a direct action wing headed by Diane Nash and a voter registration one under Charles Jones, but debates on "what we think SNCC should be" continued after the summer. Meanwhile, Moses discovered part of the solution.[12]

IN MID-JULY MOSES, who had begun corresponding with John Doar, received a letter from C. C. Bryant, the Pike County NAACP president. Bryant had read about their plans in a blurb Edward King had placed in *Jet*. Bryant was an activist much like Moore, a financially independent retired railroad worker and barber whose front yard functioned as a civil rights center. Intrigued, Moore and Moses drove to McComb. Following Ella Baker's example, Moses quickly established a family-like connection with Bryant.[13]

The three toured the McComb area. Located in southwest Mississippi, the region differed from the Delta. Unsuited for cotton plantations and less densely populated by blacks, it consisted mostly of small, poor black and white farmers who competed with one another directly. This, some whites felt, necessitated more Klan-style repression. But in McComb, a young town of 9,000 whites and 4,000 blacks, activists were slowly recovering from the mid-1950s. Some had testified in Washington for the 1957 Civil Rights Act, and the NAACP had restarted voter education meetings and organized a youth chapter. Moreover, key members in the black community, like Bryant, had organizing experience due to the Illinois Central Railroad that was so vital to the region. Connecting the South with the North, railway expansion had helped locals counter the political and economic hegemony of the Delta planters and provided employment and unionization to blacks and whites alike. Although the railroad unions were segregated, they protected black members from white economic sanctions and thereby secured their status in the black community. The trio therefore agreed to start here instead of Cleveland, and Moses moved in with Bryant.[14]

Historians have interpreted this as a conscious effort to distinguish SNCC from existing organizations that generally avoided areas as difficult or dangerous as McComb. However, the choice developed by accident rather than by design. Moses did not know enough of the state to be able to discern the level of racial violence in each area, and his commitment was less to SNCC than to Amzie Moore. "I didn't go to [SNCC] and say, 'here's my plan . . . can I get your permission?' I hooked up with Amzie [and told Jane] 'I want to . . . work on that.' But there's no contract, no money is exchanging hands, no promises made about anything. Amzie says, 'Go to McComb.' I go to McComb. So where's the group-centered leadership?" Moses had not attended SNCC meetings for a year. Without any new action to account for, he hardly even *had* a position in the organization. It was only after his chance meeting with other members in Philadelphia that SNCC began to regularly inform Moses of its plans.[15]

IN HIS ABSENCE, SNCC gave Moses the title of Special Field Secretary and agreed to staff his project. Wyatt Walker, however, claimed Moses as an SCLC worker. This worried SNCC, fearing for the McComb project's independence. Moses therefore informed Walker he would solely work as a SNCC representative. He expressed regret over the inflexibility of "the lines of communication between the organizations," but "the job needs to be done so I have made my choice. You can understand that I feel closer to the students." He nonetheless got SCLC to donate $250 for relief and transportation. It would not be the last time SNCC's precarious financial position would force the organization to beg SCLC for help, even as it criticized SCLC for projecting King.[16]

One means to counter this lack of resource was having the local communities in which SNCC worked provide financial resources, which aligned with Moses's and Baker's beliefs about local autonomy. Moses and Bryant agreed that locals had to support Moses and two other workers for a month themselves. The last two weeks in July, Moses solicited locals and church congregations for $5 or $10 contributions. Webb Owens and Jerry Gibson, two NAACP-affiliated railroad men whom locals trusted with their money, aided him. One Baptist church offered its mimeograph machine, but most aid came through black businessmen like restaurant owner Aylene Quinn, dry cleaning owner Ernest Nobles, and Burgland Supermarket owner Peter Lewis. Through Bryant and Ben Hill, both members of the Freemasons, the Masonic Temple above the supermarket was made available as a SNCC office and citizenship school. This taught Moses that "the quality of . . . the local person, that you go to work with, is everything in terms of whether the project can get off the ground." In practice, this invariably meant starting with the black middle class.[17]

Moses's dependence on this group revealed what T. R. M. Howard's biographers called the "unsung role of the black middle class." In 1950s Mississippi, black entrepreneurs sustained the movement, although whites identified the ministers or principals of black educational institutions as black leaders. The movements of the latter were often constrained by their economic ties to whites; not so with black entrepreneurs. The centrality of this group also indicates how SNCC yielded to locals' directives. It had to; not only did it lack enough money of its own, but, as historian John Dittmer observed, SNCC also needed "the support of those . . . whose word meant something in the community."[18]

In early August, Moses started the voter registration drive with John Hardy and Reginald Robinson from the Nashville and Baltimore movements, as well as five high school students Webb Owens recommended.

To optimize their chances, they knocked on the doors of everyone, including farmers and sharecroppers, whereas past NAACP drives had mainly targeted the middle class. To help put them at ease and to make their fieldwork more practical, they dressed in denim work overalls. Canvassing, however, required massive persuasive skills. To qualify to vote, one had to pay poll tax two subsequent years in advance and answer 21 questions at the county courthouse. The registrar could ask about any one of the state Constitution's 285 sections and had complete discretion in judging the interpretation. Consequently, illiterate whites regularly passed, while blacks, no matter how well educated, nearly always failed. State law also required the printing of applicants' names in local newspapers, so vigilant landlords or employers could then cut them from their homes or jobs. Finding even their parents unwilling to register, Owens motivated the teenagers with ice cream. Some interested locals nonetheless came to the nightly citizenship classes to prepare for the journey to the county courthouse. Applicants could go alone, but most, Moses noticed, felt more secure if SNCC workers came along.[19]

While registration drives were nothing new—the NAACP had prided itself in conducting them for decades—there were significant differences between Moses's program and earlier ones. SNCC workers came to McComb from outside, worked on a full-time basis for an extended time, and blended with locals by moving into their homes and sharing their exposure to Mississippi's hardships. They thus had the time for extensive local organization. In SCLC and NAACP programs, the work had been mainly executed by local activists whose time was split between family and jobs. But the SNCC workers discovered another discontinuity with past campaigns. The Freedom Rides, Moses found, had "permeated black consciousness in Mississippi." He now had an established identity. "Little kids would just look at me and say, 'There goes a Freedom Rider'"—the reverent nickname locals bestowed on *all* civil rights workers.[20]

The Rides had especially energized Mississippi's youth. Dorie Ladner, then a teenager, recounted seeing some Freedom Riders in Jackson. "I was like 'Oh my God! Here they are!' . . . I felt that I had finally found someone who thought and felt like I did." McComb high school graduate Hollis Watkins had seen the Rides on television in California during a family visit. He instantly flew home to join them. He went to the Masonic Temple to offer himself to the movement because a friend had told him that Martin Luther King Jr. was setting up a program there.

Instead, he found Moses, who simply handed him a copy of the registration test. After he completed it, Moses told him he would have qualified if he had been old enough to vote (in the 1960s, voting age was twenty-one). Now that he knew "how it's done," Moses asked, was he willing to "assist us in getting other people to register?" Watkins agreed and told some friends. The next day, they started canvassing.[21]

Moses established deep personal connections with the teenagers, which became typical of his relationships with Mississippi youth. He treated them as equals by joining rather than delegating their activities. "Bob was right there doing the same thing with us, it wasn't like you go out and do it and I'll stay here," Watkins observed. No doubt, there were discrepancies due to Moses's character, background, and age. Watkins lauded Moses's attention to details, and another emphasized how he "always helped us understand purpose." In this, Moses also surpassed most in SNCC. Marion Barry, who soon joined the McComb staff, acknowledged that most SNCC workers at this point had little sense of direction, but it was "much more clear to probably Bob Moses than anybody." Whereas they emphasized desegregation, Moses had already realized then that they were struggling to "bring Mississippi up to par with the rest of the country" on *all* levels.[22]

WITH MORE HELP, the drive became more effective. Many older blacks opened up once they discovered that the canvassers were local. The teenagers distributed flyers, invited locals to the SNCC office, and organized meetings at the Burgland Supermarket. Since classes had started on August 7, Moses accompanied four blacks to the county courthouse in Magnolia, and three qualified to vote. Three followed the next day, and two passed. On the third day, Moses accompanied another nine. The registrar, getting suspicious, only passed one.[23]

The arrival of sixteen black applicants attracted coverage in the local newspapers. This motivated black farmers in McComb's surrounding rural Amite and Walthall counties to ask Moses to set up citizenship schools there too. Although both were black-majority counties, Walthall did not have a single black registered voter while Amite had just one (McDew, however, derisively commented, "We haven't been able to find him"). But Moses lacked workers and money to branch out. Moreover, McComb residents indicated strongly that Amite would invite violence. After discussing it with Bryant, he decided to proceed anyway because "from the human point of view, they had greater needs than those people in Pike County [and] from the psychological point of view where the whole problem in Mississippi is pervaded with fear," that is, if you turned "down the tough areas [the people] would simply lose confidence in you." While they worked out the logistics of expansion, the farmers attended classes in McComb.[24]

On August 15, Moses accompanied three of them, two elderly women and one man, to the Amite County courthouse in Liberty. The registrar roughly asked why they came, and when the three recoiled in fear, Moses answered on their behalf. The startled registrar questioned him but then simply ignored them while he helped a white woman complete the answers on her test. Finally, they were allowed to apply. Meanwhile, Moses wrote afterward, the sheriff, some deputies, and clerks came "looking in, staring, moving back out, muttering." An alerted highway patrolman, W. D. Carwile, came in and observed them the entire morning. After six hours, the three had completed the test. All failed, but they considered their attempt successful. On their way home, however, Carwile followed them and pulled them over. Was Moses the New York "nigger who's come to tell the niggers how to register?" he demanded to know. Moses, who had gotten out of the car, simply responded by writing down the officer's name. Angry over such impudence, Carwile shoved him back in and ordered them to follow him to McComb. There Moses was arrested while Carwile and the county attorney frantically consulted the law books. They charged him with interfering with an arrest, but since only he was arrested, they changed it to impeding an officer in his duties. To Moses, this was an eye-opener. "Like any Black person living in America, I knew racism. What I hadn't encountered before Mississippi was the use of law as an instrument of outright oppression."[25]

Told that he would stand trial that night, Moses asked for his one phone call. Being broke, he called John Doar collect. Deliberately speaking loudly, he cited violations of the 1957 and 1960 Civil Rights Acts, as Doar had outlined in his letters, and demanded a federal investigation. Nothing would come of the FBI investigation that would be conducted the next day, but Moses's contact with the federal government likely interfered with his sentencing. Although pronounced guilty, he received a ninety-day suspended sentence and a $50 fine, which would be remitted if he paid $5 in court costs. He refused and was taken to the Magnolia jail. Two days later, Jack Young, a black NAACP-affiliated lawyer from Jackson, paid the fine and he grudgingly came out. They would fruitlessly appeal his conviction. Moses chose "jail-no-bail" on principle, he told the *Enterprise Journal*, because "I don't think I was guilty of the charges." He added another classic nonviolent tactic by refusing food while he was jailed. This indicates that Moses was acting in the spirit of SNCC's direct action wing, although he never explicitly advocated doing so as a program.[26]

News of Moses's arrest reverberated everywhere. Even the *New York Times* publicized his attempt to appeal his conviction. The story was broadcast on local radio, and John Emmerich of the *Enterprise Journal*, a white states' rights advocate who had suffered physical assaults for his moderate racial views, interviewed Moses for the first of several articles. Central in local white reports was Moses's outsider status, as was his relation with the Justice Department. One indignant editor even attempted to call the department collect but was refused and wondered "why Moses was so privileged" as to have Doar take his call. The Mississippi State Sovereignty Commission began investigating Moses too, concluding falsely that he had "objected to being stopped in a rude, verbal manner" and "refused to leave the scene" while continuing "to abuse the patrolman verbally."[27]

MOSES RETURNED TO MCCOMB on August 18. Meanwhile, over a dozen Freedom Riders released from Parchman and other SNCC workers, like Marion Barry, Travis Britt, George Lowe, and MacArthur Cotton, had joined the effort. Moses's arrest had turned McComb into the "summer's new magnet town" for them because it showed that in the Deep South, voter registration and direct action were interchangeable.[28]

The growing group continued the canvassing but also commenced organizing direct action workshops. Moses disliked this development since the local NAACP opposed direct action for fear of violence. Yet he accepted their presence in hopes of stimulating unity within SNCC. When these young people founded the Pike County Nonviolent Movement, however, Moses foresaw trouble and secretly asked Jack Young for the NAACP's aid in "any legal difficulties which may arise."[29]

Moses and Bryant felt his arrest should be used to show locals their commitment, and going back to Amite would add to his credibility. Grown in size, SNCC could now divide responsibilities: Moses returned to Amite, and Hardy, Britt, Lowe, and Cotton moved to Tylertown in Walthall. McComb was left in the hands of those who preferred to mix voter registration with direct action. That this division occurred so easily shows the efficiency of SNCC's lack of organizational structure;

although Moses had started the project, neither he nor his colleagues ever saw him as "the" leader who determined its direction. This allowed them to move flexibly along local demands rather than rigidly holding onto their own programs.

Getting started in Amite, however, proved difficult. To avoid detection, Bryant had to introduce Moses to local dairy farmer E. W. Steptoe after dark. Steptoe was the head of the Amite NAACP branch, which had operated since 1953. It had been fairly successful with 200 members, until Sheriff E. L. Caston impounded its membership rolls after the *Brown* decision. One by one, the members, threatened with economic reprisals, retreated, and the branch lived on in theory only. Like Amzie Moore, Steptoe had to appeal to outside groups to survive.[30]

Steptoe agreed to take Moses in for two weeks. They started nightly citizenship classes at his farm but soon moved them to a church in the woods when Steptoe's activist network reported an ominous surge in Citizens' Council meetings at the county courthouse in nearby Liberty. As a result, only two to five locals attended classes, whereas the classes in Walthall attracted thirty. Steptoe's neighbor Herbert Lee, another landowning farmer, came regularly, but according to Moses "did not talk much." Mostly Lee drove him and Steptoe around, since the latter lacked a car. Moses therefore asked SNCC to buy him one to cover the vast distance between the farm and church—an apt example of how resources from outside groups could facilitate the effectiveness of grassroots protest. But at the farm, Moses felt even more isolated because whites had denied Steptoe a telephone. Unsurprisingly, Steptoe, like Moore, stacked weapons everywhere. When they heard of four blacks who successfully registered on August 22, farmer Curtis Dawson and Reverend Alfred Knox were encouraged and asked Moses to accompany them to the registrar.[31]

On August 29, they left energized. "We are climbing Jacob's Ladder, higher and higher . . . ," Moses sang in his mind to bolster his courage. But before they reached the Liberty courthouse, three whites stopped them. One was Billy Jack Caston, the sheriff's cousin, who had a reputation for violence. He likely knew Moses by sight since the church where they had held citizenship classes was near his residence. Caston asked what they were up to. Before Moses could answer,[32] Caston hit him in the temple with a knife handle. Kneeling, he covered his head while Caston kept punching him. Knox tried to pull Caston off Moses, while Dawson begged him to stop. When Caston finally did, the three proceeded to the courthouse. "I felt it was important to keep going, that was the point," Moses indicated. But because Moses was bleeding profusely, the shocked registrar simply closed down.[33]

This beating magnified Moses's reputation among SNCC workers and locals. Ernest Nobles "couldn't understand what Bob Moses was. . . . He had more guts than any one man I've ever known." Historian Taylor Branch even claimed he acquired "a Christlike name within SNCC, where the story was repeated that he had clasped his hands and looked heavenward during the Caston assault, saying 'Forgive them.'" Of course, Moses was neither the first nor last civil rights worker ever beaten. But Moses's response seemed to make the difference—it symbolized *the* quality of the movement's "new wave," the refusal to be stopped by violence.[34]

Public beatings had successfully deterred past activists, including union representatives. They were designed to humiliate opponents based on the southern "code of honor," which interpreted a refusal to retaliate as cowardice. A beating could be psychologically devastating as well. For example, when a judge beat NAACP activist John Shillady in Texas in 1919, he was so shaken, he resigned. In the wake of Gandhi, Rosa Parks, the Little Rock Nine, and especially the sit-ins and Freedom Rides that took the approach to a regionwide level, however, not fighting back became seen as a means of strength and dignity. Even those who did not believe in Christian interpretations of nonviolence witnessed its effect on movement supporters and opponents. Since Moses's was probably the first known example of nonviolence during a beating while registering to vote that occurred within this "new" context, the beating by Caston underscored this sensation of discontinuity with the movement up to that date.[35]

For Moses, however, this had not been easy. He had shielded himself during the assault by going into the survival mode he had adopted at Hamilton. "I kind of separated out of my body. Like an observer." But he "tried to stick closely to the game plan." Nonviolence required a significant amount of calculation ahead of time. While Camus's philosophy had prepared Moses intellectually, emotionally it was another matter. He came to terms with it at Steptoe's. "I learned to live with my fears. Organizing myself was a necessary first step. When you're out there . . . with no electricity, no radio, no running water, everything moves very slowly and you really have time to go into yourself. I used to think, Pick one foot up and step forward, put it down and pick the next one up . . .

[you learn] the importance of a daily routine carrying you through." But nonviolence remained tricky. "The question of personal fear just has to be constantly fought," he sighed to one reporter in the 1960s. It was "an inside question" to which "I don't know if there is any answer at all."[36]

THE MEN RETURNED TO STEPTOE'S rather than McComb for medical treatment because Moses figured that just the sight of his wounds—three lacerations on his head—might deter the locals from civil rights activity forever. Dr. Anderson, a black doctor without movement ties new in town, stitched his gashes. After asking Jack Young for legal advice, Moses headed to a mass meeting in support of the Pike County Nonviolent Movement. James Bevel's fiery speech to the 200 locals in attendance led to alarmed front-page coverage in local white papers the next day, but Moses's message was equally shocking. He publicly announced his return to Liberty, because, he stated, "The law down here is law made by white people, enforced by white people, for the benefit of white people. It will be that way until the Negroes begin to vote."[37]

The following day, Moses indeed filed charges against Caston—the first time a black had done so against a white in county history. The prosecutor tried to be professional, but after it took all day to file the charges, he advised Moses to sleep on it. That night, a farmer named Weathersbee came to Steptoe's farm, saying he wanted to register if Moses accompanied him. He agreed. Joined by Travis Britt, they returned to Liberty the next day. Britt was told to wait outside the courthouse while Weathersbee registered and Moses testified at Caston's trial, which was arranged two hours after Moses had let it be known he intended to press charges.[38]

Over 100 whites carrying weapons filled the courtroom. Caston justified the beating by incredibly claiming that Moses had provoked him; Moses "brushed his shoulder and spun around into a boxing stance on the sidewalk." To underscore his status as an outsider, Caston's attorney asked Moses whether he "had participated in riots . . . in Japan or San Francisco." As the all-white jury deliberated the verdict, Moses had to wait outside with Britt. Shots were then fired into the air, and the sheriff told them to leave. The courthouse closed and Weathersbee could not finish his registration. Police escorted them to the county line while Caston was acquitted.[39]

Seeking justice elsewhere, Moses contacted John Doar. On September 1, Assistant Attorney General Burke Marshall ordered an FBI investigation, but agents even failed to photograph his wounds. It dawned on the SNCC workers that they "were out there fighting by ourselves." Moses thus ended the month having "met the Mississippi of Harlem nightmares." Yet locals like Knox, Bryant, and Steptoe had also shown him "the Mississippi of unexpected Black strength."[40]

THE LOCAL TEENAGERS were equally determined. On the day of Moses's beating, fifteen of them had planned a sit-in at the Woolworth's lunch counter.[41] Only Curtis Hayes and Hollis Watkins showed up, but they followed through and were jailed. This sparked a new grassroots insurgency: the next day, five others sat in at the bus station lunch counter, and three—Robert Talbert, Ike Lewis, and Brenda Travis—were jailed. Travis, only fifteen, had lied about her age to be allowed to participate. At the mass meeting the night before, she could not keep from staring at Moses. He believed that "the sight of my battered and bandaged head triggered some great outrage in Brenda," causing her to sit in. He knew her age, but in his absence, she had turned to SNCC's direct action proponents who believed her lie. Her arrest sparked outrage everywhere; blacks denounced whites for jailing a teenager, and whites castigated blacks for using a child. Bryant was so upset that he threatened to evict Moses and cut SNCC off from the NAACP's help. He only rescinded his threat after Moore and Steptoe intervened. The five spent over a month in jail until $5,000 in bail was raised.[42]

Moses had also been ambivalent about the sit-ins. Little direct action had occurred in the Deep South, and its consequences had yet to be discovered. But, he realized, facilitating grassroots activism meant that locals had to follow "their own ideas, not mine." Moreover, he understood that the teenagers were frustrated with his slow organizing pace. "[T]hey couldn't vote, they couldn't register, they were not old enough. And they were faced with the intransigence of the adults. They were itching to do something themselves." He therefore "couldn't have any objections . . . as long as you had local people who wanted to carry the burden and the action, then it would seem to me you were moving forward." This corresponded with Ella Baker's idea that decisions should be made by those who executed them, even if failure surely followed.[43]

Despite the resulting erosion of support, SNCC persevered. On September 5, Moses and Britt again accompanied four locals to Liberty. Told to wait outside, several whites approached them. One ranted at Moses that he "should be ashamed coming down here from New York stirring up trouble, causing poor innocent people to lose their jobs and homes." Moses asked why people should lose their homes for wanting to register, but the man kept yelling while he sat silently on the porch's stoop. "My only reaction to this in all these instances is simply to shut up, to be silent. I get very, very depressed," Moses later explained. Another man began punching Britt, hitting him fifteen times in his face before trying to choke him. The others cut off Moses as he tried to approach the sheriff's office. Both remained nonviolent, but Britt disclosed that his choice was practical; if he had retaliated, "I would have been lynched by the others. They were waiting for me to do something like that." When the man released Britt, Moses grabbed him. They and the four applicants, who were all rejected, returned to McComb. According to John Doar, the FBI could easily have identified the attackers but waited a fortnight until they could no longer ignore the Civil Rights Division's request.[44]

The other SNCC workers had similar experiences. On September 7, John Hardy took two blacks to register in Tylertown, but both were refused. When asked why, registrar John Wood hit Hardy on the head with a pistol. Bleeding, he went to the sheriff, who arrested Hardy instead, altering the charges three times. He was jailed in Magnolia, next to the sit-in students. Moses visited them for the first time and found them optimistic even though they could not take baths and one policeman had threatened Watkins with a hanging. He agreed to escort Hardy to his trial on September 22 despite being "tired and a little shook" about returning to Walthall. There they discovered that the trial had been postponed and that Hardy would be free on bail in the meantime. Nonetheless, when trying to leave, a hostile group of whites ambushed Hardy. He and Moses managed to reach their car but found the door stuck. A policeman told them to hurry. Finally getting the door open, they "backed out into the mob" and left. After that, locals refused to register. For the rest of September, Moses noted, "We just had a tough time. Wasn't much we could do."[45]

The federal government finally stepped in, blocking Hardy's trial. Unlike Moses, Hardy was beaten inside the registrar's office by the registrar, which made the connection with voter registration evident. The *New York Times* praised this unprecedented step as "an important element in the civil rights battle in the South." Black and white papers alike printed Robert Kennedy's strong support for the constitutional right to register without "fear of coercion, intimidation or physical harm. It is our responsibility to maintain that right." But state officials were unaffected;

registrar John Wood warned in *The Times* that "[t]he Federal Government, through our Attorney General, will eventually cause bloodshed between the races."[46]

Worried, the Justice Department began investigations in McComb on September 11. It found that whites had held regular meetings at which, Moses believed, the Caston and Britt beatings were orchestrated. On September 23, Doar came from Washington to investigate conditions in southwest Mississippi, a place he likened to "going back into the nineteenth century." He met Moses for the first time at Steptoe's farm. He had falsely assumed that Moses had exaggerated his injuries in his letters. Instantly reassessing the FBI's and Moses's moral fiber, Doar ordered the Bureau to finally photograph the wounds. Two months later, the Caston case was nonetheless closed without results.[47]

The incident confirmed to Moses that local agents were part of the problem rather than the solution. The FBI agent from nearby Natchez who reinterviewed Moses even tried to "convince me that I really hadn't been beaten but had fell," which he reported to Doar. When photographing his wounds, the agent warned Moses he "could shoot whoever complained about not conducting complete and thorough investigations." The agent denied this, which his colleagues conveniently corroborated. Moses later remarked that locals' faces "lit up when John Doar and the Justice Department came. . . . [It was] so different from when a local resident FBI agent came."[48]

MOSES AND STEPTOE INFORMED DOAR that they were particularly concerned about the Caston family and Steptoe's neighbor, Billy Jack's father-in-law, state representative E. H. Hurst. Several locals, including Steptoe and Lee, had been told to pay off any debts, and Knox's son-in-law had been fired. At a church revival meeting where Moses would speak, the deputy sheriff collected license plates numbers of visitors while asking repetitively about Moses's presence. Doar asked to see Herbert Lee before he flew home, but he was out. Meanwhile, one of Lee's daughters received an anonymous call at his brother's Frank's house. It warned that Lee, Steptoe, and farmer and movement supporter George Reese would all soon be killed.[49]

On the morning of September 25, Moses's worst fears came true. Hurst, driving Caston's truck, followed Herbert Lee to the cotton gin and parked next to him. Lee exited his car through the passenger side, after which Hurst ran past both trucks and started shouting. The alleged motivation for the quarrel was a $500 debt Lee owed Hurst but which was not due until December. In reality, Hurst, once a childhood friend of Lee's and Steptoe's, had resented them since their farming became more successful than Hurst considered proper. Their civil rights activism only encouraged his anger. Hurst claimed Lee then tried to attack him with a tire iron, so he hit him on the head with a pistol, which accidentally fired, killing Lee on the spot. A coroner's jury indeed exonerated Hurst the next day, claiming justifiable self-defense after Sheriff Caston and the town marshal, the first at the scene, stated they had found a tire iron under Lee's body.[50]

Moses and Charles McDew had the heavy task of identifying Lee. Upset, Moses toured the black community with Steptoe and Moore to interview witnesses—as Moore and Medgar Evers had done after Emmett Till's murder—several nights in a row even though he was terrified. He especially recalled the night riding as "really very scary. You were afraid of every headlight that came up." Since neither Moore nor Moses were familiar with the county, they feared driving onto a white farm and getting themselves killed. Moses nonetheless told Steptoe not to bring guns, or else "we just won't go."[51]

Several witnesses, including forty-four-year-old logger and veteran Louis Allen, described inconsistencies in Hurst's story. Lee had not had a tire iron, his small physique defied the logic of initiating a fight, and Hurst had evidently "lowered the gun at him." Dr. Anderson, who inspected Lee's body, confirmed that it showed no powder burns, implying he was not shot from close range. Allen stated that white officers forced him to testify that Hurst fired in self-defense. "At the coroner's jury, they asked me about the piece of iron. I said I hadn't seen no iron. 'Is this the piece of iron?' I said 'yes.'"[52]

Doar was keenly interested in the case, but despite his multiple requests, the FBI's slow bureaucracy and dependence on biased local agents ensured no action until after Lee's burial. The Mississippi State Sovereignty Commission also weighed in, insisting that Hurst shot in self-defense and that Moses had "falsified his statement to [the] Justice Department." The department nevertheless prepared suits against the sheriff, his son, three deputies, the chief of police, the town marshal, a highway patrolman, and others who encouraged intimidation of voter applicants. Yet fear of "uncontrollable violence" that would expend the department's limited resources in the state prevented these suits from ultimately being filed.[53]

On October 13, Louis Allen told Moses that he wanted to tell the truth at a grand jury hearing that examined the coroner's jury's findings. Moses asked Doar for federal protection, but the department could not vouch for Allen's safety. He then counseled Allen against testifying. Nevertheless, the FBI informed local officers that Allen had wavered. Even though he ultimately upheld his initial testimony at the grand jury, Moses knew that Allen "was just a marked man."[54]

Moses now faced the dark side of his leadership philosophy. He saw it as his rule to encourage locals to act on their own behalf. However, was his encouragement a form of manipulation if that person did not understand the implications of his or her actions? Was he complicit in what happened afterward? After the FBI leaked the information that Allen might change his testimony, whites stopped their business with him and cut off his credit. Six months later, a deputy sheriff broke his jaw with a flashlight. Harassments followed for the next two years—until whites finally killed him in an ambush in 1964.[55]

LEE'S MURDER INFURIATED the black community. Some raised money for Lee's widow, while others discussed evening the score by forming "some kind of adult violent organization." Other locals became even more afraid. Meanwhile, SNCC workers faced their own guilt about the murder. A story circulated about Lee's funeral, where his widow pounded her chest and shouted at Moses and McDew, "You killed my husband! You killed my husband!" Moses cannot remember whether this actually happened,[56] but McDew and others insist it did.[57]

SNCC workers felt responsible regardless. As Moses stated in 1964, Lee "was killed just as surely because we went in there to organize as rain comes because [of] the clouds." Yet Lee likely surfaced on whites' radars long before SNCC's arrival. Fifty-two-year-old Lee was illiterate but always felt self-empowered; he traded his dairy products in Louisiana to avoid getting cheated in local stores, shunned stores that might invite racial slurs, and refused his children's employment outside his farm. He openly belonged to the NAACP, even during the bloody 1950s. With Lee's death, Steptoe wrote Roy Wilkins, the branch "suffered a serious loss . . . Lee was one of the strongest members and had been since 1953."[58]

Moses grew angry when he read in the *Enterprise Journal* that Lee "was shot in self-defense. . . . That was it. You might have thought he had been a bum. There was no mention that Lee was a farmer, that he had a family, that he had nine kids, beautiful kids, [and had] been a very substantial citizen. It was as if he had been drunk or something and had gotten into fight and gotten shot." He then wrote a short article entitled "Another Man Done Gone" for the local NAACP bulletin. It focused entirely on Lee, who was "plain spoken, forthright, conscious of his lack of education but anxious to learn whatever was necessary . . . to register." Citing the background of his wife of twenty-two years and the education levels of his children, he stressed that one daughter now had to give up school to help her mother. With Moses's aid, SNCC helped another daughter and Steptoe's son get a scholarship.[59]

Moses's article revealed his deep respect for Lee. Even years later, his death still pained him. As he explained to one of Lee's daughters, "When one of you died, part of us died." He had begun to see locals not just as equals but as *family*. Moses felt this was the essence of the McComb experience. "Everywhere we went, [we] were adopted and nurtured, even protected as though we were family [and] that closeness rendered moot the label of 'outside agitator.'" Moses's stress on creating family connections also signaled his inherent drive for aligning with likeminded people and established a sense of continuity with previous activism among the SNCC workers. "[O]ur young generation was dynamically linked to a rooted older generation who passed on wisdom, encouragement, and concrete aid when possible. This was empowering."[60]

Throughout the 1960s, Moses carried Lee's death with him as a reminder of personal and national failure. He frequently told Lee's story to SNCC insiders and others. Many in movement leadership positions, including Martin Luther King Jr. and Stokely Carmichael, struggled with tactics that risked innocent lives. This internal stress, however, probably affected Moses even more due to his fascination with moral purity. He could not but see himself as an executioner, he told northern whites in 1964. "What does it mean to be involved in that kind of action which might precipitate that kind of [death?] . . . Camus poses it on a historical scale in terms of [whether] people who are enslaved, in order to get their freedom, have to become executioners and participate in acts of terror and death. . . . And [this] takes place on maybe a very small scale down South in terms of that kind of activity which we carry on." This moral anguish made him less suitable for the requirements of leadership, Taylor Branch argued. "King was more like General Sherman when his people were killed, and you need this toughness to keep going. It tore Moses apart." Simultaneously, it was exactly this sensitivity that drew people to him. Curtis Hayes claimed that seeing Moses "sad was ... enough for me to go and find the cat that killed Herbert Lee myself."[61]

Moses's doubts nearly immobilized him, but Camus's teachings solidified his perseverance. He resolved that the only way to soften his sense of moral responsibility over the involvement of others was to constantly inform locals of the risks and to share their exposure. "Everything that you're asking people to do, you're doing yourself." Only continuing would make Lee's sacrifice acceptable, he believed. "Lee sort of symbolized [our] signing over in blood to the struggle, so that it was clear now that they will have to kill us to get us out of here."[62]

MEANWHILE IN MCCOMB, tensions were building again. The sit-in students were bailed out on October 3 thanks to outside assistance; next to SCLC, the NAACP paid $2,500, although Roy Wilkins demanded NAACP involvement in a letter to SNCC—"otherwise the bills will have to be paid by those who plan and launch." More SNCC workers, like Charles Jones, Charles Sherrod, and Bob Zellner, had come to give momentum to McComb's growing movement. Moses, uncomfortable with Steptoe's increased dedication to self-defense and in need of "some breathing room, a place to sort out my thoughts," returned to McComb as well.[63]

Burgland High School expelled Brenda Travis and Ike Lewis the day after their release. Angered, over 100 students marched to the Masonic Temple, inviting the SNCC workers to join their march headed for the Magnolia courthouse to protest the racial status quo. Most historians consider what Taylor Branch termed a "spontaneous march" evidence of a successful grassroots-led movement. Yet the truth is that the march, like the 1960s sit-ins, had benefited more from outside assistance than the SNCC members were willing to admit. Even Moses, who in *Radical Equations* called the students' arrival a "sudden tidal surge," has privately disclosed that "we have had more responsibility for these kids than we've publicly acknowledged."[64]

The fact that other SNCC workers came to town anticipating a protest, Moses claimed, in itself suggested that the "march was planned, because Jones came down to get the publicity out." Moreover, transcripts of a 1991 reunion[65] revealed that SNCC's direct action wing used a mass meeting the night before to advise the teenagers on possible actions. Charles Jones confessed they had deliberately kept this from Moses. One participant said they had heard rumors about Brenda's possible expulsion and then decided that, if true, they would walk out. But James Bevel's speech at the meeting accelerated that decision. According to Dr. Anderson, Bevel "got the kids excited," after which they "stayed around [and] did some planning." He tellingly referred to Bevel as the "Pied Piper." SNCC workers even assisted in making signs and pamphlets. The signs were stored at the Masonic Temple that night, and the students marched there first to pick them up.[66]

As Jones had predicted, Moses and McDew opposed marching; they feared violence and the loss of adults' support and their staff to long jail sentences. Yet after speaking with some high school seniors, Moses realized he had no control over the events. Moreover, not knowing Jones and the others as well, they specifically asked for *his* support. Acquiescing to his belief that "whatever the group decides you should do," Moses, McDew, and Zellner then agreed but advised the students to march to the City Hall instead since Magnolia was eight miles away. One teenager said they were advised not to walk on the grass or beside the sidewalk but felt that "the seniors from the high school [were] leading us more so than SNCC taking over." Jones stayed behind to get the news out; to avoid arrest, he even dressed up as a butcher and called news outlets from the butcher's store.[67]

When the group reached City Hall, a white mob was already waiting. Curtis Hayes walked up the steps and asked the students to pray. After uttering "Oh, Lord," he was arrested. Hollis Watkins followed Hayes's example but suffered the same fate. This ritual continued one student after another, until police arrested all 114, including Brenda Travis, for disturbing the peace. The mob then zoomed in on Zellner. As the only white, he particularly enraged the mob. Whites began choking and punching him—one even tried to gouge his eyes out—but Moses and McDew tried to shield Zellner's body. Meanwhile, the FBI and police stood by passively. The three were kicked until police finally arrested the bloodied SNCC workers.[68]

The march caused a national uproar. The question of leadership in civil rights protests instantly became a central part of the story. Neglecting all grassroots responsibility, the *New York Times* focused chiefly on Zellner, claiming he led the students. Later articles corrected some of these details, but the general emphasis remained on the SNCC workers, with Moses now identified as "the leader." Southern whites, including the State Sovereignty Commission, also blamed the outside forces in the march. The *Enterprise Journal* worried about what was "happening to our community when children march on City Hall under the leadership of outside agitators?" The mayor insisted that until SNCC's arrival, the races "lived together peacefully in McComb"; Sheriff Simmons claimed that most students "just joined in" without knowing what they were doing. Police Chief George Guy therefore told the *New York Times* that "Moses is a pretty shrewd damn duck."[69]

The march's effect in the black community was double-edged. Many expressed anger at SNCC for using children, but the activism roused others to action. That night, another mass meeting was held, and Ernest Nobles tried, unsuccessfully, to organize a parent protest march. Even C. C. Bryant now proclaimed that he would follow "where the students lead." In subsequent days, more SNCC workers and Tom Hayden and Paul Potter of the Students for a Democratic Society (SDS) trickled into McComb, followed by northern reporters from the *New York Times*, *Newsweek*, and others.[70]

IN THE MEANTIME, Moses and the other arrested marchers faced harrowing uncertainty. The police had released Zellner to a white mob that had taken him into the countryside, carrying a noose. Police brought in local whites to curse the others in the McComb jail's basement. They specifically targeted Moses. He met this with his distinctive survival mode. "I was again, very, very quiet." At night, the students were taken upstairs, one by one, where they were aggressively questioned by local authorities. Eventually, they let ninety-seven minors go and brought the others to the Liberty jail. After thoroughly scaring him, the mob had brought Zellner to the one in Magnolia. Charles Jones, meanwhile, frantically corresponded with the Justice Department about a lynch threat that was forming against Moses, but Doar said he could do little.[71]

Jones was flabbergasted. "[H]ere was . . . the most powerful country in the history of the world, represented in the form of John Doar, and he says . . . 'ain't nothing I can do.' And that pretty much completely shook me out of any illusions . . . about the federal government." A letter from the FBI director to Burke Marshall the next day confirmed that the lynch threat had been real, but the sheriff had promised the FBI to ensure Moses's safety. Despite Jones's disillusionment, this notification that the federal government was watching likely saved his life after all.[72]

Moses meanwhile tried to accommodate to a cold and crowded Liberty cell. The toilet—a hole in the floor—had overflowed. The students took turns sitting and walking around in the water and waste until they were arraigned and charged with breach of peace. Moses and the other SNCC workers were also charged with contributing to juvenile delinquency, and Brenda Travis was sentenced to an Oakley reform school for "Negro delinquents." Pending release on bail, Moses recorded they "sang songs, we drew a chessboard on the floor, took cigarette butts, made pieces and played chess." He also taught the students math, and McDew taught history. As chairman, however, McDew bailed out early to help raise $5,000 for the rest, which Harry Belafonte donated shortly after.[73]

At Dr. Anderson's house, the SNCC workers decided to go to SNCC headquarters in Atlanta to recuperate before their trial on October 31. Only McDew stayed behind as a symbolic presence. Despite visibly patrolling Anderson's house with guns that night, the next morning, McDew found that someone taped a sign on the SNCC office proclaiming victoriously "SNCC Done Snuck" out of town.[74]

Back in Atlanta, Moses reluctantly joined the others—including Mississippi locals—in an emergency meeting to discuss SNCC's goals now that McComb was proving so costly. Executive Secretary James Forman, a northern university-trained black Air Force veteran, questioned the group's discipline and blamed McDew for staying in McComb and Moses for refusing to participate in proceedings. When everyone was asked to explain why they wanted to work full-time for SNCC, Moses merely stated he wanted to return to McComb. While this rendered SNCC's internal fissures trivial, it underscored the different priorities of SNCC's administrative forces in Atlanta and its field troops, personified in Forman and Moses. Emphasizing the need for internal organization, Forman insisted Moses should stay until SNCC had decided on its direction. Moses grudgingly stayed another day.[75]

SNCC's absence did not stop the Burgland students. Even as the black community at large, fearing violence, withdrew its support, they continued to display grassroots leadership. On October 10, the students returned to school to plead for Brenda Travis's and Ike Lewis's readmission. The authorities agreed, on the condition that the students sign an agreement to stop demonstrations. If not, they faced expulsion. The next day, authorities threatened to reduce their grades by 10 percent. Most students refused on both occasions and walked out. The students were told to return by October 16 or be expelled. Their parents asked the Board of Education, unsuccessfully, for a meeting. They demanded their children's return with a statement from the students declaring solidarity with Travis and Lewis: "we will suffer whatever punishment they have to take with them. In school we are taught democracy, but the rights that democracy has to offer have been denied to us.... However, we are children of God, who makes the sun shine on the just and unjust. So we petition all our fellowmen to love rather than hate, to build rather than tear down, to bind our nation with love and justice without regard to race, color or creed."[76]

Every day afterward, they marched to school and left after refusing to sign the slips. On October 16, 103 students marched out permanently. The *New York Times* reported they brought McComb "to the brink of a serious racial crisis." Some white residents, it noted, "conceded reluctantly that a basic change has taken place in the Negroes' attitudes, but none profess to know why." At SNCC's suggestion, Tom Hayden and Paul Potter reported on the walkouts to provoke federal attention. A white plumber then beat them while policemen looked on. Raising much publicity because the victims were white, the plumber was arrested, and Burke Marshall invited the two to Washington.[77]

Feeling responsible, Moses and the other SNCC workers upon their return from Atlanta immediately developed a "makeshift school" called Nonviolent High at the Masonic Temple. Fifty to seventy-five students attended it with Moses teaching math, McDew history, and Dion Diamond the sciences. Also included were geometry, English, French, and singing. The SNCC workers, more highly educated than the students' own teachers, discovered that their egalitarian style of teaching increased the students' confidence and stimulated their sense of themselves as leaders. On October 21, the fire department misleadingly ruled the Temple a "fire hazard." Ordered out, the school moved to a neighboring church. Considering "the circumstances [and] extreme emotional tensions in the town," Moses concluded, "we did pretty well." An MSSC investigator even indignantly documented that "Moses began to teach ... just as though it was an improved institution of education."[78]

Nonetheless, Moses and SNCC knew their school was not a viable substitute. SNCC therefore negotiated with black Campbell College in Jackson to admit the students in their high school department. By

October's end—when Nonviolent High closed because its faculty faced trial—sixty-seven had enrolled there. SNCC made several nationwide fundraising appeals, including to SCLC, to secure $30,000 for scholarships. Meanwhile, Moses, three other SNCC workers, and fifty-eight students tried to visit Brenda Travis in Oakley, but the sheriff, supported by a twenty-five-headed corps armed with guns, tear gas rifles, night sticks, and dogs, denied them admission.[79]

The trial on October 31 was swift and severe. Despite conflicting police testimonies, Moses and ten other SNCC workers were sentenced to four months and $200 in fines each. Four local students received six months' imprisonment and $500 fines each. Underscoring the issue of leadership in civil rights activism, Judge Brumfield singled out Moses and the perceived inability of local blacks "to think for themselves" in a statement that was widely circulated in civil rights circles and that represented the core of Moses's leadership dilemma. "[U]ntil this past August, we have gotten along very well. It was then that this outsider Bob Moses came. . . . Those of you who are local residents are like sheep being led to the slaughter. If you continue to follow the advice of outside agitators you will be like sheep and be slaughtered." Appeal bonds went at $1,000 each. Requiring $14,000 in total (Zellner's father bonded him out), several northern colleges organized fundraising campaigns, but $14,000 exceeded SNCC's entire annual budget. The fourteen thus had to acquiesce to jail.[80]

Confinement was not easy, Moses recorded in 1962. "Characteristic of the Mississippi jails is that you sit and rot." Not allowed to work, there was "[n]othing to do inside. They give you your meals two or three times a day; they give you your shower one or two times a week; they give you silence or nasty words otherwise." There were some moments of relief through playing chess, reading books, and writing letters home. Forman forwarded letters to Moses, and the FBI once came to interview him. The black community did its best to relieve the students' suffering, too. Alyene Quinn and others brought food daily, until the jailers limited their visits to once a week. These visits were meaningful, Moses realized, because "the community people took a stand." More than signs of support, they were of strategic importance, indicating the significance of grassroots networks. "[T]hey would smuggle in [and out] letters . . . and we had a little underground of information passing back and forth between us and the people in town." In one smuggled letter dating November 1, Moses wrote,

I am writing this note from the drunk tank of the county jail in Magnolia, Mississippi. Twelve of us are here, sprawled out along the concrete bunker. Curtis Hayes, Hollis Watkins, Ike Lewis, and Robert Talbert, four veterans of the bunker, are sitting up talking—mostly about girls; McDew ("Tell the story") is curled into the concrete and the wall; Harold Robinson, Stephen Ashley, James Wells, Lee Chester Vick, Leotus Eubanks, and Ivory Diggs [lie] cramped on the cold bunker; I'm sitting with smuggled pen and paper, thinking a little, writing a little; Myrtis Bennett and Janie Campbell are across the way wedded to a different icy cubicle.

Later on Hollis will lead out with a clear tenor into a freedom song, Talbert and Lewis will supply jokes and McDew will discourse on the history of the black man and the Jew. McDew, a black by birth, a Jew by choice, and a revolutionary by necessity, has taken the deep hates and deep loves of America, and the world, reserved for those who dare to stand in a strong sun and cast a sharp shadow.

In the words of Judge Brumfield, who sentenced us, we are "cold calculators" who design to disrupt the racial harmony (harmonious since 1619) of McComb into racial strife and rioting. . . . It's mealtime now: we have rice and gravy in a flat pan, dry bread and a "big town cake"; we lack eating and drinking utensils. Water comes from a faucet and goes into a hole.

This is Mississippi, the middle of the iceberg. Hollis is leading off with his tenor, "Michael row the boat ashore, Alleluia; Christian brothers don't be slow, Alleluia; Mississippi's next to go, Alleluia." This is a tremor in the middle of the iceberg—from a stone that the builders rejected.[81]

A religious aura pervades this letter. The last sentence referred to Psalm 118:22 ("The stone which the builders rejected has become the chief cornerstone," implying they were sanctioned by God) and Matthew 21:42 (in which Jesus called himself the stone)—famous biblical passages everyone in the local and SNCC community recognized. Published in *The Liberator*, Moses's letter became a well-known movement document, playing into the legend that cast Moses as a Christ-like figure. At the time, he must have known such language would strike a chord with locals and the religiously inclined SNCC workers. In a way, it illustrated his maturing belief in meeting people "where they are." Regardless of his intentions, it suggests that for now, Moses willingly associated himself with Christianity if it helped.[82]

Yet by including the other students' names and activities, Moses described a *collective* experience that reflected his budding leadership approach. Also noteworthy is Moses's usage of the phrase "tremor in the middle of the iceberg," which SNCC workers now consciously repeated to justify their choice of Mississippi. Deliberately going to the worst places in the South dramatized U.S. racial conditions, and if SNCC could "crack" these areas, it could "send unsettling reverberations" through the rest of the nation. Mississippi, Moses noted, "was the central place to promote the subjugation of Black people. . . . If you can do it in Mississippi, you can do it anywhere." Moreover, it solidified SNCC's recalcitrance against the established civil rights groups. Particularly the national NAACP advocated that change occurred by starting with the easier places (like border states and urban areas) and then working your way in. Even SCLC's Andrew Young once stated, "We tried to warn SNCC. . . . We knew better than to take on Mississippi."[83]

But as November progressed, Moses and the others faced bleak prospects. After visiting them, Jack Young conveyed his "very definite impression that all of them would like to be out." Yet if bond was not received in time, they had to serve their full sentences. Furthermore, Young, who had worked extensively on the cases, reluctantly wrote SNCC that he had to withdraw if his fee was not paid. SNCC then gladly accepted the $13,000 bond money needed from SCEF. The thirteen (McDew again bailed out early) were released[84] on December 6, 1961, but by then white resistance—local authorities and mobs repetitively harassed civil rights workers and a shotgun blast into a residence nearly killed John Hardy and Dion Diamond—had stopped the movement in its tracks. Upon release, Moses nonetheless proclaimed he "intended to stay in Mississippi to register more people to vote."[85]

Yet with the students at Campbell and adults afraid to register, it seemed useless to do so in McComb. About twenty-five had registered in five months of nearly forty attempts, although Moses considered any attempt "a huge breakthrough, because in the last ten years you hadn't gotten twenty people who had attempted to register." SNCC had also lost the support of the NAACP after the walk-outs, although Medgar Evers spoke at a McComb rally and attended a Lee memorial service. Privately, Evers grunted about SNCC's practice of ignoring the NAACP's wishes until it needed its money. Moreover, he charged that Lee's death and SNCC's rashness had stifled the NAACP. Bryant went so far as to ask Evers to take over the project, but other NAACP affiliates, including Moore, Steptoe, and Owens, defended SNCC. "That," Moses said, "knocked the wind out of any real effort to isolate us. Because it would be difficult for Medgar with such a small operation that he had to go against the real feelings of his key people around the state." Bryant nevertheless denied SNCC further use of the Masonic Temple.[86]

BUT MOSES DID NOT FEEL defeated. McComb had demonstrated that his slow organizing approach could be a model for successful future campaigns—so long as its lessons were applied. Its first lesson was that even though McComb had nullified the distinction between direct action and voter registration, the first was not viable in Mississippi on the long term. Direct action divided local blacks and alienated the NAACP, and SNCC lacked the money to counter excessive jail terms. Mississippi, Moses now knew, was designed to promote and reinforce racism like "a South African enclave in the United States." SNCC could not depend on federal intervention either. Voter registration in contrast, Moses claimed, was not only a viable program but also almost universally accepted. Whether willing to register or not, everybody "believed that registration would help."[87]

Second, McComb demonstrated that while entrance into local communities might be facilitated by the traditional middle class, the manpower needed to produce social change had to come from *all* in the community's social strata, including the state's vast majority of the rural poor. Young people should be especially targeted, Moses believed, since they were not tied down by jobs, families, or economic ties to whites, unlike most teachers or ministers. This was especially true in rural areas. As one Mississippi NAACP member complained to national headquarters, "We don't have the support of ministers here, we have no-one to say, 'I'll donate the NAACP a $100.00' nor do we have anyone here to say, 'I'll work for free.' We have just as much trouble with Negroes as we do [with] whites." Operating from a broad-based leadership also worked as a safety measure. This way, the movement would no longer fall victim to being reduced or stopped after the banishment or assassination of its leaders. McComb thus validated SNCC's innovative strategy of full-time field activists working on subsistence pay and establishing "family"-like connections with locals.[88]

This lesson underscores the importance of McComb as a turning point in movement history. Merely organizational presence, or individual activism, cannot define the existence of a movement. Or, as one worker stated, a movement is not a movement if it always has to depend on a few people "to keep the wheels going." "We [didn't] know nothing about [the NAACP]," another, a working-class black, agreed. "I found out later that they had been in the state for 40 years, but we sure hadn't seen 'em." Even in distributing direct aid, the NAACP had not targeted the vast majority of rural poor. Many of its beneficiaries were middle-class blacks, and since most were movement participants already, aid drives rarely functioned as a tool to enlist others.[89]

Although there had been past instances of protest, there had been no "movement" to date. Moses's strategy, aided by the Freedom Rides, not only energized local youth in a way the NAACP could not but also allowed for the inclusion of working-class and rural blacks. Because SNCC workers stayed in one place for months and emphasized the establishment of personal relationships, they were capable of sustaining long-term local involvement, especially by working-class blacks. SNCC could thus generate a local movement in McComb by drawing the "untapped sources of movement strength," ready to participate, *into* the movement, because it had the time and numbers to show them how to organize and develop their own strengths as leaders. Whereas SNCC's entrance in 1961 could only develop because it built on earlier activism, the decision to work with "ordinary" citizens alongside the middle class thus emerged pragmatically as much as philosophically precisely *because* those earlier activists historically had been unable to create the beguiling sense of movement that SNCC could. Even Aaron Henry admitted that "the arrival of Robert Moses . . . marked a high point in the Mississippi civil rights movement."[90]

Moses also found that he and his ideas thrived by SNCC's freewheeling structure. Solely the people in the field—a group of no more than twenty people—decided the project's direction in consultation with locals. This, combined with their common exposure to Mississippi brutality, fostered a unique bond among them. Unlike the campus-based sit-in students, whose approach conformed to middle-class interests, SNCC's field staff now shared Moses's budding views that the South needed "a full-scale social revolution" from the bottom up. Its acceptance of SCEF's help underscored its new militant attitude. McComb thus helped alter SNCC's function from an umbrella group to a field organization of full-time activists. This change was formalized in April 1962, when it adopted a new structure consisting of the Coordinating Committee members, the chairman, the executive secretary, two advisors, and three at large student members. In practice, however, Stokely Carmichael remembered that "whoever happened to be around . . . simply sat in and spoke his or her piece."[91]

Moses's instant fame accelerated SNCC's professionalization, too. Ironically, SNCC's effectiveness as a durable organization hinged in this period mostly on one man, James Forman. Without his administrative skills, SNCC, being over $10,000 in debt, might not have survived. Realizing how inadequate SNCC was in dealing with the media during the McComb events, he formed SNCC's Communications Department, headed full-time by Julian Bond and aided by three white students, Dottie Miller, Mary King, and Casey Hayden. To project a clear "SNCC personality" that could generate funds, he transformed headquarters, purchased a printing press, and pushed for Charles McDew's replacement with John Lewis, a charismatic Freedom Rider, as chairman. At his suggestion, SNCC opened offices in Chicago, Detroit, New York, Washington, and Philadelphia and fostered northern "Friends of SNCC" groups (FOS). Consequently, by December 1962, SNCC had raised over $50,000; in 1963, its income reached $309,000.[92]

Moses watched these developments both with glee and apprehension. While Atlanta headquarters recognized the need to consciously influence the press, he believed that the local movement itself was the main generator of sympathetic press coverage. True, Moses and others spoke regularly with reporters, but he insisted that reaching the nation at large was not yet a field concern. "It's people looking in, not us trying to project out." Nevertheless, the press and other commentators latched onto SNCC's revolutionary public image. Pamphlets like Tom Hayden's *Revolution in Mississippi* amplified the interpretation of the McComb project as SNCC's new embodiment even though its direct action wing had embraced Moses's organizing method only as another approach alongside theirs. Zellner noted that people called "from all over" and most "wanted to know about Bob."[93]

The McComb coverage transformed Moses's position in SNCC. An outsider no longer, Moses enjoyed a new and unique reputation inside SNCC. Stokely Carmichael, for instance, recalled that after the Caston beating, "my respect for Bob increased . . . I knew that sooner or later I was going to stand alongside this brother in struggle. With each new report, it kept building." Even SNCC workers themselves began to view Moses as SNCC's personification. As Carmichael put it, "He was to us . . . almost a symbol of the SNCC spirit . . . anyone who was doing the things we'd been hearing had to be not only a great leader, but more than even that, a sho-nuff *hero*."[94]

Consequently, Moses grudgingly realized, Mississippi locals and staff began to react differently to him. They began "to react to you based on what they read rather than what you had before. Which is you're reacting to people based on your interactions." He increasingly began to feel uneasy about the publicity he was generating. Throughout his life, Moses rejected implications in press and history books that he somehow "started the movement" in McComb, "because I wasn't from McComb. And as far as I know things don't get started by somebody who is not from someplace just going in cold turkey and figure that they are going to start something." Yet he realized that full-time organizers, like himself, could play transformative roles in the lives of locals. Naturally, "SNCC didn't develop Amzie," but teenagers like Hollis Watkins and Curtis Hayes developed as leaders through their connection with SNCC. "[They] were coming in and out of Mississippi, [they] were traveling with SNCC workers to other places, they're going to conferences and meetings that SNCC was holding. So that was the matrix, the Petri dish so to speak, where their own sense of themselves [evolved]."[95]

Nonetheless, the violence he had seen in McComb showed Moses the difficult aspects of this responsibility. For the time being, he put his doubts about this new leadership role to rest, but he was no longer the naive worker who had embraced Amzie Moore's challenge so optimistically a year ago. Realizing that SNCC had reached an impasse in McComb, he, Hardy, Bevel, Nash, and several local students, including Watkins and Hayes, retreated to Moore's home in Cleveland and began devising a new plan for Mississippi. Feeling accountable, Moses wanted to follow the expelled Burgland students to Jackson "to see that they got squared away." After everything, he wrote, the "movement from the rural to the urban is irresistible." But he refused to leave the area completely because locals still suffered the consequences for their activism. Seeing their withdrawal therefore merely as a "tactical relocation," the workers quietly but determinately prepared for their next offensive.[96]

CHAPTER FOUR

The Bob Moses Mystique

For Moses, the McComb experience had been double-edged. The memory of Herbert Lee was deeply painful, but the project's overall lessons seemed salvageable. From 1962 to 1963, he managed to transform them into a solid method of organizing. In the Council of Federated Organizations, a quintessential expression of his organizing views and past work, he found an instrument he could wield across Mississippi. Full-time volunteer groups moved in with locals for extended periods of time and implemented his technique of developing personal relationships with locals of all social backgrounds and helping them with whatever resources—skills, manpower, education—were lacking. Through a process of trial and error, they discovered, in Moses's words, "how you can move even if you are afraid." Realizing that an enlarged grassroots constituency was effective in the Deep South, SNCC duplicated this in other states, and other national civil rights groups raised the scale and character of support they bequeathed local ones as well. Yet Mississippi SNCC could develop the approach most consistently, in large part due to Moses.[1]

Ironically, while Moses's leadership philosophy suggested that everyone is more or less the same, the singular attributes he brought to the struggle proved crucial for SNCC's daily operations. No one could compare with Moses's hands-on organizing skills and unswerving emphasis on self-empowerment, education, and "credentializing" locals, that is, providing them with the tools they needed to become leaders in their communities irrespective of formal credentials like titles and levels of education. His ability to convey a sense of purpose in a way that crossed racial, geographical, and class boundaries spurred the Mississippi movement forward. He excelled at mixing "trial-and-error" tactics with sophisticated planning and outside facilitation. Added to these qualities were his northern background, intellectual training, boldness, and intrinsically shy character and soft speech that bolstered his message of self-effacing leadership. The foundation was being laid for what would soon became known as the Bob Moses mystique, but Moses did not see or experience his moves this way. He described himself during this time as just being "my mother's son, quietly self-circumscribed now in the space SNCC carved out in Mississippi." For the time being, these contradictions in his leadership could coexist in uneasy tension, although in practice, he already was more of a leader than he sought to be.[2]

MOSES DERIVED MUCH of his leadership from his stability, since despite his fears, he had a clear idea about how to move forward. After moving to Jackson in December 1961, he outlined his Mississippi plans in a January 27, 1962, report with Tom Gaither of CORE. The report became the blueprint for his subsequent work in the state. It proposed a concerted voter registration drive organized through a statewide coordinating group of representatives of other organizations interested in this. Its targets would be the black-majority second, third, and fourth congressional districts; the Gulf Coast area; and cities like Laurel, Meridian, and Hattiesburg. Places like Greenville, Clarksdale, Jackson, Vicksburg, and Natchez, where blacks often could vote, should receive "special consideration" since "apathy, ignorance, and long deprivation have dulled the appetite for the ballot." As in McComb, locals had to be consulted and trained so they eventually could take over the program. To staff it, Moses proposed training thirty-five Mississippi students before starting work in the summer. Such a detailed and long-term plan contrasted starkly with what some of the other name-making SNCC leaders were up to.[3]

Moses's counterparts tended to move beguilingly, if impetuously, from event to event and place to place. Most non-Mississippi SNCC workers took up voter registration only after demonstrations in Jackson and in Albany, Georgia, again had proved the futility of direct action and its inability to gain lasting, broad-based community support in the Deep South. For example, the stalwarts of James Lawson's Nashville movement, James Bevel, a flamboyant twenty-five-year-old black minister, and his wife-to-be Diane Nash, a bold twenty-four-year-old light-skinned Chicagoan, were in the midst of an attempt to revive the Jackson Non-violent Movement. With local black youth and students from nearby black colleges, such as Luvaughn Brown, Dorie Ladner, Lawrence Guyot, and Douglas MacArthur Cotton, they instigated boycotts of Jackson buses and other protests. However, as Moses anticipated from his Mc-Comb experiences, resentment among middle-class blacks grew when local authorities refused to negotiate and stopped all movement by imposing lengthy jail sentences. "Jackson is not Nashville," Moses admonished, "you don't have a Black, middle class community which is going to support you and those that might are within the NAACP [but] the NAACP is not supporting [direct action]." Moreover, locals who had businesses or family to attend to were unwilling to risk long-term prison sentences.[4]

The Bevels were unable to counter this by conveying the merits of nonviolence. To Mississippi blacks, Gandhi meant little, Moses charged, "They're into Jesus [and] carrying their guns. [What SNCC workers were] talking about has got to somehow penetrate that and it never did." Just copying a technique was insufficient, he believed. "You [need] some kind of real commitment . . . to make the people real practical, and spiritual at once." He blamed Lawson for returning to college. "I often thought about that, because . . . he didn't for some reason think that his job was to actually come *with* the students in the field." The Jackson movement's failure thereby reinforced his commitment to moral leadership by example.[5]

Moses considered the headline-grabbing 1961–1962 movement in Albany, Georgia, equally ineffectual for the long term. Although it started out as a rural voter registration project along his McComb example, it developed into something else in part due to the characters of its instigators, Charles Sherrod, a twenty-four-year-old black Virginian minister and sit-in leader, and Cordell Reagon, an eighteen-year-old black Freedom Rider from Nashville. Finding the time-consuming work Moses had done in remote rural areas too demanding, they relocated from Georgia's dangerous Terrell and Baker counties to Albany, a relatively progressive city for Georgia standards. They established promising relations with locals by hanging out at black schools and social clubs but postponed their voter registration plans when the newly formed Albany Movement—a coalition including SNCC, the NAACP, and a black ministerial alliance—began a massive direct action campaign to integrate public facilities.[6]

Month-long sit-ins and marches led to the arrest of hundreds. Soon the Albany Movement invited Martin Luther King Jr., whose brief spell in a jail cell energized locals and jumpstarted negotiations with officials, leaving SNCC's Bill Hansen to grumble that King "can cause more hell to be raised by being in jail one night than anyone else could if they bombed city hall." However, after King and other leaders posted bond, city officials reneged on their promises. The Albany Movement resumed direct action, but the city remained intransigent and the coalition was left in shambles. In the summer of 1962, King returned to Albany to face trial for his march. This renewed nonviolent protests, and SNCC watched in frustration as King resumed the spotlight. But unable to gain concessions, the Albany Movement returned to voter registration, leaving most in SNCC convinced that nonviolent moral suasion had outrun its course as a strategy.[7]

Moses refused to let the events in Albany distract him. He did not heed calls to flood Albany with SNCC workers, although he regularly spoke with the Georgia workers at Atlanta SNCC meetings.[8] Such rashness did not suit his personality and interfered with his single-minded Mississippi goals. If anything, Albany confirmed Moses's analysis of the McComb and Jackson events. Programmatic and organizational unity were vital for the fledgling Deep South movement—and they had to come through voter registration. He reasoned that the 1957 Civil Rights Act had authorized the federal government to investigate and prosecute racial discrimination in voting. This provided a theoretical "space to crawl in . . . so they can't just arrest you" without risking federal involvement. Most SNCC workers now agreed.[9]

The formation of the Kennedy administration–endorsed Voter Education Project (VEP) provided a boost for Moses's strategy. Directed by the Southern Regional Council (SRC) and funded by the Edgar Stern Family Fund and the Taconic and Field Foundations, the VEP furnished civil rights groups with money for voter registration drives. Between April 1962 and November 1964, it helped register 688,000 blacks in eleven southern states. The VEP agreed to finance part of SNCC's operations, too. It donated $24,000 in 1962 to 1963, although this was considerably less than other organizations received since SNCC's work in the unsafe rural areas promised little success.[10]

To obtain the most benefit from VEP money, Moses felt that Mississippi SNCC should create a statewide vehicle that united all national and local civil rights organizations under a common program. Mississippi's exceptionally dangerous position compared to the rest of the South meant that local blacks needed massive strength and new approaches to break it. As Webb Owens repeatedly drove home to Moses, "I belong to the NAACP. I belong to CORE. I belong with SNCC. I belong to *anything* which is going to help this Black man in Mississippi."[11]

From these realizations, the Council of Federated Organizations (COFO) was born in early February 1962.[12] In COFO, Moses's past labors and organizing views came into full flowering.

Moses was key to COFO's founding, his colleagues acknowledged. Without him, SNCC likely would not have sought cooperation; James Bevel, Diane Nash, and their roommate in Jackson, SNCC worker Bernard Lafayette, focused on the short term. They did not feel personally intertwined with the state's fate, whereas Moses's experiences in white schools, AFSC camps, McComb, and with Ella Baker and Amzie Moore primed him to search for likeminded people who prioritized their Mississippi goals over organizational commitment. He found them in Aaron Henry, Medgar Evers, CORE worker Dave Dennis, and SCLC's citizenship teacher Annelle Ponder.[13]

Fear of competition, however, was deep-seated among the organizations. While SNCC needed COFO money because movement sympathizers generally preferred donating to more conservative and familiar organizations like the NAACP, the latter feared that if money went to SNCC, it meant less for itself; eventually, only its state branch endorsed COFO. CORE, which feared anonymity, likewise initially opposed joining COFO. The interracial CORE, formed in 1941, was generally committed to nonviolent direct action, had a clear administrative structure, and had a prominent leader in James Farmer. While it looked top-down, its local branches were largely autonomous. Particularly its southern branches, mostly newly formed and black dominated, resembled SNCC in form, function, and outlook. Its members shared SNCC's age profile and sympathy for local people. But even Dave Dennis had needed some persuasion to Moses's point of view. The two first met in Baton Rouge, Louisiana, in the fall of 1961. But Dennis was not impressed. "I thought he was crazy . . . he was very quiet, [sitting] in a corner when other people talked . . . so I'm like 'what's this guy all about?'" Intrigued, he approached him. After that, they switched to voter registration in Baton Rouge. In January 1962, he and Moses reconnected; by February, Dennis had joined COFO. Dennis and Moses regularly met to see how they could ease national CORE about the cooperation. They compromised that SNCC concentrated on the first, second, third, and fifth congressional districts, and CORE on the fourth, where it already worked.[14]

Moses's ideals of unity and local ownership were reflected in COFO's structure as well. NAACP members Aaron Henry, Carsie Hall, and R. L. T. Smith were elected as president, secretary, and treasurer, respectively; Moses as program director; and Dennis as assistant program director. This gave each of the main organizations working in the state a primary responsibility. But rather than a coalition, COFO was to function merely as a framework for cooperation. Programmatic decisions were made at statewide conventions attended by all members, whose voices mattered equally. Staff, who implemented convention decisions, spread across Mississippi's congressional districts, which each had district branches. The separate organizations paid their own staff members, and funds came from the VEP and the national organizations on a volunteer basis.[15]

This framework offered the national organizations many benefits. Before this, SCLC had not had any inroads in Mississippi apart from the citizenship schools that it had inherited from the Highlander Folk School. Aaron Henry cherished "the advantage of working with the head personnel of four main groups to develop new ideas." Moses liked above all that it was a *people's* organization and that unity "spurred contributions [and] interest in Mississippi." Moreover, the established groups gave SNCC more legitimacy. Simultaneously, problems about who received credit were present from the start, Moses admitted. SNCC covered 80 percent of Mississippi's districts and COFO's budget, which effectively meant that COFO equaled SNCC. Yet between 1962 and 1963, conflicts were surprisingly minimal due to its small scope.[16]

WITH SNCC AND OTHER outside forces now on board and the desired statewide council in place, the plans Moses had proposed in January could now be realized. When COFO representatives met on February 18, 1962, to formulate a program for VEP Director Wiley Branton, Moses, anticipating the overrepresentation of the urban middle class, wrote Amzie Moore "to bring a strong group. . . . The more of the rural people come, the better chance we have of adopting the type of program you folks need." This highlights his still unwavering commitment to Moore and the poor rural black populace. At the meeting, urban middle-class leaders were indeed prominent. The NAACP's Dr. A. B. Britton, for instance, insisted on VEP money for the Jackson movement. SNCC reiterated its commitment to working in the rural counties but accepted the need to involve the middle class "for we have no leaders to spare!" COFO agreed to develop a staff along Moses's plans of native youngsters with the aid of local NAACP leaders and SCLC citizenship teachers.[17]

Recruitment occurred, for the most part, quietly over the next months. Willie Peacock, a black Rust College graduate, was leaving for Detroit when Moses and Amzie Moore, who knew his father from the RCNL, came to his house and stated that they needed him. Others joined after a meeting Moore held in Jackson. But most recruitment occurred as a side effect of other projects. Some Jackson students automatically joined COFO, whose headquarters were located in the city. This, combined with Moses's plea to leave Jackson for the rural areas, frustrated some in its Nonviolent Movement, which needed the manpower for direct action. But Moses recounted "no dramatics" between himself and James Bevel. They did not see each other often, and due to the scant progress with direct action in Jackson, Bevel had become more open to Moses's viewpoints, too.[18]

The two men even agreed on a political experiment. Believing that new approaches were needed to solve Mississippi's exceptional race problems, they encouraged blacks to run for office in the June congressional elections. Bevel moved to the Delta city of Greenwood to work on Rev. Theodore Trammell's campaign with Henry and Moore, while Moses remained in Jackson for R. L. T. Smith's campaign. But everyone knew that the black candidates had no chance of winning. Even COFO workers resisted the effort, Marion Barry noted. "They didn't understand the value or the stimulation of [Negroes running]." But winning was never the campaigns' intent. Rather, they were "an organizing tool," Moses explained, to encourage blacks to believe "that eventually they would be electing [black] people to office." The attempt therefore constituted a significant break from previous activism.[19]

Moses desired to work as a "submerged" campaign and road manager. This suited his personality and aspiration to promote local leadership but also prevented renewed "outside agitation" charges. The campaign had a small interracial volunteer staff and one paid employee, Caroline Tyler. Moses drove Smith to campaign rallies in black churches, general stores, and black colleges across the third congressional district, which allowed Moses to revisit locals in Amite and McComb in hopes of softening the blow of SNCC's departure. He also helped Tyler with her typing, distributed campaign literature, sought poll workers, and arranged speaking engagements. White lawyer Bill Higgs briefed Moses on all developments and "brought him the speeches and the legal [and] political stuff." He worked seven days a week and regularly conducted workshops himself.[20]

He held two such workshops in Claiborne County, but when fifty whites verbally abused the participants at the first meeting, only three blacks attended the second. Intimidation from local whites was a regular occurrence. In Jackson, Moses and Smith were briefly arrested while trying to desegregate the state legislature's spectators' gallery, and Smith had his house shot at and his supermarket's windows broken. Local media outlets cancelled Smith's appearances on radio and TV, although complaints to the Federal Communications Committee (FCC) forced the broadcasters to backtrack.[21]

Nonetheless, Moses discovered that politics offered new organizing possibilities. Not only would campaign coverage spread awareness, but it could be done through the projection of a local black rather than professional organizers. His head started spinning with new questions. "I first began to think through what was a political party, how does a political party get formed, what is the structure, what's the base, all those questions which had never really been real questions for me." In a letter to Smith, he proposed "training people to run for office next year the first chance we get."[22]

Political organizing, not just voter registration, was key to realizing his and Moore's ideals of concentrating black (political) power in one area. "Negroes must be trained to evaluate prospective candidates and to participate themselves in the political process," he reiterated in a memo to "interested friends and foundations." This should start with the November 1963 local elections. As preparation, he envisaged week-long Adult Education Programs at the Mt. Beulah Institute in Edwards, Mississippi, for which SNCC should recruit thirty local blacks a week who could then train others in their home communities.[23]

Tim Jenkins admitted that at this point, it was mostly only "Moses's feeling that strenuous effort had to be made to get Negroes to rethink their rightful role in the political participation." Apart from Bevel, no SNCC workers had been interested in participating in the campaigns, although it was done with full awareness of headquarters. Moses's freedom to execute his ideas again exhibits the effectiveness of individual flexibility within SNCC but also the precariousness of SNCC's overall state. Discussions on what sort of organization it wanted to be still continued. Therefore, James Forman argued, "It seemed best then to experiment and learn . . . and draw conclusions from this process." Despite the candidates' expected defeat, Moses's experiment with local politics now gradually began to determine the Mississippi movement's direction.[24]

Before anything else could happen, the rural counties of Mississippi had to be organized. This became possible when SNCC received a

Centers of Civil Rights Activity (From *Local People: The Struggle for Civil Rights in Mississippi*. Copyright 1994 by the Board of Trustees of the University of Illinois. Used with permission of the University of Illinois Press.)

$5,000 VEP grant in June 1962 to start six COFO projects on July 1. Moses could now test his method of "facilitating grassroots leadership" on a statewide level. The COFO projects, however, reaffirmed how in practice, locals and outside organizers relied on each other to be able to move in a way that black communities in the rural South otherwise might not have moved—just as Amzie Moore had predicted they would. Especially Moses's skills in mixing "trial-and-error" tactics under grassroots leadership with behind-the-scenes sophisticated planning and outside resources lifted the Mississippi movement to new grounds, even as he increasingly downplayed his own involvement. While working on the projects, he realized that what they were doing was in fact reversed physics. Unlike scientists who released energy in atoms, their job "was working with people to see how the energy of *people* was released—our own energies, other people's energies." And to do this effectively, he had to emulate what Ella Baker had done for SNCC. The key characteristic of a good organizer, he more and more believed, was "that their work emerges, and they subside."[25]

Behind the scenes, however, Moses continued to play a subtle leading role, even as COFO projects were initiated and sustained independently of his presence. Each community project and congressional district had its own director; Moses rather served as coordinator for the twenty black male SNCC workers who labored full-time on the projects. They had spread across the Delta counties: Ruleville in Sunflower, Cleveland in Bolivar, Greenville in Washington, Clarksdale in Coahoma, and Greenwood in Leflore. Hollis Watkins and Curtis Hayes worked in Hattiesburg, where they lived with NAACP president and sawmill owner Vernon Dahmer.[26]

Only Moses and two others were non-Mississippians; most were students at Rust, Tougaloo, and Jackson State College. Philosophically, SNCC *wanted* a local staff but in fact had little choice. Most outside workers, Moses admitted, simply "didn't stick." John Hardy and Reginald Robinson had left, comparing organizing in Mississippi to "deep sea diving with a lot of pressure." Robinson started a project in South Carolina and Ruby Doris Smith joined headquarters. In mid-1962, James Bevel also moved to Atlanta to become SCLC's Director of Direct Action. According to Moses, he left because he was now convinced that "we could not do voter registration in Mississippi." Nash joined him, and Bernard Lafayette started a project in Selma, Alabama.[27]

Based in Cleveland or Greenville, Moses traveled from project to project. This allowed for the native SNCC workers and locals in the projects to develop their own skills and ideas, although the native workers did not fit Moses's definition of "local leadership." By "grass-roots leadership," he solely meant people who "were publicly identified as [leaders] by the black community in which they lived." In this defi-nition, facilitating local leadership meant doing whatever to bring lo-cals, irrespective of class, gender, or political persuasion, into such a position. As Dorie Ladner reflected, locals "were putting their lives on the line to even involve themselves. So you couldn't say you want a cer-tain type [of person] first." But Luvaughn Brown remembered it somewhat differently. "No-one can say what was subconsciously done. [Generally] when one talks of developing leadership there is a natural prejudice toward people who think and act as they do."[28]

The precariousness of Mississippi activism made Moses apprecia-tive of all local leadership, but he had an overriding idea of where the COFO projects should head and was not afraid to spur this along behind the scenes when needed. The projects' goal, he wrote, was "to have several thousand Negroes apply for registration during the sum-mer." To realize this, he sought to curtail friction above all else. He invited Wiley Branton to mediate between the various groups and in-structed SNCC workers to "bend over backwards to help the NAACP." To limit internal conflicts within COFO staff and as an outreach to SNCC's direct action wing, he even accepted that staff could form a direct action group of local youth. Moses likely acquiesced since Mc-Comb showed that direct action could involve the youth's parents and because the VEP's restrictions otherwise diminished COFO's already tiny workforce.[29]

Although often portrayed as someone who avoided the pragmatic as-pects of organizing, Moses could also be an excellent hands-on manager. His behind-the-scenes work from February through September 1962, for example, underscores how the process of facilitation often depended on his singular characteristics, long-term vision, and contacts beyond the state. For instance, in March, he and Jim Dombrowski of SCEF planned a literacy project to advance voter registration. They enlisted the help of Frank Laubach, the nation's leading literacy expert, and people in Moses's organizing network. SCLC voter registration director Jack O'Dell, whom Moses knew from Harlem, offered to send Mississippi workers to SCLC's citizenship school in Dorchester, Georgia. Moses wrote Guido

Goldman, a Harvard student he had befriended at a Harry Belafonte fund-raiser, that he had also sent feelers to anyone who could help secure scholarships for Mississippi blacks to study law to increase their weight in the 1968 elections. He also helped organize citizenship workshops for his envisaged Adult Education Programs at Mt. Beulah. At these, locals discussed government structures and legal cases, outlined race and income statistics of the participants' home counties, and learned how to run tape recorders.[30]

In May, Moses arranged similar workshops at Tougaloo College for the COFO workers. These also taught cosmopolitan issues he considered important, like civil liberties and folk songs. With Myles Horton, he held additional workshops at Highlander from June 4 to 9. He insisted on bringing as many Mississippi youngsters as possible to increase their personal growth. He considered this a quintessential part of organizing. "Part of what the movement did was just . . . exposing people to all different kinds of people who were coming in and out of Mississippi [and] by taking them out of Mississippi. . . . Our job was identifying people who were good candidates to go to that training [so they feel] part of some larger movement." Participants like Hollis Watkins, Curtis Hayes, and Sam Block studied registration laws, crafted programs for their working areas, and listened to organizing advice from veteran citizenship teachers like Esau Jenkins. In October, Horton informed Moses of leads for financial help for new educational programs. By then, the Adult Education Program was halted, but, he wrote Horton, SNCC could "carry out educational programs in communities in which we are working."[31]

Ironically, Moses's desire for exposure caused the program's halt. As part of it, he helped organize and conduct a workshop series on democracy, including sessions on the Bill of Rights and its guarantees for free speech and assembly. He daringly invited Anne Braden, then still branded for her and her husband's alleged Communist Party membership, to speak because, she recorded, "Bob felt the theory of civil liberties was something very important the people should think about—especially in Mississippi." Being preoccupied, Anne's husband Carl replaced her and joined him between July 13 and 19, 1962.[32]

Two weeks later, a report Braden wrote on his trip was leaked by someone from the SCEF office to southern newspapers. The *Clarion-Ledger* alarmingly headlined, "Braden, Accused As Red, Reported Active In State"; the *Jackson Daily News* even spoke of a "secret Communist document." Upset, Moses and Bill Higgs called Braden to complain that for two days, papers printed names and places mentioned in the report, falsely describing "everybody that we contacted as part of that old Communist conspiracy." This included David Lollis, director of Mt. Beulah. Lollis was fired, and Mt. Beulah withdrew from the program. The Bradens' involvement caused such a rift in the movement that Bill Higgs and Wiley Branton even asked SCEF to withdraw from southern activism altogether. Anne retorted in a thirteen-page letter bemoaning how "the social price of McCarthyism" had been that too "many people with creative contributions to make" were driven out of the movement.[33]

The incident left COFO without a citizenship school and Moses caught in the middle. His educational efforts were halted, but he sympathized with the Bradens. Nevertheless, he was upset that Carl's report and an article by him in the *Southern Patriot* had exaggerated Braden's role in the workshops and thereby obscured local contributions. It is striking that Moses appeared to be more concerned with the media portrayal of locals than with being identified with alleged Communists—a fact that supports his genuine concern for local leadership and underscores the difference between southern indigenous leaders and northern blacks in regard to the "Communist issue." He even replied to Anne that her thirteen-page letter was "a beautiful job" and expressed regret "we all had to be so cruddy about it." He then joined SCEF's Operation Freedom program, which funded local activists who had lost their homes or jobs as a result of their activism.[34]

The Mississippi State Sovereignty Commission now increased its surveillance of Moses. Believing that the American democratic ideal of minimized government could only be safeguarded through racial purity, its investigators considered anyone advocating integration not only to be anti-southern, but anti-American, that is, Communist or at least a Communist sympathizer. Considering blacks to be easily manipulated by outsiders, they found evidence for their beliefs in the Communist Party's support for black labor and housing rights in the 1930s and 1940s and its involvement in Scottsboro and other noteworthy civil rights cases. McCarthyism then legitimized this type of terminology. But the Cold War also necessitated it as the federal government's language of democracy and support for black freedom struggles worldwide to counter the Soviet Union's global advances stimulated the civil rights movement and southern nationalists saw their historic fears about blacks' revolutionary potential materialize through the *Brown* verdict, the Montgomery bus boycott, the Little Rock crisis, and the sit-ins. The national struggle against communism and the southern one against integration thus easily morphed in segregationists' minds, even though the factual link between communism and the movement was tentative at best. Consequently, it was not hard for MSSC investigator Tom Scarborough to see the Braden incident as confirmation of Moses's subversive intentions. Moses, he argued, was probably planted by Communists. As such, a native SNCC worker like Sam Block could be no more than Moses's "leg man and stooge" so "Moses himself can remain unknown . . . until the time gets ripe for his presence."[35]

While Moses had experienced "red-baiting" in New York and Atlanta, the Braden incident showed him the difference between northern McCarthyism and the southern kind. The southern red scare distinguished itself from its national counterpart by its emphasis on race, with Mississippi being an extreme example. Despite the benefits the Cold War had for spurring the civil rights movement, it had also provided new tools to fight it. Most southern states created new anti-Communism laws and used and copied national anti-Communism organizations, like the HUAC and the Senate Internal Security Subcommittee (SISS), to harass and blemish civil rights activists through public hearings, innuendo, and spying. But Mississippi used such tactics most, and more than in other states, newspapers, politicians (most notably senator James Eastland), and the state's network of Citizens' Councils tied the movement to communism. Nonetheless, whereas the MSSC was the most extreme of all southern state sovereignty commissions, by Mississippian standards, it was fairly moderate, especially compared to the, arguably more effective, tactics violent groups like the KKK used to stop the movement.[36]

Against such fanaticism, Moses realized, the movement's past responses, like denials, the NAACP's anti-Communist resolutions, or Martin Luther King Jr.'s advice against public association with alleged Communists, were useless. Instead, the movement should simply render the issue moot by letting its actions speak for themselves. Yet he utilized his unique organizing skills and contacts to ensure they were understood correctly. For example, to counter biased southern newspapers, he became increasingly concerned with generating favorable press reports. Despite feeling that their work required a "quieter atmosphere," he realized that publicity was essential. But it should be done on *their* terms to limit the current type of depictions of himself and locals like Herbert Lee.[37]

The dismissive depiction of Lee in the *Enterprise Journal* had first alerted Moses to the workings of the media and its faceless portrayal of local blacks. While expected in the southern white press, it unintentionally became emblematic of the writings of movement supporters as well. Accounts by white liberals emphasized Lee's murder to highlight the dangerous context in which Moses and SNCC worked. They also dwelled on how SNCC workers coped with their emotions. Their portrayal of Moses as, in reporter Jack Newfield's words, "tormented by the shadows of guilt" helped to create a romantic aura around him—one that symbolized the sacrifices of the SNCC workers, rather than those of the Lee and Allen families.[38]

Determined to shift the emphasis to where he thought it belonged—with local people—Moses had then gradually begun to address the media differently. For example, when SCEF asked him to write about SNCC's McComb experiences for its February 1962 issue of the *Southern Patriot*, he wrote about Mississippi black activist Birdia Keglar[39] instead. Represented by John Doar and accompanied by Moses, she had daringly testified in court in December 1961 that the sheriff had prevented her from paying her poll tax. SCEF's editorial underscored Moses's choice to focus on Keglar rather than SNCC. "Obviously he thinks this is the key to Mississippi today—the individual courage, the lonely decisions of its citizens." Yet SCEF's editors captured both a sense of discontinuity with previous activism and the impact of full-time activists by concluding, "Perhaps he is right. But it should also be said that history will surely record the turning point in Mississippi as 1961—when a group of selfless students decided it was time for this state to rejoin the Union."[40]

Moses knew he now had to go even further. He planned a two-week news media seminar—with Carl Braden—to teach participants how to gather and present facts accurately for the news. He also befriended John Fisher of the liberal New York–based *Harper's Magazine*, arranged that the magazine would be in charge of the publicity of the COFO projects, and met a Whitney Foundation official in New York about a fellowship for a black student to write articles about SNCC's work. As he wrote Fisher, "We desperately need someone who is close to the struggle to interpret what is taking place." He even asked *Jet* magazine to put a native

Mississippi SNCC worker on its cover. He cheekily added, "We hardly ever see any Southern beauty on the cover, anyway."[41]

MOSES ALSO INFLUENCED daily life in the COFO projects by exploiting his northern connections for fundraising and other types of publicity. He used the New York publishing house of Lawrence Benenson, whose son had been a student of his at Horace Mann, for free printing and gave Benenson ideas for articles. Benenson in turn introduced Moses to Congressmen John Lindsay (R) and Emmanuel Cellar (D) in Washington, who furnished him with more contacts and helped him get money for lawyers. Moses regularly corresponded with former colleagues and friends as well; he advised one on organizing a Belafonte/King night at Harvard and asked his old roommate Bob Cohen and his New World Singers to do fundraising concerts. He wrote appeals to interested groups and visited potential donors. Most SNCC workers did such fundraising only reluctantly because it meant leaving their projects. But Moses was more alert to the advantages of trips north, especially involving New York, so he could visit his northern contacts and family. In December, for example, he mixed a visit with attending a New York Direct Action Training conference to plead for experts in nonviolence to come to Mississippi to teach the workers there. The significance of Moses's Ivy League background for advancing the movement was underscored when the Rabinowitz Foundation offered him a $15,000 grant to write a book on the student movement since he had the needed academic expertise. Moses, committed to his fieldwork, declined but suggested another well-educated black northerner, James Forman.[42]

Moses also brought the movement north through television. On August 10, he and Sam Block accompanied 25 registrants to the Greenwood courthouse before national news media, including CBS, the AP, and UPI. He even worked closely with CBS to produce the documentary *Mississippi and the 15th Amendment*, which aired on prime time on September 26. It showed SNCC workers, including himself, accompanying blacks to the Hattiesburg courthouse but highlighted the courage and determination of the *local* blacks. The documentary evoked a sympathetic response from many northern viewers. As one New Yorker wrote Moses, "[A]s I watched that TV program and observed the planning and patience that characterized your organization, I could not help but feel that what was being done, striven for, already existed [realized in you]."[43]

Moses did not view such behind-the-scenes, outside involvement as intrusive to grassroots leadership, nor was it part of a concerted drive to project or connect SNCC's work to the outside world. Distinctive as his contacts and characteristics were, in his view, he just followed opportunities, few and limited as they were, as they arose. Moreover, since Mississippi activism to date was so restricted anyway, he felt he was merely struggling to move forward in the same isolated and constricted way as the native workers and locals in the COFO projects. He was one of them, and SNCC and his contacts were merely extra instruments he brought rather than solutions or goals in themselves.

Overall, Moses and the rest of SNCC's COFO workers generally left fundraising to Atlanta headquarters, with whom they rarely had contact. Consequently, headquarters sometimes proposed rules that made sense from a public relations viewpoint but not from the fieldworkers'. For example, later that year, it created the position of state directors (Charles Sherrod became director of Georgia, Moses of Mississippi, etc.) but did so without consulting those involved. This contradicted Moses's view of letting the field staff determine who represented them, he grumbled. Yet he was too preoccupied to concern himself much with headquarters. According to him, at this stage, Mississippi staff had few contacts with the outside world, apart from the Justice Department and Friends of SNCC chapters.[44]

Moses's activities show that he and SNCC operated with relative precision even as they followed locals' initiatives. His trick was learning "everything you can about a town[,] slip in quietly, do your thing, and get out." Before going into southwest Georgia and Selma, both Charles Sherrod and Bernard Lafayette did research. Arkansas SNCC worker Worth Long likewise insisted at one meeting that workers must "study in and about our area" and "know current techniques" used elsewhere. SNCC's Research Department, founded in 1962 by Jack Minnis, helped them by providing contacts, statistics, legal briefs, and "how to" guidelines that detailed the practice of organizing. All stressed pre-research, like analyzing population shifts, key players and organizations, and areas of employment. SNCC regularly organized workshops, leadership training, and seminars to educate its members, too. It invited anyone, one document noted, "who would talk to us."[45]

SNCC'S PROJECT IN RULEVILLE exemplifies this effective blend of sophisticated planning and trial-and-error under grassroots leadership.

Moses entered Sunflower County in August to assist the project that Amzie Moore and the Bevels had instigated. By now, the COFO workers' presence had alarmed whites in the Delta. Ruleville, a black-majority town with 161 black registered voters, was particularly vigilant because Senator James Eastland's plantation was nearby. This gave the Ruleville project symbolic significance. Moses and Moore canvassed the town for two weeks, persuading six locals to register at the county courthouse in Indianola. Convinced that the project had potential, Moses drove students Charles McLaurin, Dorie Ladner, Charles Cobb, James Jones, Landy McNair, and Jesse Harris there while relating Delta history to them, as Moore had done for him two years ago. They soon opened a citizenship school, started canvassing with local youth, and accompanied potential registrants to the Indianola courthouse.[46]

Canvassing was hard and often unpleasant. Going around in the hot sun talking endlessly to locals "wasn't very romantic," Cobb recounted. "It was slow[,] dangerous [and] boring." Then they had to tell locals the negative consequences of registering, such as the risk of being fired or attacked. The key, Moses said, was to "convince them that nothing would happen [but in Sunflower County we] couldn't convince people [because] it wasn't true." Another canvasser summarized locals' inhibitions best. "If you couldn't read, couldn't bring yourself to confront a white person on any issue, couldn't find transportation for the journey to the appropriate location, couldn't believe that democracy had anything to do with folks like you, couldn't leave your obligations for more than an hour, couldn't quiet your wife who screamed in panic when you told her you intended . . . to register, couldn't think about anything except the hunger in your belly and in your children's bellies—you couldn't, wouldn't, didn't have the ballot."[47]

To overcome these hurdles, Moses found, organizers had to learn how to "slow down and get into the motion of the people [and] move with them in ways which seem meaningful to them. [Much] of what turned out to be organizing, turned out to be patience." Yet, an organizer's presence, he noticed, could also work as a catalyst.[48]

Effective organizing, Moses said, might even start with something as trivial as bouncing a ball. "You stand on a street and bounce a ball. Soon all the children come around. You keep bouncing the ball. Before long, it runs under someone's porch and then you meet the adults." This slow building of relationships meant that registration might not even be mentioned. McLaurin, for instance, spent days in front of a grocery store, just drinking sodas while its owner taught him local history. Slowing down also aided the workers' psychological survival. As Moses put it, "You can't live as though you're in very real danger every day. . . . The communities we worked in didn't live like that [so they showed us] how to take advantage of those times . . . you relaxed and deepened ties [that were] not directly connected to any specific political act," like talking on a porch or helping locals with "whatever."[49]

Doing chores for locals, such as picking cotton, scrubbing floors, and babysitting, was also a necessity for SNCC. Although VEP money made workers' living conditions easier, it was still inadequate for basic expenses. SNCC only paid its workers a weekly subsistence of $10 ($9.64 after taxes), most of which was used for project expenses, like stamps or pencils. Workers therefore often still depended on locals' generosity, even when living in SNCC-rented Freedom Houses. Conditions were sometimes dire. Sam Block, a twenty-five-year-old black Mississippi student who singlehandedly ran the Greenwood project, slept in his car for several days because he had nowhere to stay. Often SNCC workers worked for their board too. Still, SNCC viewed such chores as quintessential to its job once it noticed that working-class blacks were more open to those who took part in community life. Most SNCC workers now deliberately wore overalls to symbolize their identification with blue-collar blacks, although occasionally they went too far. Some wore overalls to church, which offended locals because, as Dave Dennis recalled, "if they *had* a suit, they *would* wear it."[50]

To overcome locals' feelings that voting seemed too abstract, workers related it to their daily problems. For example, they explained how the vote might get them paved streets. According to Hollis Watkins, canvassing was therefore "much more educational than it was political." Still, many were hesitant. "I understand what you are saying," they often responded, "except it'll get me killed." Deciding which approach to use was always tricky, as one canvasser's private writings revealed. "Maybe I should have bullied him slightly, or maybe I should have talked less. . . . Did I rush him? Should I never have mentioned registering [but] just tried to make friends?" Considering SNCC's emphasis on "letting the people decide," the issue of manipulation made canvassing even more difficult. "When you organize, you *bother* people," SNCC's Bernice Johnson said, "There is an element in the organizer that's slightly harassment."[51]

Locals also feared embarrassment over their lack of education. To register, they might have to answer questions ranging from interpreting any of the state constitution's 285 sections to one's "understanding of the duties and obligations of citizenship under a constitutional form of government." Some registrars tricked applicants with ridiculous questions—like writing a poem about the constitution—and disqualified them based on their answers. The workers' most effective canvassing technique became presenting the form and asking if the person wanted to fill it out together. In doing so, Moses argued, blacks bridged a psychological gap. At the citizenship school, they took lines from the Bible or Constitution like "there shall be no imprisonment for debt" to explain what "interpreting" meant by presenting paraphrases such as "you can't go to jail for owing some money." They also used newspapers, which helped to acquaint locals with activism elsewhere. Other activities included describing registrars' habits and building group morale, aided by speakers like Amzie Moore or Moses. Often, they just focused on teaching literacy, for which they used SCLC's literacy materials. Just taking the classes therefore could be empowering for most southern blacks, who had long been taught that education and the vote "wasn't for them"—just as Moses's classmates in elementary school had felt that taking citywide exams was "out of their range."[52]

Perhaps more than most SNCC workers, Moses became preoccupied with ideas of "credentializing" people, redefining who is qualified to do things on people's behalf, and what gives someone such a position. As his father and Ella Baker had taught him, educational titles or wealth were no such qualifiers. SNCC workers learned, in Stokely Carmichael's words, that "wisdom can come from the most unlikely of sources." For example, an uneducated elderly lady "might be highly influential simply because she was noted as a kind of personal problem-solver" within the community. Such people, Charles Sherrod explained, "don't see themselves as being leaders, although they're just natural.... We find those people out." What started from practical and philosophical reasons over time thus grew into a solid operating principle.[53]

Moses and the other SNCC workers soon discovered other innovative means of involving locals. After two weeks, the Ruleville SNCC workers, for instance, organized a mass meeting at the Williams Chapel, where Forman, Bevel, and Moses spoke. At the end, eighteen locals agreed to register on August 31. One was forty-four-year-old Fannie Lou Hamer, a stout sharecropper with a limp from polio. She later claimed that before then, she had not known much about civil rights activism, although she knew Amzie Moore, had seen the Freedom Riders on TV, and had been an informal community leader at W. D. Marlow's plantation. But she, like Moore, was not someone SNCC "discovered" or "developed"; she was innately predisposed to activism. Hamer, Moses later said, "represented what everyone was trying to . . . struggle for," namely "the promise of [those at the bottom of society] being able to find their inner spirit [and] put that to the service of a great social movement."[54]

Yet it is also important not to blur the role that full-time workers played in helping to bring the potential of locals like Hamer to the surface. As she put it, "Everything you heard us [say] nobody tell us to say that. This is what's been there all the time [but] nobody else had ever give us that chance" to express it. The meeting, which she at first declined to attend, and the presence of the SNCC workers provided a turning point. This does not mean that she, or those like her, otherwise had not become movement participants but rather that the SNCC workers accelerated the decision. The way in which SNCC workers, particularly Moses, organized mass meetings, for instance, helps explain why she embraced civil rights activism when she did.[55]

Like canvassing, mass meetings were nothing new. Blacks were used to meetings where they listened to fiery speeches by acknowledged or self-proclaimed leaders. SNCC workers, however, expanded the meetings' democratic character and provided a space, Moses said, that "demanded that Black people challenge themselves." In Mississippi, this altered function directly reflected Moses's influence. He began to see meetings as organizing tools after he noticed that at a Jackson meeting, a local teenager, Lafayette Surney, had no qualms about challenging Lawrence Guyot but was hesitant to take the floor when Moses was speaking. So "the issue really struck me [as to how] meetings become places where grassroots participants . . . feel free" to speak, so they turned them into a format in which *all* participants "were empowered. They weren't just sitting there."[56]

One strategy was giving participants responsibility by dividing them into small groups. Each group devoted itself to a problem they considered relevant to their daily lives and discussed steps to alleviate it. Then they assigned people to execute the steps and report back at the next meeting. SNCC operated this way, too; if workers were unable to solve an issue, it frequently composed a volunteer committee to research it and report their findings through an interstaff memo.[57]

Another meeting strategy became making "rights" talk less abstract. When talking about voting, SNCC workers actually distributed applications and taught participants how to fill these in, like at the meeting Hamer attended, or reviewed the form collectively. They also gave public recognition to locals by letting *them* tell their stories. This equated their strength with that of acknowledged leaders on the platform, thereby "credentializing" them. COFO meetings became organizing tools in themselves as well, as locals from different areas mingled.[58]

The key to an effective meeting, Moses discovered, was going to where participants themselves were. This required cultural knowledge, for instance, by using religion and music. It was Hamer's encounter with "freedom songs"—songs adapted from the church or the labor movement—that particularly stimulated her to join the effort. Folk singer Theodore Bikel argued that the songs now inspired action due to a change of interpretation in the relationship between religion and current events. Before, "freedom" had referred to the afterlife, whereas after the sit-ins, it was "read with an appended 'NOW.'" Bernice Johnson explained, for instance, that the biblical story of Paul and Silas in the song "Keep Your Eyes on the Prize" now had a different meaning. Ministers "preached about it like Paul and Silas were ... so unique, incredible. They were in jail and they sang until they walked out. Now, once ... you're in these cells, rocking [them with freedom] songs, and the jailers let you go because they can't stand it no more, Paul and Silas ain't got nothing on you." Even Moses's singing "Climbing Jacob's Ladder" in his mind on the way to the Liberty courthouse in 1961 reflected this development, he said. "On the one hand, it was spiritual and on the other hand it had a wider political meaning, and it was all connected in this act of driving down to the courthouse."[59]

This emphasis on religion also helps to explain why the religion-tinged "Moses legend" proved so effective in Mississippi. "[O]ne reason the Mississippi Project was one of SNCC's most successful," Stokely Carmichael stated, "was in no small part due to the fortuitous accident of Bob's last name." When Hamer addressed locals, she consciously compared him to the biblical Moses. One of her frequent phrases was that God "sent a man to Mississippi with the same name ... to tell [Governor] Ross Barnett to let my people go." Bikel likewise observed that Moses "has come to lead his people to freedom as did his namesake in Egypt. History's pun, perhaps, but was not the original Moses an 'outside agitator' too?" White liberal reporters now habitually used the imagery of a saint to describe him; Jack Newfield even called him a prophet.[60]

This made Moses increasingly uncomfortable. He began warning locals more frequently and explicitly that "if you let it, the news media will tell you who your leaders are instead of your telling the news media." He stopped using the kind of religious imagery that appeared in his Magnolia letter but continued to treat workers' and locals' religious beliefs respectfully. This left even those closest to him wonder about his own religious views, sometimes inaccurately questioning their existence. Dave Dennis said he "wouldn't know [whether Moses] went to church because he really believed in it as a way of life or [as] a tactic . . . I don't recall ever going to church with Bob, or seen Bob at church outside of the movement." Other workers have admitted that they used religion deliberately as an organizing tool. For native workers like Hamer, this came naturally, but atheists in SNCC learned to recognize and cite passages from the Bible as well.[61]

HAMER AND MOSES DEVELOPED a warm relationship that was characteristic of his familial interaction with locals; she even stated that she loved him like a son. Moses was genuinely fond of her but also instantly recognized and took advantage of her organizing potential. As with the students in McComb, he cultivated it behind the scenes by making his contacts and resources available to her. Yet what happened to Hamer and other Ruleville activists next also revealed what COFO workers were up against in 1962, reminding Moses of the shortcomings in his leadership approach.[62]

Moses first noticed Hamer on August 31, when she went with him, Charles McLaurin, Charlie Cobb, Amzie Moore, and the seventeen other locals on the voter registration trip to Indianola. None of the applicants succeeded in registering, and a highway patrolman followed them as they rode home in a bus that Moore had rented. The feeling inside the bus was ominous, but their spirits, Moses recalled, rose as soon as Hamer started to sing. The patrolman indeed stopped the bus and fined the driver $100 for having a bus "with too much yellow" on it so it might be mistaken for a school bus. Unable to pay the driver's fine, the group offered to get arrested with him. The patrolman refused, arresting only the driver. Moses, Moore, and another SNCC worker followed them to the Indianola courthouse, while the group waited as armed whites drove by. Eventually, Moses returned, saying the fine had been reduced to $32. All chipped in and the group returned home. The group's solidarity proved transformative for Hamer.[63]

That elation was soon tested when the newspapers printed the names of the "Indianola 18." Marlow evicted Hamer from his plantation, forcing her first to move in with friends Mary and Robert Tucker and later to Tallahatchie County. She returned to Ruleville two months later when Moore found her a new home. Friends and SCEF paid her utility bills after Moses had enlisted her into SCEF's Operation Freedom program, again underscoring the need for outside intervention. Moses then asked her to work full-time for COFO and invited her to a leadership conference at Fisk University in Nashville, Tennessee.[64]

Meanwhile, other locals faced similar harassments. Two black cleaners were falsely closed for "building violations," mayor Charles Dorrough cut off water and tax exemption for the Williams Chapel, and the U.S. Fidelity and Guaranty Company, located in Baltimore, cancelled the church's insurance. This indicated the extent of northern complicity in southern illegality, Moses noted coolly in a complaint letter to the Company. "The thought occurred to me that [your company] would not want to be used to help coerce minority people who seek to exercise constitutional rights." Moses was not safe either. When he and Moore walked across town, a white man in a pickup invited them to his farm. Astonished, they agreed, only to be told, "I've got a shotgun waiting for you, double barrel."[65]

The most violent reprisal came on September 10 when nightriders shot into the homes of the Tucker, McDonald, and Sisson families. Hattie Sisson had earlier attempted to register with McLaurin. Granddaughter Vivian Hillet and friend Marylene Burks were shot; Burks in the head and neck, Hillet in the arms and legs. They barely survived. Distressed, Charlie Cobb unsuccessfully called Moore for advice and then Moses, who was in Jackson. Moses suggested he informed the Justice Department and went to the hospital. There Mayor Dorrough, who also served as justice of the peace, arrested Cobb for "asking a lot of silly questions." Together they returned to the Sissons, where, one local testified, Dorrough told the sheriff on the phone, "Moses is the cause of all this." He ordered the Sisson family not to clean up the bloodstains until the FBI could determine it was human. S. D. Milam, brother of one of Emmett Till's murderers, transported Cobb to jail.[66]

The situation worsened when Moses and other workers departed Jackson at 2 A.M. to head to Ruleville in a broken car that kept stalling at slow speed. When driver James Jones fell asleep behind the wheel, they hit a road sign and came to a stop in a cotton field. Shaken but unharmed, they packed into a second car of workers behind them. The sheriff issued an arrest warrant for Moses, in whose name the car was registered, for reckless driving and leaving the scene of an accident. Represented by the NAACP's Carsie Hall, Moses and Jones later pled guilty and paid a $120 fee.[67]

When Moses and the others finally arrived in Ruleville to interview witnesses, the sheriff threatened to arrest him for interfering with a police investigation. Undeterred, the SNCC workers continued interviewing witnesses, and Moses sent detailed reports to the FBI, the media, and the Justice Department. In a news conference on September 13, President Kennedy called the shootings and other instances of violence against civil rights activists "cowardly as well as outrageous" and now openly vowed protection for registration workers. "[I]f it requires extra legislation, and extra force, we shall do that." He touted the FBI's presence and assured the assailants' prosecution, although in reality, McLaurin reported, the FBI "did more to frighten people than to help them." Despite the SNCC workers' newfound means of involving locals, after the violence, they had to spend much of September regaining the community's trust. Barely mentioning voting, they went "house to house asking people about everyday problems[,] carry them to the store downtown, help pick cotton and chop wood."[68]

ALTHOUGH SNCC'S INVOLVEMENT in Ruleville and elsewhere increasingly frustrated local authorities and even helped force the president of the United States to take a public stand, it was clear that in the face of such opposition, Moses's facilitation approach could only reach so far. But like McComb, the Ruleville story underscores how outsiders did shake up the dynamics within the black and white communities in hitherto unseen proportions. The singular attributes Moses brought to the struggle—his intelligence, audacity, (northern) resources, sense of direction, ability to mediate between the local and the national and between local blacks and local authorities, his measured speech, and self-effacing style—ensured that his approach thrived unparalleled. This is especially clear when compared to how other SNCC leaders applied the approach in Georgia and elsewhere. Even if Moses saw himself solely as a facilitator, his organizing work went beyond using one's skills and power to facilitate local groups. Emphasizing facilitation of grassroots movements alone—implying that anyone could have done what Moses did if they operated from the same humble premises—therefore cannot

adequately explain how the 1960s civil rights movement generated social change. The formation of what movement participants and observers have termed the Bob Moses mystique must be taken into account as
well. When asked whether it was enhanced in history, the majority of
SNCC veterans insist that it was real. "It was indescribable but apparent
from first meeting him," stated Julian Bond. Much to Moses's dismay, it
became a key factor in friends' and foes' projection of leadership onto
him as the months progressed.[69]

After all, Moses's distinct personality decisively influenced the nature
of the Mississippi Project, in the same way other SNCC project leaders
did theirs. For example, Georgia SNCC resembled Moses's Mississippi
project the most, but differences remained in large part to Moses's and
Sherrod's individual priorities and responses to local circumstances. As
in Mississippi, Georgia SNCC workers used nonviolence, held citizenship classes, and canvassed the working class while facing traumatizing
white harassment, including arrests, beatings, and shootings. Because
many blacks in the twenty-two rural counties they covered were too
frightened to associate with them, several painted houses or picked squash
for survival. Yet generally Georgia workers experienced less overt violence, which made it easier to involve locals and made them less in need
of developing a COFO-like vehicle. Consequently, by late 1963, Georgia
SNCC had registered a few hundred voters; in Mississippi, the number
was much lower. Of the twelve full-time workers in southwest Georgia,
only two were native blacks, and half were white. This reflected Sherrod's principled insistence on integration. While equally committed to
interracialism, Bob Zellner's beating in McComb had shown Moses that
using whites in Mississippi was counterproductive. Moreover, since
"SNCC itself had never really resolved what it meant by integration,"
he argued, "we more or less left the idea alone. . . . We talked local leadership instead."[70]

Moses's and Sherrod's personalities influenced their projects in other
ways as well. Sherrod's stress on interracialism derived from his religious
convictions, which were consistent with SNCC's Statement of Purpose.
His state directorship accordingly appealed to other religiously inclined
workers, which allowed for religion to become an integral part of their
daily life. Sherrod introduced Prayer Breakfasts each morning and, like
fellow minister James Bevel, Sherrod, one worker observed, "really gave
sermons when he spoke to people, just quoting from the Bible." As such,
Sherrod's and Bevel's flamboyant southern preacher styles contrasted

starkly with Moses's soft deposition. Sherrod could be feisty, engaging in demonstrations as eagerly as in voter registration. He sat in at Robert Kennedy's office once and when Kennedy tried to persuade SNCC away from direct action, shouted, "It is not your responsibility, before God or under the law, to tell us how to honor our constitutional rights. It's your job to protect us when we do." Simultaneously, he could be patient; he once listened for hours to a black man in Albany who kept repeating, "People treat me like a dog. . . . Do I look like a dog? Do I look like a dog?"[71]

Bevel was a different character altogether. John Lewis described him as "[w]ild. Crazy. Nuttier than nut. Brilliant. Passionate. Eccentric . . . he had an irresistible confidence about him that gave those around him . . . no choice but to pay attention." But he also listened and was open to new concepts, like the Smith campaign. Later, Bevel suffered borderline psychotic spells, but in the 1960s used rumors about them to propel the movement, saying that blacks "needed to be crazy in order to dream of freedom." As McComb demonstrated, his colorful style was highly effective in motivating locals, although it ultimately proved more suitable for SCLC's goal of mobilization than for SNCC's community organizing.[72]

Moses in turn was shy and his speech studied, which advanced his specific Mississippi organizing goals. Movement participants praised his ability to get to the point without slipping into emotional language or hollow slogans. Moses intrigued many because he was the opposite of their expectations, Luvaughn Brown added. "I anticipated a fireball. Bob certainly was not that!" Journalists noted that he spoke calmly "with the rhythms of a man crossing a stream, hopping from rock to rock." His speeches mainly featured facts, names, and dates. Some contemporaries accordingly dismissed him as a "moody, murky intellectual"; one reporter actually termed him "an outstandingly poor speaker." Even Tom Scarborough criticized Moses's slurred way of speaking, although, in a way, it was reminiscent of a southern drawl. However, while SNCC worker Worth Long's claim that "Moses deliberately rejected the role of orator because it was the traditional role of Black leadership" overstates his intent, those who knew him recognized that his style in itself carried a message. Moses's goal was to project local leadership, not drawing attention to himself. He often underscored this point, especially with uneducated audiences, by speaking from the back, engaging an audience in conversation or raising questions rather than answering them. This was a way of moral leadership by example, Casey Hayden argued. "Bob set an example through practice, gaining loyalty by listening, [which] helped individuals empower themselves."[73]

For Moses, adopting this tactic was a natural consequence of his character and upbringing. It echoed his father's teachings that everybody, however humble or lacking in education, could contribute something worthwhile if given the chance. Moreover, because Ella Baker's interest in him had motivated him, he came to see personal interaction as an organizing tool, too. Her emphasis on the significance of the individual within the movement and organizations' responsibility to care for them matched his reticent nature and ability to listen, which allowed for the other person in a conversation to open up. Because of this, workers like Julian Bond and Stokely Carmichael believed that Moses consciously or subconsciously followed Baker's example. His organizing style has regularly been dubbed as "feminine," which effectively complemented his "masculine" Mississippi fieldwork and bravery. While Moses has admitted his indebtedness to Baker, he countered that she had merely adopted that style during her 1940s work in the southern black communities. "[I]f you really want to do something with somebody else [you have to] find out who it is you are working with. All across the South you could see that in grassroots rural people. That was their style. Miss Baker [just] took this style to a sophisticated level of political work."[74]

But for those working with Moses and for (white) movement sympathizers, this style added to his appeal. "Moses was 'perhaps the most trusted, the most loved, the most gifted organizationally of any southern Negro leader' *precisely because* he seemed humble, ordinary, accessible," SDS veteran Todd Gitlin explained, "The early New Left . . . wanted elemental talk, not grand rhetoric." Instances of praise are abundant. Mary King recalled feeling her chest muscles quicken when Moses spoke, and others savored his ability to "communicate a soothing, spiritual depth." But his understatement could also be humorous. At a Mississippi meeting that whites wanted to invade, he once left his audience in stitches after ordering two guards to post the door to keep out hecklers while stating calmly, "Be gentle with them."[75]

Moses's speech was effective because it reflected *who he was*, although, Mary King admitted, he "well understood that we were engaged in certain forms of political theater." Reserve had always defined his character, and his upbringing and education had reinforced that characteristic. Apart from a safety measure, Moses's silence reflected his concern for morality and his fear of leading people, like Louis Allen, into something beyond his control. He intuitively felt that his speech should reflect the practical. As he told the *Saturday Evening Post* in 1964, "One of the things wrong with this country is that everyone is saying too much. . . . It's wrong to promise more than you can give. To accomplish something very real, you have to do something very limited."[76]

BUT EVEN IF MOSES'S self-effacing style partly resulted from caution, it helped spur the development of participatory democracy within Mississippi SNCC. Without it, Dave Dennis believed, "there would not have been a Mississippi project." Moses, SNCC advisor Howard Zinn explained, had thought about the relationship between leadership style and others' ability to thrive more than most SNCC workers. His background and age explained part of his unusual commitment to these principles. "A lack of maturity was both strength and weakness for SNCC," Mary King acknowledged, "Some may not have understood Bob's depths of commitment to raising up leaders who could speak for the oppressed, which concomitantly requires decentralization."[77]

Moreover, for Moses, exercising group-centered leadership was the only logical response to the realities on the ground in Mississippi. Within all southern state projects, key players like Moses and Sherrod and locals like Henry made decisions in unison with the other full-time fieldworkers, then with local people, and finally SNCC's national headquarters in Atlanta were notified. The latter "above," Moses believed, should never outrank the rest. Especially in dangerous Mississippi, this was a matter of principle, he argued. "How could you set up [a structure] where there's some people who have good jobs and are working somewhere safe in society, and they . . . decide policy which some other people [have to execute] for nothing at the risk of their lives? . . . I would never agree to that kind of procedure for the work that we were doing." SNCC workers therefore often laughed at outsiders' theories about their structure. "[W]e never proclaimed that [SNCC] *had* to proceed by consensus," Stokely Carmichael argued, but all "you *could* do is talk . . . because the issues are deadly serious." What emerged was then not so much a philosophy but an indispensable culture among themselves and locals to guarantee further movement.[78]

Likewise, Moses did not explicitly call to implement participatory democracy. Yet due to his shyness and experience with the Quakers, he excelled in the approach, which in turn spurred others' commitment to it. At staff meetings, he dealt remarkably consistently with conflict through consensus, although his approach was not one of anti-leadership. After all, Mary King observed, "He cared deeply about leadership and had thought profoundly about it." John Lewis recalled that Moses dealt with conflict by what religious groups like the Quakers call tarrying, that is, "almost waiting on a spirit . . . you talk and you talk with individuals and don't give up on them." When someone erred, he reacted nonviolently by not rebuking him or her. If disagreements emerged, he tried not to personalize them, even when directed at him. Yet mostly, Lewis said, workers kept disagreements private "because there was so much respect[,] affection, and love for the man." But at this stage, disputes were usually minor and the group small. Even if workers and locals were not "personally attached to him," one SNCC veteran stated in 1968, they appreciated Moses as "the quiet kind of fellow that would get things done."[79]

In practice, participatory democracy was more complicated than it seemed. Charles Sherrod, for example, personified a tendency within SNCC to impose views on locals and staff. He explicitly advised colleagues not to "let the project go to the dogs because you feel you must be democratic to the letter or carry out *every* parliamentary procedure." Stokely Carmichael likewise admitted that he did not always lead without bombast or fiat. In meetings, he occasionally took a local aside, explained the issue, and sent the person on stage to talk "as if [s]he's always known it." SNCC workers in Albany even prepared speeches for locals, and Charles Jones openly dismissed Albany Movement president William G. Anderson, a local black osteopath, as "not really a leader," arguing instead that "he must be led by the Strategy Committee."[80]

At first glance, Moses easily stands out in comparison. For example, Sherrod received much criticism from his workers for his control over which projects they could participate in. When Jean Wheeler Smith and Martha Norman wanted to leave for Greenwood but Sherrod refused, they even "waited for Sherrod to go to jail, and as soon as he went . . . we left at midnight." This contrasted starkly with Moses, who asked Smith in 1964 to go with him to Atlantic City. She declined. "He said, 'Fine,' he got back on the bus and I stayed." But Moses occasionally pushed decisions, too. "Ultimately," Dorie Ladner observed, "what he had to say, he would say." Luvaughn Brown claimed that Moses had a "quiet insistence when he felt . . . things should be approached a certain way." This included the liberty of making basic COFO decisions without consultation. Dave Dennis admitted as much when he stated that "Bob or myself . . . did sort of shove things down sometimes to get things moving in [a] certain direction that maybe was not understood at the time." This suggests that the Moses mystique might camouflage a dominant, or even manipulating, personality much like what southern segregationists accused him and other outside leaders of. But SNCC workers reject such characterizations. As Charlie Cobb explained, "We were organizers in Mississippi, not leaders, even if at moments we led. The distinction was important to us, and a practical necessity."[81]

Within the movement, Moses gained an unrivaled reputation for trying to live up to the principles of participatory democracy, grassroots leadership, and personal freedom. His distinctive habit of turning all his activities into lessons spurred this image. He often let locals do his public speaking or answer his mail after teaching them these skills. One was fifteen-year-old Greenwood prostitute Endesha Mae Holland, who became a movement regular after Moses taught her how to type. "I was so glad to be used for something. While the whole town was looking down on me, the movement said, 'You are somebody.'" She eventually became a professor. Moses's own actions were teaching moments, too. Unita Blackwell felt empowered after witnessing Moses confront state authorities. "Moses was a little bitty fella. And he stood up to this sheriff . . . I had never saw that happen before. From that day on, I said, 'Well, I can stand myself.'"[82]

How Moses involved another Greenwood fifteen-year-old, June Johnson, illustrates his slow organizing approach in practice. Having watched him for days, she finally asked him if he was a Freedom Rider. He responded by asking about her family and offered to carry her books. June then asked Moses to meet her mother. The latter disliked June's and her brother Waite's involvement but quickly became fond of Moses. According to Waite, Moses "had a special charisma with the old folks. They just seemed to trust him." Within several months, June was allowed to attend meetings—if Moses or Annelle Ponder were present. A special plea by Moses allowed her to go to Septima Clark's citizenship school in South Carolina in June 1963. June termed him "The Person Who Influenced Me Most" in an essay because he taught her "that the most important thing . . . is education and becoming a first-class citizen" and about "people who I didn't know." Everyone respected him, she noted, because he was "beaten for us." She emphasized how the full-time workers' presence bolstered local agency. "[I]f we could get more men like Bob Moses into Greenwood our problems would soon be over. . . . If he and the other workers hadn't come . . . we would be the same Uncle Toms—afraid to walk and talk for our rights."[83]

As an erudite northerner, Moses had much to learn about southern black life, too. But, as with Fannie Lou Hamer and the McComb students, he developed deep personal relations with Greenwood blacks. "Bob would actually *merge* in," Dave Dennis claimed. "He dealt with them as family. . . . It wasn't just like a strategy around them." Moses simply did not see his presence as being one of a northerner who did not need to be there; he firmly believed that his and locals' quest for freedom were inherently intertwined. "I [too] had to decide how I wanted to live in this country," he later justified his decision to come south, "I felt I was in as much of a position [to do this] as those people we were working with."[84]

Moses's closeness included looking after locals once confrontations were over, as he had done with the Burgland students. When June Johnson returned from South Carolina, she and other participants were arrested for attending a white restroom in Winona, Mississippi. In jail, she, Annelle Ponder, and Fannie Lou Hamer were brutally beaten; June lost consciousness twice. With Moses's aid, SNCC worker Marian Wright arranged for her to go to a summer camp in Connecticut to recuperate. Concerned, Moses even encouraged its director to "have her tell you about the beating," that is, "if you can get June to talk." He now often arranged such trips north for Mississippi students and helped them secure scholarships there. One was Curtis Hayes, whose "life and development," he wrote Wright, "has special meaning for me."[85]

Moses's cosmopolitan background spurred his reputation, too. Apart from his ability to utilize northern connections, he was praised for his intelligence and sense of direction. Aaron Henry admitted that Moses's "ideas usually became SNCC policy in short order," even if not everyone always agreed with him. Usually, they did, Marion Barry claimed. "It just happened that you agree once you hear [his ideas], they sound so exciting." His intelligence impressed locals even more. One revered how Moses "sees real far into the future," although "a lot of time the people . . . can't keep up with him." Yet this did not bother them. Although Moses generally waited for others to speak before he offered his own thoughts, the latter *wanted* him to speak his mind, Ladner said. "After we were finished debating for hours[,] screaming and yelling at each other, we [all would] wait for Bob to say something. . . . We were *looking* for the outside world to . . . help educate us." And Moses, many locals felt, had the ability of doing so without undermining their sense of self-esteem. Moses, sharecropper L.C. Dorsey explained, just "kept putting the questions out. 'Why do you think that is? What do you think we ought to do about that?' He'd listen to what you said and force you to think about it. That was his genius."[86]

When offering practical organizing advice about day-to-day problems, like how to involve locals, Moses often explicitly linked them to Albert Camus or other intellectuals. He regularly reread Camus's work and even carried a dog-eared copy of *The Rebel* in his pocket. Whereas Moses's frequent Camus references worried southern segregationists—one noted anxiously that a Mississippi black arrested for civil rights activism carried a copy of Sartre's *Nausea* that had "property of Bob Moses" written inside, implying that outside intellectuals were stirring up native blacks with "foreign" ideas—it impressed uneducated locals and attracted student activists. A remarkable number, especially northern whites, acknowledge Camus as a motivational source for their involvement. Not having grown up in a southern black church tradition, they tried to find a way of linking the movement's social gospel concepts to their own upbringing, as one explained. "I got involved [with French existentialism and] intellectually that had something to do with [my involvement]—the two ideas, the one that a man is defined by his acts not his words, and two, that it's not a question so much of what you accomplish as that you are doing something—the Camus idea from *Sisyphus*." Seizing upon this romantic image of the students, *New York Times* journalist Gene Roberts even characterized SNCC as a group in which "it was a must that you be able to quote Camus." This statement is exaggerated considering the many other influences that circulated in SNCC, including Frantz Fanon, Malcolm X, and the Bible. Many, in fact, learned about the existentialists through others. Undoubtedly, Moses had a major role in this with his habitual quotations from Camus. Stokely Carmichael even changed his major to philosophy because "Bob's example of clarity and rationality influenced me . . . I remember one night in a Freedom House we sat up almost till sunup discussing a tough philosophical problem. That was Bob."[87]

This focus enthralled white liberal reporters, like Jack Newfield and Ben Bagdikian, who had often had a similar academic training. By regularly mentioning Moses's connection to Camus, these writers sought him out as a black leader with whom they could identify. They did the same with Martin Luther King Jr., who quoted Georg Hegel and other (white) philosophers and theologians, at the expense of southern (religious) activists whose language bore the marks of inferior Jim Crow education, such as John Lewis or Fred Shuttlesworth. In a sense, this was a distortion of the movement, but it allowed them to use the assets of people like Moses and King to generate support for it. After all, Moses's background, language, and compassionate character formed an appealing interface between the student movement and a sympathetic national (white) audience.[88]

More significantly, Moses's cosmopolitan background gave his words extra credence with uneducated southerners despite his egalitarian approach. "I had never seen a nigga like that before," local SNCC worker MacArthur Cotton marveled. "He was definitely in a different class from anybody I'd ever know." Unita Blackwell noted the significance of having a black intellectual in their midst. "I had a good impression of a PhD. I didn't even know what they were. But they used to throw it around a lot [that] Moses had [started] a PhD. And I thought it must have been [quite] something." Trinidad-native Stokely Carmichael was even more exotic, she added. He "would talk about the Islands, and he had an accent. And that would flavor us, and then he'd tell us about African people . . . you just would sit for hours and listen [to] Stokely."[89]

He and Carmichael thus embodied what Moses believed was one of the most significant goals of the civil rights movement, that is, "exposure to ideas, to people, to places that had been closed" to locals before. He acknowledged that merely his "physical presence, as well as others from out of state, pried open this 'closed society' [and] contributed to folks' growth." As such, out-of-state workers like him rather than local stalwarts like Amzie Moore inspired Mississippi students. When Medgar Evers "would tell us that 'we wanna get our freedom someday,'" Ladner found, "I didn't really know what it meant [but] when the Freedom Riders came in, they brought that whole thing together for us." John Lewis, an Alabama native, concurred. "In many instances the people needed a spark. . . . You needed someone like a Bob Moses to come in, [or] the Freedom Riders." After all, Luvaughn Brown explained, "Coming from the outside gave Bob a perspective we did not have. His mind was free of the baggage that many of us picked up at childhood."[90]

Moses's lack of this "sense of acceptance" was a blessing, Brown believed, although—or perhaps *because*—it made him appear reckless. When Brown, Moses, and two other workers once stopped at a soda stand and its operator insisted on serving them on the backside, Moses was the only one who refused. Despite verbal abuse, Moses persisted until they got the drinks. "I just thought it was unnecessary and dangerous," Brown reflected, but "we told the story with great relish and it added to Bob's reputation."[91]

Another such incident occurred on August 16, 1962. At midnight, Sam Block called Moses in Cleveland from Greenwood's COFO office, which was surrounded by a white mob accompanied by policemen with him, Brown, and Lawrence Guyot inside. After softly advising that "it'd be a good idea to get outa there," Moses called John Doar and Burke Marshall at their Washington homes. Block then called again to say the police had left and that the whites were brandishing chains and guns. Unsure of what they could do but convinced that boldness gave him "some kind of immunity," Moses and Willie Peacock drove to Greenwood, arriving around 4 A.M. The office was empty—the three had escaped through the window and over the roof—and trashed. Moses turned on a fan and fell asleep on the couch. Convinced that its noise would get them killed, Peacock was terrified. Yet Moses's audacity empowered him, he later wrote. "I just didn't understand what kind of guy this Bob Moses is, that could walk into a place where a lynch mob had just left [and] go to sleep, as if the situation was normal. So I guess I was learning."[92]

While his director title did not give Moses any powers over others, his position as state coordinator enhanced his authority. After all, outsiders *did* respond to titles, Stokely Carmichael observed. "People were disposed to like and trust you just because." They expected that titles equated certain powers. For example, one worker whose subsistence pay had stopped complained that SNCC headquarters had no such authority. "If Bob Moses hired me, he should be the one to put me off the staff, because he is the Mississippi Project Director." John Lewis acknowledged that although SNCC "preached . . . that we didn't need leaders, [or] build up a personality . . . we did it in a way. We elected people head of a project, or Secretary, the Chair, the Field Directors." Local workers like Brown likewise denied that "SNCC had an anti-leadership view. We clearly had people who were viewed as leaders and primary decision makers. While local field secretaries made decisions based on their environment, we filed reports to [SNCC headquarters] and worked with goals set by SNCC leaders."[93]

So whether Moses wanted to or not, he was the de facto leader. Not only did he serve as the main "contact man" for everyone who came to Mississippi, including federal officials and other organizations, but all fieldworkers were required to call him daily. Sam Block wrote him repeatedly during his first months in Greenwood to ask for advice or report events. Such reports were surprisingly detailed, including budget overviews for office supplies, meals, and rent. This again underscores that Moses was aware of the projects' daily pragmatics, but he also influenced them through his responses. For instance, when Hollis Watkins and Curtis Hayes complained about working too much at Vernon Dahmer's sawmill, he made arrangements for them to move. He occasionally dealt with finances, too. When two locals wanted $20 pay instead of $10, Block directed them to Moses because "you told them to let you know if they needed any other expense money." He proposed concrete strategies to workers in letters as well. In one, he advised Guyot to expand from Greenwood to neighboring rural areas by sending small groups into different counties for a week as preparation before planning strategies. Always thinking ahead, he recommended that Guyot travel from project to project too, since this "will allow you a chance to meet students all across the state . . . for action projects in the future."[94]

Organizing in Mississippi required such wide-ranging preparations and foresight. Workers *needed* someone like Moses whose pragmatic capabilities they could trust, as their physical and mental survival depended on it. The mere fact that Moses was director in dangerous Mississippi strengthened his position, and his example in risking life and limb with them helped others in reaching the courage to risk theirs. "Mississippi represented the depths of depravity and hatred," Mary King explained, "This gave his words more echo, because the cost of poor decision making would bring the greatest reprisals to Mississippians, and he would necessarily absorb the greatest responsibility."[95]

When segregationists increasingly replicated Ruleville's violent means to stop the Mississippi movement in the winter of 1962–1963, Moses began to ponder the implications of this more and more. Although his field experiments had formed the groundwork for a long-term, increasingly political vision of social change that he summarized to the VEP as "Negro control of [the black-majority] rural counties in the Deep South," the violence prevented any significant move forward. In fact, by then, he noted distressed, a "heavy curtain seemed to have dropped down on the state, making us invisible to the nation." It dawned on Moses that the time had come for COFO's introverted, slow organizing approach to change.[96]

CHAPTER FIVE

A New Dimension

Just over a year before, Moses had come to Mississippi feeling optimistic about the possibilities for social change in the state. McComb had lowered such expectations fast. Although the campaign had offered openings for how to move forward, the memory of Herbert Lee permeated his every step. He and his colleagues had adopted an inward-looking approach that focused on the internal development of local blacks and a local movement but periodically ran into explosive situations despite their best efforts to tread carefully. By the fall of 1962, they had built his strategy into a workable approach and made effective inroads in staffing a movement. But they were still only getting incremental results, in the face of an ever-increasing risk of civilian deaths. That situation worsened after James Meredith's bloody integration of the University of Mississippi. Between fall 1962 and September 1963, what had been a relatively introverted approach would evolve, until SNCC's activities finally drew in the nation at large, forcing the Kennedy administration into action.

SNCC's inability to combat whites' violent response to the movement, and the federal government's failure to curb that violence, propelled the shift in strategy. For nearly two years, Moses wrote in February 1963, he had been caught between combating "your own fears about beatings, shootings, and possible mob violence" and trying to "stymie, by your mere physical presence, the anxious fear of the Negro community." But this proved too heavy a burden to bear. He "wrestled with life-and-death questions" that made "finding a way to deal with the still-increasing violence . . . the top of our concerns."[1]

Yet Moses continued to reject the idea that creating a more national appeal required more assertive leadership or a surrender to the will of the media or federal government. In fact, following events in upcoming months in Greenwood, Birmingham, and Jackson, he and Mississippi SNCC ingeniously succeeded in developing a national strategy that respected rather than undermined local agency. At the same time, his behind-the-scenes activities reveal the extent to which local, national, and international events intertwined in Mississippi and how full-time civil rights workers, particularly outsiders like Moses, effectively mediated between them to spur social change.

Determined to challenge the notion that the "race issue" was a southern or local problem but true to his ideals of grassroots leadership, Moses subtly guided the Mississippi movement further into political organizing by incorporating a mass direct action dimension to his slow organizing approach that involved the nation but continued to project and develop black Mississippians.

MOSES'S FEELINGS OF powerlessness in the face of white violence had built slowly but piercingly. As project director, he learned daily of incidents that hampered other workers. Telephone records and field reports from SNCC workers show rampant improper arrests, burnings, beatings, and nightly shootings between 1962 and 1963. State-sanctioned violence occurred with astounding regularity, with law enforcement often perpetrating the acts themselves. In 1963, for instance, police beat black youth Milton Hancock for joining the Greenwood COFO project and murdered black Willie Joe Lovett outside his home. They even arrested fifty-eight blacks in Itta Bena for "breach of the peace" because they had dared to ask for police protection from whites who had smoke-bombed their voter registration meeting.[2]

Despite the risks, Moses investigated many such incidents personally. When two firebombs ripped Hartman Turnbow's farm in Mileston after his registration attempt, the sheriff simply arrested Turnbow, Moses, and three other SNCC workers for arson supposedly intended to "work up sympathy" for COFO. Reporting these incidents to the Justice Department sometimes had an effect—the charges against Moses and the others in Milestone were dismissed with John Doar's help—but most appeals to the federal government came to nothing.[3]

The situation was hardly different in other states. In mid-1962, one Justice Department official asked Georgia SNCC to stay away from Baker County rather than going there himself to investigate its claims. In early 1963, a desperate Charles Sherrod even wired President Kennedy that if the department would not protect them, "our blood will be on your hands." Julian Bond regularly informed Moses about the Georgia workers' disquieting state of mind. "We're having trouble with our SW Ga. Boys," he pressed, "They're all frustrated novelists and send us reports that Forman says 'show a decided Proustian influence.' Sherrod is writing like a drunk Jack Kerouac & [John] O'Neal & [Jack] Chatfield write like drunk Sherrods." Such trauma, day after day, year after year, took its toll on Moses and the rest of SNCC.[4]

But Justice Department workers were frustrated, too. Two problems hampered their effectiveness. First, until the Supreme Court determined the federal government's role in voter registration, the Civil Rights Division was mandated to move gradually. Second, it consisted of less than two dozen lawyers, both inexperienced in southern law and overworked. The fact that southern counties often refused to hand over registration records despite federal law also led to protracted delays in gathering evidence. Moreover, the sophisticated and ever-changing methods registrars used to obstruct black applicants made the establishment of deliberate intent no easy matter.[5]

SNCC workers either were unaware of or dismissed such nuances. Whenever he could, Moses reminded the Justice Department of its powers. Alongside the 14th and 15th Amendments and Title 18 of the U.S. Code, he and other workers charged, the 1957 and 1960 Civil Rights Acts prohibited voter intimidation, allowed for the prosecution of registrars, and forced registrars to preserve their records. In practice, however, these acts demanded a protracted county-by-county, case-by-case approach against individual registrars. By late 1962, the department had filed just three lawsuits in Louisiana, three in Alabama, and seven in Mississippi. Most were stalled in court, leaving registrars, like Greenwood's Martha Lamb and Hattiesburg's Theron Lynd, free to continue rejecting black applicants. This stung, as the Kennedy administration's promotion of the VEP had raised expectations of federal involvement. SNCC's understanding was that the administration guaranteed a quid-pro-quo; if SNCC switched to voter registration, the government would protect them. Department officials deny making any such pledges, but movement insiders, like SRC's Leslie Dunbar, maintain that they did. Instead, the federal government, John Doar admitted, "refused to do more than it had to."[6]

Moses faulted the administration for bowing to politics. The Kennedys' refusal to allow U.S. Commission on Civil Rights hearings in Mississippi evidenced this. An unwillingness to challenge the Dixiecrats' power within the Democratic Party partly explains their reluctance. Moreover, at least 100 lawsuits ironically failed because of the federal judges President Kennedy had appointed to southern benches. Over a quarter were known segregationists. "I'm not favorably impressed with you," one frankly wrote John Doar, "I spend most of my time in fooling with lousy cases brought before me by your department in the civil rights field, and I do not intend to turn my docket over to your department for your political advancement." A recalcitrant FBI with under-manned southern offices, presided over by racist Kennedy nemesis J. Edgar Hoover, further hampered the department. FBI workers left the lengthy analyses of voting rolls and interviews to the overextended Justice Department, and Hoover refused to allow them to arrest whites for interfering with blacks' constitutional rights. This meant that agents often stood by when whites assaulted civil rights workers. Robert Kennedy and Burke Marshall went along with this no-arrest policy for fear that southern congressional Democrats would block even the smallest civil rights proposal.[7]

Nevertheless, Moses continued diligent cooperation with the Justice Department. SNCC assiduously collected evidence and bombarded the department with petitions, interviews, and reports. Procuring and furnishing such evidence was a vital part of its work, Moses insisted. He encouraged COFO workers to buy copies of newspapers that printed black applicants' names and send them to him because "[n]obody is recording this information but you." He even arranged with Doar that Tim Jenkins spend several days in Washington to research cases useful to the organization's work. This suggests that relations between SNCC and the department were closer than generally assumed. Moses's consensus-building character played a significant role in improving such relations. Upset as he was about the federal government's inactivity, he always prioritized trying "to understand what the process was . . . because it was there that you [had] to work out what it was that you should do." He particularly got on with John Doar and Burke Marshall. A liberal Republican, Doar sympathized with the movement, and Moses repeatedly witnessed his positive effect on black Mississippians. Rather than criticize, he therefore "concentrated more on developing a working relationship with them to get whatever help we could."[8]

While pushing the Justice Department constituted a valuable aspect of Moses's organizing, he did not consider this part of a deliberate outreach to the nation. He first began to think more strategically about "a national picture" during mid-1962 meetings of the Taconic Foundation and after James Meredith's integration of Ole Miss, the University of Mississippi in Oxford, in September 1962. Egged on by Governor Ross Barnett, local whites barred Meredith from admission. The Kennedys tried to avoid deploying troops, trusting segregationist politicians' promises to ensure order, not having learned from the 1957 Little Rock crisis the emptiness of these promises. When riots erupted on and off campus, state troops withdrew and federal troops had to restore order. One journalist and one resident were killed and 160 marshals injured before Meredith entered his first class under military protection on October 1.[9]

Moses did not at first see this crisis as a reason to alter his slow organizing methods. For him, the significance of Ole Miss was rather the realization that the political and public debate centered on the wrong premise—federal versus state power—instead of the more important principle that "being a citizen . . . was not just a formality, there was substance to it." "The country never . . . made the connection," he later explained, "between the armed struggle Mississippi terrorists waged at Ole Miss[,] the endemic Mississippi Delta sharecropper illiteracy, and the national lack of intentionality to provide a quality education for all its children." Meredith's fight and his fight were in fact identical. "SNCC and illiterate sharecroppers who [entered] into a 'registration to vote' procedure . . . made their moves from the same fundamental place as Meredith." Although Meredith's attempt had ensured federal involvement, SNCC should therefore just continue what it was doing: bringing the question of the meaning of citizenship to a head by accompanying illiterate blacks to the registrar.[10]

Yet southern whites' adamant resistance in the riots' wake made this impossible. Convinced that state politicians could not prevent another federal "invasion," an increasing number felt they had to ensure the status quo themselves. "Murderous tension thickened the air," Moses noted. Violent reprisals against COFO intensified. Subsequently, its work "proceeded by steppes instead of slopes," he wrote a northern support group. "We have been on a deep plateau all winter, shaking off the effects of the violence of August and September."[11]

Blacks celebrated Meredith's acceptance but remained wary of getting involved in the movement. This forced Moses to inform the VEP that "we are powerless to register people in significant numbers . . . until the power of the Citizens Council over state politics is broken, the [Justice Department] secures for Negroes across the board the right to register, or Negroes rise up en masse with an unsophisticated blatant demand for immediate registration." Case-by-case lawsuits were insufficient. The only solution, he insisted, was the stationing of federal marshals at the courthouse and filing "a broad suit to stop economic reprisals and physical violence to prospective registrants[,] abolish the poll tax [and] literacy test."[12]

These premises were covered in the daring January 1963 lawsuit *Moses et al. v. Robert F. Kennedy and J. Edgar Hoover.* The suit challenged the two officials based on six sections of the federal code obliging local authorities to investigate, arrest, and prosecute those preventing blacks from exercising their constitutional rights. Moses hoped it would create a precedent that indicated to Kennedy and Hoover that "their powers are immeasurably greater than they probably realized." He was not naive about the suit's outcome. As expected, department officials blocked it, arguing that this was a state responsibility. Nonetheless, it was not the kind of lawsuit that the moderate NAACP would have filed.[13]

Yet Moses characteristically denied having had much to do with the suit. It was "filed in my name, but I'm not involved in really thinking through this; it's the lawyers. They have ideas about how to attack this." Indeed, "radical" white lawyers such as William Higgs, William Kunstler, and Arthur Kinoy, known for their cooperation with Communist-suspected groups, had filed the suit. However, the fact that Moses asked Higgs to initiate the suit underscores how important outsiders like him were in mediating between the local and the national. Moses's interpretations of local realities and his ability to explain them to contacts with resources, like these lawyers, helped smooth the transition to an approach that did garner a more national appeal even as he prioritized grassroots agency. Soon enough, events in Greenwood reinforced the idea that building grassroots leadership and forging an alliance between North and South did not have to be mutually exclusive goals.[14]

GREENWOOD, MISSISSIPPI, had a remarkably hateful record toward blacks. As police commissioner Buff Hammond verbalized local sentiment, "Desegregation just won't happen until the Federal Government beats us to our knees." In 1960, fewer than 2 percent of blacks, who comprised 64.6 percent of Leflore County's population, were registered to vote; in the past seven years, only forty had dared a registration attempt.[15]

When, in mid-1962, SNCC worker Sam Block started a project in Greenwood, Moses warned Block repeatedly that he could be the next Emmett Till, who was murdered nearby. A tradition of black resistance predated SNCC's arrival, particularly among financially independent families like the McGhees, yet few among the working-class poor were willing to join their open defiance. As such, when the Mississippi State

Sovereignty Commission started investigating Block, a Mississippi native, it did not fear him as much as Moses. "Moses's presence," it predicted, "can only mean trouble."[16]

When Moses drove Block to Greenwood on June 18, the latter started his project alone and penniless. Applying Moses's slow organizing techniques and advice, he recruited local canvassers and arranged citizenship classes within two months. But after several organized courthouse trips, white opposition surged. The Citizens' Council forced blacks to evict Block, while the police, he told the *New York Times*, "threatened to knock my teeth out." Harassment increased after he filed a police brutality charge for the beating of a falsely arrested black youth. When whites beat him savagely in August, Moses heeded his requests for reinforcements in the persons of Lawrence Guyot and Luvaughn Brown. Three days later, the three were forced to escape over the rooftop from the SNCC office to circumvent a white mob.[17]

To show locals, now thoroughly intimidated, that SNCC would not leave, Willie Peacock joined Block full-time. As they succeeded in bringing a small group of locals, including NAACP leader Dewey Greene, into the project, Block felt so confident about its viability that he asked Moses if he could leave town and study in Houston for a few weeks.[18]

Because of this success, Moses pondered making Greenwood—instead of Jackson—SNCC's state headquarters. Amplified white opposition following the Ole Miss riots then made the Greenwood project the first COFO program to gain national fame. In October, Leflore and Sunflower County officials voted to stop their surplus commodities programs, which provided food and clothing to 5,000 welfare recipients throughout the year and 22,000 others during winter. Because over 90 percent of recipients were black, many viewed the cutoff as retribution for COFO. Leflore officials maintained that the reasons were financial; the *Jackson Daily News* even celebrated the ending of recipients' alleged "greed, fraud, [and] fakery." U.S. Commission on Civil Rights investigators urged the federal government to distribute surplus food, but to no avail. Meanwhile, Moses and the other COFO workers witnessed widespread poverty, including children without milk, shoes, or even clothes. Moses worried particularly about the situation in areas where the drought had cut crops because plantation owners could harvest most of it with machines, which deprived black workers of an income. "Commodities are the only way many Negroes make it from cotton season to cotton season," Charles

McLaurin and Charlie Cobb sounded the alarm bell in November. "If this is taken away . . . they have nothing at all."[19]

The cutoff affected Moses deeply. He described to SNCC's Martha Prescott how a black man's "silent hand reached over from behind" once when he was reading after finishing a bowl of stew and then took a neck bone and potatoes he had discarded. He poignantly asked her, "What the hell are you going to do when a man has to pick up a left-over potato from a bowl of stew?" Distressed, he illegitimately spent VEP money buying food for locals. VEP Director Wiley Branton reprimanded him, but Moses realized that if Mississippi did not provide for its black citizens, then COFO would have to offer a commodity drive of its own.[20]

The cutoff, Moses calculated, provided a unique opportunity for bridging the local *and* national movement. He asked Mike Miller of the Bay Area Friends of SNCC to organize a Committee to Aid Mississippi and solicited the Northern Student Movement (NSM) for money, food, clothes, and cars. He appealed for volunteers as well; anyone with "stamina and some skills, writing, preaching, singing, playing a guitar, would be good." He felt excited that "the struggle in the South rebounds into the North to bring new forces to play in that situation up there" too. Friends of SNCC groups (FOS) sprang up, and individual activists, organizations, and institutions, including churches and colleges, responded enthusiastically. Black Michigan State students Ivanhoe Donaldson and Benjamin Taylor drove trucks loaded with commodities from Detroit to the Delta twelve times. Chicago FOS sent three shipments, totaling 79,000 pounds of food. By February 1963, COFO could distribute 400 to 600 boxes a day. Harry Belafonte and black comedian Dick Gregory provided additional help. Gregory helped distribute 14,000 pounds of commodities flown in from Chicago—a dramatic picture the national media swooned over. Gregory inspired locals by teasing policemen. "Before long," Moses smiled, "everyone had a favorite Dick Gregory line." Gregory's presence strengthened SNCC's decision to stay in Mississippi but unsettled whites. The *Jackson Daily News* chastised his "cheap publicity stunt," and Governor Barnett publicly condemned northern media's gullibility in believing Gregory.[21]

Mississippi whites had clearly miscalculated the effect of the cutoff, and Moses and SNCC ingeniously exploited it to their and locals' benefit. By providing direct aid, COFO effectively set up a parallel welfare system, which it creatively turned into a novel organizing tool. Unlike earlier direct aid campaigns by the NAACP and others,

COFO's drive, which expanded to neighboring Delta counties, was also designed to organize the rural working class. "When a thousand people stand in line for a few cans of food," Moses reasoned, "then it is possible to tell a thousand people . . . they are trapped in poverty, that *they* must move if they are to escape." Before distributing commodities, he and other workers demonstrated how to fill in voter registration forms. Subsequently, he said, food became "identified in the minds of everyone as food for those who want to be free, and the minimum requirement for freedom is identified as registration to vote."[22]

While most blacks knew that the cutoff was retribution for COFO, few blamed it. With nothing left to lose, they might as well get involved—after all, COFO represented their only lifeline. This, Moses said, changed SNCC's reputation both locally and nationally, giving it "an image in the Negro community of providing direct aid, not just 'agitation.'" Nonetheless, many middle-class blacks, largely unaffected by the cutoff, remained reluctant to help. Most ministers refused involvement or usage of their churches as distribution centers. This left Moses to complain that "the lack of real cooperation from ministers is still the biggest single problem facing the local movement."[23]

Moses also worried over how the commodities should be distributed. Demand was always larger than the supply, and distinguishing the more deserving from the less was difficult. COFO staff agreed that movement participants should receive commodities first and that leftovers should be distributed on a "first-come, first-served" basis, but some argued that recipients should be required to register to vote. Fannie Lou Hamer, for instance, refused commodities until locals returned from the courthouse. Questionable as this policy was, Moses was unwilling to interfere with local agency to put a stop to it. In a similar instance, he was confronted with a minister who distributed commodities independently from COFO. Pressed by others in SNCC to either discipline or isolate him, Moses asked Aaron Henry to write him a letter requesting him to align with COFO. Such incidents indicate how thin the line was between welcoming grassroots initiatives and having them conform to SNCC's organizational preferences, even for someone as sensitive to local leadership as Moses.[24]

Most locals did not feel pressured to join the movement in exchange for food. Their participation represented something larger, Moses argued. "[Whites] could say people were hungry but they couldn't say they were apathetic [to civil rights] if for a little bit of food they were willing to risk everything." This became particularly clear when arsonists torched four black businesses near the SNCC office on February 20. Because the evening before an anonymous call had warned that the office would "be taken care of," Block believed that the businesses were burned by mistake. When local newspapers published his accusations, he was arrested for "breach of peace." Several hundred blacks packed the court-room or waited outside when Block went on trial on February 24. Most came from nearby plantations or were unemployed town dwellers. Moses watched in amazement as blacks drank from "white" water fountains and plantation workers talked back to their bosses. They "really had their chests stuck out," Willie Peacock marveled, "They came to get Sam out." Refusing a suspended sentence if he left town, Block received a six-month sentence and a $500 fine but was released on bail. Blacks celebrated this as "a personal victory." That afternoon, they tried en masse to register and then attended the largest civil rights meeting Greenwood had ever wit-nessed. "Suddenly," Moses beamed, "Greenwood had a mass movement."[25]

Moses was thrilled. The massive support for Block, unseen at prior arrests of civil rights leaders apart from Martin Luther King Jr.'s in Albany, indicated the success of his slow organizing approach through direct, unyielding commitment to civil rights on a daily basis. Block had spent eight months building relationships. A silent majority had learned to respect him as they waited to feel comfortable enough to show it. Moreover, the cutoff demonstrated SNCC's genius in directing its aid drive toward the rural poor. This, Moses believed, explained why so many locals stood with SNCC but had shunned earlier activists. He had often doubted whether his sacrifices would be worth the gains, but now their rewards were visible. "This is a new dimension," he observed, "Ne-groes have never stood en masse in protest at the seat of power in the iceberg of Mississippi politics." But, he worried, "Who knows what's to come next?" Four days later, he knew the answer.[26]

ON FEBRUARY 28, Moses invited VEP field director Randolph Blackwell to Greenwood to discuss recent events, but as they met, an untagged Buick with three whites inside parked outside the SNCC office all day. By nine, it was clear that something was wrong. Moses suggested that those workers not stationed in Greenwood return home. Unsure of what the whites in the Buick would do if they left, one worker went outside and drove around the office to test the whites' reaction. As expected, the Buick followed him. Willie Peacock therefore argued that nobody should leave, but Moses pro-posed that they break up in groups to minimize the danger.[27]

Moses, Blackwell, and Tougaloo student Jimmy Travis took a back road to reach the highway. But when they stopped for fuel, the Buick circled the gas station. For Blackwell, the experience was nerve-wracking. "I don't know how these kids are able to stand up to the strain," he commented afterward. "It seems like being in combat, where you move through the town expecting anything to happen." The other two had been in similar situations before—tales of Moses's ability to fall asleep during car chases had become legendary—but now, Blackwell told the *Chicago-Sun Times*, they "knew they would be attacked. The only question was when."[28]

Dimming the lights, Travis returned to the highway. When the traffic thinned out, the whites drove next to them and opened fire with a submachine gun. As glass shattered and the car plunged off the road, Travis fell into Moses's lap while Moses desperately tried to hit the brakes. Thirteen bullets were later recovered from the car. Miraculously, only Travis was hit, in the neck and shoulder. Doctors at the Greenwood hospital told them that the bullet in his neck was lodged behind his spine, close to a vital brain area. Had the window not slowed its impact, he would have died instantly. Travis nonetheless refused an operation because, he later testified to Congress, "I thought [the doctors] wouldn't do the best they could." He was transported to the hospital at Jackson's State University the next morning.[29]

Moses was torn. He knew that the bullets had been intended for him; he had been the number one target on the KKK's assassination list ever since McComb. He was even more alarmed to find that two of the perpetrators turned out to be well-known businessmen. If the shooters were "respectable[,] rational people" instead of "white trash," he asked a reporter, "how do you accept [and] deal with that?"[30]

FBI and local police investigations, aided by Justice Department personnel, ensured the two businessmen's arrest, but the FBI soon decided that the shooting was a local, not federal, concern and relinquished the case. The police released the two on bail and never charged anyone. In November 1964, the district attorney, a former FBI agent, dropped all charges against the two. Such incidents accordingly strengthened activists' reluctance to cooperate with the FBI and southern police.[31]

THE SHOOTING KICK-STARTED the third phase of the Greenwood project. Wiley Branton summoned activists nationwide to converge and initiate, in Moses's words, "a crash program to get as many Negroes as we could . . . to register." With the shooting, Branton wrote Governor Barnett, Leflore County had "elected itself the testing ground for democracy."[32]

Some fifty organizers answered the call. The NAACP sent Medgar Evers and Aaron Henry, CORE sent James Farmer and Dave Dennis, and SCLC Annelle Ponder and James Bevel. Branton alerted Robert Kennedy of the activists' influx "so that you can provide . . . the necessary federal protection." In subsequent weeks, John Doar repeatedly visited Greenwood, as did reporters from the *New York Times* and other northern news outlets. This escalation, the *Atlanta Journal and Constitution* predicted, "could be as important a step in voter registration as the Freedom Rides were in interstate transportation."[33]

Moses felt ambivalent about the new tactic but acquiesced as it "seemed to be the only way to answer this kind of violence." He recognized the importance of publicity and even asked Anne Braden to publicize the Greenwood story overseas. But Moses also feared long-term negative consequences for all COFO projects if SNCC workers were forced to give up their projects in other Mississippi counties. The influx might even chill the effect of Block's earlier slow organizing. Yet precisely *because of* the preceding months of building relationships and distributing aid, the influx of workers bolstered local empowerment. Mass meetings were packed and 250 locals had attempted registration by March 21. Momentum gained despite—or because of—new violence.[34]

When nightriders torched SNCC's office and shot up Dewey Greene's house, tension continued to escalate. The next day, 170 blacks gathered outside Wesley Chapel. Remembering the disruptive consequences of the McComb march, Moses was not enthusiastic when James Forman, who had briefly come down from Atlanta, suggested that they march to city hall to protest the shooting. As in McComb, however, he knew he had to follow locals' decisions. If they were to march, he argued, they should march to the courthouse and try to register. This kept the focus on voter registration and minimized the possibility of violence. They compromised on a march to the courthouse via city hall. But once there, some dozen gun-toting officers awaited them with a growling German Shepherd.[35]

Mayor Charles Sampson warned the marchers to disperse or he would release the dog. This prospect terrified Moses, who had a phobia of dogs. Yet he pressed on toward the dog and asked to speak with the police chief, which instantly enhanced his reputation of fearlessness. The police then charged into the crowd with sticks and unleashed the dog, which tore a gash in Moses's pants and bit twenty-year-old Matthew Hughes. The panicked group returned to the chapel, while the normally reserved Moses angrily proclaimed that "the dog is going to have to bite every Negro in Leflore County before we quit!" The police soon arrived at the chapel to arrest him and nine other SNCC workers, including Peacock, Guyot, and Forman.[36]

SNCC worker Cleveland Banks and Forman's wife Mildred managed to see Moses at the police station. He told them to alert sympathizing organizations to break the story. Pictures of the dog biting Hughes then spread across the nation. Reporters returned to Greenwood to witness a similar spectacle the next day, when forty blacks tried to register. On their way home, policemen with dogs again lunged into them, although they were neither marching nor protesting. Local blacks were outraged. "I never thought," sighed one, that "Greenwood peoples would treat Negroes that been around here, that nursed their children, cook for 'em and farm this land, that they would put dogs on humans . . . I will never overcome it."[37]

Meetings and citizenship classes were packed and middle-class blacks, including thirty-one ministers, now openly supported the movement. Moses estimated that local supporters numbered 600 in April. The *Greenwood Commonwealth* sniffed, "When you can draw only 400 people out of a Negro population of 30,000, you aren't stirring many folks up." Moses thought otherwise. "[A]nyone looking deeper would have seen one key transformation. Black people had learned how to stand on their feet, look the white man in the eyes, and say this is what we demand." For another week and a half, similar-sized groups went to the courthouse to register. Police kept arresting them, but with the national spotlight on Greenwood, dogs were never used again. During some trips, Dick Gregory rejoined them. To evade negative publicity, police avoided arresting him, but his presence drew massive news coverage regardless. Publicity soared when renowned civil rights leaders like Martin Luther King Jr. expressed support for Greenwood's blacks. Mayor Sampson had to defend his town on the *Today Show*. Southern journalists even investigated Moses's draft status but found, to their dismay, that army quotas were already being met.[38]

Moses's northern network instantly responded as well. Old roommate Bob Cohen urged supporters to "send five dollars a week to Bob—to ease his way." Moses's father backed his son, too. "Someone's got to fight," he proclaimed. "I'm scared to death that Bob may die [but] I want him to stay there." When Moses and the other nine went on trial on March 29, 150 local blacks gathered outside for support. Curtis Hayes and Bobby Talbert were found innocent, but Moses and the others received four months' imprisonment and $200 fines for "disorderly conduct." They refused bond, while SNCC urged its supporters to protest the sentences to federal and state authorities. Moses's New York friend Lawrence Benenson immediately requested the White House to deploy federal marshals.[39]

The time spent in jail resembled Moses's confinement in Magnolia. The group passed time reading, playing chess, singing freedom songs, and educating one another. Focusing on what their imprisonment could achieve, Moses wrote an open letter, which the others signed and SNCC published. Unlike his "Letter from Magnolia jail," it addressed national politicians, not a local audience. It asked for the enactment of legislation that provided federal protection for civil rights workers and voter registration applicants. Without such action, Moses predicted, there might be more incidents like at Ole Miss that would rock the country and cause "irreparable harm in her international affairs." Several recipients, such as California Congressman Augustus Hawkins, subsequently vowed commitment to Moses's cause.[40]

When John Doar visited the prisoners on April 3, it dawned on Moses that the stir they caused in Greenwood had moved the administration more effectively than two years of collecting evidence. The FBI had sent six agents, and Burke Marshall was now negotiating with Greenwood officials. That afternoon, President Kennedy, who faced increasing pressure from the Commission on Civil Rights and liberal congressmen, endorsed their case on television. He expressed the hope that the federal lawsuit, which the Justice Department had now filed against the city of Greenwood, "would find that there has been a denial of rights, which seems to me evident, but which the court must decide." Representing the first head-on collision with segregationists about voting rights beyond suits against individual registrars, the government requested an injunction to end interference with registration efforts and allow blacks their constitutional right of peaceful assembly and protest. Local blacks, Charles McDew wrote, saw it as a sign "for a change, that the government is on their side." News of the suit excited Moses, too. That night, Forman's diary reads, Moses was "in rare form . . . standing behind the bars singing alone, talking about freedom." He could not have anticipated what would come next.[41]

The next morning, all of a sudden, the cell doors opened—the Justice Department had arranged their release. Moses and the others left prison singing in front of dozen cameras, but their euphoria evaporated when they learned that Doar had agreed to postpone the lawsuit and cancel the hearing. The city promised to reactivate the surplus food program if the federal government funded it and to provide a bus to drive blacks to the courthouse. Whites recognized the deal as a victory because registrars could still disqualify blacks based on all the state's legal requirements; by 1964, still fewer than fifty blacks had managed to register.[42]

Moses found the deal inexplicable. How could their release supersede establishing the constitutional rights of an entire people? Doar sought out Moses, who roamed gloomily through Greenwood, in an effort to explain. Political and legal reasons were plentiful: fear of alienating the southern voting bloc, more time needed to prepare the case, and the possibility that the suit would lose or be stalled in court. The most viable reason was fear that local officials, as in Oxford, would abdicate their duties and the administration would have to ensure order by utilizing the army. But Doar knew that such explanations would sound hollow to Moses. When the latter greeted him with a desolate look, Doar kept his explanations to himself and simply said goodbye. After that, he said, "a barrier of formality" existed between them. Moses still believed years later that "we got sold out in Greenwood."[43]

GREENWOOD PROVED a turning point for Moses and SNCC. They had learned that the federal government would never be a true partner, but raising a media spectacular could nevertheless bend its will and it need not come at the expense of grassroots leadership. For Moses, this finally legitimized his plans to dramatize the Mississippi situation to unprecedented levels that had gradually been forming in his mind the preceding months.

For Moses, the events in Birmingham, Alabama, which displaced Greenwood from newspapers' covers in April, reinforced the need. SCLC had joined Fred Shuttlesworth's Alabama Christian Movement for Human Rights in a citywide desegregation campaign that culminated in mass meetings, sit-ins, and James Bevel's brainchild, the children's crusades. Police unleashed dogs and fire hoses on hundreds of children, who were then arrested. The unprecedented scenes shocked whites and blacks alike, which led to renewed negotiations with city officials. SCLC gained desegregation concessions, which, however small and tentative, were celebrated as a breakthrough for the civil rights movement. More important, they helped persuade President Kennedy to introduce a strong civil rights bill.[44]

Moses watched the effects of the Birmingham campaign with ambivalence. It had galvanized the movement everywhere. Simultaneously, it exacerbated local tensions between direct action–oriented groups like SNCC on the one hand and the NAACP on the other. For example, in Greenville, Mississippi, middle-class blacks formed an adult Negro Citizens Group that agreed to stifle direct action and encouraged "class-conscious parents" to stop their children from attending COFO meetings where they would be rubbing shoulders with "hoodlums from the pool halls."[45]

Something similar occurred in Jackson. Since late 1962, Jackson's NAACP Youth Council had been conducting a boycott against discriminating businesses. Seeing a boycott as too conservative and middle class oriented, COFO workers had been less than enthusiastic. Boycott leader John Salter even complained that Moses had done "everything he could do to pull our student activists into his projects." When white leaders refused to negotiate, Medgar Evers vowed "to move Jackson," as Moses paraphrased him, "because if people up in Greenwood could get themselves together . . . then there was just no excuse for Jackson." But the national NAACP refused all support—until Birmingham. Only then, fearing that SCLC might intervene, Roy Wilkins and Gloster Current came to Jackson. Their appearance drew more conservative blacks into the boycott strategy committee, but the leadership remained divided over demonstrations. The original boycotters—evoking Birmingham too—called for direct action, but the conservatives opposed. When the students nonetheless launched sit-ins, Wilkins appeared supportive; he even got himself arrested. Behind the scenes, however, he and Current ensured the addition of more conservative blacks to the boycott committee to stop the costly and order-disturbing protests. They finally succeeded in the first week of June.[46]

To Moses, Birmingham and Jackson underscored the methodological differences among SNCC, SCLC, and the NAACP. The Jackson movement's premature decline proved exactly why participatory democracy was the only effective approach to social change. Greenwood, where the movement continued as before when most outside activists left in mid-April, showed that out-of-state forces could not undermine grass-roots leadership if a town was united around a nondivisive strategy (voter registration) and organized along the lines of Moses's slow organizing approach. After the 1961 failure of the Bevels, neither premise was realized in Jackson. SNCC also condemned the national NAACP's timidity and criticized SCLC for its "hit-and-run" tactics, which stirred up media attention but, as in Albany, left locals at the mercy of duplicitous white officials when the group left town.[47]

During the spring and summer, Moses contemplated these lessons of Greenwood, Birmingham, and Jackson. He already noted in February that "national publicity, if correctly used and focused, is a powerful weapon in any move for change in Mississippi." He now seriously pondered marrying voter registration with mass direct action. At SNCC's Easter Conference, he praised the Greenwood events but proclaimed that "what you need is not five hundred but five thousand going down [to register]." After all, "the country is in effect asking all white people in the Delta to do something which they don't ask of any white people any place," that is, allowing blacks to vote "where they are educationally inferior but yet outnumber [whites]." He did not "for one minute think that the country is in a position or is willing to push this down the throats of white people in the Delta." But, he added in a new militant tone, "it will have to be pushed down their throats because they are determined not to have it done." Birmingham could be used as a catalyst. Mississippi's black community "before Birmingham was not ready to demonstrate en masse," he repeated in June before a War Resisters League–sponsored forum in New York, but now "it may be possible to launch this kind of thing."[48]

Moreover, Moses found that telling New Yorkers about Mississippi had become easier. "[T]hey couldn't understand [but after] Birmingham, the problem had all of a sudden become a national problem." The Mississippi movement, after all, did not occur in a vacuum. In fact, "the Negro knows from his radio and television what happened today all over the world," Medgar Evers argued, "about the new free nations in Africa [and] that a Congo native can be a locomotive engineer, but in Jackson he cannot even drive a garbage truck." The increased frequency and intensity of black protests in 1963 underscored the idea that civil rights was a national issue; between spring and summer, 930 demonstrations occurred in 115 cities in eleven southern states. Nationwide, 1963 counted 1,412 civil rights demonstrations. SNCC conducted protests in

Nashville, Greensboro, Atlanta, Knoxville, Cambridge (Maryland), and Danville (Virginia). The wave of protests influenced public opinion and intensified pressure on the Kennedys. It therefore seemed logical for Mississippi SNCC to consider a new, broader approach that fused grassroots leadership with a national movement to take advantage of the opportunity to command new federal civil rights legislation.[49]

Yet, for Moses, any approach reshaping the Mississippi movement's scope still had to be based in grassroots leadership. The national had to work for the local rather than using the local to reach national goals; any outside appeal should be rooted in the needs of Mississippi blacks, not those of national organizations, the media, or politicians. For Moses, this implied that Mississippi SNCC should expand, not abandon, its slow organizing approach. In fact, he believed in the latter's value even more. Without it—as Greenwood and Jackson showed—no mass-based political thrust could be successful; blacks would be unwilling to respond. If COFO, using a staff of more than 100 SNCC workers working in each town, could pressure the federal government to abolish the poll tax, outlaw literacy tests, and get federal referees at courthouse as well, he outlined in June, "there is a real possibility that in 1964 we can run a Negro for Congress and have a good chance of getting him elected."[50]

YET NOT UNTIL the fall of 1963 was Moses open to catering to a national constituency as a goal in itself. Between February and September of that year, he was much more focused on his indispensable role, not just as an organizer, but as a teacher. Most local blacks still did not see the value of running for elective office, and Mississippi staff remained skeptical for fear it might jeopardize relations with the nonpartisan VEP. Yet Moses felt that the readiness of Greenwood's black poor to register illustrated the potential for reshaping discussions—among blacks as well as whites—on the true meaning of citizenship and who were "credentialized" to become leaders. He therefore continued to devote much of his behind-the-scenes work on furnishing (political) education to local blacks and COFO staff and translating Mississippi realities to outsiders with resources, most of all the federal government.[51]

In this, the issue of literacy had Moses's overriding priority. President Kennedy had proposed that Congress set the literacy level for voting at the sixth grade, but Greenwood, Moses argued, showed it had to be eliminated altogether. If not, he warned, "the fight for voter registration—citizenship—would be reduced to a fight for the right of well-educated

Blacks," roughly 10 percent of black Mississippians. Moses informed Burke Marshall that COFO would continue to take illiterate blacks to register. "Under 'Equal protection of the laws,'" he asserted, they "should not be required to take *any* literacy test, since they did not have access to equal, or in some cases any, educational opportunities." A large majority of middle-class blacks actually agreed that voting was a privilege intended for the educated. Even within SNCC, some believed in literacy requirements. Moses therefore repeated his arguments to the contrary whenever possible. During a testimony before the House Judiciary Committee in Washington in May, he even bluntly stated that "the country owes it to the Negroes who have been denied the right of an education to offer them an alternative[:] either they be registered without a literacy test [or] provided with a massive education program." He reminded the committee of the stakes. Delta blacks were "not going to stand by much longer and have people shoot in their homes," he predicted. If Congress failed to act and blacks—outnumbering whites two to one—organized around self-defense, Mississippi could erupt into something "ten times worse than Birmingham."[52]

Moses believed that black unemployment caused by automation and whites' unwillingness to train sharecroppers in new technologies made universal suffrage even more crucial, since he knew from personal experience that migrating north was no solution. According to Mary King, Moses often lamented how in northern urban ghettos, "families disintegrate from economic pressure; life is filled with the stress of over-crowding, crime, unemployment; no one has any roots, nor sense of community. In Mississippi, blacks belonged. They had built the state." He had thought deeply about ways to discourage black migration. "To maintain the balance of population in the Delta," he told the New York forum, "Negroes will have to be supported through a transition era [until] there's a break in the political situation." He even proposed a system in which northern cities would each supply food for a month to Mississippi blacks. Accordingly, King asserted, "Moses stood out as one of very few individuals in the movement who tried to look at long-range goals beyond the daily circumference of the struggle."[53]

In another instance, Moses and Charles McDew wrote Negro American Labor Council leader A. Philip Randolph about their concerns for "the tight circle of slum housing, poor schooling and resulting bad jobs." They proposed meeting in New York to discuss initiatives for "broadly based action." Shortly after, Moses started correspondence with Fay

Bennett of the left-leaning National Sharecroppers Fund (NSF) about training programs for southern rural youngsters. Bennett asked Moses for advice about getting American Rental Association loans into southern rural areas, so Moses connected her with Tougaloo President Daniel Beitel and other academics he knew. Displaying a keen sensitivity to political image, he advised Bennett to seek a government representative to vouch for the NSF; this kind of cover would "dissolve the ever present communist anxieties and save weeks of letter writing."[54]

The way Moses realized his Literacy Project further demonstrates the width of his resource network, his broader strategic vision, and his ability to work with(in) white institutions. He initiated the project after he discovered that teaching illiterate black adults in Greenville was hampered by a lack of appropriate instructional material. The Literacy Project adjusted its teaching material to southern rural blacks' realities by using, for example, easy-to-read pamphlets on Social Security and job training. This way, literacy also served as an organizing tool. The project was novel too in that it used software ("programmed instruction"). After Emerson professor Benjamin Wyckoff had developed basic materials at his request, Moses tried them out in Greenville. He attended courses on programmed instruction at Hamilton College and interested his former professor, John Blyth, who now worked on techniques using technology in adult literacy programs for the New York–based Diebold Group. Moses convinced the company to make a contribution, which he used to renovate a Greenville home to house the dozen COFO workers that would work on the project. He sought funds from the Field, Ford, and Stern Foundations and tried to interest officials at the Civil Rights Commission and the Southern Regional Council. He took Blyth to Washington to meet Burke Marshall, who helped secure $80,000 from the Taconic Foundation. Marshall's involvement underscores the point that there was a closer relationship between SNCC and federal officials than hitherto recognized. After all, Moses said, "The way this government works there is the official side of everything, and then there are all these unofficial links and relationships which have formed. And people who are in power like that are always in a position to help move different things around." Until Blyth and Diebold went to court over the material's ownership in late 1964, the project proved so successful that various organizations, including the United Nations, expressed interest. To aid local blacks' quest for literacy, Moses set up library facilities in Greenville and other COFO projects, for which he organized a year-long book drive with help from magazines like *Harper's* and *Atlantic Monthly.*[55]

Moses was keen to further the education of native COFO staff as well in order to better their chances of becoming future leaders. After all, Mary King said, "To merely change the players was not what Bob [and] SNCC wanted. We did not wish to replace something bad with 'anything goes.'" At SNCC's Easter Conference, he therefore expressed his wish for a mass education program. This was necessary, he elaborated in June, because "the big danger is that three or four years from now people will step into office . . . who have not been in any way identified with the Movement." Not having "associated with the mass of people," they "could then set up an Uncle Tom–kind of relationship with the white community."[56]

To this end, Moses helped organize a conference for COFO staff at Tougaloo, got Highlander to pay part of the rent for a Greenwood building that housed various educational programs year-round, pressed for scholarships for native COFO workers, and sent Mississippi workers to conferences in Texas and at Highlander. With the New York Friends of SNCC, he planned a workshop series for civil rights workers and asked the New York Center for Programmed Instruction to develop learning materials for COFO. He envisioned training fifteen students in these, who could be stationed "in each SNCC project solely to work on the educational problems of SNCC staff [and] selected members of the local community." After he proposed that SNCC set up a tax-exempt arm to facilitate its educational work, Ella Baker organized FELD (Fund for Educational and Legal Defense), which provided scholarships for SNCC workers. Moses meanwhile masterminded the Tougaloo Work-Study Program. Dona Richards and Oscar Chase, a Yale law graduate, directed the program from Jackson. The concept was simple. SNCC workers received a $1,000 Field Foundation scholarship to spend a year at Tougaloo College after they had carried out a year of voter registration work. This construction enabled staff to deepen their understanding of the movement by attending classes on current social issues and learning from nationwide experts in the field.[57]

While working on the program, Moses fell in love with Richards. This union was not surprising; the two had much in common. Dona Richards, a twenty-two-year-old black student from New York, had attended the integrated Elisabeth Irwin High School in Manhattan, the city's first school based on John Dewey's principles of progressive education. Her education thus resembled that of Moses at Stuyvesant. In 1959, she went to the University of Chicago and received her BA in philosophy four years later. Where Moses carried books by Camus, Richards carried Whitehead, one of his Harvard analytical philosophers. Dressed in jeans, she has been described as "plucky," "guileless," and "feisty." Mary King even characterized her as "a woman of the 1990s living in the 1960s" because of her progressive feminist views. Moreover, she was devoted to grassroots leadership and displayed the same kind of bravery in her commitment to civil rights as her new boyfriend. In some ways, she was even more spirited than Moses. In July, she had joined protests in Baltimore, Maryland, where she got arrested with 282 others in an attempt to integrate Gwynn Oaks Amusement Park, and in May 1964, she daringly applied to the Law Department of Ole Miss although she was never accepted; after consulting with the MSSC, the director of admissions used bureaucratic tricks to bar her from admission.[58]

Moses liked what others termed Richards's "fierce independence," which matched his own. Being "egalitarian by nature," Moses approached gender roles, to quote Julian Bond, "more sensitively than Martin Luther King, if not perfectly free of gender bias." His mother's wish to work outside the home and the example of strong-willed women such as his aunts, Ella Baker and Fannie Lou Hamer, likely influenced his views on the potential of women in the freedom struggle and society at large, and Richards reinforced them. Generally, SNCC men, who witnessed female bravery in their projects daily, were more open to such matters than SCLC's ministers. But Moses's academic training also had something to do with this. Mary King and Casey Hayden, for instance, regularly lent him works by feminist authors like Doris Lessing. When they challenged gender roles in SNCC in late 1964, they found him and Richards among their staunchest supporters. Minutes of a SNCC meeting even note that Moses "suggested considering the substantial change in Cuba of status of women" as a model for SNCC. He and Richards soon started dating quietly; Julian Bond only realized something was up when a nervous Moses got drunk at a party where she was and hit his head, since "Moses never drunk."[59]

There was little time for romance, however, as Moses was frequently on the road. He often visited other projects as well as politicians in Washington to arrange goods for COFO's commodities drives. He got the secretary of agriculture's commitment to deliver food through an independent agency and with Congressman John Lindsay discussed a "freedom garden" project with northern urban representatives distributing seeds to Mississippi blacks. Other activities included monitoring phone bills, arranging transportation for SNCC workers, collecting the Mississippi projects' budgets, and reporting these to the VEP. His administrative work was surprisingly detailed, which underscores that he was not an idealist who abstained from nitty-gritty operations. His budget for April 1963 to March 1964, for example, compared office expenses in Greenwood, Greenville, Clarksdale, and Hattiesburg and calculated costs for gas, car maintenance, lawyers' fees, and bail. He was nonetheless often late with financial or field reports, which led Wiley Branton to withhold $1,000 in VEP funds once. SNCC's Atlanta headquarters therefore prodded him to be punctual, although they tried not "to hustle you unduly [nor] implying that you might neglect such mundane matters as reporting in favor of the more interesting problem of staying alive."[60]

Furthermore, Moses did not limit his hands-on organizing to Mississippi. He helped coordinate a Literacy Program in Selma, informed himself about conditions in other states, and pondered solutions with nationwide implications. Some examples particularly reveal the depths of his broader vision for social change and how he used his northern connections to advance it. When Peter Countryman of the NSM asked him about organizing a voter registration drive in Virginia, Moses replied that he had thought frequently about the state. Remembering his own experiences in Newport News, he advised starting the drive in the Hampton and Norfolk areas and perhaps join with students from Hampton Institute. "Given the power of Virginia in Congress," he predicted, "this could have important political effects if it were successful." He suggested contacting Virginia SNCC and his Uncle Bill to get started. When SNCC proposed building a community center in Greenwood in November, Moses similarly recommended his architect uncle as the designer. Moreover, in December, he proposed organizing black college students in the upper South. "What happens in the border states now will set the tone for what happens in the Deep South," he explained. He also advocated supporting home rule in Washington, D.C., because he believed "it would be a shame not to make a national issue of this . . . since the South uses Washington [to exemplify] the failure of integration."[61]

Moses forged North-South alliances through his love for folk music as well. In mid-1963, he asked Bob Cohen and his New World Singers for a workshop on freedom songs in Edwards "to 'teach-back' the songs that had originally come from Southern black culture." Moses thought the Singers' presence so important that he even reprimanded some local youth who were busier smacking mosquitoes than listening to the music. On July 6, SNCC organized a Delta Folk Jubilee on Laura McGhee's farm to lift movement participants' spirits. Theodore Bikel, Bob Dylan, and Moses's 1950s' inspiration, Pete Seeger, performed for black Mississippi-ans and several from neighboring Tennessee. Even some Tennessee whites dared to attend. During 1963, SNCC regularly organized festi-vals and concerts in the North to raise funds. Moses attended at least one such concert at Carnegie Hall. Although he attended merely as a fellow SNCC worker, he discussed its potential worth with organizers Joanne Grant and Ella Baker, inquired about the artists' promotional activities, and proposed hiring someone who was "Negro, Responsible, From the South" to work in SNCC's New York office with artists and other northern "sophisticates" on a permanent basis. He similarly cooperated with folk musicians Guy and Candie Carawan on a fundraising album with music and testimonies from Greenwood movement participants. He narrated its storyline because he appreciated its educational value as an "attempt at documentation" but did send recordings to interested organizations through Californian filmmaker Harvey Richards.[62]

Yet when Moses sought northern publicity, he stuck to familiar pat-terns. He regularly contacted *Harper's* John Fisher, whom he kept up-to-date on Mississippi conditions. Moses met others in the publishing business too, like *The Nation*'s owner George Kirstein, and proofread manuscripts others wrote about Mississippi. He especially used such con-tacts to publicize cases of atrocities against Mississippi blacks. By now, his preoccupation with whites' lack of interest in the value of black lives had grown almost into a personal mission. He steadfastly sought public-ity for Clyde Kennard, a black Mississippian falsely sentenced to seven years' imprisonment for stealing $5 worth of chicken feed. Moses ex-tracted a promise from *The Courier* for a cover story on Kennard and suggested that the SNCC office in Atlanta contact Kennard's mother for letters. He also sought publicity for the fifty-eight locals arrested in Itta Bena, emphasizing that "this incident cannot be ignored by the Amer-ican people." He told Fisher that he thought the case "really is a fan-tasy. Seventeen are . . . in maximum security." Along with the National

Council of Churches (NCC), whom Moses sent tapes of the story, he helped raise bail and got the Justice Department to file for their release after interviewing witnesses.[63]

The year 1963 progressed with new violence at an intensity not seen since 1955. Moses's concern over the invisibility of blacks' lives then solidified his acceptance of a more nationally oriented approach. Events in Jackson underlined the need. A sniper, Greenwood Citizens' Council member Byron De La Beckwith, assassinated Medgar Evers on his driveway on June 12—the day after President Kennedy proposed new civil rights legislation. Angry, blacks marched in the streets of Jackson, but police stopped them with violence. After Evers's funeral, 5,000 blacks marched again. When police used clubs and dogs, they retaliated with bottles and bricks. Blacks' willingness to resort to violence—as Moses had predicted in May—underscored their desperation with the racial situation. COFO workers felt a similar disillusionment with nonviolence. "I saw a cop chase women [and] beat people unmercifully," one recalled, "I stood up against a tree and just cried 'cause I couldn't do anything because I promised I wouldn't [but] I couldn't see myself preaching that to anybody." With Evers's death, the Mississippi movement lost an important mediator between its conservative forces and the new militant ones.[64]

The Jackson events angered Moses so much that he telegraphed the U.S. Commission on Civil Rights, demanding instant hearings in the state. "It is now apparent," he asserted, that the Justice Department "lacks the necessary manpower and legal equipment [to] fulfill its obligations." He particularly blamed the Federal Judiciary in Mississippi, which was "by no means able to respond to . . . the emergencies of our times with intelligent constructive judicial action" due to its close cooperation with racist law enforcers. That Evers's assassin came from Greenwood proved his suspicions that local authorities there conspired with racist extremists. It upset him especially that law officers often retaliated on blacks unaffiliated with the movement. "The country cannot demand the strong legislation needed from Congress because it . . . cannot connect these stray facts which drift through Mississippi's Cotton Curtain," he concluded. "Only a hearing of the full Commission can command the authority to present these facts to the country."[65]

Meanwhile, leaders of national civil rights, labor, and philanthropic organizations, united in the United Civil Rights Leadership Council (UCRLC), began executing A. Philip Randolph's long-cherished plans for a massive March on Washington. The event, held on August 28, 1963, is mostly remembered for King's "I Have a Dream" speech. SNCC chairman John Lewis addressed the audience as well, but only after civil rights leaders like Randolph, Rustin, and King pressured him to censure parts of his government-critical speech. This incident served to strengthen SNCC's suspicion of the federal government, mainstream civil rights organizations, and coalition politics.[66]

Prioritizing Mississippi blacks' needs at the event, Moses stayed away from the "excitement" over Lewis's speech. He attended the March with several busloads of COFO staff and black Mississippians. Some, like Herbert Lee's widow, were brought onto the Lincoln Memorial platform with entertainers like Peter, Paul, and Mary. Spotlighting them, as one worker explained, "helped them believe that they were not alone." Moreover, this was necessary because, Moses complained, "the March's organizers didn't think it important that blacks from the Deep South be present. Nor was there any attempt to foreground them [like] a banner leading a section of the march for sharecroppers denied the right to vote. [Instead] the March recruited those who already had the vote." His main activity was therefore picketing the Justice Department with a sign asking, "When There Is No Justice, What Is The State But a Robber Band Enlarged?" Afterward, he spoke with John Doar and Burke Marshall. While the picket underscores the differences between Moses and Martin Luther King Jr.—with the former exercising his Camus-inspired moral leadership by example-approach and the latter trusting inspirational speeches—Moses denied having such consciousness at the time. "King became the star of the event after his speech, not before . . . so the decision to picket could not have had anything to do with King. To suggest that is to see King through what he has become in history's eyes and to completely miss the eyes and mind-set of SNCC." After all, the picket was not Moses's intellectual property. From the start, SNCC had advocated that the March went past the Justice Department. The UCRLC had rejected the seemingly militant notion, but some SNCC workers insisted. Supporters of the "Albany Nine," a group of SNCC workers arrested for picketing the store of a juror who had acquitted a sheriff guilty of shooting an Albany black, and of four SNCC workers charged with the capital crime of sedition for marching in Americus, Georgia, therefore picketed the department that day as well.[67]

Nor was the picket a condemnation of King's methods. Moses followed what he believed was the most significant contribution he could make that day, in the same way that SNCC's flexible organizational structure allowed other SNCC workers to appear on stage or stay in their projects if they thought this more useful—or, like Malcolm X, considered the March pointless. This did not imply that he rejected others' decisions to appear in the spotlight. He recognized that that fulfilled a purpose too. He identified with organizers like Rustin. "Bayard did not organize that March so that he could himself emerge as a leader; the march was organized so that someone like King could emerge.... That's the mark of an organizer [as opposed to a leader]." In this reasoning, what Rustin did for King was the same as what Moses tried to do for Mississippi blacks. Organizing and leadership were thus not mutually exclusive domains but rather intrinsically linked complementary stages in producing social change.[68]

Despite outward appearances, Moses clearly understood how a media event like this could help the civil rights struggle. He and SNCC picketed the department knowing that the March's momentum provided extra coverage for their causes and added pressure on the administration. What is more, the March on Washington deeply influenced Moses's thinking about federal legislation and how to attain it. In another instance of the local influencing the national and vice versa, President Kennedy had proposed a civil rights bill emphasizing desegregation after the events in Birmingham and Jackson. Moses thought the bill disappointing for its failure to address voting rights, but it indicated more might be possible in the future. The March strengthened this belief. Moreover, the probability of national legislation overlapped with Robert Spike's and his National Council of Churches' efforts to lobby for congressional and senatorial civil rights votes from Midwestern states. Both the March and the NCC's actions then percolated Moses's and COFO's ideas "about what we do and the country." Moses met Spike during the March, who told him about the NCC's nascent plans for a campaign focusing on Mississippi. After Evers's death, more organizations and individuals had similar plans, such as influential white Yale graduate and Horace Mann alumnus Allard Lowenstein.[69]

It was thus *after* Evers's death, Moses said, that "things begin to heat up more." By September, it became even more clear that SNCC needed to escalate its efforts. On September 15, the KKK blew up the Sixteenth Street Baptist Church in Birmingham, Alabama, killing four black girls and wounding twenty-three others. Outrage over the inconceivable reality that children were not even safe in church spread across the nation and the COFO projects. Sam Block documented how workers' "hearts are filled with many emotions . . . I for one have not yet recovered from the shock and anger." On September 18, eight thousand people attended the girls' funeral, eulogized by Martin Luther King Jr. Among them were Moses and a busload of Mississippi blacks and COFO staff he drove there. "There was no way we were going to miss going to their 'final say,' " he recalled the bombing's impact on him. "I had never driven a bus before in my life, but if that was what it took then we were not going to miss it!"[70]

Nonetheless it were the specific conditions and limitations in Mississippi that dictated Moses's and COFO's decision to escalate its efforts in the fall. Apart from the violence, COFO worried about its ability to meet blacks' demands for assistance. Moreover, with the large concentration of SNCC workers in Greenwood, Moses was concerned over the fact that "the work in the other areas really sort of suffered," as he had already predicted beforehand. Simultaneously, while more blacks than ever had joined the movement, the vast majority had not. Less than half of Mississippi's eighty-two counties had movement centers. Movement experiences in Claiborne County, for instance, appear more typical of Mississippi movement involvement than Greenwood's. The Claiborne NAACP branch had only twenty-seven dues-paying members, and apart from Moses's unsuccessful visit during the Smith campaign, COFO did not organize the county. Despite individual acts of defiance, overall locals felt the national movement was like South Africa's anti-apartheid movement. "It's just that far away. So never ever would that upset what was going on here." Although they followed the news, which "sparked the desire," a broad-based, sustained movement did not emerge until after the 1965 Voting Rights Act. Moses admitted that most blacks "were frozen," an attitude the summer's violence aggravated.[71]

While most SNCC workers cite Greenwood as its biggest success in developing local leadership, it is unclear whether this happened due to or despite its large contingent of workers. Local leadership continued to develop after most outsiders left in April, but as time progressed, the Greenwood movement developed into a stalemate; the more workers in one place, the less effective it became. Workers failed to involve locals, morale was low, and they fought over clothing and food. Some therefore argued for the presence of cosmopolitan-educated individuals to curb the problems. "There is a need for the staff to have a conception of having a role in history," one wrote, because it is "largely because of [this] lack . . . that many of our current problems [arise]." Particularly Moses and Stokely Carmichael, he suggested, had to provide this understanding because it was "best conceived if it comes out of discussion of experience with the leadership . . . who have had the opportunity to see things in a broader perspective." Simultaneously, Wiley Branton worried that Moses already did "too much."[72]

Atlanta headquarters, for instance, asked Moses to act as a disciplinarian as part of his director job. He approached this as thoughtfully as always, but his style was not always effective in this area. It in fact strengthened SNCC workers' internal divisions. For example, in Greenwood, some locals criticized workers for their skirt-chasing, partying, occasional pushiness and failure to keep promises. Moses supported the idea of treating SNCC staff as being in "a learning and growing experience" in which "irresponsibility is handled with generosity . . . to help the person become more responsible." He characteristically operated from the premise that no one could be blamed for what one was never taught—whether it was literacy or organizing—and that individuals should be allowed to follow their own conscience. But since this had little immediate effect, Stokely Carmichael and others felt necessitated to endorse the view of SNCC as "an already disciplined group," Mike Miller documented. "After being hired, irresponsibility is not tolerated." They advocated that "staff should be cut" and "someone . . . given clear responsibility for the Greenwood project," despite Moses's repetitive calls to the contrary.[73]

Moses and COFO had clearly run up against a brick wall in Mississippi; they needed a different strategy in order to surmount their problems. Despite staff apprehensions, COFO therefore decided in September that it was time to develop Moses's plans for a large-scale protest geared toward voter registration. But this brought back Moses's leadership dilemmas with a vengeance: did this mean that he had to embrace the leadership role that was now widely thrust upon him? Or could he somehow remain "quietly circumscribed" in the state and salvage his ideals of grassroots and group-centered leadership by avoiding the use of personal power?

Bob Moses and his basketball teammates in *The Hamiltonian*, 1954.
Courtesy of Hamilton College.

Bob Moses as a member of the Honor Court in *The Hamiltonian*, 1955. Courtesy of Hamilton College.

Yearbook portrait of Bob Moses in *The Hamiltonian*, 1956. Courtesy of Hamilton College.

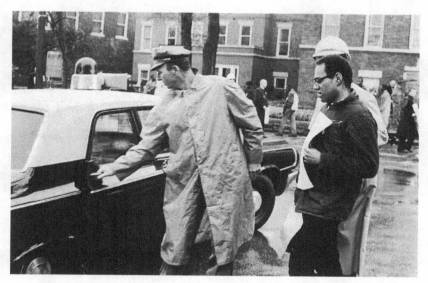

Arrest of Bob Moses in Hattiesburg, Mississippi, during Freedom Day, January
22, 1964. © Danny Lyon, Magnum Photos.

Moses contemplates the future of SNCC at Waveland, Mississippi, November 1964. © Danny Lyon, Magnum Photos.

Moses and Fannie Lou Hamer observe proceedings at the National Democratic Convention in Atlantic City, New Jersey, August 1964. © Matt Herron, Take Stock Photos.

(left) Moses addressing SNCC's 50th Anniversary Reunion, Raleigh, North Carolina, April 2010. © Laura Visser-Maessen.

(below) Moses and John Doar discuss organizing quality education initiatives at SNCC's 50th Anniversary Reunion, Raleigh, North Carolina, April 2010. © Laura Visser-Maessen.

Bob Moses talks to local woman on porch during voter registration drive, Mississippi Delta, 1963. © Danny Lyon, Magnum Photos.

CHAPTER SIX

Damned If You Do, Damned If You Don't

Between fall 1963 and spring 1964, Moses and COFO stood at a crossroads. While the March on Washington had raised expectations of a breakthrough in civil rights through federal legislation, the Birmingham church bombing and the assassination of President John F. Kennedy sapped those prospects' momentum. And Moses realized that the worst was far from over.

Yet Moses's plans for a mass-based voter registration drive formed the basis for COFO's first statewide project, the Freedom Vote. This successful campaign consolidated the Mississippi movement's convergence with the national civil rights movement. Originally a grassroots effort, it gained national significance through its controversial use of northern white volunteers. This prompted new discussions as Moses favored expanding its concept on an even bigger scale in 1964.

Preparations for this Mississippi Summer Project deeply divided the SNCC staff. To get the project accepted, Moses had to navigate between facilitating grassroots leadership and leading a national movement. This reached the core of his moral leadership dilemmas as never before. Not only did he have to persuade his colleagues of the necessity of bringing 1,000 northern whites into the state without misusing his personal power, but he also needed to salvage concerns over grassroots leadership and the knowledge that his actions would lead to more blood being spilled. For him, it was "damned if you do, damned if you don't."[1]

His singular preoccupation with breaking the never-ending cycle of violence against local blacks eventually overruled all other concerns. "It became clear that we had to do something, something big, that would really open the situation up. Otherwise they'd simply continue to kill the best among us."[2]

THE 1962 SMITH CAMPAIGN had left Moses isolated and his political organizing ideas unpopular among his fellow organizers. But by the summer of 1963, COFO workers were increasingly receptive to the idea of another political campaign, this time focused on the August 6 Democratic primaries for the gubernatorial nomination.

A new outside initiative made this strategy suddenly more appealing. When northern law students came to Jackson to research Mississippi's legal system, they uncovered a Reconstruction law designed to benefit unregistered whites, which allowed those denied the right to vote to cast affidavits as protest ballots. Local officials afterward would then have to decide whether to count them as legitimate votes. COFO decided to exploit this law for unregistered blacks. In mass meetings, workers taught blacks to write sample affidavits in Delta communities. Because the campaign was only a six-week affair, Moses looked outside Mississippi for maximum results. He asked members of Friends of SNCC groups to act as poll watchers, arranged national press coverage, and requested the presence of nationally renowned observers. The campaign provoked an unexpectedly large local black response. Some 1,000 Delta blacks cast ballots in black churches, homes, and businesses; another 600 were rejected at polls in Sunflower, Holmes, and Hinds Counties. Three weeks later an impressive 27,000 unregistered blacks cast affidavits in the primary runoff, even though all were disqualified. Paul Johnson, the most conservative candidate, won the Democrat nomination for governor.[3]

Johnson's election left Moses depressed. "It reinforces all that is bad in the state," he wrote SNCC's Executive Committee. "The full resources of the state will continue to be at the disposal of local authorities to fight civil rights gains; the entire white population will continue to be the Klan."[4]

Despite SNCC's success in generating local black involvement and substantial evidence for federal lawsuits, Moses came to the discouraging conclusion that in this way, black voter registration drives could never be effective in Mississippi. Only a drastic escalation of COFO's tactics could have any effect. "The only attack worth making," he argued in a newly militant tone, is one "aimed at the overthrow of the existing political structure[s] of the state. They must be torn down completely to make way for new ones."[5]

To do this, SNCC should prioritize the Mississippi project, he advised. Underscoring his long-term commitment to Mississippi, he argued that it should move its headquarters to Greenwood and launch a "One Man, One Vote" campaign to secure voting rights by 1964 and organize local political clubs to get a local black in Congress. Moreover, it had to explore ways to challenge James Eastland in the 1966 senatorial elections and elect "militant Negroes to local offices" in 1967. He presented his plans to SNCC in early September. SNCC refused to move headquarters but agreed to shift more personnel to Mississippi.[6]

By then, Moses's plans for the "One Man, One Vote" campaign were already on their way. Because the primary mock election had bolstered locals and SNCC workers as well as generated northern publicity, duplication of it on a statewide basis seemed a logical next step. Dubbed "the Freedom Vote," the campaign was an unprecedented, dramatic exercise in democracy. It represented continuity *and* discontinuity in movement tactics. Between November 2 and 4, COFO collected mock ballots among unregistered voters across Mississippi to elect the new governor. Participants could choose between Democrat Paul Johnson, Republican Rubel Philips (both pro-segregationists), and a COFO-backed Independent ticket of Aaron Henry with Edwin (Ed) King as his running mate. Registered blacks were encouraged to write in the Henry/King ticket during the real election on November 5. The overall goal of the Freedom Vote, Moses explained, was "to confront Mississippi people [and] the Federal Government with the issues which the politicians of the existing political machinery [are] dedicated to smothering." A projected turnout of 200,000 blacks could dramatize black electoral exclusion by disproving white politicians' claims that blacks did not vote because they did not care—a belief that, *Newsweek* claimed, 40 percent of white southerners shared.[7]

The Freedom Vote was the perfect means to further Moses's ideas about the rural black poor's inherent political abilities. Many middle-class blacks, especially black ministers, opposed the idea. They felt that a mock election wasted their time and jeopardized their jobs, businesses, and churches. Many argued that illiterate blacks should not be allowed to vote. The Freedom Vote thus became the first large-scale challenge to hegemonic ideas in both the white and black community of who is "credentialized" to run society. "We had to come to grips with this notion," Moses explained, "Who can legitimize people? How do a people get legitimate? Now these were notions that were coming out of the work itself and were slowly taking hold or growing in the workers' minds." One historian therefore called it a "revolution within a revolution" of "black 'have nots' against their former leaders, the black 'haves.'" One Holmes County black literally threatened a black grocer to participate or be boycotted.[8]

Moses knew they could benefit from the momentum that other SNCC and SCLC projects were garnering with similar projects. In Albany,

Georgia, SNCC backed two blacks running for political office and a large number of SNCC workers had joined Bernard Lafayette's voting project in Selma, where daily courthouse demonstrations had led to the imprisonment of 300 blacks. Jailed SNCC workers then conceived of a Freedom Day on October 7, which entailed amassing blacks at the courthouse to demand immediate registration. The Bevels were planning a statewide voting rights campaign with the purpose of defeating Alabama Governor George Wallace. Yet Moses succeeded in building a statewide campaign within months, whereas James Bevel's Alabama Project never really materialized. This contrast highlights the significance of individual personality and organizational leadership structures. SCLC dissipated its resources on campaigns elsewhere, and Bevel's flamboyant character alienated locals and SCLC ministers. Moses's consensus-building disposition and SNCC's flexibility and dependence on grassroots approval in turn produced a more solid campaign in Mississippi. Still, the similarity in approach underlines the fact that by the autumn of 1963, most civil rights organizations recognized an urgent need to escalate tactics.[9]

Moreover, Freedom Vote formulations converged with liberal whites' desire to become involved in the South after Birmingham, the March on Washington, and Medgar Evers's death. The South, Ella Baker observed, "became a sort of magnet.... So it wasn't just a question of developing national support [but] of providing opportunities for that drive on the part of young people . . . in the North and the West, to help with something."[10]

Arranging northern white involvement, however, was not straightforward. When one white liberal, Allard Lowenstein, proposed to enlist Yale and Stanford students' help in early September, Moses withheld an answer for weeks. Northern white involvement had never been part of his or COFO's original plan. Although CORE had used white volunteers in its Louisiana voting projects, Moses still feared that bringing them to Mississippi would invite physical danger and create psychological problems for black staff members. When SNCC headquarters pressured its Mississippi wing in the 1962–63 winter to integrate its staff, the latter had even flatly refused. Deferring to the local movement, headquarters then notified interested whites that "there are absolutely no openings to work in SNCC projects in Mississippi."[11]

Yet in a sense, Moses did not have a choice. By late 1963, a dozen whites had participated in the August primaries, and some worked full-time in Mississippi: Casey Hayden (Literacy Project), Hunter Morey (Greenville), Mike Miller and Dick Frey (Greenwood), CORE's Michael and Rita Schwerner (Meridian), and Mendy Samstein (Jackson). Mike Miller came for the Delta Folk Jubilee and instantly decided to stay. Miller recalled that Moses was hesitant to approve this decision because he feared violence. But after he, Sam Block, and James Forman "huddled, right there on Laura McGhee's farm," Moses agreed to "do a test. We'll see what happens with a white worker in the Delta."[12]

It failed miserably. Police arrested Miller shortly after, and the SNCC workers were forced to restrict white volunteers to the SNCC office. "We almost suffocated them," Moses admitted in November. "They couldn't go out in the street . . . they were wiping dishes[,] sweeping floors[,] doing all the dirty work [because] we wanted very carefully to avoid any trouble."[13]

Deploying northern whites as fieldworkers was thus highly controversial. Native blacks, like Sam Block and Willie Peacock, strenuously opposed the idea, arguing that it would endanger everyone involved. But SNCC's slow organizing approach could not accomplish a statewide enterprise within two months. Even with SNCC workers from other states, COFO needed more manpower. Equally important, Moses and the others were exhausted. Over the summer, several workers recorded witnessing, as one wrote, "the tired, tragic face of Moses." Something had to give.[14]

When Lowenstein cornered him in the Jackson office in late September, Moses agreed to his proposal with SNCC's half-hearted consent. "The need is desperate," he wrote the Yale and Stanford students, "and we would be grateful for any help you may be able to get us." Lowenstein then returned to California and helped recruit some seventy to ninety volunteers—although how the Mississippi office might ultimately decide to use them remained fluid.[15]

MOSES RATHER FOCUSED his energies on the campaign itself. From the start, it blended grassroots agency and professional coaching. On October 6, COFO organized a massive convention at Jackson's Masonic Temple. Five hundred local and full-time COFO workers from across the state—connecting them for the first time—attended. They elected Aaron Henry to head the ticket because he was well known, experienced, a Delta native, and attractive to conservative NAACP members. They approved a platform that went much further than most black Mississippians' political views, clearly reflecting SNCC influence. It advocated immediate universal suffrage, school desegregation by 1965, a crash program to improve the educational system, and the establishment of job retraining programs. Other planks included a just minimum wage, repeal of antilabor laws, and land reform. COFO then established a campaign organization in which locals and full-time organizers staffed state, district, and county committees. Aaron Henry toured the state giving a speech every night, and Jackson headquarters sought local radio and television time. The COFO office distributed 4,000 posters and 20,000 leaflets, while its Research and Publicity Department arranged transportation, prepared campaign material, and coordinated the media.[16]

Moses's role in the project gave him new stature in the national and local civil rights movement. Elected as campaign manager, he played a more visible role than usual, although much of his work took place behind the scenes. According to Aaron Henry, he was indispensable. He explained the campaign to locals and outsiders, organized press conferences, sent fundraising letters, contacted the Justice Department, and toured the state with Henry. The inclusion of Ed King on the COFO ticket, a white chaplain at Tougaloo College, directly reflected his views about integration as well as his keen insights into locals' psychology and the workings of the media. Moses, Henry, and others deliberately advocated an interracial ticket, but although Moses "preached at me," King was reluctant. He was still recovering from a car accident that he suspected to be caused by racists for his involvement in the Jackson demonstrations. But Moses was persistent. He asked him to "think of what it will be if we could show that people *are* interested in voting, and are willing to vote for black and white candidates who *ask* for their vote." Moses even argued that King's bandaged face could be used to the campaign's advantage. Although whites' involvement in King's accident was never established, Moses clearly wanted to use the idea regardless. On October 13, King agreed to join the ticket.[17]

Moses's most significant contribution lay in safeguarding the grassroots base of the enterprise and turning it into an unprecedented organizing tool. Seeing the effort as a means of ensuring long-term continuity for the movement—that is, a chance "to establish a real statewide community of leadership for Negroes"—he favored local agency whenever possible. He emphasized that community leaders should determine all election practicalities, such as opening times, and not to print the SNCC name on campaign material. He instructed workers to record people's contact information at polling places, buildings that served as meeting places, and who did what in the community.[18]

Moses nevertheless understood that national awareness helped determine the success of the Freedom Vote. He advocated the idea of celebrities and nationally known figures as poll observers and to invite entertainers at the final rally. Despite his work to drum up publicity, however, only local media attended the opening press conference on October 14. That evening's first campaign rally drew only 400 locals. Moreover, the budget was tight, and COFO needed money for so-called Vote Mobiles, twenty rented and fourteen staff cars with ballot boxes, that allowed workers to canvass remote areas faster. But it could not even pay a fifth of the proposed $20,500 budget. "We need your help— desperately," Moses wrote Lowenstein. "We will not be able to utilize the basic information media—posters, leaflets, and the news outlets— unless we can pay for them." Lowenstein subsequently approached re- nowned civil rights leaders like Martin Luther King Jr. and Roy Wilkins and media outlets such as *Life* magazine and NBC. SNCC sent out fundraising appeals and advised Friends of SNCC groups to contact newspapers in Boston, Chicago, and New York by using the "good angle" of Moses and Dona Richards, who had attended schools there. Despite sympathetic articles in the *National Guardian* and the *Village Voice*, national press coverage remained poor. However, few in COFO anticipated the publicity that the northern white volunteers would arouse upon their arrival on October 22.[19]

PUBLICITY HAD NEVER BEEN a reason for drawing upon white volun- teers. "We just wanted them to get out the vote," Moses insisted at a No- vember COFO meeting. In his view, the volunteers merely *augmented* rather than directed locals' initiatives, much like he saw his own involve- ment. "What distinguished the Mississippi movement from the foci of the other civil rights movements," he always maintained, was its grassroots-initiated "state-wide strategy," which *then* "led to a 'national picture/strategy'"—not vice versa. He never considered either Lowen- stein or the students as central to the effort. But Lowenstein saw it dif- ferently. "When I first got to Mississippi," he claimed in 1965, "everything was finished. The whites had won." He thereby advanced the idea that he and the resources he brought rescued the movement, a concept that many observers at the time and since have accepted.[20]

Having been dean at Stanford University, president of the National Student Association (NSA), and delegate to the National Democratic Convention, Lowenstein knew almost everyone of national importance, including Hubert Humphrey and other political heavyweights. Ella Baker and James Forman, who had disliked him ever since their days in the NSA, warned Moses repeatedly about his opportunism. He tended to think that since he recruited them, he controlled the volunteers, rather than having them work at locals' service. When Moses for instance told one volunteer not to go to Yazoo City because it was too dangerous, the latter complained to Forman that Lowenstein, not Moses, directed his moves. Forman exploded. "If Lowenstein told him to go to heaven and Moses said he should go to hell, then he'd better start packing his summer clothes." When Lowenstein brought a group of volunteers to Yazoo City regardless, John Lewis drove down and took them back to Jackson.[21]

The difference in Moses's and Lowenstein's leadership styles was also evident from the way they presented themselves and the movement. Lowenstein openly took credit for initiating the Freedom Vote. This greatly disturbed Moses, who always took great care to foreground locals' initiatives even as his behind-the-scenes work was vital. After all, he countered, the Freedom Vote had emerged as an "evolutionary process of looking at how to move." Discussions about running COFO-backed candidates had been ongoing since 1962. What is more, he argued, "the idea that it was important to record who first had such and such an idea is itself sort of foreign to the whole culture of the Movement."[22]

But Moses could also be pragmatic when needed. When such conflicts complicated his efforts—some in SNCC even blamed him for Lowenstein's presence—he characteristically sought consensus. He emphasized to the workers that Lowenstein had "a lot of contacts. I think we can work with him. Let's try it." According to Julian Bond, Moses nevertheless kept him "at arm's length." Not because he considered him "a bad person," but because he wanted "to take us in a direction we don't want to go." Similarly, Lowenstein admired Moses but questioned his judgments. Although he understood the need for grassroots involvement, participatory democracy was "wasting valuable time," and the absence of hierarchy meant that "who could do what was quite fuzzy."[23]

Nonetheless, the two complemented each other. "Lowenstein understood politics and America; Moses understood man and Mississippi.

Lowenstein['s task] was to see our problems from his unique perspective," Ed King explained, while Moses could "place it in a Mississippi framework." Lowenstein argued that "bitter" SNCC workers in hindsight have exaggerated conflicts between him and SNCC. Moses, he said, never felt he was undermining his leadership. In fact, Moses regularly defended him. For example, when SNCC workers were enraged over his escape from police by hiding in a segregated white restaurant, Moses pointed out that they often did the same in black ones. For the most part, Bond agreed, workers simply accepted Lowenstein as "a necessary evil."[24]

Most SNCC workers similarly appreciated the white volunteers. Since there was no time to train the whites in dealing with locals, COFO placed half of them in the Jackson and Greenwood offices. Their skills—typing, running mimeographs, and experience with political campaigns—were best utilized there, and their presence freed experienced COFO activists to work in the field. The students also brought money and contacts. They were in touch with their congressmen and hometown newspapers, and the Yale and Stanford communities raised $11,400. This helped SNCC to purchase a Wide Area Telephone Service (WATS) telephone line, which made long-distance calls much cheaper and allowed messages to be conveyed without fear of detection by whites. But some in COFO resented these "super-educated Americans." The office-field division of labor intensified resentment. As in Greenwood, it became evident that what made SNCC's group-centered leadership structure effective became its Achilles' heel when speedy decision making was required. Usually policies were determined in consultation with locals and as many COFO representatives as possible. Now the pressure of time, added to the growing scope of the project, made leisurely consultation more and more difficult. Smaller groups increasingly made decisions in the Jackson headquarters, where the white volunteers were concentrated. This fueled an unjustified suspicion among fieldworkers that the white volunteers, in Mendy Samstein's words, "were intimately involved in the decision-making process whereas they were excluded." According to Ed King, Moses appeased SNCC workers' concerns by saying "gently, 'We have to get along. This is helping us. We were able to get . . . a thousand leaflets printed that we otherwise could not have.' "[25]

When white volunteers joined the fieldworkers, the effect was just as double-edged. When experienced blacks accompanied a white volunteer during canvassing, they noticed how local blacks immediately directed themselves to the white and appeared "to agree with anything he said."

Some whites then simply *told* locals to complete the Freedom Ballot. While this increased the number of votes cast, it bypassed ideas of black empowerment. Charles Cobb noticed the same problem with COFO's few full-time white workers. Hunter Morey directed the Greenville project successfully but, Cobb complained, "Negroes are reacting to his whiteness, or completely accept the idea of a white directing Negroes. [They look at] whatever being white means today, not what it may mean after the struggle is over."[26]

The attention that northern papers lavished on the volunteers added to the resentment of some black COFO workers. Stories emphasized incidents like the beating of Yale student Bruce Payne and the false arrests of Moses and two other Yale students—one of them the nephew of a congressman—for ignoring a stop sign. Samstein sardonically recorded that during the campaign's final rally, "NBC spent most of their time shooting film of the Yalies and seemed hardly aware of the local people and full-time SNCC workers." Moses in a way catered to this as well by foregrounding former presidential candidate Norman Thomas, who toured the state on their behalf, at a press conference.[27]

Workers' resentment grew when the federal government, which publicly ignored the campaign to prevent further alienation of southern white voters, flooded Mississippi with Justice Department officials and FBI agents. Yet few agents were available in places where whites did not campaign, leaving black workers in danger. For example, when Charlie Cobb, Ivanhoe Donaldson, and Don Harris went to the Jackson airport in a rented Oldsmobile to drop Moses off for a short business trip to Memphis, a policeman arrived to question them. Because the workers had left the Oldsmobile's papers at the SNCC office, the policeman detained them. Before someone could arrive with the papers, however, the policeman released Moses to board his plane and ordered the others to leave. But as soon as the workers left, the officer, joined by two others he had summoned in the meantime, followed them and at a gas station chastised them for two hours. One falsely arrested Donaldson for having "illegal plates" and beat him twice with his gun while yelling, "Goddamned black bastards think they're going to be taking over around here. Well, you and the other goddamned Moses's niggers around here ain't gonna git nuthin but a bullet in the haid!" He placed his gun in Donaldson's face and cocked the hammer, but another policeman stopped him. "You just cain't kill that nigger, heah." They then let them go.[28]

Nonetheless, according to Stokely Carmichael, it was a revelation for Moses to see that due to the white students, overall "the violence could actually be controlled. Turned, y'know, on and off . . . at least for three weeks." Local whites mostly reacted with intimidation and arrests on trumped-up charges; sixty arrests occurred within twenty-one days on traffic violations alone (of a 200-arrest total). Many working-class blacks subsequently refused involvement, although Moses had done everything he could to ensure their safety. Because the volunteers would soon leave and COFO lacked the numbers to organize the entire state, the campaign committee, at Moses's insistence, decided not to go into all of Mississippi's counties. Rather than campaign in dangerous areas, COFO mailed 25,000 ballots to be returned anonymously. Whenever possible, workers sought white cooperation, but more often their enterprise resembled an "underground" operation. In Jackson, Meridian, and elsewhere, canvassing was done by dividing the towns into blocks, each covered by local students and headed by a community member—the "block captain"—to avoid detection and spur local agency. In Greenwood, workers canvassed in cotton fields but did so secretively in threesomes, dressed as fellow cotton pickers. One stood guard, another explained the campaign, and the third hid completed ballots in his cotton sack. In its final days, when the atmosphere surrounding the campaign reached fever pitch, COFO circumvented white hostility by campaigning during black church services. The majority of all votes obtained during the November 2 to 4 weekend came from such church collections, but blacks also voted in private homes, businesses, and social clubs. "[I]t turned out," Ed King noted, "that the people were angrier, more willing to suffer [and] fight than the leaders recognized."[29]

On Monday night, November 5, COFO workers gathered at the Masonic Temple to celebrate the results. An unprecedented 83,000 blacks voted,[30] with 99 percent voting for Henry and King. However, the numbers fell far short of COFO's goal of 200,000 votes, and a full two-thirds of the votes came from just eight counties. In twenty-five counties, fewer than 100 ballots were cast apiece, and only a fifth of the total votes came from areas with full-time COFO projects. COFO nevertheless hailed the result as a victory. "[H]ad there been no police interference," the campaign committee asserted, "Henry and King might have reached the total of more than 200,000 votes predicted . . . Governor-elect Johnson received less."[31]

For Moses, the conclusion of the Freedom Vote experiment was clear. A permanent fusion of the local and the national, albeit on grassroots terms, was the only viable direction forward for the Mississippi movement. "The measure of freedom has now been heard in every part of Mississippi because you took it there," he told the crowd, "Though we certainly can't realize it, history was being made all over the state this week." But, he went on, "We don't expect to correct the evils of Mississippi by this snail's-pace voting registration, but we do expect to build enough pressure to make it politically impossible for a federal government to remain so indifferent. . . . We expect our efforts to dissuade those who believe that anything less than federal troops will work."[32]

That night, he confirmed to the *Texas Observer*, discussions began about forming an insurgent local Democratic party that would send delegates to the Democratic National Convention in 1964. This would be part of a new plan he envisioned, the 1964 Mississippi Summer Project, another statewide project directed toward voter registration and building grassroots leadership aided by northern volunteers, albeit on a much larger scale. Moses estimated that the number of locals willing to do voter registration work had grown tenfold. COFO had expanded into new areas like Issaquena and Leake Counties, and over 60,000 Mississippi blacks had given their contact information. "Right now," Frank Smith told national SNCC, "Mississippi is [the] best organized of any SNCC project. . . . People are ready to move. A year ago [it took] 6 months to organize a town. Now we can do it in a month." Moses had finally found a way forward, but now he had to convince critics, not the least his fellow COFO workers, that his plans were not an abdication of but rather a means—the *only* means—to salvage substantial future grassroots movement.[33]

THE DECISIONS THAT ENSUED were among the most crucial of Moses's career in SNCC. Although he downplayed his own importance, his ability to think in broader terms shaped discussions over the Summer Project and ultimately decided its outcome. The incident provides a window into how Moses's leadership worked in practice, capturing perfectly how he struggled to reach a goal he saw as necessary without resorting to autocracy and through indirection approximated this ideal as closely as possible. The discussions thereby underline his consensus-building skills, while also revealing how he could skillfully utilize his charisma to wield power.

The November 11 to 17 COFO meeting in Greenville, at which the 1964 Project was first discussed, stands out. Moses assumed an unusually vocal role, but without downplaying his opponents' views and overstating his own, he coaxed the group into moving beyond their emotions by deploying pragmatic arguments and emphasizing their shared values. Usually this technique harvested admiration from his colleagues. Moses often "would hold back all of his comments until an appropriate time when he felt he could summarize and direct the entire course of the discussion," one worker reveled. "He would come in with a brilliant statement, which just clearly cut through all of the mess and all of the tangle and all of the debate, said exactly what probably three-quarters of the people wanted to have said and allowed the discussion to move on." But this time, SNCC workers were aware of what Moses was doing and resented it. Some even felt manipulated. This allegation stung him deeply and caused him to take on a self-conscious and timid role in the months that followed. When he finally asserted his leadership, he argued he did so only on behalf of local people and *after* the group-centered leadership process had yielded no satisfactory solution.[34]

When Moses arrived at the Greenville meeting, he found that the COFO staff, including his girlfriend, had already rejected most of the Summer Project plans. Of the thirty-five blacks and seven whites in attendance (mostly SNCC workers), the Project's strongest opponents—Charlie Cobb, Ivanhoe Donaldson, Hollis Watkins, Curtis Hayes, and Willie Peacock—were in the minority, as were those who favored the plan in its entirety, like Moses, Fannie Lou Hamer, and Lawrence Guyot; most were still undecided or favored only portions of it. Yet without it, Moses argued, "blacks were not going to get the vote fast enough to have significant impact as their numbers shrank." Moreover, the exhausted staff could not go on indefinitely, especially now Wiley Branton had notified him and Aaron Henry in New York shortly before the meeting that the VEP stopped financing voter registration programs in Mississippi. The cutoff, Branton explained with regret, was the result of mere arithmetic—it spent most of its money on Mississippi but harvested the least results there.[35]

Without VEP money, COFO could barely maintain the projects it had now, let alone cultivate new areas. The Freedom Vote had suppressed staff conflicts, but the disappointing turnout in Leflore County (only 1,500) revitalized frustrations and infighting in Greenwood. Jane Stembridge called the project's state "one of sadness" in which staff was "destroying each other." Petty arguments proliferated. Block walked around "telling [people] how much he doesn't care about the movement." The Summer Project might alleviate such problems, bringing onboard new donations and volunteers to offset COFO's financial problems. The ambitious program, which ranged from establishing "parallel institutions" like Freedom Schools and community centers to voter registration and the creation of the new political party, might provide enough activity to divert people from unproductive squabbling.[36]

But opposition to the Project centered on the involvement of northern whites. Moses pushed for their return from the start. In a memo he had sent beforehand, he outlined the crucial questions that needed to be decided. "1. What form should the organization of the Negro community in Mississippi take? What are the relative roles of COFO and some form of political organization? Can we avoid a personality-centered organization?" and "2. How large a force of volunteer summer workers should we recruit? 100? 1,000? 2,000?" In his view, the second question did not have to preclude the first, as long as the whites took on a facilitating role in a similar vein as COFO workers themselves had adopted.[37]

At the meeting, most of his colleagues rejected that reasoning. "It's wrong for people outside Mississippi to come in," one objected; it would be far better to train native Mississippians because they "have got to stay, after the [white] folks leave." Moses replied that SNCC was already doing this. "We shouldn't be accused of not training Mississippi people. We certainly tried. Not until last summer did the first white people come." Dona Richards questioned the value of the publicity the Yale students had brought, but Moses urged the group to consider the effect on the federal government and the upcoming presidential elections. He admitted that this would be dangerous; they had "to prepare to have several people killed." Douglas MacArthur Cotton complained that the presence of whites especially increased the danger to blacks, but Guyot countered that Cotton himself—like everyone in the room—was personally responsible for someone getting jailed or worse, too. They already were, in Camus's axiom, executioners. This stung Moses, who still struggled deeply with the moral consequences of his work. "I don't think that's fair—We [went] to work in McComb and we end up with a guy killed. Now we didn't know [that] when we started," he protested.

As he had tried to do ever since Herbert Lee's death, Moses proposed to just focus on the controllable things. "Let's start planning now—make certain people responsible for jobs they got to do." But resentment over the role of whites during the Freedom Vote soon resurfaced. Someone suggested that whites be restricted to "special projects" and not be allowed to "take over the office" again. Moses denied that they had done this. "We had a lot to do in Jackson. It was as simple as that. I wouldn't accept any blanket rule like that." He explained that the presence of whites did not necessarily have to undermine grassroots empowerment. "You have a problem of things to be done," he pointed out, "and you go ahead and see who can do what, and also train local people." That approach had failed during the mock election, Cobb countered, because whites held leadership positions in the office. "[W]e needed experienced people in the field," Moses offset the accusation. "The decision was made on the basis of the needs of the campaign. There just weren't enough people—it wasn't that we weren't thinking about training people." Dona Richards reminded him of the whites who went to Yazoo City against his advice. That had not been the fault of the volunteers, Moses stated; Lowenstein had "briefed them because *we* [did not say] who should brief them." To avoid such problems in the future, the staff listed the measures it had agreed upon the previous night: whites could not direct projects, write platforms, or operate the WATS line. Moreover, they should be screened carefully and work mainly in the white community.

Moses disagreed. "In other words," he summarized, "get rid of whites." Amid a chorus of denials, he persisted. "It seems to me that's the idea, if you're sending them to work in white communities." Richards emotionally called out her boyfriend, "That's the way *you* want to characterize it. Don't exaggerate it. They said no whites in certain leadership positions. They did not say no whites at all."

Moses would have none of this. Cutting through the rationalizations, he addressed the issue of blacks' insecurity head on. "People say if Negroes and whites work in the field, *they* are more articulate and *they're* going to do the talking. And then if you say put them in the office, they're better typists [and] you don't want them *there*. Then there's no place for them." When one worker complained that Mendy Samstein led a project, Moses urged the group to look beyond race and acknowledge the "personhood" of each individual. "[T]here's a big difference between saying a white man's on the WATS-line and *Mendy's* on the WATS-line . . . I don't think he's offensive [or] imposing on people [so] it's a dehumanizing statement to make." Moreover, he added, "we spread generalizations that are a lie—that any Negro can talk to any other Negro because he is a Negro."

Moses's unusual forcefulness unsettled the staff. Dona Richards—known as a "pretty high-powered intellectual" herself[38]—warned him that he was dominating the debate in a way that he claimed to abhor. "The tone gets to be all on one side, because after everyone speaks, you answer." Another attacked Moses's intellect. "You're perpetuating the idea of inferiority. YOU're taking the same attitude some white people take to us." Guyot verbalized the staff's confusion, "You seem to have used logic now to change the entire tone of the conversation." But when asked to state his "pitch," Moses's reply represented an apt description of his personal worldview and ability to see in the long term.

> My position all along [has been]: you try to get as many Negroes as you can to do the job [and] get white students in to the extent that it won't do harm to the Negro community . . . my feeling has been that the type of person you have is much more important than whether he's white or not, that some white people . . . can break down the depersonalization of people, that the Negroes would have to take them as people. They'd learn not to let their fears and emotions get the better of them when they talk to whites. These are the kind of people I look for when I go around and talk to people about coming down . . . I was also concerned that we *do* integrate it because otherwise we'll grow up and have a racist movement . . . if the white people don't stand with the Negroes, then there will be a danger that after [Negroes] get something they'll say, okay, we got this by ourselves. And the only way you can break that down is to have white people working alongside of you—so then it changes the whole complexion of what you're doing, so it isn't any longer Negro fighting white, it's a question of rational people against irrational people.

Several voiced agreement when he added, "The situation has to be looked at rationally. Who are the people we need? Who do we have? . . . The questions can't be couched in those terms—that no white person can be head of any project—that's a racist statement. I don't see how we can operate on that principle. We can, but I don't want to be part of an operation like that."

The issue of race, however, involved powerful emotions. "The first consciousness that Negroes have [is] of whiteness," Cobb explained. "It may be an irrational thing [but] you have to decide, is it practical . . . to have a white project director?" Ivanhoe Donaldson agreed. "I came into

SNCC and saw Negroes running the movement and I felt good [although this] might be irrational." Issues of class also came into play. As Guyot later confessed, "It was a question not only of white against black but skill versus non-skill." Many SNCC workers, he believed, would have felt equally uncomfortable with well-educated black volunteers. "It was about turf . . . you had people with us [who before joining] SNCC had led very ordinary lives. Now they were heroes. They were leaders." Curtis Hayes felt similar. "[W]e knew more about Mississippi than [northerners] did, but they had the ability to carry out these long analyses, intellectual discussions about our environment that seemed like foreign language." They therefore feared that locals would "feel inferior and fall back into the same rut that they were in before we started the grassroots organizations."[39]

But Moses persisted in depicting resentments against whites as a weakness that SNCC needed to overcome. "The one thing we can do for the country that no one else can," he stated, "is to be above the race issue." Some older locals concurred. "If we're trying to break down this barrier of segregation," Fannie Lou Hamer said, "we can't segregate ourselves." The rest of the meeting then centered on staff admissions of irrationality and reflections on their significance. "I'm a product of this irrational society. I get irrational feelings," Cobb said, but "I want to get away from all that stuff. And the question is *how?*" "Contact," replied Howard Zinn. "The only way we can handle these irrational feelings," another agreed, "is not to honor them." The meeting then closed without a final vote for *or* against the project. Further discussions were postponed to COFO's next meeting on December 15.

The fact that the plans even survived that meeting owed much to Moses's personality and reputation within SNCC. Staff members understood that if Moses—whose analyses so far had been proven correct—felt so strongly about the need for white participation, then they would have to contemplate the possibility of a SNCC without its most respected figure. "Moses put himself and his political credibility with staff on the line," Guyot emphasized in 1966. Thirteen years later, he even claimed that the opponents changed their position "because of the collective respect that all of us had for Bob Moses." Samstein agreed but nuanced that it was not "that simple. There was a lot of back and forth discussion [so] it [can't] be thought of as a cut-and-dried thing."[40]

The exceptional trust COFO workers had in Moses's insights nonetheless accelerated the Project's acceptance. "I'm certain that had such a proposal come from anywhere or anyone else, it would have been dismissed as an impractical, even dangerous fantasy," Stokely Carmichael claimed. "But this was Bob Moses talking. And he never ran his mouth loosely. *If* Bob said it could happen . . . 'Bet yo' life and live for evah.'"[41]

However, at the December 15 COFO meeting, it became apparent that their unequivocal trust had unintentional consequences as well. In Moses's absence, the staff approved the Summer Project but remained undecided over the number of participants. Dave Dennis proposed that further decisions be postponed until Moses could join the meeting. While the reluctance to speak about the project without Moses was logical given his position as Mississippi director, some staff members again openly questioned whether such dependence hampered their own empowerment. One participant criticized the implication that "someone is indispensable here," meaning that in a participatory democracy, no one's presence or absence should determine agendas or outcomes. Internal jealousy might also be a reason. Even the forceful Guyot was "mad because nobody's challenging Moses," although he emphasized that he was "attacking Moses as an institution not a person." Another staff member grumbled about "the Bob Moses mystique—we've operated as though the very word of God was being spoken."[42]

SNCC's Executive Committee meeting of December 27 to 31, 1963, rehearsed many of the arguments that had been debated in Greenville. James Forman, John Lewis, and Marion Barry stressed the Project's publicity value, arguing that SNCC had a unique opportunity to put pressure on President Johnson. Others, like Cobb and Donaldson, restated their concerns about bloodshed and the effects of an "outside invasion" on local leadership. Moses, wary about seeming to dominate the debate as he had done in Greenville, just matter-of-factly stated that his northern networks had told him that northern students were "organizing to come down. [So] SNCC has to decide whether to have a project [and] how many will be involved." Asking the group to make a decision because it was "too big a responsibility to make alone," he merely summarized the arguments for and against. Eventually, national SNCC passed a motion that in 1964, it intended "to obtain the right for all citizens of Mississippi to vote, using as many people as necessary."[43]

During the following months, Moses would explain the need for the Project but refrained from making a forceful case. By not taking a public stance, he also bought himself time to ponder its consequences. Despite his own nagging doubts, however, he remained convinced that the enlistment of white volunteers would strengthen rather than weaken local leadership. Ordinary black Mississippians *wanted* their return; Amzie Moore had been calling for outside help since 1960. "It was clear," he believed, "that if there was [a] vote put to the assembly of COFO [local blacks] would vote that the students come in." Dorie Ladner has made the point that outside help could hardly undermine grassroots leadership because in most places, the latter did not exist. "We wanted everyone who would come, to come. Because we were just a tiny, tiny, tiny little drop against this whole establishment. . . . All of us who were debating were local [but] we were not making any dent in the status quo."[44]

In a speech at Stanford University, Moses later clarified his thoughts in a way that showcased his genuine faith in locals' perceptions. "[T]he people in Mississippi did not have the reaction of the staff [and] I think in many cases the instincts of the people . . . about these things are truer, deeper, less cluttered, less bothered by personal problems . . . then the instincts of the staff." The debate over the Project therefore demonstrated "the distinctively different perspectives of organizer and community leader."[45]

FIVE DAYS AFTER the Greenville meeting, a sniper's bullet in Dallas further complicated Moses's plans. President Kennedy's death shook fieldworkers' morale; if the *president* could be killed, "then so could *they*." Moses's first reaction was similar. "Well, nobody's safe." At its biannual conference at Howard University in the Thanksgiving weekend of November 29 to December 1, 1963, SNCC tried to understand its political consequences. Moses considered this more important than joining the public outpouring of remorse that swept the nation, which he felt overshadowed genuine criticisms of the administration. "The conference may be the one place . . . where people can get together and talk about something that can be meaningful for the whole country without having to pay homage[,] which is trivial," he wrote Mary King. "It just doesn't seem that anywhere in the country we have a counter-balance to the idea that if a President dies, he was a hero . . . So if there are any real issues at the bottom of this [death] we must cover them up. . . . And see, SNCC doesn't have to go through that."[46]

The staff was unsure what Kennedy's death meant for the movement. Some felt it might serve as a unifying force that could accelerate civil rights legislation, while others feared that the murder, rumored to be a Communist plot, might renew McCarthyism. Kennedy's successor,

Lyndon B. Johnson, inspired little confidence. Although he had steered the 1957 Civil Rights Act through Congress, Johnson was not a civil rights liberal. Moreover, he instantly reached out to the traditional middle-class national black leadership. In his first days as president, he met Martin Luther King Jr., Roy Wilkins, James Farmer, Whitney Young, and A. Philip Randolph. The significance of Johnson's failure to invite John Lewis to the White House was not lost on the SNCC staff. When other civil rights groups agreed to stop demonstrations in order to allow Johnson some breathing space, SNCC refused.[47]

Looking beyond individuals, Moses did not refer to Johnson or Kennedy in his speech to the SNCC conference. Instead, he stressed the federal government's significance for the movement. Rebutting a recent *Life* article by Theodore White that accused the civil rights movement of blackmailing the administration, Moses dwelt on the need to "change the political structure of the South as we now know it." He explained SNCC's purpose for 1964 through a metaphor Leslie Dunbar used in his 1961 essay *The Annealing of the South*. "The South & the country doesn't change unless its heated up to a white hot heat first, and then while it's in the process of cooling off, it's possible to [mold it and] make some changes." This meant creating a situation that forced a confrontation between federal and state authorities. He gently urged his audience to understand that creating this confrontation was "not a lunatic move" because the current situation "*is* a national crisis." Unlike the other SNCC leadership, he even openly called to attack the power structure at its roots. The two-party system, he argued, needed to be destroyed.[48]

Moses's erudition and cosmopolitan background were on full display. He juxtaposed Plato and Ulysses, quoted Camus, and urged his colleagues to face the issue of civil liberties. Attacking lingering McCarthyism, he stated, was "the next frontier." Moses was still one of the few in SNCC who habitually pushed this question. He had recently asked the National Student Association to sponsor discussions about the topic because communist charges kept moderate whites at bay. At the conference, he urged SNCC to make its "nonexclusion" policy explicit. Afterward, he asked the Provisional Student Civil Liberties Coordinating Committee to compile a "manual on basic civil liberties questions" to distribute to all SNCC workers and called on the organization to demand the abolition of HUAC. When colleagues resisted his ideas, Moses tried to find a practical compromise. "We should . . . take a position, and close behind it. [The real disagreement is] between a principled position that political association is never relevant even when it causes turmoil, and a pragmatic one that it would have occasional relevance. . . . What we need is a criterion of flexibility without a flat statement one way or the other." SNCC agreed to adopt "a position of non-alignment"—that is, "of no political test for members"—but not to state this openly.[49]

Moses's pragmatic views on economic disparities also separated him from his colleagues. Many SNCC workers shunned the workshops that labor representatives from the AFL-CIO conducted during the Thanksgiving conference, even though unions had sponsored it. Some, like Tim Jenkins, James Forman, and Bill Mahoney and others from the SNCC affiliated Howard University's Nonviolent Action Group (NAG), had forged bonds with the labor movement. Most, however, were skeptical or indifferent. *The Nation* blamed this on the workers' limited backgrounds, although it also represented their resentment of labor's well-attested history of racial discrimination and fears that financial contributions—like at the March on Washington—meant "control of our policy."[50]

Yet after three years of working with the black poor, SNCC began to realize that racial equality would mean little if gross economic inequality persisted. This forced it to clarify its overall goals. Moses answered that challenge at its December 27 to 31 meeting in Atlanta from his faith in grassroots initiatives. He pointed to COFO's commodities drive, a self-help project in Ruleville where local women sold quilts, and to getting government programs into Mississippi to retrain unskilled laborers. Charles Sherrod stated that Georgia SNCC was helping the Koinonia community to take over a pecan factory.[51]

Some NAG members responded with attacks. Instead of engaging in futile attempts to prop up the ailing rural economy, SNCC should "take all the Negroes from the rural areas into the cities and force the revolution. Hungry people need to be massed to turn over the government. . . . Don't fight automation." Moses replied in a calm, pragmatic way. "We don't know what terms such as 'revolution' and 'revamp the economy' mean. We need to take time out from action and study with some up-to-date people. . . . It may be that no one knows the answers to the technological revolution in which we are caught." He advocated the same slow approach to economics as to voter registration. "The only way . . . is to organize the unemployed and sit on their doorsteps. We need to work on several different levels[:] education of staff on economic organization [and simultaneously] continue with programs of mass action, organizing people, development of leadership." SNCC agreed to develop a program to educate its staff on economics as well as to follow Moses's example in politics by running black candidates in all of its projects.[52]

IN BETWEEN THE MEETINGS, Moses left Mississippi for over a month, returning to New York to recuperate for a bit, even as he continued organizing. He met National Council of Churches officials, discussed a literacy training program with John Blyth, and contacted the Harlem Youth Opportunities Unlimited (HARYOU) about its educational and employment programs. At Moses's request, he, Ella Baker, and Charles Sherrod attended HARYOU's January 3 to 4 meetings, because he wanted to explore "whether such a youth program might not be possible for Southern urban areas." This underscores Moses's nonstop preoccupation with bridging the North and the South. In April 1964, he repeated his belief that changing Congress through his southern work might alleviate the explosive situation in northern ghettos, because "the preconditions for [Negro acts of terror] already exist [because] people have been blocking effective legislation in the Congress which would be able to deal with some of the serious problems we have in our cities." Job problems were inextricably tied to school and housing problems. Trouble would therefore continue until local, state, and federal authorities created agencies that could "deal with those three problems conceived as a unit." With this sharp analysis, he predicted the severe riots that erupted in Harlem three months later—the first of many nationwide in subsequent years.[53]

Meanwhile, Moses used this time to cultivate his relationship with Dona Richards. Although they had sharp public disagreements at SNCC meetings, privately their relationship had been proceeding at a quick pace—as did most relationships in SNCC, probably as a side effect of the intense and volatile conditions under which many lived. So it was perhaps not so surprising that, although they had only been dating for a couple of months, the two were married while in New York. Martin Luther King Jr. wired the couple on December 23, wishing them "a happy and long life" and calling their movement contributions "an inspiration to generations yet unborn."[54]

Reactions among staff members in Mississippi, however, verged upon churlish. The feminist Richards was "almost ostracized," Mary King claimed, for her wish to remain independent during the marriage, including by keeping her maiden name. Jealousy played another role. "Everyone wanted to marry Bob," Julian Bond stated. Such feelings were not always romantic, Dorie Ladner explained. "[The marriage] made us angry. Because we had had Bob all to ourselves . . . he was like my big brother. . . . We didn't want to share him." Dave Dennis agreed. "They thought they were some part of Bob. In Mississippi males and females did. . . . People felt that she had come in and taken Bob away." A heartfelt tribute to his personality and skills, these explanations underscore the remarkable extent to which Moses had managed to blend in with his southern coworkers and local blacks. Consequently, Bond and Dennis asserted, the marriage gave Richards "extra status [and a] bigger role in meetings," which likely aggravated the jealousy.[55]

SNCC workers' responses to the marriage therefore went much deeper than mere personal apprehensions; they came to the core of the internal debates over its inherently conflicting nature that had begun to surface within the organization. Not only did they belie the factual standing Moses—and by extension, individuals at large—had in SNCC's group-centered leadership but also the role that class and the North-South divide played in it. Apparently, the fear of skilled and erudite northerners taking over that Richards personified made the Mississippi staff self-conscious and insecure while their paradoxical embrace of Moses reflected their contradictory desire for leadership and direction.

For the newlyweds, this was not easy. Richards felt as conflicted about being thrust into prominence as her husband. Separating marriage and movement life made matters even more difficult; their first home in Hattiesburg even functioned as an extension of the SNCC office. Moses had occasionally discussed this with his fellow activists, asking, "If we're going to have families [and] different kind of jobs . . . can SNCC evolve in a way to accommodate those demands?" In practice, the answer was often no. Dennis, for instance, complained that Moses and Richards "isolated themselves a lot." He once came to the couple's second home in Jackson to discuss movement business, but "Bob sent me on this porch . . . because Dona did not want to have the movement come into her house so I left because I wasn't going to sit out there!" Others grumbled that "Moses used to be on time, but not since he got married" and that "his mail was generally unopened." Despite their marriage, moreover, Richards did not withdraw her opposition to a Summer Project that utilized white volunteers.[56]

COFO's Executive Committee meeting on January 10, 1964, revealed that concerns about the Project were still much alive. Moses repeated his argument that a national strategy would complement and strengthen local leadership. "The general situation here is that of absolute resistance on the part of the State of Mississippi," he pointed out. "We need external and internal pressure to break it." He then listed the programs the Project could sponsor and suggested ways of organizing them. Others raised the same old objections: it was too ambitious, too dangerous, and whites would take over. Moses acknowledged their concerns, but reassured everyone that in any project "[w]e argue things through until there is a consensus." By an informal vote, COFO accepted the proposal to deploy 1,000 participants without a quota for whites. The fact that half of those present abstained, however, showed that support for the Project did not approximate a genuine consensus. Charles Cobb, for example, stated that he favored the Project's "educational angle [but] can't stomach the idea of large numbers of northern whites."[57]

When discussions continued on January 24, opponents restated their skepticism. "The staff has been forced into [the] summer project," one said; "we cannot handle 1,000," stated another. Mike Sayer deplored "the exaggerated focus on Washington. Do revolutions get organized from outside anywhere? We must organize from within the state." Supporters, including Charles Sherrod and Ella Baker, cited specific programs they liked or sheer pragmatics. "We voted to set up machinery, therefore we are committed." The meeting once more ended undecided.[58]

Moses could not attend the meeting, as he was in jail in Hattiesburg in Forrest County, where demonstrations again showed that outside involvement could achieve national awareness without eclipsing grassroots agency. Compared to the Delta, Forrest County was fairly progressive, although only 12 of its 7,406 voting-age blacks were registered in 1961. In his career as registrar, Theron Lynd had accepted 1,836 whites and no blacks. The Fifth Circuit Court had ordered him to cease his discriminatory practices, but Lynd was appealing the decision. Following Moses's suggestion of a mass voting drive to test the federal government's response to Lynd's appeal, the Hattiesburg COFO staff planned a Selma-like Freedom Day on January 22. Movement stalwarts like Ella Baker, James Forman, John Lewis, Aaron Henry, Charles Evers, Annelle Ponder, and Dave Dennis came in. National news crews followed the arrival of fifty clergymen of the National Council of Churches' United Presbyterian Commission on Religion and Race, the Episcopal Society for Cultural and Racial Unity, the Rabbinical Association of America, and the Presbyterian Interracial Council. New York Rev. Robert Stone had approached Moses at the Thanksgiving conference. Inquiring whether northern clergy could help in Mississippi, he had sent him to Lawrence Guyot, Hattiesburg's project manager. The involvement of northern white clergy crystallized Bob Spike's post–March on Washington plans to seek a theater to "bear witness" to southern racial atrocities and thereby bring extra forte to their lobbying demands in Midwestern states for a new civil rights bill.[59]

The large-scale involvement of white clergy made the campaign an unprecedented event in movement history. Moreover, by converging local and national movement needs, it represented a logical move in between the Freedom Vote and the Summer Project. On January 17, Moses likewise had argued that "a full-blown effort in Hattiesburg" could function as a preamble to the Summer Project. "[W]e have to have both—a local fuss to justify major invasion from outside." If successful, it could have long-term implications, he believed. "[I]f we gain the right to picket in integrated picket lines then labor unions will [too]." The latter might "move into Mississippi [and] then . . . a whole host of other organizations [might] get to working people in Mississippi."[60]

On the morning of January 22, some 200 protesters gathered before the courthouse and auxiliary police. Yet to the crowd's confusion, the police announced that they could register. This not only kept the Justice Department at bay but the media as well, as city officials had learned the lessons of Greenwood and Birmingham that confrontations in the streets should be avoided at all costs. The press did not respond to citations of injustice but only to "blood and guts," as one *New York Times* reporter brazenly admitted. Moses attributed this behavioral change to the presence of the white clergy. "Certainly we could not have maintained our picket line . . . without their acting as an out-of-state buffer." Local officials, however, simply moved their tactics indoors; Lynd stalled registration by allowing only one applicant at the time.[61]

But SNCC had planned for Moses to get arrested if the opportunity arose. As predicted, police singled him out and ordered him to move from the sidewalk opposite the demonstration. Moses left to consult with his colleagues and returned with a picket sign to accompany two registrants toward the courthouse. The officer—ironically named John Quincy Adams—instantly arrested him for "breach of peace" and "interfering with an officer." When nearby FBI officers merely wrote down his complaint, Moses, citing Section 242 of Title 18 of the U.S. Code, declared a citizen's arrest of Adams instead. Held on a $600 bail, Moses wired Burke Marshall and demanded a civil suit against Adams and an injunction against Hattiesburg officials. He was put on trial and subjected to a fierce cross-examination. But Moses stayed his usual calm self, even softly correcting the prosecuting attorney's pronunciation. When the attorney derisively asked which law school he attended to justify disobeying Adams, he coolly answered, "[T]he First Amendment.... That's the whole point of a democracy, that the citizens ... don't have to go to law school to know what their rights are." Such bravery enlarged his reputation among the present movement workers and clergymen. He was nonetheless found guilty and sentenced to ninety days and a $225 fine. He passed his time in jail rereading Camus and discussing details of COFO projects with visiting SNCC workers, until the National Council of Churches paid his bail. He rejoined the Hattiesburg staff on January 29.[62]

With just one arrest, Freedom Day ended as a "quiet victory," so COFO decided to create a perpetual picket line. For another week, locals and clergymen marched daily, leading to 150 registration attempts. COFO duplicated Freedom Days in Canton, Greenwood, and Liberty and SNCC in Georgia. Some 100 to 350 locals showed up, but police avoided public disturbances and generally retaliated by intimidating and arresting locals and staff far from the courthouse scene. Bored reporters soon failed to show up. Despite temporary boosts in local activity, the Freedom Days barely led to more registrants (in Hattiesburg, 200 of 850 blacks had registered by May 26), but they reinforced that white outsiders brought protection for local blacks, bolstered their commitment, and enticed the nation. The NCC, converted through the experiences of its clergymen, vowed massive support for the Summer Project. This gave its proponents new ammunition, although they repeatedly stated that "COFO can call on outside help only if the local community is already moving."[63]

ON JANUARY 31, staff discussions about the Summer Project again ended without resolution. Moses observed distraught how the group "applauded with equal enthusiasm two rousing speeches advocating opposite courses." He said little else because "I was still trying to come to grips in my own mind with all the implications." But that evening, events in McComb taught the implications of *not* doing it. Hours before he was to leave Mississippi permanently, Louis Allen was murdered with three shots to the head.[64]

Ever since telling the truth about Herbert Lee, Allen had suffered economic and physical intimidations; Sheriff Daniel Jones had broken his jaw, the police had (falsely) arrested him for carrying a concealed weapon and for passing bad checks, and they even tried to frame him for domestic violence. In October 1961, he had to go into hiding after rumors that then-Sheriff E. L. Caston had instigated a plot to kill him. A week before his murder, one of Allen's sons had his car fired on. Sheriff Jones, who had forced another six locals connected to the Lee and Allen cases to leave town, denied to the *Enterprise-Journal* that "the Negro-white question [was] a ruling factor" in Allen's death and claimed that its cause would rather be found in Allen's alleged criminal past. At Burke Marshall's request, the FBI investigated the murder, but its agents, accepting Jones's explanations, dismissed the case. The murder is still unsolved today, even though the FBI admitted in 2011 that Sheriff Jones may well have been responsible.[65]

The news reached Moses the next morning by telephone. The news was so distressing, a report noted, that he "wouldn't get out of the bed to see what we were talking about . . . until he got ready." Guilt about Lee's and Allen's fate immediately resurfaced. Moses had not seen the Allens since July 1962. He instantly drove to McComb to collect witness testimonies. While driving back to Hattiesburg on February 2, he contemplated the Summer Project. Seeing Allen's widow made him realize "that we couldn't protect our own people." "[It] seemed to me like we were just sitting ducks," he verbalized his disbelief, "There was no real reason to kill him . . . they just came right up to his house [and] gunned him right down."[66]

His desire to do something, however, represented more than personal guilt. It was also an extension of his ongoing effort to publicize the recent string of atrocities against blacks, which had reached new heights during the winter as the proximity of a new Civil Rights Act loomed. Frustrated over the Citizens' Councils' inability to destroy the movement, the KKK accelerated its terror, as it had announced in an ominous leaflet. "The Ku Klux Klan is now awake from a thirty-five year sleep . . . where they see the sores of the communist-led Negro, vice and crime erupting on the people of this nation they will return, and by sinister means they will heal and bind the sore." Within days of President Kennedy's death, five black bodies were found near Natchez. Moses reported these to SNCC headquarters, but only the *New York Times'* Claude Sitton responded. Moreover, Moses told headquarters, Natchez's black community "is withdrawn, fearful, and silent. Don't even bother to try to find someone for attribution for a quotation." Shootings, cross burnings, and bombings of black churches, businesses, and homes became commonplace as 1964 commenced. In Amite and Pike Counties, six black businesses and two homes were bombed and three blacks were found dead in their car. Allen's death, Moses reasoned, was just "the latest in [this] string of murders—lynchings."[67]

Subsequent weeks reinforced this notion as Moses investigated atrocities in southwest Mississippi such as the KKK's whipping of Natchez voter registration leader Archie Curtis, the murder of black Clifford Walker, and arrests of several SNCC workers. He protested this "reign of lawlessness" to Robert Kennedy and asked the NAACP's Jack Greenberg to defend three Greenwood blacks falsely arrested for robbery. On March 5, he again demanded that the U.S. Committee on Civil Rights hold hearings on Mississippi. "The present situation parallels that which existed during the 1880's," he wrote them, "It was the failure of the federal government to interfere with the Klan then that resulted in the failure of reconstruction . . . Will the United States once again stand aside while the Klan creates its own law?" Similar crimes could only be prevented, he concluded grimly, if "the people involved are exposed and the situation brought to the nation's attention."[68]

Moses felt like being back in 1961 but realized that their organizing had not been in vain. "For me, it was as if everything had come full circle." 1964 was different, he reasoned. "You're back where you started but you're in a different place . . . you've got this whole national ferment now[,] networks in place[,] potential strategies lined up [and] some sort of opening to look at in terms of how can we respond." The Summer Project was it. As of then, he acknowledged, "I began to argue strongly" for the Project, using the mounting white terrorism as an overriding argument. Some, like Willie Peacock and Hollis Watkins, still opposed, denying that "white participation [was] essential to the survival of the Mississippi movement." But Moses contested this. "In my mind, the need for a major gesture outweighed legitimate worries of how the influx of white students would affect Black leadership." It offset his concerns over staff manipulation, too. He later admitted he "threw all my weight behind it" because "I knew [it] would . . . tip the scales." If he did not, COFO would simply continue "this deadlock . . . from one meeting to another."[69]

COFO workers eventually accepted the project because of its almost unanimous support from older locals and because of Moses's arguments. Even Cobb acknowledged that "you had to do something about this violence [but COFO] didn't have the capacity." Yet Moses denied that anyone could have determined the debate through argument alone. "It's not a debate that gets settled because of some rational argument . . . the issues really lie so much deeper in the emotional dimension of people. . . . There was just deciding whether or not we were going to move."[70]

Moses was learning firsthand that group-centered leadership was more difficult in practice than in theory; its justifications could simultaneously be used to speak up or to stay silent, and the choice between was constantly influenced by one's (informal) position in the group based on class, education, personality, and pragmatics. Having continuously fought the tension between the necessity of providing leadership and his unwillingness to impose his views, Moses eventually solved his moral dilemma by subjugating organizers' concerns to the wishes of locals like Allen who cared little for academic banter and just wanted help. Yet this subjugation had far-reaching consequences for Moses, SNCC, and COFO. Striking what Marion Barry called "a balance between efficiency and democracy" remained an ongoing challenge—and the Summer Project exacerbated it to the point of their destruction.[71]

CHAPTER SEVEN

Freedom Is a Constant Struggle

Like other great turning points in the civil rights movement—the Free-dom Rides, Moses's entry into McComb, Birmingham—SNCC's 1964 Summer Project, known as Freedom Summer, has been obscured by myth. After all, Moses agreed, it is a fascinating story "about the coming together of a number [of] historical forces," most of all the effective con-vergence of the local and national movement. He likened Mississippi to a whirlpool, which "just sucks everybody in for this one event," and "somehow [in] this process state-sponsored racism gets rooted out."[1]

The Project made the introduction of voting legislation all but inevitable. The white volunteers' experiences spurred a new cluster of social movements, including the Berkeley Free Speech, antiwar, and women's movements. It crystallized the image of the southern-based civil rights movement as an interracial one rooted in effective coalition building and local empowerment that refused to be stopped despite vio-lence. In this grand narrative, Freedom Summer was its finest moment before this broad-based coalition split apart at the Democratic National Convention in August and began its alleged "tragic epilogue," the Black Power movement.[2]

However, this idealistic story underappreciates how tentative the coalition was from the start and how dependent it was on the behind-the-scenes efforts of activists who could mediate between the sepa-rate groups, Moses in particular. The Project embodied the ultimate test of his consensus-minded leadership approach. For the summer's dura-tion, he succeeded in uniting national and local black leadership and northern white liberals around the goals of ending racial violence and democratizing the South. Yet this effort was a heavy burden. Not only did he have to fight unparalleled white opposition, but internal forces within the movement and his own mind as well.

The Project and Moses were considered synonymous. "However par-ticipatory . . . SNCC was," one worker conceded, Moses was "the real leader of Freedom Summer." This gave him unprecedented, and unso-licited, leverage in SNCC, COFO, and the national movement. This role also brought unwanted responsibility, entangling him in an all-consuming fight to prevent new bloodshed. But the Project's positive effect on black Mississippians made his constant struggle worthwhile. For Moses, Staughton Lynd said, "[t]his was what it was all about"—even if in the end, Moses admitted, "no-one comes out undamaged," including SNCC, COFO, the Democratic Party, and Moses himself.[3]

MOSES UNDERSTOOD that Freedom Summer represented a shift for SNCC. Although organizers worked toward local development, they now also simultaneously sought national attention in the style of the SCLC. The volunteers "brought the rest of the country down with them for a look and we knew Mississippi couldn't stand a hard look."[4]

That summer of 1964, SNCC had more staff in Mississippi than other organizations had in the South. But Moses did not see this as a break from past activity in itself; in fact, the slow organizing of the previous years had made its ambitious 1964 work possible. "This is what social change is about," Howard Zinn explained. "You move on to a new level and the minute you appear, the forces that defend the old situation . . . react violently. When you've established yourself there, they adapt to this, there's a period of relative peace and then you move an inch beyond that." With innovative projects like Freedom Schools and its political party, aided by hundreds of white volunteers, the SNCC-led project represented what Martin Luther King Jr. praised as "one of the most creative attempts I had seen to radically change the oppressive life of the Negro" in movement history.[5]

Moses knew that white Mississippians' responses would be extreme. According to *Newsweek*, they acted "as though Armageddon were just around the corner." During the spring, cross burnings, bombings, and beatings reached record numbers. Membership in the KKK and new white supremacist organizations, like the Americans for the Preservation of the White Race, mushroomed. In February, one KKK division from Natchez, the White Knights of the Ku Klux Klan of Mississippi, formed a statewide organization and adopted a four-stage retaliation plan, with the final stage labeled "Extermination." Its Imperial Wizard, Samuel Bowers, urged its members—estimated at 6,000 by summer—to form "swift and extremely violent" covert groups that could instantly "destroy and disrupt [our enemy's] leadership." Local authorities, many of whom had close ties to such organizations, prepared for the "invasion" in their own fashion. Jackson Mayor Allen Thompson expanded his police force and bought a twelve-man tank "with shotguns, tear-gas guns, and a sub-machine gun." The state legislature gave the highway patrol "full power in civil disorders" and permitted other cities and the governor to use "Allen's Army" as he saw fit.[6]

Moses feared that the rest of the country would be of little help. Opinion polls showed that 65 percent of Americans actually opposed the volunteers' influx because of the potential for violence. The White House was similarly appalled. It considered the COFO workers a "nuisance," understanding that their escalation plans promised to disrupt the administration's carefully staked-out position of neutrality. As one Washington official complained to the *Louisville Times*, COFO workers "would like to be killed. They want the Federal Government to occupy the state." Moreover, with the imminent passage of the new Civil Rights Act, Mississippi was already explosive. "[T]here's going to be the damnedest shootings," President Lyndon Johnson grumbled, because "[COFO's] sending them in by buses in the hundreds." Worrying about the complicity of local authorities in racial violence, he urged the FBI to increase its investigations of "fundamentally lawless activities" in Mississippi. Simultaneously, Robert F. Kennedy asked the FBI to utilize its techniques for "infiltration of Communist groups" in order to prevent bloodshed.[7]

But the FBI mainly focused on investigating the COFO workers instead. When CBS News, for instance, aired a clip of Stokely Carmichael criticizing the FBI, its agents instantly investigated him with the aim of discrediting him. Likewise, when Moses noted at a July press conference that the KKK possessed automatic firearms and hand grenades, the FBI spent more time uncovering the source of his information than on verifying the truth of his claims. J. Edgar Hoover accused Burke Marshall and the Commission on Civil Rights (CCR) Staff Director Howard Rogerson of sharing this information. Marshall denied it, although he privately admitted that "the Department had received information indicating that COFO . . . had undoubtedly been furnished information." This again suggests that the bond between federal officials and COFO was closer than hitherto acknowledged and illustrates the difficulty between the FBI and the Justice Department to act as a unified force on behalf of civil rights.[8]

McCarthyism was another major obstacle in getting moderate whites in the North and South to embrace the Project. The FBI justified targeting COFO because of its alleged Communist associations, although it found no conclusive evidence of COFO workers' or the volunteers' subversive intensions. Many white southerners were convinced that Communists were guiding COFO regardless. On July 22, Senator James Eastland even tried to convince the U.S. Senate by citing countless examples of suspect Freedom Summer participants, including Moses. The Mississippi State Sovereignty Commission, which privately characterized SNCC as a "nappy crew of un-Americans," gave him the list after Governor Paul Johnson had authorized it to bug Freedom Houses. Although SNCC workers found such accusations "faintly amusing," Hollis Watkins said that they recognized that many local blacks "didn't have no understanding of what communism was" and that the allegations accordingly could "frighten black people away."[9]

As hard as he had pushed for its acceptance, Moses therefore faced the Project with foreboding. "We may not break Mississippi," he told the *Detroit Free Press*, "but we will dent it." Within movement circles, however, he sounded less confident. During a speech in April, he candidly admitted his concerns. "[N]obody really knows what might happen . . . we're back in that same kind of dilemma [of] victims and executioners [but] when you come to deal with it personally, it still rests very heavy." By June, he was so tense that several workers documented how little he smiled. Having assumed the role of a national movement leader, he felt personally responsible for the Project's outcome.[10]

Moses began to spend more time on bureaucratic dealings and networking. Above all, he sought ways to reduce the Project's dangers. One means was ensuring that participants would have access to legal representation beyond the small group of overwhelmed local attorneys SNCC then relied on. Moses met representatives of lawyers' associations in Washington, and with lawyers from Detroit devised plans to lift the bar on the employment of out-of-state lawyers in Mississippi. Several organizations pledged support, including the NAACP's Legal Defense and Education Fund (Inc. Fund), the CORE-affiliated Lawyers' Constitutional Defense Committee (LCDC), the American Civil Liberties Union (ACLU), and the left-leaning National Lawyers' Guild (NLG).[11]

Moses reached out to more northerners with resources. He contacted the faculties of universities and colleges and asked them to serve as observers, researchers, teachers, and political advisers. With Bob Spike of the NCC, he reached out to influential union leaders such as George Meaney (AFL-CIO), Walter Reuther (United Automobile Workers), and A. Philip Randolph (Brotherhood of Sleeping Car Porters). Stressing that labor had a stake in the success of the civil rights movement, he pointed out that "the struggle for the right to vote in Mississippi has largely been a struggle for the right to organize [and] to picket." Labor could help the Project by walking picket lines with locals and sending speakers to COFO meetings. The presence of national labor officials, he added, would "be a good experience for local labor leaders and for workers." In May, he went to Detroit and Washington to discuss the Project with Reuther and other union representatives.[12]

Winning over President Johnson was of special importance. Howard Zinn had written Moses that federal protection might be secured if a group of national prominent figures met with the president. Zinn's proposal underscores the significance of activists with broader strategic visions in the movement. After all, Moses acknowledged, such a meeting was "not something [the field staff] would be concerned with. . . . That was a thousand miles away from anything that was on our minds." In April, he proposed the idea to twenty people, including the heads of the national civil rights organizations, Harry Belafonte, Marlon Brando, Ossie Davis, and Harlem rent-strike leader Jesse Gray. "The President must be made to understand that this responsibility rests with him, and him alone," he emphasized, "and that neither he nor the American people can afford to jeopardize the lives of the [summer workers] by failing to take the necessary precautions." At Ella Baker's advice, he decided that any delegation seeing the president should consist mainly of Mississippians "who can speak from personal involvement." The letter that went to the president on May 25 did not state any concrete demands apart from the meeting, despite Zinn's recommendation that Moses threaten with demonstrations in Washington if the president refused. Moses liked that idea, but nothing came of it because Roy Wilkins and Martin Luther King Jr. feared that demonstrations would put "too much pressure on the President all at once."[13]

The White House refused a meeting regardless. It informed Aaron Henry that the president's schedule was too "heavy," although the real reasons were entirely political. Presidential Assistant Lee White wrote President Johnson that he believed it was "nearly incredible that those people who are voluntarily sticking their head into the lion's mouth would ask for somebody to come down and shoot the lion."[14]

Moses refused to take no for an answer. On June 14, he wrote the president again. "Surely the number of persons who would sit down, plan, and execute" terrorist acts, he wrote coolly, "are relatively few [and] can be singled out." He now bluntly demanded the presence of the Justice Department, special FBI teams, and federal troops. "We are asking that the Federal Government move before the fact," he concluded. "I hope this is not asking too much of our country." He never got a reply, but behind the scenes, the federal government was acting. By late June, the Justice Department had established files on the KKK and other extremists, catalogued counties with frequent interference of civil rights, and sent four veteran lawyers to travel the state.[15]

Moses meanwhile devised another means of forcing federal protection. Because his requests to the Commission on Civil Rights for hearings on Mississippi went unheeded, he helped to organize unofficial, "parallel" hearings at the National Theater in Washington. On June 8, twenty-five Mississippi blacks, including Elizabeth Allen, Fannie Lou Hamer, and Jimmy Travis, testified about civil rights violations before a panel of nationally renowned figures, including novelist Joseph Heller, writer Michael Harrington, and southern-born historian C. Vann Woodward. Howard Zinn composed the panel and Moses arranged with Aaron Henry and Wiley Branton that COFO became its official sponsor. He gained endorsements from the national civil rights organizations and, after meeting Bob Spike in Washington, the National Council of Churches.[16]

"The purpose of this meeting," Moses stated in opening the hearings, "is to try to open to the country and the world some of the facts which we who work in Mississippi only know too well," facts that "have not been publicly aired and [are] very difficult to get across to the country." Afterward, the panel added its voice to SNCC's call for federal protection and for official hearings in Mississippi by the Civil Rights Commission. Two days later, the CCR indeed informed Moses that it wanted to meet in Jackson to hear from COFO representatives. It asked SNCC to keep the meeting confidential and emphasized that "this is *not* a Commission hearing, but a staff meeting for the purpose of assembling information and appraising witnesses." Still, COFO regarded it as a victory.[17]

MOSES TRIED TO DIMINISH dangers further by tightening organization in Mississippi itself. There would be forty-four individual projects statewide. Each project had an administrative council consisting of the Freedom School, Community Center, and Voter Registration directors; a lawyer; and a local minister. This was the area's "basic decision making group," but the Jackson office had "the final review" and Moses and Dave Dennis were key members in an "appeal board for decisions."[18]

The two were closely involved in the selection of summer volunteers as well. Applicants were interviewed at FOS offices ("Freedom Centers") at individual colleges, with a final review in Jackson. The Jackson screening committee included Mendy Samstein, Ivanhoe Donaldson, and Dona Richards, with Moses acting as a consultant. As director, he reserved "the right to make final decisions," allowing him to safeguard his concerns for safety and local empowerment. "There will be danger," he explained to *The Reporter*, "in accepting anyone who greatly misunderstands himself, the movement, or Mississippi." He advised recruitment centers to reject people who were arrogant or trying to be heroes and instead to identify "the willing ones (i.e., willing to do anything) and the *non-rugged individualists*" who would adhere to "strict discipline." He informed volunteers of Project specifics and suggested ways they could raise funds. He also wrote rejection letters. While they were standardized letters, they featured his distinctive emphasis on personal worth. Everyone had something worthwhile to contribute, he replied, even if only through contributions or pressuring politicians. "[Y]our role . . . will still be of critical nature . . . no revolution can continue without its supply base or support troops."[19]

Moses influenced recruitment most directly through his tours of northern colleges. As a graduate of elite white universities, he easily connected with these students. In fact, of all COFO staff, Cleve Sellers noted, "Moses communicated best with the white students." At Stanford University, for instance, he summarized the lessons he learned from Mississippi's sharecroppers in the style of philosophy classes familiar to them. "The questions that we think face the country . . . go very much to the bottom of mankind and people. They're questions which have repercussions in . . . international affairs and relations. They're questions which go to the very root of our society. What kind of society will we be?" At others, he simply held question-and-answer sessions. Louis Lomax's coverage of one such session at Queens College in New York for *Ramparts* noted how Moses constantly tried to ensure that those who were accepted understood the consequences. When the students laughed at James Forman's description of preparing for unsavory conditions like doing "your business in outhouses," Lomax stated that Moses lost his cool. "'Don't laugh,' Moses screamed. 'This is for real—like for life and death.'" While Julian Bond later wrote *Ramparts* to rectify that "Moses never screams," Lomax's embellishment does indicate a perceived shift of emotion on Moses's part that betrayed his preoccupation with preventing bloodshed.[20]

Moses's communication skills helped northern reporters better convey the Project's goals as well. Sympathetic journalists from magazines like the *Saturday Evening Post* and *The Reporter* invariably explained the Project to a national audience through him; some, like the editor of *The World*, sent reprints of their articles to him for distribution, hoping it caused "much good publicity [for] you and your cause."[21]

Despite his aversion to the spotlight, Moses accepted that such public relations work came with his position. Moreover, he understood that publicity was essential. In meetings and memoranda, he suggested that COFO get Bayard Rustin "to give the project a national focus." He asked volunteers for pictures of themselves for publicity purposes and advised recruitment centers to hold press conferences at which the accepted volunteers should call for federal protection. Yet his prime motivation in doing all this remained empowering locals, not the projection of the volunteers or himself. He still refused to be interviewed for a CBS documentary that included Governor Paul Johnson because appearing next to Johnson would spur his elevation as a leader, and, as he justified that decision at SNCC's June 9 to 11 meeting, the "concept of group leadership [is] more important than one man." Furthermore, he added, if reporters came by "following the northern kids," COFO could *then* "project local people." His insistence on temporarily moving headquarters from Atlanta to Greenwood, which SNCC finally agreed to, likewise reflected his concern for protection of locals and staff. "The move," he had argued in April, "will create greater publicity" because "local newspapers of participating workers would be more responsive to calls actually coming from inside the state."[22]

To recruit more volunteers, Moses contemplated calling on Allard Lowenstein once more. While his doubts about Lowenstein remained unaltered, he believed that his involvement was critical. He invited him to COFO meetings, including its state convention on February 9, when locals voted to endorse the Summer Project. But Lowenstein again tried to assume control. "Al," Julian Bond still grumbled in 2008, "wanted to run the Summer Project—from New York." From as early as January, he questioned SNCC's overrepresentation in COFO and in the Project. According to Ed King, Lowenstein even pondered "creating a new leadership structure for the Mississippi movement" that was more closely aligned with his moderate allies in the NAACP. Several SNCC workers, including Moses, believed that he recruited volunteers independently in order to "keep volunteers with radical views out." In February, Moses nonetheless begged for his support. "If you pull out it won't reduce any tensions absolutely, it will merely be an exchange of one set for another. You know yourself that nothing political and significant can be done without public tension—it stands to reason they won't be done without private ones also. You not only have to stay—you must."[23]

A month later, however, tension between Moses and Lowenstein reached a climax. SNCC accepted the assistance of the National Lawyers' Guild, a group that had been targeted for its nonexclusion of Communists since the 1930s. Lowenstein, a staunch anti-Communist, convinced Stanford volunteers to demand that Moses decline the NLG's offer. Jack Greenberg likewise informed Moses that the Inc. Fund, like the LCDC, "will not engage in any joint ventures . . . with the National Lawyers' Guild, and that we will not agree to any division of jurisdictional lines with them as you suggest. If SNCC or COFO enter into an arrangement with the Guild we will be unable to participate." Bob Spike wrote Moses that the NCC considered the NLG's involvement "so serious a complication" that it considered withdrawing its support. The Justice Department and the national civil rights organizations likewise condemned the move. SCLC's Andrew Young asked SNCC to reconsider, the NAACP's Roy Wilkins flatly refused cooperation, and CORE's Carl Rachlin even informed Burke Marshall and the FBI of the NLG's involvement.[24]

This backlash upset Moses. Although the NCC had agreed to pay for the volunteers' training and transportation, he was loath to repudiate the NLG's help. He begged Greenberg and others to see that the Communist issue "is not our fight. Don't make it our fight." In life-and-death cases, Moses told the *National Guardian*, the Communist issue was "irrelevant. Some of the best legal service we have received has come from the Guild. We have found the Guild willing to take cases that we could get none of the other lawyers to handle." Moreover, his critics' assumptions were patronizing and hypocritical, he later explained.

> You're trying to do what you say [Communists] want to do. I
> mean, you're going to say, "They're going to come in and tell us
> who we can associate with"—that's why you don't want them in.
> [But] you're just doing that right now . . . we're our own people

and are able to figure out who we want to associate with [so] you don't really credit us with being able to do that [as if] we are somehow people that need to be protected and you are the people to protect us.

National SNCC chose Moses's side and finally forcefully confirmed its commitment to free association. When he traveled to Stanford University in mid-April, he staunchly defended COFO's choice not to have "that whole atmosphere of the fifties injected into the movement." Furious, Lowenstein advised the students to withdraw from the Project, alleging that Moses was "run by Peking." From then on, Moses carefully avoided him; he even had Mendy Samstein covering for him. Lowenstein eventually left the project, and although he and Moses saw each other occasionally that summer, they did not speak for almost a year.[25]

With Lowenstein's departure, Moses lost not only an important recruiter with valuable political connections but also a much-needed mediator between the different civil rights groups. On the national level, the groups aligned in COFO seriously mistrusted each other, and the Project only intensified interorganizational rivalry. SNCC especially resented the fact that other organizations used COFO for their own projection but were unwilling to commit significant amounts of money and manpower. The NAACP, in turn, resented its limited role in COFO's decision-making structure and considered the Project a waste of money. As Roy Wilkins told SNCC, "The NAACP doesn't put anything into a project where it doesn't expect to get something out." The upshot, Moses noted concerned, was that SNCC faced a huge financial challenge.[26]

These rivalries seriously complicated Moses's efforts to get the Project off the ground, but he characteristically resolved such conflicts by reminding all of their common goals and to look at long-term pragmatics. For example, when James Farmer announced the Summer Project in the *Washington Post* on February 23 despite COFO's agreement to announce it at a joint press conference on March 15, he instantly sought consensus. "[I]f the national organizations insist on releasing press statements which give the impression that the entire program is their own," he explained to Farmer, "then that will inexorably lead to cynicism and demoralization of the staff which must work very closely together in the field." He assured Farmer that "it is possible to all work together" and confessed that *Newsweek* also had wrongly implied that the Project was also SNCC's. In reprimanding Farmer, his main concern was not SNCC's projection but, he continued, the damage for Mississippi blacks "who are in desperate need of a united front to give them psychological courage." In April, he therefore proposed that SNCC should "develop some means of publicizing good points of the various civil rights groups and their programs."[27]

But not all SNCC workers understood the importance of Moses's attempts to guard everyone's interests. Although SNCC's goal had always been facilitating local organizations as independent units, its fear of COFO as a competing force had only increased since it had recently adopted a constitution and held monthly meetings. At SNCC's Executive Committee meeting in June, some therefore even questioned Moses's loyalty to SNCC, because how "could Bob set up a confederation like COFO through which these other groups would . . . raise funds for their own operations and use the publicity if Bob really cared about SNCC?" As usual, he responded with calm pragmatism. "My commitment is basically as a SNCC person," he vowed, but what mattered was not SNCC's projection but that "the energy that makes COFO positive comes from SNCC." Mary King later commented that "the prospect of one thousand white volunteers . . . was what [really] was bothering people and that was why they had turned on Bob." But it was not even that, one worker confessed at the meeting, "[I]t's not whites that are feared but *death*." But there was no way back. The time for what Moses called the "final showdown" had come.[28]

MOSES'S MOST SUBSTANTIAL attempt to safeguard movement consensus was the organization of two orientation sessions for the volunteers before the Project's start. He had argued for them since January. It was essential, he asserted in June, that SNCC "set a tone at the orientation [so the] volunteers can understand . . . what they're getting into." To finance the orientation, he secured $25,000 from the NCC and, following up on a suggestion by Myles Horton, sizable donations from Chicago philanthropist Lucy Montgomery. Western College for Women in Oxford, Ohio, agreed to host the week-long sessions after Berea College in Kentucky withdrew following protests of alumni and trustees. The first session, for 300 volunteers who would work on voter registration, started on June 14 and the second, for 175 Freedom School teachers, on June 21.[29]

Moses left an indelible stamp on both sessions. He outlined the Project's goals in the keynote address and spoke regularly throughout both weeks. COFO had no money, he told the volunteers, so they should depend on local leadership. He emphasized the dangerous realities of their jobs. COFO's lawyers would help them when arrested, he reassured, but told them not to be distracted by allegations about the National Lawyers' Guild. "This kind of thing bogs us down. I don't want to get caught up in a discussion of communism in the movement. It's divisive, and it's not a negotiable issue." He urged them to avoid arrests if at all possible and to post bail if they were. Female volunteers should wear modest clothing, he advised, and avoid going to bars. "Don't come to Mississippi this summer to save the Mississippi Negro," he stressed. "Only come if you understand, really understand, that his freedom and yours are one."[30]

He warned that they should be realistic in terms of what they could achieve. "Maybe we're not going to get many people registered [or] into Freedom Schools. Maybe all we're going to do is *live* through this summer. In Mississippi, that will be so much!" One volunteer wrote that he considered merely "our spending the summer in Negro homes . . . a very important victory." When addressing the second group, Moses added, "You are not going to Mississippi to try to be heroes. . . . You are heroes enough just going into the state. This is not a Freedom Ride. . . . You have a job to do. If each of you can leave behind you three people who are stronger than before, this will be almost 3000 more people we will have to work with next year."[31]

Direct action was to be avoided. Integrated restaurants were of no interest to Mississippi's black poor, he explained, and a sit-in or "unwise individual action" in northeast Mississippi "might provoke a killing in the southwest." In a memo to the volunteers' parents, he underlined the fact that "we are specifically avoiding any demonstrations for integrated facilities, as we do not feel the state is ready to permit such activity at this time." Several COFO workers disagreed, especially now that the new Civil Rights Act, effective on July 2, begged testing. Stokely Carmichael and Bob Zellner grudgingly urged teenagers in Greenwood to follow Moses's directives, but local youth—spearheaded by Laura McGhee's son Silas—moved independently. As Moses predicted, this eventually provoked white mob violence and Silas's near-fatal shooting.[32]

Because most volunteers did not know what to expect, COFO staff lectured them on Mississippi history and law, aided by role-playing workshops. Drawing a map of Mississippi on the blackboard, Moses explained its different areas in terms of black population strengths, leniency toward civil rights, and presence of white supremacist groups. Volunteers were instructed to memorize the Inc. Fund's "If You Are

Arrested in Mississippi" pamphlet and COFO's Security Handbook. Workers read out hate mail they had received. One letter called the volunteers "morally rotten outcasts" who upon entering Mississippi deserved to "get their just dues as infiltrators of an enemy power." But not everyone appeared to understand what they were getting into, Cleveland Sellers observed. "Many of them talked about Mississippi as if it were somehow the same romanticized scenes they had read in *Gone with the Wind*."[33]

Most volunteers were white, came from urban areas in New England or California, and attended elite universities like Harvard and Berkeley. Their median family income was twice the national average. Only 10 percent were black—not a bad showing in view of the fact that blacks accounted for only 2.9 percent of the nation's college students and that very few attended the top universities where SNCC recruited. Because the volunteers had to be self-supporting and those younger than twenty-one needed parental consent, most were older than the 1960 sit-in students. In early July, about 450 volunteers were in Mississippi. They were later supplemented with another 400, but there were never more than 650 at any one time. Several hundreds of doctors, educators, and clergymen volunteered as well through organizations like the Delta Ministry and the Medical Committee on Human Rights.[34]

As Moses feared, race and class tensions emerged even before the volunteers set foot in Mississippi. Although some COFO members welcomed the volunteers—"We need you," Fannie Lou Hamer pleaded, "Help us communicate with white people"—others were openly hostile. They mistrusted the volunteers' inexperience, fearing that "that idiot in my group [will] get me killed by doing something stupid." The *New York Herald Tribune* even reported of rumors "that some of the staff disliked whites and would like to see [them] get hurt in Mississippi." It did not help that reporters swarmed around the volunteers. "*Look*-magazine is searching for the ideal naïve northern middle-class white girl," one wrote home, "For the national press, that's the big story."[35]

Tension reached a crisis on June 16 when some volunteers laughed during a showing of the documentary Moses had helped to film in 1962. Registrar Theron Lynd came across as cartoonish, while local activist Hattie Sisson, a hero to COFO workers, appeared eccentric, even as she told of the horror of the shooting that had nearly killed her granddaughter and her friend in Ruleville the previous summer. Hollis Watkins—who had risked his life exposing Lynd—exploded in rage and six other

COFO members walked out, offended and repulsed by the volunteers' naivety and insensitivity.[36]

Feeling guilty, Moses resumed his role as mediator. He was shocked to discover how large the disparity between the volunteers and staff was in understanding each other and what they were about to do. For days, he and other COFO staff had been trying to give the volunteers a sense of the southern black experience, but the incident only revealed how precarious race relations within the movement were. One volunteer documented that during the clash, "Bob and Dona Moses were both in tears." Staughton Lynd recorded that just four days earlier, Moses had stated "that if anyone was to blame for cutting off the discussion of feeling toward whites too soon, it was he." He had tended "to discourage the kind of soul-sharing Sherrod cultivated in SW Georgia" and simply put twenty of SNCC's black NAG workers in the Delta and made Stokely Carmichael district director to "eliminate staff misgivings" about whites taking over. Moreover, he had supported the white community summer projects of the Southern Student Organizing Committee, a new organization of southern whites founded by SNCC's Sam Shirah, in Jackson and Biloxi, hoping that they would diminish black-white tensions by demonstrating to black staff members that white workers would be "facing the same dangers they are, but in white communities." But COFO workers just saw the projects as a convenient way of keeping whites out of black ones.[37]

Since all these remedies clearly had proven inadequate, Moses realized that he now had to face the issue head on. So he informed the second volunteer group of COFO's endless discussions on race, of which the first group had known nothing. He used an analogy from Albert Camus's *The Plague*, in which the authorities refused to recognize the disease at great expense. The same was true for the "plague of prejudice," he said. "The country isn't willing yet to admit it has the plague, but it pervades the whole society. Everyone must come to grip with this, because it affects us all." He pleaded to "discuss it openly and honestly, even with the danger that we get too analytic and tangled up. If we ignore it, it's going to blow up in our faces."[38]

When John Doar addressed the volunteers, Moses again served as a mediator. The volunteers had just written a poignant plea to President Johnson. "[A]s we depart for that troubled state, [we ask] to hear your voice in support of those principles to which Americans have dedicated and sacrificed themselves." But when asked what protection they could expect, Doar bluntly told them, "Nothing. There is no federal police force." Angry, the volunteers started booing until Moses intervened. "We don't do that," he reprimanded. He shamed the group by observing that "we are all—the whole nation—deeply involved in the crimes of Mississippi." As an example, he used Harvard University, which was the largest stockholder in the holding company for Mississippi Power and Light "on whose board sit several White Citizens' Council leaders." He told the second group to "be polite" to Doar and reminded them of past instances when Doar had helped the movement. "Because of Moses's admonition," one volunteer recorded, "most of the muttering remained only that."[39]

Moses was decisive in the debate over nonviolence as well. For him, this was not only a practical necessity in order to minimize bloodshed but also a basic principle. Although James Lawson and John Lewis are often considered the embodiment of philosophical nonviolence in SNCC, the latter believed it was Moses. "Maybe he didn't say he was the most nonviolent person [but] he *lived* nonviolence . . . his very existence [and] rare demeanor was [all nonviolence]." By 1964, however, Moses's views were shared by a declining minority of SNCC workers. Due to whites' increased hostility, a lack of training in nonviolence, and federal inertia, workers readily accepted locals' long tradition of armed self-defense of the properties they stayed at. "No-one here has lived the life of Gandhi," Sam Block admitted at SNCC's June meeting, "Bob's too valuable to be killed in Mississippi, because there's nothing in Mississippi worth dying for! I'm not going to carry a gun but if someone else is going to protect himself, then let him protect me as well!" Some confessed to having had guns in the Greenwood office since January.[40]

To create consensus, Moses again took a pragmatic approach. While he had earlier asked locals like Steptoe not to bring guns when they went out together and had argued that "if you do nothing to change the violent beliefs of people with whom you work, then you're inconsistent with these [nonviolent] beliefs," he now prioritized the ability to work effectively over getting into divisive discussions over nonviolence and self-defense. Whenever he drove around with Steptoe, the latter now simply hid his gun and Moses pretended to find out later, because he believed that the argument in itself was useless for the work they were doing. After all, in Mississippi, the distinction was neither appropriate nor practical. Voter registration did not depend on nonviolence either as a tactic or a way of life, because it was rarely accompanied by public demonstrations and because "there is nothing in the federal government that says you have to be nonviolent to go register." But it was not served by openly carrying guns either, since that inhibited the ability to "move as quietly as possible among people so that you could work. Because the strategy was not to pick a fight and just throw yourself into the wave of mechanisms." Moreover, he maintained at the June meeting, "Self-defense is so deeply ingrained in rural southern America that we as a small group can't affect it. It's not contradictory for a farmer to say he's nonviolent and also to pledge to shoot a marauder's head off." Yet "[t]he difference is," he reminded SNCC, "that we on the staff have committed ourselves not to carry guns." The group subsequently adopted his compromise: SNCC workers and volunteers should remain nonviolent, but they should not attempt to impose their principles on locals.[41]

When the issue resurfaced at the orientation session in Ohio, Moses's views again held sway. He informed the volunteers of SNCC's decision but acknowledged its practical difficulties by citing Camus's "gray area" between victims and executioners. "If you were in a house which was under attack, and the owner was shot, and there were kids there, and you could take his gun to protect them—should you? I can't answer that. I don't think anyone can." Bayard Rustin and James Lawson—both, like Moses, pacifists—outlined the case for philosophical nonviolence, but Stokely Carmichael rebutted them. After a heated debate, Moses stood up. One volunteer described the scene in her notebook: "As he spoke—slowly, gently—a subtle [and] permanent change came over the room. He was ultimate reality and ultimate possibility. [He said:] 'In Mississippi we have two ground rules: 1) No weapons are to be carried or kept in your room. 2) If you feel tempted to retaliate, please leave.' Questions were [now] resolved. The session ended."[42]

DESPITE MOSES'S EFFORTS, fears about what lay ahead still troubled volunteers and staff. Many released their anxieties during late-night parties. Moses turned to folk dancing, which he introduced to the exhausted civil rights workers to lift their spirits. Bob Cohen recalled "Bob leading a bunch of us in a Yugoslavian line dance to a record he had brought." Similarly, Staughton Lynd noted how after leaving one "very somber" staff meeting, they saw volunteers "dancing the *hora*. Without a word, Bob put down the papers he was carrying and joined." Julian Bond underscored how remarkable this input was. "For southern black people . . . well, we don't folk dance." Yet this outside influence Moses brought enriched their lives. "We enjoyed it and it seemed like, 'Why haven't we been doing this all along?'" But the dancing did not bring Moses solace for long.[43]

On June 22, he was addressing the second group of volunteers when a SNCC staff member came in and whispered something in his ear. He crouched and stared at his feet. Then he stood and delivered the news. "Yesterday morning, three of our people left Meridian, Mississippi, to investigate a church-burning in Neshoba County. They haven't come back, and we haven't had any word from them. We spoke to John Doar.... He promised to order the FBI to act, but the local FBI still says they have been given no authority." It seemed, one volunteer recorded, as if he "was somewhere else; it was simply that he was obliged to say something, but his voice was automatic."[44]

A pale Rita Schwerner stepped in for the shaken Moses and revealed the missing men's names: her husband, twenty-four-year-old white CORE worker Michael Schwerner; twenty-one-year-old black CORE worker James Chaney from Meridian; and twenty-year-old white volunteer Andrew Goodman, whom Moses had recruited at Queens College. Dazed, the volunteers split up to contact federal officials.[45]

Moses left and sat down on the college cafeteria steps, frozen. He instinctively realized "they were dead ... I knew that in my bones." He remained there, mute and staring blankly, for the rest of the afternoon, perhaps hoping that his heartrending sight would deter the rest of the volunteers from going to Mississippi.[46]

The Chaney-Schwerner-Goodman story is the most well known of Freedom Summer. It dominated headlines for two months. After the three investigated the burning of pro–civil rights Mt. Zion Methodist Church in Philadelphia, deputy sheriff Cecil Price locked them up in sheriff Lawrence Rainey's jail for a trumped-up traffic charge. Around 10:30 P.M. Price released them, but only after contacting Ray Edgar Killen, the ring leader of one of the White Knights' covert squads. Schwerner was a pro-integrationist atheist of Jewish descent, and as such, Sam Bowers considered him "a thorn in the flesh of everyone living." Price stopped the three again outside of town, stalling until Killen's squad arrived. They killed Schwerner and Goodman with a single shot each and Chaney with three after beating him. They burned the trio's car, which local Choctaw tribe members found in a swamp on June 23. On August 4, their bodies were found in an earthen dam.[47]

Adding to Moses's grief, project critics, like columnists Rowland Evans and Robert Novak, blamed SNCC for the deaths. Journalist Joseph Alsop charged that COFO "must have wanted, even hoped for, martyrs"; the *Washington Post* charged that the government was not "so apathetic, stupid, hypocritical or cowardly that it must be constrained to act by the threat of piling martyrs' corpses on its doorstep." Even the Justice Department pursued this line.[48]

Upset, Moses tried to offset the accusations. He communicated to Burke Marshall and other "project contacts" that Freedom Summer had not caused but "simply revealed the terror" that "is a continuing fact of life." Thirty years later, the charges still angered him. "I don't think people appreciate what [that accusation] means. Because, believe me, if it had been possible in any way . . . to stop [violence] from happening, it would have been done." Dave Dennis compared it to warfare. "When you're in a war, you don't send soldiers out to be killed, you send soldiers out to win the war, hoping like hell that they're not gonna be killed." Moreover, the decision to risk participants' lives had not been made lightly; as late as June, workers grappled with the realization that "it's our hands and our minds that created a project that's going to stimulate violence." If COFO exploited anything, Moses admitted to the volunteers, it was the sad reality that "you bring with you the concern of the country. It does not identify with Negroes. It identifies with whites." The volunteers well understood this. As one wrote home, "We're not dupes . . . I am being used, but I know why and how, and will that Bob Moses so use me."[49]

The murders nonetheless had a profound impact on Moses and his coworkers. "[I]t really took [the Project] into a different emotional space [and] level of commitment," Moses recalled. "You have got to reevaluate your going into Mississippi in light of the knowledge that some in your crew are already dead before you even get there." Ed King claimed that Moses "would not, almost could not, talk about Neshoba" for days. As with Herbert Lee and Louis Allen, he could not shake his feelings of guilt.[50]

Near the summer's end, SNCC photographer Matt Herron encountered Moses in Jackson for the first time in months. "So I greeted him effusively. 'Bob, it's great to see you! How are you?' And he stopped me dead. He looked at me with these haunted eyes, and said, 'Are you kidding?' And I realized then that he carried the murders . . . with him through that whole summer. It absolutely haunted him, and colored everything that he did." As director of the Neshoba area but absent that day, Dennis felt the same. "[W]e would have been on top of it quicker if I had been there. The people . . . there just didn't know what to do."[51]

Seeing Moses upset contributed to the COFO workers' despair. "There had to be *something* more we could do to help the brothers," Stokely Carmichael verbalized their thoughts. "And for ourselves. And for Bob." On June 23, several therefore went to Neshoba. They searched for the bodies in snake-infested swamps and abandoned buildings at night while ducking the Klan. Among them was Moses's wife. She *"insisted,"* Ivanhoe Donaldson said, "and who was going to stop her?"[52]

AS AFTER HERBERT LEE's death, Moses lifted his initial immobility by deciding that fulfillment of COFO's goals was the only way to make the trio's sacrifice meaningful. Withdrawal was no option, he wrote the volunteers' parents. "Negroes of Mississippi have suffered for decades from [this] kind of incident. . . . Only our presence in Mississippi ensures the continued concern of the nation for the Negroes of that state." He joined John Lewis and James Forman in calling the federal government and asked the volunteers and their parents to do likewise. He, Forman, Henry, Guyot, and Charles Evers met Central Intelligence Agency (CIA) director Allen Dulles in Jackson on June 25. Meanwhile, FOS groups held support demonstrations in New York, Chicago, and Boston. They planned civil disobedience in Washington too, but Moses instructed SNCC to reject the plans because it implied that COFO wanted to embarrass the government, rather than exhort it to act.[53]

On June 26, Moses and other COFO members met with Arthur Kinoy and William Kunstler in Oxford. "We cannot sit here and do nothing," Kinoy recalled Moses as saying. "Think of something! We want you to do something that says loud and clear we are not running. . . . We're hitting back!" They devised an unprecedented lawsuit, *COFO v. Rainey*, on behalf of all Mississippi blacks against Lawrence Rainey and all other racist local sheriffs. Volunteer lawyers compiled affidavits from locals like Fannie Lou Hamer and outsiders like Rita Schwerner and Mario Savio. COFO distributed copies of the brief for publicity. In August, the lawyers filed a suit on behalf of Moses, Henry, Dennis, and SNCC's Hunter Morey, challenging the new state laws passed to obstruct civil rights activism, and NLG lawyer Victor Rabinowitz spoke with Moses and James Forman about lawsuits against Greenwood, Clarksdale, and Canton authorities.[54]

Moses further increased COFO's safety precautions. He insisted that nobody should travel alone without leaving details of the destination. COFO installed a two-way radio system that linked its offices and cars. Communications workers were instructed to call the Jackson office every two hours and maintain instruction boards with timelines when someone left. Moses reversed the decision to send volunteers to southwest Mississippi for the time being. A week later, however, he decided that COFO could not desert locals around McComb again. Since "anyone who goes in faces a high probability of death," he told *Newsweek*, experienced staff members went instead. "Then nobody can accuse us of sending [volunteers] in for the purpose of getting killed. Then the whole question will be whether the country will do for us and for Negro people what they have done for the volunteers." He privately admitted that this deployment also provided a means for black staff members to "escape from the volunteers." Remembering Ella Baker's lessons about looking after movement participants' long-term development, he flew to California to recruit his Harlem friend Alvin Poussaint, now an established psychiatrist, as a physician for staff and volunteers.[55]

Getting through to the volunteers was Moses's biggest concern. After the burned car was found, "I was sure they were dead," he said, but he kept this to himself for Rita Schwerner's sake. "But then there were the volunteers. They had to be told the truth." He and other staff "did their best to discourage our coming," one volunteer wrote home. "Moses said he wished they would find the bodies . . . just to make us fully realize what we were getting into." During "one long 'soul-session' discussion," another reported, "he sent us away for hours to rethink." Some volunteers were shaken. "Thoughts are going crazy," one wrote. "Moses just told us now is the time to back out. Should I? I don't know—I am scared shitless." COFO's medical staff reported a noteworthy rise in "those openly anxious, fearful or unable to sleep soundly." But for others, the murders gave Mississippi a romantic aura. Reporters' depiction of the volunteers as heroes encouraged this feeling. Across the nation, various organizations announced plans to come to Mississippi in carloads. Even the NAACP now spoke of sending in 1,000 individuals.[56]

Fearing chaos, Moses and Forman rushed to media outlets to discourage them. "People coming into Mississippi will not help the program as it has been developed and will not help black people," Moses stated. They helped best by remaining in the North, where they could "act as a force for political pressure." When people kept calling the FOS offices, he reiterated on June 27 that untrained volunteers would only hinder the effort since COFO could not "house them, supervise their activities, or protect them."[57]

After only a handful of volunteers quit, Moses addressed the group once more in a final speech that represented the quintessence of his leadership style and thereby unintentionally enhanced his reputation. One volunteer called his speech a "near sacred moment" that "increased my commitment.... The impact on me was riveting and life affecting." Another termed it "one of my most profound experiences of leadership ... I would have done anything he asked me to do—I trusted him so much."[58]

As Moses spoke, he hung his head and stared at his feet. Speaking slowly and softly, he drew an analogy from J. R. R. Tolkien's *The Lord of the Rings*. "There is a weariness from constant attention to the things you are doing, the struggle of good against evil." Drawing upon Tolkien allowed him to express his emotions while hiding behind a fictitious character. His and Frodo's struggle in resisting an unwanted corrupting power and the exhaustion of constantly battling evil were essentially the same. Invoking Tolkien, rather than the Bible, helped him to reach the northern students, as it was one of the most popular books among educated young people. He hoped it might help "to get them to understand what it was like, what SNCC workers ... were going through." It worked, one volunteer wrote home. "For those ... who knew the book, it was a great and beautiful moment and it gave us an understanding which we might otherwise never have had."[59]

Moses then said, "The kids are dead." He paused, one volunteer noted, "without regard for dramatic effect. But long enough for it to hit us." The group turned silent. "There may be more deaths," Moses added and, after another pause, "I justify myself because I'm taking risks myself, and I'm not asking people to do things I'm not willing to do." Moreover, "people were being killed already, the Negroes of Mississippi, and I feel, anyway, responsible for their deaths." He cited Herbert Lee and Louis Allen. But "[i]f you are going to do anything about it," he sighed, "other people are going to be killed. No privileged group in history has ever given up anything without some kind of blood sacrifice." He again stared silently at the floor. "Obviously," one volunteer wrote home, his rationales "don't satisfy him ... Moses almost seemed to be wanting all of us to go home." Moses then continued, "[I]n our country we have some real evil.... If for any reason you're hesitant about what you're getting into, it's better for you to leave. Because what has got to be done has to be done in a certain way, or otherwise it won't get done."

An absolute silence followed until a girl sang "They Say That Freedom Is a Constant Struggle." All stayed.[60]

FREEDOM SUMMER HAD barely begun, and yet COFO had already largely accomplished what it sought to achieve. The Project had become a defining example of successful nonviolent direct action; it invited white retaliation, but its effect on a national audience paradoxically inhibited new violence. Only after the killings did federal authorities and Mississippi's white elite finally determine to eradicate the state's terrorist groups. Yet it was perhaps the blow to the state's economy that was the most persuasive. After the murders, Gulf Coast tourism dropped by 50 percent, the state had to borrow $8 million in expenses, and its tax revenues fell. Some factories even relocated offices to Louisiana to avoid Mississippi mailing addresses. Subsequently, Governor Johnson, Senator Eastland, and Mayor Thompson publicly repudiated the violence and ordered compliance with the Civil Rights Act. "The country," Moses concluded to *Newsweek*, "unfortunately, moves only in response to acts of violence." Apart from southwest Mississippi, he stated in August that "there is little harassment of workers. . . . We interpret that as meaning that police put out the word to local citizens." Although wary of the word *success*, he pointed out that "the whole pattern of law enforcement of the past hundred years has been reversed. In some areas the police are offering protection where they never did before."[61]

Yet neither the KKK nor local authorities surrendered easily. The FBI documented that COFO nonetheless suffered 1,000 arrests, thirty-five shootings, and eight beatings during the short summer; COFO reported many more incidents of harassment. Reports taken over the WATS telephone line of a typical day in July for instance looked like this:

JULY 2: *Harmony*: Cross burned, tacks strewn in Negro community

Hattiesburg: Two vote registration canvassers followed and questioned by men describing themselves as state officials. . . . Local police stop Negro girl, five white boys en route home. Policeman curses, threatens arrest, slaps one boy

Batesville: Panola County Sheriff Carl Hubbard detains several persons housing civil rights workers

Meridian: White teenage girl throws bottle at civil rights group
    outside church, cuts leg of local Negro girl
Canton: Local police turn on sirens, play music on loudspeaker
    near COFO-office, fail to answer phone calls or highway patrol
Gulfport: Two voter registration workers threatened. . . . Man grabs
    volunteer's shirt: "I'm going to whip your ass." Workers run.

Another worker, black volunteer Wayne Yancey, died in a suspicious car crash probably caused deliberately by white racists. In McComb alone, twenty-five bombings and burnings occurred. State officials kept targeting the Project as Communist led and treated the trio's disappearance as a hoax. Senator Eastland even maintained that the three were "probably laughing it up on Moscow Gold in a New York hotel." When Rita Schwerner, Ed King, and Bob Zellner tried to see Governor Johnson, Schwerner's WATS report reads, he "slammed the door and locked it."[62]

This was not surprising considering how involved state authorities had been in the crime. The MSSC had distributed information on Schwerner to the KKK, and Sheriff Rainey blatantly refused to join the subsequent search or even to speak with the FBI. To Moses's amazement, even Governor Johnson admitted in 1970 to having known that the trio would be taken out of jail to scare them but that it had simply ended badly. COFO's compilation of its fifty calls to federal and state authorities underscored the latter's deliberate passivity. Prison employees lied about the trio's presence, and the local FBI ignored COFO's calls. The local FBI even refused action until late afternoon the next day when residential agent John Proctor "interviewed" Cecil Price while enjoying smuggled liquor together. It accordingly "took 24 hours—undoubtedly the critical 24 hours," Moses told the volunteers in Ohio, "to get the Federal Government to act."[63]

Moses was upset that the White House seemed equally aloof. Rita Schwerner saw Allen Dulles in Jackson—for two minutes. On June 29, she met an unenthusiastic Lee White in Washington. "If you wish to talk with me," White wrote President Johnson beforehand, "my secretary can get me out of the meeting." Afterward, he nonetheless brought her to the president. She asked him for "thousands of extra people," Johnson told J. Edgar Hoover, but "I told her I [had already] put [in] all that we could efficiently handle." Johnson initially refused to meet the parents of Schwerner and Goodman as well for fear "that [if] I start housemothering each kid that's gone down there and that doesn't show up . . . we'll have this White House full of people every day." He eventually agreed to see them because White reminded him that the visit was "highly publicized," but reassured the president that "it would not be necessary to endorse the project [or] blame Mississippi."[64]

The case nonetheless deeply troubled the president. The disappearance dominated his telephone calls for ten days. The calls betray his sense of powerlessness, as evidenced by his repetitive questions to each caller whether they thought the men were murdered. He tried to walk a tightrope between segregationist Mississippians and the civil rights groups. "I'm doing what I can," he sighed in one call, to "be as considerate of my fellow man as I can and still try to lead the nation." But the civil rights groups made this impossible, he complained to J. Edgar Hoover. "[We have to] show the country that we are really working [on this] because if we don't this crowd's gonna demand everything in the world."[65]

President Johnson subsequently ordered 400 Marines to drag swamps for the bodies and sent 100 additional FBI agents. He told Hoover he did not "want these Klansmen to open their mouth without your knowing." Hoover opened an FBI office in Jackson for investigations but "most certainly not," he assured *The Clarion-Ledger*, to "give protection to civil rights workers." Yet the new agents, appalled by what they inherited, infiltrated the Klan and interviewed over 1,000 Mississippians. Paid informants revealed the men's burial place, and federal authorities arrested twenty whites. In 1967, seven of the suspects, including Cecil Price, were imprisoned for depriving the trio of their civil rights (but not for murder since homicide is a state and not a federal crime). In 2005, Ray Edgar Killen was retried and sentenced to sixty years for manslaughter. The *Saturday Evening Post* reported that by January 1965, the KKK's membership in Mississippi had shrunk to 2,000. The breakup of the KKK and the resolution of the murders can largely be attributed to Johnson's order.[66]

But for Moses and other COFO workers, these successes did not outweigh the administration's initial reserve. John Lewis placed "the full responsibility for these deaths directly in the hands of the United States Justice Department and the [FBI]." Moses likewise charged at SNCC's Fall Conference that "the federal government is more willing to sacrifice the lives of Negroes . . . than it is to tamper with the structure of the government." He told *Newsweek* the federal government's weak response confirmed that the nation considered white lives more valuable than black ones. He tried to see the benefit of the uptick in attention, hoping that it would improve the lives of local people. But only a saint would not have resented the fact that suddenly the AP, UPI, NBC, ABC, and CBS called COFO headquarters twice daily, and national papers like the *New York Times* and *Washington Post* now stationed reporters in Jackson. That the search for the bodies of the civil rights workers turned up other bodies—including those of two black Alcorn student-activists missing since 1963—fueled SNCC's bitterness. "As soon as it was determined that these bodies were not the three," Dave Dennis recalled, "those deaths were forgotten."[67]

Such emotions further complicated Moses's attempts to maintain movement consensus. At James Chaney's memorial service on August 7, Dennis ventured his fury. He tearfully proclaimed that he had "a bitter vengeance in my heart tonight [and] I'm not going to stand here and ask anybody . . . not to be angry!"[68]

While Dennis did not say so out loud, he, as well as many other COFO workers, had reached "a point whereby I just could not anymore tell people to be nonviolent." Yet Moses's influence prevailed. At a Greenwood staff meeting, Stokely Carmichael went "to get the mandate from Bob" to arm himself. After the phone call, one observer documented, Carmichael returned "a different man." As "calm and thoughtful as Moses himself, Stokely said, 'What I think we ought to do is work harder on freedom registration forms.'" For the time being Moses's consensus-building approach still worked. Since both disagreed on self-defense, he convinced Carmichael to focus instead on what they could agree on, the need for voter registration.[69]

FOCUSING ON GRASSROOTS empowerment helped Moses to persevere. On August 19, he stated that the Project was "eminently successful" in its goal of "the development of local leadership and staff who will help sustain projects." Local participation, he proudly noted, "was beyond our expectation." In Leflore County, for example, where only 2 of 123 blacks managed to become registered voters that summer, 3,384 signed up for COFO's mock "freedom" registration lists. This constituted progress, Moses explained in *Pacific Scene*, "in terms of what happens to the people we are working with. . . . They don't have any participation in society but they've found freedom. They can do things that they've wanted to do for a long time. They've been able to confront people who are on their backs. They take whatever is dished out—bombings, shootings, beatings, whatever it is. After people live through that they have a scope that they didn't have before." Amzie Moore praised the Summer Project as "the best thing that's happened here since the 1940s." If measured in "numbers of people touched by the civil rights movement in Mississippi," Julian Bond agreed, "it can't be anything but a success."[70]

COFO's Freedom Schools in particular—forty-seven of them enrolled 2,500 students aged seven to seventy—brought Moses tremendous joy. Charlie Cobb had envisioned the schools in November 1963 as a prolongation of Moses's educational programs and as an attack on the "intellectual wastelands" that Mississippi's existing black schools represented. Despite the state legislature's attempts in the early 1950s to make the latter "separate but equal" to fend off the federal government, they were sometimes still housed in shabby buildings without facilities and mostly used outdated teaching material. Occasionally, the teachers were almost as poorly educated as their pupils. Black public school teachers, moreover, were notoriously reluctant to support the civil rights movement and sometimes surreptitiously undermined it. The Freedom Schools, in turn, served as parallel educational institutions but also advocated social action.[71]

Behind the scenes, Moses had worked hard to make them succeed. The schools benefited tremendously from his skills in communicating the Mississippi movement's needs to outsiders with resources, such as Broadway performers and the United Federation of Teachers. He approved Jane Stembridge's manual for the schools' prospective teachers, sent pamphlets to the volunteers so they could involve churches and other civic groups, and sought the assistance of social scientists and education specialists at Boston and Yale Universities. He met Philip Stern in Washington to discuss the schools and spoke with Myles Horton and the NCC about using Highlander and Mt. Beulah for teacher workshops. With Ella Baker and COFO's John O'Neal, he discussed screening and recruitment of the teachers. The curriculum was established at an NCC-sponsored conference in New York during March 21 to 22, which Moses attended. At his invitation, participants included Myles Horton, John Blyth, and programmed learning specialist Joan Countryman. To ensure his goal of grassroots empowerment and minimize internal conflict, he played a key role in the teachers' orientation program at Oxford, too. He advised the volunteers "to be patient" with their pupils because "there is a distinction between being slow and being stupid, and the kids in Mississippi are very, very, very slow." He knew this from experience, but he was also influenced by Frank Riessman's "slow versus dull" theories in *The*

Culturally Deprived Child, which SNCC's Mary Varela had sent him beforehand. He emphasized that the teachers should not expect too much. If they could "break off a little chunk of a problem [and] make some steps in examining it thoroughly, then [you] will have accomplished something really significant."[72]

To expose Freedom School participants to as many sources of influence as possible, Moses again appealed to his book drive donors. The French Embassy even contacted him about donating French teaching aids. The influx of books fascinated the State Sovereignty Commission, which reported nervously that those "addressed to Robert Moses" included Robert Williams's *Negroes with Guns* and C. Wright Mills's *The Marxists*. The curriculum included neither but did embrace, in one historian's words, "a radical pedagogy and a radical philosophy" that reflected Moses's thinking. The schools' essence, one volunteer explained, "was enabling the students to formulate . . . their own thoughts [and this] was certainly Moses's way." The curriculum was based on pupils' daily lives but built "up to a more realistic perception of American society, themselves, the conditions of their oppression, and alternatives offered by the Freedom Movement." This was done through questions like "How is Bob Moses like Moses in the Bible?" and "Why doesn't Mrs. Hamer stay in the North once she gets there to speak?" COFO advised the volunteers to utilize their own skills and teach what the students requested. Mirroring SNCC's decentralized structure, there were no set opening times and no traditional discipline. Under the influence of northern educators, the schools prioritized literacy and math, but leadership development was never forgotten. In typing classes, for instance, students wrote freedom newspapers, and French was used to develop grammar and phonology in English, which would benefit job searches.[73]

All schools experienced failures and successes, but overall Moses considered them one of the Project's greatest achievements. On August 6—two days after the harrowing discovery of the Chaney, Schwerner, and Goodman bodies—he attended a three-day Freedom School Convention in Meridian. Each school sent three student representatives and a coordinator. The Holly Springs school performed a play about Medgar Evers, and speakers included A. Philip Randolph and James Forman. Characteristically, Moses merely asked questions to help students "articulate what they wanted for the future." He gleefully watched as the students formed committees to formulate a platform for the Mississippi movement's new political party on topics ranging from housing and education to foreign affairs. "It was the single time in my life that I have seen Bob happiest," Staughton Lynd observed. "He just ate it up."[74]

Moses also cherished the establishment of sixteen community centers statewide as additional tools for creating a parallel society. Like the Freedom Schools, they had a dual function. They provided daycare, educational assistance, and recreation for youth and gave adults leadership training, political education, job training, and help with health and Social Security problems. Moses's own involvement was limited to enlisting his Uncle Bill to construct one center and, through Myles Horton, in recruiting two wealthy Californians to provide a building crew and job training for locals in Mileston, although he occasionally advised workers. At his suggestion, one group for example tried to cooperate with local doctors in setting up a clinic.[75]

The schools and centers were of lasting significance to the locals participating in them. Some, like the Dwight sisters and Walter Saddler, even became scholars or news anchors later in life. Several centers stayed open after the summer, but others faltered for lack of facilities, money, and local personnel. To continue them, COFO's reports confirm, it had "to find support in large doses from outside of the state." The schools did continue into the fall and were revived in the summer of 1965. "I have learned . . . much more this summer than I learned in many, many years," one teenager wrote elated. "Freedom School ment more to me then I can explain."[76]

To spur grassroots leadership further, Moses made sure to include music and drama. He helped to recruit forty New York musicians for a Caravan of Music. Bob Cohen, Pete Seeger, Bob Dylan, Judy Collins, and other singers taught musical workshops and performed spirituals at Freedom Schools and community centers statewide. To encourage locals' artistic aspirations, Moses helped organize a folk and drama festival in early August at which they could perform. Cohen served as coordinator and Sam Block and Willie Peacock as codirectors. Moses was program chair and secured the festival site. Three other SNCC workers founded the integrated Free Southern Theater and traveled the state performing Martin Duberman's play *In White America*. In Ruleville, blacks organized a Freedom Festival at which Freedom School pupils read self-written poems and performed plays, including "a puppet play in which the valiant knight Bob Moses fought the wicked witch Segregation."[77]

DESPITE SUCH SUCCESSES, Moses was sad to see that strife within some projects threatened to curtail the development of grassroots leadership. Internal racial tensions remained present throughout the summer, although many have been exaggerated after the fact. Nonetheless, "the space in the black community was really not a completely welcoming space," Moses recalled, "so [the volunteers] had to figure out how to walk through that [and it] is to their everlasting credit that they did." Culture shock added to their difficulty in adapting. "I really can't stand it here," one volunteer wrote home, "the SNCC field staff with their cold, emotionless eyes and blank, beaten faces . . . the filthy, vermin-infested living conditions in Ruleville [and blacks'] hopelessness and apathy." Yet most locals' affectionate treatment of volunteers and Moses's and other veteran staff's mediation helped keep tensions submerged for the time being.[78]

For example, during the orientation and in memoranda, COFO workers had advised the volunteers on how to handle locals. Moses stressed facilitation, while James Forman told them not to address them on a first-name basis and to help with chores. Historian-activist Vincent Harding warned them not to use locals—and each other—in an emotional or sexual way. " 'My summer Negro,' 'the White girl I made' are no different from the token Negro in the school," he said, "none are really known and experienced." Stokely Carmichael pointed out that many black southerners disapproved of alcohol and counciled the volunteers against using it. Annelle Ponder advised to respect locals' manners, costume, and faith. Others told the volunteers to "encourage people to speak up," "go slowly enough to include everyone," and "praise people freely." The training encouraged volunteers not to treat blacks, as Robert Penn Warren put it, as "an abstraction" that they could "decorate with certain self-indulgent theories, feelings, and fantasies, like a Christmas tree." Some whites nonetheless displayed attitudes that were similar to the national media's romanticized portrayal of the Project. Some even tried to become "more Negro than Negroes." Moses recalled that such whites "became objects of amusement" in COFO but also invoked "suspicion as to their motives."[79]

Veteran staff members were sometimes guilty of romanticism, too. Forman derisively called this "local people-itis," the idea that "local people could do no wrong," and that "no-one, especially somebody from outside the community, should initiate any kind of action or assume any form of leadership." When staff members could not "bear to hurt the delicate sensitivities of a group of local youths" who had disrupted the COFO office, some workers, for example, penned a furious memo that condemned this "Bourgeois sentimentality." This kind of "middle class paternalism," they wrote, implied that "we done been 'prived so long that we is not capable of observing simple rules of discipline and must be excused for anything we do." The youths' elevation to "the miraculous, the rare and into totally overwhelming sacred cows . . . bewilders and sickens us," they went on. "If you been poor you know damned well there ain't no nobility in that." Jane Stembridge likewise complained that those "who think it is glorious to put on levis and identify with the people . . . are full of shit."[80]

Lyrical words about the potential of grassroots leadership made Moses liable to accusations of romanticization too. In the *Village Voice*, he described Mississippi's "pure and uncorrupted sharecroppers" as "the greatest source of strength for the Movement." He told reporter Jack Newfield that he and his wife planned to travel Mississippi next year "teaching Negroes about themselves, those poor, simple folks on the bottom no-one trusts . . . I'll get them to write about their lives, and I'll send some of it to you because it will be so poetic." He particularly attracted criticism for his unbounded faith in Fannie Lou Hamer. "Even the usually level-headed, reserved Bob Moses," her biographer Chana Kai Lee concurred, "tended to blur the distinction between what Hamer was actually doing and the immensity of her mobilizing potential." Nevertheless, Hamer vindicated Moses's stress on grassroots movements. SNCC's Communications Department even deliberately built her up as such for the media. Hamer purposely crafted a public image of herself too by emphasizing her "triumph over destitution" while masking the stereotypical stigma of needing outside help. Northern whites swooned over stories like hers, and SNCC knew it.[81]

But unlike Moses, some volunteers believed that locals could not do it themselves or at least that they could do it *better*. "[T]here is a kind of Jesus Christ complex that many middle class whites bring to their relations with people whom they consider oppressed," one acknowledged in a letter. Another noted that the volunteers had "fresher energy than the veterans" and "less patience with a casual approach." "The inefficiency of people running their own shows tends to bug northerners," her colleague agreed, so "the tendency is to step in." Most such cases were relatively mild, volunteer Paul Lauter recalled, citing workers who had "learned a lot about black history [and] wanted to *tell* it to the [Freedom School] kids" instead of letting them "express their own thoughts." Other examples were more severe. "White college-educated Northerners have a tendency to take command of an assembly through rapid-fire parliamentary [maneuvers]," another volunteer wrote home, "which leave local people baffled and offended." In Vicksburg, a volunteer even lectured its native project director on "local problems as if they were issues that had arisen in a college seminar." The volunteer subsequently left Mississippi after Moses took the director's side.[82]

This left Moses in a bind. As during the Freedom Vote, the Project's short time span demanded the skills of educated whites but may have weakened local leadership. The volunteers' skills ensured that things could be done faster, but it hurt him to see that locals, especially native COFO workers, withdrew from the projects. Locals felt inferior, native SNCC worker Mary Lane explained. "After these people came in, you could see . . . it every day, 'the man' moving up a little more . . . and you find out that they can do a much better job of it than you could." In 1965, Ulysses Everett, another native worker, recalled his anger when he returned to the Hattiesburg SNCC office after having spent months in jail. Everything was "completely changed from what it was. And you see all these kids around, typing, you know, talking [but] I didn't understand what they was talking about, because I didn't have an education. I couldn't type [but for us] it was worth something just being in the office working." He fled to the black-dominated project in Laurel.[83]

Moreover, while Moses and COFO had predicted such strife, they had underestimated the impact of the black community's internal class differences. Locals' willingness to accept veterans' and volunteers' flaws decreased the higher one got up the social ladder. Despite Moses's calls to locate "doctors, teachers, ministers, beauticians etc. and try to involve them in the program," the Summer Project exacerbated tensions between COFO and the black middle class. Although workers adapted their behavior to middle-class mores, a minority rubbed against them through partying, inappropriately casual dress, or acting superior. Moses and Bill Hansen had to travel to the Gulf Coast projects in order to squelch locals' complaints "about sex and drinking." Laurel's NAACP president, Dr. B. E. Murph, chastised workers' "erratic irresponsibility" in an angry letter to Gloster Current. They preyed on NAACP members and displayed amoral behavior, including "vivacious looking white girls who smiled at everyone without provocation." They smoked and played dice, painted the NAACP building without permission, stocked the library with trashy novels, and left clutter. "The story . . . is the same all over the State. It is worse in some places. They have taken over the Civil Rights Program," Murph concluded dismayed. "COFO Must Go!"[84]

Other NAACP members had reached similar conclusions, although Moses kept trying to mediate. When Charles Evers, Medgar's less consensus-minded brother, for instance asked him for manpower for a citizenship school, he accepted but insisted that it should be a joint project based in participatory democracy. Believing in top-down leadership, Evers rejected such restrictions and decided to refuse involvement with COFO and Freedom Summer altogether. Meanwhile, relations between the national NAACP and SNCC also deteriorated after the mid-July race riots in Harlem, when SNCC, to President Johnson's and the moderate civil rights organizations' dismay, refused to support a moratorium on demonstrations until after his reelection. Despite outward unity, Gloster Current now frankly advised Evers to "encourage Dr. Henry to wean himself away" from COFO and to "review our relationship with that outfit at the end of the summer." When NAACP members did participate in COFO activities, SNCC sometimes resented it. In Batesville, for example, workers complained that the community center was "too exclusively of the educated people. The majority are teachers and pretty much dominate the goings and doings." Rather than welcoming such participation as evidence of local leadership, SNCC deplored it.[85]

Moses was too caught up in the summer's work to contend with the issues that were proliferating. He presumed that dealing more thoroughly with internal conflict could wait until after the summer. This would prove a costly mistake. The divide between middle- and working-class blacks and the lingering tensions between the civil rights organizations would unintentionally but catastrophically come to a head in the Summer Project's political program.

CHAPTER EIGHT

A Moment Lost

In the night of July 22 to 23, 1964, President Lyndon B. Johnson lay in bed, unable to sleep. He was mulling over the Democratic National Convention (DNC) to be held in Atlantic City between August 22 and 27. He hoped it would be a glorious moment, with flag waving and cheering crowds as Party delegations from all fifty states nominated him as their candidate for the 1964 presidential elections. But he knew COFO had different plans.[1]

For months, Moses and COFO had worked hard to build a broad-based coalition of white liberals and national movement leaders that helped the newly established Mississippi Freedom Democratic Party (MFDP), a grassroots political movement consisting mostly of poor blacks, demand to be seated at the DNC instead of the official, all-white Mississippi delegation. This forced the president into a catch-22. If he indulged the Dixiecrats, he could lose vital northern support, but rejecting them might cost him the presidency. "The only thing that can really screw us good," Johnson knew, is "that group of challengers from Mississippi."[2]

The prospect filled Moses both with excitement and apprehension. Everything he had done until now was a buildup to this moment. The Challenge was a daring yet calculated political gamble. Citing John Dewey's beliefs that education and democracy should be mutually reinforcing, he saw the MFDP as a quintessential vehicle for developing enduring grassroots leadership. "The radicalness of it is getting the people whose issue it is to actually be an integral part of the strategy, from the meetings, the policy, the actions, everything." After all, Mississippi politicians' allegations that COFO were outside agitators, stirring up an otherwise unwilling populace, could only be countered by the people themselves. What made matters even more pressing was his belief that the effectiveness of the movement at large hinged on the outcome of the Challenge. "[The political structure hasn't] been able to come up with real solutions. Everything has been patchwork," he explained in April. "How long can this go on? How long are Negroes goin' to maintain nonviolence? . . . the answer is I don't know."[3]

The Challenge represented a defining moment for his own leadership too. Moses's hands-on organizing skills and out-of-state contacts were vital for its realization, but he had to ensure that black Mississippians were not eclipsed in the process. Moreover, at the DNC, he was confronted with the authoritarian forms of power he loathed, and he had to figure out how to play along without adopting such tactics himself. But to save grassroots agency, he realized, he ironically might have to assert his own.

THE MFDP EXEMPLIFIED Moses's theory of parallel structures, that is, the concept of setting up institutions similar to those that excluded blacks but improving them. The regular state Democratic Party (the Regulars) held precinct, county, district, and state elections throughout the summer to choose its delegates for the DNC. Mississippi blacks would attempt to vote in these state elections, but if, as expected, they were excluded, party bylaws allowed them to form their own party (the MFDP) and choose their own delegates. Because MFDP elections were open to everyone of voting age regardless of race or literacy qualifications, they could claim at the DNC that their delegates truly represented the state's population and that the Mississippi seats therefore belonged to them. Evidence of exclusion would also strengthen demands for stronger voting rights legislation and facilitate federal lawsuits to nullify state election results. The Challenge paradoxically depended on a trust in the federal government that COFO workers increasingly doubted. Yet whereas the Challenge was a one-time, nationally oriented affair, the MFDP itself was founded as a lasting instrument for local empowerment. It was designed, its organizers wrote, to be a statewide "people's organization." Ordinary members would determine its leadership, which would be "responsible at all times for all its decision[s] to its people."[4]

The idea of the Challenge initially met resistance within SNCC. Stokely Carmichael recalled that "when Bob first raised the idea . . . [f]olks thought he was nuts. Or fantasizing." SNCC had backed congressional candidates in Albany, Selma, Danville, and Enfield (North Carolina), but no one had entertained the idea of a major political effort like the MFDP. This was partly because other southern state Democratic Parties at least claimed some kinship with the national Democratic Party and had "token" black representation. But most SNCC projects also lacked the manpower, finances, statewide coordination, and a cosmopolitan educated director with nationwide contacts. "No-one could develop the program Bob has," Don Harris admitted in June. Consequently, for weeks, the Challenge lived mostly in Moses's mind.[5]

But Moses was not just thinking; he was busy doing. COFO workers had spoken of the Challenge since the Freedom Vote, but nothing concrete developed until late December 1963. Memoranda and minutes of subsequent meetings confirm how much the enterprise depended on organizers with broad visions in its first stages, especially his. During SNCC's December 27 to 31 meeting, Moses broached the need for a plan centered on "the breakup of the Dixiecrats," because "[t]he money for real change, e.g. in education, has to come from the federal government, and won't without a change in Congress." It was an issue that, Moses knew from his 1950s summer camps, "had long floated in New York politics" and would likely find support there. He and James Bevel had discussed strategy and considered involving Bayard Rustin, a consummate networker who shared their desire to marginalize the Dixiecrats. SNCC declined to commit itself, but it liked the idea of capitalizing on Rustin's skills. Moses then joined Mendy Samstein in Atlanta to learn the daunting mechanics of Democratic Party elections. They researched the work of white southern lawyer Bill Higgs, known for representing James Meredith during his integration of Ole Miss and the penman of several titles in the new Civil Rights Act, and asked Rustin's white northern ally Rachelle Horowitz of the Workers' Defense League to investigate it further. During COFO's January 10 Executive Committee meeting, Moses presented her findings and set out a plan.[6]

Moses's guiding vision was much needed since most COFO workers found the goal of the Challenge confusing. As late as June 1964, several doubted its necessity. Charlie Cobb warned that blacks could be manipulated through party membership. Ivanhoe Donaldson agreed. "If we are working in a program which is completely controlled by those working against us what is the point of working within the Democratic Party? It is not a radical tool." But Moses, as always looking to the long term, asked them to consider how the Challenge could benefit black Mississippians. To help them, COFO needed a better understanding of economic and political structures, and the Challenge "should at least give us an idea of what we do or don't understand." He reassured his colleagues that the Democratic Party could usurp neither SNCC nor the MFDP. The Challenge remained radical because it would bring new, locally based leadership into play. "Note that Jackson Negroes are embarrassed that Mrs. Hamer is representing them," he said. "She is too much of a representative of the masses." The Challenge could thus help democratize Mississippi's black community. Moreover, Moses helped the workers believe in the Challenge's feasibility. At best, they believed, it could bring national publicity to the state and spur insight in and connections with the Party's liberal wing. But as the project progressed through Moses's and others' efforts on the national level, they gradually began to believe that more was possible.[7]

Since most COFO workers had no experience with cultivating national support, Moses constantly traveled in and out of Mississippi to generate as broad a coalition as possible. A May 5 letter to Harry Belafonte showcased what Mary King called Moses's "political shrewdness." After describing the Challenge as an effective means "for united action among the civil rights groups," he proposed to ensure the support from Robert F. Kennedy because of rumors that Kennedy wanted to organize against President Johnson. He based this on Kennedy's role in Pierre Salinger's Senate campaign, about which he had heard when he was in California. Moses calculated that "it would certainly be in Bobby Kennedy's interest to help the challenge to develop into as big a thing as possible." He cannily asked Belafonte to meet Kennedy and "feel him out for us." He then wrote his friend, Harvard University's Guido Goldman, asking him to see Belafonte to make sure "that the meeting with Kennedy comes off."[8]

Moses enlisted others in his northern network. Through Bayard Rustin's close friend, white labor activist Tom Kahn, he persuaded a reluctant Rustin to help. He also extracted a commitment from Roy Wilkins—no mean feat considering the latter's hostility toward SNCC. In January, he proposed forming a committee that included Tom Hayden of SDS to advise COFO. On July 23, he discussed strategy with Ella Baker, Martin Luther King Jr., James Farmer, Dave Dennis, and Bayard Rustin at Tougaloo College. To safeguard his desire for a civil rights–labor alliance, Rustin advised moderation and pressured King to refuse any commitment unless there were clear rules regarding demonstrations. Eventually, Moses agreed that there would be no call from SNCC for a mass demonstration. It was the only time he and King met to discuss the Challenge because, Moses explained, "we travelled in very different movement circles."[9]

Meanwhile, Moses had asked Casey Hayden to further develop the Challenge. She discussed it with Allard Lowenstein and closely followed discussions on the Democratic Party within the Students for a

Democratic Society, debates that, according to Mary King, deeply "influenced her thinking and discussions with Bob." In March, she contacted renowned University of Chicago historian and political scientist Walter Johnson. He recommended obtaining strong legal advice, recruiting California and Illinois Democrats, and seeking backing from the United Automobile Workers (UAW). The UAW not only was the most powerful union in the nation but also wielded considerable influence within the Michigan Democratic Party. During his visit to Stanford University, Moses indeed met influential California Democrats, who, he elatedly reported, "were enthusiastic and are making plans for seeking [MFDP] delegate support." In May, he went to Detroit to meet several Michigan Democrats and attended a fundraising party, organized by white lawyer Dean Robb at Moses's request. He wrote Solidarity House's Bill Dodd for support and asked Roy Reuther to help him obtain a meeting with his brother, UAW President Walter Reuther. In June, he also reached out to Ralph Helstein, president of the left-leaning United Packinghouse Food and Allied Workers.[10]

The most significant new person Moses enlisted was white UAW lawyer and former Americans for Democratic Action (ADA) chairman Joseph Rauh. Rauh had high political connections, including Hubert Humphrey. Moreover, he belonged to the DNC's Credentials Committee, the body that would decide the Challenge's outcome. Moses met Rauh at the March 19 to 20 National Civil Liberties Clearing House Conference in Washington, D.C. During a panel that Rauh chaired, Moses asked him what he thought their chances were. "[P]retty good," he replied, and offered his services. Two days later, they discussed the Challenge again at the UAW convention, which Moses attended with Ella Baker and James Forman. Baker claimed that Reuther had been notably cold; after Moses explained the MFDP Challenge, "Walter gets up, acting as if nothing had been said" and left. According to Rauh, Reuther recognized "it immediately as a possible confrontation with [President] Johnson." But Rauh obtained ADA support and concocted ways to get seats for civil rights supporters on the Credentials Committee. He, Moses, and Baker discussed plans again in Washington on May 20 and 21 during an ADA convention and brought labor/CORE activist Norman Hill into the meetings. Rauh then agreed to act as the MFDP's legal counsel.[11]

Rauh's presence during these preliminary stages proved vital. When Moses came "to D.C. to talk to political people," Stokely Carmichael wrote, "Rauh's name clearly opened doors." Moreover, Aaron Henry acknowledged, "without the technical guidance from Joe Rauh and his associates, we probably would have been completely overwhelmed." Bill Higgs, whom Ella Baker recruited as another legal adviser, played a crucial role as well. With lawyer Ben Smith, Moses and Jack Minnis devised plans to file a lawsuit if the MFDP were not seated. Rauh rejected this proposal, arguing that their whole case depended on telling the DNC that it "must make that decision in our favor precisely because there is no other tribunal to which we can appeal." His directive role is also evident from his dismissal of Moses's arrangements for a workshop for MFDP members at Highlander, which signaled the different end goals of the two. "We have enough of a scrap ahead," he stated; the "necessary discussions with the delegation could be held in Atlantic City." To facilitate its relationship with Rauh, the MFDP opened an office, under Baker's direction, in Washington.[12]

From raising funds and support to arranging transportation to Atlantic City, the Washington office did much of the work that helped the federal government take the Challenge seriously. At Moses's urging, Baker utilized workers from Howard University's NAG and other students to gain support from unions and to contact delegates to get their states to pass resolutions supporting the MFDP. Prathia Hall, another northern SNCC worker educated in white schools but a veteran of the Albany movement, enlisted the help of the National Council of Churches. Baker met A. Philip Randolph, Adam Clayton Powell, and other national civil rights, labor, and political leaders, but she was nevertheless wary about placing too great an emphasis on recruiting nationally prominent figures. Like Moses, she felt that the leadership and direction of the MFDP should come from Mississippians. But COFO knew it needed outside help; it simply lacked the know-how and resources.[13]

The Challenge thus epitomized the tensions between COFO's new national strategy and the old grassroots approach. In 1970, Aaron Henry stated that it was absurd to think that "country bumpkins from Mississippi" could just be "let in" at Atlantic City. "It took Whitney Young, Roy Wilkins[,] Martin Luther King [and] the power of this nation to open that door." Yet he denied that the impetus came from outside. "[L]et nobody ever feel that the [MFDP] was an idea imposed upon us—it was us!" Obviously, the efforts of black Mississippians themselves had prompted outside involvement in the first place, and these were the people who were most exposed to white retaliation. Locals *had* to make the key decisions, Moses explained, because "people will not organize that kind of seminal effort around somebody else's agenda. It's got to be internalized."[14]

BEFORE THE MFDP COULD choose its delegates for the DNC, participants first had to be "freedom registered." Moses had devised the plan of a freedom registration at the Greenville meeting in November 1963. Because official registration was impossible, he argued that they could register blacks *unofficially* in a parallel procedure similar to the mock ballots. He aimed to freedom register 200,000 to 400,000 blacks statewide. Those who were freedom registered could also vote in COFO's June 2 primaries. Like the Freedom Vote, these were mock elections held simultaneously with the official Democratic primaries. Three local blacks—Fannie Lou Hamer, James Houston, and Rev. John Cameron—ran for Congress and one, Victoria Gray, for Senate as write-in candidates for the Democratic Party. Moses regarded these mock elections as an integral part of the MFDP effort. "This campaign will provide us with heads for the [MFDP] delegation, establish us as a force actually interested in working within the Democratic Party [and] spur Freedom Registration through the publicity we get." COFO workers served as campaign managers, precinct registrars, and canvassers.[15]

Preoccupied as he was by other matters, Moses was not closely involved in the campaign. Apart from sending a memo with instructions in January, he largely left the fieldworkers to depend on their own skills. This was not always fruitful, Mendy Samstein complained to the SNCC office. "[Freedom Registration] is not getting off the ground—[workers] need the mental gymnastics done in Jackson and given to them laid out so they can proceed forth without tripping over their feet. They want directives." Still, Gray received 4,314 votes statewide, Houston 1,190 in the third congressional district, Cameron 1,071 in the fifth district, and Hamer 389 in the Delta.[16]

COFO organized new freedom registration drives in June. Through Dona Richards, the Jackson office now provided clear guidelines: one registrar was situated in each county and aided by one deputy registrar in each town, mobile registrars, and one coordinator in each project. Forty-two of COFO's forty-four projects held such drives, which underlined the projection of Freedom Summer as politically centered. Moses saw the drives as a convenient means to invite more outside forces. More bodies meant more registration campaigns and thus a greater chance of federal lawsuits. Moreover, Aaron Henry confessed, "We simply did not have enough capable Negroes and sympathetic whites in the state to organize and implement our ideas." Despite this outside involvement, one volunteer argued, COFO saw success as "finding local people who would try to get [other] people registered." In Holly Springs, one report proudly reads, "The majority of the canvassing is being done by local people already." In other projects, the volunteers did most of the work. "They have more time," one Batesville black explained. "I have to work." But most found the work frustrating. "There is tremendous potential power in the Negro community," one reported, "but it's all rocking in swings on the front porch saying 'Yassuh, yasssuh'!"[17]

By mid-July, Freedom Registration had reached only 21,431—a tenth of Moses's minimum goal. Moreover, while 200 Mississippians had officially founded the MFDP at COFO's state convention in Jackson on April 26, Moses and Aaron Henry considered the turnout disappointing. They realized that COFO needed to spend more "time to get the word around in Mississippi" because blacks needed to attend the regular state party elections before they could justify the MFDP ones.[18]

The trouble was, attending meant jeopardizing life and livelihood. Locals in several counties, including Neshoba, refused altogether, a fact that the Regulars later used to discredit the MFDP's claims that it accurately reflected the will of the state's population. To counter this, Dona Richards distributed brochures explaining the regular Party's procedures, and Moses and other workers toured black communities to encourage blacks to attend the regular elections. On July 19, Moses circulated an Emergency Memorandum among COFO workers that gave a project-by-project breakdown of registration numbers and local MFDP conditions. Revealing that they were "in a very bad shape" statewide, he instructed that "*everyone* who is not working in Freedom Schools or community centers *must* devote all their time to organizing for the convention challenge." It was the summer's top priority.[19]

He outlined several "emergency organizing" ideas, like Freedom Registration Days and Folk-Sings (registration for admission to folk singers' performances). He proposed a halt to regular voter registration activities, including taking locals to the courthouse "*unless* they *ask* to be taken. . . . After August 20th or so we will have ample opportunity to try to convince people to register—*if* we feel that the psychological value of getting a few people 'to try' is worthwhile." The latter condition indicated Moses's growing militancy and cynicism since 1961 and boded ill for what was to come after the summer's end. In the past four long years, he had been on an emotional roller coaster with intense highs but possibly even steeper depths. For every carefully treaded small step forward, he had been forced to take two giant ones back. The latest blow—the disappearance of Chaney, Schwerner, and Goodman—had almost been too much. He was exhausted and regarded the MFDP as his final bet to produce lasting social change in Mississippi. Or, as he dismally characterized it at Stanford University, "This will be a real turning point in terms of whether it will be possible to get anything out of the political structure that is meaningful in this country."[20]

Moses announced Martin Luther King Jr.'s help through tape-recorded radio spots; a television appearance with Aaron Henry, Victoria Gray, and Ed King; and a five-day speaking tour across Mississippi. Although this appeared a reversal of Moses's dependence on grassroots leadership, he considered it valid to use King to promote a COFO project. King was, after all, the head of one of its most notable organizations, and SNCC and CORE heads John Lewis and James Farmer toured Mississippi for the same reason. Moreover, despite Rustin's warnings to keep it at arm's length, King embraced the MFDP. "[N]othing had inspired me so much for some time as my tour of Mississippi," he later reflected, "I was proud to be with [COFO and the MFDP]." Yet King's presence represented something special. Some 20,000 local blacks came to hear him. Greenwood blacks, one volunteer wrote, "rushed tearfully to touch him." Most SNCC workers observed this kind of reaction with ambivalence. On the one hand, they turned such enthusiasm to their advantage. As Stokely Carmichael admitted, many locals "didn't know what was SNCC. They just said, 'You one of Dr. King's men?' 'Yes, Ma'am, I am.'" On the other hand, they could only frown at the twenty-car caravan of reporters and FBI agents, whom President Johnson had ordered, that accompanied King. The Jackson NAACP was irked with King's presence too, but it reacted more harshly to Moses. He received only "luke-cold applause," one volunteer recorded, because he spoke about "sharecroppers and people who earn fifteen dollars a week" as the new movement leadership. Appalled, most NAACP members shunned the MFDP for months.[21]

By the end of the campaign in mid-August, freedom registration reached 63,000, a disappointing figure for Moses, who had already scaled down his expectations from 400,000 to 100,000. Moreover, in most counties, only a handful of Mississippi blacks had tried to attend the Regulars' elections. The attempt was generally futile. Despite state law, three-quarters of Mississippi's 1,884 precincts held no conventions. When they did, whites often lied about their time and location or barred blacks from voting. A handful of blacks "won" election to the county conventions, but none were elected to the Regulars' state convention. These attempts were nonetheless enough to establish exclusion, which allowed the MFDP to proceed with its own precinct, district, and county elections. Only forty of Mississippi's eighty-two counties held elections due to white harassment, including (false) arrests, beatings, and burnings of meeting places. MFDP elections meticulously followed state Party rules, but, inspired by SNCC's ideal of grassroots democracy, discussions lasted until everyone understood the issues to be voted on. The MFDP was an unprecedented experiment in bottom-up leadership in another aspect, too. Its composition reflected class conditions in the black community. Barely a fifth of its members consisted of the traditional middle-class leadership of ministers, teachers, or businessmen; the rest were sharecroppers, maids, farmers, and other blue-collar workers.[22]

Despite participants' inexperience, one observer reported, "[w]ithin ten minutes they were completely at ease and had elected a chairman, secretary, [and] delegates. . . . It was tremendously interesting to watch and indicative of the innate political nature of all men"—as Moses's father had always taught him. "We haven't found a Negro yet who's heard of precinct conventions," Moses wrote excited, but "they are very eager to learn." One volunteer recounted another "Moses-style anecdote" of success when he and another worker supervised Batesville's first election. The second evening they deliberately ran late to find the meeting "in full swing without us. We didn't bother attending the third." Locals used the meetings to discuss issues like job discrimination or the need for recreational facilities. Such discussions helped define locals' stance on the regular Party, its differences with their own, and what "freedom" meant in concrete terms.[23]

The meetings, however, had a mixed record of success. In many rural areas, only a handful of people showed up, and frightened locals shunned volunteering for visible positions like chair. Unfazed, Moses emphasized the long-term nature of change. In the short term, he explained, "[t]he important thing may be to [just] draw people into a statewide organization that can support them in some way as we continue to organize those areas." He advised to "just bring them to the District or State Convention" or simply have all "come as delegates."[24]

Integrating meetings to demonstrate that the MFDP was an open party was even trickier to realize. Canvassing in white areas was not a practical proposition; it was too dangerous. The few whites who joined the MFDP came from moderate areas like Biloxi. Other participants had difficulty grasping proceedings or the MFDP's significance. "One man," an observer wrote, "said flatly that he didn't understand what the purpose of the meeting was." Another recalled how at one meeting, Martin Luther King Jr. "said a lot of fancy things, many of which—I think— were over people's heads." In countering such impediments, COFO workers played a significant facilitating role. In Pike County, delegates refused election "until Curtis Hayes took over . . . and persuaded the group of the importance of the business at hand." Dave Dennis, James Forman, Stokely Carmichael, and Dona Richards addressed MFDP meetings and taught locals how to move motions or conduct nominations. In addition, COFO held workshops to educate its staff in all political procedures, and workers distributed pamphlets explaining the MFDP in simplistic terms and memoranda with instructions outlining structural proceedings, like how to formulate resolutions and keep records, and summarizing the responsibilities of the chair and other officials.[25]

At the August 6 MFDP state convention, COFO's local and national efforts converged. Over 800 delegates and 1,700 observers from in and outside Mississippi came to Jackson's Masonic Temple. The delegates elected an Executive Committee and the delegation to the DNC. Like the regular Party, they chose forty-four delegates and twenty-four alternates. Among them were E. W. Steptoe, Dewey Greene, Charles McLaurin, Jimmy Travis, four whites, several war veterans, and two sons of slaves. Aaron Henry and Fannie Lou Hamer were elected delegation chair and vice chair and Lawrence Guyot party chairman. They pledged loyalty to the national Party, and their platform endorsed a variety of Great Society–type programs to ameliorate poverty. It also backed the United Nations and called for an end to tyranny in Africa, Hungary, and East Germany. "Man, this is the stuff democracy is made of," one observer recorded excited. "It was not a political convention, it was a demonstration that the people of Mississippi want to be let into America." But outside speakers featured prominently, too. In the keynote, Ella Baker urged locals not to elect people who "will represent themselves before they represent you," and Joseph Rauh outlined the "11 and 8" strategy the MFDP should follow in Atlantic City. First they would present their case to the Credentials Committee. If the latter rejected their case, they could bring it to the convention floor if 11 of the committee's 108 members supported them. With the endorsement of

Pamphlet explaining the MFDP. (Source: File 0362, Reel 41, Series XVI, Mississippi Freedom Democratic Party, SNCC Papers. Courtesy of the Roosevelt Study Center, the Netherlands)

Democratic National Convention

The Democratic National Convention is a very big meeting in August.

It is a very important meeting because people in the Democratic Party choose the person they want to run for President of the United States.

People in the Democratic Party from all over the country come together to talk.

Mississippi sends a group of people to this national meeting.

This summer we are going to send a Freedom group to the national meeting.

In order to choose the people that we want to go to the National meeting we will have to have four kinds of meetings here in Mississippi first.

We will have:

PRECINCT MEETINGS

How many? As many precinct meetings as we can have—all over the state.
Who can come? Everyone who is registered on the Freedom Registration books.
What will they do? They will choose people to go to the county meetings.

Democratic National Convention

State Convention

District Conventions

County Conventions

Precinct Meetings

We will have: COUNTY MEETINGS

How many? There will be 82 county meetings—one in each county in the state.
Who can come? The people who we picked at the precinct meeting.
What will they do? They will choose people to go to the district and state meetings.

We will have: DISTRICT MEETINGS

How many? There will be five district meetings—one in each district in the state.
Who can come? The people who were picked at the county meetings.
What will they do? They will choose some people to go to the national meeting.

We will have: A STATE MEETING

How many? There will be one state meeting.
Who can come? The same people who went to the district meetings.
What will they do? They will all get together and choose more people to go to the national meeting.

eight state delegations, they could request a roll-call, during which all present state delegations were forced to vote on the issue. Several had already pledged their support. The audience, Rauh said, was "shouting '11 and 8' before [my] speech was over."[26]

For Moses, the convention was a dream come true. He celebrated the MFDP as an institute in which locals truly "learned how to stand up and speak" and Atlantic City as a chance to ask "the national Democratic Party whether it would be willing to empower people in their meetings in a similar way." When he addressed the convention, however, he warned against excessive optimism. Most locals, he later explained, believed that "the Democratic Party would embrace them" and failed to comprehend "the depth to which . . . southern politicians were entwined in the Democratic Party." But as a resident from Harlem, he knew "that this process of voting and going into politics wasn't going to pull us out of the problems we were in." After all, "*my* experience with the Democratic Party so far didn't suggest that they were prepared to challenge their powerful southern wing." He told the delegates that they could expect a hearing but little else because the President feared losing the South altogether. Focusing on the long term, he argued that getting seated was less important than establishing their party "as a permanent institution that could carry on the fight for MFDP legitimacy, black rights, and fuller black enfranchisement in Mississippi." He then asked James Forman to tour Mississippi to reinforce that message.[27]

Despite locals' efforts, many critics treated the MFDP and SNCC as interchangeable. Particularly the fact that the SNCC-dominated COFO ensured that the NAACP and other middle-class blacks were not central to the MFDP spurred charges of SNCC manipulation. But Moses considered this far-fetched. "The delegation . . . reflected not so much our control as our ideals." Rural blacks, Ed King said, automatically united "to defeat 'big city' businessmen and professionals." In many counties, the NAACP had ignored them but never truly developed a base among the middle class, so they lacked strength at MFDP elections. Since the NAACP generally shunned the MFDP where it did operate, they logically were not elected to office there either. But now that the Challenge no longer appeared "crazy," conservative blacks wanted not only to join the MFDP but also, according to SNCC, to control it. Such beliefs were encouraged by field reports relating how at one meeting, "the comfortable middle-aged 'We Don't Want Any Trouble' Uncle Toms . . . monopolized the meeting and the votes. Most of the Great New Blood which pulsed through the precinct meeting was slyly siphoned out." While SNCC workers' long-felt animus for the NAACP might have influenced such reports, the MFDP's earliest participants did demand the exclusion of several middle-class moderates despite their long records as activists. This, in turn, frustrated the latter, Ed King explained. "These people had never been told 'no' by other Negroes," so when told they could "work with the Freedom Party" but not be "a delegate . . . they wouldn't."[28]

Simultaneously, SNCC workers, including Moses, consciously exploited this class animus. Already at their June meeting, they discussed which locals should be sent to the DNC. "A problem arises because people on the fringes of SNCC are not educated to what we want," Dona Richards said, acknowledging the thin line between local control and full-time workers' desires. They therefore encouraged those who were people whom SNCC knew and trusted, like Fannie Lou Hamer and E. W. Steptoe. Ella Baker even credited COFO with seeing "to it that the little people . . . were not run over [by] middle class types." Often this occurred subtly. SNCC workers, one said, "knew who were active in the different communities and this information just got around. Consequently the ones who [went to MFDP-meetings] were just about selected based on the ones that [SNCC] knew." But Moses admitted that by 1964, SNCC now sought a specific "type" of local leadership. Whereas three years earlier it had not had the luxury to distinguish between locals, it now openly supported militant ones. "There was an effort in the organizing by which to get . . . as radical a delegation as you could." Radicalism and class are not inherently related; SNCC supported militant middle-class activists like Annie Devine and Victoria Gray. But it was increasingly clear, Moses said, "that the MFDP be an organization where Mississippi's Black poor . . . could speak and make decisions." Like the Freedom Vote, he saw the MFDP as a revolution within the leftist movement to determine who was "credentialized" to run society. Yet due to time pressure and the summer's hectic events, few in COFO, he acknowledged, considered the possibility that "the class thing" might come "to a head" at the DNC. Atlantic City accordingly "marks a watershed in the movement," he gloomily noted afterward, "the end of the consensus on which the movement in Mississippi grew."[29]

THE FRAGMENTED MFDP delegation and its supporters arrived in Atlantic City feeling hopeful. Moses's warnings that they might fail swiftly faded into the background. "We had exceedingly high expectations as a result of the response that we got," one worker explained. Mississippi farmers lobbied congressmen, distributing booklets with legal precedents, pamphlets on Mississippi hate crimes, and statements of the regular Democrats criticizing the national Party. Media attention circled around the civil rights protests staged on the boardwalk outside the convention—including placards showing James Chaney, Michael Schwerner, and Andrew Goodman, as well as the remnants of their car. Moreover, the Regulars doubled down on their image as die-hard racists. State authorities had filed injunctions prohibiting the MFDP from operation, and Lawrence Guyot was arrested on a trumped-up charge to prevent him from attending the convention. The Regulars had adopted Governor Paul Johnson's plea to "refrain from taking any position regarding support of presidential and vice-presidential candidates" until the DNC rejected the MFDP. Their platform unanimously opposed the national Party's; most even openly supported President Johnson's conservative Republican opponent, Barry Goldwater. "We can't afford to turn our country over to the Reds and the red-inspired blacks," MSSC Director Erle Johnston explained. The governors of Alabama, Arkansas, Louisiana, and Florida announced that they too would boycott the DNC if it seated the MFDP. With four black delegates, reporter I. F. Stone noted, only Georgia symbolized "a new moderate South."[30]

Consequently, the MFDP believed it had right on its side. While he remained cautious, even Moses briefly allowed himself to believe that its moral case would be irresistible. If the Challenge got to the floor of the convention, the delegates would not be able to reject it. "I don't see how they possibly can," he stated at a press conference, "if they really understand what's at stake." When he boarded the bus to Atlantic City, one volunteer reported, Moses "was seen to smile."[31]

But whereas Moses's main concern was getting the Democratic Party to follow its own rules, most of the religiously inclined MFDP members understood politics "as a deeply moral, almost spiritual, affair." The MFDP's presentation to the Credentials Committee on Saturday, August 22, epitomized its moral appeal. Believing that locals could best represent their case, Moses did not speak, but he had approved Joseph Rauh's brief beforehand. Aaron Henry opened the presentation—amid large cabinets filled with locals' depositions on voter discrimination—emphasizing the MFDP's loyalty in the face of persistent and severe persecution. The issue "is not so much who sits where," he concluded, "but the taking of some constructive action to batter down the doors of prejudice within the Mississippi Democratic Party." Ed King described the fear that prevented more whites from joining the MFDP. When one committee member objected that he did not "want to listen to stories of horror," Rauh admitted they were the core of their case. Fannie Lou Hamer then testified about her beating in Winona. "Is this America, the land of the free and the home of the brave where we have to sleep with our telephones off of the hooks because our lives be threatened daily because we want to live as decent human beings?" she asked. Moses called listening to Hamer's testimony from the back of the room a "wonderful, charging experience," because "she was able to convey [the MFDP's story] in a way that most of us could not." Other speakers included Roy Wilkins, James Farmer, and Martin Luther King Jr. Farmer reminded the committee that "making a political decision on principle and on morality is also sound and viable politics," and King spoke elaborately of "the moral health of this party and this nation." "Your choice," Joseph Rauh ended the presentation, "comes down to whether you vote for the power structure of Mississippi that is responsible for the death of those three boys, or whether you vote for the people for whom those three boys gave their life."[32]

In a hollow rebuttal, the Regulars denied discrimination of blacks at their conventions and blasted the MFDP as a "group of dissatisfied, power-hungry soreheads" who were supported by "known Communists." Meanwhile, Hamer's speech had been so heart-wrenching that President Johnson had ordered an instant press conference in order to divert the news media. His ploy failed, as the TV networks replayed her speech during prime-time news. Subsequently, 416 telegrams supporting the MFDP (and only one for the Regulars) arrived at the White House. "I don't think prior to ten days beforehand many Americans knew what the [MFDP] was," Wisconsin Congressman Robert Kastenmeier explained. "It took really the dramatization at the convention . . . to bring it alive." Charles Sherrod agreed. "No human being confronted with the truth of our testimony could remain indifferent," he wrote in its aftermath. "Many tears fell." After Rauh spoke, the *New Republic* observed, "even the reporters rose and applauded." David Lawrence, the Credentials Committee chair, postponed a decision until the next day. "What do you do," one member sighed, "with 53 women on a committee?"[33]

Many white liberals found themselves torn between sympathy for the MFDP and concern for party unity. "It is, of course, entirely irrelevant . . . whether [Mississippi's] jailers beat prisoners or whether or not its

Governor insults widows," one reporter wrote. "No party manager can accept . . . that any stranger can come to a national convention and claim his right to sit and vote on no higher credentials than his courage and his suffering." Most party representatives felt likewise. Prior to the convention, the state delegations of California, Michigan, Wisconsin, Colorado, Massachusetts, Minnesota, Oregon, New York, Washington, and the District of Columbia had pledged support for the MFDP, but their reasons varied. The Michigan and New York delegations emphasized the issue of party loyalty, whereas the delegations from Minnesota and Wisconsin stressed the "opportunity to demonstrate [the Party's] devotion to justice and equal rights." The Minnesota governor nonetheless vowed to follow the president's orders. Overall, the Democratic Party was more concerned with the Regulars' disloyalty than with their racism. After all, the DNC's general counsel Harold Leventhal asked, "What southern delegation isn't truly subject to the same charge?" But he knew that the DNC could not refuse the MFDP altogether. "The contestants—while weak on their own credentials—make a case against the Regular Democrats that will seem strong and just in many quarters." In July, Leventhal had therefore suggested to David Lawrence that the Party offer the MFDP "fine spectator seats" as honored guests. When its support grew, he advocated an "intermediate solution" like "splitting the delegation on a lop-sided basis, say 4 to 1." Yet concern over a southern walkout dominated his proposals. On August 17, he even suggested solving the loyalty issue by softening delegates' pledges to a mere "affirmation that it is the present intention of the delegate to support the ticket of this Convention . . . unless future developments preclude his doing so as a matter of good conscience."[34]

President Johnson also sympathized with the MFDP's cause. As he privately stated, the Regulars "oughtn't to be seated. [They] wouldn't let those nigras vote. And that's not right." But he was bent on not seating it. He even threatened to withdraw his promise to Hubert Humphrey of a place on the presidential ticket unless the latter succeeded in defeating the Challenge.[35]

On August 19, Johnson invited Roy Wilkins, James Farmer, Bayard Rustin, and A. Philip Randolph to the White House. There he lectured them—complete with flipcharts—on the dangers of a white backlash. Johnson also recruited Walter Reuther. "There's not a damn vote that we get by seating these folks," Johnson told him. Reuther and Humphrey then pressured Joseph Rauh through multiple phone calls. Meanwhile, acting on orders from the White House, the FBI conducted electronic surveillance of Martin Luther King Jr., Bayard Rustin, Joseph Rauh, SNCC, CORE, the MFDP, and Robert F. Kennedy. When Moses later found out about the wiretaps, he thought this was incredible but he figured he "just was naïve about the way in which the FBI works." At the height of the convention, President Johnson even contemplated renouncing his nomination because he did not "want to have to *fight* to carry Texas." Although it is doubtful he was serious, the MFDP had evidently penetrated his conscience—to the extent of obsession. The MFDP's effect on politics was thus immediate *and* long term: it bolstered Johnson's determination to do something about voting rights, even if he felt that it had to wait until after the November elections because of "politics." As Johnson told Reuther on August 9, "If they give us four years, I'll guarantee the Freedom delegation . . . will be seated four years from now." On August 25, he repeated this commitment. "We're hearing 'em. . . . We passed a law back there in '57 and said it was the first time in eighty-five years that everyone was going to have a chance to vote. . . . And we're going to say it again . . . in '64."[36]

IGNORANT OF THE PRESIDENT'S machinations against them, Moses and the MFDP supporters felt jubilant after the hearing. On Sunday, the Credentials Committee proposed to seat the MFDP as "honored guests," but its supporters on the committee rejected the idea after conferring with the MFDP. Another committee member suggested offering it two seats, which briefly divided them. Since at least eleven committee members still wanted the roll call, David Lawrence postponed the decision again, until Monday. The MFDP delegation continued lobbying and tried to get as many delegates as possible to sign a statement supporting the MFDP. A group that included Moses, Dona Richards, Aaron Henry, Ed King, and Fannie Lou Hamer convinced Martin Luther King Jr. to join Robert Kastenmeier in asking Credentials Committee members to sign as well.[37]

According to Lowenstein and Rauh, Moses had told them that he would regard two seats as a victory. Moses has consistently denied this, but he clearly knew that politics implied making concessions. Ed King even claimed that Moses already asked him "in Mississippi . . . to put myself in their shoes and figure what might be thrown at us and what we might have to compromise." The MFDP meanwhile met to discuss potential compromises, too. It approved one that Oregon congresswoman and Credentials Committee member Edith Green proposed: the proportional seating of all in both Mississippi delegations who pledged their loyalty to the national Party. Discussing compromises beforehand was sound pragmatic politics, indicating that the MFDP was not as naive as often presumed afterward. The MFDP in fact expected—and even sought—the seating of both since this had been customary in the past; in 1944, the DNC had even seated two competing Texas delegations in one of which Lyndon Johnson himself had been a delegate. As such, Green's proposal, Moses always maintained, was "our bottom line as far as compromise goes."[38]

Unlike Rauh or James Forman, Moses was not a strategist trying to get as much as possible from the DNC; he considered himself solely a representative of black Mississippians. During the convention, he therefore mediated between the MFDP and national Party representatives. "Bob," Ed King said, "became a symbol as a leader of what we were saying. [He didn't want to but] he knew it was necessary." Moses was constantly "caucusing and meeting with our own delegation to get reports back" to the other state delegations. This was essential, Joseph Rauh explained, because although "you couldn't do better than [utilizing these Mississippi] people as their own advocates," they "hadn't been going around the country" like Moses. As Moses admitted, the Challenge "couldn't have happened just out of the blue. You had to have the contacts." But he did not believe that such mediation had to preclude grassroots leadership; MFDP delegates could be included in such meetings. He considered the DNC "a huge classroom" in which Mississippi blacks "were actually learning the democratic process. . . . It was a great sort of theater for empowerment." After all, "[t]hey were there, they had nothing else to do, and they could all sit, while we all talked and hashed out all the matters. . . . And the more people who were educated by that then the wider the fallout when you got back to Mississippi." Joseph Rauh and Arthur Waskow later commended Moses for doing "a superior job" in insisting "on open party processes" and "that the constituents in Mississippi be remembered." According to Mendy Samstein, Moses spent Sunday explaining to the MFDP delegates "what was at stake, what role the President was playing" and "all the different compromises and alternatives," because most "couldn't follow all the shifts in strategy." He even declined to leave an MFDP support rally, where he was scheduled to speak, for a top-level meeting in Martin Luther King Jr.'s suite. Moses sent Fannie Lou Hamer, Aaron Henry,

Annie Devine, Hartman Turnbow, and Victoria Gray instead. They likewise insisted that other MFDP delegates could listen from the hall through an open door.[39]

Many national black leaders, however, were unable to embrace Moses's challenge and accept delegates as legitimate grassroots leaders. They felt that politics was best left to the professionals. Roy Wilkins allegedly told MFDP members that he had "been in the business over twenty years [so] why don't you pack up and go home?" In a secret meeting that evening that deliberately excluded the MFDP, black representatives of northern delegations told SNCC workers they believed the MFDP should follow the president's wishes. When Annie Devine showed up uninvited and chastised them for forgetting "the people who put them there," the meeting simply closed. Afterward, black Michigan congressman Charles Diggs tricked Moses into giving up a list of the Credentials Committee members who supported the MFDP. Subsequently, all received phone calls from presidential aides, who pressured several to withdraw their support or lose benefits like loans or job offers. Presidential aide Walter Jenkins, the FBI documented, also instructed "Democratic heads [to] talk to various members of the Credentials Committee and have them change their vote."[40]

The national Party's forceful response to the MFDP reflected its class bias as much as the fear of losing the election. It preferred dealing with leaders like Roy Wilkins, whom President Johnson considered "the most rational [black] statesman." Hubert Humphrey and Walter Reuther likewise characterized the MFDP as not being "emotionally stable." During the convention, they centered all negotiations on Martin Luther King Jr., although he barely played a role in the Mississippi movement. "Everything revolved around him," Moses later complained. President Johnson found it impossible to understand why the MFDP refused to give up. "If I were a Negro," he told Wilkins, "I'd just let Mississippi sit up on the platform [and] salute the son of a bitch. Then I'd nominate Johnson for President and . . . the next four years, I'd see the promised land." This reasoning entirely missed Moses's point that blacks, particularly the working class, *could* not nominate Johnson because they were excluded from the political process.[41]

Many white liberals and national black leaders did not know what to do with Moses. They neither understood nor appreciated his role as mediator. Bayard Rustin, who had played a double game of support and opposition since the MFDP's conception, even wanted to exclude him from a high-level meeting with Hubert Humphrey on Tuesday. "There was all this negotiating going on which we were not party to," Moses later grumbled, "I spent hours waiting in [Martin Luther King Jr.'s] hotel room. No communication. No coordination . . . it was pulling teeth to get information as to what was actually happening." Yet the Democratic establishment still preferred dealing with the articulate Moses to one of the MFDP's barely literate delegates. "Moses," James Forman noted, was "singled out by the powers at Atlantic City as the person who could make the [MFDP] accept any compromise." Hubert Humphrey even told Moses that he believed that "anything you tell those people they're bound to do . . . I know you're the boss of that delegation." Moses interpreted this as a clash between Old and New Left values. "The traditional Left," he later told the *Village Voice*, "keeps talking about coalitions and leaders, but always from the top; to them Mississippi is a chess board. . . . That's part of why I keep trying not to get alienated from these [local] people by becoming one of those official leaders."[42]

Subsequent meetings had spurred such conclusions. On Monday, Moses conferred with Humphrey, several Credentials Committee members, including Rauh and Edith Green, along with Martin Luther King Jr., Henry, Hamer, and Ed King. According to Arthur Waskow, it "was a most upsetting occasion. Moses came down from it looking like death itself." Moses had insisted that the MFDP should be seated because "only Negroes can speak for Negroes in Mississippi." But Humphrey blatantly dismissed the concept of bottom-up leadership. "That meant only Russians could speak for Russians, French for Frenchmen." In tears, he explained his vice-presidency was at risk. Fannie Lou Hamer, crying as well, shamed him by asking if his "position [was] more important . . . than four hundred thousand black people's lives?" It was a revelation, Moses recounted to the *Village Voice*, to learn that the MFDP delegates "were the only people at that whole convention who were free, who made democratic decisions. The President told all the others what to do."[43]

During the Tuesday meeting—held in Humphrey's suite with Moses, Rustin, Henry, Ed King, Martin Luther King Jr., Andrew Young, and Walter Reuther—Humphrey admitted that President Johnson had said he did not want "that illiterate woman" to have any meaningful platform. Ed King claimed in 1966 that Moses then called Humphrey a racist. Moses does not remember the incident but agreed with the interpretation. He termed the overall "tone of the meeting insulting." He especially remembered Reuther, whom the president had flown in from Detroit, "telling us that even when we got the vote, we elected irresponsible people." "Being a person from Harlem, as a constituent," he said, "that really upset me."[44]

This was not what upset Moses most.

After the Monday meeting, Edith Green announced that they still had enough support on the Credentials Committee—albeit barely—to get a minority report for a roll call vote. David Lawrence then postponed a decision, yet again, until Tuesday. This gave him, Humphrey, Reuther, and Walter Mondale the time they needed to concoct a new plan: a compromise that they pressured the MFDP delegates in Humphrey's suite to accept right there and then, without referring back to their colleagues. Reuther threatened to fire Rauh and withhold funding from SCLC if they did not. Aaron Henry and Ed King were open to the offer, but Moses was not; he instead went on about the federal government's inadequate responses to the situation in Mississippi. Andrew Young and Bayard Rustin criticized SNCC for not understanding the need to get President Johnson reelected. Tensions in the room were palpable. When Humphrey impressed that "the peace of the world depends on you and what you do now," Moses quietly retorted, "We didn't come here to represent the people of the world. We are here to represent the voteless people of Mississippi."[45]

The back-and-forth came to an end when a senator's aide burst into the room, shouting, "It's over!" They rushed to an adjacent room[46] to watch a bulletin announcing that the Credentials Committee, whose meeting was deliberately scheduled simultaneously, had unanimously accepted the compromise while the people in Humphrey's suite still thought it was a negotiating matter. "You tricked us!" Moses shouted at Humphrey. He left the room, slamming the door in Humphrey's face. He later said his reaction—atypical of his calm character—"probably caught [Humphrey] by surprise too." But he was just "furious," although "the pretense at negotiation was not wholly unexpected." He was also livid with Rauh because the unanimous ruling implied his consent. Rauh had actually voted "no" but nevertheless considered Henry's endorsement as sufficient reason to embrace the compromise, believing it to be "a great victory for civil rights."[47]

The compromise proposed to seat Aaron Henry and Ed King as atlarge delegates and the rest of the MFDP as honored guests. All Regulars who signed a loyalty oath would also be seated. In addition, the compromise promised to end voter discrimination in the elections of future state delegations. The Credentials Committee ruled that "corrective action must begin" but that seating the MFDP was to "change the rules in the middle of the game." Seating the Regulars "takes care of the legal problem," Illinois Democrat Jacob Avery satisfactorily proclaimed, "and to seat the two [MFDP delegates] takes care of the emotional, I could even say, moral problem." Yet the MFDP's point, Moses countered, was to "bring morality into politics"—not vice versa. It was not even a compromise, one summer volunteer remarked, but rather "a decision made and told to the delegation." To the MFDP, this equaled the "kind of dictation" blacks were "learning to stand up against." Furthermore, Henry explained, two seats with the Democratic Party deciding who occupied them—two urban, middle-class men—was "token recognition" and "typical white man picking Black folks' leaders." "What is the compromise?" Moses snapped at an NBC reporter that night. "We are here for the people and the people want to represent themselves. They don't want symbolic token votes. They want to vote themselves."[48]

The compromise, Henry noted, was paternalistic in other ways, too. First, the promise of future reform was hollow because it prohibited discrimination against "voters," and Mississippi blacks still had little chance of becoming registered. Moses told *Pacific Scene* that when he asked Humphrey how many voters he could "guarantee us in Mississippi in the next four years," he simply replied, "We can't guarantee you any because the Democratic Party doesn't run the administration." Second, the two seats were *at large*, which meant that the MFDP would not represent Mississippi but blacks nationwide. They were two extra seats created for this purpose, so the Party cunningly would not have to take them *away* from anyone. The compromise, its concocters admitted, treated the Challenge solely as "a national, rather than a parochial problem." The MFDP countered that it was "unreasonable to ask the Mississippi delegation to bear the burden of the entire country," especially because all delegations represented their state only. Third, the compromise "offered the [M]FDP nothing in the way of permanent recognition, patronage, official status or a guarantee of participation in the 1968 convention." Above all, Victoria Gray added, accepting meant "betraying the very many people back there in Mississippi [who had] laid their lives on the line."[49]

MOSES HEADED TO THE Union Temple Baptist Church, where the MFDP was caucusing. The mood was bitter. The MFDP had learned, in the words of one volunteer, that "naked coercion [and] sneaky backroom deals" were "also 'the stuff democracy is made of.'" When Joseph Rauh, Edith Green, six other Credentials Committee members, Martin Luther King Jr., Ed King, and Aaron Henry arrived, a heated meeting ensued. The committee members voiced resentment at the charge of betrayal, but Rauh reiterated that fighting on was useless because their support had now dropped below eleven. Martin Luther King Jr. was not even allowed to speak. By a vote of hands, the delegation rejected the compromise and repeated it would not accept anything less than Green's proposal. Moses and several other COFO staff and Credentials Committee members huddled to discuss their next move. They had two more hours before the DNC formally approved the compromise, and just hours earlier they had had the support of more than eleven. Their votes could be retrieved, Moses pleaded. But the "Credentials minority" announced that it had given up.[50]

Moses was appalled. He had gone straight to the church to reassure the MFDP delegates that he had not accepted anything on their behalf without them knowing; even the thought that they for one second might think that he had willingly engaged in old-style politics too was too much. He was so averse to the establishment's blatant dismissal of his leadership philosophy that when Rauh wanted to talk privately with Martin Luther King Jr., Moses and James Forman refused to leave them because they feared another backroom deal. But despite acting as a moral agent, Moses could not conceal his resentment. Henry afterward blamed him for "forcing us into a hasty decision" because he had opposed pleas to postpone a final decision "until calmer heads might prevail." Dismissing the delegates' agency, Henry even accused him of manipulation because "Moses knew that the delegation would reject the proposal if an immediate vote was taken." Rauh likewise chastised the "hysteria out there that Moses had built against the thing." "Bob couldn't recapture himself and he fought against it 100 percent," he later grumbled. "You couldn't reason with him . . . this had struck him like a bolt of lightning." One volunteer recorded that Moses even "raised his voice and interrupted their speeches, declaring that there was no time to waste on discussing the compromise: they had all year to do that, and now must get [back] the needed signatures for the minority report." According to Ed King, however, what Moses might have said "was only what . . . most of the [Mississippi] people thought already." As such, just as during the 1963 meeting in Greenville when he had asserted himself forcefully on behalf of the Summer Project, his actions could still be considered consistent with his beliefs. "All I cared about was the insides of those 68 delegates and the future of the [M]FDP in Mississippi," Moses stated afterward. "It wasn't my responsibility to care about Humphrey or the backlash."[51]

That evening under Moses's guidance, twenty-one MFDP members, using floor passes from supporters in the Oregon, Michigan, and Colorado delegations, held a sit-in in the near-empty Mississippi section. All but four of the regular state delegation had refused the loyalty pledge, returned home, and officially endorsed Barry Goldwater. Governor Paul Johnson justified this decision by stating that the DNC's openness to the MFDP equaled "the hatred and cruelty of a modern 20th century Reconstruction . . . Mississippi's debt to the national Democratic Party is now paid in full." Because of the unit rule, these four could still cast votes on behalf of all the Regulars. This essentially meant the Regulars had won; even in their absence, they kept their seats *and* their votes. The purpose of the sit-in, Ed King explained, therefore was to demonstrate "that these were seats that belonged to the people of Mississippi, the black [and] white." But when the chair read out the compromise to all the state delegations, it passed within thirty seconds.[52]

Arthur Waskow recorded that it was "Moses essentially" who pushed the sit-in "to cope with the extreme depression and bitterness" within the MFDP; Moses in fact made several trips to the Mississippi section with the loaned floor passes to "smuggle" in a few sit-inners at a time through a side door he had found. His resort to direct action indicated the depth of his anger, although he still believed in consensus. Due to their pre-summer arguments about whether to have civil disobedience at the convention, he asked Martin Luther King Jr. beforehand "if it was okay to have nonviolent protest on the floor. And he said yes." The next day he got King to admit that the "sit-in was probably a creative response to the tension and bitterness that had erupted." But he was not seeking King's approval; he merely "wanted to make sure that I had him on record saying that he had approved of this form of response." Other national leaders were less sympathetic. The National Council of Churches condemned the sit-in, and Democratic Party officials dismissed it as additional proof of the MFDP's unreasonableness. The sit-in nonetheless generated widespread press coverage, and its participants, Waskow observed, "felt victorious."[53]

Hoping to prevent more civil disobedience, the national leadership pressed the MFDP to review their rejection. On Wednesday, Aaron Henry convened the delegates in the church to listen to Joseph Rauh, James Farmer, Allard Lowenstein, Bayard Rustin, Martin Luther King Jr., and several NCC members. Henry now supported the compromise as a means to spur further civil rights legislation. Contrary to Moses, he also felt that "the people that helped us open the door had a right to at least have something to say about what the decision ought to be." One by one, the national leaders then spoke in favor of accepting the compromise, insisting that the delegation needed to understand, in Rustin's words, the difference between "protest and politics." Martin Luther King Jr., who admitted that he would vote against it if he had been a native Mississippian, asserted that pragmatism should prevail "even in the most idealistic of situations." When Moses questioned him, he acknowledged that he "would not have rejected the proposal in the first place." Only Rita Schwerner and James Forman spoke against the compromise. The meeting accordingly underscored the difficulties of maintaining consensus in a broad coalition: strains were created because COFO workers' field experiences had added a radical bent to their perspective that was difficult for their outside allies to comprehend.[54]

Moses deliberated whether to use his influence with the delegation as a counterweight. Throughout the convention he had responded to requests for advice by telling Fannie Lou Hamer and others, "Do what you think is right," and still believed that the decision about accepting the compromise solely belonged to the MFDP. But to defend that point of view to its delegates, he realized he paradoxically would have to do what the other leaders did: speak up and risk the possibility that the delegation did what he wanted not because they agreed but because they were blinded by his charisma.[55]

His wife might have influenced him in this as well. Although she worked hard toward its realization, Dona Richards had always been ambivalent about the Summer Project for fear of what outsiders' involvement might do to black leadership. This had been her overriding priority when she opposed her husband during the 1963 Greenville meeting, and now she applied a similar logic in opposition to the national leadership. She had called in James Forman, confident that he would have less qualms about asserting his views even though he had not been privy to MFDP deliberations. "They want to try to force the people from Mississippi to change their minds," Forman recalled her as saying on the phone. "Bob's the only one that's against it. He's not sure he's going to speak [so we] want you to come down and speak for SNCC."[56]

Eventually, Moses reasoned that speaking up did not betray his ideal of grassroots leadership, because the delegates could only make an informed decision if they could "listen through *all* the arguments." But as after the Greenville meeting, he struggled with the accusations of manipulation. When his time to speak came, he therefore merely implied his opposition. He announced that the decision was solely the delegation's to make. He nonetheless advised the delegates to base it on "Mississippi and its own hopes and desires," not on wanting to gratify their established liberal allies. Despite his demure tenor, Bill Higgs noted, it "was really like listening to the Lord . . . Moses could have been Socrates or Aristotle . . . as Moses was finishing, King and everybody knew the jig was up."[57]

This led Arthur Waskow to laud Moses afterward as "an excellent politician who can manipulate when necessary but prefers to do so on behalf of ending the process of manipulation as soon as possible, and who (it seems to me) himself avoids manipulation on many occasions when he could easily use it."[58]

The delegation discussed the compromise in private and once again voted for rejection. The MFDP repeated its sit-in that night. When President Johnson addressed the convention on Thursday, sergeants-at-arms barred entrance to the rows of the Mississippi section. The delegation, again guided by Moses, then formed a circle and stood silently, carrying pictures of President Kennedy with his famed "Ask Not What Your Country Can Do for You" quotation. Meanwhile Johnson nominated Hubert Humphrey for the vice-presidency and proclaimed that the Mississippi problem had found "a fair answer to honest differences among honorable men."[59]

THE MFDP'S REJECTION of the compromise, although almost unanimous, strained the group's unity. Those who favored acceptance, Moses recalled, "were the NAACP [and the] more established people from the large cities," but the "delegates from the rural areas voted against it." According to movement folklore, the first, by far the minority, tried to overrule the latter. It was "the worse mess I've ever seen," Unita Blackwell stated. "All the big fish . . . moved in on us." But many working-class blacks were empowered by the MFDP experience and fought hard for their point of view. "We didn't come all this way for no two seats," Fannie Lou Hamer impressed, "when all of us is tired!"[60]

Yet not all MFDP delegates had been open to the national leaders' viewpoints merely because the presence of "big shots" overwhelmed them. Nor did middle-class blacks automatically dismiss working-class delegates. Several genuinely believed that accepting the compromise made political sense. Even Charles McLaurin, who had worked for SNCC since 1962, acknowledged that only after Moses spoke had he realized that "the movement was bigger than just getting some recognition." But many SNCC and COFO workers experienced the events as betrayal due to their oversensitivity to such issues. After all, the national leaders' attitude offended Moses so much precisely *because* he had always treated the MFDP as a means "to teach the lowest sharecropper that he knows better than the biggest leader what is required to make a decent life for himself." As Unita Blackwell put it, "We was ignorant [but] not stupid." But Atlantic City, Moses lamented afterward, reaffirmed that the established liberal elite "looked at the political process like it was school integration. You get a couple of well-dressed Negroes, shine their shoes, and bring them in and you've started your process." To him, it demonstrated the power structure's unwillingness to accept the nation's lower class—black as well as white—as more than "recipients of largesse."[61]

Moses had started the Challenge as an effort to save what he perceived around him—in the North and South—as an increasingly splintered movement prone to violence and uprisings. But, he later sighed, the "moment was lost" because the class bias among national civil rights leaders and white liberals only spurred the alienation of large segments of the movement from both. As Moses put it, "Atlantic City was a watershed in the movement because up until then the idea had been that you were working more or less with the support of the Democratic Party [but now you] turned around and your support was puddle-deep."[62]

Doubting the value of coalition politics for social change, Atlantic City helped propel SNCC toward Black Power. "The seating of the [MFDP] could have gone a long way toward restoring [blacks'] faith in the intentions of our government," Sherrod wrote in its aftermath. Instead, John Lewis noted, the lesson many learned was that anyone "who trusted the white man at this point was a fool, a Tom." The "betrayal" of black leaders accelerated this development. Stokely Carmichael, one of Black Power's chief proponents, had been a Bayard Rustin protégé during his time at Howard University. "One of the main things that happened to Stokely at Atlantic City," Moses observed, "is he disengages himself mentally and spiritually from Bayard . . . that's what feeds Black Power in Stokely." The embrace of Black Power, in turn, stifled SNCC's effectiveness in subsequent years as the shift alienated SNCC from poor blacks like Fannie Lou Hamer. The events left many of the white volunteers disillusioned, too. Atlantic City, Lewis believed, turned them "into radicals and revolutionaries. It fuelled the very forces of protest and discontent that would eventually drive Lyndon Johnson out of office."[63]

Furthermore, Moses bemoaned in 1983, "no-one saw the connection between [Atlantic City] and the urban situation." He had started the Challenge to help northern blacks as much as southern ones, but the Democratic Party "missed the chance." Had it included working-class blacks, he argued, it could have used that as a means to arrest the trend of urban rioting that started that summer in Harlem and that would come to dominate the late 1960s. Northern blacks had the right to vote, but since the working class was not organized enough, their representatives remained the few powerless, middle-of-the-center black politicians who worked against the MFDP in Atlantic City. Riots became inevitable, Moses believed, because it "was clear [that] there was nothing in the Democratic Party to build on." Had the Challenge succeeded, national leaders like Martin Luther King Jr. might have reached rioters by telling them "to organize like the sharecroppers did in Mississippi [and] seek the political route out of our problem." There still would have been "vicious struggle," he later said, but perhaps "not *arms* struggle." These might-have-beens, however doubtful, contributed to Moses's increasingly pessimistic worldview.[64]

The most negative immediate consequences of Atlantic City were the isolation of SNCC and the disintegration of the Mississippi movement. Afterward, SNCC workers distrusted all of its former allies. As one stated, "SNCC believed that the rest of the world . . . was corrupt [so it] began talking about serious independent political action." This further antagonized moderates. They already attacked SNCC, to whom they attributed the rejection of the compromise rather than the MFDP. The "very simple" MFDP delegates "had been rewarded more than they could reasonably have expected, but they felt cheated," the *New Republic* noted, perplexed. Bayard Rustin criticized the MFDP in *Commentary* for not understanding the need to compromise, although, Moses still grumbled years later, he failed to mention its acceptance of Edith Green's proposal.[65]

Criticism of SNCC was "much more negative" than expected, SNCC's Jim Monsonis wrote Moses in September. He correctly predicted that it cost SNCC much-needed support. Freedom Summer had turned its $40,000 deficit into a large surplus; by late 1965, SNCC again had to borrow $10,000 in order to stay afloat. Ironically, most moderates viewed SNCC's weight with the MFDP as manipulation but refused to interpret their own behavior similarly. SNCC denied the claim, although one report recognized that "it is perhaps true that without the influence of SNCC the delegation might have accepted the compromise." Still, it noted, Fannie Lou Hamer and other delegates "fought like hell to have that compromise defeated and might well have succeeded without our assistance."[66]

This confession underlines the tension that existed between Moses's conception of leadership and the reality that bottom-up as well as top-down processes had brought them all to Atlantic City. Throughout its existence, SNCC had carefully tried to balance its desire to nurture grassroots leadership—and by extension the MFDP—while not manipulating it. Although facilitation remained an ideal that could never exist in pure terms, SNCC had nonetheless found ways of building grassroots leadership that strengthened locals' autonomy. Because the MFDP was the result of an unprecedented broad-based effort on the national level that complemented grassroots initiatives in Mississippi, however, maintaining local autonomy became increasingly problematic. All involved—including SNCC—wanted a voice in the outcome. The reality that the MFDP was not a pure grassroots enterprise lay at the heart of Moses's outburst in Hubert Humphrey's suite, too. He had clearly understood the frictions between his ideals and the messy realities of politics and throughout the summer had walked a tightrope in between. Suppressing his own emotions, he had continuously sought consensus and acted calmly, deliberately, and rationally to ensure that everyone involved at least strove to approximate the ideal as closely as humanly possible. When the episode in Humphrey's suite raised the question head on, however, his allies sacrificed the ideal of grassroots democracy. Seeing his trusted allies engage in power politics in proverbial smoke-filled rooms, to the exclusion of the people they were supposed to be representing, appalled him. As Rauh put it, it was "like a white man hitting him with a whip ... everybody had ratted on him." In 1999, Moses confirmed that he had expected the Democratic Party's rejection but considered the "betrayal" of the people he had trusted the "most difficult."[67]

Bayard Rustin, Allard Lowenstein, Roy Wilkins, and Joseph Rauh went so far as to join a growing chorus of "Old Lefters" in blaming "Communist elements" in SNCC for the rejection of the compromise. Rauh wrote Humphrey that the influence of alleged Communists like Moses could only be stopped by federal recognition of the "responsible elements in Mississippi," meaning Aaron Henry and other moderate blacks. *Washington Post* columnists Rowland Evans and Robert Novak admitted that Moses was "no Communist" but repeatedly criticized him for being "dangerously oblivious to the Communist menace." They replied to a reader that their attacks belonged to an orchestrated move to return the movement to moderate control. "We believe along with many other supporters of Negro rights that the revolutionary stage has passed and now is the time for reform. Accordingly . . . leadership of the civil rights movement [must] return to the NAACP." Such attacks, however, only served the movement's opposition as the FBI renewed Communist investigations of SNCC and COFO.[68]

Moderates' version of Atlantic City could dominate public debates because SNCC refused to discuss Communist associations and because its organizational structure did not identify any apparent spokesmen for the media. Moreover, SNCC had not planned a strategy for a rejection. In hindsight, Mary King agreed, SNCC could have published "papers with quotations from local leaders." They should have used its well-educated members too, Julian Bond asserted. "If we were doing this again, we would say, 'listen, we've got this guy, Bob Moses, he's fabulous. You need to talk to him.'" In 1964, Monsonis already begged Moses to write a response in "a major magazine" because "nothing else is going [to] stop the slurs . . . the Convention clearly indicated you as the 'leader' of the delegates, whether you want it or not, and people will have to pay attention to your account of things." Moses never did; by then, he was on a plane with Harry and Julie Belafonte, James Forman, and nine other SNCC workers headed to Africa.[69]

It might not have made any difference anyway; moderates' anger at SNCC was too strong. At a meeting of the groups who participated in Freedom Summer in New York on September 18, for instance, the participants engaged in what Courtland Cox called a "diatribe against Bob and SNCC." The meeting painfully exposed their differences in organizational leadership and forced the inherent contradictions of SNCC's strategy of grassroots leadership financed by northern backing into the open. Gloster Current criticized Moses as a mumbling dictator who "left a very negative impression." He denied that the MFDP was a true grass-roots enterprise. When the SNCC workers maintained that locals controlled COFO and the MFDP, Current's assistant Jim Morsell admitted that this was equally undesirable. If locals made "decisions injurious to [the NAACP's] national interests, no matter how democratic they might be," he said, "[w]e must have a way out." Current agreed. "The NAACP is a disciplined army. No decision is made on lower levels without authorization from the top. Aaron Henry has got to get in line."[70]

Their charges against Moses as a director who told other groups to "take it or leave it" were fantastic. As Art Thomas of the National Council of Churches objected, it was "unreal" for "an ad hoc group to meet in New York and determine what should go on" in Mississippi. But the reality was, Bob Spike noted, that "Mississippi is no longer a local problem." Seeing COFO as a "confederation of national organizations" instead of "local groups plus local outlets of national organizations," they demanded an input into its decision making. Allard Lowenstein proposed a "new central body" based in "structured democracy, not amorphous democracy." When Cox insisted only a low-level meeting of Mississippians could determine future direction, Current exploded. "The more I listen to Cox the more I know we need a top level meeting. I have been listening to the crying of people from Mississippi for seventeen years. I don't want to listen to Steptoe. . . . We need a high-level meeting so we can cut away the underbrush."[71]

Strengthened by the requests from B. E. Murph and other Mississippi NAACP leaders, Gloster Current persuaded his Board of Directors that the NAACP should leave COFO. After informing COFO of the decision at its statewide conference in Jackson on March 7, 1965, Aaron Henry joined Current for a closed NAACP meeting to discuss plans for an independent summer project in Mississippi. SCLC also planned an independent summer project, SCOPE (Summer Community Organization and Political Education), in six southern states using white volunteers. Despite a reconciliation meeting that Harry Belafonte organized between SNCC and SCLC leaders, the relationship between the two organizations had further deteriorated after the Selma-to-Montgomery marches that spring,[72] so SCLC decided not to cover Mississippi in SCOPE's range.[73]

The NAACP's withdrawal and SCLC's decision to put its resources elsewhere hastened COFO's decline. National CORE pulled out after fights with its southern chapters over James Farmer's support for the compromise. SNCC then realized that its scarce resources were better spent on the MFDP than on the waning COFO. The latter, James Forman noted in April, displayed a "serious problem of leadership of project directors, poor morale, and no programs." With the MFDP ready to substitute, Moses said, COFO simply was "not indispensable anymore." Moreover, after the Challenge, the federal government, churches, labor, and other organizations now established programs in Mississippi. The Economic Opportunity Act even required "maximum feasible participation" of the poor in Johnson's post reelection Great Society programs. Moses considered this "a tremendous breakthrough" but also shared Mary King's observation that this "rendered redundant the role that SNCC and COFO had played." COFO agreed to its own abolition at a Tougaloo meeting on July 27, 1965, and, after Moses and Dennis filed bankruptcy to dissolve it legally, abdicated its resources and projects to the MFDP.[74]

Yet COFO's abolition was a mere formality; it had been defunct since Atlantic City. COFO's raison d'être had always been providing locals with an organization in which *all* black Mississippians felt represented. The withdrawal of the NAACP or the SCLC was not so important; what accordingly *was* fatal was the loss of internal unity. Since most COFO members also belonged to the MFDP, the latter's internal split over the compromise along class lines was replicated in COFO. The traditional black leadership, embarrassed by the rejection, refused to work with the MFDP. They instead joined the Loyal Democrats of Mississippi, a recently formed third Democratic Party encouraged by the federal administration that consisted of moderate blacks and whites and that was eventually seated at the 1968 Democratic National Convention as the official Mississippi delegation. This naturally angered the working-class blacks who dominated the COFO/MFDP constituencies. The NAACP's departure, justified by SNCC's "take-over" attitude and offending "Beatnik" appearances, widened the gulf. At the March COFO convention, Fannie Lou Hamer blasted Aaron Henry. "How much have the people with suits done? If they, dressed up, had been here, then the kids in jeans wouldn't." Such statements reflected the growing political awareness of some working-class blacks like Hamer. The fact that black leaders like Roy Wilkins and Martin Luther King Jr. had stayed in fancy hotels whereas many MFDP delegates had slept on the floor of the Union Temple Baptist Church, for instance, had strengthened their class-based interpretations of the DNC.[75]

But not all MFDP and COFO members were similarly radicalized. At the March meeting, several defended the NAACP, and in many cases, as in Hattiesburg, collaboration between the classes had been and continued to be possible. Moreover, most MFDP members wanted to remain a protest group within the Democratic Party rather than becoming a militant third party. Unlike SNCC, most of them had left the DNC proudly. After all, one COFO volunteer observed, "They had the president of the United States stop for them." Mississippi blacks who stayed home were similarly affected. One cheered with joy when she watched the sit-in on TV. "All the time till now I never seen no nigger in a convention, but they was there! Lots of them!" Even Lawrence Guyot dismissed "independent political organizing [as] dangerous." Many Mississippi blacks did not have any radical ideas about "freedom"; most simply wanted to attain concrete things, like cars, better jobs, and decent housing. Several COFO members accepted jobs in the new federal War on Poverty programs, which paid salaries of $125 a week. "At some point in your life," Moses explained, "you got to earn over $30 a week. Don't you?" He did not see "this as the way to go," because it made them unable "to criticize the government," but he understood that attainting middle-class status was a logical reward for their suffering. "People were trying to make good on the gains that they [had] just struggled for." Consequently, historian John Dittmer concluded, it was inevitable that Mississippi's "grassroots insurgency transformed into a more moderate reform movement, one willing to sacrifice the needs of the poor to obtain rewards for the black middle class."[76]

Yet in all social revolutions, there are periods that are experienced as setbacks but in hindsight are seen as progress. The same could be argued for the MFDP. The Democratic Party kept its promise to integrate its activities on all levels. Future delegations to the DNC had to reflect their states' racial composition and pledge loyalty to the national Party and its platform. The 1972 McGovern Rules expanded these guidelines to further ensure fair representation of minorities and women. The Challenge also spurred the acceptance of southern blacks into the political process and the Democratic Party's ranks. The MFDP strengthened President Johnson's commitment to ending black disfranchisement. Immediately after his reelection in November 1964, he ordered the Justice Department to draft appropriate legislation. The subsequent Voting Rights Act of 1965, which ruled discriminatory voting practices unconstitutional, ensured that by 1968, almost 60 percent of eligible black

Mississippians were registered to vote. Consequently, the number of black elected officials grew from 1,469 nationwide in 1968 to 9,040 in 2000; 1,628 of them lived in Mississippi and Alabama.[77]

The MFDP's continued activism—in 1979 Moses noted with pride that in some counties, the MFDP still existed—also helped force the Voting Rights Act's adoption. In 1965, the MFDP organized another national enterprise, the Congressional Challenge, which demonstrated through hundreds of depositions from locals that Mississippi's congressmen were elected illegitimately. While the bloody civil rights marches in Selma in March 1965 helped national politicians in persuading the general public to accept the act, behind the scenes, the MFDP's work had made the opening salvo. Politicians, Ed King explained, do not "pass a new law because people are in the streets . . . They need to say 'we did this with reason, with calm. We had thousands of documents.'" Simultaneously, President Lyndon Johnson's fears proved correct. His push for civil rights legislation cost the Democratic Party the South for generations. To this day, the Republican Party has effectively capitalized on the Dixiecrats' former constituencies, leading to continued blockage of numerous social reform bills at the state and federal levels.[78]

Moses was thus right when he predicted in 1964 that "it'll take about 50 years . . . for [grassroots] people to get in the Democratic Party and figure out whether it could work." All this ultimately opened the way for Barack Obama's nomination as the Democratic Party's presidential candidate. During Obama's inauguration, Moses was in Washington as well. At one radio station, he proudly credited the MFDP for setting the stage "that allowed this to happen." But it was a victory paid at SNCC's and his own expense.[79]

CHAPTER NINE
Not a Happy Time

Moses had gambled—and lost. Within the next year, he would lose every-thing dear to him. Above all, his consensus-based organizational leader-ship approach faltered through the heavy toll of Freedom Summer and Atlantic City.

A new phase was beginning in the national and local movements, and in his life. "The Movement never really recuperated from that summer," Moses acknowledged, "and the price [of] freeing Mississippi was the destabilization of SNCC." As a more and more hierarchical SNCC embraced black nationalism, and as he and SNCC found themselves in-creasingly at odds with what the grassroots leadership they had encour-aged in Mississippi wanted, Moses faced new moral dilemmas. Trying to fight off escalating bouts of depression and the extreme emotional pressure of having lived in danger for so long, he wandered the nation and globe at age thirty, desperately "looking for some kind of answers." Yet the darker his state of mind, the more he latched onto his faith in his organizational leadership approach. In his disillusion, he found a way forward that came to determine his attitude toward leadership and activism in the next phase of his life.[1]

AFTER ATLANTIC CITY, disillusioned as Moses was, it was nevertheless clear that a Voting Rights Act was in sight. "The voting registration drive was finished," Moses concluded. "That part of the movement was over." This led SNCC and other civil rights organizations into what A. Philip Randolph termed "the crisis of victory." At its highest point of achieve-ment, disenchantment eroded workers' morale; they no longer knew how to proceed.[2]

By endorsing voting rights, President Johnson paradoxically deprived SNCC of the sole program it had been able to sustain for four consecu-tive years. SNCC workers answered this challenge with the theory of "let the people decide." But faced with the reality that Atlantic City had ren-dered a unitary concept of "the people" void, it became more of a slogan than a realistic organizing strategy.[3]

Moses, too, faced the daunting question of the next step. After all, "I had said to myself and to Amzie that I would stay until we saw this [voting] program through . . . I hadn't ever committed myself to stay in Mississippi forever." Unable to find new goals, he split his time between a variety of projects. He spoke at fundraising dinners in Chicago and New York and recruited lawyers Ben Smith, William Kunstler, and Arthur Kinoy as members of a new legal advisory committee, but mostly he returned to the efforts that had brought him the most joy: developing grassroots leadership by providing exposure. He, for example, discussed SNCC's educational programs with Ella Baker and Myles Horton and arranged leadership workshops for MFDP members. He spoke to the Benton County MFDP, worked on the Radio Tougaloo Project (a "freedom radio" directed by locals), and attended the Sea Island Folk Festival to learn more about developing grassroots festivals in COFO projects. He invited folk singers to organize workshops in the Mississippi Delta and occasionally led a workshop on folk dancing himself. Meanwhile, he tried to reconstitute some feeling of movement unity, even as he gradually recognized that his approach was out of step with the *Zeitgeist*.[4]

At the heart of Moses's and his colleagues' crisis of victory lay the tension between their grassroots model for social change and reality. SNCC's philosophy masked the class differences not only within the black communities but also between rural blacks and SNCC staff. SNCC had gradually adopted a political view that was dismissive of the middle class in favor of the "uneducated masses," while the latter paradoxically moved closer to the middle class in their political orientation. As one MFDP leader explained, "Success breeds moderation." Ed Brown astutely described the contradictory situation SNCC workers found themselves in: President Johnson had "taken over our program [and] the community people . . . were overjoyed and enthusiastic about it [while] we were very satirical and very bitter about it."[5]

Moses watched the coming of the Great Society programs with ambivalence. Getting federal programs into Mississippi had always been an important objective of his, but he worried when movement initiatives like the Child Development Group of Mississippi (CDGM) were incorporated into the new federally funded Head Start programs and staffed with moderate activists. The backlash from Atlantic City put SNCC out of play. "The thing that hurt was that we didn't know anything about it being set up," he said. This was particularly sad because it meant that a new "foundation on which the movement could have regained its unity . . . was taken out from under."[6]

Rather than admitting that they might need to revise some of their political assumptions, most workers refused to alter their conception of leadership, thus widening their distance from locals. "What is needed," SNCC workers stated in one report, is "to make sure that many more people like Mrs. Hamer and Mrs. Devine emerge who are militant enough to command our confidence." Consequently, Ed Brown admitted two years later, several workers began to "force our various points of views on the community. . . . [They] only wanted local people to decide when [they decided] in accordance with what the staff thought; and when local people deviated, then they were to be ostracized." Some workers laid so much stress upon giving uneducated people a voice that it embarrassed such locals. Even Moses was guilty of this. In February 1965, he reintroduced a notion that no one with an education above the twelfth grade should become a member of SNCC's Executive Committee. Feeling patronized, Fannie Lou Hamer instantly had her name withdrawn.[7]

The differences between SNCC and locals revealed themselves most clearly over the MFDP's pro–Democratic Party direction. The MFDP kept its promise to work for President Johnson's reelection, and its Congressional Challenge was another attempt to become part of an established structure that most in SNCC no longer trusted. Workers who did support it, one admitted, only did so "to *prove* the Democrats didn't mean what they said." The MFDP's gravitation toward the Democratic Party proved especially difficult for Moses; he believed that it should become an independent political force. "We are raising fundamental questions about how the poor sharecropper can achieve the Good Life," he explained in 1965, "questions that liberalism is incapable of answering." Joseph Rauh claimed that Moses left the DNC stating, "You cannot trust the system. I will have nothing to do with the political system any longer." While that opinion is exaggerated—Arthur Waskow wrote shortly after how much Moses respected Edith Green as someone who showed "that it was possible to stay within the political system and yet be committed to a decent moral principle"—Moses did believe that working with the Democratic Party was useless. After all, "if everyone saw their own particular personal position as somehow more important [than] the long range evolution of the country . . . then it seemed like they really were devoid of any real substance." He even contended that the Party had merely used the MFDP to extract a loyalty oath from the Regulars.

Still visibly upset, he castigated the class-based thinking of the Party at a November 1964 *National Guardian* dinner. "Mrs. Hamer? How can she be seated? She's not legal. . . . Are the others legal? They had the *real* election. No they didn't! They had the mock election. We had the *real* election!"[8]

Moses feared that the Congressional Challenge would become a repetition of Atlantic City. "The President will be against us, but he will try to use us to blackmail the committee chairmen to get his legislation [passed and] in the end no-one will be for seating us . . . because to face the truth of our claim would rip this nation apart." But Moses predominantly opposed it because he regarded it as a media-based enterprise that deviated from developing MFDP members. He wanted to strengthen the party's base first by training members extensively in the political process. Many of SNCC's problems in 1965, he later stated, resulted from its decision "to go national too quick." Several Freedom Summer projects faltered after the volunteers had left because local leadership was not yet capable of taking them over. The MFDP risked making the same mistake, he sighed, because "there is only so much energy, so much money, and so much time."[9]

Having been so close to national success, most MFDP members were unwilling to adopt such a long-range view. It was hard for them "to do the same kind of thing that had been done in Mississippi before," Moses reflected. "It was more glamorous to . . . get your lawyers [and] FDP people together and take them to Washington." This glamour trend was exacerbated when Lawrence Guyot, the MFDP chair, led several marches in Jackson in which hundreds of people were arrested. Moreover, the MFDP decided to organize its own summer project in 1965 using northern white volunteers, albeit fewer than in 1964. But Moses declined to openly oppose the MFDP's plans because "there was no way to take that disagreement to the people without clashing with Guyot." His principle that locals such as Guyot should decide the MFDP's destiny outweighed rectifying what he felt was a wrong direction for the movement. Now that the MFDP carried the bulk of the work in Mississippi, he felt that SNCC could no longer justify an input in the decision making. SNCC's and "my time had run out," he stoically concluded. "I had had my shot."[10]

The MFDP's growing independence exacerbated SNCC's crisis of victory. It had developed grassroots leadership but felt disenchanted with the result. SNCC ironically felt like SCLC when the sit-in students exerted their independence but still asked for money; the MFDP was $8,000 in debt and depended on SNCC for resources. A COFO report noted that SNCC workers failed to step back because they were unable to give up their sense of importance but also believed—with some justification—that most locals were as yet incapable of continuing the work. Workers in the 1965 MFDP summer project likewise complained of locals' passivity. "There is a strong tendency in much [of what] we do to make local people errand boys," one tellingly wrote, because she believed, "we are the only ones who know what we are doing."[11]

SNCC was especially averse to seeing another influx of more white northerners; the psychological strains of an integrated movement the year before had proven to be too maddening. Whites' skills and locals' gratitude had seemed to confirm black workers' inferiority. Consequently, no meeting could occur without the race issue coming up. Blacks, Moses explained, felt that the movement was theirs because "it's their energy that made it." Some even treated whites as subordinates. This left one white to rant at a black worker, "You're a dictator, a little Caesar. You're everything I'm against in the movement!" A December 1964 COFO report noted that "white workers are often subject to severe racial abuse and even violence." Moses watched this with sadness.[12]

The fact that 200 volunteers wanted to stay in Mississippi in the fall of 1964 fueled these tensions. Because SNCC workers rarely met during the summer for long-term planning, they had not anticipated this. At a conference Moses organized at Tougaloo College between August 17 and 19, COFO workers tried to select volunteers who could stay. Eventually, it was decided that volunteers who wished to stay would constitute a SNCC-supervised but northern-financed freedom force. Essentially, they could stay but only if they remained in a vacuum. "No-one actually was thinking about trying to take the students and use them as an organized force," Moses admitted. Most workers preferred for them to go. "There wasn't enough in the black community to hold the whole," he explained in a heartrending mea culpa at a 1989 Freedom Summer reunion. "We couldn't all be in that one little space . . . we didn't see any way to strike a consensus so that you could all be together [in a way] that wouldn't tear people apart."[13]

Scholars have observed that the intensity of internal interracial conflicts often depends on the degree to which movement goals are attained. When organizers fail to see meaningful social change, outsiders are often pressured to retreat. SNCC's failure to keep up the self-evaluation sessions of its early years exacerbated this. As one worker remarked, "[I've been] on the SNCC staff for three years, and I still don't know what SNCC is." Moreover, the volunteers had not had the time to learn by trial-and-error, as SNCC workers had. As early as December 1963, several workers pleaded to "define ideology" and "establish specific goals," although these were very un-SNCC-like objectives. But Moses bore part of the responsibility for this failing too. In attempting to win support for Freedom Summer, he forestalled the discussion of what he felt would be divisive issues. "After the summer these problems of structure, philosophy, and conflict can be discussed more thoroughly," he said, quelling discussions at the June 1964 meeting. "I don't share your concern about these problems, possibly because I have a very limited idea of what we'll be able to accomplish."[14]

When Freedom Summer accomplished more than expected but revealed that getting the vote alone did not eradicate inequality, Moses's approach caught up with him. As Staughton Lynd correctly observed, "The penalty for non-ideological thinking is an undercurrent of despair." "I'm ready to die," Ruby Doris Smith, Charles Sherrod, and others stated, "but I need a program worth dying for!" They demanded that SNCC define its purpose. "As an organization we have never decided whether or not we want to be: (1) agitators (2) demonstrators or (3) organizers," one complained in November, "and we can't fool ourselves into believing that we can be all three."[15]

The need to distinguish between reform and revolution became an often-repeated charge in SNCC meetings. "Our orientation must always be towards eliminating causes rather than trying to make their effects more bearable for a few. This is what makes us different from a goddamn social welfare agency," some workers crudely asserted in a paper. Such proclamations of revolutionary purposes were eventually translated into Black Power, SNCC's first systematic definition of society's wrongs and its programmatic solutions.[16]

YET MOSES REJECTED any such ideological answers more than ever. To salvage SNCC's quest for a new goal, he always maintained, workers should have reduced "their scope back to what they were good at and what their true purpose was," that is, becoming an "organization of organizers." Returning to slow, long-range organizing could also end intraorganizational rivalry. Adopting a "different timetable gives you a different [organizing] context," he told them, and "will also get us out of the race with [Martin Luther] King, SCOPE, etc." During a September 1964 Executive Committee meeting he reiterated his idea of having a local black run against Senator Eastland in 1967. In April 1965, he proposed another long-range plan, which again underscored his political perceptiveness. Anticipating that Robert Kennedy and Hubert Humphrey would vie over the presidential nomination in 1972, he figured that the South would feature prominently in the primaries. "Between now and '72 we should organize people across the country in a network independent of the Democrats," he therefore argued, "Kennedy and Humphrey will be forced to go to this network."[17]

Moreover, a return to small-time organizing was necessary because following locals' desires led SNCC more and more into the question of economic power. One report warned that in 1965, SNCC would increasingly deal with "areas where voting is relatively easy, and facilities are ostensibly integrated, but where the poor jobs–poor education–poor conditions cycle remains unbroken." Breaking it required specialized and patient organizing techniques. In November 1964, Moses therefore repeated his beliefs to adopt the same long-term approach to the question as to voter registration. Labor unions, he argued, were only a part of the answer since they were part of the establishment and could thus "only discuss a narrow aspect of the problem: wages." Instead, the answer should be found within poor people themselves. "There are more people in this room who know more about the 1957 and 1960 Civil Rights Acts than anyone in Congress or the Justice Department, from being out in the field and trying to make use of them, from just knowing people for whom they were intended," he explained. "The same is true for the Poverty Bills."[18]

But as Moses had already observed in December 1963, SNCC workers lacked both patience and expertise. "I thought that you knew ways to tell us which way to go, who to contact," a surprised Unita Blackwell, for instance, told them when she got rebuffed in her request for help in building a hospital. At the November meeting, discussion of economic programs led nowhere because, one devastatingly admitted, "we ran out of knowledge." SNCC organized a Labor Conference at Highlander in January 1965, but, a report noted, "the discussion was at a vocabulary level far above [locals'] understanding, and we lost them." Another attempt at discussion in February was again fruitless; the reality that SNCC needed specialized, disciplined workers had led to a debate about needing a more bureaucratized structure to assess workers' efficiency rather than about social and economic programs. Eventually, SNCC helped black Mississippians run for election in the federal Agricultural Stabilization and Conservation Service (ASCS) and helped them establish the Mississippi Freedom Labor Union and the Poor People's Corporation of Mississippi, which facilitated black-owned cooperatives. But since SNCC lacked an overarching vision of social and political change, the overall result, as one worker already predicted in November, was "the development of a series of separate institutions that don't relate to one another."[19]

Moses again found himself at odds with his colleagues. Most were unwilling to retreat into obscurity and allow locals to replace them. "People were not willing to just say, okay, we had [Freedom Summer], we got certain benefits from it [and] we can now go back under and pick up where we left off," he later sighed. In October 1964, Courtland Cox frankly asserted that SNCC should "get at the roots of power . . . in counties which affect the national power structure. We must stop being parochial." Moses viewed this development as one of the unintended consequences of Freedom Summer. Workers developed a desire for "taking the kind of charisma that had developed around the Summer Project and making it a kind of permanent part of SNCC," which, he argued, contributed to its embrace of Black Power. This underscored the contrast between Moses and many of the younger southern black SNCC workers. The latter, Jane Stembridge observed, now "turned to people who seemed more militant, who talked louder, who seemed to talk with more anger in their voices, who perhaps were more angry than Bob. A kind of get-up-and-go kind of person. 'This is what we're going to do. Let's go and do it now.' Whereas Bob would outline much more basic long-range crucial goals. They were harder for [them] to grasp. . . . [They wanted to] act right now."

James Forman catered to this desire by advocating plans for a Black Belt Project, a new southwide summer project using black volunteers bent on the creation of a visible black political unit that could compete for power within the national political system. Unlike Moses, Forman concluded that Freedom Summer underscored his growing belief that only a revolutionary mass-based student movement led by "a strong, centralized organization"—meaning a more hierarchical SNCC—could overcome racial inequality.[20]

Moses was again left in a bind. A SNCC that acted as an entity of its own would only further compromise its ability to act as the servicing tool for local blacks he had always used it as, but by fighting for his views, he would paradoxically spur its existence as a unitary mechanism. Yet its internal divisions *had* to be resolved somehow. For the Mississippi movement, COFO's disappearance and the abdication of its programs to the unsteady MFDP were ultimately perhaps worse than SNCC's internal struggles, but the latter was not unrelated to the former. SNCC's infighting, coupled with negative publicity, led to its growing inability to finance and staff COFO and MFDP projects. In retrospect, Moses thought that to regain consensus in SNCC and the Mississippi movement, COFO should have been resurrected on a common issue that benefited the entire black community in the way that voter registration had done—like his educational projects or the new poverty programs—and SNCC could then exist in its service. But, he lamented, SNCC workers were too distracted to think so far ahead.[21]

THE MOST SERIOUS DISTRACTION Moses and his colleagues faced was their physical and mental burnout. "When I look back it feels like 20 years folded into four," he often reflected. This was a universal SNCC problem. One worker desired a transfer from Arkansas after only five months because "working long periods in the same area . . . tends to lead each of us into a kind of rut—stagnation: we lose perspective." The summer's disillusioning events accelerated such feelings. Workers and volunteers could not but evaluate America through the lens of their Mississippi experiences. "When you're in Mississippi, the rest of America doesn't seem real. And when you're in the rest of America, Mississippi doesn't seem real," Moses related. But the events in Atlantic City convinced many that there *was* no dichotomy between Mississippi and America. As Ed King said, "Moses said that 'Mississippi is a mirror to America,' and we discovered to our horror that that was true."[22]

Moses had tried to prepare Mississippi blacks for rejection at the DNC, but what "we didn't count on," he said, "was the need to educate the SNCC staff about what happened." Consequently, cynicism and demoralization set in. Workers in other states shared this. In Georgia, one wrote, SNCC's unsuccessful desegregation campaigns left them "demoralized, immobile, and disgusted." Such frustrations led to a growing inability to function effectively. "I become petty and chauvinistic about my particular work, unable to get along with people in other fields, and slightly inhuman in my own," another wrote. Theft and delinquency occurred increasingly often in SNCC offices. Many workers suffered from what psychiatrist Robert Coles called battle fatigue, a state of mind comparable to shellshock or posttraumatic stress disorder. They experienced "clinical signs of depression" like "exhaustion, weariness, despair, frustration, and rage." Others sought relief through alcohol and marijuana or suffered from insomnia and ulcers due to tensions, bad living conditions, and malnutrition. One worker in Belzoni described his project head as a "shell . . . he's twenty-one [but the] guy is wasted."[23]

Living in constant fear of violence was the most nerve-wracking. In the *Student Voice*, Mendy Samstein poignantly described witnessing the McComb bombings. Everyone "instantly knows what that sound means [and] the moments of torment that follow—whose house, who is dead? It's not mine. Then who? My neighbor, my friend—my mother, my brother, my son, or maybe SNCC again. Who? And one's stomach aches with pain and the pain seeps up into the chest and the head and comes out of every [pore]." Veterans like Stokely Carmichael suffered multiple breakdowns following years of racial violence. Even Alvin Poussaint, whom Moses had invited to help them cope, returned from Mississippi needing therapy. In an extreme case, the tensions that volunteer Dennis Sweeney suffered aggravated his psychoses, leading him to eventually murder Allard Lowenstein in 1980. Sweeney had been a close friend of Moses; he and Dona Richards were two of only five friends at Sweeney's wedding to Mary King in late 1964. Within a year, the two divorced due to Sweeney's increasing emotional breakdowns. Indicative of what watching his colleagues fall apart did to him, a guilt-ridden Moses spoke extensively and caringly at the 1989 Freedom Summer reunion about Sweeney "as someone whom the Movement had failed."[24]

Having been in Mississippi longer than any SNCC worker, Moses inevitably suffered from battle fatigue, too. He now fell back into his periodic spells of depression. "No one, black or white, can endure what Bob has without becoming at least as bitter as he," one colleague told the *Village Voice* that summer. "That is the nature of Mississippi." As director, he could not escape dealing with death and destruction in the fall either. He visited Andrew Goodman's parents, investigated the McComb bombings, and visited workers in Natchez, where police had played Russian roulette with one. "I remember watching the changes in Bob," Connie Curry related in the mid-1970s. "It broke his heart . . . he used to get hurt everytime anybody would look mean at him, literally. [So] you could imagine that kind of sensitivity in Mississippi where people wanted to kill him."[25]

The summer's reaffirmation that white lives were more valuable than black ones spurred Moses's disparaging analysis of American society.

During the *National Guardian* dinner, he called the Neshoba killings "the most political murder" in American history because they raised "basic questions that the society and the national administration are not prepared to answer." In April 1965, he similarly decried the lack of interest in the Alcorn students whose bodies were found during the Chaney/ Schwerner/Goodman search. "Nobody knows about them. And nobody asks why did that grand jury let [their killers] off . . . on the same day that they indicted [those who] killed the other three." Moses developed what he called his murderers' jury theory: just as the prejudiced jury could not convict the racist sheriff, society at large could not condemn itself for its own indifference. Apathy, he argued, occurred because the "country refuses to look at Mississippi . . . as like them." He referred to a picture of the trial in *Life* in which the suspects were laughing "as though they were morally idiots." Society accordingly saw them "as people who are in no way like most Americans," and "therefore they analyze the problem wrongly [and] look for wrong solutions." This "problem is so deep," he sighed, that "all you can do is raise these questions."[26]

Moses groped for direction. He revisited Albert Camus and his belief that if men could give history no meaning, then "they could always act so their own lives have one." Blacks needed to determine their own objectives by continuing to build parallel institutions, even if it entailed staying outside the system forever. "Why can't we set up our own schools?" he pondered, because "when you come right down to it, why integrate their schools? . . . Many of the Negroes can learn in it, but what can they do with it? What they really need to learn is how to be organized to work on the society to change it." He even contemplated establishing a "shadow government" because, he told *Pacific Scene* in February 1965, "what is the government? Who sets it up? The people set it up. . . . Why can't we set up our own government? So that in 1967, if we get organized enough between now and then, we can set up our own government and declare the other one no good." Such dramatizations of his belief in grassroots leadership—bordering on nationalism—betrayed Moses's despair. Sparse in his expressions as always, he later appraised the period simply as "It wasn't a happy time."[27]

BUT MOSES WAS NOT THE ONLY ONE whose personal frame of mind, cloaked with intellectual musings, directly affected his ideas of leadership and forthcoming activism. To flee movement strains—and the volunteers—many looked outside Mississippi and the South to regain their focus. Veterans like Hollis Watkins, Sam Block, Charles Sherrod, and Dave Dennis resumed their studies, while others traded Mississippi for Alabama. Stokely Carmichael directed a project in Lowndes County, where SNCC worked with locals to build an independent political party, the all-black Lowndes County Freedom Organization. Its symbol was a snarling black panther. But most SNCC workers moved north.[28]

By late 1966, only a third of SNCC worked in the rural South; the rest could be found in Atlanta and in northern cities.[29] Simultaneously, many mentally leaped across the globe for inspiration. A growing number of workers tapped into the nationalist philosophies that had always been an undercurrent in SNCC. Workers increasingly read Frantz Fanon, accepted rapprochements with Malcolm X, and forged pan-African connections. Kenya's leader Oginga Odinga's visit to the Atlanta office in December 1963 had accelerated this interest. "Black people at that time had a need to get together by themselves and I think that has to be analyzed in terms of a worldwide perspective," Moses later explained, because "why would you expect that what is sweeping around the rest of the world should not also sweep through this country?" The same occurred in organizations like CORE and in SNCC projects that had not experienced a massive influx of whites. In Arkansas, for example, Ben Grinage replaced white Bill Hansen as director because its workers felt that blacks needed to be in leadership positions. Likewise, when Charles Sherrod left the Georgia Project in 1965, his successor Don Harris recalled, whites "drifted out and we just didn't take any others in." Interest in nationalism was a natural outgrowth of workers' experiences in the South, but in the 1964 to 1965 winter, it also provided a welcome diversion. Blacks "began to look for ideologies in Africa, Cuba, China," one black scholar argued, "rather than [learning from] what we had just experienced."[30]

A SNCC delegation's trip to Africa between September 11 and October 4, 1964, spurred such identifications. Guinean President Sekou Toure had asked Harry Belafonte to invite a group from SNCC to discuss organizing techniques with Guinean youths. But the question of *which* workers should go worsened internal fissures. Should the most sophisticated go to best fulfill the trip's political purposes or those who most deserved a break? And what about uneducated Mississippians? SNCC had an obligation to them, Moses reminded his colleagues. How could it argue in Atlantic City that sharecroppers were equal to professionals and now exclude them in favor of intellectuals? When Forman announced that he, John Lewis, and Courtland Cox had acted as a committee (albeit with a mandate from a small staff meeting at Tougaloo College) that selected himself, Lewis, Julian Bond, Ruby Doris Smith, and project representatives of Alabama, Georgia, and Mississippi (Prathia Hall, Don Harris, and Moses and Dona Richards) to go, other workers angrily questioned this selection process and the fact that this was an all-black group. Moses insisted that he and Richards would go with their own money so locals could take their spots. Eventually, SNCC agreed to include Fannie Lou Hamer, Matthew Jones, and Bill Hansen. Nevertheless, the argument left bad feelings all round. Like Forman, Moses later called the trip a mistake that diverted from the "immediate concentration on the transition back to normal."[31]

Yet once they were in Guinea, the workers quickly forgot their troubles. They stayed in President Toure's private seaside villas, dined in his palace, and attended front-row performances of his dancing crew. They witnessed the opening of a stadium and visited a match factory, a printing plant, and markets in Conakry. With the president, his advisors, and students, they discussed social change and read socialist literature. Despite sickness, Moses enjoyed the experience. He especially marveled at the tropical vegetation and Hamer's discovery of a new world. "She didn't speak a word of French," he smiled, but "she would just grab people and talk to them and talk to them." Watching Guinea's poverty gave him an appreciation of Guineans' struggles in the wake of its decolonization from France in 1958. For all, it was a revelation to see blacks, in Hamer's words, "doing everything that I was used to seeing white people do." The delegation, Dona Richards wrote afterward, "felt a kind of belonging that most of us had never felt." News distributed by the U.S. government on African Americans increased skepticism about their homeland. When Guineans showed Moses a picture of himself sitting on a counter with a white man to show "how the South had progressed in integration," Hamer recalled, he got "very angry." When he returned to Africa in 1965 and saw an article in the U.S. government magazine *Topic* that described how Moses "had won representation for black Mississippians" in Atlantic City, his confidence in the government reached a new low. Guineans also confronted them for not opposing U.S. intervention on the continent enough. When locals approached them with the question "American?" Richards wrote, "We were ashamed, and answered in very broken French, 'Oui, mais revolutionaries.'"[32]

Moses recalled that President Toure advised the SNCC workers to "hold onto your resources and develop your people." Other Guineans repeated this message. While Moses saw it as an affirmation to continue grassroots organizing, it rather strengthened his colleagues' interest in pan-Africanism. Ruby Doris Smith contemplated establishing worldwide Friends of SNCC groups, and James Forman dreamed of creating an African Bureau. In September 1965, Dona Richards asked SNCC to initiate an Africa Project, which included a library, pamphlets explaining African liberation movements, and a conference. As motivation, she referred to the meetings with the Guinean students who "had something which we have been taught not to have[:] a cultural heritage to learn about and to be proud of." This discovery radicalized her views of white American society in a different manner than her husband's. President Johnson, she believed, deliberately stymied blacks' sense of pride. "Johnson is now trying to tell us that our family structure is the *cause* of our exploitation and what we need is to have a father like his. The result of this propaganda (a premeditated result, I'm sure) is that we lose what little pride we had in ourselves *as Negroes*, as we desperately try to emulate white cultural habits as much as possible." Yet "through identification with the African heritage we can find the strength with which to fight Johnson's plan." It was therefore high time, she felt, to "expand our borrowed cry of 'ONE MAN, ONE VOTE' to 'SELF-DETERMINATION and DIGNITY, throughout the world!!!'"[33]

THE TRIP ALSO SPURRED the divide between Moses and Forman. "[C]areful attention must be given to the selection of leaders because the people judge an organization by them," Toure impressed on Forman. This encouraged Forman's views on organizational leadership. "An organization that is seeking revolution," he now agreed,[34] "cannot afford weak or vacillating leadership." An October emergency meeting in Atlanta to discuss the volunteer freedom force, for which the delegation returned home early, convinced him that SNCC's adoption of a more centralized structure could not wait. Some eighty-five volunteers wanted to join SNCC permanently. This would double SNCC's size. Between 1961 and spring 1964, paid staff had fluctuated between 20 and 130, including about 20 whites, but it was now set to reach almost 200, of whom nearly half would be white. Because this would drastically alter SNCC's racial, geographical, and class composition, most workers, particularly Forman, rejected the plan. But with no clear SNCC structure, their opposition could not be translated into binding mandates. After all, workers asked, when was one actually on staff? If one was on the payroll? Or were criteria like the willingness to work or amount of time spent in the field more important? Who decided which workers could stay? Project directors? Did Forman's resistance imply that he wanted the Atlanta office to determine what happened in the field? *Were* there any criteria for hiring or firing staff? *Could* staff even be fired?[35]

The question clearly involved more than providing a satisfactory context for the volunteers. "How does one determine who the good people are, and who the good people are who will decide who the good people are?" Moses philosophically summarized the issue at the meeting—expressions that Forman later termed "vague hang-ups" over power questions that were irrelevant for the pragmatic-minded fieldworkers. Rather than apply strict administrative criteria, Moses argued, the volunteer question should be determined flexibly. The staff should be expanded a few at a time in thorough deliberations with project directors based on careful consideration of "the color question, the sophistication of the volunteer, [and] possible fall-out" in the projects. Forman pleaded for the maintenance of the freedom force. He later wrote he was defeated in a vote, although historian Wesley Hogan has observed that minutes of the meeting do not mention a vote, and several workers recalled simply receiving a memo with the names of the volunteers who remained, implying that the issue was indeed resolved locally.[36]

The meeting's other topic, approval of the Black Belt Project, sharpened the debate over structure. Its supporters were mostly cosmopolitan-educated workers like Forman, Carmichael, and Samstein. Despite its national angle, Moses had supported it too when it came under discussion at a September Executive Committee meeting. He emphasized southwide speaking tours for MFDP members, residential Freedom Schools, libraries run by locals, and literacy programs as the Project's greatest aims—unlike Forman's stress on building a black political force. But now Moses stayed silent. "It was useless to try and go into another student project like we had," he explained in hindsight, "because of the problems with the staff . . . we just couldn't handle that." Several workers, particularly Lawrence Guyot and Frank Smith, demanded to know "who made [the] decision," implying that its supporters wanted to impose a top-down style of management. Supporters, in turn, asked why SNCC's "leadership is not fighting for this proposal. Leadership has to fight for what it wants. Who is Frank Smith, to try and sabotage this program?" This was especially pertinent because Smith had worked for SNCC since 1962 but was not an official staff member. Guyot left the meeting angry. The Project was never discussed again.[37]

Forman later judged the failure to adopt the Project as "a crucial defeat. There are moments in history when an idea is ripe for implementation and can change the destiny of many." This interpretation, however, ignored the valid points raised against it. Several questioned whether SNCC had the financial resources and personnel and, if so, how to distribute them equally. Others argued that SNCC should complete its responsibilities to its existing programs before expanding. "Are we interested in building a political empire for SNCC, or in building local leadership?" Smith retorted, "[These] two types of organizations are not compatible. We must discuss what SNCC is." Guyot opposed because the Project meant fewer resources for Mississippi. Workers from Arkansas, Alabama, and Georgia supported him; they already felt they were "at the bottom of the list." Freedom Summer had only exacerbated that situation. As one disgruntled worker said in June, "We've got beatings and murders in Arkansas, too, you know." They were proven right; southwest Georgia, for instance, had only two cars, whereas several Mississippi projects now had two each. This "was unintentional [but] inescapable," Julian Bond noted, because "Mississippi *demanded* this kind of effort."[38]

Fieldworkers were becoming increasingly concerned that headquarters were acting in a high-handed and arbitrary way. No one but Forman knew how much money came in and how and why it was spent, whereas fieldworkers had to account for all their spending. "We are broke and hungry," one wrote headquarters upset. "I have been spending all my subsistence money for the last seven weeks on nothing but needs in the field, so if we ever spend a dollar or fifty cents of SNCC money for food, don't give us no shit!" The problems increased after Freedom Summer. Now the staff had doubled, SNCC had to raise $30,000 in salaries per month next to general expenses, while its income was declining. Understandably, headquarters wanted to check where money went, especially when they heard of workers who just "sat around" waiting for locals to initiate something or who squandered resources by, for example, wrecking cars when speeding. Moreover, the question which workers could be fired meant that field staff had to accept office workers' interpretation of what "work" entailed.[39]

Many fieldworkers, mostly northerners, rebelled against Forman's push for bureaucratization. If SNCC created new, viable programs, they argued, discipline problems would automatically diminish. Another group of fieldworkers, generally southern blacks, used the situation to demand a *more* rigid structure. Workers who stole, drank, or otherwise misbehaved hampered their projects. "Why [are people] left in projects long after their project directors have complained and complained about them?" one wondered frustrated. The lack of top-down guidelines accelerated local offices' ineptitude. "You have stood us up," another worker wrote the Jackson office annoyed. "We are sick and tired of [inefficiency]." Subsequently, Howard Zinn summarized in November 1964, SNCC workers were caught in a vicious circle that allowed for leaving "decisions to a few people at the top, or to individuals in the field acting on their own, in other words, both too much localism and too much dictation."[40]

THESE REALIZATIONS COMPLICATED Moses's leadership dilemmas. "People began to question what happened within the organization. And once that was raised," he knew, "that process had to [be gone] through." But acknowledging the process meant acknowledging his views for SNCC. Remembering what had happened in Greenville, he therefore opted for doing so only in a subtle way that still allowed him to avoid taking a formal leadership stance.[41]

A retreat in Waveland, Mississippi, which he and Forman arranged between November 6 and 12, 1964, became the testing ground for their approaches. A fluctuating staff of 80 to 140 discussed structure and program proposals in workshops and through anonymous position papers. Moses appreciated the papers as an exercise in democracy because it prevented disagreements based on personality. The workshops also safeguarded participatory democracy: small groups discussed a single issue and afterward presented their conclusions for discussion with the entire group. SNCC had always worked this way, but now, he discovered, "there's this fear that there's something going on that you're missing." Forman wanted concrete results and wanted them *now*. He traveled from workshop to workshop, Moses grumbled. "He couldn't ... discipline himself to accept the process [and get] in one area of discussion." Forman repetitively asked Moses to spur things along. When Moses replied that "things will start working out in a while," he became increasingly frustrated.[42]

Forman opened the meeting with his call for a centralized structure, with a coordinating committee consisting of the whole staff (a recognition of fieldworkers' desire for input) that decided policy three times a year through voting and a program secretary who oversaw the implementation of programs in the field. Forman's tactic of opening a meeting with a formal speech and his call to let programs flow from structure ignored SNCC's normal way of proceeding. "Where's our dialogue?" some criticized. When they proceeded to discuss programs, Forman pressed for his structure plan each day and tried to force a vote on it, even when attendance fell to 50 percent of the staff. On the fourth day, he finally succeeded in moving the discussion to structure.[43]

True to form, Moses opposed Forman only implicitly in an anonymous position paper. "We are on a boat in the middle of the ocean. It has to be rebuilt in order to stay afloat," he wrote, but it "also has to stay afloat in order to be rebuilt. Our problem is like that. Since we are out on the ocean we have to do it ourselves." Moses was referring to Austrian philosopher Otto Neurath's metaphor about a scientist in a leaking boat who tried to assemble a precise language of science from the ocean of ordinary language around him to prevent it from sinking. Yet he could not dock his boat to get his language of science in order because the ocean's ordinary language was constantly rebuilt. SNCC, Moses implied, should not focus too much on precise language—a specific structure or a particular ideology. SNCC had to be flexible, avoiding looking to models from the past (its own or someone else's), while instead finding its own answers suited for that moment in time because the urgency of staying afloat meant it simultaneously had to act.[44]

SNCC, he clarified, should engage in self-evaluation but not "be hung up" over questions like decision making. Evoking the famous Buddhist parable of the blind men and their elephant, he urged his colleagues to recognize that all truth was subjective and as such, to let different perspectives coexist and choose a pragmatic way forward. Just as the blind men learned that it was impossible to discover the function or nature of an elephant by touching it in the dark—those touching its trunk identified it is a water pipe while others, touching its ears, as a fan—SNCC could not define its function by pinpointing individual parts. Instead of discussing what SNCC *is*, they should try to "reach wider agreement on how to use it." After all, it was better to have a worker who did not know what SNCC was but knew how to use it to run a Freedom Day than vice versa. Structures did not have to be explicit to be used effectively. "Certain logical structures are so everywhere that almost nobody can see them," but "you can use them without knowing what they are and feel fine."[45]

He proposed to divide SNCC's conundrums in three areas: crucial problems central to their work, everyday problems on the edge, and the working problems in between. Crucial problems, like the months-long debates over Freedom Summer, should be dealt with through patience and everyone's input, while working problems could be circulated among all, with discussion of their solutions limited to "staff who are interested. . . . When it's over they disband." Everyday problems could be solved instantly "by the person responsible in [a] forum with himself or whoever." Essentially, Moses proposed to continue the intangible decentralized structure he had always applied in Mississippi. To underscore his words, he ended with a warning from philosopher Alfred Whitehead: "The fixed man for the fixed duty is a public danger."[46]

Despite his effort at anonymity, Moses's erudition betrayed his identity and thereby sharpened the conflict with Forman. As Howard Zinn said, "No-one can tell me that when Jim Forman came across that metaphor he didn't know who wrote it. We all deal with metaphors, but some deal with them more than others." Forman indeed counterattacked in his opening speech. Referring to "someone" comparing SNCC to a boat, Moses summarized, he said, "I don't like the metaphor. I think we don't want to say that it's an ocean. We need to get some direction in it and say that our boat is on a river, that it's moving someplace." Forman even stated that SNCC was "on a river *of no return*," meaning that it was committed to a certain direction and could not be hamstrung on questions like structure; it had to adopt one so it could fulfill that direction. "The longer we take to deal with this question, the longer we fail to give the kind of service to the people that we could," he stressed. Thus, both men were calling for an end to theoretical debates, but whereas Moses argued that structure was irrelevant, Forman insisted that structure was indispensable.[47]

Forman later wrote that he then realized that SNCC was in "a factional fight" between those wanting a decentralized structure—the Moses faction—and those who wanted a tight structure—the Forman faction. The latter, the so-called hardliners, indiscriminately termed the former floaters or the Freedom High faction, although they did not, in fact, constitute a coherent or organized group. Some, like Moses, wanted a loose structure because their field experience had shown it was the only viable approach for grassroots leadership and survival. Others, mostly the "Christian idealists" from SNCC's early days, wanted it on principle; if equality were unattainable in society at large, then they should at least practice it among themselves. Not a few, generally northern whites, elevated personal freedom above all else. Becoming "high on freedom," they combined Moses's existentialist philosophy with the attitude from the spiritual "Go where the Spirit says 'Go.'" Highly articulate, this group was disproportionally vocal, which left many southern-born hardliners convinced that northerners wanted to take over SNCC through overintellectual analyses about power and leadership. Even though many floaters were northern blacks just looking for a meaningful program, hardliners characterized everyone "at Waveland who don't want structure [as] white, intellectuals, and not doing a specific job," as one wrote in February. Freedom High became a derogatory term for anyone engaged in "rambling and inconclusive discussion which will leave us all spiritually purged but still in organizational chaos."[48]

However, these terminologies—which did not surface until spring 1965—did not accurately describe what happened at Waveland. Forman's analysis has dominated historical discussions of that staff meeting and thereby turned it into the complete opposite of what Moses had wanted it, and his role in the meeting, to be. As one SNCC veteran complained, "When I read the history books I deduce that I was considered part of a faction at Waveland, the 'anti-structure' people. That's interesting. . . . The point wasn't whether we were pro- or anti-structure, but rather what kind of structure we needed." The many memoirs of other SNCC workers, generally hardliners, reinforced these interpretations. Cleveland Sellers, for instance, described how he interrupted a secret floater meeting at which Moses was present. The group's discussion moved into "abstract, philosophical areas," so he chastised the "little Bobs": "Stick with reality! . . . What we ought to be discussing is strategy and programs. Where are your programs?" John Lewis similarly described them as people unwilling to accept responsibility to "anything other than his or her own spirit."[49]

Floaters *and* hardliners thus took aspects of Moses's ideas to justify their own actions and thereby contributed to his—and the meeting's—mythification. Moses's definition of power and how to attain it simply differed from Forman's. He cared deeply about leadership, believing that "the only difference between the leader and the led was a matter of becoming." He recognized that certain degrees of discipline and organization were necessary, as his stress on screening and his meticulously detailed memoranda indicate. The Waveland meeting likewise belies his depiction as an impractical idealist. Although he occasionally drifted into philosophy, overall he provided pragmatic solutions, like the need to establish pilot programs on economic issues.[50]

Moses therefore always rejected the Freedom High interpretation of what he wanted to do. "I don't want to be called a person who doesn't want to work," he grumbled at a February 1965 SNCC meeting. "I [just] asked what or who do we organize? Do we build a SNCC machine or do we organize people?" In the field, he explained in retrospect, SNCC "*had* a network [and] basis for a structure. But we didn't have a *theory* about the structure we had. And so it got thrown overboard with the idea well, it's freedom high and people are just going to do whatever they want." Moreover, what took root in Mississippi under SNCC's influence derived from Amzie Moore's insights, and "Amzie certainly wouldn't think of himself either as a floater, a hardliner, [or] Christian idealist." Neither did he appreciate the term *Moses faction*. "I was not, like Jim, trying to actively lead SNCC. . . . It was clear for me, all along, that you couldn't sit down and think through how to put something like SNCC together [because] SNCC evolved through many twists and turns."[51]

Forman's position, however, derived naturally from his daily operations, too. He had spent time in the field, including in Monroe, Danville, Greenwood, and Albany, but he never stayed long enough to obtain what Wesley Hogan termed the "experientially grounded insight" of workers like Moses. What mattered for Forman's job was efficient administration and the projection of SNCC to donors, government officials, and the general public. This orientation logically influenced his perception of what was needed to produce social change. "There is no social revolution which can survive without organization," he already argued in 1962. "It may *arise* spontaneously, but it cannot survive unless it is encouraged." At Waveland, Forman therefore reiterated Jim Monsonis's point that a designated spokesman could improve SNCC's troubled fundraising. He pressured Moses, but the latter predictably replied that he was not available. Moses recognized the need for fundraising—in meetings, he proposed multiple ideas—but overall he lacked durable alternatives. What his colleagues failed to understand, he later said, was that "the resources were part of SNCC because of what it was that SNCC stood for; and if they changed what it stood for, the resources would disappear."[52]

Yet Forman was not merely motivated by office needs. Like Moses, he cared deeply about building leadership but believed that people learned how to act by participating in a structure. This was not the same as desiring power in itself, although these ideas were easily confused. Forman admitted that he fought hard to have his ideas implemented.

Consequently, some hardliners used that to justify their own power quests. "Too many of our leaders are not seriously concerned about building an organization that is going to be something other than an instrument to enable them to inflate their super-conceited egos," one complained. Some southern blacks, Jane Stembridge agreed, "wanted positions, titles, identity, never having had any." In subsequent years, newcomers to SNCC, mostly urban blacks influenced by Malcolm X, stimulated this politicking trend. Combined with the departure of veterans experienced in participatory democracy, this accelerated SNCC's rift from southern rural blacks. When Fannie Lou Hamer questioned its late 1966 proposal to expel whites from the organization (although only a handful were left), she was dismissed as "no longer relevant." This departure from rooting SNCC's organizing in community people played a major role in its eventual rapid decline.[53]

SNCC'S TRAGEDY WAS that the incompatibilities of Forman's and Moses's views, combined with the clustering of groups around certain personalities that separated workers from their collective experience, led to an either/or thinking that had been contained before Freedom Summer. SNCC's success, after all, was based in *both* views. Ella Baker recognized this. "Moses and his role in Mississippi benefited [from] the fact that you had a Jim Forman who was philosophically developed enough to recognize . . . that going to people getting money was a form of providing them with an opportunity to develop." This balance could be maintained due to the goal of voter registration. In its absence, workers struggled to re-create consensus, and "the process," Moses lamented, was "short-circuited because of impatience."[54]

The Waveland meeting is a case in point. When discussing incidents of stealing, Moses for instance approached it as symptomatic of the loss of SNCC's atmosphere of genuine interhuman living. "What bothers me," he said, "is that people steal my time because they don't really talk of themselves, from the center, they talk from the periphery. They steal because there isn't enough time to go around, and the needs of people don't get answered. . . . In our society, we steal whole people's lives away." But hardliner Ed Brown dismissed this as philosophic mumbo-jumbo: he was not interested in "the motivations that cause people to steal . . . we have got to deal with priorities. If it means that you lock your doors, then you must, but let's get on with real business at hand for the future of the organization." Moses and Brown raised two aspects that each believed were central to SNCC's survival: trust and expediency. But the desire for both prevented the realization of either.[55]

SNCC's expansion accelerated this destructive paradox. When the meetings were small, Carmichael said, office workers had "sat in with the field staff and left feeling deeply involved at a frontline level." But now, Don Harris noted, "there were too many people in the field versus too few people in Atlanta operating too inefficiently to adequately deal with everything we were doing." Participatory democracy became impractical. Especially the length of discussions spurred frustrations. In the past, Charles McDew recalled, "somebody may have spoken 8 hours, and 7 hours and 53 minutes was utter bullshit, but 7 minutes was good. [Baker] taught us to glean out the 7 minutes." But in such a large group, workers increasingly began to accept motions because they were tired of talking, not because they agreed. "It was not democracy because it was the people who could stay awake the longest who became the winners," one later complained. In 1966, for example, John Lewis defeated Stokely Carmichael in a vote for the position of chair, but after his supporters had left the meeting exhausted, another vote was forced that Carmichael won.[56]

Another downside of participatory democracy in the post-1964 climate was that "whoever could articulate the plan best" became the "leader." These generally were the whites and northern middle-class blacks like the Howard University group. Lower-class southern blacks feared, one wrote, that the former used the Atlanta office to "push grand intellectual schemes about what we will do with the local people." Race and class accordingly became another stake in the structure debate. Hard-liners used the "intimidation" of lower-class blacks to demand voting power for field staff, whereas floaters used it to argue *against* a voting-dominated structure because then a minority could impose their will even more. SNCC's desire to retain its redemptive qualities at a time when its growing nationalist political perspective increasingly determined its direction inevitably enhanced its deadlock; it essentially crippled itself by obsessing about internal inequities. Racial tensions made constructive discussion near impossible. The now oft-repeated suggestion that "whites and blacks should be used according to the functions which they best serve"—that is, each within their own community—foreshadowed the 1966 expulsion of whites. At Waveland, working-class blacks still adopted a self-imposed inhibition. Their inability to follow discussions—"I don't talk 'cause I don't understand the words that you-all use!" one shouted—caused most to simply avoid workshops or leave them early.[57]

Overall, SNCC workers still favored a decentralized, consensus-based organizing approach. On the last day, they discussed Forman's structure proposal and two alternatives. Time constraints ended discussions prematurely, but staff agreed that SNCC should not "alter our definition of ourselves for the people who give us money." Forman later wrote that the discussions collapsed over the question of firing workers. Confusion therefore existed as much on the last day as on the first. The only thing everyone recognized was the sad truth of Mendy Samstein's statement that "we are a lot of different people from different backgrounds. We are not brothers just because we have been put on pay-roll." In subsequent months, morale and discipline further declined. More workers left or abandoned responsibilities for new projects, and tolerance of white workers continued to decrease. This left the remaining SNCC workers increasingly open to Forman's centralization proposals, while it pushed Moses more and more into the opposite direction.[58]

AS 1965 APPROACHED, Moses struggled with the growing realization that in this climate, he could not contribute anything worthwhile without embracing his leadership role. Yet this he was unwilling to do. He resigned as COFO director in December 1964 because his role "was too strong, too central, so that people who did not need to, began to lean on me, to use me as a crutch." But this did little to change his reputation; Freedom Summer had turned him into a national civil rights leader. Magazines and papers like the *Saturday Evening Post* accompanied articles with large pictures of him. Mississippi blacks hung such pictures in their homes, next to images of Jesus; rumors circulated that even Governor Johnson had a blown-up picture of Moses in his office, as if he personified everything he considered evil in Mississippi. Many volunteers treated Moses, in Sellers's words, as "a cultural hero" and copied his speech and clothing. Volunteer Mario Savio, later spokesman of the Berkeley Free Speech movement, was so impressed he "wanted to be like Bob Moses. I wanted to *be* Bob Moses if could do it." In letters home, others lauded him as "someone you read about in novels" and "as great a man as any generation could produce." Moses "is more or less the Jesus of the whole project," one concluded, "Not because he asks to be, but because of everyone's reaction to him." Even veteran workers copied his mannerisms, especially his rolling hand as he spoke. "We thought we were smarter if we did that," Julian Bond laughed.[59]

This only deepened Moses's depression and battle fatigue. His treatment as "the all-perfect and all-holy and all-wise leader," John Lewis noted, "made him so uncomfortable he felt like climbing out of his own skin." Indicative of his downcast state of mind, Moses reprimanded the 1,000-strong audience that gave him a standing ovation at the *National Guardian* dinner. "This is absurd," he sniped. "You're acting like you're part of the establishment." He left the event depressed. Forman recalled how Moses bemoaned the fact that no one ever called him a motherfucker. Lacking any moral alternatives, he increasingly withdrew into the passive role of observer he had pioneered at Hamilton. This too was part of his silence during the Black Belt Project discussions, although he communicated his thoughts to Forman in private. But his "silence created even *more* reverence for him. It was maddening," Lewis wrote, "You could see him almost starting to crack under all these pressures."[60]

For the hardliners, Moses's attitude was incomprehensible. "My position was that you just stand up and say, 'Mother-fucker, fuck you,' and you'll be one of the guys then," Forman later reflected. "But you don't abdicate leadership." He blamed the floaters. "[Moses] was made to feel guilty [primarily by] the middle class element, who constantly sniped at him about his supposedly excessive influence." This explanation, however, underrates Moses's capacity for self-criticism and guilt, as well as the sincerity with which he approached his philosophical entanglements with his leadership position. To Forman's warnings that if he abdicated leadership, "this thing will collapse," Moses merely retorted, "At what point do you turn over leadership?" He similarly retreated from the secret floater meeting after the hardliners' invasion. "Bob could have won the confrontation if he had wanted to," Sellers noted. "He was smart enough to tie [us hardliners] into philosophical knots. He didn't do it because he realized that he would have had to become what he abhorred, a manipulator."[61]

During SNCC's February 12 to 19, 1965, meeting at Atlanta's Gammon Theological Seminary, Moses again stayed silent as hardliners pushed through Forman's proposals. The field staff was added to the Coordinating Committee (originally two representatives from each state), and only paid staff could now make decisions, through majority vote rather than consensus. A new "secretariat" constituted the executive secretary (Forman), chairman (Lewis), and a program secretary (Sellers). Forman and Lewis received authority to make formal policy decisions in between meetings. The Executive Committee, expanded to twenty-one members, became dominated by hardliners, too. Forman celebrated this as a victory for the working class but acknowledged that the meeting was traumatic, with many abstaining from voting "out of confusion or dislike for the general atmosphere."[62]

Having always opposed subordination to majority vote for the life-threatening work they did, Moses finally spoke up. "If you want to keep a slave, give a man the vote and tell him he's free," he said. But his attempt to show his colleagues that they were being manipulated under the pretense of democracy was lost on the meeting. But Moses declined to fight the hardliners any longer.[63]

Realizing that his leadership dilemmas had reached an impossible crisis, Moses withdrew further in himself. His colleagues looked on with concern. "It was as if all the strife of the entire movement was playing itself out inside his skin, inside his soul, and his head," John Lewis recalled. Moses searched desperately for an exit, concluding that he could only find one if he literally became someone else. A few nights later, near the end of the week-long meeting, he walked into the room where the group was gathering. After inviting his colleagues to drink from the bottle of wine he had brought and eat some of the cheese that someone else happened to have with him, he announced that he had changed his name to Bob Parris and would leave Mississippi. "It was clear to me that they couldn't make me into such a [leading or media] figure, if they couldn't use my name," he later explained. "Just the fact that you have to stop and say that Robert Parris is in fact Robert Moses, is enough to confuse a lot of people."[64]

The name change ceremony provides further insight into how Moses's gloomy state of mind influenced his leadership. He said he was strained and needed a break. His name change was "the only way to cope" because then he could change from "Moses the Myth" to "Robert [Parris] the Man." He looked directly at others with strong leadership positions in SNCC like Lewis, Forman, and Carmichael and said, "It's time for you to leave." They too, he implied, were "becoming creatures of the media, contending for power." Throughout, Moses pretended to be drunk, although he clearly was not. When the bottle of wine returned to him, he simply left with his wife. He never played a directive role in national SNCC meetings again.[65]

Most bystanders, being less educated in symbolism than Moses, looked at him like Alice looked at the rambling Mad Hatter in Wonderland. Cleve Sellers called his monologue "a complicated existential exposition" that "was too heavy." "People were stunned. Dead silent. No-one knew what exactly to make of this," Lewis agreed. "But everyone knew it was hugely significant." His departure has therefore been mythologized in movement circles as much as his entry into Mississippi. Some enjoyed calling him Parris and revered his act, in James Miller's words, as "one of the most striking gestures of self-abnegating democratic (anti-) leadership in the Sixties." Others thought he had succumbed to a mental breakdown. Forman called it the meeting's "most difficult and confusing hour."[66]

Because Moses never explained his actions—doing so implied asserting leadership—the idea that his disillusionment had taken the best of him was allowed to spread. In subsequent years, as he made more decisions few understood, workers mourned him as another movement casualty. "One thinks of Bob with a heavy sense of possibilities lost, roads not taken, hopes unnecessarily destroyed," Staughton Lynd for instance wrote in 1970.[67]

Yet Moses never did anything without meaning. What seemed an incoherent, abstract ramble was actually his strongest indictment of the hardliner policy to date. The whole name change ceremony, he finally explained years later, was a reaction against SNCC's power seeking. Although his might be a post facto rationale, even Sellers acknowledged that while Moses had seemed "on the verge of hysteria, he appeared to be in complete control of himself." The wine and cheese helped Moses's point because onlookers interpreted it as a last supper that symbolized his equation with Jesus. But since the bottle was nearly empty, he implied that with him "no-one should expect miracles."[68]

Even the passing of the wine and pretending to be drunk were gestures heavily laden with symbolism. That afternoon, one uneducated southern black had drunk whiskey to get the courage to address SNCC's key members. Because he had been drinking, some hardliners denied him speaking time. The fact that less "qualified" workers felt they needed to "rev themselves up" before exercising their right to speak and then having disciplinary rules curb that right, Moses said, "got to me." Clearly, "the willingness of people to . . . speak for themselves was under threat." By passing the wine, he dramatized *everyone's* right to speak. He pretended to be drunk "to see if they would put *me* down" too, and since no one did, he exposed the hypocrisy of the hardliners' rules. The ceremony had thus allowed him to express his views without imposing them; it was moral self-effacing leadership at its best—even if his colleagues missed the point.[69]

The significance of Moses's withdrawal has been intensely debated among movement participants and historians. The overriding view is that his absence hastened SNCC's decline. Some attributed an enormous personal power to him that questions the degree of group-centered leadership in SNCC. The movement "split first of all because Bob Moses has left," one worker already stated in 1965. "Since then most of the people have said . . . we certainly should have supported Moses [and] toned down Forman." John Lewis also believed that Moses's departure fatally damaged SNCC. "If there was one thread that might have held it all together, it would have been Bob Moses. . . . But he absolutely refused to fill that role, and we would all suffer because of it." Such interpretations, however, neglect SNCC's daily realities in 1965. As Julian Bond argued, "It wasn't as if we bam! just threw up our hands and said 'Oh what will it be' . . . we lost an important figure [but] that doesn't mean we slipped into disarray." One December 1964 report already noted that Moses was "taking no part in key day to day decisions," indicating he had abdicated leadership well before his physical withdrawal. Some even credited him for leaving. "If he had stayed and become institutionalized," one worker acknowledged, "whatever value Bob had to the movement would have been lost."[70]

Moreover, Moses's closest colleagues stuck to his organizing approach. For several months, SNCC veterans like Charlie Cobb continued to oppose centralization. Stokely Carmichael felt "a responsibility to carry on the work Bob had given so much of himself of." In Alabama, he used the slow organizing technique Moses popularized in Mississippi. "I just got into that Bob Moses bag," he said, "I had to see what I could do in the place no-one else would go." Until the murder of a white worker in August 1965, he had opposed restraints on whites' presence in the project, using the same reasoning Moses had used to sanction Freedom Summer. John Cumbler, 1965 summer volunteer, stated that COFO workers often started arguments with "if Moses were here he would argue we should. . . ." Although Bond suspected that some "just made things up that they wanted to do," the fact that they did so for months sustains Cumbler's claim that Moses "continued to permeate the best part of the Movement. . . . His spirit was still there."[71]

There is little to support the assumption that if Moses had stayed, SNCC's outcome would have been any different. Many SNCC workers would have left regardless. When they lamented his absence after the fact, they were merely expressing a sense of personal loss. "If Bob would get into this, then we'd see more clearly," Bond paraphrased their thinking. Lewis agreed that there was little personal ill-feeling because the philosophy of nonviolence called for allowing individuals to go "only as far as their conscience would go." Mary King concurred. "One must be loath in making judgments about another human being's decisions about self-assertion or when is the right time to leave."[72]

But Moses had never intended to leave SNCC permanently. "Basically I was waiting on SNCC; that's what I [did] for almost two years . . . I wasn't looking for SNCC to provide us with a program, but I was waiting for SNCC to resolve the basic problems that had surfaced as a result of '64. And I felt that it was worth whatever amount of time it took to resolve them." Taking an active role in debates would have mattered little. "There wasn't anything I could say that would be helpful. The problems that we were trying to grapple with weren't of the kind that could be dealt with in one meeting. It would take what people weren't willing to give, which was time."[73]

ON THE FIRST DAY of the Selma-to-Montgomery march, Moses and his wife moved to Birmingham to see what organizing in an urban area was like. They were still on SNCC's payroll but had not reported to Alabama Director Silas Norman. This upset SNCC's Executive Committee, which convened on April 12, 1965, to curb such lapses in discipline. The meeting soon dissolved into an attack on all floaters. In a fashion far removed from SNCC's early spirit, the group evaluated each worker to decide whether SNCC should be "shaping [them] up or shipping out." Moses's and Richards's actions could not be ignored either. "I will not look for them," Norman complained. "They must contact me." "Someone should find out what they are doing," Ruby Doris Smith agreed. "They can't say their work is irrelevant to SNCC." Marion Barry objected that "if it was anybody else, we'd be raising hell." Forman concurred. "All should be subject to discipline. If Bob is above discipline, he should be project director." Although Stokely Carmichael disliked the fact that Moses was given too much slack, he opposed personal attacks. "People here are incapable of dealing with the real problem, which is lack of programs. That is why people 'float.' Dealing with floaters deals with symptoms rather than the cause." But Forman said he liked discussing individuals. "This is the first time in this organization that we have [done] some constructive work on the individual level." The committee continued evaluating individuals for two days.[74]

Two weeks later, Moses and Richards appeared at a small SNCC meeting in Alabama, where he underscored the growing divide between himself and his colleagues. In a final attempt to let his colleagues focus on the long term, Moses softly pointed out that SNCC wanted "to create an atmosphere that is best for the workers [but] is it best for the people? . . . Remember the people don't have our frustrations." He even drew mathematical charts outlining various relations between organizers and locals to show that a movement of different community groups could only be created if the organizer removed himself as the reference point. This could be realized, he stressed, by implementing the Executive Committee's recent proposal of organizing People's Conferences. But many SNCC workers now considered such meetings, where locals could talk without a deadline and workers' guidance, as too close to the freedom high spirit. They agreed to organize the conferences, perhaps in reverence to Moses, but without his active leadership—he insisted that the point was for locals "to let it snowball from there"—they never materialized.[75]

Meanwhile, the Vietnam War increasingly diverted Moses's attention. His Mississippi experiences had strengthened his pacifism. Already at James Chaney's memorial service on August 6, 1964, he raised a newspaper headlining the recent Gulf of Tonkin incident and declared, "The same kind of racism that killed these young men is going to kill a lot more people in Vietnam." After all, he later explained, "The country [was] unable to see Vietnam for exactly the same reasons . . . they didn't see us." The government defended freedom in Vietnam but not in Mississippi, he had told the volunteers in Ohio. "The guerrilla war in Mississippi is not much different from that in Vietnam. But when we tried to see President Johnson, his secretary said that Vietnam was popping up all over his calendar and he hadn't time to talk to us." Moses saw this as the same hypocrisy that "sent me [to Mississippi] in the first place," namely, "all the hue and cry about Eastern Europeans and the right to vote in the '50s." Moreover, he had met North Vietnamese citizens in Africa. "That was the first time," he said, "I could actually get in touch with, and see them as people without the whole propaganda in this country."[76]

Moses first expressed his views on a national level after Tom Hayden came to Birmingham and asked him to speak at SDS's April 17 antiwar protest in Washington. Before 20,000 demonstrators—nearly all of them white—Moses indicted "the prosecutors of the war" as "the same people who refused to protect civil rights in the South." During the May 21 to 22 Vietnam teach-ins at Berkeley, he addressed a largely white audience of 10,000 people. His speech captured perfectly how Moses merged his cosmopolitan background and organic experiences in Mississippi into a philosophy that treated his roles in the civil rights and peace movements as inseparable. Introducing himself as a Third World member, he told his listeners that if they wanted to do anything about Vietnam, they had "to learn from the South." "I saw a picture in an AP release," he explained. "It said, 'Marine captures Communist rebel.' Now I looked at that picture and what I saw was a little colored boy standing against a wire fence with a big huge white Marine with a gun in his back. But what I knew was that the people in this country saw a Communist rebel." If his audience used the South "as a looking glass, not a lightening rod," Moses said, it could "offer a different reality" to the nation. "If you can begin to understand . . . why you don't move when a Negro is killed the same way you move when a white person is killed, then maybe you can begin to understand this country in relation to Vietnam and the Third World." He repeated his murderer's jury theory. "You can learn when it is that a society gets together and plans and executes and allows its members to murder and then go free. And if you learn something about that, then maybe you'll learn something about this country and how it plans and executes murders elsewhere in the world." He told them to write Hazel Palmer, a black maid who became an MFDP leader. Through her, they could learn about similar "faceless leaders" in the Third World as persons instead of political labels.[77]

Many civil rights movement supporters disliked Moses's antiwar activities. When he and Staughton Lynd, another devout pacifist, talked to John Bennett, dean of Union Theological Seminary, after the April rally, the latter questioned Moses's presence. He argued that black involvement in the antiwar effort jeopardized the black struggle. "That really got me," Moses said. "I got angry." Critics like Bennett believed that the peace movement diverted attention, energy, and President Johnson's goodwill from the cause of racial equality. Even Lynd acknowledged the inherent difficulties in combining the goals of different movements. "Moses condemned America's action in bombing North Vietnam," he wrote in 1964. "Yet at Atlantic City Moses's party pledged alliance to the man who ordered the bombing. The dilemma of victim and executioner is literal and cruel." Moses's wife also questioned his growing concern for the (white) antiwar movement while she and SNCC increasingly looked to Africa. She adamantly opposed the war but felt that becoming involved in the peace movement increased Communist charges against SNCC and thus threatened the fundraising needed for building black political power. "We can't do anything to help the Vietnam situation," she wrote in September 1965, "[but] we can hurt ourselves by trying."[78]

Many southern blacks shared such misgivings. SNCC perceived intense resentment against the war in black communities but little interest in action. It did not formerly oppose the war until 1966; Martin Luther King Jr. not until 1967. Blacks' unwillingness to follow Moses confirms sociologist Max Weber's theory that for a charismatic leader like him to attain—or maintain—influence, the existence of a (perceived) crisis situation is indispensable. "The war," Moses admitted, just "was not something that people were concerned about." Black conservatives even considered opposition to the war as unpatriotic. When McComb teenagers opposed the draft in an MFDP newsletter, Charles Evers and others denounced the MFDP as Communist. The MFDP then refused to endorse the statement. Moses "is completely out of touch with the people [and what they] can and will do," one worker concluded. Yet Moses felt that black involvement in the peace struggle would *benefit* their own. Feeling connected to a broader movement might help COFO workers cope with battle fatigue. In addition, now blacks had the franchise, he told the *Southern Patriot*, they had to make it meaningful. "People need a chance to vote on real issues. That [includes] debate on foreign policy." Blacks were *obligated* to speak up; just as they had helped the South see that its "basic problem lies not with outsiders but itself," they now had to help the nation awake from the myth that all its problems were caused by extremists, be they urban rioters or communist nations. To mitigate the criticism, Moses nonetheless asked a leave of absence from SNCC.[79]

Moses then joined a British labor organizer he had met at the April rally in contacting traditional peace groups. He even attended Allard Lowenstein's Encampment for Citizenship, a New York summer camp for peace activists, and phoned Bayard Rustin. But Rustin, like most traditional peace organizers, refused involvement for fear of jeopardizing the Great Society programs. Realizing that only the New Left could raise momentum against the war, Lynd, Moses, and pacifist David Dellinger planned a Washington Summer Action Project. Moses and Richards moved to New York, where he worked with white pacifist A. J. Muste, and then to Washington. The Project's highlight was a four-day Assembly of Unrepresented People, with workshops ranging from foreign policy to community organizing. Participants included SDS, the National Council of Churches, the War Resisters League, artists, lawyers, and professors. Most were white, but Moses brought thirty black Mississippians. SNCC did not participate, despite Moses's request "to break [its] isolation" and start working in a movement centered "on the entire American public" rather than just "the Negro ghetto." On August 6, the anniversary of the Hiroshima bombing, a prayer vigil was held near the White House. There Moses denounced the fierce reaction to the McComb statement as racism since the White House openly accepted a similar Declaration of Conscience by Muste. On August 9, the Nagasaki bombing anniversary, some 800 marched to the Capitol to present Congress with Declarations of Peace composed in the workshops, but American Nazis threw red paint on Moses, Lynd, and Dellinger, just before they and 300 other marchers were arrested.[80]

AFTER HIS RELEASE ON BAIL, Moses spoke again with Lowenstein. Interpreting the war as one directed at China, the latter proposed taking a group of students there. Tom Hayden was thinking of inviting another group to Vietnam. Moses briefly thought about going on either one of the trips but instead accepted an offer to stay at the house of Bill Sutherland, of the War Resisters League, in Tanzania's then capital Dar es Salaam. Moses went because he wished to gain "insight about the world situation, because [I] really believed it was going to be 50 years before the mistakes within the movement and the Democratic Party . . . could be regained." Meanwhile, the climate of suspicion in SNCC had increased. In May, his wife had barely escaped injury when a frightened cook accidentally threw a meat cleaver after some floaters brought knives to a conflict with hardliners. After this, Sellers observed, "the Hardliners were in control of SNCC." He notified workers that if they failed to satisfactorily report on their activities, they would be fired. In Africa, Moses hoped to regain "some sense of direction" for the movement and "some hope and inspiration . . . as Malcolm X" had found there a year earlier.[81]

But the trip had a different effect on Moses than on his wife. In October, they flew to Ghana and, via Tanzania, went to Egypt to visit W. E. B.

DuBois's son and widow and returned home after staying in Paris and London in early 1966. In Ghana, they attended a conference of the pan-Africanist organization OAU (Organization of African Unity). Kwame Nkrumah, the first African leader to declare independence in 1957, hosted it in Accra. Richards marveled at the country's quick industrial development and the street banners everywhere proclaiming "Africa Must Unite." Conference attendees were mostly black nationalists. "These people are engaged in actual fighting in their, yet unfree, countries," she reported admiringly to SNCC. The trip accordingly strengthened her interest in pan-Africanism. She noted that Africans begged for information on the American civil rights movement and that SNCC could help provide this through articles and SNCC films. SNCC, in turn, could "gain from the Africans ... a different and more satisfying approach to our problems." African Americans should especially adopt Africans' nondefensiveness about whites now that integration "has become, for us, meaningless." The only way forward, she reiterated, was starting to think "in terms of how western civilization ... has always related to the colored people of the world."[82]

Moses did not wholly share his wife's excitement. American blacks, he acknowledged in hindsight, "never did really grasp Africa." Identification with Africans blinded them to the realities on the continent; when Ruby Doris Smith clothed herself in African attire during the 1964 Guinea trip, Toure's advisors, for instance, dismissed such makeovers as naive. Moses and Richards now met several revolutionaries whom Malcolm X had visited who were still spirited, but Moses could not fail to notice that "the mood on the whole continent ... had soured significantly." This only added to his troubled worldview. "Africa was falling apart. They were fighting each other, regimes were toppling," including Nkrumah's.[83]

Yet because SNCC still had no clear direction upon their return and because he too identified with Third World struggles, Moses was willing to keep pursuing the avenues his wife was exploring. This included the organization of an all-black conference on decolonization called *Roots*, held in New Orleans. Richards recruited the group who organized the event, including CORE activists Rudy Lombard and Jerome Smith and several other black women, like Don Harris' wife Tina and Janet Jemmott. They raised the money for the conference by organizing a dance that featured Jemmott's brother Jerry, a well-known guitarist, at a ballroom in Harlem owned by a friend of Richards's mother.[84]

The women at the conference presented a paper that explored the idea of black consciousness. This resulted as much from their experiences in Mississippi as world events. Whites' presence had complicated black women's struggles with their femininity and self-image. Most black female workers resented what Alvin Poussaint termed the "white African queen complex"—white female volunteers' "repressed fantasy of the intelligent, brave, and beautiful white woman leading the poor, downtrodden, and oppressed black man to freedom." They also resented white women's prominence in SNCC and their close proximity to black male workers. This threatened everyone's physical safety, and interracial dating problematized internal relationships. Apart from competition and threatening black women's self-worth—already judged by white standards of beauty and virtue—they feared that white women used black men (and vice versa). Their growing pro-black emotions, Moses explained, therefore did not represent "a nationalist perspective" like Black Power but rather a "very deep psychological perspective that was mixed with politics. . . . [This] was what I was responding to [with *Roots*. These women] were saying we need to do this."[85]

The women asked Moses to attend because his presence would draw in others. He "went along, trying to see if there was some way, something to do," but he had nothing to do with the paper. Most historians and contemporaries nonetheless ascribe the conference and the paper to him. This is likely explained by contemporary denigrating views of female agency and the national incomprehension of the movement's pro-black course. It was more fascinating to attribute both to Moses, beside Martin Luther King Jr., *the* symbol of the 1960s integrationist movement. They played up his disillusionment with white liberals and described him as a tragic hero, the idealist turned sour, like the movement itself.[86]

His brief decision to stop speaking to whites, which he announced shortly after the conference, spurred this interpretation. John Lewis, Roy Wilkins, and Joseph Rauh claimed that he already "left Atlantic City vowing never to speak to a white man again." Others, like Taylor Branch and Stokely Carmichael, stated that he announced the decision at his name change ceremony. Both are unlikely given his later involvement with the peace movement. Moreover, in *Pacific Scene* in February 1965, Moses stated his unaltered "faith principle" that if whites "were presented with real information about people and how they live . . . they would [not] consciously choose to isolate other people." Despite pondering the idea of a shadow government, he still hoped that both races could overcome their differences. "The less overlay of bitterness, the more possible to work out a reconciliation."[87]

Many references to Moses's embrace of black nationalism depend on hearsay. In interviews with SNCC workers, rumors about Moses being "extremely negative in terms of white people" are rampant, yet none provide factual details. Stanley Wise, SNCC's executive secretary during its Black Power period, claimed that Moses's Africa trip convinced him to sever his relationships with whites. "These were people he cut away in one fell swoop," Wise stated without naming any. Others, like Dorie Ladner, refused to sacrifice their beloved image of Moses and denied he ever made the decision. Or, like Mary King, described it as a passing phase caused by temporary emotional stress. "He was probably emotionally, spiritually, and physically depleted . . . [it] was not directed at his personal associates but was a rejection of his acculturation and the overwhelming and downpressing constructs of white culture. At that moment, the world—the white world—was too much with him." This, too, SNCC worker Janice Goodman said, was "part of the Moses myth, particularly among whites—he could do no wrong." Some blamed his wife. "One could understand that coming from Dona, as many of us supposed, but not from Bob," one said. "[Moses] is not Stokely, he is not Rap,"[88] Goodman explained, "so it must have been the influence of Lady MacBeth."[89]

Yet the realities of human behavior are often complex, and this was certainly true for Robert Moses. He promoted black nationalism in the Booker T. Washington self-help sense, as his proposals for parallel institutions demonstrate. The MFDP, Julian Bond argued, even "served as a prototype for the model of Black Power advocated [by] Carmichael." Furthermore, as Goodman asserted, it is "difficult to believe anyone could influence Moses to do that in which he does not sincerely believe or thought was ethically or morally wrong." Moses confirmed that he had had no "problem trying to see where [his wife's views] would lead." Considering the sacrifices SNCC people made, he thought it was "a little much for people to say, well, 'you can't explore this avenue.'"[90]

Yet the accusation of his wife's influence was not wholly far-fetched. Shortly after the *Roots* conference, their relationship had cooled, partly over Moses's overemphasis on the war and partly because she and Rudy Lombard were, in Moses's words, "trying to work out some type of relationship." Moses's relationship with Richards had always been as intense and volatile as life in SNCC itself. When the organization began to falter, it became increasingly difficult for the two to ignore the ever present differences within their own union as well. In part, looking into nationalism became a way of trying to retrieve what was left of their marriage. "I was really following what my then wife, Dona, wanted to do," he confessed years later.[91]

In retrospect, Moses claimed he was more exhausted by his leadership role than hostile to whites' presence. He had escaped leadership in the black community but now felt pressured into a similar role in the peace movement. Yet it was time, he felt, "for them to develop their own strategies and thoughts." He always denied that his decision was directed at all whites. "I never decided to stop speaking to white people. I decided not to speak to Staughton Lynd and Mendy Samstein," meaning whites who leaned on him. "There were plenty of white people I was speaking to. So that was not the issue." Yet his decision was perhaps more extensive than he suggested. Janice Goodman, for instance, remembered how she and black SNCC worker Mike Thelwell once saw him in Washington. They had not seen him in months and thus did not lean on him. But "Moses simply turned his back and walked away," she said, and "it was my [white] presence that was the sticking point" because Moses spoke with Thelwell when he left her side. For her and whites who heard similar stories irrespective of the actual circumstances, this was traumatizing. "It hurt very deeply, because any one of us would have been literately willing to take the bullet for Bob," one explained.[92]

But Moses was again looking on the long term. He supported separate black conferences because it was the only way for SNCC to recuperate. "Whatever energy I had, I needed to put it into the black movement and the black community, and nationalism and the problems we were having, and to stay with that and ride it through," he said, implying that he suspected Black Power to be a passing phase. "There's a real need for black people to meet by themselves . . . SNCC meetings dragged on interminably [because] people never could say what they felt." Integrated meetings perpetuated the situation where blacks attacked whites and vice versa. Moses therefore saw *Roots* as a means to provide this space: he wanted to provide a pragmatic—as opposed to an ideological—solution, for the sake of *both* races. He even claimed that "part of my involvement in the peace movement was . . . just a way of helping the white students get out of the civil rights movement." Outsiders, he lamented, analyzed this wrongly. "In this country, it's inevitable that you interpret [something like *Roots*] as anti-white . . . it's impossible [to] have an interpretation that people are searching for an identity, which is not necessarily to be geared at cutting down somebody else's identity."[93]

Moses's idea of nationalism therefore did not equal the politics of rage that SNCC or the Black Panthers turned it into with Black Power. In fact, he witnessed SNCC's unveiling of Black Power with great apprehension. When Stokely Carmichael first announced the phrase during the Meredith March in June 1966, Moses was staying with Amzie Moore. He saw Carmichael in Jackson at the end of the march, but, he recalled, "you couldn't talk to him. He was, you know, caught up." Carmichael was preoccupied with the media, which delved into his slogan with fascination and condemnation alike. Moses rejected Carmichael's and other black nationalists' playing to the media by means of incendiary rhetoric. "Once SNCC got a charismatic media person, Stokely and then Rap, the dynamics within the organization shifted," he later stated. "The organizers stopped organizing because it was more glamorous to do what Stokely was doing." Moreover, his unwavering commitment to nonviolence was incompatible with the Black Power line of self-defense. He deplored the way black nationalism seemed to encourage rioting in urban black communities. When Carmichael "yelled 'Black Power,'" he said, "that was it. We lost the ability to speak to the inner city." Black Power, he concluded, was a "departure from what we [had been] doing in Mississippi" and "wasn't able to sustain a movement."[94]

Few of his colleagues, however, saw the difference between what Moses intended to do and the Black Power movement around them. "You got Stokely working in Lowndes [and] Moses [and] his conference," Ed Brown summarized in 1967, and this explained "how you get Black Power." Because Moses fled the country shortly after, gossip about his whereabouts and activities—ranging from welfare worker in Harlem to leading guerilla bands in Africa—took over. The mysteries surrounding his disappearance accordingly strengthened rather than diminished his legendary image. But Moses knew nothing of this as he recuperated abroad from his movement experiences. A decade later, he returned an even more fervent believer in his approach for social change, whose wisdom he reaffirmed in a revived organizing career that successfully combined his cosmopolitan and organic experiences into a new bottom-up movement for racial equality that is still in existence today.[95]

Epilogue

After the *Roots* conference, Moses retreated to Cleveland, Mississippi, for about four months in the spring of 1966 to think about his marriage and future. In the course of just over a year, he had lost all that had identified him in the past years: his organization, his movement, his life partner, even his own name. That he returned to Amzie Moore in one of his most difficult hours in his personal life and activist career is telling. Having found his purpose there once, he might find it again. But this was not simple, and his battle fatigue did not make it easier. According to Moore, Moses "didn't speak to anybody hardly." He occasionally encountered Mississippi SNCC workers, but overall he felt invisible. This was a relief.[1]

Now that so few sought his advice, he changed his name back to Moses, less than a year after he had assumed it. This indicated that the name change had never been more than a coping mechanism, indicative of the stress he was under, rather than a full-swing conversion in the vein of many of his coworkers in SNCC and other blacks who in this period began to adopt African names or black Muslims who adopted Islamic ones. For many of them, such as Stokely Carmichael, H. "Rap" Brown, Malcolm X, and boxer Cassius Clay, these were lifelong commitments, born from a mix of deep-seated psychological, historical, and/ or religious factors.

There was not much for Moses to do in Mississippi. He and Moore talked regularly about Vietnam, but since Moses had cut short his relations with the antiwar movement, Moore said, he was "out of touch with whites." Moore now headed the Bolivar County Head Start program, and federal officials swerved in and out his home. Moses thought this was all right but thought it unwise for SNCC organizers to get involved. With nine other Mississippi workers, he went on another two-week retreat in Alabama in July 1966 to rethink their next moves now that Black Power had taken over SNCC. But essentially, he had reached an emotional and organizational dead end. It was clear that he and his unaltered organizing ideas would not find a way back into SNCC any time soon.[2]

Unforeseen events then rendered a return impossible. In Alabama, Moses received a notice to report for the draft in New York City on September 1. Since he had already passed the legal draft age of twenty-six by five years, he suspected that the FBI had pressured the draft board as retribution for his antiwar activities. This was certainly plausible considering the selective means through which the draft was being applied. Many draft protesters or movement participants who spoke out against the war, like John Lewis, suddenly found their draft status revoked or reclassified. Considering this politicization of the draft, Moses had every expectation that the issue would not disappear until he was safely locked away.[3]

Moses did not want to report for duty but, having already spent enough time in jail, did not relish that prospect either. He also feared that returning to jail would revive media interest in his persona, turning him into a symbol once more. Yet becoming a draft evader meant returning to a life of being chased, constantly looking over his shoulder, thinking one step ahead. Moreover, it meant giving up any hope of reviving his relationship with Dona Richards.[4]

Moses returned to New York to figure out what to do. Dona Richards and Janet Jemmott were working at a nursery school there, along with two other drafted black movement workers, a young Mississippian and a New Orleans CORE worker, whom Moses knew from the Alabama meeting. The two were preparing to join the ranks of the 30,000 Americans who would flee the country in the next decade to avoid being enlisted. Moses and Richards were still on speaking terms, despite her failed attempt at a relationship with Rudy Lombard. After it became clear, however, that his marriage could not be saved, he decided to join the Mississippian and CORE worker in fleeing the country. The nursery job became a cover where the three could work "incommunicado" until they "got ready to leave." Because the draft board already trailed the other two, Moses traveled to Montreal, Canada, and rented a place for them. They went up, while he returned to New York for the rest of August to prepare for the trip, including arranging the divorce from Richards.[5]

When September arrived, Moses borrowed money from his brother Gregory and followed the others to Montreal. He changed his name again, living under the name Robinson. Because he spoke French, he had no trouble fitting in and obtaining the paperwork he needed for his new life. Until June 1968, he earned a meager living doing a variety of jobs like night watchman, janitor, and department store salesman. He sold newspapers over the telephone and worked at the airline service, packing food on trays.[6]

It was a difficult time for Moses, being as he was "really thrown out on your own resources." He had no contact with anyone in the United States or with the other refugees for fear of alerting the Canadian authorities. Feeling isolated, he had the time to pose himself various hypotheticals. He mulled over his relationship with Richards and his time in the movement. Indicative of his still troubled state of mind, he even wondered whether the assassinations of John F. Kennedy and Malcolm X might not actually "represent the opening salvo of a systematic right-wing offensive to decapitate the movement." He made a long list of key figures that might be the next targets. His shortlist included Martin Luther King Jr., Robert Kennedy, James Farmer, Bob Spike, and Taconic Foundation executive Stephen Currier. Within two years, four of them would indeed be killed.[7]

Eventually, Moses befriended a West Indian family named Williams with four children who adopted him as Uncle Bob. This made life easier because it allowed him to go into the city; in the 1967 summer, he frequently visited the Canadian Expo with the Williams children. Meanwhile, Janet Jemmott, the only one who knew the trio's hiding place, put him in touch with his ex-wife. He then briefly snuck back into the United States to "check on Dona, to see how she was doing." The visit ended any lingering doubts about their relationship, and it was the last time he saw her. After completing an MA and PhD in anthropology at New School University, she became a professor in African Studies at Hunter College, remarried, and changed her name to Marimba Ani. Her most well-known work is *Yurugu: An Afrikan-Centered Critique of European Cultural Thought and Behavior* (1994), which denounces the destructive influence of Europeans on blacks across the globe.[8]

In late 1967, Jemmott visited Moses in Canada. In the past three years, she and Moses had become good friends through her friendship with Richards. Like Richards, Jemmott was an independent, strong-willed woman. Raised in the South Bronx, she was deeply influenced by her mother, a strong woman formed by the terror she had felt as a child in South Carolina when her half-blind father risked being lynched after he accidentally bumped into a white woman. After two years of picketing Woolworth stores in New York, Jemmott had left her job teaching social sciences in Harlem to come to Mississippi in 1964 as one of the few black summer volunteers. She worked in SNCC's all-black project in dangerous Natchez, where she experienced several arrests and once only narrowly escaped violence when the FBI intercepted a group of Klansmen just before she and a number of black Mississippians entered the courthouse to register to vote. Local blacks' warmth—and commitment to self-defense—she later wrote, helped her find "deliverance from my fears." She then joined several Mississippi Delta projects. In Selma, Alabama, she organized workshops to educate farmers on the ASCS elections and started work on the Lowndes County Freedom Organization. Having lived under the same strain as a SNCC fieldworker and having gotten to know him during the most difficult years of his life, she understood Moses better than anyone. In early 1968, they became an item and married later that year.[9]

By this time, Moses had applied for a Canadian passport under his pseudonym because he still did not feel safe and wanted to flee to Africa with his new wife. They chose Tanzania, because it was the only African country without internal turmoil and the only one prepared to accept draft resisters. Just as they were about to embark, the FBI was in the midst of combing through Canadian passport applications to capture James Earl Ray, Martin Luther King Jr.'s assassin who had fled to Canada. After a "nerve-wracking flight," Moses and Jemmott safely arrived in Tanzania via Uganda. However, in order to enter Tanzania, one needed to show a return ticket. Because they lacked both a return ticket and the money to buy one, the Tanzanian immigration authorities refused them entry. The airlines flew them to Egypt, the only country willing to accept them. They stayed in Cairo for nine months, living on money Jemmott's mother sent and what money they earned working for David DuBois's radio station. In late 1969, they were finally allowed to enter Tanzania, after Bill Sutherland vouched for them. Moses turned in his false passport and got asylum under his own name without the American Embassy's knowledge.[10]

Moses called the next seven years of life in Tanzania "a blessing." He loved his new family life with Jemmott, their daughter Maisha, and sons Omowale and Tabasuri. Being in a place where "nobody knew his past," he could live "as just another person.... That helped me get grounded again." They settled in a two-bedroom home surrounded by mountains and open land in a remote area outside Same, some six hours from the capital Dar es Salaam. "It just seemed calmer[,] slower paced," Maisha later described the impact on her father. "That kind of space and openness, living without pressure, was healing." But despite daily swimming, meditation, and yoga sessions—which he maintained throughout his life—the brutality of Mississippi had left a permanent imprint on his character. "He's very serious and focused," Maisha said. "He doesn't do a lot of chit-chat. Sometimes it's hard because sometimes you want to joke around." After each child was born, Jemmott's mother stayed with them for six months. But Moses's family knew nothing of their whereabouts because he feared that the FBI would harass them. Moses's father died in 1970; according to Aunt Doris, "he drank himself to death in grief." Moses sent home an African cane to be placed in his casket.[11]

The family joined the small local community of Wa Negro, African Americans living in Africa. In between cooking and changing diapers, Moses spent his time coaching a basketball team, learning Ki-Swahili, and "gaining some insight into Africa, its problems and its potentials." Having been in hiding for so long in Canada, Moses now longed to be in touch with the outside world and become involved in something to alleviate its problems; despite his emotional trauma, his love for his fellow men and community had never disappeared. Bill Sutherland introduced him and Jemmott to President Julius Nyerere. Mixing socialism with pan-Africanism, Nyerere had opened his country to countless black intellectuals and revolutionaries from across the globe, such as Malcolm X, Che Guevara, and fugitive Black Panthers. This had led Dar es Salaam and its surrounding areas to become a thriving, stimulating place to be for civil rights activists, and Moses reveled in the contact he had with government officials, locals, and other Wa Negro, including his former SNCC friend Charlie Cobb, who lived in the capital for two years as a journalist.[12]

President Nyere had helped them settle and secured positions for Moses and Jemmott at the Ministry of Education. They taught math and English at Same Secondary School and in 1975 at a school in Kibaha, outside Dar es Salaam. Same Secondary School had about 300 students, all from different tribes, and a staff of thirteen teachers. Here Moses discovered "what it meant for a school *system* to be committed to its children." Unlike his experiences within the American system, the Tanzanian one "was absolutely dedicated to every student. Because the country needed them," he noted. Many students walked miles each day to be able to attend school, where community solidarity was imprinted through having all students work together in the school garden. To overcome the language barrier with his Ki-Swahili–speaking students, Moses developed games as educational tools. In Mississippi meeting style, he asked them to read their instruction books, talk among themselves about it, and then translate their discussions into symbolic representations on the blackboard so everyone understood the issues involved.[13]

By 1975, the Moses family increasingly thought about returning to the United States. Among American blacks, there had been much "romanticizing about what it would be like to live in Africa," Moses explained, but they had quickly learned their boundaries in transferring "into African culture and to feel comfortable."[14]

Had the country made them feel more welcome, they might have stayed. However, seeing the "politically sophisticated American blacks" as a threat to tribal culture, Tanzanian authorities withheld citizenship from the Moses family and other Wa Negro. After African Americans smuggled guns into Tanzania during the 1974 Pan Africanist Conference in Dar es Salaam, they were subjected to police searches. "They came in our place and searched [it. This happened] all over the country," Moses recalled. "Wherever they found the least thing that scared them . . . they put people in jail."[15]

Jemmott's mother began sending clippings about Jimmy Carter's presidential campaign promise of amnesty for draft evaders, and Moses started inquiries about returning to Harvard to complete his PhD in philosophy. With Alvin Poussaint's and Robert Coles's help, he obtained a National Fellowship Fund for Harvard and accommodation in Cambridge, Massachusetts. They moved back to America in May 1976. Other movement friends founded the Bob Moses Fund to help the struggling family—a fourth child, daughter Malaika, was born shortly after their return—as Moses completed his dissertation and Jemmott attended Boston University medical school before she became a pediatrician at the Massachusetts Institute of Technology.[16]

MOSES'S TIME ABROAD was not merely part of a healing process to recover from the traumas of Mississippi. Aged thirty-one in 1966, he increasingly thought about settling down and raising a family of his own. "The real choice" in deciding to flee, he said, "in hindsight was leaving and doing family versus staying and doing more movement." He had watched his coworkers' struggle with their love lives—most who married fellow activists, like himself, ended up divorced—and he knew that "it would have been hard to stay and do family." In the end, Maisha confirmed, "Being a father to us was always the most important thing to him." Moreover, even in his darkest moments—when movement observers and participants assumed his emotional breakdown had destroyed him—he never gave up on his core ideas. Having learned in Mississippi that social change was the sum of experiential learning in combination with sophisticated planning and, most of all, patience, he once again looked to the long term. He never gave up the idea of resuming his activist career or his faith in organizing from the bottom up. But just as he could not do his dangerous work in Mississippi before having faced his own fears, organizing *himself*, and recuperating, was the first step.[17]

Once he returned home, recovered from his trauma, the search came for a consensus goal around which to unite a community and doing the research around it before starting to organize. Resuming his PhD was part of that process. Moses hoped that it would again enable him "to give service to my people as they take their place in the Nation and in the International community," he wrote in his 1975 application for the fellowship. "I feel now that I could personally benefit by a period of research and reflection."[18]

It was not strange that his quest for a new activist career should involve teaching. It combined his lifelong concern for education and exposure with his love of mathematics and philosophy. From his work with the Tanzanian students, it had become clear "that they needed another language besides English to get any kind of concept about what was going on underneath these symbols" to give them practical meaning in their daily lives. This spurred his thoughts about looking at the language of math from a philosophical perspective so it could become a tool for social change. "I am attracted by this tool," he continued in his application, "how one learns it; how one teaches it; how one uses it for the growth and regeneration of a concept, a person, a people, a nation." In his dissertation, he therefore investigated what the language of math entailed by comparing whether the nature of the evidence for mathematics and logic differed from the evidence in other subjects like physics through tracing how renowned mathematicians and philosophers, like Immanuel Kant and Felix Klein, had addressed that issue from the nineteenth century onward. While working on this, he became fascinated by the ideas of Professor Willard Quine of Harvard's Mathematics Department. In Quine's suggestion that "mathematics gets off the ground through ordinary events described in ordinary language," Moses found the scientific and philosophic framework for the work he had developed in Tanzania. "That is, you take ordinary language and straight-jacket it, so to speak. And you come out with a conceptual language which no-one speaks, but which underlies the symbolic representations that appear in the logic and math." Having done the research, he could now start "fishing around for a kind of movement."[19]

Moses found his new movement while tutoring his oldest daughter and two classmates in algebra. Inner-city public school children were not offered algebra in the 1970s and 1980s. Just as in the 1950s, children in these schools were confined to a tracking system that steered them into classes designed to prepare them for vocational school. Maisha was only assigned to college preparatory classes in math and science after her mother forced her to demand enrollment. Unlike most middle-class families, Moses had consciously put his children in public school because he wanted them to be exposed to the inner-city culture he had known as a child. As a result of the tutoring, for which Moses used his own experimental algebra assignments, Maisha and the other two became the first in the school's history who passed a citywide algebra test that enabled them to take honor courses in math and science; Maisha went on to receive a BA in psychology at Harvard and an MA in mathematics at Southern Illinois University. But 40 percent of the student population at her school, Martin Luther King Open, were black pupils from low-income families who were not getting the same benefits. Rejecting the elitism of a system that handpicked students who qualified for the tutoring, Moses therefore pondered a means to reach *all* students, including those considered incapable of learning algebra. The tutoring thus reemphasized his PS-90, Mississippi, and Tanzania experiences: *all* their classmates needed to be looked upon as "an investment for the whole society."[20]

The parallel with the 1960s was clear. "Kids," Moses said, "are being told that algebra is not for them just like sharecroppers were told that voting was not for them." In the same way that the civil rights movement had found consensus around the idea of "one man, one vote," he reasoned, the country could now unite around the proposition that "all children can learn, and that all children deserve the best education."[21]

In the 1960s, he had emphasized literacy—reading and writing—as the means for this goal, but in the information age, he believed, it had to be *math* literacy. This was the solution to the "poor jobs–poor education–poor conditions cycle" that he had been seeking for decades, especially for the inner-city communities that had never left his thinking. Whereas literacy had helped provide political access, math literacy could now be the organizing tool to spur *economic* access. "Industrial technology created schools that educated an elite to run society, while the rest were prepared for factory work," he said, reviewing his historic understanding of his own education. But the advent of the computer age made education even *more* elitist. As such, "[n]ew technology demands a new literacy—higher math skills for everyone, urban and rural." This was particularly necessary for minorities. "Math illiteracy is not unique to Blacks the way the denial of the right to vote in Mississippi was. But it affects Blacks and other minorities much, much more intensely, making them the designated serfs of the information age just as the people that we worked with in the 1960s on the plantations were Mississippi's serfs then." The patchwork solutions to the resulting problems in urban communities—violence and criminalization—that imploded into the riots in the 1960s were still the same, he believed. They were "Band-Aid solutions—build more jails, put more police on the street. That is working at the problem from the back end."[22]

The experiments at King Open, Moses said, were thus "consistent with my needs in terms of family, work, and movement." A prestigious MacArthur Genius grant, which he received in 1982, enabled him to develop the Algebra Project (AP), an alternative, bottom-up egalitarian educational program for underprivileged children that Moses, now in his eighties, still directs. In 1984, the program was offered to all the seventh graders of King Open, and a year later, it became an official part of the curriculum. After the MacArthur Grant expired in 1987, Moses was able to bring the project to more schools in Boston with the help of other community organizers and black ministers and the financial backing of several charities. From there, the project was expanded to schools in Chicago, Los Angeles, the Midwest, and San Francisco. Numerous grants from among others the National Science Foundation enabled further expansions and improvements to the curriculum, with the aid of some of the nation's most renown mathematicians and math educators. The AP is now successfully implemented at over 100 schools across thirteen states in the North and South and has scientifically been proven to increase the number of college acceptances of underprivileged children, especially those with black, Latino, and Appalachian origins. It "has had an extremely beneficial effect on students—particularly on their attitudes, motivation, problem solving, and ability to articulate and share mathematical ideas," one study found. Another lauded it as "empowering and inclusionary" and argued that its promotion would "help the

United States maintain its technological advantage in math-related fields relative to other industrial countries." Spin-offs of the AP are the Young People's Project (YPP), initiated by Moses's own children and on whose advisory board is his wife, and his Quality Education as Constitutional Right (QECR) campaign, which tries to get quality education adopted as a constitutional amendment. Other related projects are Finding Our Folk, which documented the impact of Hurricane Katrina, and Training of Trainers, a workshops series aimed at teaching civil rights organizing traditions to southern high school students.[23]

THE AP SHOULD NOT BE CONSIDERED a mere afterthought to Moses's time working in the movement. Since he has been working on it for over thirty years and worked for SNCC for a mere five years, it might even be more apt to consider his time in the movement to be the prelude and the AP the core of his life's work. After all, the AP embodies the essence of his leadership, ideas, worldview, character, and driving forces of his entire life. It combines Quine's and Moses's Tanzania lessons of symbolic representations and games as educational tools with his father's, Ella Baker's, and the Mississippi movement's notions of "credentializing," personhood, and ownership of learning. Its central goal is self-empowerment, which makes it a quintessential "continuation of what we did in the '60s." As with voter registration, the motivation for seminal change had to be internalized. "Taking responsibility for your own life, your own learning, can change a person," he explained, "Fannie Lou Hamer was the symbol of that philosophy, and it's an important part of the Algebra Project. If math has no relevance to a student's life, he won't learn it." Just as in the Freedom Schools, AP participants are therefore taught to see the conceptual language of math behind daily occurrences they meet in their everyday lives. For example, students are shown the math behind clapping games on the basketball court, they go on subway trips to learn the idea of displacement, or they make lemonade to learn deductions by mixing the ingredients. They might then draw out or rap about their experiences to capture their new mathematical language in symbolic representations that have meaning for them. The program thus meets them "where they are." Using math, in Moses's words, as a "tool for liberation" therefore is perhaps even more radical than direct action, one scholar observed. Although the AP aims to incorporate the oppressed into an existing system, it exudes Ella Baker's definition of radical as "getting down to and understanding the root cause. It means facing a system that does not lend itself to your needs and devising means by which you change that system." The "key word here is *you*," Moses emphasized, "the kind of systemic change necessary to prepare our young people for the demands of the twenty-first century requires young people to take the lead in changing it."[24]

To facilitate that process, Moses has applied his life lessons to the AP. The workshop style of the Mississippi meetings became its model, he said, since "classrooms are just [like] meeting places" that can "be structured as a tool for empowering the people." Another central aspect in the participants' learning experience is teamwork, because without consensus, "moving the country into systematic change . . . becomes almost impossible." Just as Moses brought local Mississippians to his citizenship workshops—and the MFDP delegates into the meetings at Atlantic City—with the idea that they would go home and teach others, the AP revolves around the concept of "each one teach one." This goes for the students, who have to collaborate to solve mathematical problems, and their supervisors. AP teachers, instructed in John Dewey's theories, seek consensus by involving the participants' parents, making it foremost "a community organizing project rather than a traditional program of school reform." Like SNCC organizers, they immerse themselves in the community's life, "learning its strengths, resources, concerns, and ways of conducting business." As such, they have to "present themselves as learners" who don't answer students' questions but "help students find questions that will lead them to discover their own answers."[25]

The teachers essentially serve as the facilitators that he and SNCC workers were in their early years before they "went national"—and before Moses's fame crippled his ability to lead effectively. He called those years the "crawl space" in which their slow organizing approach was allowed to develop. The AP finds itself in a similar space, his oldest daughter argued. "The movement in the early 1960s was the culmination of all this energy that had been building for years that sort of came to a head and erupted. But it was relatively short-lived. The work we're doing now is in that building phase of gathering energy that may culminate in a similar type of movement." It allowed Moses to be the leader again he had always striven to be: a guiding force who applied his organizing skills and extensive networks and resources behind the scenes on behalf of others' development. Even as he moved into national circles again by, for instance, addressing Congress about the need to institutionalize quality education, he foreground those for whom the work is intended. In SNCC style, he might divide audiences at public events into groups that each hash out a particular aspect of quality education and having representatives of each present their conclusions to the entire room for discussion. Or, as he did when he received an award from *Essence* magazine for his educational work, he might simply ask his students to come on stage and perform a rap song about math. In such a "crawl space," Moses's organizing talents come out best.[26]

In a way, the AP also rectifies the failures of SNCC and the Mississippi movement to secure long-term movement due to internal rifts and the lack of a secure economic base. AP members are in a similar state of "guerilla warfare" with the establishment as SNCC workers were, Moses argued. "You're looking for an opening. You're looking for a soft spot, trying to find out where you can penetrate. And you are working with and against various structures. You're in them, but you're working against them at various levels." Potential donors, as AP board member Alvin Poussaint observed, could often be frustrated with Moses's reluctance to do fundraising—even refusing to wear tuxedos because this is "a way the upper classes pull rank on the lower classes"—and with his rejection of donations that do not permit the AP to involve community people in designing how the funds should be spent. This cost the AP a grant at least once. Some participants find the emphasis on consensus through endless meetings exhausting.[27]

Having learned from the post-1964 period in Mississippi, however, Moses refused to let "hardliners" take over and took his initiative from listening to community people even more. In fact, the AP instituted his insight from SNCC that locals have to take time to develop economic bases, networks, and organizations of their own. The Young People's Project, for instance, is run by students who grew up in the AP and over time have found their own financial base. This helps empower them. "The beauty of the YPP is that its members are in the schools, but organizationally it is not part of the school system. YPP members have carved out their own crawl space in the schools that allows them to operate and get some presence, some visibility there, some legitimacy. That's a big step for young people," Moses noted. "They're not going to be easy to dislodge."[28]

The AP also brought Moses south again. He had returned to Mississippi only twice since his time in SNCC. In 1982, he had brought his family to the funeral of Amzie Moore, for whom he had set up a trust fund through the Bradens after Moore's health began to decline in 1980.

Seven years later, he attended a workshop in Jackson held to discuss movement workers' outrage over the movie *Mississippi Burning*, which turned the FBI in the Schwerner/Chaney/Goodman case into heroes. He saw Dave Dennis, then a successful lawyer, for the first time in twenty-four years and convinced him of the need to implement the AP at southern schools. In 1992, Dennis started the AP's Southern Initiative, funded by the Southern Regional Council, and has been its director ever since.[29]

Once the AP's program was up and running, it brought Moses back to Mississippi for a much more sustained engagement with the state. In the mid-1990s, he lived in Jackson four days a week to set up the AP at Brinkley Middle School and Lanier High School. This was much needed. Despite the movement's gains, Mississippi remains the poorest state in the country. According to *The Nation*, its black jobless rates rose from 7.9 to 15.9 percent between 1960 and 1990, black population strength dropped by 7 percent, and integration triggered an exodus of white students from public schools. Jackson counted fewer than sixty whites among 20,000 pupils. Moses returned to Mississippi because it was the best "theater where we can lift our program out of the 'let's teach math better'-box and take it to the country as a Civil Rights issue." The AP is now in several dozen schools across the Mississippi Delta. At the annual Achievement Tests, math scores of the students at Brinkley Middle School who participated in the AP are 13 percent higher than those who did not, while discipline problems have dropped by 90 percent. Lacking a subway system to learn math with, Moses took students on bus tours that stop at civil rights museums and other places that have movement significance, such as Medgar Evers's home and Tougaloo College.[30]

MOSES'S RETURN TO MISSISSIPPI became a new period of healing as he gradually "began to feel that [Mississippi] was a good place for me" again. He contacted former movement comrades like C. C. Bryant and Dr. Anderson and made amends with Joseph Rauh and John Doar. Having heard rumors that he was in Tanzania, the two had sent letters to him seeking some sort of absolution. Doar had been determined to reach Moses because "I had such admiration for him that I wanted him to understand that he had his facts wrong." Rauh's letter went over the events at Atlantic City in detail. Because the letters were sent to the American Embassy, Moses never replied for fear of drawing attention. But after his return to the United States, Rauh visited Moses and "finally straightened out the chronology of [Atlantic City] and how he had been misled." Moses and Doar also reconciled. The two cooperated on Moses's QECR campaign, and in 2011, Moses spoke extensively at a gathering sponsored by the Justice Department to honor Doar and his legacy in the Civil Rights Division. Until Doar's death in November 2014, the two remained close friends.[31]

The AP returned Moses to mainstream acceptance. Since its inception, he has received numerous awards and fellowships honoring his educational, civil, and human rights work. These included the Peace Award from the War Resisters League (1997), the Heinz Award for the Human Condition (1999), the Puffin/Nation Prize for Creative Citizenship (2001), the Mary Chase Award for American Democracy (2002), and the James Conant Bryant Award from the U.S. Education Commission (2002). He has received honorary degrees and visiting professorships from Swarthmore College, the University of Michigan, Cornell University, Princeton University, and the University of Florida. Even the Mississippi legislature acknowledged his contributions to the state by proclaiming May 2 to 3 "Bob Moses Day." Moses began reaching out to his former SNCC comrades and allies as well. Having avoided them for two decades, he has taken part in reunions again and used his former networks to advance his AP and QECR campaigns. Facing his past again was a difficult process. "For a long time, I didn't read anything about myself," he stated in 2004, but "I've gotten to the point where I can read things and not let them affect me."[32]

Yet he insisted that today's projection of the movement and its leadership remains flawed. He lamented how the historical awareness of today's generation has been shaped by documentaries like *Eyes on the Prize* that project the movement "as a series of protest marches." Amzie Moore and the Mississippi Freedom Democratic Party are largely unknowns. "[T]here is a great deal they don't understand yet for 'our' stories in our words are largely absent from the historical canon," he observed. This worried him deeply, because "these stories are more important than just remembering some old times. We need to use them." If they are not, it remains "difficult for ordinary people to see themselves as being central to making change." This is why he finally decided to write down part of his experiences in *Radical Equations*, helped Phil Alden Robinson make the movie *Freedom Song* about the McComb movement, and occasionally gave interviews and commentaries at conferences again. In them, he reiterated his message from the 1960s. "I never thought about the [civil rights] movement in terms of King," he for instance provocatively stressed at one 1986 symposium celebrating Martin Luther King Jr. "It never occurred to me to think about the movement in terms of King. I lived and breathed the *movement*."[33]

But his idea of a "movement" is complex. He recognized it as a long-term endeavor. "We didn't create the civil rights movement we were part of and helped to shape. You can't say that any single person actually put that movement together. What we did then was create a network that helped sustain and advance the movement.... Movement history came into existence when the first African walked off the first slave ship in chains. It shaped events long before our involvement as young people in the 1960s." Yet he underscored the idea that the 1960s were an exceptional period in history. As he and his daughter noted, "the crawl space" was a building phase, which by definition culminates into *something* that is an end, a result. This is his dream for the AP, too.

> If "student power" can take root, nurture itself, receive critical support, evolve, and grow over the next fifty or seventy-five years ... the YPP and other such networks defined by young people can become important in establishing a culture of math literacy in the targeted population.... The work of the Algebra Project can become institutionalized through the kids who come back and take our work into the community. And you don't need all of them coming back. All you need is a critical network, a few, three or four out of a hundred.... There may be a "movement" starting or reflected in this if all over the place little groups of people begin to spring up.[34]

The question remains, then, when one can speak of an "end" or a "result" and what role that "critical network" plays in fostering social change. Are they facilitators or initiators? To complicate matters, an inherent part of Moses's philosophy for social change rested on the world outside the own community. Both in the 1960s and in the AP, success depended on participants' ability to attract key allies with resources and, as one AP pamphlet acknowledged, by presenting "themselves in a way that convinces people who are not directly affected by the outcome of the struggle" that theirs is "an earned insurgency." These realities should not be forgotten when establishing the legacy of Moses and SNCC. In *Radical Equations*, Moses glossed over most of his behind-the-scenes organizing and networking activities described in the previous pages here. These activities spurred the movement and were vital; what emerged in Mississippi, the most difficult state of all, under Moses's directorship is an astounding achievement and confirms Amzie Moore's wisdom regarding the necessity of outside help. "Without Bob Moses and the grassroots movement he inspired, there would have been no 'Freedom Summer' in 1964. Nor any Voting Rights Act passed into law in 1965," one scholar said in capturing his significance. Such generalizations miss the complexity of what actually happened and how much (the decision to have) Freedom Summer and the Voting Rights Act were a cumulative result of countless individuals and factors, but the conclusion is not wholly farfetched. The level of truth in the statement depends on one's definition of facilitation. Whereas it is Moses's opinion that his work was all in locals' service, someone else's might be that it was induction.[35]

In a similar vein, Moses's forcefulness during the 1963 meeting in Greenville that kept plans for the summer project alive or his actions in response to the "compromise" at the DNC might be considered subtle manipulation. Or was it subtle *education?* The moral line in between is hard to establish. After all, manipulation implies something negative, doing something to help advance one's own personal position. Although Moses got the group in Greenville to do what he wanted, such was never his goal; he did what he did for what he genuinely believed was to the benefit of all. Yet as one of the few who had a helicopter view of what they were doing, he had an obligation to speak up; responsible decision making, *agency*, could only be achieved when exposed to *all* views at stake in a debate, especially when it concerned matters of life and death. But the irony of Moses's leadership was that he tried to voice his opinion as one in many but that his acquired position in the movement as a result of his exceptional qualities made his opinion count for more than one. Moses wrestled with these realizations on a daily basis and did not come out with a satisfying moral answer either way. Even when he stayed silent, he indirectly voiced his opinion. Perhaps the fact that he recognized this and was troubled by it is all one needs to know about his moral anchor and significance for a movement that strove for democracy all around.

In the end, Moses was neither the existentialist hero nor the unassuming facilitator he has been celebrated as. This means that within the multiple factors involved in understanding the production of social change, the importance of full-time facilitation of local people, particularly by outsiders like Moses, should neither be exacerbated nor minimized. In explaining his views at the 1986 Martin Luther King

Jr. symposium, Moses likened the movement to an ocean. And just as oceans are the sum of numerous waves, the movement should be understood as the collective endeavor of numerous, faceless people. "Let us shift our attention from the wave to the ocean," he therefore argued, "because the wave is not the ocean. Even if it's a tidal wave [like King], it has no meaning apart from that ocean." But acknowledging the truth of this does not automatically mean that individual leaders had minimal significance. The implied assumption—that although a facilitator like Moses brought unique organizing skills, but since he applied them in humility and therefore that anyone who operated from the same premises could have accomplished the same—is flawed reasoning. As historian Nathan Irvin Huggins already critiqued in 1987, "Individuals do make a difference," so "it is foolish to imagine that the individual actors were interchangeable parts and that, without [their] particular personality . . . someone else would have served as well." The same goes for Moses. Regardless if one typifies his behavior at the Greenville meeting or Atlantic City as subtle manipulation or subtle education, he had a clear and powerful vision for the direction of the Mississippi movement and advanced it behind the scenes, even if only as a teacher and a guide. Moses was both an organizer *and* a leader, and to get a full understanding of the 1960s civil rights movement, these mutually reinforcing roles must be acknowledged and examined further.[36]

Judgments on the effectiveness of Moses's and SNCC's organizational leadership approach therefore should neither be cast in "either/or" terms. Those who were not there especially must be loath to make judgments at all; the fact that movement participants like Moses risked their lives perhaps earned them that privilege. Just as he termed Freedom Summer, Moses's idea of leadership was by definition "a double-edged sword," one that was always "damned if you do, damned if you don't." Participatory democracy was an ideal and, as such, could never exist in pure form; it could only be approximated. It was precisely this striving for an ideal that gave him and SNCC their great moral power, but it was unavoidable that this moral ethos could not be sustained forever. SNCC's paradox of simultaneously rejecting and desiring leadership and structure inevitably hampered its future effectiveness. Similarly, it was inevitable that Moses's success invited his projection.[37]

Moses's and SNCC's inherent inability to keep up their moral ethos demonstrates the necessity of recognizing "ends"—or rather "breaks" or "transitions"—in movements despite continuities in players, objectives, organizational longevity, or methods. In 1968, when James Forman was still trying to build SNCC as a mass-based organization by forging political alliances with the Black Panther Party and other (pro)black organizations, Ella Baker recognized the occurrence of a break in movement continuity aptly. "I don't think that enough was [done by SNCC], and yet I would have to qualify this by saying that what was done maybe was as much as could be expected."[38]

Moses essentially acknowledged this transition period too when he left SNCC. Not only did disillusion exacerbated by physical and mental exhaustion prompt his departure but also the common sense recognition that his utility in the organization had run out. His approach depended on flexibility, in which the recognition of "end" points is inherent, too. In effect, his boat metaphor in his 1964 Waveland position paper—which called to determine SNCC's strategies on the forever altering social contexts in which they worked rather than (past) models or theories— foreshadowed the wisdom that sociologists Francis Fox Piven and Richard Cloward demonstrated in 1979 when they argued that "[i]f there is a genius in organizing, it is the capacity to sense what is possible for people to do under given conditions. . . . Both the limitations and opportunities for mass protest are shaped by social conditions." But this is not negative, Moses believed. New movements will always emerge as long as underneath the philosophy for social change that he developed "on the ground, running" in Mississippi is encouraged. "The main thing is not to set out with grand projects," he still adamantly proclaimed in the later years of his life. "Everything starts at your doorstep. Just get deeply involved in something. . . . You throw a stone in one place and the ripples spread."[39]

Robert Parris Moses and Leadership in Civil Rights Movement Historiography

> Who is telling the story defines the historic "truth" and accuracy of the story. So there is a character called Bob Moses in many of the history books that discuss Mississippi's civil rights movement of the 1960s. I read about him. I sympathize with him. Sometimes he seems like me, and then sometimes I am confused by him and want to understand him better.
>
> —ROBERT PARRIS MOSES, 2001

To understand Bob Moses and his significance for the Mississippi and overall civil rights movement, it is necessary to admit that he is indeed a "character," created by other movement participants, scholars, observers, *and* himself.[1]

From his first days in the movement until today, Moses has fought against the mythology of the "outside agitator" that was projected in contemporary media outlets and early historic works. In this rendering of history, full-time civil rights workers, especially those not native to the South, are depicted as those who instigated, and ultimately saved, the struggling southern-based civil rights movement. In later works, influenced by SNCC veterans' agitation against their historic depiction, Moses is described in the way he would have preferred himself, as a mere facilitator of local leadership.

Yet in tearing down the "outsider agitator" claim, scholars must be careful not to create a new mythology, one that treats grassroots civil rights leaders as all-knowing and thereby minimizing the unique contributions individuals like Moses made. The treatment of Bob Moses in civil rights historiography illustrates the need for new, more in-depth assessments of leadership dynamics within southern communities that fully appreciate how outside/full-time organizers and local blacks worked in mutually reinforcing ways without romanticizing or belittling the contribution of either. To do this effectively, scholars must not only combine top-down and bottom-up approaches for explaining social change during the civil rights era, but also take oral history and movement workers' insights seriously.

QUESTIONS ABOUT THE ROLE of leadership and organizations in the generation of social change have always been at the center of movement studies. Generally speaking, however, movement historiography can be divided into two streams, a "classical" and a "revisionist" phase. The first two decades following the movement's peak in the early to mid-1960s represented the first phase and the last two/three decades the second, although there are notable exceptions to this generalization, and this shift has been gradual rather than abrupt.[2] The first books on the civil rights movement, written in the 1960s and early 1970s, reflected analyses of how the movement was viewed at the time of its heyday, that is, "as spontaneous and discontinuous with previous struggles." Its participants were presented as saint-like figures, distinct from ordinary blacks. Their heroism was even more apparent in the midst of the gun-toting Black Power militancy and race riots that had swept the country by this time. Both found little understanding from a national audience.[3]

David L. Lewis's 1970 biography of Martin Luther King Jr., although written to undercut his romanticization, set the pattern of viewing the movement through King's life. For a long time, the dominant master narrative—and the term *civil rights movement* itself—referred to the years 1954 to 1965. To scholars of the 1970s and 1980s, King and his like were attractive because their "sacrifices to transform their country . . . contrasted sharply with the prevailing Reagan-era mentality that glorified . . . personal wealth and ignored community health." Between the late 1960s and late 1980s, historians therefore tended to focus on the events, organizations, and leaders that drew national media attention. As historian Steven Lawson put it, they "conceived of the civil rights struggle as primarily a political movement that secured legislative and judicial triumphs," echoed by the word *rights* in its name. Numerous studies pinpointed specific organizations and leaders or local cases that had national significance.[4,5]

In the mid-1980s, following William Chafe's 1980 work on Greensboro and Robert Norrell's 1985 study of Tuskegee, scholars began to challenge this narrative. This led to a body of works, pioneered by sociologist Aldon Morris, that stressed the resource mobilization theory, that is, how "preexisting indigenous African American social networks and organizations," like the black church, historically black educational institutions, and black business and civic organizations formed the basis from which the 1960s movement sprung. It also produced an abundance of studies on specific cities or states,[6] including several works that treated civil rights struggles in the North.[7] By emphasizing local communities, previously unknown or little known local leaders, and historical black institutions, scholars found that their stories often had to start well before 1955 and continue well past 1965. Some noted that nationalism and self-defense were already evident during the movement's classical phase, which led to a new appraisal of the Black Power era, exemplified in the works of Timothy Tyson, Lance Hill, and Joseph Peniel. Others, like Jacqueline Dowd Hall, contended that the movement's origins were to be found in the 1930s and 1940s. As such, she turned the activism of the Old Left into the "decisive first phase" of the modern civil rights movement. Scholars highlighting this trend[8] emphasized the so-called civil rights unionism or Black Popular Front of the 1930s and 1940s. What emerged was thus a large body of literature that differentiated older studies that put the responsibility for social change on exceptional individuals and specific organizations from ones that recognize the "black freedom struggle," in Clayborne Carson's words, as a bottom-up, "locally based mass movement" with a multiplicity of agents, voices, and goals.[9]

Discussions of Robert Moses within civil rights movement historiography have generally followed a similar pattern. They have consistently emphasized at least one of three points: (1) his representation as a legendary figure (stressing the

Bob Moses mystique), (2) his personification of SNCC's public's image of group-centered leadership, and (3) his embodiment of the community organizing tradition. Studies also tend to portray him as a tragic hero, an idealist so unhappy with the hero worship of his persona that he stopped speaking to whites and left for Africa. As such, his life is almost a parable of SNCC's and the overall movement's demise.

Books that appeared in the mid-1960s generally highlight the Bob Moses mystique. Yet this aspect of Moses's activism seems particularly prominent in the work of northern white middle-class authors, in contemporaneous times but also in the 1980s, 1990s, and 2000s. White liberal authors in the 1960s generally identified with the student movement. They connected SNCC to the overall emergence of young people as a major political force in the 1960s, as exemplified by the National Student Association and other groups. Several, like historians Howard Zinn and Staughton Lynd and journalist Ben Bagdikian, were activists themselves, and some even closely linked to SNCC, which gave their work a certain level of authority. Nonetheless, to promote SNCC's politics, they followed a particular pattern of how to view the movement, stressing the students' youth, idealism, and spontaneity at the cost of previous generations. Consequently, local activists and continuity in activism were hardly present in their work, and the SNCC students were romanticized.[10]

Within this student body, however, Moses was singled out as exceptionally heroic. In *Who Speaks for the Negro?* (1965), southern-born novelist Robert Penn Warren—a onetime defender of racial segregation—for instance stressed the "powerful appeal of [Moses's] personality," illustrated by a story of how Moses had just fallen asleep during a car chase by armed whites. Howard Zinn in *SNCC: The New Abolitionists* (1965) and journalist Jack Newfield in *A Prophetic Minority* (1966) pictured him as an almost larger-than-life, modern-day Lucky Luke on a mission down South. He emerged as an existentialist hero, resembling figures like Albert Camus, who had cult status among white liberals. Newfield idealized him as the personification of Camus's concept of action; he described his first trip to Mississippi as "the most creative and heroic single act anyone in the New Left has attempted." Newfield even claimed that act to be the basic inspiration for the New Left as a whole.[11]

However, these writers' work did not offer any analysis of his daily activities or the influences from the black community that shaped Moses's ideas. It seems that what made Moses appear exceptional to these writers was his northern and elite academic background; they were less interested in the nuts-and-bolts of his activism than in the fact that he gave up a relatively comfortable life for a dangerous mission. Moses embodied what Staughton Lynd called the ideal of the scholar-activist in the tradition of American heroes like Ralph Emerson who followed, as C. Vann Woodward said, the credo that "the intellectual must not be alienated from the sources of revolt" and had "thrown themselves into the popular movements of their day."[12]

Moses's leadership received a more extensive analysis in the 1980s to 1990s, when the publication of several SNCC veterans' memoirs[13] and the appearance of studies that treated SNCC in depth offered renewed interest in the organization. Clayborne Carson's *In Struggle* (1981), Emily Stoper's *The Student Nonviolent Coordinating Committee* (1989), and Taylor Branch's *America in the King Years* trilogy (1989, 1998, 2006) all highlighted Moses as the personification of SNCC and its ideals. According to Carson, Moses's approach was "the most singular part of SNCC's legacy." Its departure from this for a more hierarchical structure and a racially exclusive ideology, he believed, was an understandable yet regrettable mistake. This view is echoed in later studies like Charles Payne's *I've Got the Light of Freedom* (1995) and Wesley Hogan's *Many Minds, One Heart* (2007).[14]

By depicting Moses as *the* symbol of leadership by example, some writers overemphasized his existentialist quest for individual freedom. Branch asserted that he "was a mystical purist. He valued SNCC for the succor it provided to likeminded people, but he remained aloof from the more pragmatic functions of an organization, such as fund-raising, discipline, and publicity." Stoper even described him as an "exponent of anarchist ideas," a characterization that would surely come as a surprise to Moses himself. In typifying Moses as an anti-leader, all three writers dwelled upon his ambivalence about the "worshipful cult" he acquired. Branch recorded how Moses "tumbled through doubts that his anti-leadership convictions merely shielded him from inevitable responsibility" and how "his self-effacing reluctance enlarged his mystique and the hunger of people to follow him." All three emphasized this as the main reason why Moses left the organization in 1965. In doing so, they attributed immense personal influence to him.[15]

Moses thus continued to be depicted as *the* driving force behind the production of social change in Mississippi; he holds the initiative, rather than a two-way stream of others influencing him and vice versa. The only biography of Moses to date, *And Gently He Shall Lead Them* (1994) by attorney Eric Burner, reinforced this image. Burner's interest is in how Moses's "presence and leadership style offer an entrance . . . into a decade that set radicals to pursuing purity and to practicing, at times, a democracy of incessant action." Although he conceded that Moses could be pragmatic, he emphasized Moses's embodiment of group-centered leadership and attributed epic characteristics to him: he represented "a leader who encouraged but did not command" and who sought "not to be reborn but simply to do right" by "working unobtrusively and with unostentatious courage among the wretched." This depiction is further enhanced by his general exclusion of other (local and professional) activists—except King and Lowenstein, who were both marginal players in the Mississippi movement. Burner's account of how social change is produced thus seems to revolve around exceptional individuals.[16]

Local studies of the Mississippi movement, most notably John Dittmer's *Local People* (1994) and Charles Payne's *I've Got the Light of Freedom* (1995), altered the established image of Moses. By emphasizing the activism of dozens of professional or ad hoc local organizations and individuals in Mississippi from the 1940s to the 1980s, these studies found that SNCC's and Moses's experiences were hardly unique. They demonstrated that civil rights activism existed before, during, and after SNCC's presence. This implied that although Moses's departure may have weakened SNCC, it did not mark the end of the Mississippi movement.

While providing new insight into Moses's daily activities, Dittmer and Payne portrayed him less as a leader than a facilitator of local activism, treating his decisions predominantly as an outgrowth of his commitment to grassroots leadership. Payne especially expanded this reading of Moses and SNCC, which he captured as a group that "built on and elaborated that legacy" of organizational and intellectual continuity that local activists supplied. SNCC's job is shown as "simply building relationships," and therefore the "proper measure of [its] work is the extent to which the people they helped bring into political activity became leaders themselves." While Payne admitted that "for many people in Mississippi, attachment to the movement meant attachment to the particular individuals who represented it" and that Moses "was responsible for much of what made the Mississippi movement distinctive," he is described as bringing unique organizing skills but applying them in humility. Moreover, Payne and others presented him as a product of the black community and have relatively little to say about the cosmopolitan influences on his life. Since local studies by their format generally exclude SNCC projects and civil rights activism in other states, however, the image of the decentralized, community organizing Mississippi branch of SNCC as representative of *overall* SNCC is maintained. By extension, since Moses played a visible role in the Mississippi movement, he hence continues to represent (the best of) SNCC's public image. Yet what's different is that he and SNCC are no longer placed in the forefront of social change; they are "following" more than "leading."[17]

This view of Moses as a facilitator contrasts starkly with the picture that emerges from many of the memoirs of SNCC veterans. These more resemble earlier 1960s accounts, burnishing the image of a respected and trusted leader who had a clear vision for the movement. Moses, Cleveland Sellers indicated, was "a special SNCC person" who had "something about him . . . that seemed to draw all of us to him." James Forman recollected how his "admiration for Bob Moses and his band of guerrilla fighters swelled up," and Stokely Carmichael noted he was "influenced by him in fundamental and lasting ways." When Moses asked him to be the director of Mississippi's second congressional district, he "was moved, overwhelmed as much by the responsibility as by Bob's confidence. To be appointed to that job, and by Bob? I couldn't believe it." Mary King described feeling "a sudden rush of exhilaration" whenever she saw Moses. "He inspired me and touched me. I trusted Bob implicitly and felt deep affection for him. He was only thirty years old but I considered him prophetic." These memoirs accordingly suggest that Moses's personal presence was for a long time a quintessential aspect of the organization in Mississippi, whose unity was sustained through Moses's charisma and foresight, as well as the respect and admiration they harvested. Their words accordingly cannot be disregarded when assessing Moses's leadership.[18]

IRONICALLY, SNCC WORKERS' memoirs and oral history accounts have helped create an image of Moses that they reject for themselves. From the 1960s onward, they have adamantly tried to foreground grassroots leadership and downplay their own in publications, conferences, and other public manifestations. As a result, an even more complex rendering of history has emerged. Civil rights autobiographies in particular "offer evidence of a dense intertwining of individual and collective narratives in formation over time," scholar Kathryn Nasstrom has argued. Apart from the question of reliability due to memory lapses, protection of veterans' current and past positions, and settling old scores (James Forman's and Cleveland Sellers's come to mind), disputes in memoirs and oral histories have centered "on everything from points of fact to broad interpretations of the movement" as well as their depictions within popular and academic accounts of the movement.[19]

This, in turn, shapes the work of scholars who listen to them as well. Both Dittmer and Payne have been accused of uncritically adopting movement participants' point of view. Payne's book is in part a response to workers' insights and demands in oral histories and memoirs to present "the collective, multi-faceted nature of leadership" that existed in the movement. His is a deliberate effort to live up to Moses's plea to prevent that "the men and women better than presidents [are] largely forgotten, which may make it more difficult to produce any more like them." In making the case for his book, he even cites Moses's understanding of the movement as having two traditions, the community-mobilizing and the community-organizing tradition. He wants to emphasize the latter as an antidote to Moses's complaint that the former is "the only part of the movement that has attracted sustained scholarly attention," the complaint Moses repeated in *Radical Equations* (2001). Payne's own interview with Moses in 1993 might have strengthened these interpretations, in a similar vein as it is not unlikely that John Dittmer's 1983 interview with him might have influenced the writing of *Local People* since both books quote from these interviews extensively.[20]

While skepticism is always warranted, this does not render participants' viewpoints as useless or something to be used in the periphery in serious scholarship. The latter, after all, is not free from subjectivity either. As historian Emilye Crosby has argued, "Disregarding or downplaying the accounts of SNCC workers and their local allies is as political as the decision to listen to them." Therefore, she asserted, participants' accounts are *central* resources for the goal of bridging top-down and bottom-up approaches in understanding social change. They provide "a useful blueprint and way of rethinking the intersections between various movement approaches and philosophies (and the ways that people understood them on the ground). These insights, this nuance, belong at the heart of our scholarship (not because it comes from activists, but because it is effective) and must be part of any attempt at synthesis."[21]

Crosby's analysis could also be applied to the question as to how Moses himself has helped influence concepts of the movement and himself, as well as how and to what extent scholars should take his views into account. Caution is necessary; the fact that he did not give any interviews for nearly fifteen years in between his 1965 departure from SNCC and his return from Africa helps him present a fairly consistent trajectory of his work and organizing views. This is epitomized in *Radical Equations*, a book that likewise does not tell a story of an exceptional individual but solely of an instrument for indigenous leadership whose potential had always been present. Moreover, some of his explanations warrant extra caution; the extent to which he says he stopped speaking to whites, for example, is contradicted by the words of other movement participants.

But if one evaluates the interviews from his later years to the ones he gave in the 1960s, overall there is a remarkable, and informative, consistency in the way he presents himself and the message he reiterates. For instance, the Moses in the 1966 Anne Romaine interview hardly differs from the one in *Radical Equations* or my own interviews with him, and this must be considered. Moses's thoughtful analyses are key to understanding who he is and how and why he moved, what kind of a leader he was, and add valuable nuances and insights into what were his and SNCC's objectives and thus what the movement did or did not accomplish.

Crosby cites the example of Moses's observation that nonviolence and self-defense were neither antithetical to, nor necessary for, the voter registration work they were doing. But there are plenty more. For instance, Moses's own accounts of what he wanted to achieve help remind us how much the civil rights movement was *not* about civil rights but about *human* rights, about intangible goals such as self-empowerment and agency. Moreover, without them, it would be easy to equate his name change and departure from SNCC with a mental breakdown—a touch of madness even—rather than rational decisions, to interpret SNCC's internal struggles during and after the Waveland meeting as a mere factional fight, or to reduce the movement toward Black Power as self-defeating. Moses's nuance of the latter makes clear that black nationalism *in itself* was not what inhibited the post-1965 movement but the way its advocates *used* it. By emphasizing that they abandoned the slow organizing approach on which the Mississippi movement was built, he implies both a continuity and discontinuity in activism worthy of consideration for scholars interested in Black Power. Making black nationalism "glamorous" was a new dimension, but by suggesting that his slow community organizing approach and nationalism could have coexisted (or been mutually reinforcing), he confirms the idea that black nationalism (and self-defense) was never a stranger to the black community. His explanations about the *Roots* conference also add valuable nuances and complexities to our understanding of black nationalism, and the role black women played in it illuminates the need for more scholarship on their views and experiences. His analysis of the significance of economics in forcing the movement's and SNCC's hand is another topic that might be a valuable blueprint for more scholarly attention.[22]

Yet what is particularly noteworthy and problematic is the consistency in what Moses does *not* discuss in either his written or oral histories. He consistently avoids detailing how his own, behind-the-scenes activities spurred the Mississippi movement. Whether done intentionally or because he genuinely believes these activities to be of secondary importance, not discussing or downplaying them influences the way the movement is understood. As I have tried to show in the previous pages, incorporating such behind-the-scenes activities and the personal views, preconceptions, skills, and background influences that guided them are needed to provide a more realistic assessment of him and of leadership dynamics in the movement. Furthermore, an overemphasis on local activism implies that blacks in the South disposed of sufficient resources themselves—organizational, financial, political—to wage the civil rights struggle with minimal outside assistance. The contrary, in fact, was the case. The presence of *full-time* civil rights workers—indigenous or not—made a decisive difference; to argue that a leader like Moses or a national organization like SNCC merely had to facilitate grassroots leaders begs the question why facilitation was needed to begin with. Even Moses admits that such "critical networks" are vital to advance any type of movement—be it for civil rights or math literacy—but in what way exactly and to what extent needs further analysis.

Moses's activism and leadership, as well as his own depictions of them (or lack thereof), thus validate Crosby's plea for rooting any such quest in a multifaceted source base of oral history attached to archival evidence *and* "traditional" scholarship. This will also help us understand the complex relationship between the origins of ideas and subsequent activism better. Compared to most SNCC workers, Moses came from an atypical background: while his political development had strong roots in the black community of his childhood, his exposure to the white world as an adolescent helped determine the accents of his later civil rights activism.

Yet by stressing indigenous black institutions, revisionist historians have emphasized organic influences over cosmopolitan ones. While earlier accounts of Moses highlighted his attraction to French existentialism and downplayed black stimuli on his thinking, later ones made the opposite mistake. In a similar way, Steven Lawson argued, books on Martin Luther King Jr. have "create[d] an either/or proposition that lines up a predominantly Western intellectual tradition against an African-American religious heritage" rather than "a both/and situation." The same observation can be applied to some leaders in SNCC that most defined its direction apart from Moses, like James Forman, and, to a lesser extent, James Lawson and Tim Jenkins. They not only were older than most rank-and-file members but had also been exposed to international experiences, life in the North, secular or nontraditional Christian viewpoints, and high-quality education in the white world. Even the SNCC students from black Howard University combined their organic experiences with intellectual theorizing spurred by visits from cosmopolitan-educated (black) activists like Bayard Rustin. As Moses acknowledged, the Howard students were "radicalized on the one hand by the movement and they're radicalized on the other hand by intellectuals who are interested in these kinds of movements." This contrasts starkly with SNCC leaders like John Lewis, Charles Sherrod, and Fannie Lou Hamer, who were reared in impoverished southern towns, were highly religious, and had either an average to low-quality (black) college education, a limited high school education, or no formal education at all.[23]

Revisionist accounts of the civil rights movement focus on this second cultural strand in SNCC at the expense of the first. Noteworthy is that in his public assertions after his return from Africa, Moses rarely emphasized the cosmopolitan influences on his thinking and activism either; in *Radical Equations* he does not even mention Albert Camus once. Whereas Camus and other Western and Eastern philosophers and thinkers featured prominently in his speeches and newspaper interviews in the 1960s, he now roots his life's work firmly in the black community, most notably in Amzie Moore's and Ella Baker's model. They were his *Fundi* in community organizing, he noted in the introduction to the book, the Tanzanian word for those who mastered the art of passing on knowledge through example and direct contact. "Borrowing from another African tradition," he continued in a telling tribute, "I feel the need to speak the names of at least some of these important adult Black grassroots leaders who quietly shaped not only Mississippi's civil rights movement, but the southern civil rights movement as a whole: Amzie Moore, Fannie Lou Hamer, Hartman Turnbow, Irene Johnson, Victoria Gray, Vernon Dahmer, Unita Blackwell, Henry Sias, Aylene Quinn, C. O. Chinn, C. C. Bryant, Webb Owens, E.W. Steptoe, Annie Devine, and Hazel Palmer. Their work, which also educated me and other young people, changed the political terrain of a state, and of the nation. What they were is who we are now."[24]

Yet the unprecedented presence of the first cultural strand in local movements was part of what distinguished the 1960s movement from previous ones. The period from 1955 to 1965 saw civil rights activism developing new ideas, styles, and methods. Two new organizations, SCLC and SNCC, transformed the civil rights struggle in the South and gave it a fresh dynamism; Moses's presence in McComb stands as testimony. Without him and SNCC, it is impossible to imagine a Freedom Summer. Despite all its explanatory value, stressing the indigenous southern base of the civil rights movement downplays the fact that cosmopolitan influences were crucial, not just in bringing practical skills, resources, and contacts but also in the articulation of a wider political vision, in terms of ideas and strategies, and this must be acknowledged. For example, when Moses in interviews dismissed his reaching out to lawyers and journalists like John Fisher as something other than facilitation because his impetus was southern based, or in *Radical Equations* discussed the MFDP predominantly as an exercise in the empowerment of the Mississippi poor, he deemphasized how much changing the idea that racism was a local problem propelled his activities. Yet minutes of SNCC meetings and his 1960s speeches indicate how much the situation in the North was present in his thinking and spurred his activism; his forceful reaction to the events in Atlantic City cannot be understood without looking at his *national* goals and hopes either.

Moreover, historians' treatment of Moses as the personification of grassroots activism downplays how atypical he really was for Mississippi's grassroots realities. In an unconscious echo of the "outside agitator" theme so beloved by white southerners, Mississippi NAACP leader Aaron Henry emphasized this disconnect in *his* autobiography. "SNCC spokesmen, particularly Bob Moses, reasoned that as long as the upper and middle class held the wealth of the country, the poor people would never get their share. This thinking did not emerge from the cotton fields of Mississippi. These were theories brought into the state by various highly educated people."[25]

It would be impossible to render Moses's truth more accurate or trustworthy than Henry's or vice versa. This illuminates a related point that Crosby makes, namely, "how much diversity there was *within* the movement." In utilizing participants' insights, scholars must thus be aware of which "*particular subset* of activists" they quote, and to avoid the political stigma attached to each "subset" must include a broad section of them. But, although awareness is good and necessary, perhaps we should not take this idea that "all history . . . is political" too far. After all, neither Moses nor Henry are being dishonest; nor is the recognition that French existentialism was relevant to Moses's thinking per definition evidence of elitist or white-oriented history writing. All three interpretations can coexist without undermining or obliterating the message or truth of either, and this should be reflected in our history writing.

The accent here on an individual leader is thus not to contribute to his romanticization or to belittle the role of ordinary people as the movement's foot soldiers. Rather, it is a plea to sharpen the arguments made by Payne and Dittmer in recognizing how much local and outside/full-time organizers needed each other and thereby further the development of the "interactive synthesis" Emilye Crosby has called for, "one that seriously engages the collective insights of local studies, while simultaneously considering the full range of movement-related scholarship," *including* top-down studies of leaders and local *and* full-time activists' own accounts.

What this case study of Moses's leadership has attempted to show is that within the multiple factors involved in understanding the generation of social change, the existence of a continuous and mutually reinforcing process of leading and organizing, in which individuals like Moses can simultaneously lead and follow, must be recognized and analyzed in more depth to avoid an imbalanced account of movement history. Moses illustrates the significance of his and SNCC's self-negating leadership approach in developing grassroots leadership *and* the significance of the individual in generating social change. The recognition that Moses was a creative instigator of social change does nothing to detract from his assertion that "it was when sharecroppers, day laborers, and domestic workers found their voice . . . that the Mississippi political game was really over."[26]

Notes

List of Abbreviations

AFSC • American Friends Service Committee, Philadelphia

ALP • Allard Lowenstein Papers, Southern Historical Collection, University of North Carolina

AMP • Amzie Moore Papers, State Historical Society Wisconsin

ARP • Anne Romaine Papers, Southern Historical Collection, University of North Carolina

ASAA • Archive Stuyvesant Alumni Association, New York City

CABP • Carl and Anne Braden Papers, State Historical Society Wisconsin

CL • *Jackson Clarion-Ledger*

COFO Panola County Office Records • Council of Federated Organizations Panola County Office Records, State Historical Society Wisconsin

CORE Records • Congress of Racial Equality Records, State Historical Society Wisconsin

DGFOIAC • David J. Garrow Freedom of Information Act Collection, Schomburg Center for Research in Black Culture, New York City

DJCRD • Records Department of Justice Civil Rights Division, Roosevelt Study Center, Middelburg, the Netherlands

EBP • Ella Baker Papers, Schomburg Center for Research in Black Culture, New York City

HCL • Hamilton College Library, Clinton, NY

HRECR • Highlander Research and Education Center Records, State Historical Society Wisconsin

HRMP • Hunter R. Morey Papers, State Historical Society Wisconsin

HU • Howard University, Washington, D.C.

HZP • Howard Zinn Papers, State Historical Society Wisconsin

IGFSC • Iris Greenberg/Freedom Summer Collection, Schomburg Center for Research in Black Culture

JDN • *Jackson Daily News*

JFK Papers • Civil Rights during the Kennedy Administration, Papers of John F. Kennedy, Roosevelt Study Center, Middelburg, the Netherlands

LBJ Papers • Civil Rights during the Johnson Administration, Papers of Lyndon B. Johnson, Roosevelt Study Center, Middelburg, the Netherlands

LC • Library of Congress, Washington, D.C.

LVP • Lise Vogel Papers, State Historical Society Wisconsin

MCEJ • *McComb-Enterprise Journal*

MFSR • Mississippi "Freedom Summer" Review, 1979, conference, State Historical Society Wisconsin

MKP • Mary E. King Papers, State Historical Society Wisconsin
MOHP • Mississippi Oral History Project, University of Southern Mississippi
MSP • Mendy Samstein Papers, State Historical Society Wisconsin
MSSC Online • Mississippi State Sovereignty Commission Online
NAACP Records • National Association for the Advancement of Colored People Records, Library of Congress
NYT • *New York Times*
RBC • Ralph J. Bunche Collection, Howard University
Records SCLC • Records Southern Christian Leadership Conference, Roosevelt Study Center, Middelburg, the Netherlands. Also available at King Center, Atlanta.
RSC • Roosevelt Study Center, Middelburg, the Netherlands
SCRBC • Schomburg Center for Research in Black Culture, New York City
SHSW • State Historical Society Wisconsin, Madison, Wisconsin
SLP • Staughton Lynd Papers, State Historical Society Wisconsin
SNCC Papers • Student Nonviolent Coordinating Committee Papers, Roosevelt Study Center, Middelburg, the Netherlands. Also at King Center, Atlanta.
TBP • Taylor Branch Papers, Southern Historical Collection, University of North Carolina
UNC • University of North Carolina, Chapel Hill, N.C.
USM • University of Southern Mississippi, Jackson, Miss.
WHP • William Heath Papers, State Historical Society Wisconsin

Epigraph

Ladner, Dorie. "Band of Brothers," December 22, 1964.

Preface

1. Carson, "Civil Rights Reform," 29.
2. Nasstrom, "Between Memory and History," 325–64.
3. Moses interview with author, November 2013 (hereafter cited as Moses, November 2013).
4. Nasstrom, "Between Memory and History," 325–64.
5. Moses interview with author, April 2010 (hereafter cited as Moses, 2010); Moses, November 2013.
6. Ibid.
7. William Heath to author, email, July 24, 2014.

Introduction

1. Moses, "Commentary," 74.
2. Payne, *I've Got the Light of Freedom*, 4.

3. Taylor Branch in *New York Times Magazine*, February 21, 1993, qtd. in Podesta, "Robert Parris Moses," http://www.answers.com/topic/robert-parris-moses; Moody, *Coming of Age*, 274; MFSR, 1979, Session 2, SHSW.

4. William Chafe to author, email, October 29, 2013; Newfield, "Moses in Mississippi."

5. Carmichael and Thelwell, *Ready for Revolution*, 311–12.

6. Moses and Cobb, *Radical Equations*, 85–87.

7. Bagdikian, "Negro's Youth's New March"; Greenberg, *Circle of Trust*, 183.

8. Cagin and Dray, *We Are Not Afraid*, 423–24.

9. Moses, 2010.

10. King, *Freedom Song*, 483–84; Stoper, "The Student Nonviolent Coordinating Committee," 14–15; Ansbro, *Martin Luther King*, 90, 187.

11. Cagin and Dray, *We Are Not Afraid*, 179.

12. "Paper on the Salary Structure of the Student Nonviolent Coordinating Committee," no date, Box 2, Folder 1, Samuel Walker Papers, SHSW.

Chapter One

1. Rose C. Feld, "Harlem Riot Attributed to Many Economic Ills," *NYT*, March 24, 1935; Naison, *Communists in Harlem*, 144–45.

2. Naison, *Communists in Harlem*, 32; Biondi, *To Stand and Fight*, 1; Grossman, *Land of Hope*, 28–29, 37, 57; Sugrue, *Sweet Land of Liberty*, 13.

3. Sugrue, *Sweet Land of Liberty*, 13, 175, 202; "Negro Rents Held Artificially High," *NYT*, December 15, 1937; Greenberg, *"Or Does It Explode?"* 5, 14, 30–31, 44–45, 174; Naison, *Communists in Harlem*, 23.

4. Greenberg, *"Or Does It Explode?"* 184; "PWA Harlem Rent Set at $7 a Room" and "11,500 Seek, 574 Get Model Apartments," *NYT*, March 31, 1937, and August 19, 1937; Moses interviews Jay, 2014. Applicants' numbers for the Harlem River Houses vary from 11,500 to 14,000 to 20,000. Moses's brother Gregory was born in November 1933.

5. During the world-famous Scopes trial, John Scopes faced prosecution for teaching the evolution theory, which was against Tennessean law. William Moses's views on the trial were published in the *Norfolk Journal and Guide* and in the *Pittsburgh Courier*.

6. Moses interviews by Paul Jay, June 2014 (hereafter cited as Moses interviews Jay, 2014); Burner, *And Gently*, 9, 226; Moses, November 2013; Doris Moses, interview by Taylor Branch, August 1, 1993, and Robert Parris Moses, interview by Taylor Branch, August 10, 1983, Box 108, Folder 1, TBP, UNC (hereafter cited as Doris Moses interview Branch, 1993; Moses interview Branch, August 10, 1983).

7. Moses interviews Jay, 2014; Burner, *And Gently*, 9, 226; Moses, November 2013; Doris Moses interview Branch, 1993; Moses interview Branch, August 10, 1983.

8. Why Gregory Moses did not pursue a higher education is unknown; according to Bob Moses, no records exist that clarify what happened to his father between 1922, when he graduated from high school, and 1932, when he married

Moses's mother. Although in the 1983 Branch interview Moses related his father's unease to his Grandfather's illness, he denied that link in 2013. Instead, he suggested that the move from Philadelphia to New York might have been unsettling for his father, but this is a mere guess (Moses, November 2013).

9. Louise Parris's mother, Georgia Elam (Grandma Johnson), did marry a Pullman porter named Johnson (Louise never knew her real father) who ran a New York–Florida route. Moses was named after one of the three children the two had together (Moses, November 2013).

10. Ethel Moses worked as a hostess at the Cotton Club; Lucia and Julia worked there as chorus dancers. Lucia became famous for her dancing roles in the Broadway productions *Shuffle Along*, *Keep Shuffling*, and *Showboat* and was seen as a sex symbol due to her roles in Oscar Micheaux's films, Ethel for her role in the movie *The Scar of Shame* (Alicia T., "Ethel Moses," www.imbd.com; Adrienne Wartts, "Moses, Lucia Lynn," http://www.blackpast.org/aah/moses-lucia-lynn-c-1906).

11. Branch, *Parting the Waters*, 325; Burner, *And Gently*, 9–10; Moses, November 2013; Robert Parris Moses, interview by Charles Payne, August 1993 (hereafter cited as Moses interview Payne, 1993); Russell, *Black Genius*, 328; Moses and Cobb, *Radical Equations*, 27; Doris Moses interview Branch, 1993; Moses interview Branch, August 10, 1983; Warren, *Who Speaks for the Negro?* 90; Howe, "Come to the Fair!" 315.

12. Greenberg, *"Or Does It Explode?"* 9; Moses, March 2011 and November 2013.

13. Greenberg, *"Or Does It Explode?"* 200; Biondi, *To Stand and Fight*, 3, 10; Moses, March 2011.

14. Moses interviews Jay, 2014.

15. Ibid.; Greenberg, *"Or Does It Explode?"* 10; Doris Moses interview Branch, 1993; Robert Parris Moses, interview by Clayborne Carson, March 29–30, 1982 (hereafter cited as Moses interview Carson, 1982); Moses and Cobb, *Radical Equations*, 32–33.

16. Greenberg, *"Or Does It Explode?"* 58, 103; Harvey, *Redeeming the South*, 46, 123, 214; Grossman, *Land of Hope*, 157–60; Myrdal, *An American Dilemma*, 2:863, 875, 877; Cone, *Black Theology*, 108.

17. Burner, *And Gently*, 12–13; Moses interview Carson, 1982; Moses, March 2011; U.S. Department of Justice, Southern District of New York, "Resume of the Inquiry Conscientious Objector Robert Parris Moses," March 21, 1962, Mississippi Department of Archives and History, USM (hereafter cited as "Resume of the Inquiry," 1962); Dave Dennis, interview by author, 2010 (hereafter cited as Dennis interview author, 2010); Peggy Quinn to author, 2010; Sugrue, *Sweet Land of Liberty*, 262. Moses attended Sunday school at St. Mark's United Methodist Church at 138th Street and St. Nicholas Avenue.

18. Moses, November 2013.

19. Julia and Lucia Moses often told of a trip they undertook with their mother, Julia Trent, to the latter's birth place. The caretaker, however, refused to believe them until they showed him a secret passage serving as evidence that Trent's mother and the slave master's son had "lived after the Civil War in the open 'as family'" (Moses, November 2013).

20. Ibid.; Burner, *And Gently*, 19, 228; Moses and Cobb, *Radical Equations*, 40; Alicia T., "Ethel Moses," www.imdb.com.

21. Moses and Cobb, *Radical Equations*, 40; Moses, November 2013; Moses interviews Jay, 2014.

22. Moses interviews Jay, 2014; Burner, *And Gently*, 10; Moses interview Payne, 1993; Lemann, *The Promised Land*, 99; Gitlin, *The Sixties*, 170; Warren, *Who Speaks for the Negro?* 90–91; Naison, *Communists in Harlem*, 32; Greenberg, *"Or Does It Explode?"* 63; Alvin Poussaint, interview by author, October 2010 (hereafter cited as Poussaint interview author, 2010); Myrdal, *An American Dilemma*, 2: 980.

23. Moses interview Payne, 1993; Warren, *Who Speaks for the Negro?* 90–91; Moses, November 2013; Moses and Cobb, *Radical Equations*, 40, 223; Payne, *I've Got the Light*, 234.

24. Moses interview Payne, 1993; Warren, *Who Speaks for the Negro?* 90–91; Moses, November 2013; Moses and Cobb, *Radical Equations*, 40, 223; Payne, *I've Got the Light*, 234.

25. Moses interviews Jay, 2014; handwritten notes Taylor Branch, January 16, 1999, Box 108, Folder 1, TBP, UNC (hereafter cited as Notes Branch, 1999); Dittmer, *Local People*, 457n; Burner, *And Gently*, 10; Howe, "Come to the Fair!" 314–17; Moses, November 2013.

26. Moses interviews Jay, 2014; Russell, *Black Genius*, 328; Myrdal, *An American Dilemma*, 2:704; Naison, *Communists in Harlem during the Depression*, 214; Sugrue, *Sweet Land of Liberty*, 164, 188; Warren, *Who Speaks for the Negro?* 89.

27. Doris Moses interview Branch, 1993; Moses, March 2011 and November 2013; Russell, *Black Genius*, 328.

28. Hayes, "I Used the Term 'Negro,'" 160–61. The teacher's name could also be spelled "Mrs. Stewart." The poem is also called *Abu Ben Adhem*.

29. Sugrue, *Sweet Land of Liberty*, 258.

30. Moses interview Branch, August 10, 1983.

31. Norton et al., *A People and a Nation*, 534, 536, 539–44; Biondi, *To Stand and Fight*, 173, 175.

32. *Indicator*, Yearbook 1952, ASAA; Meyer, *Stuyvesant High School: The First 100 Years*, 10–17. The number of black students in Moses's graduating year might be higher, as not all students listed in the yearbook were accompanied by pictures.

33. Moses interview Branch, August 10, 1983; Poussaint interview author, 2010; Moses interviews Jay, 2014.

34. Poussaint interview author, 2010; Moses interviews Jay, 2014; Cagin and Dray, *We Are Not Afraid*, 87; Ransby, *Ella Baker*, 251; Moses interview Carson, 1982; Robert Parris Moses, interview by Taylor Branch, August 11, 1983, Box 108, Folder 1, TBP, UNC (hereafter cited as Moses interview Branch, August 11, 1983).

35. Poussaint interview author, 2010; Moses interviews Jay, 2014; Cagin and Dray, *We Are Not Afraid*, 87; Ransby, *Ella Baker*, 251; Moses interview Carson, 1982; Moses interview Branch, August 11, 1983.

36. Doris Moses interview Branch, 1993; Moses interview Carson, 1982; Moses interview Branch, August 11, 1983; Poussaint interview author, 2010; "Fiery Cross in Jersey," *NYT*, August 14, 1948; Van Slyck, "Summer Camps," http://www.faqs.org/childhood/So-Th/Summer-Camps.html.

37. Moses interview Carson, 1982; Moses interview Branch, August 11, 1983; Burner, *And Gently*, 10; Cagin and Dray, *We Are Not Afraid*, 87; Hammerback and Jensen, "Working in 'Quiet Places,'" 3; Hammerback and Jensen, "'Your Tools Are Really the People,'" 127. In this sense, Moses's approach foreshadowed the 1960s New Left. The latter was characterized by its break with this self-restraining mentality regarding cooperation with alleged Communists, although it rejected Marxism. Moses has accordingly been viewed as one of its defining faces. Moses, however, always rejected the New Left label. He first saw the term in *Newsweek*, which had "a kind of mixed metaphor on the cover [that] said, 'In Orbit on the Left.' And the idea that you were orbiting in some kind of elliptical fashion like a planet but that you were orbiting on the Left struck me as not really that useful" in determining human behavior. He defined the New Left as consisting of white liberal groups like SDS and black nationalists after 1965. Yet in his activism, Moses and currents of the New Left flowed interminably through one another. So did further connections to and breaks with the Old Left, although he never joined any Old Left groups. What is striking from Moses's answer then is not whether or not he fitted conceptions of the New Left but that he did not recognize himself in the image others held of him, a recurrent issue in Moses's life. (Agger, *The Sixties at 40*, 182–83, 187–88.)

38. Burner, *And Gently*, 11; Branch, *Parting the Waters*, 325; Moses interview Branch, August 10, 1983; Moses interviews Jay, 2014.

39. Burner, *And Gently*, 11; Branch, *Parting the Waters*, 325; Moses interview Branch, August 10, 1983; Moses interviews Jay, 2014.

40. Burner, *And Gently*, 11–12, 14; "Resume of the Inquiry," 1962; *Hamilton Alumni Review* 21 (1956): 125, and *The Hamiltonian*, Yearbook 1953, 1954, 1955, 1956, HCL.

41. Branch, *Parting the Waters*, 325–26; Moses interview Branch, August 10, 1983.

42. McKay et al., *A History of Western Society*, 916–17.

43. Stoper, *Student Nonviolent Coordinating Committee*, 117. Nonetheless, Stoper correctly claimed, it "was not . . . Camus that made SNCC value small, democratic groups; it was its own experience both internally and in relation to other organizations." (Ibid.)

44. Carson, *In Struggle*, 46; Camus, *The Rebel*, 100–11, 125–32, 279–82 (quotes pp. 102 and 281); Warren, *Who Speaks for the Negro?* 94–95; Agger, *The Sixties at 40*, 184.

45. Bond and Lewis, *Gonna Sit at the Welcome Table*, 722; *The Hamiltonian*, Yearbook 1956, 126, HCL.

46. Moses interview Branch, August 11, 1983; "Required Reading Now Is Done Voluntarily," *NYT*, November 13, 1955.

47. Burner, *And Gently*, 6.

48. Lynd and Lynd, *Nonviolence in America*, xii–xiii; Anderson, *Bayard Rustin*, 65.

49. Moses, 2010; "Resume of the Inquiry," 1962; Moses interview Branch, August 11, 1983.

50. Moses and Cobb, *Radical Equations*, 29; Anderson, *Bayard Rustin*, 60–61, 98–99, 183–96, 239–64.

51. Moses and Cobb, *Radical Equations*, 29; Burner, *And Gently*, 14; Branch, *Parting the Waters*, 326; Moses, 2010; "Resume of the Inquiry," 1962; Moses, October 2010; Robert Parris Moses, interviews by Anne Romaine, September 1966 and November 14, 1987, ARP, UNC (hereafter cited as Moses interviews Romaine); Moses interview Branch, August 11, 1983; Moses interviews Jay, 2014.

52. Burner, *And Gently*, 12; Moses interview Branch, August 11, 1983; Poussaint interview author, 2010.

53. Burner, *And Gently*, 12; Moses interview Branch, August 11, 1983; Branch, *Parting the Waters*, 326; Dennis interview author, 2010.

54. Burner, *And Gently*, 12; Moses interview Branch, August 11, 1983; "Resume of the Inquiry," 1962; Robert Parris Moses, interview by Taylor Branch, July 31, 1984, Box 108, TBP, UNC (hereafter cited as Moses interview Branch, July 31, 1984).

55. Moses interview Branch, August 11, 1983; Burner, *And Gently*, 14; Branch, *Parting the Waters*, 326; Moses, 2010; "Friends International Work Camps," brochure, 1956, AFSC.

56. "Orientation Program," June 3–8, 1955, and "Notes to Volunteers," January, February, April, May, 1955, AFSC. The AFSC paid travel expenses and insurance, but volunteers had to contribute $470 (although the AFSC offered financial aid if necessary).

57. Moses, 2010; "Moses Speaks to I.R.C. Monday on Summer in European Camps," and "Moses Describes European Travels to IRC Meeting," *The Spectator*, October 21 and 28, 1955, HCL.

58. Moses, 2010; "Moses Speaks," and "Moses Describes European Travels," *The Spectator*, October 21 and 28, 1955, HCL; Burner, *And Gently*, 14.

59. Moses, 2010.

60. Ibid.; Branch, *Parting the Waters*, 326; Burner, *And Gently*, 14–15; Cagin and Dray, *We Are Not Afraid*, 87; Moses interview Branch, August 11, 1983.

61. Branch, *Parting the Waters*, 326; Moses, 2010.

62. Moses interview Branch, August 10, 1983. See also Branch's handwritten notes accompanying the interview; Burner, *And Gently*, 13, 15; Warren, *Who Speaks for the Negro?* 90, 98–99; "Murrow to Be Honored," and "Warren at Hamilton," *NYT*, March 13, 1954 and June 4, 1956; Moses, March 2011; Moses interviews Jay, 2014.

63. Moses interviews Jay, 2014; Burner, *And Gently*, 11, 14; Warren, *Who Speaks for the Negro?* 90, 97–99; Moses and Cobb, *Radical Equations*, 27–28, 36–37.

64. Robert Wright, interview by John Britton, July 28, 1968, RBC, HU; Lewis, *Martin Luther King*, 28.

65. Wright, *Uncle Tom's Children*, 5–15; Moses and Cobb, *Radical Equations*, 27–28; Sugrue, *Sweet Land of Liberty*, 425.

66. Warren, *Who Speaks for the Negro?* 97; Payne, *I've Got the Light*, 234.

67. Moses interview Branch, August 10, 1983; "Resume of the Inquiry," 1962.

68. Moses interview Branch, August 10, 1983; Branch, *Parting the Waters*, 326–27.

69. Ibid.

70. Ibid.; Moses interview Carson, 1982; Moses interviews Romaine; Heath, *The Children Bob Moses Led*, 6–7.

71. Burner, *And Gently*, 16; Branch, *Parting the Waters*, 327; Moses to Dorothy Miller, no date, JFP, LC*; King, *Freedom Song*, 145; Poussaint interview author, 2010; Moses, March 2011. *When I researched the James Forman Papers in 2008, these had not been catalogued yet. It is therefore impossible to record box and folder numbers as they are no longer up to date.

72. Burner, *And Gently*, 16; Branch, *Parting the Waters*, 327; Moses interview Branch, August 10, 1983; Myrdal, *An American Dilemma*, 2: 979–82.

73. Moses interviews Branch, August 10, 1983, and July 31, 1984; Robert Parris Moses, interview by Taylor Branch, July 30, 1984, Box 108, TBP, UNC (hereafter cited as Moses interview Branch, July 30, 1984); Moses and Cobb, *Radical Equations*, 27.

74. Moses interviews Branch, August 10, 1983, July 30 and July 31, 1984; Warren, *Who Speaks for the Negro?* 90; Robert Parris Moses, interview by William Chafe, October 7, 1989, ALP, UNC (hereafter cited as Moses interview Chafe, 1989, ALP, UNC). In 1959, Lowenstein was unknown to Moses, and they did not interact personally.

75. Burner, *And Gently*, 16–17; Notes Branch, 1999; Lemann, *The Promised Land*, 99; Moore, "A SNCC Blue Book," 328.

76. Sugrue, *Sweet Land of Liberty*, 179; Moses, March 2011; Bob Moses, "Speech" (West Coast Civil Rights Conference, April 23, 1964), USM (hereafter cited as Moses speech West Coast Civil Rights Conference, 1964).

77. Oppenheimer, *The Sit-In Movement*, 80, 85–98; Bond and Lewis, *Gonna Sit at the Welcome Table*, 388–91; Emanuel Perlmutter, "Sit-Ins Backed by Rallies Here," *NYT*, March 6, 1960; Carson, *In Struggle*, 9–18; Zinn, *SNCC*, 16–28. See also Chafe, *Civilities and Civil Rights*.

78. Moses and Cobb, *Radical Equations*, 3; *Freedom on My Mind*, directed by Field and Mulford, 1994 (hereafter cited as *Freedom on My Mind*, 1994); Burner, *And Gently*, 17; Bagdikian, "Negro Youth's New March."

79. Moses and Cobb, *Radical Equations*, 3; *Freedom on My Mind*, 1994; Burner, *And Gently*, 17; Moses interview Carson, 1982; Carmichael and Thelwell, *Ready for Revolution*, 140; Carson, *In Struggle*, 17; DuBois, *The Souls of Black Folk*, 5.

80. Greenberg, *Circle of Trust*, 25; Zinn, *SNCC*, 29.

81. Morris, *The Origins of the Civil Rights Movement*, 200, 203; Oppenheimer, *The Sit-In Movement*, 43, 44, 49; Fairclough, *To Redeem the Soul of America*, 65; Zinn, *SNCC*, 26.

82. Burner, *And Gently*, 18–19; Moses and Cobb, *Radical Equations*, 27–28; Moses interview Carson, 1982; Moses interviews Romaine; Bagdikian, "Negro Youth's New March"; Cagin and Dray, *We Are Not Afraid*, 86.

83. Burner, *And Gently*, 18–19; Moses and Cobb, *Radical Equations*, 27–28; Moses interview Carson, 1982; Moses interviews Romaine; Branch, *Parting the Waters*, 300–1.

84. Moses interview Carson, 1982; Moses, 2010; Moses and Cobb, *Radical Equations*, 28.

85. Moses interview Carson, 1982; Moses, 2010; Moses and Cobb, *Radical Equations*, 28; Moses, "Constitutional Property," 79–80; Moses and Cobb, *Radical Equations*, 28; Branch, *Parting the Waters*, 575, 850–51; Moses interview Branch, August 10, 1983; Moses interviews Romaine.

Chapter Two

1. Moses interview Carson, 1982; Moses, "Foreword"; *Freedom on My Mind*, 1994.

2. Fairclough, *To Redeem the Soul of America*, 33, 45; Andrew Johnson to Gloster Current, April 22, 1964, and Aaron Henry to Current, April 25, 1964, Group III, Box C-74, Part 27, NAACP Records, LC; "SCLC Organizational Structure," founding document, no date, Files 00428–00430, Reel 5, Part 4, Series I, Records of Andrew J. Young, SCLC Records.

3. Fairclough, *To Redeem the Soul of America*, 4, 33–34, 38, 45, 57, 61, 171; Branch, *Pillar of Fire*, 92; Branch, *Parting the Waters*, 203; Garrow, *Bearing the Cross*, 153.

4. Fairclough, *To Redeem the Soul of America*, 4, 33–34, 38, 45, 57, 61, 171; Branch, *Pillar of Fire*, 92; Branch, *Parting the Waters*, 203; Garrow, *Bearing the Cross*, 153; Moses interview Carson, 1982.

5. Garrow, *Bearing the Cross*, 132; Ella Baker, interview by John Britton, June 19, 1968, RBC, HU (hereafter cited as Baker interview Britton, 1968, HU); Rubin, *Student Nonviolent Coordinating Committee*, 20–21; Carson, *In Struggle*, 20–21, 22–24; Claude Sitton, "Dr. King Favors Buyers Boycott" and "Negro Criticizes NAACP Tactics," *NYT*, April 16 and 17, 1960.

6. Morris, *The Origins of the Civil Rights Movement*, 203; Baker interview Britton, 1968, HU; Charles McDew, interview by Katherine Shannon, August 24, 1967, RBC, HU (hereafter cited as McDew interview Shannon, HU); Claude Sitton, "Students Impatient with Old Efforts," *NYT*, April 24, 1960.

7. Hogan, *Many Minds*, 27, 35–36; Carson, *In Struggle*, 22–24, 25, 154.

8. Hogan, *Many Minds*, 27, 35–36; Carson, *In Struggle*, 22–24, 25–26, 154; King, *Freedom Song*, 274–75; Greenberg, *Circle of Trust*, 34; Sellers and Terrell, *River of No Return*, 35; Lynd and Lynd, *Nonviolence in America*, xli–xlii, 222; Stoper, *Student Nonviolent Coordinating Committee*, 27; Julian Bond, interview by author, October 27, 2008 (hereafter cited as Bond interview author, 2008); Ransby, *Ella Baker*, 248, 252.

9. Moses and Cobb, *Radical Equations*, 29; Moses interviews Romaine; Branch, *Parting the Waters*, 575; Curry et al., *Deep in Our Hearts*, 10, 11, 15.

10. Moses and Cobb, *Radical Equations*, 34–36; Marsh, *God's Long Summer*, 102–3; Jane Stembridge to David Forbes, August 14, 1960, File 0810, Reel 4, Series IV, Ex. Sec. Files Jane Stembridge, SNCC Papers; Raines, *My Soul Is Rested*, 105; Ransby, *Ella Baker*, 252–53.

11. Moses interview Carson, 1982; Moses and Cobb, *Radical Equations*, 33; Baker interview Britton, 1968, RBC, HU; Payne, *I've Got the Light*, 93; Mary King, interview by author, December 8, 2009 (hereafter cited as Mary King interview author, 2009).

12. Moses interview Carson, 1982; Sugrue, *Sweet Land of Liberty*, 13; Ransby, *Ella Baker*, 15–21, 64–104, 105–47, 303; Payne, *I've Got the Light*, 86; Moses and Cobb, *Radical Equations*, 33.

13. Branch, *Parting the Waters*, 558, 801, 898–99; Branch, *Pillar of Fire*, 92, 195–97, 286, 552; Garrow, *Bearing the Cross*, 450, 463–64; Fairclough, *To Redeem the Soul of America*, 64.

14. Garrow, *Bearing the Cross*, 118, 131; Baker interview Britton, 1968, RBC, HU; Carson, *In Struggle*, 20–21; Rubin, *Student Nonviolent Coordinating Committee*, 20–21; Ella Baker, "Bigger Than a Hamburger," in *The Southern Patriot*, May 1960, in *Gonna Sit at the Welcome Table*, eds. Bond and Lewis, 406–7; Hogan, *Many Minds*, 35, 42; Ransby, *Ella Baker*, 281, 303; Lewis and D'Orso, *Walking with the Wind*, 85–86; Morris, *The Origins of the Civil Rights Movement*, 218; Zellner, *Wrong Side of Murder Creek*, 101–3.

15. Moses interview Carson, 1982.

16. Ibid.

17. Ibid.; Raines, *My Soul Is Rested*, 86, 87, 102; Lefever, *Undaunted by the Fight*, 45–46, 48, 51.

18. Burner, *And Gently*, 24; Moses interview Carson, 1982; Fleming, *Soon We Will Not Cry*, 55–56, 60; Moses and Cobb, *Radical Equations*, 30; Bond interview author, 2008. On average, the COAHR students were at least five years younger than Moses, which might have contributed to their lack of determination. Nonetheless, eighteen-year-old Ruby Doris Smith regularly picketed the A&P by herself as well.

19. Moses and Cobb, *Radical Equations*, 30; Bond interview author, 2008; Sellers and Terrell, *River of No Return*, 41–42; King, *Freedom Song*, 145.

20. The union's name, and whether it was its national office or one of its locals, which made the demand has never been established, although accounts vary from the United Auto Workers to the United Packing Workers. These are odd considering their own left-wing orientations. Considering Rustin's altered stance on Communism and close relationship with anti-Communist A. Philip Randolph, Jane Stembridge was therefore probably correct to suspect that Rustin's homosexuality was much to blame. (Ransby, *Ella Baker*, 263.)

21. Burner, *And Gently*, 25–26; Moses interview Carson, 1982; Woods, *Black Struggle*, 9–10; Sellers and Terrell, *River of No Return*, 43; Ransby, *Ella Baker*, 248, 263; Carson, *In Struggle*, 9; Forman, *Making of Black Revolutionaries*, 219.

22. Newfield, "Moses in Mississippi"; Bagdikian, "Negro Youth's New March."

23. King, *Freedom Song*, 45; Baker interview Britton, 1968, HU; Sellers and Terrell, *River of No Return*, 38–39.

24. Moses and Cobb, *Radical Equations*, 30; Moses interview Branch, July 30, 1984; Moses interviews Romaine; Woods, *Black Struggle*, 29–31, 44–45, 104–5, 107–8, 123–24; Branch, *Parting the Waters*, 122.

25. Moses and Cobb, *Radical Equations*, 30; Moses interview Carson, 1982.

26. Moses and Cobb, *Radical Equations*, 30–31; Branch, *Parting the Waters*, 325, 328–29.

27. Moses and Cobb, *Radical Equations*, 30–31; Branch, *Parting the Waters*, 325, 328–29; Biondi, *To Stand and Fight*, 167–70; Arnesen, "Reconsidering the 'Long Civil Rights Movement,'" 32–33.

28. Branch, *Parting the Waters*, 328; Moses interview Carson, 1982.

29. Branch, *Parting the Waters*, 325; Carson, *Autobiography of Martin Luther King*, 15–16; Ansbro, *Martin Luther King*, 187; Lewis and D'Orso, *Walking with the Wind*, 303; Moses and Cobb, *Radical Equations*, 32–33; Moses interview Carson, 1982.

30. Moses interview Carson, 1982; Moses, "Foreword."

31. Hogan, *Many Minds*, 42.

32. Moses and Cobb, *Radical Equations*, 32; Moses interview Carson, 1982; Lefever, *Undaunted by the Fight*, 105, 107; Jane Stembridge to Anne Braden, June 16, 1960, File 1012, Reel 4, Series IV, Ex. Sec. Files Jane Stembridge, SNCC Papers; Ransby, *Ella Baker*, 10, 234–35.

33. Bond interview author, 2008; Woods, *Black Struggle*, 167.

34. Bond interview author, 2008; Sellers and Terrell, *River of No Return*, 41–42, 45; Bond and Lewis, *Gonna Sit at the Welcome Table*, 412–13; Halberstam, *The Children*, 403.

35. Moses interview Carson, 1982; Moses and Cobb, *Radical Equations*, 31; Branch, *Parting the Waters*, 328.

36. Moses interview Carson, 1982; Moses and Cobb, *Radical Equations*, 35; Moses interview Branch, August 10, 1983; Stembridge to Committee Members SNCC, August 10, 1960, File 0919, to David Forbes, letter, August 14, 1960, File 0810, and Jane Stembridge to Committee Members SNCC, August 10, 1960, File 0918, Reel 4, Series IV, Ex. Sec. Files Jane Stembridge, SNCC Papers.

37. Moses interview Carson, 1982; Moses interview Branch, August 10, 1983; "Oct. Conference," in *The Student Voice*, August 1960, in Carson, *The Student Voice*, 6; "Announcements Sent to Following," report, July 25, 1960, File 0044, and Jane Stembridge to Bob Moses, letter, July 25, 1960, File 0048, Reel 1, Series I, Marion Barry Chairman Files, SNCC Papers; Moses and Cobb, *Radical Equations*, 36–37; Grant, *Ella Baker*, 134; Ransby, *Ella Baker*, 252, 261–62.

38. Moses and Cobb, *Radical Equations*, 20, 38; Stembridge to Moses, August 16 and 25, 1960, Files 0816 and 0835–0836, and Moses to Stembridge, no date, Files 0836–0837, Reel 4, Series IV, Ex. Sec. Files Jane Stembridge, SNCC Papers; Bond interview author, 2008.

39. Moses interview Carson, 1982; Moses and Cobb, *Radical Equations*, 37–38.

40. Moses and Cobb, *Radical Equations*, 37–38.

41. Stembridge to Fred Shuttlesworth and to Jesse Walker, August 11, 1960, File 0807, and Stembridge to Amzie Moore, August 15, 1960, File 0811, and Stembridge to Forbes, August 14, 1960, File 0810, and Stembridge to Philip Pennywell, August 19, 1960, File 0827, Reel 4, Series IV, Ex. Sec. Files Jane Stembridge, SNCC Papers.

42. Stembridge to Patricia Drayton, September 1, 1960, File 0847, and Stembridge to Moses, August 18, 1960, File 0819, and Stembridge to Beverly Moore, August 19, 1960, File 0820, and Moses to Stembridge, no date, Files 0821 and 0828, Reel 4, Series IV, Ex. Sec. Files Jane Stembridge, SNCC Papers.

43. Stembridge to Patricia Drayton, September 1, 1960, File 0847, and Stembridge to Moses, August 18, 1960, File 0819, and Stembridge to Beverly Moore, August 19, 1960, File 0820, and Moses to Stembridge, no date, Files 0821 and 0828, Reel 4, Series IV, Ex. Sec. Files Jane Stembridge, SNCC Papers.

44. Moses and Cobb, *Radical Equations*, 38.

45. Moses interview Carson, 1982; Moses and Cobb, *Radical Equations*, 38.

46. Moses and Cobb, *Radical Equations*, 38; King, *Freedom Song*, 133–34.

47. Crosby, *A Little Taste of Freedom*, 15; Dittmer, *Local People*, 19–20, 125; Zinn, *SNCC*, 64; Cobb, *The Most Southern Place*, 254.

48. Dittmer, *Local People*, 10, 19; Lemann, *The Promised Land*, 11; Cobb, *The Most Southern Place*, 196–198, 263, 264 (for more on the effect of the Great Depression and technological advancement on Delta blacks, see Chapter 8); Payne, *I've Got the Light*, 16–18.

49. Dittmer, *Local People*, 20–23, 68–69; Stembridge to Moses, August 25, 1960, File 0835, Ex. Sec. Files Jane Stembridge, SNCC Papers.

50. Payne, *I've Got the Light*, 17–21; Dittmer, *Local People*, 10.

51. Payne, *I've Got the Light*, 21–28. Quote Jackson newspaper on pp. 27.

52. Ibid., 29–34; Burner, *And Gently*, 29; Forman, *Making of Black Revolutionaries*, 280–81.

53. Hampton and Fayer, *Voices of Freedom*, 141.

54. Stembridge to Moore, August 15, 1960, File 0811, and Moses to Stembridge, no date, Files 0883, 0833, and 0834, Reel 4, Series IV, Ex. Sec. Files Jane Stembridge, SNCC Papers; Moses and Cobb, *Radical Equations*, 38–39; Raines, *My Soul Is Rested*, 236; Cagin and Dray, *We Are Not Afraid*, 136–37.

55. Moses and Cobb, *Radical Equations*, 40–41; Moses interviews Romaine.

56. Moses and Cobb, *Radical Equations*, 40–41; Moses interview Payne, 1993; Moses, "Comments," Conference on Ethics and Morality, 1980.

57. Amzie Moore, interviews by Michael Garvey, March 29 and April 13, 1977, MOHP, USM; Cagin and Dray, *We Are Not Afraid*, 134–35.

58. Moses interview Carson, 1982; Moses and Cobb, *Radical Equations*, 41–42; Hampton and Fayer, *Voices of Freedom*, 140.

59. Moses and Cobb, *Radical Equations*, 41–42; Hampton and Fayer, *Voices of Freedom*, 140.

60. Moses to Stembridge, no date, 1960, File 0835, and Stembridge to Moses, August 25, 1960, File 0836, and Stembridge to Moore, September 1, 1960, File 0847, Reel 4, Series IV, Ex. Sec. Files Jane Stembridge, SNCC Papers. See also Branch, *Parting the Waters*, 330–31.

61. Cagin and Dray, *We Are Not Afraid*, 137–38.

62. Moses interview Carson, 1982; Stembridge to Moses, August 25, 1960, and Moses to Stembridge, no date, File 0836, Reel 4, Series IV, Ex. Sec. Files Jane Stembridge, SNCC Papers.

63. Moses and Cobb, *Radical Equations*, 42; Moses to Stembridge, no date, 1960, Files 0835–0836, and Stembridge to Moore, September 1, 1960, File 0847, Reel 4, Series IV, Ex. Sec. Files Jane Stembridge, SNCC Papers; Cagin and Dray, *We Are Not Afraid*, 137; Moses interviews Romaine.

64. Stembridge to Moses, August 18, 1960, File 0819, August 25, 1960, File 0835, and Moses to Stembridge, no date, Files 0837 and 0883, and Stembridge to Alfred Cook and to Walter Williams, August 29, 1960, File 0839, Reel 4, Series IV, Ex. Sec. Files Jane Stembridge, SNCC Papers.

65. That year, Simpkins's and McCain's ideas did impact another young Louisiana activist, Dave Dennis of CORE, Moses's future comrade in Mississippi (Dennis interview author, 2010).

66. Moses to Stembridge, no date, Files 0837, 0838, and 0882–0885, Reel 4, Series IV, Ex. Sec. Files Jane Stembridge, and Stembridge to Patrick Jones, August 31, 1960, File 0753, Reel 3, Series III, Staff Meetings, SNCC Papers; Dennis interview author, 2010.

67. Stembridge to Moses, August 16 and 25, 1960, Files 0816 and 0835, Reel 4, Series IV, Ex. Sec. Files Jane Stembridge, and "General Report Since August 1, 1960," no date, File 0752, Reel 3, Series III, Staff Meetings, SNCC Papers.

68. Cohen, "Sorrow Songs," 178; Moses interview Carson, 1982; Newfield, *A Prophetic Minority*, 73.

69. Newfield, *A Prophetic Minority*, 73; Moses interview Branch, August 11, 1983; Anonymous FOR member to Stembridge, October 1, 1960, File 0499, Reel 11, Series V, SNCC Conferences, SNCC Papers; Moses interviews Romaine; Amzie Moore to Bob Moses, December 22, 1960, Box 1, Folder 2, AMP, SHSW.

70. Newfield, *A Prophetic Minority*, 73; Moses interviews Romaine; Moses interview Carson, 1982; Moses to Ed King, March 11, 1961, and King to Moses, March 13, 1961, Box 108, Folder 3, TBP, UNC; Cagin and Dray, *We Are Not Afraid*, 138–39; "Attention! Join Our Own Peace Corps of the South," April/May 1961, in Carson, *The Student Voice*, 44.

Chapter Three

1. "McComb Negroes Unable to Think for Themselves . . . Says Judge," *The Liberator* 1, no. 2 (November 17, 1961): 3–4, private collection Joan Mulholland.

2. Amzie Moore to Moses, December 22, 1960, and Moore to friends, January 26, 1961, Box 1, Folder 2, AMP, SHSW; Moses and Cobb, *Radical Equations*, 44; Dittmer, *Local People*, 103; Moses interview Carson, 1982; Moses interview Branch, July 31, 1984; Robert Parris Moses, interview by John Dittmer, August 15, 1983 (hereafter cited as Moses interview Dittmer, 1983).

3. Dittmer, *Local People*, 33, 53; Beito and Beito, *Black Maverick*, 70, 93; Crosby, *A Little Taste of Freedom*, 15, 55.

4. Dittmer, *Local People*, 59, 70–71; Dittmer, "The Politics of the Mississippi Movement," 68; Crosby, *A Little Taste of Freedom*, 64, 66; "Declaration of Constitutional Principles: The Southern Manifesto," March 12, 1956, in *Debating the Civil Rights Movement*, Lawson and Payne, 59–64; "Mississippi" and "Mississippi Code," report, no date, File 0233, Reel 3, Files W. Wilson White, and "Constitutional Law of Mississippi as Adopted February 29, 1956," report, no date, File 0788, Reel 4, Burke Marshall Records, DJCRD Records, RSC; Woods, *Black Struggle*, 95–97. See also Katagiri, *The Mississippi State Sovereignty Commission*.

5. Dittmer, *Local People*, 70, 73, 86–87, 101; Amzie Moore to James P. Kizart, letter, December 20, 1955, qtd. in Cobb, *The Most Southern Place on Earth*, 222; Ransby, *Ella Baker*, 302; Beito and Beito, *Black Maverick*, 153–54, 162, 181.

6. Aaron Henry to Ella Baker, April 5, 1958, File 00358, Reel 1, Part 2, Series II, Correspondence Ella J. Baker, Records SCLC; Moses interview Payne, 1993; Hampton and Fayer, *Voices of Freedom*, 50, 52; Moses interview Dittmer, 1983; Moses interview Branch, August 10, 1983.

7. Lawson and Payne, *Debating the Civil Rights Movement*, 181; Moses interview Carson, 1982; Moses interviews Romaine; Moses to Mr. Sheenfeld, June 25, 1961, and G. V. Ward to Moses, July 17, 1961, Box 108, Folder 3, TBP, UNC.

8. Moses interviews Branch, August 10, 1983, and July 30, 1984.

9. In February, 1961, SNCC volunteers Ruby Doris Smith, Diane Nash, Charles Jones, and Charles Sherrod were jailed in Rock Hill, South Carolina, to dramatize the plight of a CORE group who chose "jail-no-bail" after a sit-in, but their example failed to inspire others. See Carson, *In Struggle*, 32.

10. At Parchman, the activists were placed in filthy cells in its maximum-security unit. After they started singing freedom songs, their belongings and mattresses were confiscated, and cold wind was blown into the cells. Guards used electric prods on them, and several were placed in sweatboxes, unvented, dark units of only six feet that were often placed in the hot sun—a practice that has now been defined as torture. (Zinn, *SNCC*, 54–57; Branch, *Parting the Waters*, 482–85.)

11. "The First Year," report, no date, File 0786, and Minutes of SNCC Meeting, November 25–27, 1960, Files 0780–0781, Reel 3, Series III, Staff Meetings, SNCC Papers; Carson, *In Struggle*, 27–32. See also Arsenault, *Freedom Riders*.

12. Carson, *In Struggle*, 31–32; Minutes of SNCC Meeting Baltimore, July 14–16, 1961, File 0790, and Minutes SNCC Meeting Louisville, June 9–11, 1961, Files 0792–0795, Reel 3, Series III, Staff Meetings, SNCC Papers; Robert Parris Moses, interview by Taylor Branch, March 13, 1988, Box 108, Folder 1, TBP, UNC (hereafter cited as Moses interview Branch, March 1988); Branch, *Parting the Waters*, 486.

13. Payne, *I've Got the Light*, 112–13; Moses interview Dittmer, 1983; C. C. Bryant, interview by Jimmy Dykes, November 11, 1995, MOHP, USM; Cass, "The Moses Factor."

14. Payne, *I've Got the Light*, 112–13; Cagin and Dray, *We Are Not Afraid*, 14; Dittmer, *Local People*, 100; Moses and Cobb, *Radical Equations*, 24; Cobb, *The Most Southern Place*, 141.

15. Moses, 2010 and March 2011; Moses interview Dittmer, 1983; Stoper, *Student Nonviolent Coordinating Committee*, 188; Branch, *Parting the Waters*, 486; Moses interview Branch, July 30, 1984; Moses interviews Romaine.

16. "SNCC Office Report," File 0304, Reel 3, Series II, Executive and Central Committee Files, and Minutes of SNCC Meeting Baltimore, July 14–16, 1961, Files 0792–0795, Reel 3, Series III, Staff Meetings, SNCC Papers; Burner, *And Gently*, 38–39; Moses interview Carson, 1982; Moses to Wyatt T. Walker, August 3, 1961, Box 108, Folder 3, TBP, UNC; Ed King to Wyatt T. Walker, July 24, 1961, and August 28, 1961, Files 00316–00317, and Walker to SNCC, July 11, 1961,

File 00314, Reel 4, Part 2, Series III, Wyatt T. Walker Correspondence, Records SCLC.

17. Moses and Bryant, "Comments," 1983; Payne, *I've Got the Light*, 115; Moses and Cobb, *Radical Equations*, 45; Dittmer, *Local People*, 100–4; Moses interview Dittmer, 1983.

18. Dittmer, *Local People*, 104; Beito and Beito, *Black Maverick*, xi, xiv–xv.

19. Lynd, "Mississippi: 1961–1962," 7–17*; Payne, *I've Got the Light*, 115; Moses and Cobb, *Radical Equations*, 46; Dittmer, *Local People*, 70–71, 105; Cagin and Dray, *We Are Not Afraid*, 141; Moses interview Branch, July 30, 1984; Moses interview by Blackside, Inc., May 19, 1986, for *Eyes on the Prize* (hereafter cited as Moses interview *Eyes on the Prize*, 1986). *Lynds's article is a transcript of Howard Zinn's interview with Moses of June 20, 1962 (Box 2, Folder 10, HZP, SHSW).

20. Hogan, *Many Minds*, 50–51; Moses interviews Romaine; Notes Taylor Branch, March 13, 1988, Box 108, Folder 1, TBP, UNC; Hammerback and Jensen, "Working in 'Quiet Places,'" 6; Moses, 2010.

21. Dorie Ladner interview author, November 16, 2009 (hereafter cited as Ladner interview author, 2009); Luvaughn Brown, interview by author, January 13, 2011 (hereafter cited as Brown interview author, 2011); Payne, *I've Got the Light*, 118–19; Hollis Watkins, interview by Robert Wright, August 5, 1968, RBC, HU (hereafter cited as Watkins interview Wright, 1968, HU); Cobb, *On the Road to Freedom*, 283; Branch, *Parting the Waters*, 493; Hollis Watkins, interview by John Rachal, October 1996, MOHP, USM (hereafter cited as Watkins interview Rachal, 1996, MOHP, USM).

22. Hollis Watkins, interview by Blackside, Inc., November 9, 1985, for *Eyes on the Prize* (hereafter cited as Watkins interview *Eyes on the Prize*, 1985); Gitlin, *The Sixties*, 148; Marion Barry, interview by Howard Zinn, December 18, 1965, Box 3, Folder 10, HZP, SHSW (hereafter cited as Barry interview Zinn, 1965, HZP, SHSW); Moses interview Dittmer, 1983.

23. Branch, *Parting the Waters*, 493; Cobb, *On the Road to Freedom*, 285; Watkins interview Rachal, 1996, MOHP, USM.

24. Branch, *Parting the Waters*, 493–94; Dittmer, *Local People*, 105; Zinn, *SNCC*, 67, 77; Moses interview Dittmer, 1983; Lynd, "Mississippi: 1961–1962," 8.

25. Branch, *Parting the Waters*, 494–95; Moses interview Branch, July 30, 1984; Moses and Cobb, *Radical Equations*, 47–48, 58; Tom Hayden, *Revolution in Mississippi*, pamphlet, January, 1962, USM; Field Report Bob Moses, no date, qt. in Forman, *Making of Black Revolutionaries*, 226–27.

26. Hayden, *Revolution in Mississippi*, USM; Moses and Cobb, *Radical Equations*, 47–48, 58; Doar and Landsberg, "The Performance of the FBI"; Moses interview Branch, July 30, 1984; Lynd, "Mississippi: 1961–1962," 9–10; Burner, *And Gently*, 46–47; Hammerback and Jensen, "Calling Washington Collect," 139–40; Payne, *I've Got the Light*, 117–18, 123; John Emmerich, "New York Negro Refuses to Pay $5 Court Costs," *MCEJ*, August 16, 1961.

27. Moses and Cobb, *Radical Equations*, 48; "Negro Plans Appeal" and "Southern 'Dynamite' John Oliver Emmerich," *NYT*, August 25, 1961, and December 4,

1961; John Emmerich, "New York Negro Refuses to Pay," and "Jailed Negro Pays Fine, Continues Voter School," *MCEJ*, August 16 and 18, 1961; A. L. Hopkins, "Robert Moses, Colored Male," report, April 19, 1962, MSSC Online.

28. Branch, *Parting the Waters*, 496; Carson, *In Struggle*, 50.

29. Moses interview Dittmer, 1983; Cagin and Dray, *We Are Not Afraid*, 145; Moses and Cobb, *Radical Equations*, 52; Watkins interview Rachal, 1996, MOHP, USM; Dittmer, *Local People*, 85; Bob Moses to Jack Young, August 18, 1961, File 0558, Reel 42, Series XVII, Other Organizations, SNCC Papers.

30. Dittmer, *Local People*, 105–6; Moses and Cobb, *Radical Equations*, 49; Payne, *I've Got the Light*, 113–14; Branch, *Parting the Waters*, 494–96; Eldridge W. Steptoe Jr., interview by Jimmy Dykes, November 14, 1995, MOHP, USM (hereafter cited as Steptoe Jr. interview Dykes, 1995, MOHP, USM).

31. Dittmer, *Local People*, 105–6; Payne, *I've Got the Light*, 113–14; Moses interview Branch, July 30, 1984; Lynd, "Mississippi: 1961–1962," 10; Moses, 2010; Moses to Forman, October 2, 1961, File 1348, Reel 69, Appendix A: MFDP Papers, SNCC Papers.

32. An FBI report and a field report written by Moses confirm this, although in *Radical Equations*, Moses mentioned that the beating started without a word and all three whites participated ("Statements Moses to FBI," report, September 9, 1961, Box 108, Folder 2, TBP, UNC; Moses and Cobb, *Radical Equations*, 26; Moses Field Report, no date, qt. in Forman, *Making of Black Revolutionaries*, 223–24).

33. Moses and Cobb, *Radical Equations*, 26; Forman, *Making of Black Revolutionaries*, 223–24; Lassiter and Crespino, *Myth of Southern Exceptionalism*, 127; Branch, *Parting the Waters*, 497–98; Moses interviews Branch, July 30, 1984, and March 13, 1988; Notes Branch, 1999, TBP, UNC.

34. Branch, *Parting the Waters*, 500; Gitlin, *The Sixties*, 148; Hammerback and Jensen, "Working in 'Quiet Places,'" 7.

35. Hogan, *Many Minds*, 82; Sullivan, 86–87.

36. Moses and Cobb, *Radical Equations*, 55; *Freedom on My Mind*, 1994.

37. Lynd, "Mississippi: 1961–1962," 10; Newfield, *A Prophetic Minority*, 76; Branch, *Parting the Waters*, 498–99; Affidavit Robert Parris Moses, September 27, 1961, File 0186, Reel 40, Series XV, State Project Files, SNCC Papers; C. L. McGowan to Mr. Rosen, September 28, 1961, Box 106, TBP, UNC; Moses interview Branch, July 30, 1984; Burner, *And Gently*, 52; Hayden, *Revolution in Mississippi*, 11–12, USM.

38. Branch, *Parting the Waters*, 498–99.

39. Ibid.; Forman, *Making of Black Revolutionaries*, 229; Claude Sitton, "Negro Vote Drive in Mississippi Is Set Back as Violence Erupts," *NYT*, October 24, 1961.

40. Doar and Landsberg, "The Performance of the FBI"; Burke Marshall to FBI Director, September 1, 1961, and "Statements Moses to FBI," September 9, 1961, and FBI Director to local SAC, September 5, 1961, Box 106 and Box 108, Folder 3, TBP, UNC; Hammerback and Jensen, "Calling Washington Collect," 141–42; Moses and Cobb, *Radical Equations*, 26.

41. SNCC first recommended the library but watchful personnel closed it down. Hollis Watkins said that they "were told" to go there by SNCC's direction wing (Watkins interview Wright, 1968, HU).

42. Dittmer, *Local People*, 106–8; Payne, *I've Got the Light*, 119–20; Moses and Cobb, *Radical Equations*, 52–53; Lynd, "Mississippi: 1961–1962," 10–11; Moses interview Carson, 1982; Moses interview Branch, July 30, 1984; Cagin and Dray, *We Are Not Afraid*, 151.

43. Dittmer, *Local People*, 106–8; Moses and Cobb, *Radical Equations*, 52–53; Moses interview Dittmer, 1983.

44. Forman, *Making of Black Revolutionaries*, 229–30; Travis Britt, Affidavit, File 0191, no date, Reel 40, Series XV, State Project Files, SNCC Papers; Fred Halstead, "Trying to Vote in the Delta Takes Nerve," February 26, 1962, private collection Joan Mulholland; Doar and Landsberg, "The Performance of the FBI."

45. Forman, *Making of Black Revolutionaries*, 228, 230–31; Lynd, "Mississippi: 1961–1962," 11–12; John Hardy, "Racist Violence Increasing as Students Push Civil Rights Effort in South," *New University News*, 1962.

46. Doar and Landsberg, "The Performance of the FBI"; Claude Sitton, "Negro Vote Drive in Mississippi Is Set Back," and Anthony Lewis, "Negro Vote Drive Wins a Court Test," *NYT*, October 24 and 30, 1961; "U.S. Seeks to Curb Vote Interference," *Afro*, September 26, 1961; " 'Bobby' Moves Against Walthall Vote Officials," *CL*, September 21, 1961; Branch, *Parting the Waters*, 507–8.

47. Forman, *Making of Black Revolutionaries*, 230–31; Doar, "The Work of the Civil Rights Division," 4; O'Reilly, *"Racial Matters,"* 68; Branch, *Parting the Waters*, 509; Hammerback and Jensen, "Calling Washington Collect," 141–42.

48. SAC New Orleans to Director FBI, November 24, 1961, and A. Rosen to Mr. McGowan, November 30, 1961, and SA to SAC, New Orleans, November 22, 1961, and C. L. McGowan to Mr. Rosen, September 28, 1961, Box 106, TBP, UNC; Moses interview Branch, August 11, 1983.

49. Moses to FBI from Pike County Jail, November 6, 1961, Box 106, TBP, UNC; Moses interview Branch, July 30, 1984.

50. Branch, *Parting the Waters*, 510; Payne, *I've Got the Light*, 121–23; FBI report, October 2, 1961, Box 106, TBP, UNC; Fred Halstead, "Trying to Vote in the Delta Takes Nerve . . . Interview with Travis Britt," February 26, 1962, private collection Joan Mulholland.

51. *Freedom on My Mind*, 1994; Steptoe Jr. interview Dykes, 1995, MOHP, USM; Moses and Cobb, *Radical Equations*, 50.

52. *Freedom on My Mind*, 1994; Steptoe Jr. interview Dykes, 1995, MOHP, USM; Moses and Cobb, *Radical Equations*, 50; "Mississippi Negro Witnessed Slaying," SNCC newsletter, February 2, 1964, File 0096, Reel 14, Series VII Communications Department, Public Relations, SNCC Papers.

53. Branch, *Parting the Waters*, 510–11, 520–22; A. L. Hopkins, "Conference with Sheriff E. L. Caston, Amite County, Attorney T. F. Badon, and District Attorney regarding the death of Herbert Lee," September 26, 1961, MSSC Online; Doar, "The Work of the Civil Rights Division," 6–7.

54. Doar, "The Work of the Civil Rights Division," 6–7; Moses interview Branch, August 11, 1983.

55. Newsletter SCEF, August 9, 1962, private collection Joan Mulholland.

56. Moses included the story in *Radical Equations* (p. 50), but he denied remembering the event in his July 30, 1984, interview with Taylor Branch. This raises important questions regarding the value of oral history, in terms of the accuracy of memory, and regarding SNCC's abilities to shape its own history.

57. Fred Halstead, "A Man Is Killed in Cold Blood," March 5, 1962, private collection Joan Mulholland; Branch, *Parting the Waters*, 510; McDew interview Shannon, 1967, HU; Phil Alden Robinson, interview by author, April 30, 2010 (hereafter cited as Robinson interview author, 2010).

58. Moses speech West Coast Civil Rights Conference, 1964; Payne, *I've Got the Light*, 121; E. W. Steptoe to Roy Wilkins, no date, Reel 10, Group III, Box C-73, Part 27, Records NAACP.

59. Payne, *I've Got the Light*, 121; Moses interview *Eyes on the Prize*, 1986; McDew interview Shannon, 1967, HU; Lynd, "Mississippi: 1961–1962," 12–13; Robert Parris Moses, "Another Man Done Gone," *The Informer*, no date, WHP*, SHSW; Gloster Current, request, no date, Reel 10, Group III, Box C-73, Part 27, Records NAACP. *William Heath kindly let me research his papers at his home in 2008. They have since been moved to the State Historical Society Wisconsin and recatalogued. It is therefore impossible to record box and folder numbers as they are no longer up to date.

60. Robinson interview author, 2010; Moses and Cobb, *Radical Equations*, 18, 56; Payne, *I've Got the Light*, 128–29; Moses interview Payne, 1993; Brown interview author, 2011.

61. King, *Freedom Song*, 146, 150; Newfield, *A Prophetic Minority*, 81; Bond interview author, 2008; Moses speech West Coast Civil Rights Conference, 1964; Branch qt. in Cass, "The Moses Factor"; *Freedom on My Mind*, 1994.

62. *Freedom on My Mind*, 1994; Moses interview Branch, July 30, 1984; Moses and Cobb, *Radical Equations*, 51; Russell, *Black Genius*, 331; Blake, *Children of the Movement*, 43–44.

63. Lynd, "Mississippi: 1961–1962," 13–14; Branch, *Parting the Waters*, 511; Dittmer, *Local People*, 112; Evers-Williams and Manning, *Autobiography of Medgar Evers*, 238. Wilkins qtd. in Dittmer, 112.

64. Branch, *Parting the Waters*, 511–12; Moses and Cobb, *Radical Equations*, 51–53; Robinson interview author, 2010; Zellner, *Wrong Side of Murder Creek*, 151–52.

65. The reunion was organized for the movie *Freedom Song* between June 27 and 30, 1991. Moses, who read several drafts of the script, had advised director Phil Alden Robinson to make the movie about the McComb locals rather than him. Instead of creating a Hollywood production, he asked Robinson to "sign onto our process" by letting locals "tell what happened and go with that." With some exceptions, all locals and SNCC workers that played a role in the 1961 events attended. To make sure no one profited from the movie, Robinson and Moses organized the Mississippi Community Foundation to which the locals signed off their story rights, and the studios in turn paid the foundation. Nonetheless, the

purist Moses insisted that the movie was set in a fictional town, because he could not guarantee who accurately had said or done what in 1961 (Robinson interview author, 2010).

66. Robinson interview author, 2010; Moses interview Carson, 1982; *Freedom Song* reunion, transcripts; Hayden, *Revolution in Mississippi*, 17, pamphlet, USM; Dittmer, *Local People*, 110.

67. Dittmer, *Local People*, 110; Moses interview Dittmer, 1983; McDew interview Shannon, 1967, HU; Stoper, *Student Nonviolent Coordinating Committee*, 191.

68. Dittmer, *Local People*, 110; Moses interview Dittmer, 1983; McDew interview Shannon, 1967, HU; Stoper, *Student Nonviolent Coordinating Committee*, 191; Moses interview Branch, July 30, 1984; Branch, *Parting the Waters*, 512–13; Zellner, *Wrong Side of Murder Creek*, 157, 160–61.

69. "114 Students Arrested," "Hard-Core Segregationist City in Mississippi Is Nearing Crisis," and "Negro Vote Drive Is Set Back as Violence Erupts," *NYT*, October 5, 21, and 24, 1961; "McComb Police Jail Racial Marchers," *MCEJ* October 5, 1961, private collection Joan Mulholland; "Jail 114 in Mississippi Who Protested Race Segregation," *Jet*, October 19, 1961; A. L. Hopkins, "Investigation of Negro Student Demonstrators," report, October 20, 1961, and "Robert Moses, Colored Male," report, April 19, 1962, MSSC Online.

70. Cagin and Dray, *We Are Not Afraid*, 157; Dittmer, *Local People*, 111–12; Branch, *Parting the Waters*, 513–14; Cobb, *On the Road to Freedom*, 286–87.

71. Zellner, *Wrong Side of Murder Creek*, 163–67; McDew interview Shannon, 1967, HU; Lynd, "Mississippi: 1961–1962," 14; Stoper, *Student Nonviolent Coordinating Committee*, 40, 192.

72. McDew interview Shannon, 1967, HU; Stoper, *Student Nonviolent Coordinating Committee*, 40, 192; Director FBI to Burke Marshall, October 5, 1961, Box 106, TBP, UNC; Branch, *Parting the Waters*, 513.

73. McDew interview Shannon, 1967, HU; Lynd, "Mississippi: 1961–1962," 14; Moses interview Branch, July 30, 1984; News Release, May 21, 1962, Files 0007–0008, Reel 13, Series VII, Communications Department, Public Relations, SNCC Papers.

74. McDew interview Shannon, 1967, HU; Branch, *Parting the Waters*, 514, 518–19; Forman, *Making of Black Revolutionaries*, 234–35.

75. Branch, *Parting the Waters*, 514, 518–19; Forman, *Making of Black Revolutionaries*, 234–35.

76. Forman, *Making of Black Revolutionaries*, 232; "McComb, Mississippi," File 0891, Reel 22, Series VIII, Research Department, SNCC Papers; Parents Burgland students to Board of Education, October 13, 1961, and statement Burgland Students, WHP, SHSW; Lynd and Lynd, *Nonviolence in America*, 246.

77. "2 Beaten in Mississippi," and Claude Sitton, "Hard-Core Segregationist City in Mississippi Is Nearing Crisis," *NYT*, October 12 and 21, 1961; "Workman Claims Newsman Cursed," "Man Brags 'We Stole the Film,'" and "McComb Victims Ask Aid," *Jackson State Times*, October 12 and 13, 1961; "Pray, Walk, Fight," *Newsweek*, October 23, 1961.

78. Lynd, "Mississippi: 1961–1962," 14; Dittmer, *Local People*, 112–13; Payne, *I've Got the Light*, 125; Branch, *Parting the Waters*, 521–22; "'Non-Violent' Building

Condemned in McComb," *Jackson State Times*, October 21, 1961; A. L. Hopkins, "Robert Moses, Colored Male," report, April 19, 1962, MSSC Online.

79. "Brenda Travis Denied Visitors," *The Liberator* 1, no. 2 (November 17, 1961): 1, private collection Joan Mulholland; Charles McDew to Wyatt T. Walker, January 5, 1962, File 0448, Reel 9, Series IV, Ex. Sec. Files James Forman, SNCC Papers; Travis Britt, interview by James Mosby, September 24, 1968, RBC, HU.

80. "McComb Negroes Unable to Think for Themselves" and Bob Moses, "Letter from Magnolia Jail," *The Liberator* 1, no. 2 (November 17, 1961): 3–4, private collection Joan Mulholland; Dittmer, *Local People*, 111, 113; Zellner, *Wrong Side of Murder Creek*, 170; Cagin and Dray, *We Are Not Afraid*, 160; Phil Curry, Oberlin McComb Committee, to SNCC, November 10, 1961, File 0765, Reel 5, Series IV, Ex. Sec. Files James Forman, SNCC Papers; Payne, *I've Got the Light*, 126.

81. Dittmer, *Local People*, 113; Moses, "Letter from Magnolia Jail"; Lynd, "Mississippi: 1961–1962," 14; Forman to Moses, November 20, 1961, File 1148, Reel 69, Appendix A: MFDP Papers, and "Fact Report 1961–1962," File 0500, Reel 8, Series IV, Ex. Sec. Files James Forman, SNCC Papers; Moses interview Carson, 1982.

82. Branch, *Parting the Waters*, 500; Carson, *In Struggle*, 78, 140; *Freedom on My Mind*, 1994; Halberstam, *The Children*, 403; Marsh, *God's Long Summer*, 46; King, *Freedom Song*, 469; Forman, *Making of Black Revolutionaries*, 233.

83. Marsh, *God's Long Summer*, 10; Hammerback and Jensen, "Calling Washington Collect," 136; Zinn, *SNCC*, 228; Stoper, *Student Nonviolent Coordinating Committee*, 19–20, 258; Davis, "'Sisters and Brothers All,'" 57n.

84. On May 21–22, 1962, the thirteen appealed their convictions for the October march. At the hearing, Moses pronounced a keen understanding of the stakes. "We are not in Mississippi fighting for civil rights as such, but for those civil liberties that provide an alternative to an armed struggle." They were nonetheless all found guilty. But in 1965, the Mississippi Supreme Court overturned his conviction despite "the contempt which many may have for Moses," since he was not "guilty of violent, loud, offensive or boisterous conduct" but rather had behaved like "a hen mothering her brood." (News Release, May 21, 1962, File 0008–0009, Reel 14, Series VII Communications Department, Public Relations, and Bob Moses to Mr. Benenson, May 15, 1962, File 0378, Reel 5, Series IV, Ex. Sec. Files James Forman, SNCC Papers; "Pike Court Opens 19 'Rider' Appeal Trials," "Second Leader of SNCC Is on Trial in Magnolia," *MCEJ*, May 21 and May 22, 1962; "SNCC Staffers Sentenced in Mississippi," June 1962, in Carson, *The Student Voice*; "Negro's Sentence Overruled in McComb Demonstrations," and "Court Throws Out Moses's Conviction," *CL*, October 12, 1965.)

85. Jack Young to SNCC, November 14, 1961, File 0097, Reel 10, and SCEF to SNCC, November–December 1961 and June 30, 1962, Files 0503, 0510, and 0593, Reel 9, Series IV, Ex. Sec. Files James Forman, and Newsletter SNCC, December 6, 1961, File 1070–1071, Reel 13, Series IV, Communications Department, Public Relations, SNCC Papers; Woods, *Black Struggle*, 201–2; Dittmer, *Local People*, 114; Branch, *Parting the Waters*, 559–60; Zinn, *SNCC*, 77.

86. Dittmer, *Local People*, 112; Moses interviews Romaine; Moses interview Carson, 1982; Moses interview Dittmer, 1983; "NAACP Invites JFK, Brother to Visit

State," *State Times*, October 11, 1961; Medgar Evers to Roy Wilkins et al., October 12, 1961, and Evers to Alfred Baker Lewis, February 1, 1962, qt. in Evers-Williams and Manning, *Autobiography of Medgar Evers*, 235–39, 243–44; Medgar Evers report, October 31, 1961, Reel 10, Group II, Box C-75, Part 27, Records NAACP.

87. Moses interview Carson, 1982; Moses interviews Romaine. Moses and Bryant, "Comments," 1983; *Freedom on My Mind*, 1994; Hammerback and Jensen, "Calling Washington Collect," 136; Moses interviews Branch, July 30, 1984, and February 15, 1991, TBP, UNC; Carson, *In Struggle*, 54.

88. Moses and Cobb, *Radical Equations*, 45–46, 55–56; Hammerback and Jensen, "'Your Tools Are Really the People,'" 134; Andrew Johnson to Gloster Current, April 22, 1964, Group III, Box C-74, Part 27, Records NAACP; Lynd, "Mississippi: 1961–1962," 14–15.

89. MFDP orientation, KZSU Project South, 1965, LC; Unita Blackwell, interview by Robert Wright, August 10, 1968, HU (hereafter cited as Blackwell interview Wright, 1968, HU); Wilkins to Evers, December 21, 1955, qt. in Evers-Williams and Manning, *Autobiography of Medgar Evers*, 43–44; Beito and Beito, *Black Maverick*, 146.

90. Moses and Cobb, *Radical Equations*, 55; Moses and Bryant, "Comments," 1983; Henry and Curry, *Aaron Henry*, 11.

91. Carson, *In Struggle*, 5, 50–51, 69–71; Murphree, *The Selling of Civil Rights*, 30; Rothschild, "Northern Volunteers," 16; Carmichael and Thelwell, *Ready for Revolution*, 301–2.

92. Murphree, *The Selling of Civil Rights*, 30, 39, 43–45, 51; Forman, *Making of Black Revolutionaries*, 271; Stoper, *Student Nonviolent Coordinating Committee*, 96; Hogan, *Many Minds*, 65.

93. Moses, 2010; Branch, *Parting the Waters*, 519; Greenberg, *Circle of Trust*, 48; Agger, *The Sixties at 40*, 184.

94. Moses interviews Romaine; Carmichael and Thelwell, *Ready for Revolution*, 241–42, 310.

95. Moses interview Payne, 1993; Moses and Bryant, "Comments," 1983; Moses, 2010.

96. Moses interviews Romaine; Dittmer, *Local People*, 114; Stoper, *Student Nonviolent Coordinating Committee*, 195; Burner, *And Gently*, 69.

Chapter Four

1. Moses, "Questions Raised by Moses," April, 1965, qt. in Bond and Lewis, *Gonna Sit at the Welcome Table*, 722–24; "Freedom Summer Planned in Miss.," Special Issue (Spring 1964), in Carson, *The Student Voice*, 133, 135.

2. Moses interview author, March 10, 2011.

3. Gaither and Moses, "Voter Registration—A Projected Program," January 27, 1962, Box 6, EBP, SCRBC; Payne, *I've Got the Light*, 129–30.

4. Cobb, *On the Road to Freedom*, 290; Moses and Cobb, *Radical Equations*, 56–57; Dittmer, *Local People*, 116–18, 123; Moses interview Dittmer, 1983; Moses interviews

Romaine; Moses interview Payne, 1993; Moses interview Branch, July 30, 1984; Moses interview Carson, 1982.

5. Moses interview Dittmer, 1983; Moses interviews Romaine; Moses interview Payne, 1993; Moses interview Branch, July 30, 1984; Moses interview Carson, 1982.

6. Carson, *In Struggle*, 56–65; Branch, *Parting the Waters*, 524–61; Charles Sherrod, interview by author, April 16, 2010; Charles Sherrod, interview by Blackside, Inc., December 20, 1985, for *Eyes on the Prize* (hereafter cited as Sherrod interview *Eyes on the Prize*, 1985); Bill Hansen to SNCC, July 1962, and SNCC Staff Meeting, minutes, June 3, 1962 (private collection Adam Fairclough); Garrow, *Bearing the Cross*, 173–219.

7. Carson, *In Struggle*, 56–65; Branch, *Parting the Waters*, 524–61; Bill Hansen to SNCC, July 1962, and SNCC Staff Meeting, minutes, June 3, 1962 (private collection Adam Fairclough); Garrow, *Bearing the Cross*, 173–219.

8. Sherrod and Moses frequently talked one on one, and "there was always cross-currents of thoughts." The Albany SNCC office's front door even featured a poster of Moses (Sherrod interview author, 2010; Holsaert, "Resistance U," 185).

9. Moses interviews Romaine; Barry interviewd Zinn, 1965, HZP, SHSW; Moses interview Branch, July 30, 1984; Moses interview Carson, 1982.

10. Polletta, "Strategy and Identity," 115; Watters and Cleghorn, *Climbing Jacob's Ladder*, 29, 44–50.

11. Rothschild, "Northern Volunteers," 17; Moses interview Branch, March 13, 1988; Moses interview Carson, 1982; Moses and Cobb, *Radical Equations*, 55; Moses interview Payne, 1993; Moses interview Chafe, 1989; Moses interview Dittmer, 1983.

12. Unknown to Moses, COFO already existed: it was founded in May 1961 as an ad hoc group of local blacks to negotiate the Freedom Riders' release from Parchman with Governor Ross Barnett. Barnett had refused to meet NAACP officials, so Henry and Evers tricked him by going as COFO (Moses interviews Romaine).

13. William Higgs, interview by Howard Zinn, December 19, 1965, Box 3, Folder 10, HZP, SHSW (hereafter cited as Higgs interview Zinn, 1965, HZP, SHSW); Stoper, *Student Nonviolent Coordinating Committee*, 199–200; Dennis interview author, 2010; Rothschild, "Northern Volunteers," 17; Evers-Williams and Manning, *Autobiography of Medgar Evers*, 88–89.

14. Forman, *Making of Black Revolutionaries*, 266–69; Lewis and D'Orso, *Walking with the Wind*, 186–87; Moses interview Branch, 1983; Cagin and Dray, *We Are Not Afraid*, 180; Meier and Rudwick, *CORE*, 8, 10, 18; Stoper, *Student Nonviolent Coordinating Committee*, 69–70; Dennis interview author, 2010.

15. Stoper, *Student Nonviolent Coordinating Committee*, 61; Henry and Curry, *Aaron Henry*, 108–9, 115; Dittmer, *Local People*, 118–19; "Mississippi: Structure of the Movement," no date, File 0048, Reel 6, Series IV, Ex. Sec. Files James Forman, SNCC Papers; King, *Freedom Song*, 309.

16. Dittmer, *Local People*, 118–19; Cobb, *On the Road to Freedom*, 267; Moses interview Payne, 1993; Greenberg, *Circle of Trust*, 63; Aaron Henry, interview by Robert Wright, September 25, 1968, and Baker interview Britton, 1968, RBC, HU; Moses interview Carson, 1982.

17. Moses to Moore, February 7, 1962, Box 1, Folder 2, AMP, SHSW; Carsie Hall to COFO, February 5, 1962, and "First Draft of Report to Council of Federated Organizations," no date, and "Report to Council of Federated Organizations," February 18, 1962, and "Mississippi: Structure of the Movement," no date, Files 0016A, 0033–0034A, 0017–18, and 0048, Reel 6, Series IV, Ex. Sec. Files James Forman, SNCC Papers.

18. Payne, *I've Got the Light*, 152; Moses interview Branch, March 13, 1988; Burner, *And Gently*, 67; Moses interview Carson, 1982; Branch, *Parting the Waters*, 560; Cagin and Dray, *We Are Not Afraid*, 174, 180; Branch, *Pillar of Fire*, 55; Moses and Cobb, *Radical Equations*, 57, 66.

19. Moses and Cobb, *Radical Equations*, 71; Marion Barry, Bill Higgs, and R. L. T. Smith, interviews by Howard Zinn, December 18, 19, and 30, 1965, Box 3, Folder 10, HZP, SHSW; R. L. T. Smith, interview by Robert Wright, July 10, 1969, RBC, HU; "Negro to Run in Primary for Congress," *CL*, December 17, 1961. When Trammell died of a heart attack, Bevel worked for his replacement, Rev. Merrill Lindsay.

20. Marion Barry, Bill Higgs, and R. L. T. Smith, interviews by Howard Zinn, December 18, 19, and 30, 1965, Box 3, Folder 10, HZP, SHSW; Moses to Smith, no date, File 0328, Reel Series IV, Ex. Sec. Files James Forman, SNCC Papers; Forman, *Making of Black Revolutionaries*, 263; Moses, 2010; Moses interview Dittmer, 1983; Cagin and Dray, *We Are Not Afraid*, 174; Higgs interview Zinn, 1965, HZP, SHSW; "Recent Progress of the Jackson Nonviolent Movement," no date, Box 6, EBP, SCRBC.

21. Crosby, *A Little Taste of Freedom*, 79; Burner, *And Gently*, 67–68.

22. Moses to Smith, no date, File 0328, Reel Series IV, Ex. Sec. Files James Forman, SNCC Papers; Moses interviews Romaine.

23. Moses to Interested Friends and Foundations, no date, JFP, LC.

24. James Forman and Tim Jenkins, interviews by Howard Zinn, November 12 and December 18, 1965, Box 3, Folder 10, HZP, SHSW; Forman, *Making of Black Revolutionaries*, 238; Moses to Interested Friends and Foundations, no date, JFP, LC.

25. Moses, Address at 75th Birthday Celebration, 1978; Hammerback and Jensen, "Your Tools Are Really the People," 131–32.

26. Ivanhoe Donaldson, interview by Anne Romaine, March 23, 1967, ARP, UNC; Payne, *I've Got the Light*, 128–29; Moses and Cobb, *Radical Equations*, 57.

27. "Supp. Material from SNCC Exec. Meeting, Nov. 1963," Box 2, Folder 21, HZP, SHSW; Moses interview Branch, 1999.

28. Moses, 2010; Ladner interview author, 2010; Brown interview author, 2011.

29. Moses to John Fisher, May 12, 1962, File 0870, Reel 6, Series IV, Ex. Sec. Files James Forman, SNCC Papers; SNCC Meeting, minutes, June 1–2, 1962, File 0812–0813, Reel 11, Series V, SNCC Conferences, and Moses to Smith, no date, File 0328, Reel 9, and Moses to Workers in the VEP, no date, File 1010, Reel 10, Series IV, Ex. Sec. Files James Forman, SNCC Papers; Branch, *Pillar of Fire*, 55; Dittmer, *Local People*, 124; Branch, *Parting the Waters*, 634; Stoper, *Student Nonviolent Coordinating Committee*, 11.

30. Branch, *Parting the Waters*, 518, 634; Burner, *And Gently*, 90, 207; Jim Dombrowski to Frank Laubach, March 12, 1962, Box 1, Folder 2, AMP, SHSW; Moses to Guido Goldman, October 22, 1962, File 0662, Reel 6, Series IV, Ex. Sec. Files James Forman, SNCC Papers; Moses to Governing Board of the Miss Adult Education Program, 1962, Box 14, CORE Records, SHSW.

31. Payne, *I've Got The Light*, 142–44; Moses to Myles Horton, May 15, 1962, File 0928, and Horton to Moses, no date, File 0931, Reel 6, Series IV, Ex. Sec. Files James Forman, SNCC Papers; Moses to Horton, August 13, 1962, October 10, 1962, and Horton to Moses, no date, November 15, 1962, and Moses to A. D. Beittel, May 29, 1962, Box 21, HRECR, SHSW; Moses interview Payne, 1993.

32. Anne Braden to Wiley Branton, September 23, 1962, Files 0671–0677, Reel 5, Series IV, Ex. Sec. Files James Forman, SNCC Papers.

33. "Braden, Accused as Red, Reported Active in State," *CL*, September 1, 1962; "Secret Communist Document Is Bared," *JDN*, August 31, 1962; Woods, *Black Struggle*, 157–59; Carl Braden to Jim Dombrowski and John Coe, September 2, 1962, and Carl Braden to Bill Higgs and Moses, September 7, 1962, Box 55, Folder 13, CABP, SHSW.

34. Anne Braden to Moses, September 25, 1963, and Carl Braden to Moses and Aaron Henry, September 12, 1962, and Moses to Carl Braden, October 8, 1962, Box 55, Folder 13, CABP, SHSW; Burner, *And Gently*, 140–41.

35. Woods, *Black Struggle*, 2–48, 95; Tom Scarborough, "Mt. Beulah or Southern Christian Institute, Edwards, Miss.," July 23, 1962, "Bolivar County—Aaron Henry and James Bevel," May 21, 22, and 23, 1962, "Leflore County—Samuel Block and Robert Moses," August 9–10, 1962, MSSC Online.

36. Woods, *Black Struggle*, 2–48, 85–111, 143–49.

37. Moses interview Branch, August 10, 1983.

38. Newfield, *A Prophetic Minority*, 81.

39. Birdia Keglar was a long-time activist. She opened her home to the SNCC workers but also initiated the first NAACP branch in Tallahatchie County in 1963. In 1966, she died in a car crash widely believed to have been caused by the KKK.

40. Bob Moses, untitled story for *The Southern Patriot*, February 1962, and editorial comments, Files 0884–0886, Reel 9, Series IV, Ex. Sec. Files James Forman, SNCC Papers.

41. Moses to John Fisher, May 12, 1962, File 0870, Reel 6, Series IV, Ex. Sec. Files James Forman, and SNCC Meeting, minutes, June 1-2, 1962, File 0812–0813, Reel 11, Series V, SNCC Conferences, and Moses to Larry Still, October 3, 1962, File 0979, Reel 12, Series VII, Communications Department, Public Relations, SNCC Papers.

42. Moses to Benenson, May 15, 1962, and no date, Files 0378 and 0491, Reel 5, and James Forman to Russell Lasley, May 9, 1962, File 0592, Reel 10, and Moses to Harry Belafonte, no date, File 0561, Reel 5, and Moses to Guido Goldman, October 22, 1962, File 0660, and Goldman to Moses, File 0662, Reel 6, unknown sender to Forman, June 11, 1962, File 0232, Reel 8, William Miller to Forman, July 20, 1962, File 0945, Reel 7, and Moses to Hermann Rottenberg, no date, File 1219, Reel 8, and Forman to Moses, June 11, 1962, File 0572, Reel 9, and "Report of Proceed-

ings Conference on Direct Action Training," File 0536, Reel 8, Series IV, Ex. Sec. Files James Forman, SNCC Papers.

43. Burner, *And Gently*, 75; "Registration Efforts in Mississippi Continue Despite Violence and Terror," *The Student Voice* 3, no. 3 (October 1962), in Carson, *The Student Voice*, 58; Murphree, *The Selling of Civil Rights*, 42; New Yorker to Moses, October 31, 1962, Files 1081–1082, Reel 11, Series VI, Bookkeeping Department, Financial Records, SNCC Papers.

44. Moses interview Carson, 1982; Hogan, *Many Minds*, 65; Moses interviews Romaine; Robert Parris Moses, interview by Joe Sinsheimer, December 5, 1984, Box 108, Folder 1, TBP, UNC (hereafter cited as Moses interview Sinsheimer, 1984, TBP, UNC); Forman to Lester McKinnie, February 26, 1962, File 0844, Reel 7, Series IV, Ex. Sec. Files James Forman, SNCC Papers; Agger, *The Sixties at 40*, 171, 184–85.

45. Hogan, *Many Minds*, 69; Hammerback and Jensen, "Working in 'Quiet Places,'" 10; Cagin and Dray, *We Are Not Afraid*, 321; Forman, *Making of Black Revolutionaries*, xii; Stoper, *Student Nonviolent Coordinating Committee*, 196; Georgia meeting, minutes, December 14, 1962, File 0110, Reel 6, Series IV, Ex. Sec. Files James Forman, SNCC Papers; Murphree, *The Selling of Civil Rights*, 23; Untitled SNCC Document, Box 6, EBP, SCRBC.

46. Branch, *Parting the Waters*, 635–36; Lee, *For Freedom's Sake*, 31; Moye, *Let the People Decide*, 92–97.

47. Charles Cobb, interview by John Rachal, October 21, 1996, MOHP, USM; King, *Freedom Song*, 130; Mosely, "A Reminiscence," 10–11; Marsh, *God's Long Summer*, 14.

48. Moses interview *Eyes on the Prize*, 1986; Lynd, "Mississippi: 1961–1962."

49. Sutherland-Martinez, *Letters from Mississippi*, 80–81; Payne, *I've Got the Light*, 243; Moye, *Let the People Decide*, 103; Moses and Cobb, *Radical Equations*, 68; Charles McLaurin, "Notes on Organizing," no date, Files 0053–0055, Reel 40, Series XV, State Project Files, SNCC Papers.

50. Hammerback and Jensen, "Calling Washington Collect," 144; Carson, *In Struggle*, 71; Dittmer, *Local People*, 120; Hogan, *Many Minds*, 79; Untitled SNCC Document, Box 6, EBP, SCRBC; Carson, *In Struggle*, 81; Lewis and D'Orso, *Walking with the Wind*, 187, 267; Forman, *Making of Black Revolutionaries*, 365; Dennis interview author, 2010.

51. Polletta, "Strategy and Identity," 117–18; "Ruleville," report by Charles McLaurin, August 18–31, 1962, Files 0954–0956, Reel Series IV, Ex. Sec. Files James Forman, SNCC Papers; Hollis Watkins and Charles Cobb, interviews by John Rachal, October 23, 29, and 30, 1996, and October 21, 1996, MOHP, USM; Greenberg, *Circle of Trust*, 122.

52. Watkins and Cobb interviews Rachal, 1996, MOHP, USM; Moses and Cobb, *Radical Equations*, 46; "Mississippi Voter Registration Test," in *Student Nonviolent Coordinating Committee 50th Anniversary*, Rubin, 58–59; Payne, *I've Got the Light*, 149; Branch, *Parting the Waters*, 634.

53. Moses speech West Coast Civil Rights Conference, 1964; Carmichael and Thelwell, *Ready for Revolution*, 109; Watters and Reese, *Climbing Jacob's Ladder*, 106; Sherrod interview *Eyes on the Prize*, 1985; Payne, *I've Got the Light*, 247–49.

54. Moye, *Let the People Decide*, 97–100; Lee, *For Freedom's Sake*, 25; *Freedom on My Mind*, 1994; Moses and Cobb, *Radical Equations*, 79–80.

55. Moye, *Let the People Decide*, 97–100; Lee, *For Freedom's Sake*, 25; Payne, *I've Got the Light*, 154; Robnett, *How Long? How Long?* 149.

56. Moses and Cobb, *Radical Equations*, 71, 81, 87; Moses, 2010.

57. Moses and Cobb, *Radical Equations*, 71, 81, 87; Moses, 2010; Payne, *I've Got the Light*, 259–61.

58. Moses and Cobb, *Radical Equations*, 71, 81, 87; Payne, *I've Got the Light*, 259–61; Lee, *For Freedom's Sake*, 25.

59. Payne, *I've Got the Light*, 259–63; Carmichael and Thelwell, *Ready for Revolution*, 292; Greenberg, *Circle of Trust*, 110–25, 190; Marsh, *God's Long Summer*, 26–27; Reagon, "Women as Culture Carriers," 401–2; Theodore Bikel, "We Shall Overcome," *Hootenanny*, January–February 1964, Files 0565–0568, Reel 5, Series IV, Ex. Sec. Files James Forman, SNCC Papers; Lassiter and Crespino, *The Myth of Southern Exceptionalism*, 127; Moye, *Let the People Decide*, 100.

60. Marsh, *God's Long Summer*, 25, 32, 163; Reagon, "Women as Culture Carriers," 401–2; Bikel, "We Shall Overcome," *Hootenanny*, January–February 1964; Carmichael and Thelwell, *Ready for Revolution*, 31, 93–94, 289–91; King, *Freedom Song*, 146; Newfield, *A Prophetic Minority*, 73.

61. Cagin and Dray, *We Are Not Afraid*, 179; Hammerback and Jensen, "Robert Parris Moses," 264; Greenberg, *Circle of Trust*, 77; Dennis interview author, 2010; Heather Tobis Booth, interview by author, November 2009.

62. Stoper, *Student Nonviolent Coordinating Committee*, 307.

63. Lynd, "Mississippi: 1961–1962"; Moye, *Let the People Decide*, 98–101; Lee, *For Freedom's Sake*, 27–37; Branch, *Parting the Waters*, 636–39; Burner, *And Gently*, 78, 80; *Freedom on My Mind*, 1994.

64. Moye, *Let the People Decide*, 98–101; Lee, *For Freedom's Sake*, 27–37; Branch, *Parting the Waters*, 636–39; Amzie Moore to SCEF, 1962, Box 55, Folder 13, CABP, SHSW; Marsh, *God's Long Summer*, 17.

65. News release, September 17, 1962, File 0146, Reel 10, Series IV, Ex. Sec. Files James Forman, SNCC Papers; Watters and Cleghorn, *Climbing Jacob's Ladder*, 139.

66. Moses and Cobb, "Shooting Incident in Ruleville," October 8, 1962, Files 00365–00371, and Cobb, "Report," 1962, Files 00372–00373, Reel 5, Part 4, Series I, Records of Andrew J. Young, Records SCLC; Lynd, "Mississippi: 1961–1962."

67. Lynd, "Mississippi: 1961–1962"; Burner, *And Gently*, 82–84; Branch, *Parting the Waters*, 638–39.

68. Burner, *And Gently*, 82–84; Branch, *Parting the Waters*, 638–39; Russell, *Black Genius*, 332; Joseph A. Loftus, "Kennedy Decries Church Burnings in Racial Dispute," and "Transcript of the President's News Conference on Foreign and Domestic Matters," *NYT*, September 14, 1962; Moye, *Let the People Decide*, 102–3.

69. Bond interview author, 2008.

70. Stoper, *Student Nonviolent Coordinating Committee*, 28; "SNCC Field Work in Mississippi," spring 1963, Files 0057–0058, Reel 10, Series IV, Ex. Sec. Files James Forman, SNCC Papers; "SNCC Field Work in Southwest Georgia," spring 1963, in *Student Nonviolent Coordinating Committee*, ed. Rubin, 38; Carson, *In Struggle*,

75–77; Hogan, *Many Minds*, 67–68, 151; Greenberg, *Circle of Trust*, 56; Bill Hansen to SNCC, June 26, July 6, July 23, and August 1, 1962, private collection Adam Fairclough; MFSR, 1979, Session 2, SHSW; King, *Freedom Song*, 71, 497, 505; Sherrod interview author, 2010.

71. Hogan, *Many Minds*, 74–75; Greenberg, *Circle of Trust*, 56; Murphree, *The Selling of Civil Rights*, 31; Untitled paper on Terrell County, no date, Box 1, Folder 13 and Report Guy Carawan, Box 2, Folder 9, HZP, SHSW; "NAG Plans May 17 Demonstrations in DC," *The Student Voice* 3, no. 1 (April 1962): 3, in Carson, *The Student Voice*, 51; King, *Freedom Song*, 158.

72. Lewis and D'Orso, *Walking with the Wind*, 60–61, 177; Branch, *Pillar of Fire*, 54; Branch, *Parting the Waters*, 480.

73. Brown interview author, 2011; Warren, *Who Speaks for the Negro?* 48–49; Hogan, *Many Minds*, 188; Carmichael and Thelwell, *Ready for Revolution*, 310–13; Hammerback and Jensen, "Your Tools Are Really the People," 126–40; Gitlin, *The Sixties*, 148; Halberstam, *The Children*, 402; Tom Scarborough, "Leflore County—Samuel Block and Robert Moses," August 14, 1962, MSSC Online; Payne, *I've Got the Light*, 333; Hammerback and Jensen, "Robert Parris Moses," 263.

74. Hogan, *Many Minds*, 42, 241; Carmichael and Thelwell, *Ready for Revolution*, 305; Moses and Cobb, *Radical Equations*, 32; Moses interview Payne, 1993; Bond interview author, 2008; Lawson, "Freedom Then," 469.

75. King, *Freedom Song*, 146; Warren, *Who Speaks for the Negro?* 48–49; Hogan, *Many Minds*, 188; Hammerback and Jensen, "Your Tools Are Really the People," 126–40; Gitlin, *The Sixties*, 148.

76. Mary King interview author, 2009; Moses and Cobb, *Radical Equations*, 40; James Atwater, "If We Can Crack Mississippi," *Saturday Evening Post*, July 2, 1964; Moses interview Payne, 1993.

77. Branch, *At Canaan's Edge*, 30; Mary King interview author, 2009.

78. Howard Zinn, interview, November 11, 1965, Box 3, Folder 10, HZP, SHSW; Moses interview Carson, 1982; Greenberg, *Circle of Trust*, 134, 185–86.

79. Zinn interview, 1965, HZP, SHSW; Dennis interview author, 2010; John Lewis, interview by author, November 16, 2009 (hereafter cited as Lewis interview author, 2009); Mary King interview author, 2009; Robert Wright, interview by John Britton, July 28, 1968, RBC, HU.

80. Sherrod interview *Eyes on the Prize*, 1985; Hogan, *Many Minds*, 60, 75, 79; Payne, *I've Got the Light*, 318, 335; Greenberg, *Circle of Trust*, 90; Polletta, "Strategy and Identity," 175; Sherrod interview author, 2010; "Southwest Georgia," 1963, File 1016, Reel 9, Series IV, Ex. Sec. Files James Forman, SNCC Papers; Carmichael and Thelwell, *Ready for Revolution*, 385–86; Murphree, *The Selling of Civil Rights*, 31; SNCC Staff Meeting, minutes, June 3, 1962, private collection Adam Fairclough.

81. "Southwest Georgia," 1963, File 1016, Reel 9, Series IV, Ex. Sec. Files James Forman, SNCC Papers; Hogan, *Many Minds*, 151; Greenberg, *Circle of Trust*, 137–38; Brown interviews author, 2011; Ladner interview author, 2009; Cobb interview Rachal, 1996, MOHP, USM; Meier and Rudwick, *CORE*, 394; Dave Dennis, interview by Blackside, Inc., November 10, 1985, for *Eyes on the Prize* (hereafter

cited as Dennis interview *Eyes on the Prize*, 1985); Cobb, "Organizing Freedom Schools," 134.

82. Payne, *I've Got the Light*, 334; *Freedom on My Mind*, 1994; Carmichael and Thelwell, *Ready for Revolution*, 313, 320–21; Hampton and Fayer, *Voices of Freedom*, 180.

83. Branch, *Pillar of Fire*, 68–69; Payne, *I've Got the Light*, 226, 240; June Johnson, "The Person Who Influenced Me Most," no date, WHP, SHSW.

84. Moses interviews Jay; Ladner interview author, 2009; Dennis interview author, 2010.

85. Payne, *I've Got the Light*, 227–28; Moses to Jay Stager, July 6, 1963, and Stager to Moses, no date, Files 1192 and 1347, Reel 69, and Moses to Professor Lonero, February 16, 1964, 0462, Reel 64, Appendix A: MFDP Papers, and Moses to Marian Wright and Jim Forman, no date, Files 0032–0033, Reel 6, Series IV, Ex. Sec. Files James Forman, SNCC Papers. Moses loaned $100 from SNCC for Hayes to get started in Chicago. Months after leaving McComb, SNCC workers tried to get Brenda Travis released from Oakley. Eventually, Ella Baker became her guardian. ("Getting Miss Brenda Travis out of a Mississippi jail," April 1962, File 1203, Reel 6, Series IV, Ex. Sec. Files James Forman, SNCC Papers; Charles B. Gordon, "White Teacher No Longer Has Custody on Negro Girl," *CL*, July 27, 1962; Dittmer, *Local People*, 171–73.)

86. Henry and Curry, *Aaron Henry*, 115; Barry interview Zinn, 1965, Box 3, Folder 10, HZP, SHSW; Ladner interview author, 2009; King, *Freedom Song*, 146; George Raymond, interview by Robert Wright, September 28, 1968, RBC, HU; Cass, "The Moses Factor."

87. Cagin and Dray, *We Are Not Afraid*, 147, 179; Burner, *And Gently*, 5, 15, 213; Anonymous White Male, interview KZSU Project South, 1965, LC; King, *Freedom Song*, 110, 162; Greenberg, *Circle of Trust*, x; Agger, *The Sixties at 40*, 92; Stoper, *Student Nonviolent Coordinating Committee*, 117; Cagin and Dray, *We Are Not Afraid*, 147; Carmichael and Thelwell, *Ready for Revolution*, 310–11.

88. Payne, *I've Got the Light*, 401–2.

89. Ladner interview author, 2009; Brown interview author, 2011; Robert E. Wright, interview by John Britton, July 22, 1968, and Douglas MacArthur Cotton, interview by Robert Wright, August 5, 1968, RBC, HU; Unita Blackwell, interviews by Michael Garvey, April 21 and May 12, 1977, MOHP, USM. The fact that workers with resources were present on a full-time basis was more important than whether they were outsiders, as one black said about local SNCC worker Lawrence Guyot. "We didn't know what a workshop was. So he taken us to a workshop [and that's really] what made me want to stay in the movement. I was understanding some of these things [movement people] was talking about." (Ulysses Everett, interview KZSU Project South, 1965, LC.)

90. Lewis and Ladner interviews author, 2009; Brown interview author, 2011; Moses and Cobb, *Radical Equations*, 74–75.

91. Brown interview author, 2011.

92. Payne, *I've Got the Light*, 151; Branch, *Parting the Waters*, 633–34; Burner, *And Gently*, 1, 53, 75–76; Willie Peacock, "Comments," Panel Discussion, Session "From

Student Activists to Field Organizers," SNCC's 50th Anniversary Reunion Conference, Shaw University, Raleigh, N.C., April 15, 2010.

93. Lewis interview author, 2009; Brown interview author, 2011; Carmichael and Thelwell, *Ready for Revolution*, 358–61; Nick Hampton, Report, March 1963, Box 1, Folder 3, COFO Panola County Office Records, SHSW.

94. Block to Moses, June 23, July 11, 22, and 27, 1962, and Moses to Lawrence Guyot, August 11, 1962, JFP; Moses interview Branch, 1991; Will Henry Jr., interview by Robert Wright, June 29, 1969, RBC, HU.

95. Mary King interview author, 2009.

96. Polletta, "Strategy and Identity," 115; Moses and Cobb, *Radical Equations*, 61.

Chapter Five

1. Moses and Cobb, *Radical Equations*, 59–61.

2. Branch, *Parting the Waters*, 781–82; Burner, *And Gently*, 106–7; Cobb, *The Most Southern Place*, 242; "SNCC Worker Beaten, Jailed," SNCC News Release, no date, private collection Joan Mulholland; Moses, "On the Death of Willie Joe Lovett," no date, File 0754, Reel 38, Series XV, State Project Files, and Moses to John Fisher, July 26, 1963, File 0876, Reel 6, Series IV, Ex. Sec. Files James Forman, SNCC Papers.

3. Branch, *Parting the Waters*, 781–82; Burner, *And Gently*, 106–7; Cobb, *The Most Southern Place*, 242; Burke Marshall to Adam C. Powell, March 31, 1964, File 0544, Reel 5, Series IV, Ex. Sec. Files James Forman, SNCC Papers.

4. Bill Hansen, "Albany and Southwest Georgia," June 25–July 6, 1962, Albany City Archives, private collection Adam Fairclough; "S.W. Georgia Voter Program Continues Despite Legal Losses," *The Student Voice*, April 1963, in Carson, *The Student Voice*, 66; Bond to Moses, December 6, 1962, Box 2, Folder 9, HZP, SHSW; Moses and Cobb, *Radical Equations*, 70–71.

5. Doar, "The Work of the Civil Rights Division," 1–4, 6, 10–11; Doar and Landsberg, "The Performance of the FBI," 3, 5–6, 14–15; Garrow, *Protest at Selma*, 15–18.

6. Doar and Landsberg, "The Performance of the FBI," 3, 5–6, 14–15; Stoper, *Student Nonviolent Coordinating Committee*, 41; Burner, *And Gently*, 47–49; *Robert Moses, et al. versus Robert F. Kennedy and J. Edgar Hoover*, lawsuit, January 1963, Files 0649–0668, Reel 23, Series VIII, Research Department, SNCC Papers; "Federal Inaction Challenged," *The Student Voice*, September 23, 1964, in Carson, *The Student Voice*, 193; Navasky, *Kennedy Justice*, 127–28; O'Reilly, *"Racial Matters,"* 66–67; Dittmer, *Local People*, 119–20; Carson, *In Struggle*, 70; John Doar, conversation with author, April 14, 2010.

7. Burner, *And Gently*, 48; Dittmer, *Local People*, 194–98, Carson, 85–86; "Voter Registration Drive Moves Forward Painfully," *The New American*, February 6, 1963; Hammerback and Jensen, "Calling Washington Collect," 146–47; King, *Freedom Song*, 292–97; Doar, "The Work of the Civil Rights Division," 10–11; Garrow, *Protest at Selma*, 22–24; O'Reilly, *"Racial Matters,"* 49–77; Doar and Landsberg, "The Performance of the FBI," 59–61.

8. O'Reilly, *"Racial Matters,"* 64–65; Stoper, *Student Nonviolent Coordinating Committee*, 41; Moses to Workers in the VEP, no date (likely August 1962), File 1010, Reel 10, Series IV, Ex. Sec. Files James Forman, SNCC Papers; Moses interview Branch, July 30, 1984; Moses interview Sinsheimer, 1984, TBP, UC; Moses to the Civil Rights Division, July 6, 1962, and Moses to Tim Jenkins, February 24, 1963, JFP, LC; Carson, *In Struggle*, 85.

9. Moses, 2010; Dittmer, *Local People*, 138–42; see also Eagles, *The Price of Defiance*.

10. Moses, "Report to Voter Education Project," no date (likely December 1962), private collection Joan Mulholland; Moses interview author, May 2, 2011 (hereafter cited as Moses, May 2011).

11. Moses, "Report to Voter Education Project," no date (likely December 1962), private collection Joan Mulholland; Moses, May 2011; Dittmer, *Local People*, 138–42; Payne, *I've Got the Light*, 153; Moses and Cobb, *Radical Equations*, 58–59.

12. Dittmer, *Local People*, 138–42; Payne, *I've Got the Light*, 153; Moses and Cobb, *Radical Equations*, 58–59; "Bob Kennedy, Hoover Sued," in Ann Arbor Friends of SNCC Bulletin, no date, File 1191, Reel 7, Series IV, Ex. Sec. Files James Forman SNCC Papers; "Voter Registration Drive Moves Forward Painfully," *The New American*, February 6, 1963.

13. Carson, *In Struggle*, 86; Burner, *And Gently*, 89–90; Branch, *Parting the Waters*, 712–13; *Moses v. Kennedy and Hoover*, lawsuit; Burke Marshall to John Pemberton, March 13, 1963, Files 0489, Reel 4, Burke Marshall Records, DJCRD, RSC.

14. Moses, 2010; Moses to Higgs, December 4, 1962, JFP, LC.

15. Cobb, *The Most Southern Place on Earth*, 232, 237, 239.

16. Payne, *I've Got the Light*, 133–34, 144; Zinn, *SNCC*, 83–84; Constancia Romilly, "Report on Leflore County," no date, Files 0700–0702, Reel 8, Series IV, Ex. Sec. Files James Forman, SNCC Papers; Tom Scarborough, "Leflore County—Samuel Block and Robert Moses" and "Leflore County—Further Investigation on Samuel Block and Robert Moses," August 14 and September 12, 1962, MSSC Online.

17. Payne, *I've Got the Light*, 141–53; Dittmer, *Local People*, 128–35; "Mississippi Negro Alleges a Beating," *NYT*, August 16, 1963.

18. Payne, *I've Got the Light*, 141–53; Dittmer, *Local People*, 128–35; Block to Moses, July 27, 1962, JFP, LC.

19. Dittmer, *Local People*, 143–45; Payne, *I've Got the Light*, 158–59; James Ward, "For Leflore: Alms or Arms," *JDN*, March 21, 1963; Burke Marshall to Raymond Blanks, May 29, 1963, Files 00540–00541, Reel 5, Part 1, JFK Papers, RSC; McLaurin and Cobb, "Preliminary Survey," November 19, 1962, File 0136, Reel 38, Series XV, State Projects Files, SNCC Papers; Moses to Peter Countryman, November 7, 1962, JFP, LC.

20. Moses and Cobb, memorandum, December 21, 1962, and Moses to Martha Prescott, JFP, LC; Burner, *And Gently*, 93.

21. Countryman to Moses, October 29, 1962, and Moses to Countryman, November 7, 1962, JFP, LC; Moses to Mike Miller, letter, March 20, 1963, File 0934,

Reel 7, Series IV, Ex. Sec. Files James Forman, SNCC Papers; Dittmer, *Local People*, 145–146; Payne, *I've Got the Light*, 158–60; Moses and Cobb, *Radical Equations*, 63–64; Gregory and Lipsyte, *Nigger*, 161; "Another Cheap Publicity Stunt" and "Ross Says 'Race Agitators' Could Halt Food Program," *JDN*, February 6 and 15, 1963.

22. Moses and Cobb, *Radical Equations*, 59–60; Carson, *In Struggle*, 80.

23. Carson, *In Struggle*, 80; Payne, *I've Got the Light*, 158–60; Dittmer, *Local People*, 146; Cagin and Dray, *We Are Not Afraid*, 190; Polletta, "Strategy and Identity," 141.

24. Payne, *I've Got the Light*, 158–60; Dittmer, *Local People*, 146; Cagin and Dray, *We Are Not Afraid*, 190; Mike Miller to Moses and Charles McDew, March 16, 1963, and Miller to Moses, March 17, 1963, File 0938, and Anonymous SNCC worker to Miller, March 20, 1963, File 0934, Reel 7, Series IV, Ex. Sec. Files James Forman, and Charlie Cobb, telephone report, February 18, 1964, File 0702, Reel 38, Series XV, State Project Files, SNCC Papers; Lee, *For Freedom's Sake*, 64–65.

25. Moses and Cobb, *Radical Equations*, 62; Dittmer, *Local People*, 146–47; Payne, *I've Got the Light*, 161–62; "SNCC Staff Jailed," *The Student Voice*, April 1963, in Carson, *The Student Voice*, 65, 68.

26. Payne, *I've Got the Light*, 176, 238; Murphree, *The Selling of Civil Rights*, 49–50; Moses to Chicago FOS, February 24, 1963, qt. in Moses and Cobb, *Radical Equations*, 59–60.

27. Payne, *I've Got the Light*, 162–63; Dittmer, *Local People*, 147–48.

28. Payne, *I've Got the Light*, 162–63; Dittmer, *Local People*, 147–48; "How Nonviolent Warrior Feels on Firing Line in Rural Dixie," *The Chicago-Sun Times*, May 20, 1963, Box 1, Folder 14, HZP, SHSW; Forman, *Making of Black Revolutionaries*, 294–95; Warren, *Who Speaks for the Negro?* 403; Hammerback and Jensen, "Robert Parris Moses," 264–65.

29. Payne, *I've Got the Light*, 162–63; Dittmer, *Local People*, 147–48; *The Story of Greenwood*, 1965; Washington Civil Rights Hearings, 1964, Box 2, Folder 5, HZP, SHSW.

30. Notes Branch, 1999; *The Streets of Greenwood*, 1962; "Two Shots Hit Voter Worker," *The Delta Democrat-Times*, March 1, 1963.

31. Lee White to Roy Wilkins and James Farmer, March 20 and 21, 1963, Reel 5, Part I, Files 00481 and 00487, Reel 5, JFK Papers, RSC; Burner, *And Gently*, 96–98; "SNCC Staff Jailed," *The Student Voice*, April 1963, in Carson, *The Student Voice*, 65, 68; Dittmer, *Local People*, 150; Payne, *I've Got the Light*, 163–64; "Charges Dropped Against Two Held in '63 Shooting," SNCC News Release, November 29, 1964, File 0082, Reel 14, Series VII, Communications Department, Public Relations, SNCC Papers.

32. Dittmer, *Local People*, 148–49; "Notes on Bob Moses," Box 1, Folder 14, HZP, SHSW; "Negroes Threaten 'Test' of Leflore," *JDN*, March 2, 1963.

33. Dittmer, *Local People*, 148–49; Fred Powledge, "Negro's Shooting Spurs Voter Drive," *The Atlanta Journal and Constitution*, March 3, 1963.

34. Dittmer, *Local People*, 148–51; *The Story of Greenwood*, 1965; Payne, *I've Got the Light*, 163, 165, 167–68; Anne Braden to Forman, March 10, 1963, File 0728, Reel 7, Series IV, Ex. Sec. Files James Forman, and "Moses Vows Program Will

Continue," SNCC News Release, March 1963, File 0970, Reel 13, Series VII, Communications Department, Public Relations, SNCC Papers.

35. Dittmer, *Local People*, 151–57; Payne, *I've Got the Light*, 170–74; Branch, *Parting the Waters*, 719–25; Burner, *And Gently*, 99–103; Forman, *Making of Black Revolutionaries*, 296–304; Moses interview Branch, July 30, 1984.

36. Dittmer, *Local People*, 151–57; Payne, *I've Got the Light*, 170–74; Branch, *Parting the Waters*, 719–25; Burner, *And Gently*, 99–103; Forman, *Making of Black Revolutionaries*, 296–304.

37. Forman, *Making of Black Revolutionaries*, 296–304; Cleveland Banks, "Report on Voter Education in LeFlore County," no date, File 00449, Reel 5, Part 4, Series I, Records of Andrew J. Young, Records SCLC; *The Story of Greenwood*, 1965.

38. Forman, *Making of Black Revolutionaries*, 296–304; Dittmer, *Local People*, 151–57; Payne, *I've Got the Light of Freedom*, 170–74; Branch, *Parting the Waters*, 719–25; Moses and Cobb, *Radical Equations*, 65; "U.S. Acts in Negro Vote Case," *The Evening Star*, Washington, D.C., March 30, 1963; "U.S. Court Denies Negro Voter Suit" and "Cruelty in South Is Laid to Police," *NYT*, April 2 and 7, 1963; James Ward, "An Incredible Coincidence and Headlines on Greenwood," *JDN*, April 5, 1963; "Bob Moses Denied Objector Exemption," newspaper unknown, April 3, 1963, private collection Joan Mulholland. *Greenwood Commonwealth* qt. in article *Evening Star*.

39. Bob Cohen to Judy Richardson, letter, no date, William Heath Papers; "Urgent," memorandum, no date, and "Greenwood, Mississippi," SNCC News Letter, April 1, 1963, File 0025, Reel 14, Series VII, Communications Department, Public Relations, SNCC Papers; "SNCC Staff Jailed," *The Student Voice*, April 1963, in Carson, *The Student Voice*, 65, 68; Lawrence Benenson to The President, March 28, 1963, Papers John F. Kennedy, Digital Archive John F. Kennedy Library, http://jfklibrary.org.

40. Forman, *Making of Black Revolutionaries*, 299–303; "Jailed SNCC Staff Sends Open Letter," News Release, April 3, 1963, File 1037, Series VII, Communications Department, Public Relations, and Augustus Hawkins to Moses and to Dorothy Miller, April 5 and 10, 1963, File 0896, Reel 6, Series IV, Ex. Sec. Files James Forman, SNCC Papers.

41. Dittmer, *Local People*, 154–57; Payne, *I've Got the Light*, 173–74; Branch, *Parting the Waters*, 721–25; Claude Sitton, "Mississippi Town Seizes 19 Negroes," *NYT*, April 4, 1963; Forman, *Making of Black Revolutionaries*, 303.

42. Forman, *Making of Black Revolutionaries*, 303; Branch, *Parting the Waters*, 724–25; Cobb, *The Most Southern Place on Earth*, 233; Moses and Cobb, *Radical Equations*, 64–65; "U.S. Court Denies Negro Voter Suit," *NYT*, April 2, 1963.

43. Branch, *Parting the Waters*, 724–25; Moses interview Branch, July 30, 1984.

44. Branch, *Parting the Waters*, 673–802. See also McWorther, *Carry Me Home*.

45. Lewis and D'Orso, *Walking with the Wind*, 198; Charles Cobb, "Re: Greenville, Mississippi," November 8, 1963, Files 0964–0969, Reel 5, Series IV, Ex. Sec. Files James Forman, SNCC Papers.

46. Bob Moses, "Speech" (New York, June 3, 1963), transcript in *The Southern Patriot*, June 18, 1963, Box 108, Folder 3, TBP, UNC (hereafter cited as Moses,

"Speech," June 3, 1963, TBP, UNC); Dittmer, *Local People*, 157–69; Moses and Cobb, *Radical Equations*, 70.

47. Dittmer, *Local People*, 157, 169, 173–74; Payne, *I've Got the Light*, 174–75.

48. Dittmer, *Local People*, 194; Moses to John Blyth, February 24, 1963, File 1159, Reel 69, Appendix A: MFDP Papers, SNCC Papers; Bob Moses, "Speech" (SNCC Easter Conference 1963); *The Making of Black Revolutionaries*, 305–7; Moses, "Speech," June 3, 1963, TBP, UNC.

49. Moses speech West Coast Civil Rights Conference, 1964; Carson, *In Struggle*, 90–91; Sugrue, *Sweet Land of Liberty*, 302; Salter, "Medgar Evers Speaks," 36–37.

50. Moses and Cobb, *Radical Equations*, 65–66; Moses, "Speech," June 3, 1963, TBP, UNC.

51. Moses, 2010; "Executive Committee Meeting," report, January 1, 1963, File 0808, Reel 3, Series III, Staff Meetings, SNCC Papers; Hammerback and Jensen, "Calling Washington Collect," 145–46; Moses and Cobb, *Radical Equations*, 68–69; Forman, *Making of Black Revolutionaries*, 305–7.

52. Moses and Cobb, *Radical Equations*, 68–69; Forman, *Making of Black Revolutionaries*, 305–7; Moses to Burke Marshall, February 24, 1963, JFP, LC; Moses, "Report to Voter Education Project," no date (likely December 1962), private collection Joan Mulholland; Lawrence Guyot, interview by John Rachal, September 7, 1996, MOHP, USM; Hammerback and Jensen, "Robert Parris Moses," 267; Burner, *And Gently*, 107–8; Carson, *In Struggle*, 88–89.

53. Cagin and Dray, *We Are Not Afraid*, 182; Moses, "Speech," June 3, 1963, TBP, UNC; King, *Freedom Song*, 151–52; Zinn, "The Battle-Scarred Youngsters," *The Nation*, October 5, 1963.

54. Charles McDew and Bob Moses to A. Philip Randolph, January 21, 1963, Box 6, Folder 3, EBP, SCRBC; Moses to Fay Bennett, February 21, 1963, File 0324, and Bennett to Moses, February 24, 1963, File 0325, Reel 8, Series IV, Ex. Sec. Files James Forman, SNCC Papers.

55. Dittmer, *Local People*, 478n; Burner, *And Gently*, 91–93; King, *Freedom Song*, 402, 483; Moses interview Sinsheimer, 1984, TBP, UNC; Moses interview Branch, February 15, 1991, TBP, UNC; Moses interview Dittmer, 1983; "Memorandum on Programmed Learning for Illiterates," no date, Files 1338–1340, and Moses to Blyth and Blyth to Moses, February 15, 22, 24, and 26, 1963, Files 1149, 1153, 1159, 1162, and 1170, and Moses to Dr. Pitts, Valida Diehl, and Vaughn Albertson, February 24 and March 6, 1964, Files 0149, 0130, and 0133, Reel 64, and Blyth to Daniel Beittel, Jane Eddy, and Benjamin Wyckoff, February 15, 18, and 26, 1963, Files 1150–1151 and 1167, and Moses to Les Dunbar, Walter Brown, Fay Bennett, and Julian Bond, February 23 and 24, 1963, Files 1154, 1155, 1161, and 1162, Reel 69, Appendix A: MFDP Papers, and Casey Hayden to Mrs. Sterling, May 11, 1963, File 0210, Reel 9, and Moses to John Fisher, July 26, 1963, File 0876, Reel 6, Series IV, Ex. Sec. Files James Forman, SNCC Papers; Jerry Tecklin to Burrill Crohn, February 24, 1964, Box 1, Folder 1, Jerry Tecklin Papers, SHSW; Dave Dennis, "Field Report," March 1–March 31, 1963, Box 14, Folder 1, CORE Records, SHSW.

56. King interview author, 2009; Forman, *Making of Black Revolutionaries*, 307; Moses "Speech," June 3, 1963, TBP, UNC.

57. Moses to Myles Horton, May 19, 1963, and Moses to Mrs. McAdoo, and Horton to Moses, September 24, October 18, 1963, and no date, and Forman to Horton, November 22, 1963, Box 21, HRECR, SHSW; Vivien Franklin to James Forman, November 25, 1962, File 0433, Reel 6, and "New York Friends training weekend," Theodore Olson to Forman et al., April 4, 1963, File 0530, Reel 8, Series IV, Ex. Sec. Files James Forman, and "Moses Phone Call," September 20, 1963, File 0062, Reel 16, Series VII, Communications Department, Internal Communications, and "Progress Report on Civil Rights Leadership Institute," Constance Curry to Paul Potter et al., May 9, 1963, Files 0812–0813 Reel 3, Series III, Staff Meetings, and Moses to John Gilmore, February 24, 1963, Files 1164–1165, and Moses to Bob Horne, letter, August 8, 1963, File 1197, Reel 69, and Dona Richards to Maxwell Hahn, no date (likely fall 1963), Files 0771–0772, Reel 70, Appendix A: MFDP Papers, and Richards, "Tougaloo Work-Study Project," no date (likely early 1964), Files 1011–1011A, Reel 39, Series XV, State Project Files, SNCC Papers; Grant, *Ella Baker*, 157.

58. Notes Taylor Branch, March 13, 1988, Box 108, Folder 1, TBP, UNC (hereafter cited as Notes Branch, 1988, TBP, UNC); J. W. Bunkeley to Richards, May 2, 1964, File 1122, Reel 64, Appendix A: MFDP Papers, SNCC Papers; King, *Freedom Song*, 76–77, 463; Mary King interview author, 2009; Bond interview author, 2008; Ladner interview author, 2009; Erle Johnston to Jack Doty, letter, August 25, 1964, and Virgil Downing, "Dona Richard Moses," report, May 22, 1964, and Dona Richards, "Application for Admission to the School of Law," April 10, 1964, MSSC Online.

59. King, *Freedom Song*, 76–77, 463; Mary King interview author, 2009; Bond interview author, 2008; SNCC meeting at Waveland, November 6–12, 1964, minutes, Files 0935–0957, Reel 11, Series V, SNCC Conferences, SNCC Papers (hereafter cited as Minutes Meeting SNCC, November 6–12, 1964, SNCC Papers).

60. Forman to Clarence Jones, September 23, 1963, File 0612, and Casey Hayden to John Fisher, July 9, 1963, File 0874, and Moses to Aaron Henry, no date (likely January 1963), File 0918, Reel 6, Series IV, Ex. Sec. James Forman Files, and "Moses Phone Call," September 20, 1963, File 0062, Reel 16, Series VII, Communications Department, Internal Communications, SNCC Papers; Forman, *Making of Black Revolutionaries*, 305; Moses to Martha Prescott, December 11, 1962, and Moses to Branton, February 22, 1963, JFP, LC; Burner, *And Gently*, 93–94.

61. Moses to Peter Countryman, November 7, 1962, File 0683, Reel 8, and James Forman to William Moses, November 20, 1963, File 0672, Reel 7, Series IV, Ex. Sec. Files James Forman, and "Meeting of the SNCC Executive Committee," minutes, December 27–31, 1963, Files 0313–0328, Reel 3, Series II, Executive and Central Committees, Executive Committee, SNCC Papers.

62. Cohen, "Sorrow Songs," 177–89; SNCC News Release, July 1963, Box 2, Folder 3, HZP, SHSW; Burner, *And Gently*, 109; Moses, 2010; Murphree, *The Selling of Civil Rights*, 47–48; Guy and Candie Carawan, conversation with author, April 15, 2010; Harvey Richards to Dear Friends, March 5, 1963, File 0032, Reel 9, and Moses to Dottie Miller, no date (likely January 1963), File 0276, Reel 7, Series IV, Ex. Sec. Files James Forman, SNCC Papers.

63. "Miss. Story Told," *The Student Voice*, April 1963, in Carson, *The Student Voice*, 67; Dorothy Miller to Rose Daly, March 28, 1963, File 0873, and Moses to John Fisher, July 9 and 26, 1963, Files 0874 and 0876, Reel 6, Elizabeth Sutherland to Forman, File 0271, Reel 9, Moses to Dottie Miller and Miller to Moses, January 24, 1963, and no date, Files 0274 and 0276, and Bertha Gober to Victoria Gray, January 24, 1963, File 0274, Reel 7, Series IV, Ex. Sec. Files James Forman, and John Clarke to Moses, 21 October 1963, File 0008, Reel 65, Appendix A: MFDP Papers, and John Fisher to Moses, July 3, 1963, File 0002 and Fisher to Philip Stern, July 3, 1963, File 0003, Reel 40, Series XV, State Project Files, SNCC Papers; Marion Palfi to Amzie Moore, July 16, 1963, Box 1, Folder 5, AMP, SHSW; Moses to Forman, no date (likely mid-December 1963), private collection Joan Mulholland.

64. Dittmer, *Local People*, 165–69, 173; Robert E. Wright, interview by John Britton, July 28, 1968, RBC, HU; Evers-Williams and Manning, *Autobiography of Medgar Evers*, 259–60.

65. Moses to Berl Bernhard, no date, File 0137, Reel 10, Series IV, Ex. Sec. Files James Forman, SNCC Papers.

66. Carson, *In Struggle*, 91–95; Lewis and D'Orso, *Walking with the Wind*, 194–95.

67. Carson, *In Struggle*, 91–95; Lewis and D'Orso, *Walking with the Wind*, 194–95; Moody, *Coming of Age in Mississippi*, 334; Moses interview author, August 20, 2011 (hereafter cited as Moses, August 2011); Branch, *Parting the Waters*, 864–75; Burner, *And Gently*, 113–14.

68. Moses, "Commentary," 74; Moses, 2010; Dittmer, *Local People*, 199.

69. Burner, *And Gently*, 108–9, 114; Moses, 2010, and August 2011; *Oh Freedom over Me*, Moses interview by John Biewen for American Radio Works, 1994 (hereafter cited as Moses interview Biewen, 1994); Murphree, *The Selling of Civil Rights*, 62.

70. Moses, 2010, and August 2011; Branch, *Parting the Waters*, 888–92; Moody, *Coming of Age in Mississippi*, 345–49; Sam Block, "Greenwood, Mississippi," September 26, 1963, File 0107, Reel 17, Series VII, Communications Department, Internal Communications, SNCC Papers; Branch, *Pillar of Fire*, 140.

71. Henry and Curry, *Aaron Henry*, 129; Moses interviews Romaine; Crosby, *A Little Taste of Freedom*, 67, 83, 91; "Voter Registration Drive Moses Forward Painfully," *New American*, February 6, 1963.

72. Payne, *I've Got the Light*, 167, 241, 335; Sam Block, "Greenwood, Mississippi," September 26, 1963, File 0107, Reel 17, Series VII, Communications Department, Internal Communications, and Mike Miller, "The Greenwood Operation and Related Questions," August 9, 1963, File 0797–0798, Reel 38, Series XV, State Project Files, SNCC Papers.

73. Mike Miller, "The Greenwood Operation and Related Questions," August 9, 1963, Files 0797–0798, Reel 38, Series XV, State Project Files, SNCC Papers; Ruby Doris Smith to "Whom It May Concern," September 17, 1963, File 0104, Reel 17, Series VII, Communications Department, Internal Communications, SNCC Papers.

Chapter Six

1. Cade, "Mississippi Summer Twenty-five Years Later," 421–22.
2. Carmichael and Thelwell, *Ready for Revolution*, 354–55.
3. Dittmer, *Local People*, 200–7; Payne, *I've Got the Light*, 290–94, 424; Moses to Dear Friend, August 2, 1963, File 1196, Reel 69, Appendix A: MFDP Papers, SNCC Papers; Sinsheimer, "The Freedom Vote of 1963," 223–24.
4. Moses to SNCC Executive Committee, "SNCC Mississippi Project," no date, JFP, LC.
5. Ibid.
6. Ibid.; Report by Ex. Sec., September 24, 1963, Box 5, Folder 1, SLP, SHSW.
7. Cobb, *The Most Southern Place on Earth*, 233–34; Moses, "Statement of Purpose of the Freedom Ballot," no date, Files 0476–0477, Reel 41, Series XVI, Mississippi Freedom Democratic Party, and "Mississippi 'Freedom Vote' Campaign," File 0349, Reel 38, Series XV, State Project Files, SNCC Papers; Payne, *I've Got the Light*, 294–95; Sinsheimer, "The Freedom Vote of 1963," 223.
8. Moody, *Coming of Age in Mississippi*, 361–62; Willie Blue, "Plans for Attack," report, October 2, 1963, File 0108, Reel 17, Series VII, Communications Department, Internal Communications, SNCC Papers; Sinsheimer, "The Freedom Vote of 1963," 225, 234–36.
9. Garrow, *Bearing the Cross*, 287–356; Branch, *Parting the Waters*, 892–93, 899–900; Branch, *Pillar of Fire*, 141, 144–45, 190, 212, 245–46, 285–86.
10. Ella Baker, interview by Anne Romaine, March 25, 1967, ARP, UNC.
11. Cagin and Dray, *We Are Not Afraid*, 212–13; Rothshild, "Northern Volunteers," 22–23; Moses interview Carson, 1982; Moses and Cobb, *Radical Equations*, 72–73; Ruby Doris Smith to George Goss, May 17, 1963, File 1020, Reel 9, Series IV, Ex. Sec. Files James Forman, SNCC Papers.
12. Moses and Cobb, *Radical Equations*, 72–73; Mike Miller, interview by author, April 15, 2010 (hereafter cited as Miller interview author, 2010).
13. Moses and Cobb, *Radical Equations*, 72–73; Miller interview author, 2010; Minutes SNCC Meeting in Greenville, November 1963, Box 2, Folder 10, HZP, SHSW.
14. Moses interviews Romaine; Hogan, *Many Minds*, 149–50; Bob Johnson to James Forman, June 27, 1963, File 0131, Reel 7, and Casey Hayden to Guido Goldman, July 2, 1963, File 0665, Reel 6, Series IV, Ex. Sec. James Forman, SNCC Papers; Moses and Cobb, *Radical Equations*, 73; Ed King, interviews by William Chafe, March 10 and October 30, 1988, ALP, UNC; Sinsheimer, "The Freedom Vote of 1963," 229–30.
15. Sinsheimer, "The Freedom Vote of 1963," 229–30; Cagin and Dray, *We Are Not Afraid*, 212–14. Moses to Yale and Stanford students qtd. in Sinsheimer.
16. Sinsheimer, "The Freedom Vote of 1963," 226–28; Dittmer, *Local People*, 201–2; Joan Bowman, "Report," October 23, 1963, Files 0117–0118, Reel 15, Series VII, Communications Department, Internal Communications, and State Executive Committee to Elect Aaron Henry Governor, "Organizational Framework," no date, Files 0373–0374, and "Mississippi Freedom Vote Henry," October 1963, File

0346, and "Mississippi 'Freedom Vote' Campaign," no date, File 0349, Reel 38, Series XV, State Project Files, SNCC Papers.

17. "Organizational Framework," no date, Files 0373–0374, Reel 38, Series XV, State Project Files, and Wiley Branton to Moses, October 23, 1963, File 0454, Reel 64, Appendix A: MFDP Papers, SNCC Papers; Aaron Henry, interview by Howard Zinn, December 28, 1965, Box 3, Folder 10, HZP, SHSW; Ed King, interview by author, April 14, 2010 (hereafter cited as Ed King interview author, 2010); Sinsheimer, "The Freedom Vote of 1963," 227.

18. Moses to Campaign Workers, "Urgent Top Priority," no date, Box 1, Folder 20, HZP, SHSW; State Office to District Managers and Field Workers, "Election Procedures," October 25, 1963, File 0733, Reel 68, Appendix A: MFDP Papers, SNCC Papers.

19. Moses to Dear Sir, October 1963, File 0461, Reel 41, Series XVI, Mississippi Freedom Democratic Party, and WATS report, no date, File 0063, Reel 15, Series VII, Communications Department, Internal Communications, and Julie Prettyman to Moses, October 1963, File 0026, Reel 65, Appendix A: MFDP Papers, and Mary King to Bob Rogers, October 24, 1963, File 1180, Reel 8, Ex. Sec. Files James Forman, SNCC Papers; Mike Sayer, "WATS–notes," October 30, 1963, Box 1, Folder 1, MKP, SHSW; Moses to Allard Lowenstein, October 17, 1963, WHP, SHSW; Burner, *And Gently*, 123.

20. SNCC Meeting in Greenville, minutes, November 1963, Box 2, Folder 10, HZP, SHSW; Moses interview Chafe, 1989, ALP, UNC; Moses, August 2011; Chafe, *Never Stop Running*, 188, 202–5; Payne, *I've Got the Light*, 424.

21. Ed King, interviews by William Chafe, March 10 and October 30, 1988, ALP, UNC; Hogan, *Many Minds*, 146; Forman, *Making of Black Revolutionaries*, 356–57; Sinsheimer, "The Freedom Vote of 1963," 237.

22. Moses interview Chafe, 1989, ALP, UNC; Chafe, *Never Stop Running*, 202–3; Allard Lowenstein, interview by Robert Wright, March 30, 1970, RBC, HU.

23. Chafe, *Never Stop Running*, 188, 202–8; Bond interview author, 2008; Moses interviews Romaine; Allard Lowenstein, interview by Anne Romaine, March 4, 1967, ARP, UNC (hereafter cited as Lowenstein interview Romaine, 1967, ARP, UNC); Allard Lowenstein, interview by Clayborne Carson, May 17, 1977, ALP, UNC.

24. Sinsheimer, "The Freedom Vote of 1963," 222, 229; Chafe, *Never Stop Running*, 188, 202–8; Bond interview author, 2008.

25. Sinsheimer, "The Freedom Vote of 1963," 231–32, 234; Joan Bowman, "Report," October 23, 1963, Files 0117–0118, Reel 15, Series VII, Communications Department, Internal Communications, SNCC Papers; Chafe, *Never Stop Running*, 185; Hogan, *Many Minds*, 148; Mendy Samstein, "Notes on Mississippi," no date 1963, Folder 1, MSP, SHSW (hereafter cited as Samstein, "Notes on Mississippi," 1963, MSP, SHSW); Ed King interview author, 2010.

26. Hogan, *Many Minds*, 151; Charles Cobb, "Re: Greenville, Mississippi," November 8, 1963, Files 0964–0969, Reel 5, Series IV, Ex. Sec. Files James Forman, SNCC Papers; Mendy Samstein, interview by Anne Romaine, September 4, 1966, ARP, UNC.

27. Sinsheimer, "The Freedom Vote of 1963," 232, 234, 238–39; Dittmer, *Local People*, 203–5; John Herbers, "50 Yale Men Aid Mississippi Negro," *NYT*, October 30, 1963; Samstein, "Notes on Mississippi," 1963, MSP, SHSW.

28. O'Reilly, *"Racial Matters,"* 158; Ivanhoe Donaldson, "Another Incident of Brutality in Mississippi," October 30–November 5, 1963, Files 1090–1092, Reel 7, Series IV, Ex. Sec. Files James Forman, SNCC Papers.

29. Carmichael and Thelwell, *Ready for Revolution*, 353–54; "Miss. Workers Face Police Harassment," June 2, 1964, in Carson, *The Student Voice*, 157; Sinsheimer, "The Freedom Vote of 1963," 232, 234, 238–39; Dittmer, *Local People*, 203–5; Lowenstein interview Romaine, 1967, ARP, UNC; Miriam Cohen, "Field Report," October 23–30, 1963, Files 0992–0993, Reel 5, Series IV, Ex. Sec. Files James Forman, SNCC Papers; Dona Richards to L. D. Rayfield, October 30, 1963, Box 3, Folder 4, HRMP, WSHS; Ed King, interview by James M. Mosby, May 28, 1970, RBC, HU.

30. Estimates, however, range from 72,000 to 92,000.

31. Sinsheimer, "The Freedom Vote of 1963," 240–42; Dittmer, *Local People*, 206; · Committee to Elect Aaron Henry Governor to Congress, "A Petition," November 25, 1963, Box 1, Folder 20, HZP. SHSW.

32. Dittmer, *Local People*, 206; Sinsheimer, "The Freedom Vote of 1963," 241–43.

33. Dittmer, *Local People*, 206–7; *The Texas Observer*, November 15, 1963, WHP, SHSW; Minutes meeting SNCC Washington Conference, no date, Box 1, Folder 21, HZP, SHSW; King, *Freedom Song*, 240–41, 246–47; Frank Smith, "Re: First Congressional District," November 11, 1963, Files 0122–123, Reel 17, Series VII, Communications Department, Internal Communication, SNCC Papers.

34. Stoper, *Student Nonviolent Coordinating Committee*, 291–92.

35. Moses interview Carson, 1982; Zinn, *SNCC*, 186–89; Rothshild, "Northern Volunteers," 26–29; Branton to Aaron Henry and Moses, November 12, 1963, File 0955, Reel 10, Series IV, Ex. Sec. Files James Forman, SNCC Papers; Dittmer, *Local People*, 212–13; Howard Zinn, "Notes on Mississippi Staff Meeting, Greenville, Nov. 14–16, 1963," and partial typed minutes of the meeting, Box 2, Folder 10, HZP, SHSW. All quotes in subsequent paragraphs about the meeting were taken from Zinn's notes and the typed minutes, unless indicated with a new endnote.

36. Dittmer, *Local People*, 212–13; Jane Stembridge, "Field Report, Greenwood, Mississippi," November 20, 1963, File 0123, Reel 17, Series VII, Communications Department, Internal Communications, SNCC Papers.

37. Moses, "Memo to Mississippi Staff," no date, WHP, SHSW.

38. Lisa Anderson Todd, interview by author, October 23, 2008.

39. Lawrence Guyot, interview by Anne Romaine, November 23, 1966, ARP, UNC; Lawrence Guyot, interview by John Rachal, September 7, 1996, MOHP, USM; Hogan, *Many Minds*, 150–51.

40. MFSR, 1979, Session 7, SHSW; Raines, *My Soul Is Rested*, 286–87.

41. Carmichael and Thelwell, *Ready for Revolution*, 350.

42. "Minutes COFO-meeting December 15 [1963]," Files 0553–0558, Reel 42, Series XVII, Other Organizations, SNCC Papers; Branch, *Parting the Waters*, 193.

43. "Minutes of the Meeting of the SNCC Executive Committee," December 27–31, 1963, Files 0313–0328, Reel 3, Executive and Central Committees, Executive Committee, SNCC Papers (hereafter cited as Minutes SNCC meeting December 27–31, 1963, SNCC Papers).

44. Moses interview Biewen, 1994; Moses and Cobb, *Radical Equations*, 74–75; Branch, *Pillar of Fire*, 194; Moses interview Carson, 1982; Ladner interview author, 2009.

45. Moses speech West Coast Civil Rights Conference, 1964.

46. Moses interview Biewen, 1994; Lewis and D'Orso, *Walking with the Wind*, 245–47; Notes Branch, 1999, TBP, UNC; King, *Freedom Song*, 242–43; Mary King to Forman, November 25, 1963, Box 3, Folder 5, MKP, SHSW.

47. Lewis and D'Orso, *Walking with the Wind*, 245–47; Branch, *Pillar of Fire*, 174–79; Beschloss, *Taking Charge*, 28–30, 128–30.

48. Branch, *Pillar of Fire*, 165; "Bob Moses Talk at SNCC's Washington Conference," November 30, 1963, Box 4, Folder 12, SLP, SHSW; *The Nation*, January 6, 1964, 30–33, Box 1, Folder 7, HZP, SHSW.

49. "Bob Moses Talk at SNCC's Washington Conference," November 30, 1963, Box 4, Folder 12, SLP, SHSW; *The Nation*, January 6, 1964, 30–33, Box 1, Folder 7, HZP, SHSW; Moses, "Civil Rights and Civil Liberties," no date, Box M85–587, Folder 3, Pamela P. Allen Papers, SHSW; Paul Goodberg to Moses, December 3 and 6, 1963, File 1129, Reel 70, and File 1200, Reel 69, Appendix A: MFDP Papers, SNCC Papers; Minutes SNCC meeting December 27–31, 1963; Carson, *In Struggle*, 106–7.

50. *The Nation*, January 6, 1964, 30–33; Bond interview author, 2008; Carson, *In Struggle*, 103–4; "Report on Meeting With Union Leaders," December 2, 1963, File 0011, Reel 49, Series III, Other Organizations, Washington Office, SNCC Papers.

51. Minutes SNCC meeting December 27–31, 1963, SNCC Papers.

52. Ibid.

53. Ibid.; Moses speech West Coast Civil Rights Conference, 1964.

54. Notes Branch, 1988, and Martin Luther King to Bob and Dona, telegram, December 23, 1963, Box 108, Folder 3, TBP, UNC.

55. King, *Freedom Song*, 463; Dennis interview author, 2010; Ladner interview author, 2009; Bond interview author, 2008.

56. Zinn, *SNCC*, 103; Blake, *Children of the Movement*, 41; Paul Lauter, conversation with author, March 25, 2009; Dennis interview author, 2010; Warren, *Who Speaks for the Negro?* 88; "Moses Phone Call," September 20, 1963, File 0062, Reel 16, Series VII, Communications Department, Internal Communications, and Rachelle to Gail Hershberger, January 4, 1963, File 0440, Reel 63, Appendix A: MFDP Papers, SNCC Papers.

57. "Minutes of the COFO Staff Executive Committee Meeting," January 10, 1964, "Minutes of Committee on Student Summer Project Meeting," January 13, 1964, and Summer Project Committee to COFO Executive Committee, "Plans and Procedures for Summer Project," January 17, 1964, JFP, LC.

58. "Minutes of Meeting, January 24, 1964" in Hattiesburg, JFP, LC; Branch, *Pillar of Fire*, 220–21.

59. "150 Try to Register" and "Hattiesburg Fact Sheet," *The Student Voice*, January 20, 1964, in Carson, *The Student Voice*, 105, 107–8; Dittmer, *Local People*, 179–80; Zinn, *SNCC*, 111–12; Branch, *Pillar of Fire*, 179, 214–20; "Minutes of the COFO Convention," February 9, 1964, JFP, LC; Mendy Samstein, "On the Hattiesburg Situation," report, no date, File 0551, Reel 38, Series XV, State Project Files, SNCC Papers.

60. Mike Miller, "Comments on the Hattiesburg Freedom Day," no date, File 0551, Reel 38, State Project Files, SNCC Papers; "Notes on Staff Executive Meeting," January 17, 1964, JFP; Moses speech West Coast Civil Rights Conference, 1964.

61. "Minutes of the COFO Staff Executive Committee Meeting," January 10, 1964, and "Notes on Staff Executive Meeting," January 17, 1964, JFP, LC; Dittmer, *Local People*, 220–21; Branch, *Pillar of Fire*, 214–24.

62. Dittmer, *Local People*, 220–21; Branch, *Pillar of Fire*, 214–24; Zinn, *SNCC*, 102–22; Moses to George Meaney, May 1, 1964, Files 0801–0803, Reel 70, Appendix A: MFDP Papers, and COFO, "Hattiesburg Report," no date, and "Information from Atlanta Georgia," no date, File 0758, Reel 38, and File 0202, Reel 39, Series XV, State Project Files, and "Hattiesburg, Mississippi," report, January 27, 1964, File 0203, Reel 15, Series VII, Communications Department, Internal Communications, SNCC Papers.

63. Dittmer, *Local People*, 221–24; Branch, *Pillar of Fire*, 219–20; "Hattiesburg Report," no date, File 0758, Reel 39, Series XV, State Project Files, and "Supplement to Hattiesburg Report," no date, File 0603, Reel 23, and File 0572, Reel 21, Series VIII, Research Department, SNCC Papers; "Minutes of COFO Convention," February 9, 1964, JFP, LC.

64. Branch, *Pillar of Fire*, 221–23; Moses interview Branch, July 30, 1984; Moses and Cobb, *Radical Equations*, 75–76.

65. Payne, *I've Got the Light*, 299–300; Moses, "Report Concerning the Louis Allen Case," no date (likely February 1964), Files 0497–0499, Reel 20, Series VIII, Research Department, SNCC Papers; Charles Gordon, "Ambush Killing of Negro, 44, Puzzles Amite Officers," *MCEJ*, February 2, 1964; A. Belmont to A. Rosen, memorandum, February 3, 1964, Box 106, TBP, UNC; *60 Minutes*, "Cold Case."

66. "McComb, Mississippi," report, February 1, 1964, Files 1143–1146, Reel 16, Series VII, Communications Department, Internal Communications, SNCC Papers; Moses interview Branch, July 30, 1984; Moses interview Dittmer, 1983; Moses and Cobb, *Radical Equations*, 76; Moses interview *Eyes on the Prize*, 1986.

67. Dittmer, *Local People*, 215–17; KKK leaflet qtd. in Moses and Henry to A. B. Britton, March 5, 1964, WHP, SHSW; King, *Freedom Song*, 243.

68. Moses and Henry to A. B. Britton, March 5, 1964, WHP, SHSW; Dittmer, *Local People*, 215–17; "Klan Beats Miss. Negro," *The Student Voice*, February 18, 1964, and "Mayhem in Miss.," *The Student Voice*, March 3, 1964, in Carson, *The Student Voice*, 121–22, 129, 132; Burke Marshall to John Lewis and Moses, February 28, 1964, File 0525, Reel 1, Series I, Chairman Files John Lewis, and Moses to Jack Greenberg, March 4, 1964, Files 0007–0008, Reel 7, Series IV, Ex. Sec. Files James Forman, SNCC Papers.

69. Carmichael and Thelwell, *Ready for Revolution*, 355; Moses interview Dittmer, 1983; Moses interview Biewen, 1994; Dittmer, *Local People*, 219; Moses and Cobb, *Radical Equations*, 76; Moses interview Carson, 1982.

70. Moses interview Biewen, 1994; Cobb interview Rachal, 1996, MOHP, USM; Warren, "Two for SNCC"; Branch, *Pillar of Fire*, 223–24.

71. Minutes SNCC meeting December 27–31, 1963.

Chapter Seven

1. Moses interview Branch, 1991.

2. McAdam, "Let It Shine," 487–91; Lynd, "Freedom Summer," 484–86; Nasstrom, "Between Memory and History," 325–64.

3. Moses interview Branch, 1991; Paul Lauter, interview by author, April 13, 2009 (hereafter cited as Lauter interview author, 2009); Dittmer, *Local People*, 260.

4. O'Reilly, *"Racial Matters,"* 158.

5. "Progress Report I," *The Student Voice*, July 15, 1964, in Carson, *The Student Voice*, 169–70; Carson, *Autobiography of Martin Luther King*, 249; Howard Zinn, interview, 1965, HZP, SHSW.

6. Marsh, *God's Long Summer*, 64–66; Dittmer, *Local People*, 215–17; "Mississippi: Allen's Army," *Newsweek*, February 24, 1964, File 0031, Reel 10, Series IV, Ex. Sec. Files James Forman, SNCC Papers; O'Reilly, *"Racial Matters,"* 161–63; "Mississippi Prepares for Summer Project," *The Student Voice*, June 9, 1964, in Carson, *The Student Voice*, 159–60; "1964 New Mississippi Laws," report, no date, File 0788, Reel 4, Burke Marshall Records, DJCRD, RSC.

7. Rothshild, "Northern Volunteers," 35; "Rights Fight Heading for a Bitter Summer," *Louisville Times*, April 29, 1964; O'Reilly, *"Racial Matters,"* 159, 161–63; Beschloss, *Taking Charge*, 312–13, 420–41; Robert Kennedy to Lyndon Johnson, June 5, 1964, and Lee White to Lyndon Johnson, April 8, 1964, Files 00085–00087 and 00082–00083, Reel 7, Part I, LBJ Papers, RSC; Cartha DeLoach to J. Edgar Hoover, June 8, 1964, Box 101, DGFOIA, SCRBC.

8. O'Reilly, *"Racial Matters,"* 178–79; M. A. Jones to C. DeLoach, July 8, 1964, and SAC New Orleans to J. Edgar Hoover, July 31, 1964, and Hoover to Burke Marshall and Howard Rogerson, July 2 and 13, 1964, and A. Rosen to Mr. Belmont, July 10, 1964, Box 101, Folder 62-109384, DGFOIA, SCRBC.

9. Woods, *Black Struggle*, 147, 154, 199–200, 207–10; King, *Freedom Song*, 289; SAC New Orleans, June 23, 1964, and Hoover to W. C. Sullivan and to SAC Jackson, November 24 and 25, 1964, Box 101, Folder 62-10938, DGFOIA, SCRBC; James Eastland, "Communist Infiltration in the So-Called Civil Rights Movement," July 22, 1964, transcript in *The Congressional Record*; Watkins interviews Rachal, 1996, MOHP, USM; Tom Scarborough, "Lafayette County" and "Lafayette—Marshall Counties," reports, May 5 and 19, 1964, MSSC Online, accessed November 22, 2007.

10. *The Detroit Free Press*, June 22, 1964; Moses speech West Coast Civil Rights Conference, 1964; Lauter interview author, 2009; Belfrage, *Freedom Summer*, 24; Watson, *Freedom Summer*, 29.

11. Dittmer, *Local People*, 229–30; Casey Hayden to Jon Regier, February 14, 1964, File 0020, Reel 6, and Mary Varela to Forman, September 24, 1963, February 3, 1964, and no date, Files 0858–0859, 0869, and 0872, Reel 10, Series IV, Ex. Sec. Files James Forman, SNCC Papers; Hunter Morey, "The Problem of Legal Aid in Mississippi," Box 3, Folder 1, and Jack Greenberg to Moses, letter, April 6, 1964, and John Kiefer to Moses, letter, March 18, 1964, Box 3, Folder 4, HRMP, SHSW.

12. Moses et al. to Dear Faculty Member, April 8, 1964, File 0021–0022, Reel 6, Series IV, Ex. Sec. Files James Forman, and Moses to Robert Spike, May 1, 1964, File 0800, and Moses to George Meaney, A. Philip Randolph, James Carey, Walter Reuther, no date, Files 0800–0806, Reel 70, Appendix A: MFDP Papers, and Minutes SNCC Executive Committee Meeting, May 10, 1964, Files 0993–0997, Reel 3, Series III, Staff Meetings, SNCC Papers (hereafter cited as Minutes SNCC Meeting, May 10, 1964, SNCC Papers).

13. Zinn to Moses, "To Prevent or Minimize Violence," no date, Box 2, Folder 6, HZP, SHSW; Moses to Friends of Freedom in Mississippi, April 6, 1964, Files 1225–1226, Reel 38, Series XV, State Project Files, and Aaron Henry et al. to Lyndon Johnson, May 25, 1964, File 0142, Reel 14, Series VII, Communications Department, Public Relations, SNCC Papers; Minutes SNCC Meeting, May 10, 1964, SNCC Papers; Dittmer, *Local People*, 239; Minutes SNCC Executive Committee Meeting, April 18–19, 1964, Box 6, Folder 2, EBP, SCRBC (hereafter cited as Minutes SNCC Meeting, April 18–19, 1964, EBP, SCRBC); Moses to Martin Luther King et al., May 17, 1964, JFP, LC.

14. Dittmer, *Local People*, 239; Lee White to Lyndon Johnson, June 17, 1964, Reel 7, Part 1, LBJ Papers, RSC.

15. Moses to Lyndon Johnson, June 14, 1964, Files 0160–0161, Reel 14, Series VII, Communications Department, Public Relations, SNCC Papers; Doar and Landsberg, "The Performance of the FBI," 43.

16. Minutes SNCC Meeting, April 18–19, 1964, EBP, SCRBC; Julian Bond to John Pratt, June 2, 1964, File 0190, Reel 8, Series IV, Ex. Sec. Files James Forman, and Washington hearings, Files 0641–0644, Reel 42, Series XVII, Other Organizations, SNCC Papers; Mike Thelwell to Howard Zinn, May 19, 1964, and "Lyndon Johnson and the Mississippi Summer," report, 1964, Box 2, Folder 5, HZP, SHSW.

17. Washington hearings, Files 0641–0644, Reel 42, Series XVII, Other Organizations, SNCC Papers; Michael Finkelstein to Moses and Bob Weil, June 10, 1964, Box 3, Folder 4, HRMP, SHSW; COFO Legal Coordinator to All Project Directors and Law Students, July 28, 1964, Box 1, Folder 12, COFO Panola County Office Records, WSHS.

18. "Mississippi Summer Project," no date, Files 0034–0036, Reel 64, Appendix A: MFDP Papers, and SNCC Executive Committee Meeting, June 9–11, 1964, minutes, Files 0975–0992, Reel 3, Series III, Staff Meetings, SNCC Papers; Burner, *And Gently*, 149–50.

19. Woodley, "It Will Be a Hot Summer"; Moses, "Memo to Freedom Centers," no date (likely April 1964), and Moses, Rejection letter, no date, USM; Minutes SNCC Meeting, April 18–19, 1964; John Maguire to COFO and Moses, May 11,

1964, Files 0849–0850, Reel 69, Appendix A: MFDP Papers, and Moses to accepted volunteers, no date, File 0804, Reel 39, Series XV, State Project Files, SNCC Papers.

20. Woodley, "It Will Be a Hot Summer"; Sellers and Terrell, *River of No Return*, 82; Branch, *Pillar of Fire*, 295–96; Louis E. Lomax, "The Road to Mississippi," *Ramparts*, Special Edition 1964, 8–23, Box 1, Catherine Clarke Civil Rights Collection.

21. Julian Bond to Edward Keating, November 3, 1964, File 0524, and William Kreger to Moses, March 26, 1964, Reel 12, Series VII, Communications Department, Public Relations, SNCC Papers; James Atwater, "If We Can Crack Mississippi . . . ," *Saturday Evening Post*, July 25–August 1, 1964, 15–19.

22. Murphree, *The Selling of Civil Rights*, 64–65; "Notes on Staff Executive Meeting," January 17, 1964, JFP, LC; Moses to accepted volunteers, no date, WHP, SHSW; Moses, "Memo to Freedom Centers," no date, USM; Minutes SNCC Meeting, April 18–19, 1964, EBP, SCBRC; Hogan, *Many Minds*, 370, 37n; SNCC Executive Committee Meeting, June 9–11, 1964, Handwritten and typed minutes, Files 0887–0909 and 0975–0992, Reel 3, Series III, Staff meetings, SNCC Papers (hereafter cited as Minutes Meeting SNCC, June 9–11, 1964, SNCC Papers).

23. "Minutes of the COFO Convention," February 9, 1964, JFP, LC; Dittmer, *Local People*, 232–34; Bond interview author, 2008; Chafe, *Never Stop Running*, 189–92, 206; Moses interview Chafe, 1989; Moses to Allard Lowenstein, no date (likely February 1964), WHP, SHSW.

24. Dittmer, *Local People*, 230, 233–34; O'Reilly, *"Racial Matters,"* 181–84; Greenberg and Spike to Moses, April 7 and 27, 1964, Folder 4, HRMP, SHSW; Carl Rachlin to Marvin Rich et al., April 13, 1964, Box 22, CORE Records, SHSW.

25. Branch, *Pillar of Fire*, 273–74; Moses interview Chafe, 1989; *National Guardian*, June 27, 1964; Minutes SNCC Meeting, April 18–19, 1964, EBP, SHSW; Dittmer, *Local People*, 233–34; Moses interview Chafe, 1989; Ed King, interview by William Chafe, March 30, 1988, ALP, UNC; Chafe, *Never Stop Running*, 189, 192–94; Moses interview Carson, 1982; Samstein, "Notes on Mississippi," 1963.

26. Moses to Lowenstein, no date, WHP, SHSW; Minutes SNCC meeting December 27–31, 1963, SNCC Papers.

27. Moses to James Farmer, March 2, 1964, File 0582, Reel 42, Series XVII, Other Organizations, SNCC Papers; Minutes SNCC Meeting, April 18–19, 1964, EBP, SCBRC.

28. Dittmer, *Local People*, 236; Minutes SNCC Meetings, December 27–31, 1963, and June 9–11, 1964, SNCC Papers; King, *Freedom Song*, 309–10.

29. Woodley, "It Will Be a Hot Summer," 30; Minutes SNCC Meeting, April 18–19, 1964, EBP, SCBRC; Minutes SNCC Meeting, June 9–11, 1964, SNCC Papers; Casey Hayden to Jon Regier, February 14, 1964, File 0020, Reel 6, Series IV, Ex. Sec. Files James Forman, SNCC Papers; COFO Staff Executive Committee Meeting, January 10, 1964, minutes, and Summer Project Committee to COFO Staff Executive Committee, memorandum, January 17, 1964, JFP, LC; Myles Horton to Moses, April 17, 1964, Box 21, HRECR, SHSW; Greenberg, *Circle of Trust*, 201.

30. Belfrage, *Freedom Summer*, 9–11; Lise Vogel, "Notes of 1964 Orientation," LVP, SHSW (hereafter cited as Vogel Orientation Notes, LVP, SHSW); Burner, *And Gently*, 155–56.

31. Belfrage, *Freedom Summer*, 9–11; Vogel Orientation Notes, LVP, SHSW; Burner, *And Gently*, 155–56; Sutherland-Martinez, *Letters from Mississippi*, 13.

32. Vogel Orientation Notes, LVP, SHSW; Belfrage, *Freedom Summer*, 9–11, 170–77; "Rights Workers Off for Mississippi to Register Negro Voters," *NYT*, June 21, 1964; Moses to Parents Volunteers, no date, WHP, SHSW; Payne, *I've Got the Light*, 210–14.

33. Vogel Orientation Notes, LVP, SHSW; Belfrage, *Freedom Summer*, 9–11, 170–77; Sutherland-Martinez, *Letters from Mississippi*, 15; Sellers and Terrell, *River of No Return*, 82–83; Charles Benner to John Lewis, June 16, 1964, File 1096, Reel 38, Series XV, State Project Files, SNCC Papers.

34. Dittmer, *Local People*, 244–45; Bond, "1964 Mississippi Freedom Summer," 78–84. See also McAdam, *Freedom Summer*.

35. Dittmer, *Local People*, 244–45; Belfrage, *Freedom Summer*, 7; Carson, *In Struggle*, 112–13; Watson, *Freedom Summer*, 30, 33; Sutherland-Martinez, *Letters from Mississippi*, 22; "Preparing for Mississippi," *The New York Herald Tribune*, June 18, 1964.

36. Dittmer, *Local People*, 244–45; Belfrage, *Freedom Summer*, 7; Carson, *In Struggle*, 112–13; Watson, *Freedom Summer*, 30, 33.

37. Watson, *Freedom Summer*, 30–31; *Freedom on My Mind*, 1994; Terri Shaw, "Freedom Summer Recollections," no date, USM; Moses and Cobb, *Radical Equations*, 79; Staughton Lynd to Howard Zinn, June 12, 1964, Box 2, Folder 7, Howard Zinn Papers; Belfrage, *Freedom Summer*, 11; Minutes SNCC Meeting, April 18–19, 1964, EBP, SCRBC; Carson, *In Struggle*, 102–3, 118–19; Lewis and D'Orso, *Walking with the Wind*, 250. Moses supported the white community projects in Biloxi and Jackson out of idealism *and* political realism. Since one-third of Mississippi's poor was white, they should unite with their black counterparts because it "was the only way I saw out of the impasse we came to politically in this race question," he later clarified (Moses interview Carson, 1982).

38. Belfrage, *Freedom Summer*, 11.

39. Ibid., 22–23; Volunteers to President Johnson, June 17, 1964, File 0161, Reel 14, Series VII, Communications Department, Public Relations, SNCC Papers; Carmichael and Thelwell, *Ready for Revolution*, 369–71; Anne Braden, draft article, 1964, Box 56, Folder 1, CABP, SHSW.

40. Lewis interview author, 2009; Warren, *Who Speaks for the Negro?* 91; Minutes SNCC Meeting, April 18–19, 1964, EBP, SCRBC; Minutes SNCC Meeting, June 9–11, 1964, SNCC Papers; King, *Freedom Song*, 311–25; Payne, *I've Got the Light*, 204–5.

41. Minutes SNCC Meeting, April 18–19, 1964, EBP, SCRBC; Minutes SNCC Meeting, June 9–11, 1964, SNCC Papers; Crosby, "It Wasn't the Wild West," 202–3.

42. Belfrage, *Freedom Summer*, 10; Sutherland-Martinez, *Letters from Mississippi*, 15, 34–35; Vogel Orientation Notes, LVP, SHSW; Eilen Barnes, "Account of Ori-

entation at Western's Campus," File 23, Reel 2, Microfilm, Lucy Montgomery Papers, SHSW.

43. Terri Shaw, "Freedom Summer Recollections," and Terri Shaw, interview by Stephanie Scull Millet Shaw, June 7, 1999, MOHP, USM; Cohen, "Sorrow Songs," 177–89; Lynd, "Mississippi: 1961–1962," 8; Bond interview author, 2008.

44. Belfrage, *Freedom Summer*, 11–12; Cagin and Dray, *We Are Not Afraid*, 320–21; Dale Minor and Chris Koch for Pacific Radio, "Whatsoever a Man Soweth," June 27, 1964, Files 0362–0372, Reel 20, Series VIII, Research Department, SNCC Papers.

45. Belfrage, *Freedom Summer*, 11–12; Cagin and Dray, *We Are Not Afraid*, 320–21.

46. *Freedom on My Mind*, 1994; Carmichael and Thelwell, *Ready for Revolution*, 373.

47. Cagin and Dray, *We Are Not Afraid*, 1–46, 278–301; Marsh, *God's Long Summer*, 66–72.

48. "Mission to Mississippi," *The Washington Post*, June 25, 1964, Pamela P. Allen Papers, SHSW; Moses interview Branch, July 30, 1984; Alsop qtd. in "Mississippi—Summer of 1964," *Newsweek*, July 13, 1964, Catherine Clarke Civil Rights Collection, SCRBC.

49. Moses interview Branch, July 30, 1984; Moses to "Mississippi Summer Project Contacts," June 27, 1964, File 0648, Reel 42, Series XVII, Other Organizations, SNCC Papers; Dennis and Moses interviews *Eyes on the Prize*, 1985, 1986; King, *Freedom Song*, 318; "Last Summer in Mississippi," *Redbook Magazine*, November 1964, WHP, SHWS; Eugene Nelson, letter, June 26, 1964, Eugene Nelson Letters 1964, SHSW.

50. Moses interview Biewen, 1994; Burner, *And Gently*, 158.

51. Matt Heron conversation with author, April 17, 2010; Dittmer, *Local People*, 248–50.

52. Carmichael and Thelwell, *Ready for Revolution*, 373, 377; Sellers and Terrell, *River of No Return*, 81–93.

53. Russell, *Black Genius*, 334; Moses to parents volunteers, no date, WHP, SHSW; Belfrage, *Freedom Summer*, 15; O'Reilly, *"Racial Matters,"* 167; King, *Freedom Song*, 388–90.

54. MFSR, 1979, Session 8, SHSW; Cagin and Dray, *We Are Not Afraid*, 384–85; "Omnibus Rights Suit Filed Against Miss.," *The Student Voice*, August 19, 1964, in Carson, *The Student Voice*, 187, 190; Affidavits *COFO vs. Rainey* lawsuit, Files 0187–0195, Reel 63, and 0703–0704 and 0721, Reel 66, Appendix A: MFDP Papers, SNCC Papers; Victor Rabinowitz to Arthur Kunstler et al., August 5, 1964, Box 3, Folder 4, HRMP, SHSW.

55. Lewis and D'Orso, *Walking with the Wind*, 265; Murphree, *The Selling of Civil Rights*, 66; Jim Kates and Alvin Poussaint, interviews by author, May 25, 2009, and October 2010; Cagin and Dray, *We Are Not Afraid*, 386; "Mississippi—Summer of 1964," *Newsweek*, July 13, 1964, Catherine Clarke Civil Rights Collection, SCRBC; Moses interview Branch, August 10, 1983; Moses interview Dittmer, 1983.

56. Zoya Zeman, interview by John Rachal, April 18, 1996, MOHP, USM (hereafter cited as Zeman interview Rachal, 1996, MOHP, USM); Jan Handke, report,

June 29, 1964, USM; Moses interview *Eyes on the Prize*, 1986; Kates, "June 1964" and "August 1964"; "Last Summer in Mississippi," *Redbook Magazine*, November 1964, and Robert Coles and Joseph Brenner, "American Youth in a Social Struggle," report, no date, WHP, SHSW; Sutherland-Martinez, *Letters from Mississippi*, 38–39.

57. King, *Freedom Song*, 394–95.

58. Joseph Ellin, June 28, 1964, USM; Tobis Booth interview author, 2009; *Freedom on My Mind*, 1994.

59. Belfrage, *Freedom Summer*, 25–26; Moses interview Branch, 1991; Sutherland-Martinez, *Letters from Mississippi*, 28–29, 36–37; Seth and Dray, *We Are Not Afraid*, 352–53; McAdam, *Freedom Summer*, 72; Branch, *Pillar of Fire*, 374.

60. Belfrage, *Freedom Summer*, 25–26; Moses interview Branch, 1991; Sutherland-Martinez, *Letters from Mississippi*, 28–29, 36–37. Also for preceding paragraph.

61. Carson, *In Struggle*, 123; Watson, *Freedom Summer*, 235; "Mississippi—Summer of 1964," *Newsweek*, July 13, 1964; "Mississippi Feels Pinch on Economy," *The Sunday Gazette-Mail*, December 20, 1964, Box 56, Folder 1, CABP, SHSW; Martin and Victoria Nicolaus to friends, February 19, 1965, Folder 1, Martin and Victoria Nicolaus Papers, SHSW.

62. O'Reilly, *"Racial Matters,"* 160, 166–67; Eastland in Rubin, ed., *Student Nonviolent Coordinating Committee*, 83, 91; Sellers and Terrell, *River of No Return*, 103–6; Rita Schwerner, "Attempts to See Governor," June 25, 1964, File 0346, Reel 16, and "Mississippi Summer Project Running Summary of Incidents," June 16–July 16, 1964, Files 0139–0142, Reel 17, Series VII, Communications Department, Internal Communications, SNCC Papers; Dittmer, *Local People*, 265–71.

63. Chaney, "Schwerner, Chaney, and Goodman"; Paul Johnson, interview, September 18, 1970, Files 00432–00446, Reel 2, Part 3, Oral Histories, LBJ Papers, RSC; Moses interview Dittmer, 1983; Cagin and Dray, *We Are Not Afraid*, 336–65, 407–8; "COFO Contacts with Neshoba County Law Enforcement Officers," June 21–June 24, 1964, Files 0365–0366, Reel 16, Series VII, Communications Department, Internal Communications, and "Missing Mississippi Summer Project Workers," report, June 26, 1964, Files 0163–0167, Reel 14, Series VII, Communications Department, Public Relations, SNCC Papers.

64. O'Reilly, *"Racial Matters,"* 166–67; Lee White to Lyndon Johnson, June 23 and 29, 1964, Files 00099 and 00100, Reel 7, Part 1, White House Central Files, LBJ Papers, RSC.

65. Lyndon Johnson to Lee White, John McCormack, Nicholas Katzenbach, James Eastland, Paul Johnson on June 23, 1964, to Russell Long on July 20, 1964, and to J. Edgar Hoover on June 23, 24, 26, 29, and July 2, 1964, in Beschloss, *Taking Charge*, 425–27, 430–41, 444–45, 448–49, 458–59.

66. Lyndon Johnson to J. Edgar Hoover on July 2, 1964, in Beschloss, *Taking Charge*, 448–49; Jerry DeLaughter, "FBI Director Tells Plans for Our State," *CL*, July 11, 1964; Doar and Landsberg, "The Performance of the FBI," 47–48; Harold Martin and Kenneth Fairly, "We Got Nothing to Hide," *Saturday Evening Post*, January 30, 1965, 27–33, Catherine Clarke Civil Rights Collection, SCRBC.

67. O'Reilly, *"Racial Matters,"* 176, 192; "Mississippi—Summer of 1964," *Newsweek*, July 13, 1964; Burner, *And Gently*, 163; Murphree, *The Selling of Civil Rights*, 67; Dennis interview *Eyes on the Prize*, 1985.

68. Dennis, "Oration for Funeral of James Chaney," 360–63.

69. Dennis interview *Eyes on the Prize*; Belfrage, *Freedom Summer*, 182–83.

70. "Moses in Mississippi Raises Some Universal Questions," *Pacific Scene*, February 3, 1965; "Statement of Robert Moses," August 19, 1964, File 0699, Reel 43, Series XVII, Other Organizations, and "Mississippi Summer Project Ends," August 29, 1964, File 0196, Reel 13, Series Communications Department, Public Relations, SNCC Papers; King, *Freedom Song*, 482–83; Julian Bond, interview by John Britton, January 22, 1968, RBC, HU.

71. Payne, *I've Got the Light*, 301–6; Cobb interview Rachal, 1996, MOHP, USM; Moses speech West Coast Civil Rights Conference, 1964; Dittmer, *Local People*, 259; Charlie Cobb, "Prospectus for a Summer Freedom School Program," November 1963, Files 0022–0024, Reel 20, Series VIII, Research Department, and Cobb to SNCC Executive Committee, "Summer Freedom Schools in Mississippi," January 14, 1964, File 0456, Reel 63, Appendix A: MFDP Papers, SNCC Papers.

72. King, *Freedom Song*, 441; Moses to accepted volunteers, no date, WHP, SHSW; Moses to Dick Parrish, March 10, 1964, File 1225, Reel 9, Moses to Philip Stern and Robert Cohen, May 1, 1964, File 0486, Liz Fusco to Myles Horton, September 2, 1964, File 0465, Matthew Holden to Moses, May 21, 1964, File 0265, and Mary Varela to Moses, no date, File 0574, Reel 67, and "People Invited to the Curriculum Conference," no date, File 0605, Reel 64, Appendix A: MFDP Papers, and Moses et al. to "Theatre Group for SNCC," no date, File 1020, Reel 1, Chairman Files John Lewis, SNCC Papers; Ransby, *Ella Baker*, 326–28; Cagin and Dray, *We Are Not Afraid*, 353.

73. Ransby, *Ella Baker*, 326–28; Moses to Valida Diehl, March 6, 1964, File 0130, Reel 64, and Edouard Morot-Sir to Moses, September 11, 1964, File 0466, Reel 68, Appendix A: MFDP Papers, and Liz Fusco, "Freedom Schools in Mississippi, 1964," no date, Files 0005–0008, Reel 39, and Staughton Lynd, "Mississippi Freedom Schools," July 26, 1964, Files 0332–0337, Reel 38, Series XV, State Project Files, SNCC Papers; Tom Scarborough, "Lafayette—Marshall Counties," report, May 19, 1964, MSSC Online; Lauter interview author, 2009; Rothshild, "Northern Volunteers," 115–27, 138–40.

74. Rothshild, "Northern Volunteers," 115–27, 138–40; Dittmer, *Local People*, 260–61; Branch, *Pillar of Fire*, 441–42; Emery, *Lessons from Freedom Summer*, 278–97.

75. Dittmer, *Local People*, 260–61; Branch, *Pillar of Fire*, 441–42; Zeman interview Rachal, 1996, MOHP, USM; "The COFO Community Centers," report, no date, Files 0707–0717, Reel 21, Series VIII, Research Department, and "Progress and Problems of the COFO Community Centers," report, Summer 1964, Files 0558–0559, Reel 63, Appendix A: MFDP Papers, SNCC Papers; Myles Horton to Moses, February 26, 1964, and Penny Patch to Horton, March 18, 1964, Box 9, Folder 23, HRECR, SHSW.

76. Dittmer, *Local People*, 260–61; Branch, *Pillar of Fire*, 441–42; Bessie Mae Herring, "What the Summer Project Ment to Me," no date, File 0576, Reel 68, Appendix A: MFDP Papers, SNCC Papers; Community Center Staff, July 8, 1964, Box 1, Folder 3, COFO Panola County Office Records, SHSW; "Project Proposal for Mississippi for the Summer of 1964," no date, JFP, LC.

77. Cohen, "Sorrow Songs," 177–89; Chilcoat and Ligon, "Developing Democratic Citizens," 107–137; "Folk Festival in Mississippi," News Release, File 0720, Reel 3, Series III, Communications Department, Public Relations, and Judy Walborn, "Freedom School Report," July 15, 1964, File 0502, Reel 67, Ralph Ford, James Betts, and Lewis Flagg to Moses, July 20, 22, and 24, 1964, Files 1246–1247, Reel 69, Appendix A: MFDP Papers, SNCC Papers; Moses to Ben Griffin, July 18, 1964 and Erle Johnston, "COFO Musical and Dramatics Festival," July 20, 1964, MSSC Online.

78. Moses interview Biewen, 1994; Wally to Staughton Lynd, July 11, 1964, File 0242, Reel 68, Appendix A: MFDP Papers, SNCC Papers; Dittmer, *Local People*, 264; Payne, *I've Got the Light*, 301, 306–15; Carson, *In Struggle*, 116–17.

79. Rothshild, "Northern Volunteers," 67; "The Volunteers for Mississippi Learn Some Vital Do's and Don'ts," *New York Herald Tribune*, June 17, 1964; Vogel Orientation Notes, LVP, SHSW; Annelle Ponder, "Adult Program," no date, Box 1, Folder 3, COFO Panola County Office Records, SHSW; Belfrage, *Freedom Summer*, 42; "Techniques for Field Work," no date, Box 1, Folder 2, Catherine Clarke Civil Rights Collection, SCRBC; Warren, *Who Speaks for the Negro?* 120; Lynd, "Freedom Summer," 484; Stoper, *Student Nonviolent Coordinating Committee*, 101.

80. Forman, *Making of Black Revolutionaries*, 422; "SNCC's Goals and Sentimentality," no date, Folder 2, Stuart Ewen Papers, SHSW; Jane Stembridge to Mary King, letter, April 21, 1964, Box 3, Folder 3, MKP, SHSW.

81. Newfield, "Moses in Mississippi"; Lee, *For Freedom's Sake*, 42, 72–73; Bond interview author, 2008.

82. Dittmer, *Local People*, 261–63; Edith Black and Jay Lockard interview KZSU Project South, 1965, LC; Lauter interview author, 2009; Martin and Victoria Nicolaus to Friends, December 9, 1964, Folder 1, Martin and Victoria Nicolaus Papers, SHSW; Sutherland-Martinez, *Letters from Mississippi*, 235.

83. Mary Lane, interview by Robert Wright, July 12, 1969, RBC, HU; Payne, *I've Got the Light*, 335–36; Ulysses Everett interview KZSU Project South, 1965, LC.

84. Payne, *I've Got the Light*, 241; "Notes from Bob Moses," no date, JFP, LC; "Letters from Mississippi with regard to sexual tensions," report, WHP, SHSW; Minutes 5th District Meeting, November 25, 1964, Box 14, Folder 1, CORE Records, SHSW; B. E. Murph to Stephen Gill Spottswood, no date, Reel 10, Group III, Box C-74, Part 27, Records NAACP, LC.

85. Dittmer, *Local People*, 178, 274–79; Crosby, *A Little Taste of Freedom*, 85–88, 214–16; Charles Evers to Moses, July 13, 1964, File 1240, and Moses to Evers, no date, File 1242, Reel 69, Appendix A: MFDP Papers, SNCC Papers; "SNCC, CORE Refuse Action Moratorium," August 5, 1964, in Carson, *The Student Voice*,

179, 182; Claire O'Connor, Community Center Batesville, report, August 6, 1964, Box 1, Folder 3, COFO Panola County Office Records, SHSW.

Chapter Eight

1. Lyndon Johnson to John Connally, July 23, 1964, in Beschloss, *Taking Charge*, 466–67; Visser-Maessen, "We Didn't Come for No Two Seats," 93.

2. Lyndon Johnson to Walter Reuther, August 9, 1964, in Beschloss, *Taking Charge*, 510–11; Visser-Maessen, "We Didn't Come for No Two Seats," 93.

3. Agger, *The Sixties at 40*, 184; Russell, *Black Genius*, 334–35; Moses speech West Coast Civil Rights Conference, 1964; Moses interview Dittmer, 1983.

4. Report on MFDP, no date, Folder 1, MSP, SHSW; Hogan, *Many Minds*, 176–77.

5. Carmichael and Thelwell, *Ready for Revolution*, 400; Stoper, *Student Nonviolent Coordinating Committee*, 14; Minutes SNCC Meetings, April 18–19, 1964, EBP, SCRBC; Minutes SNCC Meeting, June 9–11, 1964, SNCC Papers.

6. Minutes SNCC Meeting, December 27–31, 1963, SNCC Papers; Moses interviews Romaine; COFO Staff Executive Committee Meeting, January 10, 1964, minutes, JFP, LC.

7. Minutes SNCC Meeting, June 9–11, 1964, SNCC Papers; Convention Committee to COFO Staff Executive Committee, "Plans for Action at National Democratic Convention," January 16, 1964, JFP, LC.

8. Ed King interview author, 2009; Moses to Harry Belafonte, May 5, 1964, Files 0809–0810, and Casey Hayden to Guido Goldman, May 5, 1964, File 0810, Reel 70, Appendix A: MFDP Papers, SNCC Papers; Lyndon Johnson to Walter Reuther and Walter Jenkins, August 24 and 25, 1964, in Beschloss, *Taking Charge*, 489, 523–27, 531–35.

9. Moses to Joseph Rauh, May 1, 1964, File 0799, Reel 70, Appendix A: MFDP Papers, and Casey Hayden to Norm and Velma Hill et al., April 15, 1964, Files 0242–0243, Reel 41, Series XVI, Mississippi Freedom Democratic Party, SNCC Papers; Convention Committee, January 16, 1964, and "Preliminary Notes on Primary Elections and Democratic Party Convention," January 5, 1964, JFP, LC; Moses, August, 2011; Moses interviews Taylor Branch, August 11, 1983, and February 15, 1991.

10. Moses to Joseph Rauh, May 1, 1964, File 0799, Reel 70, Appendix A: MFDP Papers, and Casey Hayden to Norm and Velma Hill et al., April 15, 1964, Files 0242–0243, Reel 41, Series XVI, Mississippi Freedom Democratic Party, SNCC Papers; Moses to Lowenstein, no date, WHP, SHSW; King, *Freedom Song*, 329; Moses to Bill Dodd, Robert Spike, Dean Robb, Larry Landry, Roy Reuther, and Mildred Jeffrey, April 30, 1964, Files 0796–0798, Moses to Jeffrey, May 15, 1964, File 0812, and Casey Hayden, "Notes on Conversation with Al Lowenstein," July 15, 1964, File 1346, Reel 69, Appendix A: MFDP Papers, SNCC Papers; Moses to Ralph Helstein, June 1964, JFP, LC.

11. Moses to Joseph Rauh, May 1, 1964, File 0799, Reel 70, Appendix A: MFDP Papers, SNCC Papers; Ransby, *Ella Baker*, 332–33; Minutes SNCC Meeting,

May 10, 1964, SNCC Papers; Cagin and Dray, *We Are Not Afraid*, 403–5; Davis, "'Sisters and Brothers All,'" 80–81; Ella Baker and Joseph Rauh, interviews by Anne Romaine, March 25 and June 16, 1967, ARP, UNC; Joseph Rauh interview *Eyes on the Prize*, October 31, 1985.

12. Ransby, *Ella Baker*, 332–33; Carmichael and Thelwell, *Ready for Revolution*, 403; Moses interviews Romaine; Henry and Curry, *Aaron Henry*, 166, 187; Jack Minnis to Ben Smith, April 20, 1964, and Rauh to Moses, June 30, 1964, Box 1, Folder 15, Benjamin E. Smith Papers, SHSW.

13. Ransby, *Ella Baker*, 333, 335–36; Davis, "'Sisters and Brothers All,'" 91; Minutes SNCC Meeting, April 18–19, 1964, EBP, SCRBC; Baker and Walter Tillow, interviews by Anne Romaine, March 25 and September 4, 1967, ARP, UNC; SNCC Meeting, minutes, May 5, 1964, Box 1, Folder 1, Walter Tillow Papers, SHSW; Ed King interviews William Chafe, 1988, ALP, UNC.

14. Aaron Henry, interview, September 12, 1970, Files 00170–229, Reel 2, Part 3, LBJ Papers, RSC; Moses and Cobb, *Radical Equations*, 20.

15. Minutes SNCC Meeting, November 14–16, 1963, SNCC Papers; "Miss. Negro Vote Curtailed in Congressional Primary," June 9, 1964, in Carson, *The Student Voice*, 159, 161; Moses to Belafonte, May 5, 1964, Files 0809–0810, Reel 70, Appendix A: MFDP Papers, SNCC Papers.

16. "Miss. Negro Vote Curtailed in Congressional Primary," June 9, 1964, in Carson, *The Student Voice*, 159, 161; "Notes from Bob Moses," no date, JFP, LC; Mendy Samstein, WATS report, March 22, 1964, Box 1, Folder 1, MKP, SHSW.

17. "Miss. Negro Vote Curtailed in Congressional Primary," June 9, 1964, in Carson, *The Student Voice*, 159, 161; "Notes from Bob Moses," no date, JFP, LC; Richards, "Freedom Registration," memorandum, no date, Files 0152–0154, Reel 67, and Moses to Belafonte, May 5, 1964, Files 0809–0810, Reel 70, Appendix A: MFDP Papers, and Hardy Frye, "Holly Springs Registration Drive," report, August 19, 1964, Files 1068–1069, Reel 7, Ex. Sec. Files James Forman, SNCC Papers; Todd interview author, 2008; Hogan, *Many Minds*, 177–78; Cobb interview Rachal, 1996, MOHP, USM; Terri Shaw, "Freedom Summer Recollections," USM; Henry and Curry, *Aaron Henry*, 164; Robert Miles interview KZSU Project South, 1965, LC.

18. Henry and Curry, *Aaron Henry*, 166–67.

19. Joseph Rauh, "Brief submitted by the MFDP," no date, Box 2, Folder 1, Roberta Yancy Civil Rights Collection, SCRBC (hereafter cited as Rauh, "Brief submitted by MFDP"); Moses, "Emergency Memorandum," July 19, 1964, Files 0062–0068, Reel 40, Series XV, State Project Files, SNCC Papers (hereafter cited as Moses, "Emergency Memorandum").

20. Moses, "Emergency Memorandum"; Dittmer, *Local People*, 272–73; Moses speech West Coast Civil Rights Conference, 1964.

21. Moses, "Emergency Memorandum"; Branch, *Pillar of Fire*, 408, 412–14; Carson, *Autobiography of Martin Luther King*, 249–50; COFO Executive Meeting, July 10, 1964, minutes, Box 3, Folder 1, HRMP, SHSW; Belfrage, *Freedom Summer*, 164–67; Carson, *In Struggle*, 164; Jan Handke, July 26, 1964, Jan Handke Papers, USM; O'Reilly, *"Racial Matters,"* 170–71; "En Route on United Air

Lines," File 00375, Reel 5, Part 4, Series I, Records of Andrew Young, Records SCLC, RSC.

22. Watson, *Freedom Summer*, 235; Davis, " 'Sisters and Brothers All,' " 83–88; Mendy Samstein, interview by Anne Romaine, September 4, 1966, ARP, UNC; Rauh, "Brief submitted by MFDP"; King, *Freedom Song*, 338–39; "MFDP Precinct Meetings," June 16, 1964, WHP, SHSW.'

23. Davis, " 'Sisters and Brothers All,' " 83–88; Sutherland-Martinez, *Letters from Mississippi*, 248; Moses to Mildred Jeffrey, May 27, 1964, File 0814, Reel 70, Appendix A: MFDP Papers and "Lafayette County Convention of MFDP," July 31, 1964, File 1072, Reel 8, Series IV, Ex. Sec. Files James Forman, SNCC Papers; Roberts, "All My Days."

24. Dittmer, *Local People*, 280; Moses, "Emergency Memorandum."

25. Sutherland-Martinez, *Letters from Mississippi*, 247, 252–54; "What to Do at a FDP Precinct Meeting" and "What to Do at a FDP County Convention," no date, File 0276, Reel 41, Series XVI, Mississippi Freedom Democratic Party, and "Convention Challenge," no date, File 1293, Reel 39, Series XV, State Project Files, and WATS report, July 8, 1964, File 0550, Reel 16, Series VII, Communications Department, SNCC Papers; "Precinct and County Meetings for Freedom Democratic Party" and "Parliamentary Procedures and Rules of Order for FDP Precinct Meetings," no date, Box 1, Folder 14, COFO Panola County Office Records, SHSW.

26. "Platform and Principles MFDP" and "Loyalty Resolution," no dates, Box 1, Folder 4, IGFSC, SCRBC; Dittmer, *Local People*, 281–83; Marsh, *God's Long Summer*, 34–35; Joseph Rauh, interview by Anne Romaine, June 16, 1967, ARP, UNC.

27. Moses and Cobb, *Radical Equations*, 79–81; Moses interview *Eyes on the Prize*, 1986; Rothshild, "Northern Volunteers," 84; Moses interview Carson, 1982; Forman, *Making of Black Revolutionaries*, 385.

28. Moses and Cobb, *Radical Equations*, 79; Dittmer, *Local People*, 282–83; Emma Sanders, interview by Robert Wright, July 8, 1969, RBC, HU (hereafter cited as Sanders interview Wright, 1969, RBC, HU); Ed King interview Romaine, 1966, ARP, UNC.

29. Moses and Cobb, *Radical Equations*, 79; Dittmer, *Local People*, 282–83; Sanders interview Wright, 1969, RBC, HU; Minutes SNCC Meeting, June 9–11, 1964, SNCC Papers; Moses interview Dittmer, 1983; Polletta, "Strategy and Identity," 144–45; Hogan, *Many Minds*, 187–88.

30. Edward Brown, interview by Harold O. Lewis, June 30, 1967, RBC, HU (hereafter cited as Brown interview Lewis, 1967, RBC, HU); Dittmer, *Local People*, 285–87; Watson, *Freedom Summer*, 241–42; Davis, " 'Sisters and Brothers All,' " 89–90, 93–94; "Freedom Democratic Party injunction," no date, Box 1, Folder 15, COFO Panola County Office Records, SHSW; "Mississippi State Democratic Party in Convention Assembled July 28, 1964," report, Box 4, Folder 13, SLP, SHSW; "Platform and Principles of the Mississippi State Democratic Party," June 30, 1964, and "Address by Governor Paul B. Johnson," no date, and "Resolution[s]," July 28, 1964, Files 1125–1133, Reel 40, Series XVI, Mississippi

Freedom Democratic Party, SNCC Papers; I. F. Stone, "Why We Support Johnson and Humphrey," *I.F. Stone's Weekly*, September 7, 1964.

31. Dittmer, *Local People*, 286–87; *Freedom on My Mind*, 1994; Hogan, *Many Minds*, 195; Watson, *Freedom Summer*, 235.

32. *Freedom on My Mind*, 1994; Hogan, *Many Minds*, 190, 237; Dittmer, *Local People*, 288–89; Davis, " 'Sisters and Brothers All,' " 94–97; Rauh interview Romaine, 1967, ARP, UNC; "Partial Proceedings of the Democratic National Convention 1964 Credentials Committee," August 22, 1964, Box 29, Joseph Rauh Papers, LC; Moses and Cobb, *Radical Equations*, 79–80; Martin Luther King Jr., "Statement before the Credentials Committee," August 22, 1964, Files 00254–257, Reel 20, Part 1, Series II, Manuscripts and Appointment Calendars, Records SCLC, RSC; Rauh, "Mississippi Freedom Democratic Party," 309–12.

33. "Partial Proceedings," August 22, 1964, Box 29, Joseph Rauh Papers, LC; Dittmer, *Local People*, 288–89; Robert Kastenmeier, interview by Anne Romaine, August 23, 1967, ARP, UNC; Sherrod, "Mississippi at Atlantic City," and Kempton, "Conscience of a Convention," WHP, SHSW.

34. Kempton, "Conscience of a Convention," WHP, SHSW; "State Democratic Resolutions in Support of the FDP," no date, Box 1, Folder 15, COFO Panola County Office Records, SHSW; Dittmer, *Local People*, 290; Davis, " 'Sisters and Brothers All,' " 92–93; Harold Leventhal to David Lawrence, August 5, 1964, and Harold Leventhal to John Bailey and David Lawrence, August 17, 1964, WHP, SHSW.

35. Dittmer, *Local People*, 286, 290–93; Lyndon B. Johnson to Hubert Humphrey, May 23, in Beschloss, *Taking Charge*, 353–55.

36. Lyndon Johnson to John Connally, July 23, to Hubert Humphrey, August 14, to Cartha DeLoach and Roy Wilkins, August 15, to James Rowe, July 23, to Walter Jenkins, August 25, and to Walter Reuther, August 9 and 25, 1964, in Beschloss, *Taking Charge*, 467–69, 485, 510–11, 515–18, 523–27, 531–35; Moses interview Dittmer, 1983; Burner, *And Gently*, 172; O'Reilly, *"Racial Matters,"* 186–90.

37. Arthur I. Waskow, "Notes on the Democratic National Convention, Atlantic City, August 1964," confidential report, fall 1964, Box 1, Folder 23, HZP, SHSW (hereafter cited as Waskow report, 1964); Dittmer, *Local People*, 289, 293.

38. Gitlin, *The Sixties*, 156n; Joseph Rauh, interview by Katherine Shannon, August 28, 1967, RBC, HU (hereafter cited as Rauh interview Shannon, 1967, RBC, HU); Chafe, *Never Stop Running*, 198; Watson, *Freedom Summer*, 250; Henry and Curry, *Aaron Henry*, 183–84; Moses interview Carson, 1982; Ed King interview author, 2010.

39. Ed King interview author; Rauh interview Shannon, 1967, RBC, HU; Rauh, Moses, and Samstein interviews Romaine, 1966 and 1967, ARP, UNC; Moses interview Carson, 1982; Hogan, *Many Minds*, 189–90; Waskow report, 1964; Lee, *For Freedom's Sake*, 90.

40. Hogan, *Many Minds*, 192–94; Waskow report, 1964; Dittmer, *Local People*, 289–90, 294–96; Cartha DeLoach to Mr. Mohr, August 24, 1964, Box 103, "MFDP-File 62–109555," DGFOIAC, SCRBC.

41. Lyndon Johnson to Roy Wilkins, August 15, to Hubert Humphrey, August 14, Walter Reuther, August 9 and 25, and to Walter Jenkins, August 24, 1964, in Beschloss, *Taking Charge*, 510–11, 515–18, 523–27, 531–35; Notes Taylor Branch, January 16, 1991, TBP, UNC; Moses interview Branch, August 11, 1983.

42. Notes Taylor Branch, January 16, 1991, TBP, UNC; Moses interview Branch, August 11, 1983; Dittmer, *Local People*, 293, 297; Moses interviews Romaine; Forman, *Making of Black Revolutionaries*, 388; Gitlin, *The Sixties*, 158; Newfield, "Moses in Mississippi."

43. Newfield, "Moses in Mississippi"; Dittmer, *Local People*, 293–98; Moses interview Branch, August 11, 1983; Ed King and Rauh interviews Romaine, 1966 and 1967, ARP, UNC; Waskow report, 1964; Lee, *For Freedom's Sake*, 93–96; Branch, *Pillar of Fire*, 465–66, 468–71; Ed King interview author, 2010.

44. Dittmer, *Local People*, 293–98; Moses interview Branch, August 11, 1983; Branch, *Pillar of Fire*, 465–66, 468–71.

45. Dittmer, *Local People*, 293–98; Lee, *For Freedom's Sake*, 93–96; Branch, *Pillar of Fire*, 465–66, 468–71; Ed King interview author, 2010; Henry and Curry, *Aaron Henry*, 189; MFSR, 1979, Session 7, SHSW.

46. It is unclear how the news of the Credentials Committee's decision was broken. Some accounts mention that a TV was rolled in. Moses does not recall a TV but a group of reporters outside Humphrey's room telling them of the decision. Others mention that the news bulletin did not announce the committee's acceptance, but the MFDP's, and that Moses shouted, "You cheated!" to Humphrey.

47. Dittmer, *Local People*, 296–98; Moses and Cobb, *Radical Equations*, 81–82; Rauh interview *Eyes on the Prize*, 1985; Samstein and Rauh interviews Romaine, 1966 and 1967, ARP, UNC.

48. Dittmer, *Local People*, 296–98; Davis, "'Sisters and Brothers All,'" 100, 103; Kempton, "Conscience of a Convention"; Forman, *Making of Black Revolutionaries*, 393; Henry and Curry, *Aaron Henry*, 187; Lisa Anderson Todd conversation author, 2009; "The Convention Challenge," no date, Files 0273–0274, Reel 41, Series XVI, Mississippi Freedom Democratic Party, SNCC Papers.

49. "The Convention Challenge," no date, Files 0273–0274, Reel 41, Series XVI, Mississippi Freedom Democratic Party, SNCC Papers; Davis, "'Sisters and Brothers All,'" 100; Henry and Curry, *Aaron Henry*, 190; "Moses in Mississippi Raises Some Universal Questions," *Pacific Scene*, February 3, 1965; Victoria Gray Adams interview *Eyes on the Prize*, November 9, 1985.

50. Watson, *Freedom Summer*, 256–257; Waskow report, 1964; Dittmer, *Local People*, 298; Lee, *For Freedom's Sake*, 96; Samstein, King, and Rauh interviews Romaine, 1966 and 1967, ARP, UNC; Joseph Rauh interview *Eyes on the Prize*, October 31, 1985.

51. Samstein, King, and Rauh interviews Romaine, 1966 and 1967, ARP, UNC; Joseph Rauh interview *Eyes on the Prize*, October 31, 1985; Waskow report, 1964; Henry and Curry, *Aaron Henry*, 193; Robnett, *How Long?* 156; Belfrage, *Freedom Summer*, 242; Burner, *And Gently*, 198.

52. Dittmer, *Local People*, 299; Davis, "'Sisters and Brothers All,'" 109–10; Ed King interview Romaine, 1966, ARP, UNC.

53. Waskow report, 1964; Courtland Cox interview *Eyes on the Prize*, May 14, 1979; Notes Branch January 16, 1991, TBP, UNC; Moses interview Branch, August 11, 1983; Moses interview Chafe, 1989, ALP, UNC; Davis, "'Sisters and Brothers All,'" 114; Moses interviews Jay.

54. Moses interview Branch, August 11, 1983; Waskow report, 1964; Dittmer, *Local People*, 299–302; Burner, *And Gently*, 186–87; Henry and Curry, *Aaron Henry*, 196–97; Aaron Henry, interview, September 12, 1970, Files 00170–229, Reel 2, Part 3, Oral Histories, LBJ Papers, RSC.

55. Unita Blackwell, interview by Robert Wright, August 10, 1968, RBC, HU; Lee, *For Freedom's Sake*, 94, 97–99; Moses interview Branch, August 11, 1983; Moses interview *Eyes on the Prize*, 1986.

56. Forman, *Making of Black Revolutionaries*, 390–93; Dona Richards and "SNCC orientation," SNCC Staff Meeting October 11, 1964, minutes, Files 1016–1021, Reel 3, Series III, Staff Meetings, SNCC Papers (hereafter cited as Minutes Meeting SNCC, October 11, 1964, SNCC Papers).

57. Moses interview Branch, August 11, 1983; Waskow report, 1964; Annie Devine, interview by Anne Romaine, November 22, 1966, ARP, UNC; Sellers and Terrell, *River of No Return*, 109; Lee, *For Freedom's Sake*, 97–99; Burner, *And Gently*, 186–87.

58. Waskow report, 1964.

59. Beschloss, *Taking Charge*, 541.

60. Dittmer, *Local People*, 300–302; Moses interview Dittmer, 1983; Blackwell interview Wright, 1968, RBC, HU; Ed King interview Romaine, 1966, ARP, UNC; Davis, "'Sisters and Brothers All,'" 4, 106–7, 235–36.

61. Moye, *Let the People Decide*, 140–41; Unita Blackwell, interviews by Michael Garvey, April 21, 1977, MOHP, USM; *Freedom on My Mind*, 1994; Hogan, *Many Minds*, 236; Burner, *And Gently*, 198; Dittmer, *Local People*, 363.

62. Moses interview Chafe, 1989, ALP, UNC; Moses interview Carson, 1982; Notes Branch January 1991, TBP, UNC.

63. Sherrod, "Mississippi at Atlantic City"; Polletta, "Strategy and Identity," 151–53; Moses interviews Romaine; Lewis and D'Orso, *Walking with the Wind*, 291–92; Anderson, *Bayard Rustin*, 279, 285; Moses interview Branch, February 15, 1991; Robert Morquand, "Up the Opportunity Ladder With Algebra," *The Christian Science Monitor*, 1989, Box 135, Folder 31, CABP, SHSW.

64. Moses interview Dittmer, 1983; Moses interview Chafe, 1989, ALP, UNC; *Freedom on My Mind*, 1994; Waskow report, 1964.

65. Brown interview Lewis, 1967, RBC, HU; Carson, *In Struggle*, 169, 173; Kempton, "Conscience of a Convention"; Moses interview Branch, August 11, 1983; Moses interview Carson, 1982.

66. Monsonis to Moses, September 5, 1964, File 0838, Reel 54, Series I, Administrative Files, Washington Office, SNCC Papers; Report on MFDP, no date, Folder 1, MSP, SHSW.

67. Rauh interview *Eyes on the Prize*, 1985; Rauh interview Romaine, 1967, ARP, UNC; Notes Branch, 1999, TBP, UNC.

68. Davis, "'Sisters and Brothers All,'" 113; Woods, *Black Struggle*, 216–18, 235; Rowland Evans and Robert Novak, "Inside Report: Civil Rights–Danger Ahead" and "Inside Report: SNIC Out in the Cold," *The New York Herald*, December 2, 1964, and March 28, 1965; Robert Novak to Princeton summer volunteer, letter, April 12, 1965, Box 1, Folder 23, Rowland Evans Jr. and Robert D. Novak Papers, SHSW; SAC New Orleans to J. Edgar Hoover, January 14 and April 1, 1965, Box 101, Folder 62-109384, DGFOIAC, SCRBC.

69. Monsonis to Moses, September 5, 1964, File 0838, Reel 54, Series I, Administrative Files, Washington Office, SNCC Papers; Bond and Mary King interviews author, 2008 and 2009.

70. Meeting National Council of Churches, September 18, 1964, minutes, Box 55, Folder 15, CABP, SHSW; Carson, *In Struggle*, 137; Dittmer, *Local People*, 315–17.

71. Meeting National Council of Churches, September 18, 1964, minutes, Box 55, Folder 15, CABP, SHSW; Carson, *In Struggle*, 137; Dittmer, *Local People*, 315–17.

72. SNCC had been working in Selma since February 1963. SCLC arrived in January 1965, after invitations from the local leadership. It started direct action projects, leading to the massive jailing of local blacks. On March 7, SCLC organized a march from Selma to Montgomery. SNCC did not participate but allowed individuals like John Lewis to join. On the Selma bridge, state troopers greeted the 600 marchers with sticks and tear gas and let their horses trample on those fallen to the ground. On March 10, SCLC renewed its attempt, now strengthened by hundreds of sympathizers, including an enraged SNCC. After Martin Luther King Jr. escorted the marchers to a police barricade, he led them into prayer and told them to turn around because federal officials had agreed that no violence would erupt if the march were aborted. SNCC saw this as meekness and hypocrisy. Eventually, the march was completed under federal protection between March 16 and 24. SCLC then left Selma to SNCC. (See David Garrow's *Protest at Selma*.)

73. Dittmer, *Local People*, 341–43; Moses interview Branch, August 11, 1983.

74. Dittmer, *Local People*, 342–343, 347–348; Moses interview Chafe, 1989, ALP, UNC; SNCC Executive Meeting, July 12–13, 1965, minutes, File 0427, Reel 3, Series III, Executive and Central Committees, Executive Committee, SNCC Papers; Moses interviews Romaine; King, *Freedom Song*, 523.

75. Dittmer, *Local People*, 342–43, 347–48; Lee, *For Freedom's Sake*, 100, 116–17; Martin and Victoria Nicolaus, December 9, 1964, Martin and Victoria Nicolaus Papers, SHSW; Gitlin, *The Sixties*, 159; Davis, "'Sisters and Brothers All,'" 93–94.

76. Mr. and Mrs. Henry to Dave Dennis, no date, Box 4, Folder 5, Robert Beech Papers, SHSW; Todd interview author, 2008; Lawrence Guyot and Don Chapman interviews KZSU Project South, 1965, LC; Stoper, *Student Nonviolent Coordinating Committee*, 42, 110; Sutherland-Martinez, *Letters from Mississippi*, 259; Moses interview Branch, July 31, 1984; Dittmer, *Local People*, 429.

77. Bositis, "Black Elected Officials"; Hogan, *Many Minds*, 194; Bell Gale Chevigny, "The Fruits of Freedom Summer," *The Nation*, August 8–15, 1994; Marsh, *God's Long Summer*, 43–44.

78. Marsh, *God's Long Summer*, 43–44; Payne, *I've Got the Light*, 318; Dittmer, *Local People*, 338–41, 351–52; Ed King interview author, 2010.

79. Moses interview Branch, February 15, 1991; Watson, *Freedom Summer*, 298.

Chapter Nine

1. Cade, "Mississippi Summer Twenty-five Years Later," 421–25; Moses interview author, 2010.

2. Moses interviews Romaine; Meier and Rudwick, *CORE*, 329–30.

3. Stoper, *Student Nonviolent Coordinating Committee*, 42; Polletta, "Strategy and Identity," 151–52, 177–78.

4. Moses interviews Romaine; Moses to Eleanor Holm et al., September 9, 1964, Box 3, Folder 4, HRMP, SHSW; Tapes "Freedom School Workshop March 27–April 7 [1965]," Reel 2, Lucille Montgomery Papers, SHSW; Horton to Baker, October 2, 1964, and Liz Fusco to Horton, letter, September 2, 1964, Box 9, Folder 23, HRECR, SHSW; David Finkelstein to Moses, January 4, 1965, File 0842, and "Summary of Status of Radio Tougaloo Project," December 7, 1964, File 0843, Reel 14, Series VII, Public Relations, and Ralph Rapoport to Bob and Dona Moses, letter, September 21, 1964, File 1131, Reel 38, and "Moses to Speak at Tuesday's Meeting," *Benton County Freedom Train*, December 21, 1964, File 1228, Reel 37, Series XV, State Project Files, SNCC Papers; Carawan, "Carry It On," 148.

5. Polletta, "Strategy and Identity," 154–55, 178; Willie Johnson interview KZSU Project South, 1965, LC; Ed Brown interview Lewis, 1967, RBC, HU.

6. Moses interview Dittmer, 1983. For more on CDGM, see Dittmer, *Local People*, chap. 16.

7. Ed Brown interview Lewis, 1967, RBC, HU; Report on MFDP, no date, Folder 1, MSP, SHSW; Lee, *For Freedom's Sake*, 137–38; Forman, *Making of Black Revolutionaries*, 438.

8. "Loyalty Resolution," no date, Box 1, Folder 4, IGFSC, SCRBC; Stoper, *Student Nonviolent Committee*, 282; Dittmer, *Local People*, 318, 320–21; Jack Newfield, "The Liberals' Big Stick," *Cavalier*, June 1965; Anderson, *Bayard Rustin*, 278; Waskow report, 1964; Moses interview Dittmer, 1983; Bob Moses, "Speech at *National Guardian* dinner November 24, 1964," File 0810, Reel 59, Series III, Other Organizations, Washington Office, SNCC Papers (hereafter cited as Moses speech *National Guardian*, 1964, SNCC Papers).

9. Newfield, "Moses in Mississippi"; Dittmer, *Local People*, 326; Moses interview Dittmer, 1983; Moses interview Carson, 1982; Moses interview Sinsheimer, 1984, TBP, UNC; Moses, 2010.

10. Moses interview Dittmer, 1983; Dittmer, *Local People*, 326, 344–46; Moses interview Sinsheimer, 1984, TBP, UNC; Moses, 2010. Moses interview Branch, February 15, 1991.

11. John Lewis, "Relations between SNCC and the MFDP," no date, Files 1195–1196, Reel 1, Series I, Chairman Files John Lewis, SNCC Papers; Report on MFDP, no date, Folder 1, MSP, SHSW; Mary Brumder, no date, Box 1, Folder 6, Samuel Walker Papers, SHSW.

12. Moses interview Dittmer, 1983; "Black and White Together: The Freedom Summer Experience," report, November 13, 1980, WHP, SHSW; Hunter Morey, "Cross Roads in COFO," December 3, 1964, File 1050, Reel 42, Series XVII, Other Organizations, SNCC Papers (hereafter cited as Morey, "Cross Roads in COFO," 1964, SNCC Papers).

13. Forman, *Making of Black Revolutionaries*, 374, 420; Moses to COFO Staff, August 1964, JFP, LC; Moses interview Sinsheimer, 1984, ALP, UNC; Cade, "Mississippi Summer Twenty-five Years Later," 420–21.

14. Marx and Useem, "Majority Involvement in Minority Movements," 81–104; Minutes SNCC meetings December 27–31, 1963, and June 9–11, 1964, SNCC Papers; Hogan, *Many Minds,* 215–16; Stoper, *Student Nonviolent Coordinating Committee,* 106.

15. Staughton Lynd, "SNCC: The Beginning of Ideology," essay, August 1964, Box 1, Folder 3, MKP, SHSW; Lynd to Zinn, June 12, 1964, Box 2, Folder 7, HZP, SHSQ; Charles Sherrod, position paper, Box 6, Folder 1, and "Semi-Introspective," Folder 6, EBP, SCRBC.

16. "SNCC's Goals and Sentimentality," no date (likely fall 1964), Box 1, Folder 2, Stuart Ewen Papers, SHSW.

17. Moses interviews Branch, February 15, 1991, and Sinsheimer, 1984, TBP, UNC; SNCC Executive Committee Meeting, September 4, 1964, minutes (hereafter cited as Minutes Meeting SNCC, September 4, 1964, MKP, SHSW), and Alabama SNCC Workshop, April 21–23, 1965, minutes, Box 1, Folder 3, MKP, SHSW.

18. Workshop Proposal, no title, no date, Box 1, Folder 2, Stuart Ewen Papers, SHSW; Minutes Meeting SNCC, November 6–12, 1964, SNCC Papers.

19. Minutes Meeting SNCC, November 6–12, 1964, SNCC Papers; Hershel Kaminsky to Walter Tillow, February 10, 1965, and SNCC Labor Conference, Box 1, Folder 2, Walter Tillow Papers, SHSW; Roy Shields, "Overall Report, Southwest Georgia," February 1965, Files 0344–0349, Reel 19, Series VIII, Research Department, SNCC Papers; Stoper, *Student Nonviolent Coordinating Committee,* 15–16, 35; Dittmer, *Local People,* 333–35.

20. Stoper, *Student Nonviolent Coordinating Committee,* 253; Moses interview Sinsheimer, 1984, TBP, UNC; Minutes Meeting SNCC, October 11, 1964, SNCC Papers; Forman, *Making of Black Revolutionaries,* 412, 416–17, 424–25.

21. Dittmer, *Local People,* 343–44; Moses interview Carson, 1982.

22. Moses and Cobb, *Radical Equations,* 21; Iris Greenberg to Ruby Doris Smith, April 17, 1964, Box 1, Folder 1, IGFSC, SCRBC; Newfield, *A Prophetic Minority,* 69; MFSR, 1979, Session 5, SHSW.

23. Moses interview Carson, 1982; "Semi-Introspective," Folder 6, EBP, SCRBC; Shields, "Overall Report, Southwest Georgia," 1965; Morey, "Cross Roads in COFO," 1964, SNCC Papers; Dittmer, *Local People,* 327; O'Reilly, *"Racial Matters,"* 75–76; Belfrage, *Freedom Summer,* xvi; King, *Freedom Song,* 178; Carson, *In Struggle,* 149; Eugene Turitz interview KZSU Project South, 1965, LC.

24. Mendy Samstein, "The Murder of a Community," September 23, 1964, in Carson, *The Student Voice,* 192–93; Williams, *My Soul Looks Back,* 130–33; King,

Freedom Song, 510–15; Allen, "Bibliography," 518. See also Doug McAdam's *Freedom Summer* and Carmichael and Thelwell's *Ready for Revolution*.

25. Moses interview Branch, February 15, 1991; Carmichael and Thelwell, *Ready for Revolution*, 435–36; Newfield, "Moses in Mississippi"; Moses interview Dittmer, 1983; Raines, *My Soul Is Rested*, 107–8; Hogan, *Many Minds*, 228.

26. Moses speech *National Guardian*, 1964, SNCC Papers; Bob Moses, "Questions Raised by Moses," April 1965, in Bond and Lewis, *Gonna Sit at the Welcome Table*, 722–24; Moses interview Branch, July 30, 1984.

27. Camus, *Resistance, Rebellion, and Death*, 106; Newfield, "Moses in Mississippi"; Gitlin, *The Sixties*, 162; "Moses in Mississippi Raises Some Universal Questions," *Pacific Scene*, February 3, 1965; Dittmer, *Local People*, 325–26; Cass, "The Moses Factor." Moses carried Camus's *Resistance, Rebellion, and Death* with him to the 1964 *Village Voice* interview.

28. Dittmer, *Local People*, 324–27; Carmichael and Thelwell, *Ready for Revolution*, 440. See also Hasan Kwame Jeffries's *Bloody Lowndes*.

29. The surge in race riots in northern cities accelerated this development. Even Moses, citing an American Medical Society report, encouraged his colleagues in April 1965 to organize northern blacks along their southern model for grassroots leadership to "channel off frustrations and tensions that make people act violently." But northern urban communities had a larger scope, and blacks were already integrated into the power structure. They required more time for developing contacts and research in uncovering the power relations in each neighborhood. Most workers—many of whom were militant black northerners who had only recently joined SNCC—were not as wedded in these methods as the old SNCC veterans had been. Impatient, they used the flamboyant rhetoric and tactics they knew from black nationalists, which divided black communities, inhibited fundraising, and spurred the organization's decline until it disappeared in the early 1970s. (Minutes Alabama SNCC Workshop, April 21–23, 1965, MKP, SHSW; Polletta, "Strategy and Identity," 278–81; Carson, *In Struggle*, 215–303.)

30. Moses interview Carson, 1982; King, *Freedom Song*, 165–70; Malcolm X to James Forman, July 31, 1963, File 0657, Reel 7, Series IV, Ex. Sec. Files James Forman, SNCC Papers; Stoper, *Student Nonviolent Coordinating Committee*, 70, 162–63; Clayborne Carson qtd. in MFSR, 1979, Session 2, SHSW.

31. Minutes SNCC meeting, September 4, 1964, MKP, SHSW; Branch, *Pillar of Fire*, 480–82; Fleming, *Soon We Will Not Cry*, 145–48; Moses interview Carson, 1982; Forman, *Making of Black Revolutionaries*, 427. Moses felt that SNCC either should have postponed the trip or sent others like those who could take photographs and do tape recordings and thereby could have made a real "cultural impact" on SNCC (Moses interview Carson, 1982).

32. Branch, *Pillar of Fire*, 480–82; Fleming, *Soon We Will Not Cry*, 145–48; Moses interview Carson, 1982; Forman, *Making of Black Revolutionaries*, 406–10; Bond interview author, 2008; Lee, *For Freedom's Sake*, 103–7; Hayes, "I Used the Term 'Negro,'" 225–26; Richards, "SNCC African Project," August 1965, Box 2, Folder 11, HZP, SHSW; Fannie Lou Hamer, interviews by Neil McMillen, April 14,

1972/January 25, 1973, MOHP, USM; Hammerback and Jensen, "Working in 'Quiet Places,'" 11.

33. Hayes, "I Used the Term 'Negro,'" 225–26; Richards, "SNCC African Project," August 1965, Box 2, Folder 11, HZP, SHSW; Fleming, *Soon We Will Not Cry*, 148; Forman, *Making of Black Revolutionaries*, 411; Richards, "Report on the Beginnings of the African project," no date, Box 6, Folder 10, EBP, SCRBC; Wilkins, "The Making of Black Internationalists," 468.

34. In his 1972 autobiography, Forman's interpretation of 1964 events seems influenced by his late 1960s black nationalist perspective. Wesley Hogan has argued convincingly that Forman gave "an orderly trajectory" to events and his own actions that rather provided an "ex post facto . . . rationale for his centralizing project" (Hogan, *Many Minds*, 211–12).

35. Dittmer, *Local People*, 319–20; Hogan, *Many Mindt*, 370n39; Forman, *Making of Black Revolutionaries*, 410, 413, 420–26; Minutes Meeting SNCC, October 11, 1964, SNCC Papers.

36. Dittmer, *Local People*, 319–20; Hogan, *Many Mindt*, 370n39; Forman, *Making of Black Revolutionaries*, 410, 413, 420–26; Minutes Meeting SNCC, October 11, 1964, SNCC Papers.

37. "Black Belt Program," Files 0779–0782, Reel 20, Series VIII, Research Department, SNCC Papers; Minutes SNCC meeting September 4, 1964, MKP, SHSW; Moses interview Carson, 1982; Dittmer, *Local People*, 318–19; Forman, *Making of Black Revolutionaries*, 417–18.

38. Forman, *Making of Black Revolutionaries*, 417–18; Minutes SNCC meetings June 9–11 and October 11, 1964, SNCC Papers; Arkansas Field Report, January 12, 1964, Box 1, Folder 1, IGFSC, SCRBC; Stoper, *Student Nonviolent Coordinating Committee*, 152–53, 211–12; John Perdew, "Southwest Georgia—Problems and Solutions," December 23, 1963, Box 2, Folder 9, HZP, SHSW; Bond interview author, 2008.

39. Stoper, *Student Nonviolent Coordinating Committee*, 77–78, 247–48; James Forman, no date, Box 8, Folder 1, EBP, SCRBC; Carson, *In Struggle*, 133, 139; Hogan, *Many Minds,* 202–3; Willie Ricks, Report, March 15, 1964, File 0496, Reel 7, Series IV, Ex. Sec. Files James Forman, SNCC Papers; SNCC Staff Institute, May 10–15, 1965, minutes, Box 3, Folder 4, MKP, SHSW.

40. Stoper, *Student Nonviolent Coordinating Committee*, 77, 293–94; Hogan, *Many Minds*, 202, 216–17; Barbara Schwartzbaum, no date, Files 0670–0671, Reel 70, Appendix A: MFDP Papers, SNCC Papers; John Bradford to Jackson office, no date, Box 1, Folder 6, Samuel Walker Papers, SHSW; Howard Zinn, position paper, no date, Box 2, Folder 11, HZP, SHSW; Minutes Meeting SNCC, October 11, 1964, SNCC Papers.

41. Moses interview Sinsheimer, 1984, TBP, UNC.

42. Moses interview Sinsheimer, 1984, TBP, UNC; Forman, *Making of Black Revolutionaries*, 433, 435; Hogan, *Many Minds*, 199–202, 216, 273–76, 280–82; Moses, "Commentary," 71–72.

43. Minutes SNCC meetings June 9–11 and November 6–12, 1964, SNCC Papers.

44. Moses, "Commentary," 71–72; Hogan, *Many Minds*, 201, 217; Bob Moses, position paper, November 1964, Box 1, Folder 2, Stuart Ewen Papers, SHSW (hereafter cited as Moses position paper); Carson, *In Struggle*, 141.

45. Moses position paper.

46. Ibid. The exact quote by Alfred Whitehead is: "The fixed person for the fixed duties who in older societies was such a godsend, in future will be a public danger." ("Epilogue: The Training of Professionals" in Alfred North Whitehead's *Science and the Modern World*, 1953.)

47. Moses, "Commentary," and Howard Zinn, "Commentary," in Albert and Hoffman, *We Shall Overcome*, 71–72, 78; "James Forman's Speech at Waveland, November 1964," in Hogan, *Many Minds*, 273–75.

48. Forman, *Making of Black Revolutionaries*, 425, 436; Polletta, "Strategy and Identity," 181, 183–84; Stoper, *Student Nonviolent Coordinating Committee*, 78–79, 270; King, *Freedom Song*, 446–48, 483–85; Mary Varela, "Some Basic Considerations for the Staff Retreat," no date, Box 8, Folder 1, EBP, SCRBC.

49. Adams, "From Africa to Mississippi," 325; Sellers and Terrell, *River of No Return*, 134–35; Lewis and D'Orso, *Walking with the Wind*, 303; Hogan, *Many Minds*, 212–14, 370–71; Carson, *In Struggle*, 139; Branch, *Pillar of Fire*, 480, 506.

50. Hogan, *Many Minds*, 212–14, 370–71; Minutes SNCC Meeting November 6–12, 1964, SNCC Papers; Lewis, *Shadows of Youth*, 186. Scholars like Emily Stoper and David Chappell, for instance, have mistakenly described Moses as an "exponent of anarchist ideas" with "a near pathological aversion" to power, although he considered both antithetical to effective organizing. (Stoper, *Student Nonviolent Coordinating Committee*, 106–7; Chappell, *A Stone of Hope*, 78–80.)

51. SNCC Meeting, February 1965, minutes, WHP, SHSW; Moses interviews author, April 15 and October 25, 2010; Agger, *The Sixties at 40*, 186–87.

52. Hogan, *Many Minds*, 208–10, 220–21, 365; Minutes SNCC Meeting September 4, 1964, MKP, SHSW; Moses interview Carson, 1982; Moses interview Branch, August 11, 1983; Moses, 2010.

53. Forman, *Making of Black Revolutionaries*, 431; Carson, *In Struggle*, 139; "Semi-Introspective," Folder 6, EBP, SCRBC; Stoper, *Student Nonviolent Coordinating Committee*, 78, 171, 252; Payne, *I've Got the Light*, 368–90.

54. Jim Kates, interview by author, May 25, 2009; Baker interview Britton, 1968, RBC, HU; Hogan, *Many Minds*, 211; Moses interview Sinsheimer, 1984, ALP, UNC.

55. Minutes SNCC Meeting, November 6–12, 1964, SNCC Papers.

56. Minutes SNCC Meeting, November 6–12, 1964, SNCC Papers; Stoper, *Student Nonviolent Coordinating Committee*, 157, 161; Carmichael and Thelwell, *Ready for Revolution*, 428–29; Grant, *Ella Baker*, 137; Booth interview author, 2009; Agger, *The Sixties at 40*, 206–7; Carson, *In Struggle*, 199–204.

57. Carson, *In Struggle*, 143–45; Ladner interview author, 2009; Brown interview Lewis, 1967, RBC, HU; Stoper, "The Student Nonviolent Coordinating Committee," 17; Hogan, *Many Minds*, 203–7; Forman, *Making of Black Revolutionaries*, 434–35; Minutes SNCC meeting, November 6–12, 1964, SNCC Papers.

58. Minutes SNCC meeting, November 6–12, 1964, SNCC Papers; Mary King to John Lewis, January 10, 1965, File 0650, Reel 1, Series I, Chairman Files

John Lewis, SNCC Papers; Hogan, *Many Minds*, 213, 216–18, 373; Carson, *In Struggle*, 146.

59. William Heath to author, October 29, 2013; Carson, *In Struggle*, 156; Sellers and Terrell, *River of No Return*, 82–83; Belfrage, *Freedom Summer*, 25, 74; Moses interview Dittmer, 1983; Cohen, *Freedom's Orator*, 52; Volunteer to Diane and Susan, June 26, 1964, USM; Sutherland-Martinez, *Letters From Mississippi*, 19; Bond interview author, 2008; for *The Saturday Evening Post*, see Files 0288–0292, Reel 20, Series VIII, Research Department, SNCC Papers. To become "SNCCY," Bond mocked workers' deference to informal hierarchies in 1965, one had to use "the Moses two-finger punch," a "forward jabbing motion of the first two fingers of the right hand, used to punch holes in other people's arguments" and say things like "what I think is . . ." but then paraphrase something "you heard Moses and Forman say at lunch" (Bond, "How to Be SNCCY," in Rubin, *Student Nonviolent Coordinating Committee*, 52–53).

60. Lewis and D'Orso, *Walking with the Wind*, 239–40, 302, 305; Forman, *Making of Black Revolutionaries*, 419–20; Moses interview Carson, 1982; Carson, *In Struggle*, 138–40.

61. Forman, *Making of Black Revolutionaries*, 419–20, 435–36; Sellers and Terrell, *River of No Return*, 133–37.

62. Forman, *Making of Black Revolutionaries*, 437–39; Carson, *In Struggle*, 151–52; SNCC Meeting, February 1965, minutes, WHP, SHSW; Stoper, *Student Nonviolent Coordinating Committee*, 80, 96.

63. Forman, *Making of Black Revolutionaries*, 437–39; SNCC Meeting, February 1965, minutes, WHP, SHSW; Moses interview Branch, July 31, 1984.

64. Forman, *Making of Black Revolutionaries*, 437–39; Moses interview Carson, 1982; Lewis and D'Orso, *Walking with the Wind*, 305; Lewis, *Shadows of Youth*, 187–88.

65. Moses interview Branch, July 31, 1984; Sellers and Terrell, *River of No Return*, 137–39; Branch, *Pillar of Fire*, 589–90; Lewis and D'Orso, *Walking with the Wind*, 366.

66. Moses interview Branch, July 31, 1984; Sellers and Terrell, *River of No Return*, 137–39; Branch, *Pillar of Fire*, 589–90; Lewis and D'Orso, *Walking with the Wind*, 366; Hammerback and Jensen, "Working in 'Quiet Places,'" 10; Pat McGauley interview KZSU Project South, 1965, LC; Forman, *Making of Black Revolutionaries*, 439.

67. Lynd, "Mississippi: 1961–1962," 7.

68. Moses interview Branch, July 31, 1984; Gitlin, *The Sixties*, 170.

69. Moses interview Branch, 1984.

70. McGauley interview Project South, 1965, LC; Burner, *And Gently*, 206; Lewis and D'Orso, *Walking with the Wind*, 303; Bond, Lewis, and Mary King interviews author, 2008 and 2009; Morey, "Cross Roads in COFO," 1964, SNCC Papers; Mary King to John Lewis, January 10, 1965, Box 3, Folder 1, MKP, SHSW; Fred Mangrum, interview by Robert Wright, July 8, 1969, RBC, HU.

71. Carson, *In Struggle*, 157; Carmichael and Thelwell, *Ready for Revolution*, 437; John Cumbler, interview by author, March 28, 2008; Bond interview author, 2008.

72. Bond, Lewis, and Mary King interviews author, 2008 and 2009.

73. Moses interview Carson, 1982; Moses interviews Taylor Branch, July 31, and Sinsheimer, 1984, TBP, UNC.

74. Moses interview Sinsheimer, 1984, TBP, UNC; Executive Committee Meeting, April 12–14, 1965, minutes, Files 0410–0426, Reel 3, Series II, Executive Committee, SNCC Papers; Carson, *In Struggle*, 169–70.

75. Carson, *In Struggle*, 170–71; Minutes Alabama SNCC Workshop, April 21–23, 1965, MKP, SHSW; Zinn, *SNCC*, 268; "'People's Conference' Will Decide Program," *The Student Voice* 5, March 1965, in Carson, *The Student Voice*, 207; Branch, *At Canaan's Edge*, 213.

76. Roberts, "All My Days"; Moses interview Branch, February 15, 1991; Belfrage, *Freedom Summer*, 9–11; Moses interview *The Story*, America Public Media radio station University of North Carolina, February 11, 2009; Moses interview Carson, 1982.

77. Moses interviews Branch, July 30 and 31, and interview Sinsheimer, 1984, TBP, UNC; Moses, "Speech," in *We Accuse* (Berkeley, Calif.: Diablo Press, 1965), ed. James Petras, 149–53, TBP, UNC; Branch, *At Canaan's Edge*, 223–24; Gitlin, *The Sixties*, 183; "On Peace and Civil Rights," *The Southern Patriot*, 1965; Carson, *In Struggle*, 184–85.

78. Moses interviews Branch, July 30 and 31, 1984; Lynd, "SNCC: The Beginning of Ideology," August 1964; Carson, *In Struggle*, 187–88; Lewis, *The Shadows of Youth*, 240–42.

79. Willner, *The Spellbinders*, 51; John Buffington, Eugene Turitz, Anonymous White Male, and Pat McGauley interviews KZSU Project South, 1965, LC; Branch, *At Canaan's Edge*, 278, 385–86; "One Freedom's Worker's Views—A Talk with Bob Parris," *The Southern Patriot*, October 1965; King, *Freedom Song*, 495; Carson, *In Struggle*, 185. In the *Southern Patriot*, Moses mentions that the SNCC's Executive Committee agreed with him that a leave of absence was unnecessary because organizations "must maintain the right of [its people] to function as individuals," yet from this time onward, Moses was no longer on SNCC's payroll, implying that he took the leave nonetheless.

80. Moses interviews Branch, July 30 and 31, and interview Sinsheimer, 1984, TBP, UNC; Moses interview Chafe, 1989, ALP, UNC; Branch, *At Canaan's Edge*, 278–79; "Summer Activities of Various Groups Attending Washington Conference," "Call for an Assembly of Unrepresented People," and "We Declare Peace," Box 12, Folder 8, Students for a Democratic Society Papers, SHSW; Moses to Walter Tillow, no date, Box 1, Folder 2, Walter Tillow Papers, SHSW.

81. Moses interviews Branch, July 30 and 31, and interview Sinsheimer, 1984, TBP, UNC; Moses interviews Romaine; Notes Branch, 1991, TBP, UNC; Sellers and Terrell, *River of No Return*, 142–46.

82. Moses interviews Branch, July 30 and 31, 1984; Notes Branch, 1991, TBP, UNC; Dona and Bob Moses to "SNCC People," letter, October 10, 1965, Box 6, Folder 10, EBP, SCRBC; Richards, "SNCC African Project," August 1965, Box 2, Folder 11, HZP, SHSW.

83. Moses interview Carson, 1982; Fleming, *Soon We Will Not Cry*, 145–48.

84. Moses, 2010; Carson, *In Struggle*, 201.

85. Moses interview Carson, 1982; Moses, 2010; Moses interview Branch, July 31, 1984; Fleming, *Soon We Will Not Cry*, 116–40; Alvin Poussaint, "The Stresses of the White Female Worker in the Civil Rights Movement in the South," October 1966, WHP, SHSW.

86. Moses, 2010; Lewis, *Shadows of Youth*, 188, 241–42.

87. Lewis and D'Orso, *Walking with the Wind*, 292; Wilkins and Mathews, *Standing Fast*, 306; Rauh interview *Eyes on the Prize*, 1985; Branch, *Pillar of Fire*, 590; Carmichael and Thelwell, *Ready for Revolution*, 435; "Moses in Mississippi Raises Some Universal Questions," *Pacific Scene*, February 3, 1965; Hammerback and Jensen, "Robert Parris Moses," 266–67.

88. H. "Rap" Brown, SNCC's chairman in 1967, was a black nationalist known for his violent rhetoric. Under his chairmanship, SNCC changed its name to Student National Coordinating Committee and briefly tried an alliance with the Black Panther Party. (See Carson's *In Struggle* and Brown's *Die, Nigger, Die*.)

89. Brown interview Lewis, 1967, RBC, HU; Carson, *In Struggle*, 201, 330n11; Greenberg, *Circle of Trust*, 80, 240; Ladner interview author, 2009; Janice Goodman, interview by author, June 2, 2012; King, *Freedom Song*, 530.

90. Bond, Moses, and Goodman interviews author, December 4, 2008, April 15, 2010, and June 2, 2012; Julian Bond, "Reflections on SNCC's Political Legacy," in Rubin, *Student Nonviolent Coordinating Committee*, 114–15; Moses interview Carson, 1982.

91. Moses interview Carson, 1982; Moses, 2010; Lewis, *Shadows of Youth*, 242.

92. Goodman interview author, 2012; Moses interview Carson, 1982; Sheila Michaels, interview by author, May 6, 2012. See also interview Michaels with Goodman, May 18, 2005, in Columbia University's Oral History Records.

93. Moses interview Carson, 1982; Hogan, *Many Minds*, 201.

94. Moses interviews Branch, August 11, 1983, July 31, 1984, and February 15, 1991; Moses interview Sinsheimer, 1984, TBP, UNC; Agger, *The Sixties at 40*, 183–84, 186–87; Hayes, "I Used the Term 'Negro,'" 160–61; Payne, *I've Got the Light*, 377–78; Moses, 2010; Morquand, "Up the Opportunity Ladder With Algebra," *The Christian Science Monitor*, 1989, Box 135, Folder 31, CABP, SHSW.

95. Brown interview Lewis, 1967, RBP, HU; Lynd, "Mississippi: 1961–1962," 7; Newfield, *Bread and Roses Too*, 35.

Epilogue

1. Burner, *And Gently*, 216; Lewis, *Shadows of Youth*, 242.

2. Moses interview Branch, July 31, 1984; Moses, 2010; Branch, *Pillar of Fire*, 612; Moses interview Dittmer, 1983.

3. Lewis, *Shadows of Youth*, 242–43.

4. Moses interview Branch, July 31, 1984; Moses interview Carson, 1982; Lewis, *Shadows of Youth*, 243–44.

5. Moses interview Branch, July 31, 1984; Moses, 2010; Moses interview Carson, 1982; Cagin and Dray, *We Are Not Afraid*, 452–53.

6. Moses interview Branch, July 31, 1984; Moses interview Carson, 1982; Cagin and Dray, *We Are Not Afraid*, 452–53; Notes Branch, 1991, TBP, UNC; Burner, *And Gently*, 220.

7. Moses interview Branch, July 31, 1984; Moses interview Carson, 1982; Cagin and Dray, *We Are Not Afraid*, 452–53; Notes Branch, 1991, TBP, UNC; Burner, *And Gently*, 220; Carmichael and Thelwell, *Ready for Revolution*, 436–37.

8. Notes Branch, 1991, TBP, UNC; Moses interview Carson, 1982; Branch, *Pillar of Fire*, 612.

9. Moses interview Carson, 1982; Moses, "If We Must Die," 266–69; Jeffries, *Bloody Lowndes*, 127.

10. Notes Branch, 1991, TBP, UNC; Moses interview Carson, 1982; Branch, *Pillar of Fire*, 612.

11. Blake, *Children of the Movement*, 37–45; Cass, "The Moses Factor"; Branch, *Pillar of Fire*, 612–13; Doris Moses interview Branch, January 8, 1993, TBP, UNC; Moses interview Carson, 1982.

12. Blake, *Children of the Movement*, 37–45; Lewis, *Shadows of Youth*, 244–45; Moses Inquiry to Robert Coles, October 1975, WHP, SHSW (hereafter cited as Moses Inquiry to Coles, 1975, WHP, SHSW).

13. Blake, *Children of the Movement*, 37–45; Lewis, *Shadows of Youth*, 244–45; Moses interview Carson, 1982; Moses and Cobb, *Radical Equations*, 94–95, 223–24; Russell, *Black Genius*, 336.

14. Moses interview Carson, 1982.

15. Ibid.

16. Ibid.; Russell, *Black Genius*, 336–37; Bond interview author, 2008; Blake, *Children of the Movement*, 44; Poussaint interview author, 2010; Morquand, "Up the Opportunity Ladder With Algebra," and Vincent Harding, November 3, 1980, Box 135, Folder 31, CABP, SHSW; Russell, *Black Genius*, 336–37; Holsaert, "Resistance U," 269.

17. Blake, *Children of the Movement*, 43, 45.

18. Moses Inquiry to Coles, 1975, WHP, SHSW.

19. Ibid.; Moses interview Carson, 1982; Moses and Cobb, *Radical Equations*, 97; Russell, *Black Genius*, 336–37; Watson, "A Freedom Summer Activist Becomes a Math Revolutionary," 114–25; Cass, "The Moses Factor."

20. Russell, *Black Genius*, 336–37; Moses and Cobb, *Radical Equations*, 93, 95–97; Gong, "The Algebra Project"; Blake, *Children of the Movement*, 39.

21. Moses and Cobb, *Radical Equations*, 5–12; Russell, *Black Genius*, 326–28, 335–43.

22. Moses and Cobb, *Radical Equations*, 5–12; Russell, *Black Genius*, 326–28, 335–43.

23. Russell, *Black Genius*, 326–28, 335–43; Moses and Cobb, *Radical Equations*, vii–xv, 3–22, 91–220; Lewis, *Shadows of Youth*, 290–92; Blake, *Children of the Movement*, 39–41; Holseart, *Hands on the Freedom Plow*, 269; Nelson, "A Case Study Analysis," 107–8, 114; Jodi Wilgoren, "Algebra Project," *NYT*, January 7, 2001; Wahman, "'Fleshing Out Consensus,'" 7–16; "The Algebra Project (AP) in the San Francisco Bay Area"; See also http://www.qecr.org/ and Theresa Perry et al., *Quality Education as a Constitutional Right*.

24. Russell, *Black Genius*, 326–28, 335–43; Moses and Cobb, *Radical Equations*, vii–xv, 3–22, 91–220; Lewis, *Shadows of Youth*, 290–92; Blake, *Children of the Movement*, 39–41.

25. Russell, *Black Genius*, 326–28, 335–43; Moses and Cobb, *Radical Equations*, vii–xv, 3–22, 91–220; Lewis, *Shadows of Youth*, 290–92; Payne, *I've Got the Light*, 410–11.

26. Blake, *The Children of the Movement*, 40–41; Moses and Cobb, *Radical Equations*, 92; Dumas, *African-American Biographies*, 59: Moses at 50th Anniversary Reunion Conference, Raleigh, N.C., April 2010.

27. Moses and Cobb, *Radical Equations*, 17; Cass, "The Moses Factor"; Watson, "A Freedom Summer Activist Becomes a Math Revolutionary"; Agger, *The Sixties at 40*, 185; Lewis, *Shadows of Youth*, 292–93. See also R. Moses, M. Kamii, S. Swap, and J. Howard, "The Algebra Project: Organizing in the Spirit of Ella," *Harvard Educational Review* 59 (November 1989): 423–443; Alexis Jetter, "Mississippi Learning," *New York Times Magazine*, February 21, 1993.

28. Moses and Cobb, *Radical Equations*, 17.

29. Moses to Anne Braden, October 9, 1980, Box 135, Folder 31, CABP, SHSW; Moses and Cobb, *Radical Equations*, vii–xv; Russell, *Black Genius*, 339–40; Lewis, *Shadows of Youth*, 290–91.

30. Lewis, *Shadows of Youth*, 290–91; Cass, "The Moses Factor"; Watson, "A Freedom Summer Activist Becomes a Math Revolutionary"; Bell Gale Chevigny, "The Fruits of Freedom Summer" and "Still It's a Fight for Power," *The Nation*, August 8–15 and August 22–29, 1994.

31. Cass, "The Moses Factor"; Lewis, *Shadow of Youth*, 291; John Doar interview *Eyes on the Prize*, 1985; Moses interview Branch, August 11, 1983; MFSR, 1979, Session 7, SHSW; John Doar, conversation with author, April 14, 2010.

32. Branch, *Pillar of Fire*, 613; Blake, *Children of the Movement*, 41; Dumas, *African-American Biographies*, 59.

33. Moses and Cobb, *Radical Equations*, x–xi, 83–84, 106, 137, 171; Moses, "Commentary," 72–73.

34. Moses and Cobb, *Radical Equations*, 173–74.

35. "The Algebra Project (AP) in the San Francisco Bay Area"; Russell, *Black Genius*, 326.

36. Moses, "Commentary," 72–73; Huggins, "Martin Luther King, Jr.," 478.

37. Russell, *Black Genius*, 325.

38. Baker interview Britton, 1968, RBC, HU.

39. Francis Fox Piven and Richard A. Cloward, *Poor People's Movements: Why They Succeed, How They Fail* (New York: Vintage, 1979), 32, 36, qtd. in *Local People*, Dittmer, 429; Payne, *I've Got the Light*, 411.

Appendix

1. Moses and Cobb, *Radical Equations*, 84.

2. For example, see William Chafe's local study of Greensboro, North Carolina, as early as 1980 (*Civilities and Civil Rights*) and Wesley Hogan's close-up

research of SNCC as late as 2007 (*Many Minds, One Heart*). Other historians have explored both avenues; Adam Fairclough wrote a study of SCLC (*To Redeem the Soul of America*) and a study of the movement in Louisiana (*Race & Democracy*). Clayborne Carson is known for his close-up analysis of SNCC (*In Struggle*) but was also one of the first historians to plead for a bottom-up approach to the movement. See also the bibliographic essay in Charles Payne's *I've Got the Light of Freedom* and Emilye Crosby, "The Politics of Writing and Teaching Movement History," in Crosby, *Civil Rights History from the Ground Up*, 3–26.

3. Cha-Jua and Lang "The 'Long Movement' as Vampire," 266; Carson, "Civil Rights Reform," 21; Nasstrom, "Between Memory and History," 325–64; Crosby, "The Politics of Writing and Teaching Movement History," 5.

4. Examples are August Meier and Elliott Rudwick's 1973 study of CORE, Carson's 1980 history of SNCC, Mark Tushnett's 1987 work on the NAACP, and a large body of works on King and SCLC (e.g., David Garrow's 1986 *Bearing the Cross*, Taylor Branch's trilogy, Thomas Peake's history of SCLC [1987], and biographies of King by Lewis, Lerone Bennett [1968], Stephen Oates [1982], and others). Examples of local studies with national significance include David Garrow's *Protest at Selma* (1978), David Colburn's study of St. Augustine (1985), and Joan Beifuss on Memphis (1985).

5. Lawson, "Freedom Then, Freedom Now," 456–57; Eynon, "Cast upon the Shore," 560; Cha-Jua and Lang, "The 'Long Movement' as Vampire," 266; Fairclough, "State of the Art," 393; Crosby, "The Politics of Writing and Teaching Movement History," 5.

6. Examples are John Dittmer's *Local People* (1994), Charles Payne's *I've Got the Light of Freedom* (1995), J. Mills Thornton's *Dividing Lines* (2006), Adam Fairclough's *Race & Democracy* (1995), Todd Moye's *Let the People Decide* (2004), Emilye Crosby's *A Little Taste of Freedom* (2005), Hasan Kwame Jeffries's *Bloody Lowndes* (2009), and the essay-collections *Groundwork: Local Black Freedom Movements in America* (2005), edited by Jeanne Theoharis and Komozi Woodard, and *Civil Rights History from the Ground Up* (2011), edited by Emilye Crosby.

7. Examples are Martha Biondi's study of postwar New York City (2003) and Thomas Sugrue's *Sweet Land of Liberty* (2008). In extending their purview to the North, some even placed the "black freedom struggles for fair employment, open housing, quality education, and equitable criminal justice outside the South at the forefront" of the overall struggle. Historians Joseph Crespino and Matthew Lassister, for instance, openly called to reject "the framework of Southern exceptionalism" that treats "southern history in false opposition to an idealized national standard" (Cha-Jua and Lang, "The 'Long Movement' as Vampire," 267, 268; Lassiter and Crespino, *The Myth of Southern Exceptionalism*, 8–12).

8. Examples are Maurice Isserman's *If I Had a Hammer* (1987), Michael Honey's *Southern Labor and Black Civil Rights* (1993), Roger Horowitz's *"Negro and White Unite and Fight!"* (1997), Bruce Nelson's *Divided We Stand* (2001), Robert Korstad's *Civil Rights Unionism* (2003), and Glenda Gilmore's *Defying Dixie* (2008). Hall's concept of the "long civil rights movement," however, has since been critiqued heavily. See Cha-Jua and Lang, "The 'Long Movement' as Vampire," 265–88;

Arnesen, "Reconsidering the 'Long Civil Rights Movement,'" 31–34; Eagles, "Toward New Histories of the Civil Rights Era," 815–48; Fairclough, "State of the Art," 387–98; Lawson, "Freedom Then, Freedom Now," 456–71; and Crosby, *Civil Rights History from the Ground Up*, 7–14.

9. Lawson, "Freedom Then, Freedom Now," 457; Morris, *The Origins of the Civil Rights Movement*, xii; Cha-Jua and Lang, "The 'Long Movement' as Vampire," 265, 267–68; Crosby, "The Politics of Writing and Teaching Movement History," 5–8; Hall, "The Long Civil Rights Movement," 1233–63; Carson, "Civil Rights Reform and the Black Freedom Struggle," 23–26, 28; Albert and Hoffman, *We Shall Overcome*, 6. See also works by Jeffrey Ogbar, Komozi Woodard and Jeanne Theoharis, and Lance Hill's *The Deacons for Defense: Armed Resistance and the Civil Rights Movement* (2006); Timothy B. Tyson's *Radio Free Dixie: Robert F. Williams and the Roots of Black Power* (1999); and Joseph Peniel's *The Black Power Movement: Rethinking the Civil Rights—Black Power Era* (2006).

10. Zinn, *SNCC*, 2, 10, 13, 15, 62, 65; Bagdikian, "Negro's Youth's New March."

11. Zinn, *SNCC*, 2, 10, 13, 15, 62, 65; Bagdikian, "Negro's Youth's New March"; Warren, *Who Speaks for the Negro?* 48–49, 114, 403; Newfield, *A Prophetic Minority*, 73, 78.

12. Lynd, "SNCC: The Beginning of Ideology," August 1964. Lynd quotes from C. Vann Woodward's 1959 essay "The Populist Heritage and the Intellectual."

13. These include James Forman's *The Making of Black Revolutionaries* (1985), Mary King's *Freedom Song* (1987), Cleveland Sellers's *The River of No Return* (1990), and Sally Belfrage's *Freedom Summer* (1990).

14. Branch, *Parting the Waters*, 519; Branch, *At Canaan's Edge*, 30; Carson, *In Struggle*, 303.

15. Stoper, *Student Nonviolent Coordinating Committee*, 78, 83–84, 107; Carson, *In Struggle*, 140, 156–57, 242, 303; Branch, *Pillar of Fire*, 55, 222; Branch, *Parting the Waters*, 518–19; Branch, *At Canaan's Edge*, 30.

16. Burner, *And Gently*, 4, 8, 31, 47, 53–4, 69–70, 90, 92–3, 105, 112, 206–7.

17. Dittmer, *Local People*, 319; Payne, *I've Got the Light*, 3–4, 180, 238, 243, 332.

18. Sellers and Terrell, *River of No Return*, 82–3, 194; Forman, *Making of Black Revolutionaries*, 278, 419–20; Carmichael and Thelwell, *Ready for Revolution*, 310–14; Lewis and D'Orso, *Walking with the Wind*, 302–3; King, *Freedom Song*, 146.

19. Nasstrom, "Between Memory and History," 325–64.

20. Payne, *I've Got the Light*, 3–4, 418, 441; Crosby, "The Politics of Writing and Teaching Movement History," 17–22.

21. Crosby, "The Politics of Writing and Teaching Movement History," 17–22.

22. Ibid., 22.

23. Lawson, "Freedom Then, Freedom Now," 460–61; Dittmer, *Local People*, 429; Hayes, "I Used the Term 'Negro,'" 160.

24. Moses and Cobb, *Radical Equations*, 4.

25. Henry and Curry, *Aaron Henry*, 201–2.

26. Crosby, "The Politics of Writing and Teaching Movement History," 13, 20; Moses and Cobb, *Radical Equations*, 20.

Bibliography

Manuscript Collections

Library of Congress, Washington, D.C., USA
  James Forman Papers, 1848–2005
  National Association for the Advancement of Colored People Records,
    1842–1999
  Joseph L. Rauh Papers, 1913–1994
Schomburg Center for Research in Black Culture, New York City, New York,
  USA
  Ella Baker Papers, 1926–1986
  Catherine Clarke Civil Rights Collection, 1962–1969
  Robert Fletcher Civil Rights Collection, 1962–1967
  David J. Garrow Freedom of Information Act materials on the Civil Rights
    Movement Collection, 1958–1969
  Iris Greenberg/Freedom Summer Collection, 1963–1964
  Roberta Yancy Civil Rights Collection, 1960–1972
University of North Carolina, Chapel Hill, North Carolina, USA
  Southern Historical Collection
      Taylor Branch Papers, 1865–2009
      Allard Lowenstein Papers, 1924–1995
      Anne Romaine Papers, 1935–1995
State Historical Society of Wisconsin, Madison, Wisconsin, USA
  Pamela P. Allen Papers, 1967–1974
  Lee Bankhead Papers, 1962–1971
  Robert Beech Papers, 1963–1972
  Carl and Anne Braden Papers, 1928–1990
  Congress of Racial Equality (CORE) Records, 1941–1967
  Council of Federated Organizations (COFO) Panola County Office Records,
    1963–1965
  Rowland Evans Jr. and Robert D. Novak Papers, 1948–2008
  Stuart Ewen Papers, 1961–1965
  Fannie Lou Hamer Papers, 1964–1967
  William Heath Papers, 1963–1997
  Highlander Research and Education Center Records, 1917–2005
  Mary E. King Papers, 1962–1999
  Mary Lane Papers, 1965, 1967
  Staughton Lynd Papers, 1938–1997
  Lucille Montgomery Papers, 1963–1967

Amzie Moore Papers, 1941–1970
Hunter R. Morey Papers, 1962–1967
National Coordinating Committee to End the War in Vietnam Records,
    1964–1967
Eugene Nelson Letters, 1964
Martin and Victoria Nicolaus Papers, 1964–1965
Mary Aickin Rothschild Papers, 1965–1974
Mendy Samstein Papers, 1963–1966
Charles M. Sherrod Papers, 1964–1967
Benjamin E. Smith Papers, 1955–1967
Students for a Democratic Society (SDS) Records, 1958–1970
Jerry Tecklin Papers, 1964
Walter Tillow Papers, 1962–1966
Lise Vogel Papers, 1964–1965
Samuel Walker Papers, 1964–1966
Dorothy M. and Robert Zellner Papers, 1960–1979
Howard Zinn Papers, 1956–1994
American Friends Service Committee, Philadelphia, Pennsylvania, USA
    Overseas Work Camps Materials, 1955–1956
Hamilton College Library, Clinton, New York, USA
    The Spectator, 1955–1956
    The Hamiltonian (yearbooks), 1953–1956
    Hamiltonian Alumni Review, 1956
Stuyvesant Alumni Association, New York City, USA
    The Indicator (yearbook), 1952
Roosevelt Study Center, Middelburg, the Netherlands
    Records of the Southern Christian Leadership Conference, 1954–1970
    Student Nonviolent Coordinating Committee Papers, 1959–1972
    Civil Rights during the Kennedy Administration, 1961–1963
        Papers of John F. Kennedy
    Civil Rights during the Johnson Administration, 1963–1969
        Papers of Lyndon B. Johnson
    FBI File on the Student Nonviolent Coordinating Committee
    Records of the Department of Justice's Civil Rights Division, 1958–1973:
        Files of W. Wilson White; Files of Joseph M. F. Ryan Jr.; Records of Burke
        Marshall; Files of St. John Barrett; Records of John Doar; Records of
        David L. Norman

Oral History and Interviews

Interviews conducted by author, in author's possession:
    Julian Bond, D.C., in person, October 27, 2008, Washington, D.C.
    Julian Bond, email, December 4, 2008
    Luvaughn Brown, in person conversation, April 15, 2010, Raleigh, N.C.

Luvaughn Brown, email, January 13 and 31, 2011

Bell Chevigny, in person, November 2009, New York City

John Cumbler, in person, March 28, 2008, Nijmegen, the Netherlands

David (Dave) Dennis Sr., in person, April 17, 2010, Raleigh, N.C.

John Doar, in person conversation, April 14, 2010, Raleigh, N.C.

Janice Goodman, email, June 2, 2012

Matt Herron, in person conversation, April 17, 2010, Raleigh, N.C.

Jim Kates, email, May 25, 26, 28 and June 2, 2009

Mary King, email, December 8, 2009

Ed King, in person, April 14, 2010, Raleigh, N.C.

Dorie Ladner, in person, November 16, 2009, Washington, D.C.

Paul Lauter, email, April 13, 2009

John Lewis, in person, November 16, 2009, Washington, D.C.

Sheila Michaels, email, May 6, 2012

Mike Miller, in person, April 15, 2010, Raleigh, N.C.

Robert Parris Moses, in person, April 15, 2010, Raleigh, N.C.

Robert Parris Moses, email, October 25, 2010, March 9–10, 2011, May 2, 2011, August 20 and 26, 2011

Alvin Poussaint, email, October 2010

Peggy Quinn, in person conversation, April 17, 2010, Raleigh, N.C.

Phil Alden Robinson, telephone and email, April 30, 2010

Charles Sherrod, in person, April 16, 2010, Raleigh, N.C.

Heather Tobis Booth, email, November 2009

Lisa Todd Anderson, in person, October 23, 2008, Washington, D.C.

Interviews in author's possession

Clayborne Carson, interview with Robert Parris Moses, March 29–30, 1982

John Dittmer, interview with Robert Parris Moses, August 15, 1983

Charles Payne, interview with Robert Parris Moses, August 1993 (see also Stephen F. Lawson and Charles Payne, *Debating the Civil Rights Movement, 1945–1968* [Lanham, Md.: Rowman & Littlefield, 2006], 170–86)

Online Databases

Mississippi Oral History Project and Civil Rights Movement in Mississippi Collection. Mississippi Digital Library, University of Southern Mississippi. http://www.msdiglib.net

Eyes on the Prize Interviews: The Complete Series, Washington University Digital Gateway http://digital.wustl.edu/eyesontheprize/ (see also *Eyes on the Prize: America's Civil Rights Years (1954–1965)*, Film and Media Archive, Henry Hampton Collection, Washington University Libraries, St. Louis, Missouri)

Recordings and Radio Interviews

The Story, episode "Dedicated to the Proposition: The March to Equality," interviews with Robert Parris Moses and Wallace Roberts, February 11, 2009, American Public Media, WUNC-FM Radio, University of North Carolina. Recording obtained through Wallace Roberts, in author's possession

Oh Freedom over Me, John Biewen, interview with Robert Parris Moses, 1994, American Public Media, American Radio Works. Accessed July 25, 2011, from http://americanradioworks.publicradio.org/oh features/oh_freedom/interview_index.html

The Story of Greenwood, Guy Carawan, Folkways Records, Album No. FD #5593, 1965

"Reality Asserts Itself: Interviews with Bob Moses" by Paul Jay, June 2014, *The Real News Network*, transcripts in author's possession, obtained through Mike Miller. See also http://therealnews.com/t2/index.php ?option=com_content&task=view&id=731

Howard University, Manuscript Division, Moorland Springarn Research Center, Washington, D.C., USA

    Ralph J. Bunche Collection, interviews:

        Ella Baker, Unita Blackwell, Julian Bond, Mary Boothe, Travis Britt, Ed Brown, Douglas MacArthur Cotton, Annie Devine, Betty Garman, Aaron Henry, Ed King, Peter Kirchheimer, Mary Lane, Allard Lowenstein, Fred Mangrum, Charles McDew, Silas McGhee, Emma Sanders, Charles Scattergood, R. L. T. Smith, Vera Pigee, George Raymond, Joseph Rauh, Will Henry Rogers, Wyatt Walker, Hollis Watkins, Robert Wright, Dorothy Zellner

Library of Congress, Washington, D.C., USA

    Project South: Interviews with Civil Rights Workers conducted by Stanford University Radio Station KZSU, 1965 (Microform)

State Historical Society Wisconsin, Madison, Wisconsin, USA

    Mississippi's "Freedom Summer" Reviewed: A Fifteen Year Perspective on Progress in Race Relations, 1964–1979

    Howard Zinn Papers, interviews:

        Marion Barry, James Forman, Jesse Harris, Aaron Henry, William Higgs, Tim Jenkins, Allard Lowenstein, Robert Parris Moses, R. L. T. Smith, Howard Zinn

University of North Carolina, Chapel Hill, North Carolina, USA

    Anne Romaine Papers, interviews:

        Ella Baker, Annie Devine, Ivanhoe Donaldson, Lawrence Guyot, Fannie Lou Hamer, Robert Kastenmeier, Ed King, Sandy Leigh, Allard Lowenstein, Robert Parris Moses, Joseph Rauh, Mendy Samstein, Walter Tillow

    Allard Lowenstein Papers:

        Interviews William Chafe:

            Julian Bond, Courtland Cox, Ivanhoe Donaldson, Lawrence Guyot, Aaron Henry, Ed King, Robert Parris Moses

    Taylor Branch Papers:

        Interviews Taylor Branch:

            Joyce Ladner, Doris Moses, Robert Parris Moses

        Interview Joe Sinsheimer:

            Robert Parris Moses

Private Collections

Adam Fairclough
Joan Mulholland

Newspapers and Periodicals

Atlanta Journal and Constitution; Chicago-Sun Times; Commentary; Delta Democrat-Times; Evening Star; Greenwood Commonwealth; Hootenanny; I. F. Stone's Weekly; Jackson Clarion-Ledger; Jackson Daily News; Jackson State Times; Jet Magazine; Liberation; Life; Louisville Times; McComb-Enterprise Journal; Nation; National Guardian; New American; New Republic; New University News; Newsweek; New York Herald Tribune; New York Times; Pacific Scene; Reporter; St. Louis Post Dispatch; Southern Patriot; Student Voice; Sunday Gazette-Mail; Texas Observer; Village Voice; Washington Post

Online Databases and Sources

Algebra Project. www.algebra.org.

Bositis, Davis A. "Black Elected Officials: A Statistical Summary 2000," abstract, January 2001, Joint Center for Political and Economic Studies. http://www .jointcenter.org/research/black-elected-officials-a-statistical-summary-2000. March 12, 2012.

Cass, Julia. "The Moses Factor." *Mother Jones*, May/June 2002. http:// motherjones.com/politics/2002/05/moses-factor. May 12, 2008.

Civil Rights Movement Veterans, 2000–2006. http://crmvet.org/.

John F. Kennedy Presidential Library and Museum. http://jfklibrary.org. June 10, 2011.

Mississippi Digital Library and Mississippi Department of Archives and History, University of Southern Mississippi. www.msdiglib.net.

Mississippi State Sovereignty Commission (MSSC) Online. http://mdah.state.ms.us /arlib/contents/er/sovcom. November 22, 2007.

Quality Education as a Constitutional Right. http://www.qecr.org/.

Podesta, James J. "Robert Parris Moses." Gale Contemporary Black Biography, entry posted 2006. http://www.answers.com/topic/robert-parris-moses. September 16, 2007.

Presidential Recordings Program, Miller Center, University of Virginia. http://millercenter.org/academic/presidentialrecordings. May 3, 2009.

60 Minutes. "Cold Case: The Murder of Louis Allen," April 7, 2011. http://www .cbsnews.com/stories/2011/04/07/60minutes/main20051850.shtml?tag =contentMain;contentBody. September 7, 2012.

T. Alicia. "Ethel Moses." www.imbd.com. December 3, 2013.

Van Slyck, Abigail A. "Summer Camps," Gale Group, entry posted 2008. http://www.faqs.org/childhood/So-Th/Summer-Camps.html. December 19, 2009.

Wartts, Adrienne. "Moses, Lycia Lynn," BlackPast.org. http://www.blackpast
.org/aah/moses-lucia-lynn-c-1906. December 3, 2013.

Dissertations

Davis, Vanessa Lynn. "'Sisters and Brothers All': The Mississippi Freedom
Democratic Party and the Struggle for Political Equality." Ph.D. diss.,
Vanderbilt University, 1996.
Hayes, Robin J. "'I Used the Term 'Negro' and I Was Firmly Corrected':
African Independence, Black Power and Channels of Diasporic Resistance."
Ph.D. diss., Yale University, 2006.
Nelson, Theardis. "A Case Study Analysis of Bob Moses' Algebra Project:
A Mathematics Program for African-American Middle School Boys." Ph.D.
diss., University of San Francisco, 1997.
Polletta, Francesca A. "Strategy and Identity in 1960's Black Protest: The
Activism of the Student Nonviolent Coordinating Committee, 1960–1967."
Ph.D. diss., Yale University, 1997.
Rothschild, Mary Aickin. "Northern Volunteers and the Southern 'Freedom
Summers,' 1964–1965: A Social History." Ph.D. diss., University of
Washington, 1974.

Documentaries and Film

Eyes on the Prize, directed by Henry Hampton. Blackside, USA. Release Date:
1987.
Freedom on My Mind, directed by Connie Field and Marilyn Mulford. Clarity
Educational Productions, Inc., USA. Release Date: June 22, 1994.
Freedom Song, directed by Phil Alden Robinson. Turner Films Inc., USA.
Release Date: February 27, 2000.
The Streets of Greenwood, directed by Jack Willis, John Reavis Jr., and Fred
Wardenburg. Brandon Films, USA. Release Date: 1964.

Unpublished Documents, in author's possession

Doar, John, and Dorothy Landsberg. "The Performance of the FBI in Investigating
Violations of Federal Laws Protecting the Right to Vote—1960–1967."
Freedom Song reunion, transcripts, McComb, June 27–30, 1991.
Hayden, Tom. *Revolution in Mississippi*. Pamphlet. Mississippi Digital Library
and Mississippi Department of Archives and History, University of Southern
Mississippi.
Kates, Jim. "June 1964." Essay.
———. "August 1964." Essay.
Ladner, Dorie. "Band of Brothers," poem, December 22, 1964.
Miller, Mike. "The Movement Unraveled: Why? Were There Other
Possibilities?" Essay, August 2011.

Moses, Robert Parris, and C. C. Bryant. "Comments," at Mississippi Voices of the Civil Rights Movement Conference, McComb, Mississippi, July 9, 1983.

Moses, Robert Parris. "Comments," Conference on Ethics and Morality, Washington, D.C., February 3, 1980.

———. Address at 75th Birthday Celebration for Ella Jo Baker, December 9, 1978, Carnegie International Center, New York City.

Roberts, Wallace. "All My Days: Memories of Mississippi Freedom Summer." Essay, 1969–2006.

Rubin, Larry, ed. *Student Nonviolent Coordinating Committee 50th Anniversary.* Conference Booklet, April 15–18, 2010.

"The Algebra Project (AP) in the San Francisco Bay Area: An Introduction for Community and Labor Organizations and Organizers, and Concerned People." Pamphlet, 2015.

Articles and Essays

Adams, Emmie Schrader. "From Africa to Mississippi." In *Deep in Our Hearts*, by Curry et al., 289–332. Athens: University of Georgia Press, 2002.

Allen, Pamela Chude. "Bibliography: The Mississippi Summer Project." In *Freedom Is a Constant Struggle*, edited by Susie Erenrich, 511–20. Montgomery, Ala.: Black Belt Press, 1999.

Arnesen, Eric. "Reconsidering the 'Long Civil Rights Movement.'" *Historically Speaking* 10, no. 2 (April 2009): 31–34.

Bagdikian, Ben H. "Negro's Youth's New March on Dixie." *Saturday Evening Post*, September 8, 1962.

Berg, Manfred. "Black Civil Rights and Liberal Anticommunism: The NAACP in the Early Cold War." *Journal of American History* 94, no. 1 (June 2007): 75–96.

Bond, Julian. "1964 Mississippi Freedom Summer." In *Freedom Is a Constant Struggle*, edited by Susie Erenrich, 78–84. Montgomery, Ala.: Black Belt Press, 1999.

Cade, Cathy. "Mississippi Summer Twenty-five Years Later." In *Freedom Is a Constant Struggle*, edited by Susie Erenrich, 421–25. Montgomery, Ala.: Black Belt Press, 1999.

Carawan, Guy, and Carawan, Candie. "Carry It On: Roots of the Singing Civil Rights Movement." In *Freedom Is a Constant Struggle*, edited by Susie Erenrich, 143–51. Montgomery, Ala.: Black Belt Press, 1999.

Carson, Clayborne. "Civil Rights Reform and the Black Freedom Struggle." In *The Civil Rights Movement in America*, edited by Charles W. Eagles, 19–32. Jackson: University of Mississippi Press, 1986.

Chafe, William H. "The Gods Bring Threads to Webs Begun." *Journal of American History* 86, no. 4 (March 2000): 1531–51.

Cha-Jua, Sundiata Keita, and Clarence Lang. "The 'Long Movement' as Vampire: Temporal and Spatial Fallacies in Recent Black Freedom Studies." *Journal of African American History* 92, no. 2 (March 2007): 265–88.

Chaney, Ben. "Schwerner, Chaney, and Goodman: The Struggle for Justice." *Human Rights Magazine* 27, no. 2 (Spring 2000).

Chilcoat, George W., and Jerry A. Ligon. "Developing Democratic Citizens: The Mississippi Freedom Schools." In *Freedom Is a Constant Struggle*, edited by Susie Erenrich, 107–137. Montgomery, Ala.: Black Belt Press, 1999.

Cobb, Charlie. "Organizing Freedom Schools." In *Freedom Is a Constant Struggle*, edited by Susie Erenrich, 134–38. Montgomery, Ala.: Black Belt Press, 1999.

Cohen, Bob. "Sorrow Songs, Faith Songs, Freedom Songs: The Mississippi Caravan of Music in the Summer of '64." In *Freedom Is a Constant Struggle*, edited by Susie Erenrich, 177–89. Montgomery, Ala.: Black Belt Press, 1999.

Crosby, Emilye. "It Wasn't the Wild West." In *Civil Rights History from the Ground Up*, edited by Emilye Crosby, 194–240. Athens: University of Georgia Press, 2011.

———. "The Politics of Writing and Teaching Movement History." In *Civil Rights History from the Ground Up*, edited by Emilye Crosby, 3–26. Athens: University of Georgia Press, 2011.

Dennis, Dave. "Oration for Funeral of James Chaney." In *Freedom Is a Constant Struggle*, edited by Susie Erenrich, 360–63. Montgomery, Ala.: Black Belt Press, 1999.

Dittmer, John. "The Politics of the Mississippi Movement." In *The Civil Rights Movement in America*, edited by Charles W. Eagles, 65–93. Jackson: University of Mississippi Press, 1986.

Doar, John. "The Work of the Civil Rights Division in Enforcing Voting Rights under the Civil Rights Acts of 1957 and 1960." *Florida State University Law Review* 25, no. 1 (Fall 1997): 1–16.

Dudziak, Mary L. "Desegregation as a Cold War Imperative." *Stanford Law Review* 41, no. 61 (November 1988): 61–120.

Eagels, Charles W. "Toward New Histories of the Civil Rights Era." *Journal of Southern History* 66, no. 4 (November 2000): 815–48.

Eynon, Bret. "Cast upon the Shore: Oral History and New Scholarship on the Movements of the 1960s." *Journal of American History* 83, no. 2 (September 1996): 560–70.

Fairclough, Adam. "State of the Art: Historians and the Civil Rights Movement." *Journal of American Studies* 24, no. 3 (December 1990): 387–98.

Gong, Wei-Ling. "The Algebra Project." *Southern Changes* (January, 1991).

Hall, Jacquelyn Dowd. "The Long Civil Rights Movement and the Political Uses of the Past." *Journal of American History* 91, no. 4 (March 2005): 1233–63.

Hammerback, John C., and Richard J. Jensen. "Working in 'Quiet Places': The Community Organizing Rhetoric of Robert Parris Moses." *Howard Journal of Communications* 11, no. 1 (2000): 1–18.

———. "'Your Tools Are Really the People': The Rhetoric of Robert Parris Moses." *Communications Monograph* 65, no. 2 (June 1998): 126–40.

———. "Calling Washington Collect: Robert Parris Moses and the Kennedy Administration." In *Civil Rights Rhetoric and the American Presidency*, edited by James Arnt Aune and Enrique D. Rigsby, 134–54. College Station: Texas A&M University Press, 2005.

———. "Robert Parris Moses." In *African-American Orators: A Bio-Critical Sourcebook*, edited by Richard W. Leeman, 261–69. Westport, Conn.: Greenwood Press, 1996.

Howe, Mentor A. "Come to the Fair!" *Phylon (1940–1956)* 1, no. 4 (4th quarter, 1940): 314–22.

Huggins, Nathan Irving. "Martin Luther King, Jr.: Charisma and Leadership." *Journal of American History* 74, no. 2 (September 1987): 477–81.

Jetter, Alexis. "Mississippi Learning." *New York Times Magazine*, February 21, 1993, 28–72.

Kempton, Murray. "Conscience of a Convention." *New Republic*, September 5, 1964.

Korstad, Robert, and Nelson Lichtenstein. "Opportunities Found and Lost: Labor, Radicals, and the Early Civil Rights Movement." *Journal of American History* 75, no. 3 (December 1988): 786–811.

Lawson, Steven F. "Freedom Then, Freedom Now: The Historiography of the Civil Rights Movement." *American Historical Review* 96, no. 2 (April 1991): 456–71.

Lynd, Staughton. "Freedom Summer: A Tragedy, Not a Melodrama." In *Freedom Is a Constant Struggle*, edited by Susie Erenrich, 484–86. Montgomery, Ala.: Black Belt Press, 1999.

———. "Mississippi: 1961–1962." *Liberation* 14 (January 1970): 7–17.

Marx, Gary T., and Michael Useem. "Majority Involvement in Minority Movements: Civil Rights, Abolition, Untouchability." *Journal of Social Issues* 27, no. 1 (Winter 1971): 81–104.

McAdam, Doug. "Let It Shine, Let It Shine, Let It Shine." In *Freedom Is a Constant Struggle*, 487–91. Montgomery, Ala.: Black Belt Press, 1999.

Moore, Jane Bond. "A SNCC Blue Book." In *Hands on the Freedom Plow: Personal Accounts by Women in SNCC*, by Faith S. Holsaert et al., 326–31. Chicago: University of Illinois Press, 2010.

Mosely, Patricia. "A Reminiscence." In *Freedom Is a Constant Struggle*, edited by Susie Erenrich, 9–11. Montgomery, Ala.: Black Belt Press, 1999.

Moses, Janet Jemmott. "If We Must Die." In *Hands on the Freedom Plow*, edited by Holsaert et al., 266–69. Chicago: University of Illinois Press, 2010.

Moses, Robert P., M. Kamii, S. M. Swap, and J. Howard. "The Algebra Project: Organizing in the Spirit of Ella." *Harvard Educational Review* 59, no. 4 (November 1989): 423–43.

Moses, Robert P. "Commentary." In *We Shall Overcome: Martin Luther King, Jr. and the Black Freedom Struggle*, edited by Peter J. Albert and Robert Hoffman, 69–76. New York, N.Y.: Da Capo Press, 1993.

———. "Foreword." In *Delta Time: Mississippi Photographs*, by Ken Light. Washington, D.C.: Smithsonian Publishing, 1995.

———. "Constitutional Property v. Constitutional People." In *Quality Education as a Constitutional Right*, by Theresa Perry et al., 70–92. Boston, Mass.: Beacon Press, 2010.

Nasstrom, Kathryn L. "Between Memory and History: Autobiographies of the Civil Rights Movement and the Writing of Civil Rights History." *Journal of Southern History* 74, no. 2 (May 2008): 325–64.

Newfield, Jack. "Moses in Mississippi: The Invisible Man Learns His Name." *Village Voice*, December 3, 1964.

Ouchi, William G., and Alan L. Wilkins. "Organizational Culture." *Review of Sociology* 11 (August 1985): 457–83.

Rauh, Joseph L. "Mississippi Freedom Democratic Party before the Credentials Committee of the Democratic National Convention." In *Freedom Is a Constant Struggle*, edited by Susie Erenrich, 309–12. Montgomery, Ala.: Black Belt Press, 1999.

Reagon, Bernice Johnson. "Women as Culture Carriers in the Civil Rights Movement: Fannie Lou Hamer." In *Freedom Is a Constant Struggle*, edited by Susie Erenrich, 396–408. Montgomery, Ala.: Black Belt Press, 1999.

Salter, John. "Medgar Evers Speaks—May 1963." In *Freedom Is a Constant Struggle*, edited by Susie Erenrich, 36–39. Montgomery, Ala.: Black Belt Press, 1999.

Sherrod, Charles. "Mississippi at Atlantic City." *Grain of Salt*, October 12, 1964.

Sinsheimer, Joseph A. "The Freedom Vote of 1963: New Strategies of Racial Protest in Mississippi." *Journal of Southern History* 55, no. 2 (May 1989): 217–44.

Stoper, Emily. "The Student Nonviolent Coordinating Committee: Rise and Fall of a Redemptive Organization." *Journal of Black Studies* 8, no. 1 (September 1977): 13–34.

Visser-Maessen, Laura. "We Didn't Come for No Two Seats: The Mississippi Freedom Democratic Party and the 1964 Presidential Elections." *Leidschrift* 27, no. 2 (September 17, 2012): 93–113.

Wahman, Jessica T. "'Fleshing Out Consensus': Radical Pragmatism, Civil Rights, and the Algebra Project." *Education & Culture* 25, no. 1 (2009): 7–16.

Warren, Robert Penn. "Two for SNCC." *Commentary*, April 1965.

Watson, Bruce. "A Freedom Summer Activist Becomes a Math Revolutionary." *Smithsonian Magazine*, February 1996, 114–25.

Wilkins, Fanon Che. "The Making of Black Internationalists: SNCC and Africa before the Launching of Black Power, 1960–1965." *Journal of African American History* 92, no. 4 (Fall 2007): 467–90.

Woodley, Richard. "It Will Be a Hot Summer in Mississippi," *The Reporter* 30, no. 11 (May 21, 1964).

Books

Agger, Ben. *The Sixties at 40: Leaders and Activists Remember & Look Forward.* Boulder, Col.: Paradigm Publishers, 2009.

Albert, Peter J., and Ronald Hoffman, Ronald, eds. *We Shall Overcome: Martin Luther King, Jr. and the Black Freedom Struggle*. New York, N.Y.: Da Capo Press, 1993.

Allen, Robert. *Reluctant Reformers: Racism and Social Reform Movements in the United States*. Washington, D.C.: Howard University Press, 1983.

Anderson, Jervis. *Bayard Rustin: Troubles I've Seen*. Berkeley: University of California Press, 1998.

Ansbro, John J. *Martin Luther King, Jr. The Making of a Mind*. Maryknoll, N.Y.: Orbis Books, 1986.

Arsenault, Raymond. *Freedom Riders: 1961 and the Struggle for Racial Justice*. New York, N.Y.: Oxford University Press, 2006.

Aune, James Arnt, and Enrique D. Rigsby, eds. *Civil Rights Rhetoric and the American Presidency*. College Station: Texas A&M University Press, 2005.

Beito, David T., and Linda Royster Beito. *Black Maverick: T. R. M. Howard's Fight for Civil Rights and Economic Power*. Chicago: University of Illinois Press, 2009.

Belfrage, Sally. *Freedom Summer*. Charlotte: University Press of Virginia, 1990.

Beschloss, Michael R., ed. *Taking Charge: The Johnson White House Tapes, 1963–1964*. New York, N.Y.: Simon & Schuster, 1997.

Biondi, Martha. *To Stand and Fight: The Struggle for Civil Rights in Postwar New York City*. Cambridge, Mass.: Harvard University Press, 2006.

Blake, John. *Children of the Movement: The Sons and Daughters of Martin Luther King, Jr., Malcolm X, Elijah Muhammad, George Wallace, Andrew Young, Julian Bond, Stokely Carmichael, Bob Moses, James Chaney, Elaine Brown, and Others Reveal How the Civil Rights Movement Tested and Transformed Their Families*. Chicago, Ill.: Lawrence Hill Books, 2004.

Bond, Julian, and Andrew Lewis, eds. *Gonna Sit at the Welcome Table*. Mason, Ohio: Thomson Learning Custom Publishing, 2002.

Branch, Taylor. *At Canaan's Edge: America in the King Years, 1965–68*. New York, N.Y.: Simon & Schuster, 2006.

———. *Pillar of Fire: America in the King years, 1963–65*. New York, N.Y.: Simon & Schuster, 1998.

———. *Parting the Waters: America in the King Years, 1954–63*. New York, N.Y.: Simon & Schuster, 1989.

Brown, H. Rap. *Die, Nigger, Die: A Political Autobiography of Jamil Abdullah Al-Amin*. Chicago, Ill.: Chicago Review Press, 2002.

Burner, Eric R. *And Gently He Shall Lead Them: Robert Parris Moses and Civil Rights in Mississippi*. New York: New York University Press, 1994.

Cagin, Seth, and Philip Dray. *We Are Not Afraid: The Story of Goodman, Schwerner, and Chaney, and the Civil Rights Campaign for Mississippi*. New York, N.Y.: Nation Books, 2006.

Camus, Albert. *The Rebel: An Essay on Man in Revolt*. New York, N.Y.: Vintage International, 1991.

———. *Resistance, Rebellion, and Death*. New York, N.Y.: Knopf, 1961.

Carmichael, Stokely, and Ekwueme Michael Thelwell. *Ready for Revolution: The Life and Struggles of Stokely Carmichael (Kwame Ture)*. New York, N.Y.: Scribner, 2003.

Carson, Clayborne. *In Struggle: SNCC and the Black Awakening of the 1960s*. Cambridge, Mass.: Harvard University Press, 1981.

———, ed. *The Autobiography of Martin Luther King, Jr.* New York, N.Y.: Warner Books, Inc., 1998.

———, ed. *"The Student Voice" 1960–1965: Periodical of the Student Nonviolent Coordinating Committee*. Westport, Conn.: Meckler, 1990.

Chafe, William H. *Civilities and Civil Rights: Greensboro, North Carolina, and the Black Struggle for Freedom*. New York, N.Y.: Oxford University Press, 1981.

———. *Never Stop Running: Allard Lowenstein and the Struggle to Save American Liberalism*. New York, N.Y.: Basic Books, 1993.

Chappell, David L. *A Stone of Hope: Prophetic Religion and the Death of Jim Crow*. Chapel Hill: University of North Carolina Press, 2004.

Charron, Katherine Mellen. *Freedom's Teacher: The Life of Septima Clark*. Chapel Hill: University of North Carolina Press, 2009.

Cobb, Charles E., Jr. *On the Road to Freedom: A Guided Tour of the Civil Rights Trail*. Chapel Hill, N.C.: Algonquin Books of Chapel Hill, 2008.

Cobb, James C. *The Most Southern Place on Earth: The Mississippi Delta and the Roots of Regional Identity*. New York, N.Y.: Oxford University Press, 1992.

Cohen, Robert. *Freedom's Orator: Mario Savio and the Radical Legacy of the 1960s*. New York, N.Y.: Oxford University Press, 2009.

Cone, James H. *Black Theology and Black Power*. Minneapolis, Minn.: Seabury Press, 1969.

Crespino, Joseph. *In Search of Another Country: Mississippi and the Conservative Counterrevolution*. Princeton, N.J.: Princeton University Press, 2007.

Crosby, Emilye, ed. *Civil Rights History from the Ground Up: Local Struggles, a National Movement*. Athens: University of Georgia Press, 2011.

———. *A Little Taste of Freedom: The Black Freedom Struggle in Claiborne County, Mississippi*. Chapel Hill: University of North Carolina Press, 2005.

Curry, Constance, Joan C. Browning, Dorothy Dawson Burlage, Penny Patch, Theresa Del Pozzo, Sue Trasher, Elaine DeLott Baker, Emmie Schrader Adams, and Casey Hayden. *Deep in Our Hearts: Nine White Women in the Freedom Movement*. Athens: University of Georgia Press, 2002.

Dittmer, John. *Local People: The Struggle for Civil Rights in Mississippi*. Champaign: University of Illinois Press, 1994.

DuBois, W. E. B. *The Souls of Black Folk*. New York, N.Y.: Penguin Books, USA Inc., 1989.

Dumas, Bianca. *African-American Biographies: Robert Parris Moses*. Chicago, Ill.: Raintree, 2004.

Eagles, Charles W. *The Price of Defiance: James Meredith and the Integration of Ole Miss*. Chapel Hill: University of North Carolina Press, 2009.

————, ed. *The Civil Rights Movement in America*. Jackson: University of Mississippi Press, 1986.

Emery, Kathy, Linda Reid Gold, Sylvia Braselmann, and Howard Zinn. *Lessons from Freedom Summer: Ordinary People Building Extraordinary Movements*. Monroe, Maine: Common Courage Press, 2008.

Erenrich, Susie, ed. *Freedom Is a Constant Struggle: An Anthology of the Mississippi Civil Rights Movement*. Montgomery, Ala.: Black Belt Press, 1999.

Evers-Williams, Myrlie, and Marable Manning, eds. *The Autobiography of Medgar Evers: A Hero's Life and Legacy Revealed through His Writings, Letters, and Speeches*. New York, N.Y.: Basic Civitas Books, 2005.

Fairclough, Adam. *To Redeem the Soul of America: The Southern Christian Leadership Conference and Martin Luther King, Jr.* Athens: University of Georgia Press, 1987.

Fleming, Cynthia Griggs. *Soon We Will Not Cry: The Liberation of Ruby Doris Smith Robinson*. Lanham, Md.: Rowman & Littlefield Publishers, Inc., 2006.

Forman, James. *The Making of Black Revolutionaries*. Seattle: University of Washington Press, 1985.

Garrow, David J. *Bearing the Cross: Martin Luther King, Jr. and the Southern Christian Leadership Conference*. New York, N.Y.: Vintage Books, 1988.

————. *Protest at Selma: Martin Luther King, Jr. and the Voting Rights Act of 1965*. New Haven, Conn.: Yale University Press, 1978.

Gilmore, Glenda Elizabeth. *Defying Dixie: The Radical Roots of Civil Rights, 1919–1950*. New York, N.Y.: W. W. Norton & Company, 2008.

Gitlin, Todd. *The Sixties: Years of Hope, Days of Rage*. New York, N.Y.: Bantam Books, 1987.

Grant, Joanne. *Ella Baker: Freedom Bound*. New York, N.Y.: John Wiley & Sons, Inc., 1998.

Greenberg, Cheryl Lynn, ed. *A Circle of Trust: Remembering SNCC*. New Brunswick, N.J.: Rutgers University Press, 1998.

————. *"Or Does It Explode?" Black Harlem in the Great Depression*. New York, N.Y.: Oxford University Press, 1991.

Gregory, Dick, and Robert Lipsyte. *Nigger—An Autobiography*. New York, N.Y.: Pocket Books, 1964.

Grossman, James R. *Land of Hope: Chicago, Black Southerners, and the Great Migration*. Chicago, Ill.: University of Chicago Press, 1989.

Halberstam, David. *The Children*. New York, N.Y.: Random House, 1998.

Hampton, Henry, and Steve Fayer. *Voices of Freedom: An Oral History of the Civil Rights Movement from the 1950s through the 1980s*. New York, N.Y.: Bantam Books, 1991.

Harvey, Paul. *Redeeming the South: Religious Cultures and Racial Identities among Southern Baptists, 1865–1925*. Chapel Hill: University of North Carolina Press, 1997.

Heath, William. *The Children Bob Moses Led: A Novel of Freedom Summer*. Minneapolis, Minn.: Milkweed Editions, 1995.

Henry, Aaron, and Constance Curry. *Aaron Henry: The Fire Ever Burning.* Jackson: University of Mississippi Press, 2000.

Hill, Lance. *The Deacons for Defense: Armed Resistance and the Civil Rights Movement.* Chapel Hill: University of North Carolina Press, 2006.

Hogan, Wesley C. *Many Minds, One Heart: SNCC's Dream for a New America.* Chapel Hill: University of North Carolina Press, 2007.

Holsaert, Faith S. "Resistance U." In *Hands on the Freedom Plow,* edited by Faith Holsaert et al., 181–94. Chicago: University of Illinois Press, 2010.

Holsaert, Faith S., Martha Prescod Norman Noonan, Judy Richardson, Betty Garman Robinson, Jean Smith Young, and Dorothy M. Zellner, eds. *Hands on the Freedom Plow: Personal Accounts by Women in SNCC.* Chicago: University of Illinois Press, 2010.

Honey, Michael K. *Southern Labor and Black Civil Rights: Organizing Memphis Workers.* Urbana: University of Illinois Press, 1993.

Horowitz, Roger. *"Negro and White Unite and Fight!" A Social History of Industrial Unionism in Meatpacking, 1930–90.* Urbana: University of Illinois Press, 1997.

Huie, William Bradford. *Three Lives for Mississippi.* Jackson: University Press of Mississippi, 2000.

Isserman, Maurice. *If I Had a Hammer: The Death of the Old Left and the Birth of the New Left.* New York, N.Y.: Basic Books, Inc., 1987.

Jeffries, Hasan Kwame. *Bloody Lowndes: Civil Rights and Black Power in Alabama's Black Belt.* New York: New York University Press, 2009.

Katagiri, Yasuhiro. *The Mississippi State Sovereignty Commission: Civil Rights and States' Rights.* Jackson: University of Mississippi Press, 2001.

King, Mary E. *Freedom Song: A Personal Story of the 1960s Civil Rights Movement.* New York, N.Y.: Quill, William Morrow and Company, Inc., 1987.

Klehr, Harvey. *The Heyday of American Communism: The Depression Decade.* New York, N.Y.: Basic Books, Inc., 1984.

Korstad, Robert Rodgers. *Civil Rights Unionism: Tobacco Workers and the Struggle for Democracy in the Mid-Twentieth Century South.* Chapel Hill: University of North Carolina Press, 2003.

Lassister, Matthew D., and Joseph Crespino, eds. *The Myth of Southern Exceptionalism.* New York, N.Y.: Oxford University Press, 2010.

Lawson, Steven F., and Charles Payne, eds. *Debating the Civil Rights Movement, 1945–1968.* Lanham, Md.: Rowman & Littlefield Publishers, Inc., 2006.

Lee, Chana Kai. *For Freedom's Sake: The Life of Fannie Lou Hamer.* Chicago: University of Illinois Press, 2000.

Leeman, Richard W., ed. *African-American Orators: A Bio-Critical Sourcebook.* Westport, Conn.: Greenwood Press, 1996.

Lefever, Harry G. *Undaunted by the Fight: Spelman College and the Civil Rights Movement, 1957–1967.* Macon, Ga.: Mercer University Press, 2005.

Lemann, Nicholas. *The Promised Land: The Great Black Migration and How It Changed America.* New York, N.Y.: Vintage Books, 1992.

Lewis, Andrew B. *The Shadows of Youth: The Remarkable Journey of the Civil Rights Generation.* New York: N.Y.: Hill & Wang, 2010.

Lewis, David Levering. *Martin Luther King: A Critical Biography*. London: Penguin Press, 1970.

Lewis, John, and Michael D'Orso. *Walking with the Wind: A Memoir of the Movement*. San Diego, Calif.: Hartcourt Brace & Company, 1998.

Lynd, Staughton, and Alice Lynd, eds. *Nonviolence in America: A Documentary History*. Maryknoll, N.Y.: Orbis Books, 1995.

Marsh, Charles. *God's Long Summer: Stories of Faith and Civil Rights*. Princeton, N.J.: Princeton University Press, 1997.

McAdam, Doug. *Freedom Summer*. New York, N.Y.: Oxford University Press, 1988.

McKay, John P., Bennett D. Hill, John Buckler, Clare Haru Crowston, and Merry E. Wiesner-Hanks. *A History of Western Society*. Boston, Mass.: Houghton Mifflin Company, 2008.

McWorther, Diane. *Carry Me Home: Birmingham, Alabama, the Climactic Battle of the Civil Rights Revolution*. New York, N.Y.: Touchstone Books, 2001.

Meier, August, and Elliott Rudwick. *CORE: A Study in the Civil Rights Movement, 1948–1968*. New York, N.Y.: Oxford University Press, 1973.

Meyer, Susan E. *Stuyvesant High School: The First 100 Years*. New York, N.Y.: The Campaign for Stuyvesant/Alumni(ae) & Friends Endowment Fund, Inc., 2005.

Moody, Anne. *Coming of Age in Mississippi: The Classic Autobiography of Growing Up Poor and Black in the Rural South*. New York, N.Y.: Bantam Dell, 1968.

Morris, Aldon D. *The Origins of the Civil Rights Movement: Black Communities Organizing for Change*. New York, N.Y.: The Free Press, 1984.

Moses, Robert P., and Charles E. Cobb Jr. *Radical Equations: Civil Rights from Mississippi to the Algebra Project*. Boston, Mass.: Beacon Press, 2001.

Moye, Todd. *Let the People Decide: Black Freedom and White Resistance Movements in Sunflower County, Mississippi, 1945–1986*. Chapel Hill: University of North Carolina Press, 2004.

Murphree, Vanessa. *The Selling of Civil Rights: The Student Nonviolent Coordinating Committee and the Use of Public Relations*. New York, N.Y.: Routledge, 2006.

Myrdal, Gunnar. *An American Dilemma: The Negro Problem and Modern Democracy*. Vol. 1. New Brunswick, N.J.: Transaction Publishers, 1996.

———. *An American Dilemma: The Negro Problem and Modern Democracy*. Vol. 2. New Brunswick, N.J.: Transaction Publishers, 1996.

Naison, Marc. *Communists in Harlem during the Depression*. Chicago: University of Illinois Press, 1983.

Navasky, Victor S. *Kennedy Justice*. New York, N.Y.: Atheneum, 1977.

Nelson, Bruce. *Divided We Stand: American Workers and the Struggle for Equality*. Princeton, N.J.: Princeton University Press, 2001.

Newfield, Jack. *Bread and Roses Too*. New York, N.Y.: Dutton, 1971.

———. *A Prophetic Minority: The American New Left*. London: Anthony Blond, Ltd., 1966.

Norton, Mary Beth, David M. Katzman, Paul D. Escott, Howard P. Chudacoff, Thomas G. Paterson, William M. Tuttle Jr., and William J. Brophy. *A People and a Nation: A History of the United States.* Brief ed. Boston, Mass.: Houghton Mifflin Company, 1999.

Oppenheimer, Martin. *The Sit-In Movement of 1960.* Brooklyn, N.Y.: Carlson Publishing Inc., 1989.

O'Reilly, Kenneth. *"Racial Matters": The FBI's Secret File on Black America, 1960–1972.* New York, N.Y.: The Free Press, 1989.

Payne, Charles M. *I've Got the Light of Freedom: The Organizing Tradition and the Mississippi Freedom Struggle.* Berkeley: University of California Press, 1997.

Perry, Theresa, Robert P. Moses, Ernesto Cortes Jr., and Lisa Delpit. *Quality Education as a Constitutional Right: Creating a Grassroots Movement to Transform Public Schools.* Boston, Mass.: Beacon Press, 2010.

Raines, Howell. *My Soul Is Rested: Movement Days in the Deep South Remembered.* New York, N.Y.: Penguin Books, 1977.

Ransby, Barbara. *Ella Baker & the Black Freedom Movement: A Radical Democratic Vision.* Chapel Hill: University of North Carolina Press, 2003.

Robnett, Belinda. *How Long? How Long? African-American Women in the Struggle of Civil Rights.* New York, N.Y.: Oxford University Press, 1997.

Russell, Dick. *Black Genius and the American Experience.* New York, N.Y.: Carrol & Graf Publishers, Inc., 1998.

Sellers, Cleveland, with Robert Terrell. *The River of No Return: The Autobiography of a Black Militant and the Life and Death of SNCC.* Jackson: University Press of Mississippi, 1990.

Stoper, Emily. *The Student Nonviolent Coordinating Committee: The Growth of Radicalism in a Civil Rights Organization.* Brooklyn, N.Y.: Carlson Publishing, Inc., 1989.

Sugrue, Thomas J. *Sweet Land of Liberty: The Forgotten Struggle for Civil Rights in the North.* New York, N.Y.: Random House, 2009.

Sullivan, Patricia. *Lift Every Voice: The NAACP and the Making of the Civil Rights Movement.* New York, N.Y.: The New Press, 2009.

Sutherland-Martinez, Elizabeth, ed. *Letters from Mississippi: Personal Reports from Civil Rights Volunteers of the 1964 Freedom Summer.* Brooklyn, N.Y.: Zephyr Press, 2002.

Thornton, J. Mills. *Dividing Lines: Municipal Politics and the Struggle for Civil Rights in Montgomery, Birmingham, and Selma.* Tuscaloosa: University of Alabama Press, 2006.

Tyson, Timothy B. *Radio Free Dixie: Robert F. Williams and the Roots of Black Power.* Chapel Hill: University of North Carolina Press, 1999.

Warren, Robert Penn. *Who Speaks for the Negro?* New York, N.Y.: Vintage Books, 1965.

Watson, Bruce. *Freedom Summer: The Savage Season That Made Mississippi Burn and Made America a Democracy.* New York, N.Y.: Viking Press, 2010.

Watters, Pat, and Reese Cleghorn. *Climbing Jacob's Ladder: The Arrival of Negroes in Southern Politics.* New York, N.Y.: Harcourt, Brace & World, Inc., 1967.

Wilkins, Roy, and Tom Mathews. *Standing Fast: The Autobiography of Roy Wilkins.* New York, N.Y.: Viking Press, 1982.

Williams, Juan. *My Soul Looks Back in Wonder: Voices of the Civil Rights Experience*. New York, N.Y.: Sterling Publishing Co., Inc., 2004.

Willner, Ann Ruth. *The Spellbinders: Charismatic Political Leadership*. New Haven, Conn.: Yale University Press, 1984.

Woods, Jeff. *Black Struggle Red Scare: Segregation and Anti-Communism in the South, 1948–1968*. Baton Rouge: Louisiana State University Press, 2004.

Wright, Richard. *Uncle Tom's Children*. New York, N.Y.: Perennial, 2004.

Zellner, Bob. *The Wrong Side of Murder Creek: A White Southerner in the Southern Freedom Movement*. Montgomery, Ala.: New South Books, 2008.

Zinn, Howard. *SNCC: The New Abolitionists*. Boston, Mass.: Beacon Press, 1965.

Index

roots in, 11; Moses's relation to, 14, 322 (n. 17); and civil rights movement, 88, 136. *See also* Harlem; Migration

Black Belt Project, 260, 267–268, 277

Black nationalism: and black women, 287, 315; in movement historiography, 186, 310, 315; and Moses, 263, 286–290, 291, 315; and SNCC, 9, 153, 245–246, 253, 258, 260, 264, 290, 291, 308

Black Panther Party for Self-Defense, 290, 295, 308, 381 (n. 88)

Black Power Movement

Blackwell, Randolph, 137–138

Blackwell, Unita, 122, 125, 244, 245, 259, 317

Block, Sam, 103, 127, 155, 161, 200, 213, 264; and Greenwood movement, 105, 107, 110, 126, 133–137, 139, 170

Blyth, John W., 30–31, 147, 178, 211

Bolivar County, Miss., 101, 291

Bombings, 129, 184, 210; in Birmingham, 52, 154–155, 157; of Hartman home, 129; and Freedom Summer, 187, 208; in McComb area, 184, 208, 262. *See also* Violence

Bond, Julian, 211, 248, 268, 288; in Atlanta student movement, 42–43; on Lowenstein, 164, 165, 193; on Moses, 43, 47–48, 49, 117, 119, 149, 164, 179, 192, 201–202, 277, 280–281; and 1964 Africa trip, 265; and SNCC, 39, 90, 129, 379 (n. 59)

Boston, Mass., 32, 163, 204, 299

Boston University, 29, 46, 211, 296

Bowers, Samuel, 187, 202

Boycotts, 54; Jackson, 143; Montgomery Bus, 33, 37, 38, 105

Braden, Anne, 44, 47, 103–104, 139, 302

Braden, Carl, 44, 47, 103–104, 105, 106, 302

Branch, Taylor, 72, 80, 287; *America in the King Years* trilogy, 312

Brando, Marlon, 190

Branton, Wiley, 97, 102, 104, 135, 138–139, 150, 156, 169, 191

Britt, Travis, 70, 73; beating of, 74–75, 76

Britton, A. Benjamin (A.B.), 97

Brotherhood of Sleeping Car Porters. *See* Randolph, A. Philip

Brown, Ed, 254, 255, 274, 290

Brown, H. 'Rap' (Jamil Al-Amin), 288, 290, 291, 381 (n. 88)

Brown, Luvaughn, 93, 102, 118, 121, 125–126, 134

Brown, Rev., 51

Brown vs. Topeka Board of Education, 26, 27, 28, 29, 105; backlash of, 62, 71

Brumfield, Robert (Judge), 61, 85, 86

Bryant, Curtis Conway (C.C.), 74, 303, 317; background of, 64–65; and McComb 1961 movement, 61, 68, 70, 71, 74, 82, 88

Buber, Martin, 40

Buddhism, Moses and, 28, 270. *See also* Lao-Tse

Burks, Marylene, 115, 198

Burner, Eric, 24, 43; *And Gently He Shall Lead Them*, 312

Cambridge, Mass., 30, 296; civil rights activism in, 145

Cameron, John, 224

Campbell College (Jackson), 58, 84, 87

Camus, Albert, xiv–xv, 5, 31, 34–35, 40, 43, 60, 61, 149, 153, 170, 176; background of, 22, 27; Moses influenced by, 3, 22–24, 30, 36, 72, 79, 80, 124, 182, 199, 201, 263, 316, 376 (n. 27); philosophies of, 22–24; and SNCC, 124, 324 (n. 43); and white liberals, 124–125, 311. *See also* Existentialism

Canton, Miss., 182, 208

Canvassing. *See* Voting rights

Carawan, Candy, 151

Carawan, Guy, 151

Harlem: black nationalism and self-help tradition in, 10, 11, 13, 14, 17–18, 19; churches in, 13; Cotton Club, 11, 322 (n. 10); and Harlem River Houses, 11, 12, 13, 14, 321 (n. 4, Chapter 1); and Harlem Youth Opportunities Unlimited (HARYOU), 178; Moses's childhood in, 11, 12, 13, 14, 17–18; in 1930s and 1940s, 10–11, 12, 13, 15; political life in, 10, 41; riots in, 10, 11, 12, 178, 217; schools in, 17–18; and Workers Education Project, 41; and Young Negroes' Cooperative League, 13, 46–47

Harmony, Miss., 207

Harper's Magazine, 106, 148

Harrington, Michael, 191

Harris, Don, 166, 220, 264, 265, 275, 286

Harris, Jesse, 109

Harris, Tina, 286

Harvard University, 12, 34, 19, 29, 103, 107, 149, 221, 298; complicity in southern racism, 200; Moses at, 30–31, 32, 163, 296–297; and white student activist volunteers, 198

Hattiesburg, Miss., 51, 93, 101, 107, 150, 179, 183, 207, 216, 250; and Freedom Day, 180–182

Hawkins, Augustus, 141

Hayden, Casey (Sandra Cason), 90, 119, 149, 160, 221

Hayden, Tom, 82, 84, 90, 221, 282, 285

Hayes, Curtis, 91, 101, 103, 127, 141, 228; and McComb movement, 74, 80, 81, 86, 91; Moses's affection for, 123, 346 (n. 85); opposes Freedom Summer, 169, 173

Head Start. *See* Antipoverty programs

Hegel, Georg, 124

Heller, Joseph, 191

Helstein, Ralph, 222

Henry, Aaron, 49, 50, 98, 120, 136, 139, 169, 180, 190, 191, 204, 248, 317–318; and COFO, 96, 97, 217, 249, 250, 340

(n. 12); early Mississippi activism of, 62, 63; and Freedom Vote, 159, 161, 162, 167; and MFDP, 223, 225, 226, 228; on Moses, 98, 123, 162, 241, 317; at 1964 National Democratic Convention, 232, 235, 236, 238, 239, 240, 241, 243; and SNCC, 63

Herron, Matt, 203–204

Higgs, William (Bill), 98, 103–104, 133, 220, 223, 244

Highlander Folk School, 42, 44, 97, 103, 148, 211, 223, 259

Hill, Lance, 310

Hill, Norman, 222

Hillet, Vivian, 117

Hogan, Wesley, 267, 273, 312, 377 (n. 34)

Holland, Endesha Mae, 122

Holly Springs, Miss., 212, 225

Holman, Carl, 47

Holmes County, Miss., 158, 159

Hoover, J. Edgar: FBI directorship of, 131; and Freedom Summer, 188, 208, 209; Moses's lawsuit against, 133; and surveillance of civil rights movement, 188. *See also* Federal Bureau of Investigation (FBI)

Horace Mann high school (New York), 34, 107, 154; Moses at, 32, 33

Horne, Lena, 15

Horowitz, Rachelle, 220

Horton, Myles, 42, 103, 196, 211, 213, 254

House Un-American Activities Committee (HUAC), 43, 44, 105, 176

Houston, James, 224

Howard, T.R.M., 62, 63, 66

Howard University, 175; and NAG, 177, 199, 223, 275, 316; and Carmichael, 245

HUAC. *See* House Un-American Activities Committee

Huggins, Nathan Irving, 307

Hughes, Matthew, 140

Humphrey, Hubert, 164, 222, 242, 248, 259; and MFDP, 234, 237; Moses slams door in face of, 239, 247; and 1964 Democratic National

Keglar, Birdie, 105, 342 (n. 39)
Kennard, Clyde, 151
Kennedy, John F., 116, 129, 141, 176,
    183, 244, 259, 293; death of, 157, 175,
    183; and integration of Ole Miss.,
    131; Moses and SNCC criticism of,
    129, 130–131; and 1964 Civil Rights
    Act, 143, 145, 152, 154. *See also* Civil
    Rights Act (1964); Federal govern-
    ment
Kennedy, Robert F., 75–76, 118, 131,
    139, 145, 184, 188, 221, 235, 259, 293;
    Moses's lawsuit against, 133
Kennedy administration. *See* Federal
    government
Killen, Ray Edgar, 202, 209
King, Edward (Ed), 60, 64
King, Edwin (Ed), 261; and Freedom
    Summer, 193, 203, 208; and Freedom
    Vote, 159, 162, 165, 167; and MFDP,
    226, 230, 231, 252; and 1964 Demo-
    cratic National Convention, 233,
    235, 236, 238, 239, 241, 242
King, Lonnie, 42, 45
King, Martin Luther, Jr., 4, 33, 37, 67,
    107, 140, 155, 163, 176, 178, 246, 258,
    287, 293, 294, 312; and Albany
    movement, 94–95, 137; and
    anticommunism, 45, 47, 105; Baker's
    criticism of, 40–41; charisma of,
    45–46, 226; and community-
    mobilizing tradition, 1, 46; educa-
    tion and philosophies of, 7–8, 23,
    24, 29, 31, 46, 124–125, 316; and
    Freedom Summer, 187, 190;
    leadership projection of, 35, 36, 37,
    38, 40–41, 124–125; and March on
    Washington, 153; and MFDP, 221,
    223, 226, 228; Moses's first meeting
    with, 45–46, 48; vs. Moses's leader-
    ship philosophy, 153–154; Moses on
    movement significance of, 305–307;
    in movement historiography, 310,
    316; and 1964 Democratic National
    Convention, 233, 235, 236, 237, 238,

241–244, 250; opposes Vietnam War,
    284; and SCLC, 38–39, 41; and
    Selma movement, 373 (n. 72);
    sexism of, 149; struggles with
    leadership, 41, 45–46, 79–80; and
    student movement, 38, 42, 66
King, Mary E., 90, 175, 196, 222, 248,
    250; on Dona Richards, 149, 178;
    marriage to Sweeney, 262; on
    Moses, 119, 120, 121, 127, 146, 148,
    221, 281, 288, 313
Kinoy, Arthur, 133, 204, 254
Kirstein, George, 151
Klein, Felix, 297
Knox, Alfred (Reverend), 71, 74, 76
Knoxville, Tenn., 145
Korean War, 25
Ku Klux Klan, 62, 65, 105, 138, 158,
    187, 188, 191, 204, 209; racial
    violence by, 154, 183, 184, 207, 208,
    294, 342 (n. 39). *See also* Violence;
    White Knights of the Ku Klux
    Klan of Mississippi
Kunstler, William, 133, 204, 254

LaBauve, John (Father), 56, 57, 58, 60,
    61
Labor movement, 24, 35, 42, 44, 113,
    152; and civil rights movement,
    189–190, 221–223, 53, 118, 162, 250,
    310; Moses and, 26–27, 146, 189–190,
    221–223, 259, 284; and SNCC, 43,
    177, 259–260, 328 (n. 20); racism in,
    65, 177. *See also Names Individual
    Labor Organizations/Unions and
    Leaders*
Ladner, Dorie, 67, 93, 102, 109, 121,
    123, 125, 175, 179, 288
Lafayette, Bernard, 39, 64, 96, 101, 108,
    160
Lamb, Martha, 130
Lane, Mary, 216
Lao-Tse, 21, 23, 31
Laubach, Frank, 102
Laurel, Miss., 58, 93, 216

Lynd, Staughton, 258, 289, 311; on Moses, 187, 199, 201, 213, 279; and Vietnam War, 283–285
Lynd, Theron, 130, 180–181, 198

Magnolia, Miss., 68, 69, 75, 80, 81, 82, 86, 141
Mahoney, Bill, 177
Malcolm X, 29, 36, 154, 285, 286, 291, 293, 295; and SNCC, 124, 264, 274
Marches: in Birmingham, 142; in Greenwood, 139–140; in Jackson, 152, 256, 290; in McComb, 80–82, 83–84, 139; on Washington, 24, 25, 152–154, 157, 160, 177, 181; Meredith March, 290; Selma-to-Montgomery, 249, 252, 281, 373 (n. 72)
March on Washington (1963), 25, 152–154, 157, 160, 177, 181; Lewis's speech at, 153; Moses and, 153–154
March on Washington movement (1941), 24
Marshall, Burke, 126, 131, 141, 146, 153, 182, 183, 194, 203; and McComb movement, 73, 82, 84; Moses's relationship with, 131, 147, 188
Marxism, 45, 324 (n. 37)
Mass meetings, 6, 158; in Birmingham, 142; in Greenwood, 139; in McComb, 73, 74, 82; Moses changes format of, 112–113; in Ruleville, 111–113
McCain, James (Jim), 59, 331 (n. 65)
McCarthy, Joseph, 18, 28
McCarthyism, 18, 104, 105, 175, 176, 188. *See also* Anticommunism
McComb, Miss., 63, 92, 94, 98, 114, 186, 205; bombings in, 184, 208, 262; lessons learned from movement in, 88–89, 95; marches in, 80–82, 83–84, 139; movement in, 61, 63, 64–91, 106, 116, 117, 118, 123, 128, 170, 182–183, 284–285, 304; as movement turning point, 88–89, 186, 304. *See also* Allen, Louis; Lee, Herbert

McDew, Charles (Chuck), 44, 63, 64, 90, 141, 146, 275; and McComb movement, 68, 77–78, 81, 83, 84, 86, 87
McDonald family, Ruleville, 115
McGhee family, Greenwood, 133; Laura, 151, 161; Silas, 197
McLaurin, Charles, 134–135, 245; and Ruleville movement, 109–110, 114–116
McNair, Landy, 109
Meaney, George, 189
Medical Committee on Human Rights, 198
Meredith, James: integration of Ole Miss, 128, 131–132, 133, 220; Meredith March, 290
Meridian, Miss., 161, 167, 202, 208, 212
MFDP. *See* Mississippi Freedom Democratic Party
Middle class. *See* Social class
Migration: changes northern blacks' relation with southern heritage, 35; churches and, 13; Great Migration, 10, 11, 12, 53; and Mississippi blacks, 53; Moses's emphasis on reversing trend of, 146; Moses's family roots in, 11
Milam, S.D., 115
Milestone, Miss., 129
Miller, Dorothy (Dottie). *See* Zellner, Dorothy Miller (Dottie)
Miller, James, 279
Miller, Michael (Mike), 135, 156, 161
Mills, C. Wright, 212
Minnis, Jack, 108, 223
Mississippi: geopolitics of, 53, 65; hill countries vs. Delta, 65; life in Mississippi Delta, 52–53; mechanization and decline of cotton plantation economy, 52–54, 134, 146; political structure of, 53; poverty in, 52–53, 54, 134–135, 303; racist reputation of, 4, 49, 127; sharecropping and tenant farming, 52; state-sponsored racism

Moses, Maisha (daughter), 294, 295, 296, 298
Moses, Malaika (daughter), 296
Moses, Omowale (son), 294
Moses, Robert Parris (Bob)
—activism of: and Atlanta movement, 40–48; and Atlantic City, 231–256 passim; and Birmingham movement, 49, 50, 51–52, 142, 143–144, 155, 281; behind-the-scenes organizing of, 98, 102, 105–107, 126–127, 128, 131, 135, 140, 145–152, 158, 162–163, 189–196 passim, 204–206, 211–214, 219–226 passim; and Freedom Vote, 157–168; and fundraising, 107–108, 274; and Greenwood movement, 107, 122–123, 126, 133–142, 144, 145, 147, 150, 151, 152, 155–156, 158, 184, 193, 204; and Hattiesburg Freedom Day, 180–182; and Jackson movement, 91, 93–94, 98; and March on Washington, 153–154; and McComb movement, xi, 61, 64–91, 92, 95, 96, 98, 106, 114, 117, 123, 128, 138, 139, 170, 182–183, 186, 205, 262, 304; and nonviolent direct action, 35, 37, 44–45, 49–50, 69–70, 74, 99, 102, 153, 144, 221, 242, 244; and Ruleville movement, 109, 111, 114–116; anti-Vietnam War views and activism of, 8, 282–285, 291; voter registration and political organizing of, 56–60, 68, 69, 98–99, 107. See also Citizenship schools; Freedom Summer (1964); Mississippi Freedom Democratic Party (MFDP); Workshops; Names of Individual SNCC and COFO Projects
—and Africa: xiii, 2, 9; and life in Tanzania, 294–296, 297, 298, 300, 303, 317; 1964–1965 trips to, 265–266, 285–286; on pan-Africanism, 264, 286, 295, 296
—and anticommunism: emphasizes civil liberties, 5, 103–104, 105,

176–177, 194–195, 197, 338 (n. 84); personal experiences with 20–21, 43–45, 47, 103–105, 189, 194–195, 248
—beliefs of: conscientious objection and draft, 25–26, 32, 64, 140, 292–294, 296; pacifism and nonviolence of, 3, 23–25, 26, 28, 40, 50, 57, 60, 70, 72–73, 77, 80, 121, 200–201, 218, 242, 290; moral and linguistic purity of, xiii, 23, 120; murderers' jury theory of, 263, 283; women, xiv, 149
—childhood and background of: family background of, 8, 11–12, 13, 321 (nn. 4, 5, 8, Chapter 1), 322 (nn. 9, 10, 19); Harlem childhood of, 11, 12, 13, 14; Harlem black culture impact on, 3, 5, 14, 16, 17, 18, 19, 25
—education of, 3, 17–31; AFSC trips abroad of, 26–28, 96, 325 (n. 56); and mathematics, 17; and philosophy, 21–23, 25, 28, 30–31, 40; and white middle class educational institutions, 3, 5, 8, 18–31 passim, 32. See also Existentialism; Hamilton College, N.Y.; Harvard University; Horace Mann High School (New York); Peter Stuyvesant High School (New York); PS-90
—and federal government: and FBI, 20, 69, 73–76, 85, 116, 181–182, 190, 292, 294, 295; and Justice Department, 69–70, 83, 130–132, 141–142, 147, 153; reaches out to, 60, 64, 73, 83, 115, 116, 126, 129, 130–132, 152, 153–154, 162, 176, 184, 190–191. See also Doar, John; Johnson, Lyndon B.; Kennedy, John F.; Marshall, Burke
—influences on: family, 14–17, 22, 24, 26, 31, 35, 36, 17, 93, 149; folk music and dancing, 20, 25, 59, 103, 151, 201–202, 213, 225, 254; sit-ins, 33–35, 36, 44, 56. See also Allen, Louis; Baker, Ella Jo; Camus, Albert; Lee,

Herbert; Moore, Amzie; *Names of Individual Philosophers and Family Members*

—and interracial relations of: double consciousness of, 30, 34; experiences with white liberalism, 19–21, 29–30, 32; views of, 29, 32, 59, 170–173; and white volunteers, 161, 163–164, 170–173, 192, 198–199, 206–207

—leadership of: appearance and demeanor of, 8, 23, 24, 50, 59, 68, 93, 118–120, 206–207; Bob Moses mystique, 2, 3, 92, 117, 122, 174, 311, 312; cult status and hero-worship of, 2, 49, 72, 90–91, 106, 138, 140, 182, 206–207, 276–277; departure from movement, xii–xiii, 9, 308; and discipline, 8–9, 136, 156, 216; formal recognition of, 304; as guide and teacher, xii, 145–148, 151, 307; hands-on organizing skills of, 8, 9, 48, 51, 92, 105, 127, 145–151; importance academic credentials and cosmopolitan background for, 3, 8, 54, 123–126, 156, 201–202, 206–207; importance of mix organic and cosmopolitan influences for, 3, 8, 316–317; importance of outsider status of in, 69–70, 74, 81, 85, 125–126; inherent contradictions in leadership of, 3–9, 92–93; internal struggles with, 2, 5, 61, 78–80, 85, 90, 106, 114, 120, 128, 138, 156, 157, 169, 170, 174, 183–185, 186–187, 189, 202–210, 243–244, 247, 269, 276–280, 306; legacy of, xiv–xv, 280–281, 305–308; as Mississippi state project director, 108, 126–127, 129; as national movement leader, 9, 162, 186, 189, 276; responses southern black poor to, 7, 8, 72, 122–125; sense of direction and broad and long-term vision of, 8, 47–48, 68, 93, 96, 99, 102, 123–124, 145, 146, 150, 158–159, 162, 181, 219–221, 227,

258–259, 297; rhetorical skills and style of, 8, 73, 118–120, 168–173; singular attributes of, xiii, 2, 6, 7, 8, 47–48, 92, 102, 116, 219–220; universal projection of leadership on, 8, 121, 173–175; withdrawal from leadership, 280–281, 315

—leadership and organizing philosophy, 1, 3, 4, 14, 23, 36, 57, 61, 74, 81, 87, 88–89, 90, 92, 94, 98, 99, 102, 121, 128, 133, 136, 139, 144, 153–154, 162, 164, 218, 236–238, 256, 269–273, 300–301, 305–308, 378 (n. 50); and group-centered leadership, 3–4, 65, 120–122, 185; on organizing vs. leading, 1, 46, 121, 154, 175, 307; and visit to Newport News, 35–36, 41

—and leftist politics: introduction to leftist politics, 19–21, 324 (n. 37); and labor movement, 26–27, 146, 189–190, 221–223, 259, 284; and New Left, 2, 119, 238, 311, 324 (n. 37); and Old Left, 5, 20, 47, 238, 324 (n. 37)

—as mediator and networker: consensus and coalition-building by, 4, 5, 6, 8, 70, 95–97, 102, 120, 121, 131, 160, 164, 165, 168–173, 180, 186, 189–201 passim, 200, 210, 217, 219–223, 242, 247, 253, 257, 261, 297, 298, 302; mediator between local and national, 6, 116, 124–125, 128–129, 131, 133, 145–146, 148–152, 186, 192–193, 206–207, 236–237; mediator within movement, 8, 102, 129, 186, 196–201, 214, 217, 237–238; and networks, 9, 21, 27, 36, 50–51, 55, 58–59, 102, 104, 140–141, 147, 174, 184, 189, 221, 273, 301, 302, 304, 305, 316. *See also* Council of Federated Organizations (COFO); National Association for the Advancement of Colored People (NAACP); Southern Christian Leadership Conference (SCLC)

Moses, Robert Parris (Bob) (cont.)
—movement goals of: federal protection, 95, 128–129, 132–133, 141–142, 152, 168, 190–191, 204; national movement goals of, 5, 129, 133, 146, 154, 176, 178, 218, 220, 226, 230, 246, 317; political organizing, 99, 146, 57; universal voting rights, 2, 56–57, 59, 88, 95, 98, 131–132, 145–146
—and nationalism: and Black Power, 289–290, 315; identification with, 263, 286–290; not speaking to whites, 288–289, 315; and *Roots*-conference, 286–287, 288, 289–290, 291, 315
—and the North: preoccupation with urban ghettos in, 146–147, 178, 246, 290, 299, 376 (n. 29); travels the urban black North, 32–33
—opposition and criticism against: beatings of, 71–73, 76, 81, 90, 99, 180–182, 334 (n. 32); arrests and imprisonment of, 45, 69–70, 82–83, 85–87, 129, 140–142, 285, 338 (n. 84); harassment experienced by, 73, 74–75, 85, 115, 140; and Travis shooting, 137–138; liberal and conservative critiques of, 5, 23, 164, 248–249. *See also* Mississippi State Sovereignty Commission (MSSC)
—organizing emphases and techniques of: 'credentializing,' 7, 92, 111, 113, 145, 159, 300; education and exposure, 7, 16, 92, 102, 124, 125, 145, 147–148, 151, 211–214; escalation in tactics, 128–129, 132–133, 139, 142, 144–145, 154, 155, 156, 157, 158, 161, 168, 176, 187; facilitation, xiii, 1, 2, 5, 9, 71, 74, 80–82, 91, 92, 101, 102, 108, 116, 148, 157, 214, 247, 301, 305, 306, 307, 309, 313, 316, 317; grassroots agency, 14, 16, 24, 25, 34, 122, 128, 133, 136, 162, 219, 306, 315; literacy, 102, 132, 145–146, 147, 150, 178; ownership, 7, 14, 51, 57, 96, 300; parallel structures, 135, 170, 191, 211,

213, 219, 224, 263, 288; personal interaction and relationship building, xiii, 7, 61, 68, 91, 119, 123; preventing black armed uprisings, 23, 146, 152, 178, 218, 245, 246, 290, 299, 338 (n. 84), 376 (n. 29); preventing and ending white racial violence, 127, 128, 129–133, 139, 151–152, 155, 157, 167, 183–185, 186–206 passim, 338 (n. 84); reversing migration trend, 146; and rural areas, 48, 51, 56–57, 97, 98; sees locals as family, 7, 65, 79, 88, 114, 122, 338 (n. 84), 346 (n. 85); slow organizing approach of, 4, 9, 61, 74, 88, 109–110, 122, 127, 129, 132, 134, 137, 144, 161, 187, 259–260, 280, 301, 315; self-empowerment and moral leadership by example, 2, 13, 17, 22, 34, 92, 94, 112–113, 118–119, 122, 126, 171, 174, 192–193, 210, 211, 230, 236, 299–302, 315; trial-and-error tactics, 61, 92, 101, 108
—personal life of: battle fatigue of, 9, 261–263, 277, 291; and Dona Richards, 148–149, 178–179, 288–289, 292, 293; emotional life of, 2, 9, 75, 128–129, 130, 135, 138, 140, 152, 155, 158, 161, 183, 189, 199, 202–210 passim, 218, 225–226, 241–242, 246–247, 253–256, 265, 293, 295, 296–297; and Janet Jemmott, 292, 293–296; life in Canada, 292–294; name change of, 2, 278–280, 291, 315; post-movement career of, 290, 297–305; privacy of, xi, xii–xii, xiv. *See also* Algebra Project
—and religion: religious aura of, 72, 86, 113; religious views of, 13–14, 18, 24, 25–26, 28, 36, 144, 322 (n. 17); uses religion, 49, 55, 86–87, 114. *See also* Buddhism; Quakers (Society of Friends)
—and representation: of civil rights movement, 304–305; and history

National Association for the
Advancement of Colored People (cont.)
    McComb movement, 64, 65, 66, 69,
    70, 74, 78, 79, 80, 87–88; and
    MFDP, 226, 230–231, 244; in
    Mississippi, 1, 6, 37, 62–63, 71, 88,
    89, 94, 155, 342 (n. 39); moderate
    stance of, 38–39, 70, 87, 94, 133,
    143–144, 194, 248; Moses's outreach
    to, 58–59, 64–65, 70, 79, 102, 217;
    organizational structure of, 37–38;
    relation with southern branches,
    37–38, 41, 62–63, 88, 143; and
    SNCC, 38–39, 62, 63, 87, 88, 94,
    143–144, 217, 231; and SCLC, 143,
    226; and social class, 6, 88, 89, 94,
    97, 143, 244, 250–251, 317; voter
    registration drives of, 65, 67; Youth
    Councils of, 58, 63, 143, 216–217. *See
    also Names of Individual Members*
National Baptist Convention, 11
National Council of Churches
    (NCC), 154, 178, 180, 182, 191, 223,
    242, 249, 285
National Guardian, 163, 193, 263, 267
Nationalism. *See* Black Nationalism
National Lawyers' Guild (NLG), 189,
    194, 197, 204
National Sharecroppers Fund, 146
National Student Association (NSA),
    38, 40, 164, 176
Nausea (Sartre), 124
NCC. *See* National Council of
    Churches
Neshoba County, Miss., 202–204, 225,
    263. *See also* Freedom Summer
    (1964)
Neurath, Otto, 270
New Deal. *See* Great Depression
Newfield, Jack, 106, 113, 124, 215, 311
New Left, 238, 284; and Moses, 2, 119,
    311, 324 (n. 37)
Newport News, Va., Moses's visit to,
    35–36, 41, 150
New Republic, 233, 246

Newsweek, 82, 159, 187, 195, 205, 207,
    209, 324 (n. 37)
New York City, N.Y., 11, 12, 25, 26, 37,
    40, 60, 63, 69, 74, 106, 163, 178, 193,
    234, 285, 292; anticommunism in,
    18, 20, 105; civil rights activism in,
    33, 293; and FOS, 90, 148, 151, 204;
    and liberal politics, 18, 20, 220;
    mental institutions in, 31; Moses's
    civil rights meetings in, 107, 144,
    146, 147, 169, 178, 192, 211, 254;
    Moses returns to, 59, 61, 178, 285,
    292; segregation in, 10, 18, 29;
    World War II impact on, 12. *See also*
    Harlem
New York Herald Tribune, 198
New York Times, 70, 75, 81, 82, 84, 124,
    134, 139, 181, 184, 210
New York University Medical
    Library, 19, 21, 23, 31
Niebuhr, Reinhold, 40
Nkruhmah, Kwame, 286
Nobles, Ernest, 66, 72, 82
Nonviolence, 24, 61, 117, 281; and
    direct action, 39, 50, 64, 94–95, 207;
    and Gandhi, 23, 24, 40, 94; growing
    criticism of, 152, 200–201, 210;
    religious base of, 23–24; and
    self-defense, 52, 57, 94, 200–201; and
    SNCC founding, 39; tactic vs. way
    of life, 24, 39, 72, 75; training in, 35,
    39, 107; and voter registration,
    200–201, 315. *See also* Boycotts;
    Sit-ins
Nonviolent High, Pike County. *See*
    Freedom Schools
Norman, Martha, 121
Norman, Silas, 281
Norrell, Robert, 310
Northern Student Movement (NSM),
    135, 150
Novak, Robert, 203, 248
NSA. *See* National Student Associa-
    tion
Nyerere, Julius, 295

Race riots, 310; Moses's preoccupation
with, 178, 217, 299, 376 (n. 29); at
Ole Miss, 132, 134. *See also* Harlem
Rachlin, Carl, 194
Racial terrorism. *See* Violence
Radical Equations (Moses and Cobb),
xiii, 80, 304, 305, 314–317
Rainey, Lawrence, 202, 204, 208
Ramparts, 192
Randolph, A. Philip, 24, 146, 152, 153,
176, 212, 223, 234, 253, 328 (n. 20);
and Brotherhood of Sleeping Car
Porters, 10, 189
Rauh, Joseph, 255, 287; and MFDP,
222–223, 228, 230; and relationship
with Moses, 239, 247, 248, 303–304; at
1964 National Democratic Conven-
tion, 232–236, 238–239, 241, 243
RCNL. *See* Regional Council of
Negro Leadership
Reagan, Ronald, 310
Reagon, Bernice Johnson, 110, 113
Reagon, Cordell, 94
Red-baiting. *See* Anticommunism
Redmond, Rev., 51
Reese, George, 76
Regional Council of Negro Leader-
ship (RCNL), 54, 62, 98
Regulars. *See* Mississippi Democratic
Party ('the Regulars')
Republican Party, 64, 252. *See also*
Goldwater, Barry
Resistance, Rebellion, and Death
(Camus), 324 (n. 43)
Reuther, Roy, 222
Reuther, Walter, 189, 190, 222, 234,
235, 237, 238, 239
Richards, Dona (Marimba Ani), xiv,
163, 215, 235, 262, 278, 281, 282, 285,
288; activism of, 148, 192, 224, 225,
228, 231, 285, 204; and Africa, 265,
266, 286; feminist views of, 149, 178;
marriage and relationship with
Moses of, 148–149, 178–179,
288–289, 292, 293; at 1964 Demo-

cratic National Convention,
243–244; and *Roots* conference, 286
and Vietnam War, 284; views of
Freedom Summer, 170–172, 179, 243
Richards, Harvey, 151
Richardson, Channing, 24, 25, 26
Riessman, Frank, 211–212
Robb, Dean, 222
Roberts, Gene, 124
Robeson, Paul, 20
Robinson, Jackie, 12, 15
Robinson, Phil Aldon, 304, 336–337
(n. 65)
Robinson, Reginald (Reggie), 66, 101
Robinson, Ruby Doris Smith. *See*
Smith (Robinson), Ruby Doris
Rock Hill, S.C., jail-ins, 64, 332 (n. 9)
Rogerson, Howard, 188
Roosevelt, Franklin D., 14, 24, 34
Roots (conference), 286–287, 288,
289–290, 291, 315
Rudd, J.M., 51
Ruleville, Miss., and movement in,
101, 108–109, 111, 114–116, 127, 177,
198, 213–214
Russell, Bertrand, 60
Rust College, 97, 101
Rustin, Bayard, 36, 37, 40, 41, 45, 153,
193, 201, 234, 248, 284, 316; back-
ground of, 24–25; and Carmichael,
245–246; invitation withdrawn of,
43, 60, 328 (n. 20); and MFDP, 220,
221, 226, 246; Moses's first meeting
with, 25; Moses identifies with, 154;
at 1964 Democratic National
Convention, 235, 238–239, 243

Saddler, Walter, 213
Salinger, Pierre, 221
Sampson, Charles, 139, 140
Samstein, Mendy, 161, 173, 192, 195,
224, 262, 267, 276, 289; and Freedom
Vote, 165, 166; and MFDP, 220, 236;
Moses on, 171
Sartre, Jean-Paul, 124

52, 98, 101, 128, 144–145, 153, 158, 159, 176, 185, 291, 300, 302, 305, 307, 308. *See also Names of Individual Members and SNCC and COFO Projects*
—organization of: appeal of, 4, 6, 7, 67–68, 88, 110; Atlanta headquarters, 40, 48, 83, 90, 95, 99, 108, 120, 150, 151, 156, 160, 193, 264, 267, 275; and Baker, 38, 40, 42, 44, 46, 47, 48–49, 101, 275; centralizing course and structure debate of, 253, 257–258, 266–282 passim, 285; and Christianity/religious base of, 39–40, 114; Communications Department of, 90, 215; decline of, 246, 274, 376 (n. 29); economic base of, 6, 49, 66, 85, 95, 110, 268; foundation of, 36, 38–40, 42, 44; informal leadership in, 7, 8, 126, 179, 379 (n. 59) (*see also* Moses, Robert Parris (Bob)); and Nashville group, 39–40, 42; as 'new wave,' 6, 38–39, 49, 65, 67; North-South divide in, 34, 38, 43–44, 173, 179; organizational structure and culture of, 7–8, 9, 22, 42, 46, 63–64, 65, 66, 68, 70–71, 89–90, 99, 112, 120, 154, 156, 159, 248, 277–278, 324 (n. 43); stages of development, 2, 9, 38–40, 56, 64, 89–90, 93, 95, 145, 156–157, 253, 275–276, 290; race and class conflicts within, 6, 117, 160–161, 165–166, 171–173, 179, 198–199, 257, 275–276; Research Department of, 108; two wings of, 64, 70, 81, 90, 102, 335 (n. 41)
—interorganizational relations of: and COFO, 96, 97, 193, 195–196, 226, 230–231; and FELD, 148; and King and SCLC, 38, 39, 40, 41, 57, 65–66, 87, 144, 249, 373 (n. 72); and NAACP, 38–39, 62, 63, 87, 88, 94, 143–144, 217, 231; and 1964 National Democratic Convention, 220, 231, 246–247, 254

—beliefs and tactics of: Africa trip of, 264–266; alienation of local people, 246, 254–255, 274; and anticommunism and civil liberties, 43, 45, 47, 60, 177–178, 195, 248, 328 (n. 20); and battle fatigue, 261–263; black nationalist course of, 9, 153, 245–246, 253, 258, 260, 264, 290, 291, 308; and direct action, 4, 39, 46, 56, 61, 63–64, 74, 81, 98; and economic inequality, 177–178, 259–260; and media and history writing, xii, 61, 84, 313–314, 336 (n. 56); and nonviolence and self-defense, 23–24, 39–40, 152, 200–201, 210; northern urban projects of, 264, 376 (n. 29); organizing approach and techniques of, 1, 5, 6, 7, 50, 51, 67, 88, 89, 101, 102, 110, 111, 121, 253–255; trial-and-error tactics of, 64, 99; and voting rights, 56–58, 60, 61, 63–64, 67, 93, 95; and Vietnam, 284; and women, xiv, 249
—conferences and meetings of: Atlanta Gammon Theological Seminary meeting of, 277–280; December 1963 meeting of, 177–178; June 1964 meeting of, 193, 196, 201; October 1960 conference of, 48, 51, 56, 58, 59, 61; 1963 Thanksgiving Conference of, 175–177; and Waveland meeting, 269–276, 315
Students for a Democratic Society (SDS), 82, 211, 221–222, 282–283, 285, 324 (n. 37). *See also* Hayden, Tom
Stuyvesant. *See* Peter Stuyvesant High School (New York)
Sugrue, Thomas, 30, 33, 384 (n. 7)
Sunflower County, Miss., 101, 109, 134, 158. *See also* Ruleville, Miss.
Surney, Lafayette, 112
Sutherland, Bill, 285, 294, 295
Sweeney, Dennis, 262